Integrated Marketing Communications

EUROPEAN EDITION

Integrated Marketing Communications

EUROPEAN EDITION

Hans Ouwersloot and Tom Duncan

The **McGraw·Hill** Companies

London Boston Burr Ridge, IL Dubuque, IA Madison, WI New York San Francisco
St. Louis Bangkok Bogotá Caracas Kuala Lumpur Lisbon Madrid Mexico City
Milan Montreal New Delhi Santiago Seoul Singapore Sydney Taipei Toronto

Integrated Marketing Communications
Hans Ouwersloot and Tom Duncan
ISBN-13 9780077111205
ISBN-10 0077111206

Published by McGraw-Hill Education
Shoppenhangers Road
Maidenhead
Berkshire
SL6 2QL
Telephone: 44 (0) 1628 502 500
Fax: 44 (0) 1628 770 224
Website: www.mcgraw-hill.co.uk

British Library Cataloguing in Publication Data
A catalogue record for this book is available from the British Library

Library of Congress Cataloguing in Publication Data
The Library of Congress data for this book has been applied for from the Library of Congress

Acquisitions Editor: Melanie Havelock
Development Editor: Hannah Cooper
Senior Marketing Manager: Alice Duijser
Senior Production Editor: James Bishop

Cover design by SCW Ltd
Typeset by Wearset Ltd, Boldon, Tyne and Wear
Printed and bound in Italy by Rotolito Lombarda

ISBN-13 9780077111205
ISBN-10 0077111206

The **McGraw·Hill** Companies

Dedication

This book is dedicated to Rob, Martine and Gerben for all the joy they bring into my life.

Hans Ouwersloot

Brief table of contents

Detailed table of contents

Overview of the European edition

Integrated Marketing Communication (IMC) is about the coherent, consistent and clear use of the company's communication options. As you will understand from reading the text, everything communicates, but this book focuses predominantly on communication initiated by the company.

Communication becomes an issue when a company wants to send a message. For example, a beverage company wants to communicate that it has developed a new drink. To communicate this message, decisions have to be made concerning three topics. Firstly, the form of communication has to be determined—these are called the communication functions (advertising, sales promotions, etc.). When you advertise, you rely on the ad to be seen and processed by the end consumer; when you choose sales promotion you try to induce trial behaviour. The second decision is about the content of communication—this is the message. Take a sales promotion: is the offer buy one, get one free? Or is it a premium? And what kind of premium then: a toy, a tooth brush, or a glass to drink the new product? The final decision concerns the media required to connect the customer to the company. Is the sales promotion distributed nationally, or in local newspapers only? Will it be made available via the company's website? IMC considers all these questions in combination with the ultimate objective to deliver a message that is understood how it was intended, and with such impact that it persuades the consumer to behave in a way that benefits the company.

To make the right decisions in the area of IMC, the use of a model is helpful. In this book, the IMC planning model connects all of the elements that are discussed separately in individual chapters. The IMC planning model, introduced in Chapter 5, is therefore the backbone of the text. Before this planning model can be understood, however, the three building blocks of IMC need to be introduced. These are branding, communication theory and consumer behaviour (covered in Chapters 2, 3 and 4 respectively).

Communication in the first place informs customers about the brand or brands of the company. Although communication also has other functionalities, in the marketing context it is a reasonable assumption to understand communication primarily as a way to learn about brands. Consequently a proper understanding of the fundamentals of branding is required. Similarly, a fundamental understanding of communication theory is indispensable. Finally, since all IMC intends to influence consumer behaviour, it is necessary to look at some basic concepts in this stream of theory.

The IMC plan next connects these basics to the execution of the communication needs of the company. The plan displays how objectives can be defined and what steps and decisions are needed to finally arrive at the execution of an IMC plan. It also makes clear that planning should be evaluated, in order for the company to learn and adapt its IMC activities as necessary. The core of the IMC plan is threefold: how to create messages, what communication functions to employ, what media to use.

Message creation is a highly creative task that has both a strategic and an execution dimension. These two dimensions are discussed in Chapters 6 and 7 respectively. To make effective plans to use media, the characteristics of traditional media are discussed in Chapter 8. Chapter 9 highlights the use of interactive media, the Internet in particular. Use of interactive media is both closest to the ideals of marketing communication and is becoming real practice ever more, not only via the Internet, but also with the possibilities mobile telephony offers. Subsequently, various planning tactics are covered in Chapter 10.

IMC is about all communications tools available to companies. Advertising is perhaps the one best known and understood, and therefore it drives much of the practice of marketing communicators. Chapters 6 and 7 therefore primarily are about advertising, but the principles and lessons displayed here are often applicable to the use of other tools too. Similarly, the discussions of media in Chapters 8 to 10 are easiest understood with advertising in mind, but the lessons equally apply to other tools as well.

Chapters 11 to 15 cover the communication functions in detail. Special emphasis will be given to examining the strengths of the various functions with respect to building brands. IMC essentially connects brands to consumers by means of information. It does not take place in a vacuum, but in the real world. Hence it is subject to the rules and laws of the society within which it takes place. Social, legal and ethical issues (Chapter 16) have their impact on the possibilities and limitations of the communication function, but also on the effectiveness of certain communication activities. Similarly, communication is not restricted by national boundaries. Either because companies actively adopt internationalization strategies, or because media (in particular the Internet, TV and magazines) have become highly international, national borders have lost much of their relevance for marketers. Understanding international topics should be in the backpack of every IMC student, and Chapter 17 addresses these.

The book concludes by discussing how IMC activities can, and should, be evaluated.

Guided tour

Chapter perspective

Each chapter opens with an introduction,
outlining the key themes of the discussion
to follow.

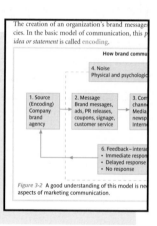

The creation of an organization's brand message
cies. In the basic model of communication, this *p
idea or statement* is called encoding.

Figure 3-2 A good understanding of this model is ne
aspects of marketing communication.

Figures and tables

Each chapter provides a number of figures
and tables to help you to visualize the various
IMC models, and to illustrate and summarize
important concepts.

IMC in action case studies

Each chapter features IMC in Action case studies,
which apply the theory of IMC to real marketing
situations within the context of the chapter topic.

Final note

This chapter summary briefly reviews and
reinforces the main topics you will have
covered in each chapter to ensure you
have acquired a solid understanding of
the key issues.

Check the key points

Key point 1: More than a product

a What is a brand? Why is a brand more than

b Explain how brands work to transform pro

c Explain how brands work to create value.

d Define brand equity. To what extent do
   concept is related to brand valuation metho

e What are the different levels of brand awaren

f What is the role of associations in branding

g Describe the associative network model.

h Explain what various stages exist for cons
   Keller's brand equity pyramid is more impo

Key point 2: Brand-building steps

a List and explain the brand-building steps.

b What is a brand position?

c In choosing a brand name and symbols, wh

Check the key points

Following on from the Final Note, these key points reinforce the major learning points from the chapter for handy reference and test understanding of the chapter topic.

Chapter Challenge

Writing assignment

Pick a company, and identify what things it do
tain a good relationship with customers. M
company's relationship-building practices.

Presentation assignment

Select four car brands (e.g. Fiat, Volkswagen, R
they take in the market. On what are their p
can you identify? Present a map that displays
sions that you think best captures the market si

Internet assignment

Visit the IKEA website and go to the country
and what the IKEA brand stands for. Then e
website—its design, contents, navigation poss
characterized the IKEA brand.

Case assignment

Chapter challenge

This end-of-chapter feature is the perfect way to practise the techniques you have been taught and apply the methodology to real-world situations. There are a variety of challenges to suit different aspects of learning.

ⓘ Key terms

associations Everything that is related to a bra

associative network Representation of brand
nected by links.

benefits Advantages that allow a product to sat

brand awareness Whether or not consumers k

brand community Collections of customers w
to each other, learning from each other, and sh
well as getting help in solving brand-related pro

brand elements Brand names; symbols; logos;

brand equity The intangible value of a brand b

brand extension The application of an establish

brand identity What the brand stands for, h
terms, to which all other characteristics and act

Key terms

These are highlighted at the end of the chapter, with accompanying definitions for reference as you progress through the book.

Further reading

Aaker, David A. and Erich Joachimsthaler (2000)

Austin, Jon R., Judy A. Siguaw and Anna S. Matt
   of the Aaker brand personality measurem
   Vol. 11–2, pp. 77–92.

Hayes, J. Bryan, Bruce L. Alford, Lawrence Süver
   ing consumer-brand relationships", *Journa*
   pp. 306–15.

Kay, Mark J. (2006) "Strong brands and co
   Vol. 40–7/8, pp. 742–60.

Keller, Kevin L. (2003) *Strategic Brand Managem*

Ouwersloot, Hans and Gaby Odekerken-Schröe
   and Why", *European Journal of Marketing*, for

Riezebos, R. (2003) *Brand Management—a theo*
   Prentice Hall.

Volkner, Franziska and Henrik Sattler (2006) "D
   keting, Vol. 70 (April), pp. 18–34.

Further reading

The Further Reading list at the end of each chapter provides useful references for you to deepen your knowledge of the chapter topic as required.

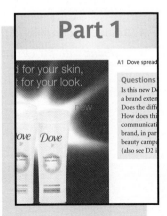

Part 1

A1 Dove spread

Questions

Is this new D
a brand exten
Does the diffe
How does thi
communicati
brand, in par
beauty campa
(also see D2 i

Colour inserts

There are two colour sections situated after Parts 2 and 4 of the text, containing an array of advertisements with questions asking you to analyse IMC at work.

Technology to enhance learning and teaching

Online Learning Centre (OLC)

After completing each chapter, log on to the supporting Online Learning Centre website. Take advantage of the study tools offered to reinforce the material you have read in the text, and to develop your knowledge of IMC in a fun and effective way.

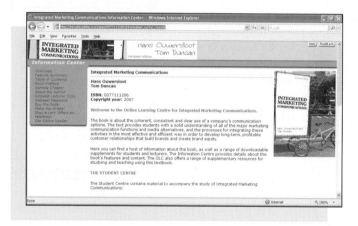

Resources for students include:

- *Video advertisements with accompanying questions*
- *Case studies*
- *Web links*
- *Self-test questions*

Also available for lecturers:

- *PowerPoint slides*
- *Lecture outlines*
- *Answers to questions in the book*
- *Testbank with MCQ/true/false and essay questions*

Visit **www.mcgraw-hill.co.uk/textbooks/ouwersloot** today

EZ Test

EZTest, a new computerized testbank format from McGraw-Hill, is available with this title. EZTest enables you to upload testbanks, modify questions and add your own questions, thus creating a testbank that's totally unique to your course! Find out more at:
http://mcgraw-hill.co.uk/he/eztest/

Custom Publishing Solutions: Let us help make our content your solution

At McGraw-Hill Education our aim is to help the lecturer find the most suitable content for their needs and the most appropriate way to deliver the content their students Our **custom publishing solutions** offer the ideal combination of content delivered in the way which suits lecturer and students the best.

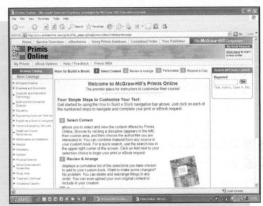

The idea behind our custom publishing programme is that via a database of over two million pages called Primis, *www.primisonline.com* the lecturer can select just the material they wish to deliver to their students:

Lecturers can select chapters from:

- textbooks
- professional books
- case books - Harvard Articles, Insead, Ivey, Darden, Thunderbird and BusinessWeek
- Taking Sides - debate materials

Across the following imprints:

- McGraw-Hill Education
- Open University Press
- Harvard Business School Press
- US and European material

There is also the option to include material authored by lecturers in the custom product - this does not necessarily have to be in English.

We will take care of everything from start to finish in the process of developing and delivering a custom product to ensure that lecturers and students receive exactly the material needed in the most suitable way.

With a Custom Publishing Solution, students enjoy the best selection of material deemed to be the most suitable for learning everything they need for their courses – something of real value to support their learning. Teachers are able to use exactly the material they want, in the way they want, to support their teaching on the course.

Please contact your local McGraw-Hill representative with any questions or alternatively contact Warren Eels **e:** *warren_eels@mcgraw-hill.com.*

 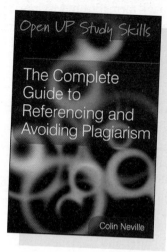 

Acknowledgements

Our thanks go to the following reviewers for their comments at various stages in the text's development:

Tino Bech-Larsen, Aarhus School of Business
Chris Blackburn, Oxford Brookes University
Anick Bosmans, Tilburg University
Sally Chan, University of Leeds
Sverre Christensen, University of Southern Denmark
Angela Hall, Manchester Metropolitan University
Sally Laurie, Northampton University
Harold Miesen, Tilburg University
Dan Petrovici, Kent Business School
Stefan Schwarzkopf, Queen Mary, University of London
Janet Ward, Newcastle University
John White, University of Plymouth

For the provision of case studies, we'd like to thank:

Pamela Adams, Franklin College, Switzerland
Merel Badenhop, Maastricht University
Lydie Coolen, Maastricht University
Edwina Luck, Queensland University of Technology

And for permission to use the colour advertisements:

Nielsen Media Research
Corbis
Ads of the World
Coca-Cola
Apple Marketing
Second Life
David Lee/howstrange.com
Tupperware

Author's acknowledgements

Books like these cannot be written without the help of many people. They deserve a sincere "thank you" and that's what they get, right here.

The team at McGraw-Hill was lovely to work with, especially Hannah Cooper who has done a wonderful job by communicating a tremendous amount of positive energy and encouragement across the North Sea and demonstrating a degree of confidence in the project that dragged it through some of its difficult phases. In an earlier stage Rachel Crookes did the same. Melanie Havelock, Alice Duijser, James Bishop, Michael Monaghan, each in their own way, are also responsible for this project to have come to completion.

Much help was also received in the production of the IMC in action case studies. A lot needed to be done here to make the feature attractive to a European and international audience. Merel Badenhop and Lydie Coolen did an awesome job in producing large numbers of small case studies (and a few larger ones) that are found throughout the book. Pamela Adams and Edwina Luck further contributed by delivering a few outstanding case studies, and also the contributions of Louise Verheij van Wijk of Philips, and Ernst Boekhorst of ABN AMRO deserve to be mentioned.

Finally, the direct or indirect support of colleagues has been very important. Roger Pruppers, Michael Güllich, Ko de Ruyter, Jos Lemmink, Ed Rohof (Bovil advertising agency), Charles Pahud de Mortanges, Hans Kasper, Bas Creemers, all have been sources of inspiration during this project. Finally a thank-you goes to Jan van Vilsteren, Jeroen Bos and many other students who have sharpened our insights in the world of IMC while writing their master theses on various topics in the fascinating world of marketing communications.

Obviously, no one of the persons mentioned here is responsible if any error or mistake would be found in this text; that's only with the authors.

PART 1

Part contents

Marketing communication builds brands

LEARNING OBJECTIVES

After reading this chapter, you should:

- ☑ Be able to describe Integrated Marketing Communications (IMC) and the main terms involved.
- ☑ Understand what needs to be integrated when adopting IMC.
- ☑ Be able to list the most important IMC tools.
- ☑ Understand why internal marketing is essential in IMC.
- ☑ Know with whom companies work together in IMC.

CHAPTER PERSPECTIVE
The changing world of advertising

No industry is more creative, exciting, rewarding, and challenging than advertising! This industry is unique because it puts everything it does on stage for the world to see and respond to—loving it, hating it, being moved by it. Its biggest challenges are to be found in the integration of advertising with the many other marketing communication tools available. Marketing communications is best known for advertising, but it encompasses much more.

Not long ago most client companies and agencies cared only about creating and sending brand messages in order to sell products. Today, companies also engage in dialogue with their customers, and increasingly customers themselves initiate these conversations. Companies realize that building a relationship and trust are more likely to boost sales and profits than simply "talking at" customers and prospects. Selling additional products to current customers is significantly less costly than selling to a new customer for the first time.

Another change is the increasing amount of new information and communication technology. New media, such as the Internet, mobile phones, and wireless computing, make marketing communication programmes ever more complex. That is why it is useful to approach advertising—and promotion in a general sense—from the integrated marketing communications (IMC) perspective.

The most important things that you will learn from this chapter are that successful companies use many types of communication, not only to win new customers but also to keep them, and that communication—the sending and receiving of messages—is at the heart of all relationships, including our relationships with our favourite brands. Furthermore, you will be shown how all this is realized: which people are involved in the communications process, both within and outside the company.

Welcome to the new integrated world of advertising and promotion.

All around the world
ABN AMRO

At the end of the Volvo Ocean Race 2005–2006, campaign CEO Jan Berent Heukensfeldt stated: "ABN AMRO decided in October 2003 to participate in this race. ABN AMRO considered it an excellent platform for marketing and communications, but also for getting 100 000 employees excited about the race and communicating that to their clients. For us it was a tragic accident with the loss of Hans Horrevoets. When we started this race we knew this was a risky venture. We said at the beginning we wanted to share the values of the bank with the world: professionalism, teamwork, integrity and respect. The success of the campaign took on a very dark tinge. But if you look at the performance of the sailing and the marketing teams, this project has been successful. We think we will get to the targets we set before the campaign in terms of media value."

Background

ABN AMRO is an international bank founded in 1824 in the Netherlands. The bank ranks number 8 in Europe and number 13 in the world, based on its €999 billion assets (30 September 2006). Over 110 000 employees worldwide serve four principal segments: personal banking, private banking, business and commercial, and corporate and institutional. Internally, ABN AMRO maintains four corporate values that drive its business: respect, integrity, teamwork and professionalism. From a communication perspective, the company's brand image is based on four specific brand values: leading, stylish, personal and ambitious. These four values connect well with the main target audiences: preferred banking clients, young professionals, students and the upper echelons of small and medium-size companies.

Sponsorship is an important marketing communication function for communicating the brand. ABN AMRO sponsors several projects, with the emphasis on sports (80 per cent, e.g. the Volvo Ocean Race) and cultural events making up the remaining 20 per cent of the sponsorship portfolio (e.g. exhibitions in museums). Sponsorship in these areas connects well to the interests of the (potential) clients. The bank does not sponsor any project of a political or religious

IMC in Action

nature, because it does not wish involvement in these controversial fields. The bank also refuses to sponsor individuals or student parties, since this can cause negative publicity when one of the individuals misbehaves. Finally, ABN AMRO does not sponsor any projects that conflict with environmental or its own corporate values (respect, integrity, teamwork and professionalism). The idea of being a sponsor in the Formula 1 race was therefore rejected, since this race is in conflict with the bank's corporate values (durability).

The Volvo Ocean Race

One of the events that ABN AMRO has sponsored is the Volvo Ocean Race. Organized every four years, the Volvo Ocean Race is an around-the-world yacht race. Normally it starts in England, but in the year 2005 the race started in Spain. It is 57 000 kilometres and it takes eight months to complete. The route is divided into nine legs, taking the crew in 2005 to Cape Town, Melbourne, Rio de Janeiro, Baltimore and Rotterdam, to finish in June 2006 in Gothenburg (Sweden). The crew may face bad weather conditions, especially when they are on open sea. The course is interrupted seven times in ports around the world, where the competition will include short, one-day races. These inshore races are a perfect opportunity to show the boats and teams to both public and sponsors. Furthermore, the longer stages are broken down by pit stops for the sailors so that they can rest and prepare for the next leg. Of course, all these stops are also ideal opportunities for local media exposure.

The Volvo Ocean Race was an outstanding chance to carry the brand name and logo into some of the bank's most important markets, such as Brazil and the US. Other reasons for participating in this race were the relatively low cost, the duration of the race and the natural affinity of ABN AMRO's board with sailing in general. The race fits pretty well with other sponsorships by the bank, and the sport is relatively popular among the wealthier classes of society where the bank finds its main target groups.

Team ABN AMRO ONE and ABN AMRO TWO

After considering the effects of sponsoring a team in such a worldwide yacht race, ABN AMRO decided to sponsor two teams (each consisting of ten sailors). Having two boats that communicate the brand name, logo and tag line (Making More Possible) would be more effective in reaching media objectives. Increasing brand awareness was the major communication objective. This was of course enormously helped by Team ONE being the overall winner of the race (also see colour insert C14). The decision to own teams, rather than sponsor them, was motivated by Ernst Boekhorst (Head of Sponsorships BU NL): "The fact that we owned two teams results in more enthusiasm and involvement among the employees and clients of our bank. They are coming to Rotterdam to watch the race and they can follow the race everywhere. Participating, rather than sponsoring, increased the involvement of our employees. Through our participation, we also constructed a larger marketing campaign."

Where (integrated) marketing communication comes in

By participating in the race with two teams, it is obvious that ABN AMRO creates brand awareness worldwide. But what about the associations with either corporate values or the brand image? Professionalism, flexibility, teamwork and innovation are important elements in such a sporting event, matching perfectly with the culture of the bank. Moreover, one boat consists of

▶ only professional sailors, while the other consists of four professionals and eight "young professionals", being in line with the target group of ABN AMRO. Research indicated that the evoked associations with the sponsorship are mostly "winner mentality" and "international". Next to this, associations like "not for everybody" and "talked-about" are mentioned, corresponding to ABN AMRO's image.

In order further to support the sponsorship, ABN AMRO decided to use other marketing communication functions in addition. First, two TV commercials were made. One was broadcast in advance of the race to inform the public about the bank's participation; the second ran while the race was in full swing. Besides commercials, the bank advertised in newspapers, especially to celebrate victories. The first victory was shared with readers of newspapers by sending a wallpaper of their boats to the first 2000 readers who responded to an ad. For the marketing targets, the company started interactive presentations for young professionals and prepared its own Hyves account for students, where exclusive videos of the race were shown. In order to reach the sales targets, ABN AMRO made use of premiums (clothing and miniature boats) and sweepstakes (e.g. a trip for two to New York). The bank shops were also used to promote the race, e.g with large point-of-sale displays.

Although this kind of sport sponsorship can create a lot of positive associations, the sponsor always runs the risk of something going wrong or the team not performing as expected. This might communicate negative messages to the public. In fact, ABN AMRO did face such an incident during the Volvo Ocean Race. One member of team ABN AMRO TWO, Hans Horrevoets, was swept overboard and died while the boat was on its way to Portsmouth. This tragic accident could have a negative influence on the corporate brand image of the bank. Proper crisis management, however, will not only mitigate the negative associations that come with such a tragedy, but may even prove in the end to have further strengthened the sponsor's image of a responsible, professional and capable organization. This is exactly what ABN AMRO did. According to Ernst Boekhorst, there had been some discussion about aborting the participation of ABN AMRO in the race shortly after the death of Hans Horrevoets. In the end the crew and the bank decided to go on, since they were almost finished and they felt it was what Hans Horrevoets would have wanted. The bank managed the incident well, e.g. by arranging a special place where people could remember him. Besides this, the celebrations in Rotterdam were relatively muted when the boats arrived there.

The SponsorRing sport

The success of the campaign was acknowledged when ABN AMRO received the SponsorRing in the sport category on 17 November 2006. This is a Dutch award given to sponsorships that were clearly different from other campaigns that year. The jury report states: "Team ABN AMRO in the Volvo Ocean Race 2005–2006 was superbly set up and carried out in an integrated way. The effects of this campaign have been detailed, measured and it has nearly achieved all objectives." Moreover, the company fulfilled four out of five categories: match (the fit with the brand and the sponsorship), goals and achievement (the goals were clear and achieved), execution and activation (in the way the sponsorship was interpreted in the marketing and corporate communication) and relationship sponsor vs. sponsorship (what the collaboration has delivered).

Has the sponsorship of the Volvo Ocean Race been effective?

> " The Volvo Ocean Race has been our most successful campaign.
> *(Ernst Boekhorst, ABN AMRO, 2007)* "

Naturally, ABN AMRO NL has evaluated the effectiveness of its participation in the Volvo Ocean Race. Despite measurement difficulties, ABN AMRO evaluates all its sponsorship activities, including their participation in the Volvo Ocean Race, every month. These assessments focus, on the one hand, on the media exposure that is created and, on the other, on the effects on awareness and attractiveness. The actual research is outsourced to specialist agencies, who measure the effectiveness both inside and outside the company. A common way to measure the effectiveness of a sponsorship is to assess the media exposure (how many times the sponsorship has been on TV) and to compare this with what such exposure would have cost in advertising time. The research agency Kobalt has estimated that the media exposure accounted for about €60 million. Compared to the out-of-pocket expenses of about €40 million, participation in the Volvo Ocean Race can be called successful.

Before the campaign began, the business unit of the bank in the Netherlands formulated objectives in the fields of brand awareness, the fit of the sponsorship and the interest to follow the event in the media. These were considered key measures for assessing the effectiveness of the project. Furthermore, the bank wanted to reach 75 per cent of the media target group (20–49 age group and upper class) at least one time. The TV commercial was enough in itself (reach of 87 per cent) to realize this target. After the race brand awareness was measured. Eighty-three per cent of the target audience did know about the participation of ABN AMRO in the Volvo Ocean Race, meeting the target of 75 per cent. Concerning fit, 42 per cent of the target audience found that there was a fit between the company and the event which was slightly below the 50 per cent target. However, interest in the race was only 18 per cent, which was far below the 50 per cent objective.

Internally the sponsorship was even more successful. Research showed that after the race, 97 per cent (target: 70 per cent) of the employees in the Netherlands knew that ABN AMRO had participated in the race. Their enthusiasm about the participation of the bank has risen from 29 per cent before the race to 63 per cent after the race (target: more than 50 per cent). According to the employees, all the corporate values are found to be matching with the sailing event, where teamwork and professionalism are ranked highest.

Will ABN AMRO participate again in the future? According to Ernst Boekhorst the answer will be no. "There is no need any more for a worldwide platform, so the bank can invest its money in a better way (e.g. the KLM open golf tournament). Today, the emphasis of sponsorship is on the local rather than the worldwide."

Think about it

Would the effectiveness of the sponsorship have been different if ABN AMRO had sponsored the whole race event instead of the teams? What about the decision to continue the race after the incident with Hans Horrevoets? To what extent does the corporate value of integrity play a role here?

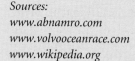

Sources:
www.abnamro.com
www.volvooceanrace.com
www.wikipedia.org

Ernst Boekhorst (ABN AMRO), Head of Sponsorship BU Netherlands. Personal interview 7 March 2007.

Jan van Vilsteren (2006) "ABN AMRO sponsorship of Volvo Ocean Race", Master Thesis, University of Maastricht.

P. de Pelsmacker, M. Geuens and J. Van den Bergh, (2001) Marketing Communications, *Harlow, England: Pearson Education Limited.*

Marketing communication: the building of a brand

When you think about Mercedes, Virgin, or Shell, what comes to mind? If you're like most people, it's a certain image, feeling, or impression. This is because a brand is *a perception resulting from experiences with, and information about, a company or a line of products.* What many people fail to understand is that brands live in the heads and hearts of customers—not on the side of a package. What marketing communications (and this book) are all about is how to create, deliver, manage, and evaluate brand messages—*all the information and experiences that impact how customers and other stakeholders perceive a brand.*

Brand messages in the very first place create awareness of the brand. Obvious as it seems, this is a crucial step in building a brand. Without brand awareness, there essentially is no brand, because a brand lives in the heads and hearts of consumers. But creating awareness of a brand name is only the first part of building a brand. Customers want to know what to expect from a brand—how they will benefit from using the brand, what the brand stands for, how the brand will make them feel when they use or own it, what recourse they have if they don't like the brand, as well as how much the brand costs and where it can be purchased. This is the second major purpose of marketing communications: helping to create the brand in all its dimensions. The information and imagery that are communicated about a brand, along with how the product performs, help customers form an opinion of a brand—a brand impression—that determines to what extent they will purchase and repurchase it. Generally speaking, the number of customers and how much they buy determines the extent to which a brand is successful—and contributes to business profits.

This book will help you understand how brand messages and product experiences—the building blocks of a brand—come together to create an impression about a brand in your mind and in the minds of millions of other people. It will explain strategies and practices used by marketers to create and deliver brand messages. This book will also explain what you would be doing if you decided to be a marketing or marketing communication professional.

Marketing communication

Marketing is all about the activities companies undertake to bring their products (tangible goods or intangible services) to the market. This includes both a strategic component and tactical decision making. For its tactical operations, marketers have many instruments at their disposal. In the marketing universe they are traditionally summarized and referred to as the four

Ps, taught in every basic marketing course—*product, price, place,* and *promotion* (Kotler and Keller, 2006). (Modern trends in marketing encompass topics like relationship management, value creation and marketing metrics, by which is meant that marketing should make clear what the added value is. The American Marketing Science Institute, www.msi.org, regularly publishes lists with most contemporary topics in marketing.) Although all four say something about a brand (see Chapter 3), promotion contains the marketing communication functions, which, along with media, are the primary focus of this book.

Marketing communication (MC) is *a collective term for all the various types of planned messages used to build a brand*—advertising, public relations, sales promotion, direct marketing, personal selling, packaging, events and sponsorships, and customer service. These types of messages are called MC functions, or tools, or instruments. For decades most of the emphasis was on one of these functions, namely advertising; however, the twenty-first century is seeing a shift: more of the marketing communication tools are being used strategically to complement and reinforce one another. MC functions need media, *vehicles through which marketing communication messages are carried to (and from) target audiences,* to be executed. The media that marketers use most frequently include TV, radio, newspapers, magazines, outdoor boards, Internet, mail, and the telephone.

Building brands is the overall objective of all marketing communication as well as of marketing. Generally speaking, the more successful a company is at building its brand or brands, the more profits it will make and the greater its brand equity will be. Brand equity is *the intangible value of a brand*—value added to a product or service that derives from a perception in customers' minds (this concept is explained more fully in Chapter 2).

MC functions and media help build a brand by connecting a company with customers. Brand messages also add value to a brand for both customers and the company. Customers gain value by learning about what problems a brand can solve or what opportunities it offers and where it can be purchased, as well as answers to specific questions. In the case of non-profit organizations, MC messages provide information about how to support a good cause. Customers can also gain value when they purchase a brand that is well known and has a good reputation.

As psychologists have pointed out, people (and companies) use brands to help define themselves (Hong and Zinkhan, 1995). Wearing a Rolex watch says something different about a person than if they wear a Swatch watch. Also, buying a well-known brand provides many people with peace of mind from knowing that the product is of good quality and the company will stand behind the product if there is a problem.

The applicability of the concept of marketing communications is broad, and extends beyond the borders of marketing. For example, governments apply MC practices to communicate ideas (be careful in the fight against terrorism), try to induce publicly desirable behaviour (stop smoking), or simply try to increase appreciation for their roles (tax-collecting bodies). This is not at odds with the branding focus that is adopted in this text, however. In all these instances there is an entity (the public body/the brand) that uses communication tools to gain awareness or to induce positive associations, attitudes or even behaviour.

The functional areas of marketing communication

What makes marketing communication so exciting and challenging is that there are so many tools from which to choose—such as advertising, sales promotion, direct marketing, publicity, and packaging, and the creativity each of these tools requires. Each MC tool is a functional area of communication expertise and specialization. When used skilfully, each can significantly impact on how customers think about a brand.

One of the important strategic decisions marketers must continually make is what mix of MC functions and media would be best for their brands. A **marketing communication mix** is *the selection of MC functions used at a given time as part of a marketing programme.* Besides selecting the mix, marketers must also decide to what extent each function will be used. An MC mix is like a cake that can be made from a variety of ingredients, the most commonly used ingredients being eggs, salt, milk, sugar, and flour, plus some type of flavouring. Just as the amount of each of these varies from recipe to recipe, the amount of advertising, sales promotion, and other MC functions varies from one MC mix to another.

In this section, eight MC functions are introduced. In addition to providing examples of how each tool can be used, the profiles provide a definition and a summary of each one's primary use in building brands. As you read about what these functions can do, imagine yourself as the marketing communication manager for a major brand. With this responsibility in mind, keep asking yourself this question:

> How would I go about determining which MC functions and media I should use to create a marketing communication campaign for my brand?

Advertising

Advertising is *non-personal, paid announcements by an identified sponsor.* It is used to reach large audiences, create brand awareness, help differentiate a brand from its competitors, and build an image of the brand. Advertising can quickly increase brand awareness and brand knowledge but its success greatly depends on the creative level. When advertising is not very creative (and much advertising is not) it has a hard time making a lasting impression. Because most advertising is designed to create brand awareness and an image for a brand, its impact is difficult to measure. There is a famous quote in the advertising world that is attributed to at least half a dozen persons: "I know half of my advertising is a waste, the problem is, I don't know which half." Advertising has historically been the dominant communication choice for many companies; however, that is changing. At Adwatch: Outlook 2002, a meeting of 400 advertising industry executives, much of the conference buzz centred on the use of marketing communication functions other than traditional advertising.[1] Recently the three largest advertising agency conglomerates (companies that own many different types of marketing communication agencies) reported that the majority of their revenues now come from providing marketing communication functions other than advertising.[2]

Sales promotion

In the mid-1800s patent medicines were one of the most widely advertised products. Because so many brands competed for consumers' attention, some brands began using sales promotion to get attention and acquire new customers. Sales promotion works by adding extra value, such as a price discount or a free trial, to an offer to stimulate consumers to try or buy a product.

Over 150 years later marketers are still using sales promotion to give customers an extra reason to buy. Pick up any local newspaper and you will find many ads containing coupons and sales promotions offers: "0% Financing on all Ford Mondeos." "Buy one pair of shoes and get the second for half price at Foot Locker." "Stay three nights at a Novotel and get the fourth night FREE." One type of sales promotion that is gaining in popularity is the frequent-buyer or customer-loyalty programme. Sometimes such programmes are offered by a number of (non-competing) organizations from different industries such as the Dutch Air-Miles programme, in which three Dutch giants, Albert Heijn, Shell and ABN Amro, collaborate together with many smaller companies. In these programmes the promotional idea (adding value) is connected to the concept of relationship marketing: the extra value is only acquired when the customer stays loyal for some time.

Because there are so many brands in each product category, and because so many of the products in a category are similar, marketers offer customers reduced prices, coupons, small gifts, and other incentives in an effort to gain attention and motivate buying. Sales promotion is *a short-term, added-value offer designed to motivate an immediate response.* Although generally used to motivate a buying decision, sales promotion is also used to move people through the buying process toward a particular brand. For example, some car dealers give customers free hot dogs and soft drinks just for visiting the dealer's showroom.

Although sales promotion has helped build brands and, even more important, helped brands keep customers from switching to competing brands, the overuse of promotional offers can actually harm a brand. Sales promotion must be combined with other MC functions and used strategically, as discussed in Chapter 13.

Direct marketing

Dell Computer Corporation is an example of how direct marketing can be the primary MC function used to build a successful brand. Michael Dell started the company when he was a student at the University of Texas. His strategy was to market directly to customers and build the exact computer that each customer wanted. Today, the primary medium that Dell uses to interact with customers is its website. Go to the Dell website (www.dell.com). How quickly can you find a page describing a laptop computer that you would be interested in buying (see colour insert B6)?

What differentiates direct marketing from other MC functions? Direct marketing is *an interactive, database-driven MC process that uses a range of media to motivate a response from customers and prospects.* As the name implies, no retailers or other members of the distribution channel are involved in *direct* marketing (although some retailers use this form of selling in addition to retail sales). It was exactly this elimination of other channel members that was later employed by Dell in its limited traditional advertising.

Publicity and public relations

Perhaps it is a surprise, but some of the best-known brands in the world never advertise. Take for example The Body Shop. Founded by Anita Roddick in 1976, one of the hallmarks of the company was that it would not waste a single pound on advertising. Instead the organization used its unique positioning in the market of skin and body care products to generate publicity, including word-of-mouth, largely helped by the charismatic and photogenic Mrs Roddick. Today it is one of the best-known brands in the world, with over 1900 outlets in 50 countries.[3]

Another example of the use of public relations to build a totally new brand is the story of Viagra. How to explain a medicine to treat erectile dysfunction posed a communication challenge. Pfizer, the maker of Viagra, determined that the best MC function to use initially was public relations. The resulting media buzz (brand publicity) and word of mouth generated by the publicity efforts prompted Pfizer to call the public relations effort "something of a cultural phenomenon".[4] Acclaimed as the fastest-selling new drug in history, the brand was launched in 40 countries, and 200 000 physicians wrote 7 million prescriptions for Viagra—all because of the brand-building introductory publicity.

The terms *public relations* and *publicity* are often used interchangeably. They are not synonymous, however. Publicity means *stories and brand mentions delivered by the mass media without charge.* It is only one aspect of public relations. Public relations means *efforts to generate and control publicity* in an effort to gain the support and co-operation of those publics.

Because publicity is "unpaid"—the media do not charge for using brand stories as they do for advertising—it is frequently used to increase brand awareness and make news announcements about brands and companies. Publicity is also used to communicate with hard-to-reach audiences (such as executives who are not heavy TV viewers and also have people who screen their mail and calls). One of the most important uses of publicity is to build brand credibility (see colour insert C4). Why this is possible is explained in Chapter 12 on PR and publicity.

Personal selling

Personal selling is *interpersonal communication in which a salesperson uncovers and satisfies the needs of a customer to the mutual benefit of both.*[5] Although usually the income of most sales representatives is based on how much they sell, more and more companies are basing compensation on how successful salespeople are at building and maintaining relationships with customers. In many business-to-business (B2B) categories, personal selling is the dominant MC function. Personal selling is often associated with the legendary salesman ringing at the door and putting a foot in the door. But personal selling techniques—often more subtle and acceptable than foot-in-the-door—can be applied in many situations where salespeople have direct contact with prospects, for example in car showrooms. Tupperware probably is the best example of a company that has become big mainly by relying on personal selling techniques (see colour insert C10).

Packaging

One of the greatest breakthroughs in marketing came in 1879 when Procter & Gamble launched Ivory soap.[6] It was a breakthrough because Ivory was a branded product inside a distinctive package at a time when soap was a commodity and was sold unbranded out of a barrel or box. Packaging helped build the Ivory brand. The success of Ivory helped create the concept of "packaged goods", which eventually led to the system that P&G designed to manage its many branded products.

One brand that uses its distinctive package design extensively is Absolut Vodka. The bottle, or something that recalls the specific shape of the bottle, has appeared in hundreds of communication outings, billboards, commercials, postal cards (see colour insert C13). In the Netherlands the brandy brand Bokma comes in square bottles, which inspired the brand to use the slogan "often round is better, sometimes square".

A package is *a container and conveyor of information.* A package can help in brand building by presenting various kinds of brand information—everything from ingredients to recipes that suggest multiple uses. Like sales promotion, packaging can add value to a product.

Events and sponsorships

Events are *highly targeted brand-associated activities designed to actively engage customers and prospects and generate publicity.* Public relations departments and agencies often use events to generate brand publicity as the opening case of ABN AMRO demonstrates (also see colour insert C14). Harley-Davidson is an internationally recognized brand that has become a cultural icon in part by sponsoring events. When thinking of a Harley owner, an image of "outlaw" Hell's Angels bikers wearing chains and black leather jackets often comes to mind. Behind that somewhat distorted image, however, is a subtle brand-building effort that leverages the Harley mystique and camaraderie. The Harley Owners Group, known as HOG, constitutes a worldwide community of Harley owners; the organization and its events have been strategically nurtured by the Harley-

Davidson company over the years. Red Bull is another brand that very effectively applies events to build a unique brand image, as described in the IMC in Action box in Chapter 11.

Most events are sponsored—that is, they are identified with one or more brands. But sponsorship goes beyond events. **Sponsorship** is *financial support of an organization, person, or activity in exchange for brand publicity and association.* Sponsorship is used not only to increase brand awareness but also to help define a brand through association. Vodafone was shirt sponsor of Manchester United, not principally because they like the team, but because Manchester United is British, successful, and big, everything Vodafone also wants to be. The increasing number of Asian players, mainly from South Korea and Japan, in the major European football leagues is sometimes attributed to the commercial interests of the sponsors of the teams in the Asian market.

Customer service

For many years, until the beginning of the 1990s, exceptional service was something that customers expected only at expensive restaurants, at high-priced hotels, or while shopping in exclusive stores. Good customer service was a product attribute that seemed to be available only to the very rich. Today, in contrast, customers have a choice of many brands in almost every product category, and how a company treats customers can be the major reason for choosing one brand over others. As you watch TV and read newspapers and magazines, notice how many companies say that they are "customer focused" or that they "put customers first". Even though their follow-through is often less than desired, these ads show that companies recognize how important customer service is in building brands.

Customer service is *a company's attitude and behaviour during interactions with customers.* At first glance, it may seem strange that customer service is a marketing communication function. The reason is that interactions with customers send some of the most powerful messages that customers receive about a brand. If the interactive experience is positive, it will strengthen the customer relationship. If it is negative, it can weaken or even kill a brand relationship.

The media of marketing communication

Nobody will deny that the media landscape has changed dramatically in the past couple of decades. Just think of the following: in 1980 Ted Turner said there was a market for a 24-hour news service. Nobody believed him. Now his CNN News Group is one of the largest and most profitable news and information operations in the world. More than 1 billion people worldwide have access to at least one of CNN's services, which are delivered through eight cable and satellite television networks, two radio networks, 10 websites, and CNN News Source, the world's most widely syndicated news service.[7]

Although TV, radio, newspapers, magazines, outdoor boards, the Internet, mail, and the telephone are the predominant MC media, marketers have devised other creative ways to deliver brand messages and connect to customers (see colour insert A6). One of the fastest growing is product placements in movies and TV shows. Another is retail store design. IKEA and Starbucks are just two examples of brands that effectively use their retail outlets to actively support their brands.

Besides the proliferation of media alternatives, there has been a major increase in the use of two-way communication between customers and companies. Brand messages initiated by customers take the form of complaints, enquiries, suggestions, and compliments. The poster child for this interactive, two-way dialogue is, of course, the Internet. Amazon.com® has made extraordinary use of this medium to build its brand. When used for direct marketing, the Internet makes it possible to run a retail operation 24 hours a day, seven days a week. It also extends a company's reach around the world. Because the Internet is computer and database driven, companies such as Amazon.com® can remember what customers order and tailor follow-up communication to appeal to individual interests predicted by products previously purchased.

Each of the marketing communication functions and all the media are discussed in greater detail in later chapters. They are introduced here to provide an overview of the communications that marketers use and to indicate why marketing communication and brand building require a disciplined and strategic approach to choosing and co-ordinating MC functions and media.

The integrated marketing communication (IMC) concept

Although MC functions and media have been used for decades, how they are selected and employed has changed significantly over the years. Recent changes are thanks to the widespread use of computers, databases, new communication technology (such as the Internet and wireless devices), and the wider array of brand choices. Deciding which MC functions to use, and how much of each, is quite a responsibility.

Added to this responsibility, however, is the need to manage the creation and delivery of these messages as well as respond to enquiries, complaints, and suggestions from customers and prospects.

Earlier in this chapter you were asked how you would go about determining which MC functions and media to use to build your brand. If you are a successful marketing manager, here is what you would probably say: *Use an integrated marketing communication (IMC) approach.*

Integrated marketing communication (IMC) *is a concept that directs the processes for planning, executing, and monitoring the brand messages that create brand–customer relationships.* IMC is about synergy (discussed below) and creativity, integration, and communication. Although many companies have co-ordinated and focused their marketing communication to a certain extent, an example of what IMC essentially means is described in the IMC in action opening case on ABN AMRO.

IMC as such does not alter the processes and procedures that are in place in companies, but it does lay the foundation on which these processes are grounded. Adopting the IMC concept poses one very fundamental question to every decision that has to be made: how does this decision relate to all the other decisions we have made, and are going to make. Approaching decisions consistently from the IMC perspective guarantees that the planning, execution and monitoring of the communications activities all relate to the same goals, and to each other.

A second major effect of adopting the IMC concept is the recognition that every time a company is in touch with its customers, something is communicated. Hosts at the reception desks not only help visitors find their way in the building, but are the first people such visitors come in touch with. When the visitor has to visit the washroom and sees a plumber fixing the toilet, he is in touch with a person that—in his perception—tells him something about his hosts. All such *touch points* are integrated in a truly IMC approach. And this notion extends to non-personal contacts. The very architecture of the building is an impression made on the customer. The design of the interior can make you feel comfortable, or not. The very location, availability of parking slots, or public transport facilities—everything communicates. Chapter 3 elaborates on this idea.

The effect of adopting the IMC concept is that communication efforts are co-ordinated and result in maximum clarity and effectiveness. Co-ordination in this sense is both with respect to the contents of the message, and to the timing of messages. No messages contradict, but rather support or complement each other, and redundancy is limited to the level that is deemed appropriate (see Chapter 3).

Integration produces synergy

To understand what *integrated* means in the context of the Integrated Marketing Communication concept, it is useful to think about integration and synergy together. **Integration** is *the combining of separate parts into a unified whole.* One outcome of integration is **synergy,** which is *the interaction of individual parts in a way that makes the integrated whole greater than the sum of its parts.* This interaction is sometimes expressed as $2 + 2 = 5$. When brand messages reinforce each other, synergy is produced. When the messages are all different, they can be confusing, which actually distracts from a coherent impression of a brand and fails to produce synergy.

Achieving integration and synergy, however, requires more than making brand messages look and sound alike, what some call "one voice, one look". Integration needs to occur in all areas where a customer comes in contact with a brand—such as customer service and product performance. Otherwise, the marketing communication messages, no matter how consistent and integrated, will ring hollow.

> It is a fundamental shift in the role and purpose of marketing, from manipulation of the customer to genuine customer involvement: from telling and selling to communication and sharing of knowledge.
>
> *Regis McKenna, relationship marketing expert*

Companies benefit in many ways from integrating their marketing communications. IMC helps brands differentiate themselves from competitors by being more customer focused. It improves accountability because relationships can be tracked in relation to sales and profits. It increases brand trust because emphasis is placed on customer retention rather than on single transactions. It fosters internal co-ordination and focus. These benefits are explained in detail in later chapters.

Relationship building applies to all stakeholders

Although a marketer's job is to build relationships with customers, he or she must be aware that marketing is part of a company and that the entire company must build relationships with *all* stakeholders. Any group of stakeholders can affect a company's sales and profits, and therefore every group of stakeholders should be taken into consideration when brand messages are created and sent. What a company does affects them, and what they do can affect the company.

From a marketing perspective, the most important group is customers (end users), followed by employees (Figure 1-1). Then come all the other groups whose relative importance varies by industry and by situation: suppliers, the media, MC agencies (for those companies that use agencies), government regulators, the communities in which a business is located, the financial community and investors, and special-interest groups. The IMC in Action box 'IKEA and the test of time' illustrates what this means for the Swedish giant.

Customers are important because they create sales. Employees are important because they produce (or acquire) the goods and services a company sells, and because those who interact

Relative importance of stakeholders to the success of a brand

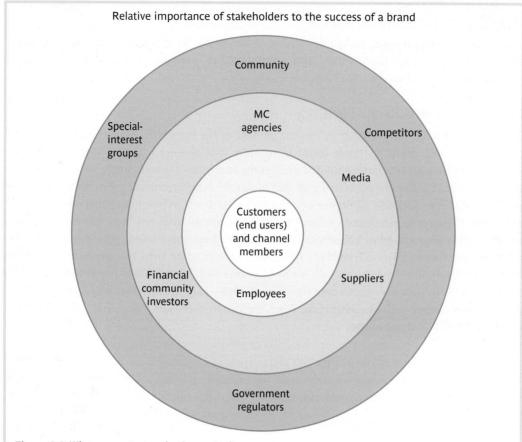

Figure 1-1 Why are customers in the centre?

directly with customers are perceived by customers as "being the company". Some executives, especially in the service industry, believe that employees, not customers, should be a company's number-one priority. The rationale is that, unless employees know their jobs, feel they are being treated fairly by the company, are members of a team and find meaning in their work, they are not going to provide excellent service to customers. Employees' treatment of customers is one of the most critical brand messages that can be sent. As one management consultant said: "It's impossible to build a loyal book of customers without a loyal employee base."[8]

As companies increasingly encourage and facilitate customer interactivity, more customers will be talking with more people in a company, and companies that ignore employees will pay a heavy cost. One study found that 46 per cent of employees in the companies surveyed argued with customers, 22 per cent did slow or sloppy work on purpose, 20 per cent came to work hung-over, and 11 per cent damaged property while joking around.[9] IMC uses internal marketing to help keep employees informed of marketing programmes and to boost employee morale and involvement in MC programmes.

IKEA and the test of time

IKEA is one of the largest furniture manufacturers and retailers in the world. Its reputation is based on stylish and innovative furniture designs, offered at low prices so that as many people as possible can afford them. With sales of €14.8 billion (2005) and 84 000 employees working in 44 countries, you can imagine that this company is successful. One important aspect of its success is its integrated marketing communication strategy. The company's vision "to create a better everyday life for many people" underlines this strategy, because the word "people" is used in the broadest sense: customers, employees and the community.

A basic marketing assumption is that the customer is always right. IKEA understands that well, and builds on a relationship with this customer by adapting in several ways to their needs. The IKEA concept for example communicates the message that by using inexpensive materials in a novel way and minimizing production, distribution and retail costs, customers can benefit from low prices. Functionality of the products and the associated quality are other examples of key messages. Moreover, the IKEA catalogue is used as a main marketing tool and provides the customer with all the available products. Since 1951 this catalogue has proved the most important communication channel for reaching customers, although this role has recently been taken over by IKEA's website. Both catalogue and website inspire people to visit the store and at the same time reinforce the IKEA brand. Finally, the company has probably caught your attention at some time with its blue/yellow retail stores, where "the customer can buy everything under one roof".

In addition to communication with customers, IKEA lays great emphasis on internal marketing communication. Employees' creativity and the diversity of cultures are highly valued. Employees are empowered by receiving broad instructions (instead of detailed ones) concerning their job activities and behaviours. All of them are allowed to choose their own methods of achieving objectives, within reasonable limits of ethical behaviour and costs. Thanks to the absence of a clearly defined job hierarchy, opinions and ideas can be expressed directly to top management. In turn, top management learns what customers need, adapts to these needs and can finally better satisfy its customers.

Other stakeholders, such as advertising agencies and the media, are used in the communication of the IKEA brand. Advertising agencies are sometimes used to design multi-media campaigns, for example in September 2006, when IKEA worked together with Interpublic Group's Deutsch. The agency launched a campaign that aimed to alter the perception that IKEA merchandise is best suited to college students and recent graduates, because the IKEA concept builds on "creating a better everyday life for many people". Regarding the use of different media, IKEA now increasingly uses TV, radio and the Internet after a long period of using only print media. The website especially is a source of information and provides a great deal of customer service. Next to ordering the latest catalogue, interactivity with the customers is created by the fact that they can create their own kitchen or workplace here!

As we have seen from the above, IKEA uses different stakeholders and integrates them to communicate its brand.

Think about it

Do you know other companies that have such an integrated marketing communication? What are the advantages of the catalogue and the website to the customers? To IKEA?

Sources:
www.ikea.com

Marketing VOX: The Voice of Online Marketing (2006).

"Ikea and Deutsch: Reunited and It Feels So Good". Retrieved 4 October 2006, from www.marketingvox.com/archives/2006/09/21/ikea_and_deutsch_reunited_and_it_feels_so_good/

Dutta, S. and Regani, S. (2005). "Ikea's innovative human resource management practices and work culture" (reference 405-020-1). Published by: ICFAI Centre for Management Research. Retrieved 4 October 2006, from www.ecch.com/casesearch/view_pdf.cfm?id=54706&folder=20054&ref=405-020-1

IMC and internal marketing

Everything communicates, but employees are the most important party in communicating to the company's environment and first of all its customers. Besides that, the employees are often in two-way contact with the customers: not only do they communicate to customers, employees in general are the receivers of messages from those same customers. Managing this two-way flow of information in which the employee is the key person is an important objective of **internal marketing,** which is *an ongoing effort to involve employees in the planning process and then communicate the finalized plan back to them to get their buy-in and support.* The essence of internal marketing is that marketing is not only the responsibility of the marketing department, but is a company-wide task, from CEO to the student intern.

One useful approach to reach this is to think of employees, especially those "touching the customer", as customers. Imagine what a customer would like to know, and you get an idea of what your employees *at least* must know. The more employees are informed and made to feel a part of the company's effort to build customer relationships, the more they will satisfy customers. Companies can increase morale and productivity by keeping employees informed so they are not embarrassed when asked about certain programmes, for example. Also, giving employees a sneak preview of advertising and promotional materials before they begin running makes them feel that they really are members of "the team". Internal marketing can also enhance employee loyalty. Reducing employee turnover means lower training costs and an overall increase in experience throughout the company. A study of employee loyalty found that it is possible to generate commitment among employees with good communication, opportunities for personal growth, and workplace flexibility.[10] Most important, however, internal marketing can help create internal understanding of, and respect for, the company's core values, which are the essence of its brands.

Like external marketing, internal marketing is dependent on communication, and problems arise when employees are not kept informed. There are three basic aspects of internal marketing communication: informing employees, empowering them, and listening to them.

Informing employees

Customer service, brand building, relationship marketing: whatever approach a company adopts, it has to be made real by the people inside the organization. If those people do not know what the strategy is, how can they help to carry it out? The execution of any strategy begins by informing those who have to execute it; and since the IMC approach makes clear that everything and everyone communicates, everyone in the company has to be informed.

Just as a company uses many different MC functions and media to communicate with customers, so it should also use a variety of messages and channels of communication to reach employees. Like customers, employees have their preferred methods of receiving information. For this reason, good internal marketing makes use of company intranets, newsletters, e-mail, voice mail, bulletin boards, and face-to-face meetings with employees. An intranet is a *computer network that is accessible only to employees and contains proprietary information.* Intranets facilitate communication (e-mail, messaging), collaboration (shared databases, conferencing), and the co-ordination of work flow (work-flow applications integrate messaging and databases). Extranets are another valuable "internal" communication channel as they help keep outside MC agencies informed. An extranet is a *limited-access website that links suppliers, distributors, and MC agencies to the company.*

Empowering employees

Because internal marketing provides employees with information, it enhances employee empowerment, which means *giving employees the resources to make decisions about problems that affect customer relationships.* As companies downsize and shift responsibility to lower levels, service employees on the front line of customer contact are making more decisions that affect customer relations. Generally, the more information these employees have, the better the decisions they will make.

Empowerment programmes must be supported by training and information about company policies—a communication challenge. Automaker Nissan requires all dealer employees (including clerks and receptionists) for its flagship models to attend six-day training programmes designed to teach employees how to recognize and address legitimate customer problems. A support programme with the objective of creating empowered and responsive employees has these goals:

- To inform employees about their role in satisfying customers.
- To inform employees about their role in the company's success.
- To reward employees on the basis of their individual performance and the company's overall performance.
- To listen to employees when they have ideas about how to better serve customers—even when the ideas involve other areas of operations.
- To give employees easy access to customer information files and other databases that enable them to make quick and knowledgeable responses.

Listening to employees

Like external marketing, internal marketing depends on two-way communication. If an internal marketing programme only sends messages, employees will see it as propaganda. If company messages are going to have integrity, internal marketing must encourage and facilitate employee feedback, which will let managers know whether employees understand and agree with the internal marketing messages and are willing to support the various MC programmes.

Even more important, listening to employees can provide valuable real-time customer research that helps in budgeting, planning, and adjusting MC plans. A justified criticism of some MC plans is that they are made in corporate office "ivory towers". Such plans fail to address the real problems and opportunities in the marketplace. Customer-contact employees can be a valuable source of competitive and product performance information.

Customer-contact employees vary from industry to industry. In some industries, such as office machines and automobiles, service personnel are the employees most likely to have ongoing contact with customers. The people who deliver grocery products—soft drinks, snacks, processed meats, dairy products—directly to the stores are important contact points. They are often responsible for shelving the products or setting up merchandising materials, so they are constantly in the stores mingling with actual customers. These delivery people are often the first employees to be aware of product or marketing communication problems or other customer concerns. Internal marketing that facilitates employee input about customers' needs can improve MC planning (also see IMC in Action "Using employee input in MC planning" in Chapter 5).

One example of internal communication gone wrong comes from Wild Oats, a chain of natural foods stores known for social responsibility and sensitivity to employees. Customers, employees, and the media were amazed when they one day learned that the Wild Oats CEO had ordered managers to search employees' bags twice a day as part of an anti-theft policy. Several managers resigned in protest, and negative stories appeared in the local media. In response, the CEO wrote a letter to the local newspaper admitting that the store's "infamous loss-control memo was not well thought out, impossible to enforce, and, in retrospect, just plain Dilbertesque". (The latter is a reference to the well-known comic strip "Dilbert", which lampoons poor management practices.) The CEO concluded that the ruckus had caused the company to conduct "a comprehensive internal review of how we communicate to our staff members and the need to think more completely about the consequences of our actions".[11] This company learned the hard way that everything it does and says, including in-house staff policies, sends a brand message to all its stakeholders—and to customers in particular.

Who are the IMC partners?

Integrated marketing communication not only requires internal co-ordination of marketing efforts, but external partners also need to be brought into line. Co-ordination with the partners that are involved in the marketing communication function is crucial. In fact, it is often those specialists that are hired to help a company define and execute its brand communications that play a crucial role in developing an IMC strategy. Who are those IMC partners?

In accordance with one of the basic principles of economics and business as defined by Adam Smith—that specialization pays off—the communication function has witnessed a high level of functional specialization. Many players can be seen in the marketing communications arena, but basically they can be grouped in three types: (1) MC agencies, (2) the media, and (3) the companies and brands behind the marketing communication, which include non-profit organizations, government bodies, and all other entities that have something to sell. Companies can exist only if enough people are persuaded to buy their products and services or, in the case of non-profit organizations, to donate time or money.

In order to tell customers about their products, services, and causes, most companies hire marketing communication (MC) agencies to create and place brand messages in the media (the exceptions are businesses, mostly quite small, that do everything in-house). The more a company spends on marketing communication, the more likely it is to use one or more MC agencies.

The lion's share of the revenue earned by most media comes from advertising and the media could not exist without it. But the media can sell advertising only if they have significant numbers of readers, listeners, or viewers—the more they have, the more they can charge.

Clearly, companies, agencies, and media are interdependent, coexisting in what is sometimes called marketing's *golden triangle* (see Figure 1-2). The triangle of partners in IMC is shown surrounding customers and other company stakeholders (all those who can affect or be affected by a company or brand) to illustrate the customer-centric nature of IMC.

Companies are the leading party in this game. After all, they provide the euros for all activities of the agencies and the media. In the marketing communication context, this role is nevertheless restricted to deciding on the branding strategy. The branding strategy is the input for the agency to work on, and all too often agencies are instrumental in defining the brand strategy as well. Branding is discussed in Chapter 2. The media are the vehicles that the agencies use for disseminating the messages that evolve from the branding strategy and the efforts to translate this in communicable messages. The role of media is covered in Chapters 8 and 9. The remainder of the book essentially deals with the work of the agencies. What will be discussed below is what kinds of agencies exist, and how they work.

How do agencies work?

There are many types of MC agencies. The most common types of agencies are those that specialize in mass media advertising, public relations, direct marketing, sales promotion, and packaging/corporate identity. Most MC agencies have between 20 and 40 clients (also called *accounts*). To avoid conflicts of interest, most agencies handle only one company in a particular product category.

Many large corporations not only work with a variety of MC agencies but also, when the budget is extremely large, use two or more agencies within a speciality area such as advertising. In these cases the competing agencies handle different brands, product lines, or geographical regions.[12]

Although every agency has its own unique organization, job titles, and departments, there are commonalities among agencies. Some provide a full range of services to clients; others specialize in certain types of work. The single largest number and type of MC agencies, especially in terms of MC euros handled, are advertising agencies.

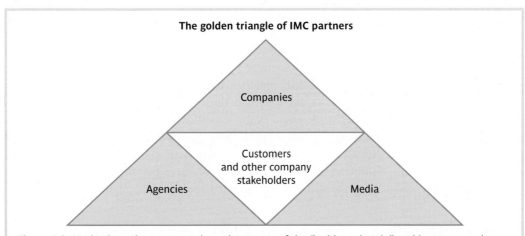

The golden triangle of IMC partners

Companies

Customers and other company stakeholders

Agencies

Media

Figure 1-2 Notice how the customer is at the centre of the "golden triangle" and how companies, agencies, and media are all connected to each other.

Full-service advertising agencies

A **full-service agency** is *one that provides all or most of the services needed in its area of MC specialization.* In advertising, a full-service agency provides research services, creative development of brand messages, media planning and buying, and account management (which involves strategic planning). The term *full-service* does not mean that an agency provides expertise in all the MC functional areas. Also, full-service agencies do not actually make final print and broadcast ads. Instead, they create rough drawings, layouts, and story boards (for TV commercials), and they write scripts and ad copy. They then oversee the production of the ads and commercials by specialists outside the agency.

Creative boutiques and freelancers

A **creative boutique** is *an agency of creative specialists, usually writers and designers, who work for clients and other agencies.* These organizations are similar to the creative departments in full-service agencies. Creative boutiques usually work on a project basis, turning over finished work to another agency for media placement and buying. Boutiques are often started by creative people, such as a copywriter/art director team, who worked for a full-service agency, did very well, and decided to be their own bosses. To demonstrate how creative they are, agencies promote themselves with brand messages.

Freelancers are *independent creative people who are self-employed and take on assignments from an agency or a marketer on a project-by-project basis.* Freelancers can be considered one-person boutiques; they specialize in copywriting, art direction, photography, or artwork. They usually work for small clients who cannot afford an outside agency, or they do work that a client's ad agency would charge too much for doing. They also take assignments from large agencies when these agencies need extra help or when no one at an agency knows how to (or is willing to) do such things as creating a brochure, a menu, or a product directory.

Media buying services

As the name implies, **media buying services** are *agencies that specialize in buying time and space—that is, placing brand messages in the media.* Media buying services developed as small and medium-sized companies when advertising agencies realized they were paying a higher price for media because they were buying in relatively small quantities. By buying for many different clients, media buying services can have the same buying clout as the large full-service agencies. Media buying agencies generally receive a commission of 2 to 4 per cent of the media euros they manage. (The idea of media placement is also important in public relations; some companies specialize in distributing publicity materials to the media.)

Among the fastest-growing media agencies are those that handle product placements. **Product placements** are *paid verbal or visual brand exposures in entertainment programming.* Rather than buying time and space for their clients, these agencies negotiate with producers of movies, TV shows, and other entertainment events to have their clients' brands appear or be mentioned in these entertainment products. The price of these placements depends on the extent of a brand's presence and the size of the anticipated audience.

In-house agencies

Some companies feel they can save money and have more control over their marketing communication by doing much of the work themselves. To do this, they set up an **in-house ad** agency, *a department within a company that is responsible for producing some or all of that company's marketing communications.* In-house agencies are commonly used in retail advertising and are found in the headquarters of grocery and drugstore chains that must create new ads every week. The retail in-house agency must work closely with the chain's buyers and store managers to provide promotions within tight deadlines. It also must be aware of quantities of products that have been purchased to ensure that, when customers respond to promotional offers, the stores have enough product on hand to satisfy demand.

Upscale marketers, such as Calvin Klein or Ralph Lauren, handle their own marketing communication in-house because they believe they can best control the creative effort and bind it closely to their brand image. Marketers use in-house agencies to control both costs and the creative product, eliminate the expensive overhead of external agencies, and take advantage of commissions offered by the media. Also, companies that do not have a large enough budget to attract the interest of outside marketing communication agencies do their own marketing communications, working with freelance copywriters, artists, and publicists. Depending on the type of business, an in-house agency may also do brand publicity, sales promotion, and direct marketing as well as advertising.

Although economies can be made by having an in-house agency, there are also drawbacks. First, in-house control is often won at the expense of creativity. Because in-house agency people work on only one account—their company—they do not have the benefit of interacting with, and learning from, people working in other types of businesses. Second, working for an in-house agency instead of for an independent one is often a second choice for creative professionals, particularly in advertising, so the talent pool lacks depth. Third, because an in-house agency is buying only its own media space and time, it has less bargaining power than an advertising agency that is buying media for dozens of companies and, therefore, its media costs are likely to be higher.

Other MC agencies and suppliers

Much of the previous discussion focused on advertising agencies; however, there are also agencies that specialize in other areas of marketing communication. It is no exaggeration to say that specialized agents exist for every MC tool. Even within these areas agencies can be found that specialize in certain niches.

Agencies and IMC

Not until the 1980s did agencies begin to talk about integration and recognize that their clients needed a way to better manage and co-ordinate their marketing communications. The agencies, however, had no idea how to satisfy this need. Some of the large ones did offer services such as "Whole Egg" (Young & Rubicam) and "Orchestration" (Ogilvy & Mather), but these were primarily efforts to obtain a larger portion of their clients' MC assignments rather than to provide a practical process for integrating brand messages and building brands. The services soon faded away.

Those early IMC approaches focused on "one-voice, one-look" advertising and failed to take into consideration the fact that everything a company does has the potential to send a powerful brand message. Only in recent years have advertising agencies made progress in offering IMC services. They are still experimenting, however, to find the best way to accomplish this for their clients. Interestingly, when a sample of agency and client executives was asked, "Who directs the integration effort?", 74 per cent of the agency respondents said agencies do, while 94 per cent of the client respondents said clients do.[13] The reality, confirmed in other research studies, is that integration is driven by clients. Because clients pay the bills, they call the shots.

How agencies respond to integration

TBWA is a worldwide-operating communications agency. It is also a conglomerate of a number of different larger and smaller agencies. TBWA clearly illustrates both the strengths and limitations of integration. Let us look at how the Dutch branch of TBWA is organized.

In the Netherlands TBWA consists of five individual agencies, each with their own profile and speciality: advertising, design, brand experience, PR and new media. These agencies have their own shareholders, and did not organically originate from the womb of TBWA, but instead joined the group from outside at different times. This suggests that integration is not an issue at TBWA but this is just a small part of the truth. The five agencies are located under one roof (literally) and share their ideas from the earliest stages of contact with the account. Often an account is developed taking in contributions from the various agencies. As Simon Neefjes, CEO of TBWA\Neboko, the biggest and most successful of the five agencies, explains: "When we had the idea of the Heineken megaphone hat, we sat together in the common room and started to brainstorm on ideas how to use this central, big idea. One of the ideas was to send the hats to opinion leaders, and this ended up as an item in the nationwide eight o'clock news show with anchorman Philip Freriks." Further, Neefjes argues that the structure of five largely independent agencies offers flexibility to adapt to changes in the environment. When more attention is required for specific expertise, TBWA can react by reallocating its resources to the most appropriate agency.

In other countries TBWA has similar structures, with small concessions to local circumstances. Hence on a national level, synergies are created, but internationally, integration of activities is modest. Nevertheless, all national agencies have adopted a technique which is developed at TBWA headquarters, called disruption. In this way, there is a common core in the way TBWA-related companies work. TBWA thus shows both the possibilities and the limitations of working in an integrated way.

Think about it

What benefits does TBWA's approach offer clients? How important is international integration in the European context of many relatively small countries with different backgrounds and cultures?

Source:
www.TBWA.nl

A final note: IMC cuts through message clutter

Marketplace confusion arises from the proliferation of brands and products. Forty years ago, the average grocery store carried about 8000 items, counting all the brands and their different sizes and flavours. Today that number is closer to 30 000. Such proliferation is not limited to items available in food, drug, and mass merchandising stores. The number of services has also grown. When you look in the Yellow Pages, you find dozens of competing companies in most service categories. Consumers suffer from brand-choice overload.

They also suffer from brand-communication overload. The average person watches TV four hours a day, has a choice of over 50 channels, and is exposed to 42 000 TV commercials every year, even with zipping and zapping (see colour insert A4). Factor in commercials on rented videotapes, radio commercials, ads in newspapers and magazines, ads on packages, billboards, direct-mail offers, telemarketing calls, and commercial e-mails, and you have an avalanche of brand messages.

By co-ordinating marketing communications and fine-tuning message strategies, IMC makes brand messages more relevant, more effective, more sensitive, and less wasteful of media and personal time. An example is the trend in radio commercials that typically try to attract attention by focusing on one key benefit and refer the listener to a website for further information. In this way two objectives are reached. Through self-selection only those potential customers with an above-average interest in the brand are going to receive the most extensive information about the product, with the result that it makes sense to be more explicit about the brand, and more detailed than a radio commercial could ever be. And this means that communication becomes significantly less wasteful and more cost-effective.

🔑 Key terms

advertising Non-personal, paid announcements by an identified sponsor.

brand A perception resulting from experiences with, and information about, a company or a line of products.

brand equity The intangible value of a brand.

brand messages All the information and experiences that impact how customers and other stakeholders perceive a brand.

creative boutique An agency of creative specialists, usually writers and designers, who work for clients and other agencies.

customer service A company's attitude and behaviour during interactions with customers.

direct marketing An interactive, database-driven MC process that uses a range of media to motivate a response from customers and prospects.

employee empowerment Giving employees the resources to make decisions about problems that affect customer relationships.

events Highly targeted brand-associated activities designed to actively engage customers and prospects and generate publicity.

extranet A limited-access website that links suppliers, distributors, and MC agencies to the company.

freelancers Independent creative people who are self-employed and take on assignments from an agency or a marketer on a project-by-project basis.

full-service agency An agency that provides all or most of the services needed in its area of MC specialization.

in-house ad agency A department within a company that is responsible for producing some or all of that company's marketing communications.

integrated marketing communication (IMC) A concept that directs the processes for planning, executing, and monitoring the brand messages that create brand–customer relationships.

integration The combining of separate parts into a unified whole.

internal marketing An ongoing effort to involve employees in the planning process and then communicate the finalized plan back to them to get their buy-in and support.

intranet A computer network that is accessible only to employees and contains proprietary information.

marketing communication (MC) A collective term for all the various types of planned messages used to build a brand.

marketing communication mix The selection of MC functions used at a given time as part of a marketing programme.

media Vehicles through which marketing communication messages are carried to (and from) target audiences.

media buying services Agencies that specialize in buying time and space for placing brand messages in the media.

package A container and conveyor of information.

personal selling Interpersonal communication in which a salesperson uncovers and satisfies the needs of a customer to the mutual benefit of both.

product placements Paid verbal or visual brand exposures in entertainment programming.

publicity Stories and brand mentions delivered by the mass media without charge.

public relations Efforts to generate and control publicity.

sales promotion A short-term, added-value offer designed to motivate an immediate response.

sponsorship Financial support of an organization, person, or activity in exchange for brand publicity and association.

synergy The interaction of individual parts in a way that makes the integrated whole greater than the sum of its parts.

Check the key points

Key point 1: MC and MC functions

a   What is the core objective of Marketing Communication?
b   What is advertising, and what is its primary use?
c   What does sales promotion do?
d   What is direct marketing, and how is it used?
e   What is the difference between publicity and public relations?
f   What is the primary advantage of personal selling?
g   Why is packaging considered a marketing communication tool?
h   What benefits are derived from using events and sponsorships?
i   Why is customer service included in the list of functional areas of marketing communication?
j   What is a marketing communication mix?

Key point 2: Key elements in the IMC definition

a   How is IMC defined? What are the key elements in the definition?

b   Explain the difference between a stakeholder and a customer.

c   Why do marketers care about building relationships with their customers?

d   What does synergy mean? How does synergy relate to marketing communication?

e   What is the scope of integration, with respect to the IMC concept? In other words, what is integrated in a true IMC approach?

Key point 3: IMC and internal marketing

a   What is the key idea of internal marketing?

b   What are the three key aspects of internal marketing?

c   Why is empowering employees important?

Key point 4: IMC partners

a   What is the golden triangle of IMC partners? Who is/are in the centre of this triangle?

b   Explain why there are so many different kinds of agencies. What is your opinion on in-house agencies in the light of this argument?

c   How does IMC cut through message clutter? Choose a major brand, and develop a list of the marketing communication tools it uses in its marketing communication mix. Is the brand using a one-voice, one-look strategy?

Chapter Challenge

Writing assignment

Identify a product that you think needs to work on its brand image. Look at how each element of the marketing communication mix is delivering a message, and recommend how the effectiveness of the communication could be improved.

Presentation assignment: ABN AMRO

Develop a short survey to investigate the effectiveness of ABN AMRO's participation in the Volvo Ocean Race. Interview 10 people of different ages and occupations and both genders. Ask whether they have been aware of the event, what settings they remember, and whether they like or dislike the sponsorship and why. Finally, determine whether they understand the essence of the campaign. Prepare for class a presentation that summarizes your findings.

Internet assignment

Go to the websites of Bertelmans-online (www.bol.com) and Amazon.com (www.amazon.com), and compare their operations. Pretend you are going to buy a book, and analyse the differences in the way the two companies handle your transaction and attempt to create a relationship with you.

Notes

[1] Mercedes Cardona, "Big Guns Predict Smaller Ad Role", *Advertising Age*, 1 July 2002, pp. 1, 19.

[2] Bradley Johnson, "Moving Sideways", *Advertising Age*, 6 May 2002, p. 4.

[3] Source: www.thebodyshopinternational.com

[4] Thomas Harris, "Viagra Keeps It Up", *MRP Update*, May 1999, p. 2.

[5] Barton Weitz et al., *Selling* (Burr Ridge, Il: Irwin, 1995), p. 6.

[6] Laurie Freeman, "The House That Ivory Built", *Advertising Age*, 20 August 1987, pp. 1–14, 162–200.

[7] "CNN", *The Future of Brands: Twenty-five Visions*, ed. Rita Clifton and Esther Maughan (New York: New York University Press and Intergrand, 2000), p. 53.

[8] Ronald Henkoff, "Service Is Everybody's Business", *Fortune*, 27 June 1994, p. 52.

[9] Kathy Boccella, "Study: Grocery Employees Steal More Than Customers Do", *Denver Post*, 27 March 1994, p. 7I.

[10] "Employees Can Create Loyalty", *Tampa Tribune*, 7 May 1999, p. 5.

[11] Mike Gilliland, "CEO Admits Mistake, Changes Store Policy", *Boulder Daily Camera*, 14 March 2000, p. 6A.

[12] Tobi Elkin, "Branding Big Blue", *Advertising Age*, 20 February 2000, pp. 42, 44.

[13] Claire Atkinson, "Integration Still a Pipe Dream for Many", *Advertising Age*, 10 March 2003, p. 1.

Further reading

Gould, Stephen J. (2004) "IMC as Theory and as a Poststructural Set of Practices and Discourses: A Continuously Evolving Paradigm Shift", *Journal of Advertising Research*, Vol. 44–1, pp. 66–70.

Holm, Olof (2006) "Integrated marketing communication: from tactics to strategy", *Corporate Communications: An International Journal*, Vol. 11–1, pp. 23–33.

Hong, Jae W. and George M. Zinkhan (1995) "Self-concept and advertising effectiveness: The influence of congruency, conspicuousness and response mode", *Psychology and Marketing*, Vol. 12–1, pp. 53–77.

Kapferer, Jean-Noël (1994) *Strategic Brand Management*, New York: The Free Press.

Kitchen, Philip J., Don E. Schultz, Ilchul Kim, Dongsub Han and Tao Li (2004) "Will agencies ever 'get' (or understand) IMC?", *European Journal of Marketing*, Vol. 38–11/12, pp. 1417–36.

Kliatchko, Jerry (2005) "Towards a new definition of Integrated Marketing Communications (IMC)", *International Journal of Advertising*, Vol. 24–1, pp. 7–34.

Kotler, Philip and Kevin L. Keller (2006) *Marketing Management*, Upper Saddle River: Prentice Hall.

Papasolomou, Loanna and Demetris Vrontis (2006) "Building Corporate Branding through internal marketing: the case of UK retail bank industry", *Journal of Product & Brand Management*, Vol. 15–1, pp. 37–47.

Peltier, James, John A. Schibrowsky, Don E. Schultz and Debra Zahay (2006) "Interactive Integrated Marketing Communication: Combining the power of IMC, the new media, and database marketing", *International Journal of Advertising*, Vol. 22–1, pp. 93–115.

PART 2

Part contents

Brands and brand relationships

After reading this chapter, you should:

- ☑ Understand the main branding concepts, in particular brand equity.
- ☑ Understand how brands are strategically managed.
- ☑ Know how brands are operationally built.
- ☑ Appreciate why a brand can be seen as a relationship.
- ☑ Know how a strong brand can be leveraged.

CHAPTER PERSPECTIVE
Companies make products, but they sell brands

In many companies, the main marketing priority is to create customers. As management consultant Peter Drucker explained many decades ago, when this effort succeeds, the company is rewarded by making sales. According to Drucker, building **customer relationships**—*a series of interactions between customers and a company over time*—will produce more sales and profits than will focusing on sales transactions alone. This is why more companies are placing greater emphasis on retaining customers.

Branding consultant and professor at Berkeley, California, David Aaker has emphasized that it is rather the brand to which customers relate. Brands are a company's marketing instruments for building relationships. Brand relationships benefit both the customer and the company. Brand loyalty is the ultimate reward to the company, ideal customer behaviour that is the result of combined marketing efforts, among which IMC is one of the most important.

IMC seeks to maximize the positive messages and minimize the negative ones that are communicated about a brand, with the objective of creating and sustaining brand relationships, but that is only one reason why companies practise IMC. When used to build long-term relationships, IMC also builds and strengthens the brand itself. The stronger a brand is, the more value it has. Positive brand relationships generate profits.

This chapter explains what a brand is, describes how brands and brand relationships are created, and looks at how the strength of a brand can in the end be leveraged.

Philips turns into a market-driven organization
History

The foundations of what was to become one of the world's biggest electronics companies were laid in Eindhoven, in the Netherlands, in 1891.

Philips began by making carbon-filament lamps and by the turn of the century, was one of the largest producers in Europe. In 1918 it introduced a medical X-ray tube. This marked the beginning of the diversification of its product range and the moment when it began to protect its innovations with patents in areas stretching from X-ray radiation to radio reception. Innovation was the key driving factor for Philips, and has remained so. Table 1 gives an overview of some of the milestones in Philips' history, including the major innovations that have emerged from Philips Laboratories.

1925	Experimentation with television
1927	Production of radios
1933	Production of X-ray equipment in US
1939	Introduction of electric shaver
1963	Introduction of compact audio cassettes
1965	Start production of integrated circuits
1969	Optical disc
1983	Compact disc
1997	Introduction of DVD

Table 1 Milestone events in Philips' history

Despite its impressive technological achievements the Philips company has been a relatively modest commercial success. By the beginning of the 1990s the Philips management had come to realize that, while technology may be a sound basis for a healthy company, it must be supported by skilful marketing. The company had to transform from a technology-driven company to a market-driven one. The first modest step in this process was witnessed in 1990 when Philips launched its first single global theme line.

The efforts to transform Philips into a truly market-driven, customer-centric organization have resulted in considerable activity across a broad front. The drive to build a strong brand reached a major milestone in September 2004 with the launch of a new brand positioning, encapsulated in the brand promise "Sense and Simplicity". The advertising campaign that launched it illustrates the transformation into a healthcare, lifestyle and technology company. The campaign represents a significant marketing investment that is intended to drive preference for Philips over time. Philips was becoming a brand. But how was this brand developed?

The need for brand positioning

The Philips brand, which consumers and customers have known for over a century, had the potential to be a key driver of growth and a powerful competitive tool. However, Philips had not yet succeeded in giving the brand a relevant and distinctive character, while the most powerful global brands, by contrast, are based on the ownership of a territory—a space in consumer and customer minds that makes the brand different and preferred over the competition.

Having a brand position is important, therefore, because it will give customers and consumers a specific reason for buying Philips products rather than those of its competitors, and it will also give the organization a clear and visible point of reference for its activities. Accordingly, in order to give the Philips brand a relevant and distinctive meaning and make it a key driver for growth and a powerful competitive tool, a brand positioning was developed as the centrepiece of Philips' commercial activities, and as a filter for strategic decisions.

Strategy development—defining the brand positioning

To define a brand positioning for Philips, the company sought to combine two fundamental insights. First it asked: what is the true DNA of Philips? In other words, who are we, what makes us the way we are, what makes us different from other companies. The second insight resulted from extensive market research among customers and consumers, with the main question: what do you expect from a technology company in general, and Philips in particular? The result of this eight-month process was Philips' first-ever brand positioning which is structured in such a way that it can be used as a decision-making tool for marketing strategy and, more importantly, one that appeals to the heads and hearts of consumers.

The underpinning of this brand positioning consists of three essential pillars that should be used together in everything that is done. The first pillar requires that any activity must be guided by insights of how consumers experience the benefit of technology. One of the consequences is, for example, that aesthetic and functional designs must be based on satisfying end-user needs. The second pillar is that products and services must be convenient and easy to experience in order to remove the hassles often associated with technology. A very concrete example is that with every product the question is asked: is a manual essential to be able to use the product? The third pillar demands that products and services must continue to deliver the benefits associated with advanced innovation. Something is truly advanced when it improves the lives of people. A key question to prove this point is: is the product adaptable, future-proof, and interoperable?

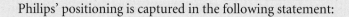

Philips' positioning is captured in the following statement:

> Technology is there to help us, make our lives easier and more productive. So why is it so often such a hassle, full of complexity and frustration?
>
> We are convinced that no matter how complex and advanced a product or solution is, you should be comfortable using it. It is this very simplicity that transforms a task into an opportunity, a burden into a pleasure.
>
> Which is why Philips is committed to delivering products and solutions that are easy to experience, advanced, and designed around you. We keep it simple for you, no matter how advanced the technology.

Within the company, brand positioning is seen as a key driver of necessary change, helping Philips in the transformation to One Philips and becoming a more market-driven company. For external purposes the brand positioning is stripped down to its essence: "Sense and Simplicity".

> Positioning has ultimately to be used as a filter to all the Company's activities. Final objective should be to embed Positioning in the way of working of all our employees.
>
> *Gerard Kleisterlee, CEO Philips in 2004*

Philips' brand positioning as filter for all company activities

Philips uses the new brand positioning in three ways: internal marketing, marketing communications and strategic decisions.

Internal marketing

Brand positioning is about standing out from the crowd in today's increasingly competitive global marketplace—and Philips' brand positioning will allow the company to do just that. But it is then crucial that all employees around the world make it happen.

As Gerard Kleisterlee, CEO, phrased it at the internal introduction of the brand positioning:

> Creating a powerful brand comes down to you and me, each individually. Each of us, every day, asking ourselves a few very simple questions:
>
> – Are we focused on the customer?
> – Are we easy to deal with?
> – Do we use advanced processes and technology?
>
> If we constantly ask ourselves these three questions, if we challenge ourselves to deliver on the promise of the Brand Positioning, then each of us will make a valuable contribution to make the Philips brand one of the most powerful brands in the world.

Marketing communications

An intrinsic part of the development of the brand campaign was to develop a brand promise that clearly and concisely captured the essence of the three pillars. While a number of alternatives were researched, "Sense and Simplicity" was found to be the ideal expression of the brand positioning.

The inspiration for "sense" is found in the "Designed Around You" pillar. All activities should be driven by insights into how stakeholders experience the benefits of technology.

Understanding consumers and customers is the key to manufacturing products, services, and solutions that make sense. The feeling of consumers that products make sense is considered to be a condition to deliver on the promise of simplicity. In addition to being the over-arching theme of all three pillars, the word *simplicity* naturally communicates "easy to experience".

Brand architecture

To support the brand positioning a new brand architecture and naming structure was implemented that has the three pillars as a starting point. The key objective was to make sure that the way the Philips brand name was used "makes sense". For example, this means that the first question for a new product or solution is: does the offer fit the Philips brand positioning? If this is not the case, the product will not be branded Philips.

Other proof points

Apart from these strategic areas, the promise of simplicity is also carried through in literally every aspect of the company's operations. For instance, Consumer Electronics has simplified its user interfaces and manuals and Lighting is standardizing its more than 40 different remote controls. Internet and intranet sites are updated and simplified—a major undertaking. There is the 10-slide presentation policy in Sales & Marketing. This could save a billion slides a year within Philips, so imagine the savings in time and paper. Not to mention simpler, more effective meetings.

External recognition

Philips' efforts have been recognized externally too. In 2005 Philips jumped 12 positions in the BusinessWeek Top 100 Global Brands list, climbing to number 53. And the estimated value of the brand has increased from US$4.4 billion to US$5.9 billion. This improvement is explicitly attributed to the introduction of brand positioning. For Philips, simplicity really makes sense!

Source:
This case has been written in collaboration with Louise Verheij van Wijk, at the time of writing Director Global Branding at Philips

What "brand" means

When tobacco giant Philip Morris acquired Kraft Foods several years ago, it paid six times the value of Kraft's physical net assets. The Philip Morris CEO said his company needed a portfolio of brands with strong customer relationships that could be leveraged to enable the tobacco company to diversify itself, especially in the retail food industry.[1] Philip Morris was willing to pay billions of dollars for a set of customer and trade brand relationships. Likewise, the former CEO of automaker Chrysler once explained that the future success of his company was not determined by its past sales and profits but rather by Chrysler's brand relationships with its dealers and customers.

So brands are important, but what is a brand? In Chapter 1, a *brand* is defined as "a perception resulting from experiences with, and information about, a company or a line of products". According to Interbrand, one of the top brand consulting firms in the world, a brand is "a mixture of tangible and intangible attributes, symbolized in a trademark, which, if properly managed, creates influence and generates value".[2]

Why does one brand have twice the share of another when there is no difference in product attributes or performance and both brands sell for the same price? The answer is—a difference in perceptions. A brand is basically more of a perception than a logo on the side of a package. A brand exists predominantly in people's heads. In the marketplace, perceptions are the collective result of everything a customer or other stakeholder sees, hears, reads, or experiences about a company and its brands. A perception can be influenced through positive (and negative) communication experiences, but not controlled. According to a creative director for Chrysler's in-house MC agency, the auto industry has a lot of *parity products* (products with few distinguishing features). In such a situation, perceptions become very important: "Practically the only difference that's left is the perception of what the car feels like and how it's gonna make you feel when you drive it."[3]

Brand managers try to achieve a certain differentiation. The way they want to make this differentiation is determined by the brand identity to which they aspire. The brand "identity" is very much like any other identity. A **brand identity** is *what the brand stands for, how it is described in most fundamental terms, to which all other characteristics and actions can be traced back.* Brand identity resides with the company, but the brand image resides in the heads and hearts of the customers. **Brand image** is most easily described as *the customer's perception of brand identity.* One measure of successful brand management is the degree to which brand identity and brand image overlap. Philips long used the slogan "Let's make things better" to express their commitment to helping improve people's lives by making them easier, using Philips products. But when customers started to interpret the slogan to mean that Philips had to make better things, there was a big discrepancy between Philips' identity and its image. Keep in mind that both companies and products have identities and images that differentiate them from competitors, so in this book the word *brand* is used in discussions of both products and companies. Furthermore, you should remember that brands are just as important in business-to-business marketing and not-for-profit marketing as they are in marketing consumer products.

A brand differentiates a product from its competitors and makes a promise to its customers. On the customers' side, brands function as a short-cut in decision making. A brand conveys a lot of meaningful information that helps a customer to choose a product from the shelves. For the firm, brands function as organizing devices—not only in administrative matters but, more important, the brands are the entities that can be loaded with meaning. Everything the firm wants to communicate about its products is done in terms of brands. In this way, brands function as the unique interface between company and customers.

A brand is thus more than just a product. Cars, bank accounts, chocolate bars, shoe repair, computers, and medical care are all products. What differentiates one car or one bank account from another, however, is the brand. Take football clubs. In their most basic form they all offer the same product—football. They all have eleven players on the field that try to score, and prevent the opponent from scoring. Yet, despite these commonalities, there are major differences among them. These differences are determined by the quality of the players and coaches, the policies of the presidents, the heritage of the clubs, the stadiums and cities in which they are located, among other things.

Branding, *the process of creating a brand image that engages the hearts and minds of customers*, is what separates similar products from each other. What comes to mind when you think of each of the following: Manchester United, Inter Milan, Barcelona and PSV Eindhoven? You probably don't think about their football alone. Rather, you also think about things such as biggest club in the world (Manchester United), unattractive *catenaccio* (Inter Milan), Catalunya (Barcelona), small but sympathetic (PSV).

Customers and prospects are influenced by a wide variety of messages that are sent by both the tangible and the intangible attributes of a brand. *Tangible* attributes are characteristics you can observe or touch, such as a product's design, performance, ingredients/components, size, shape, and price (see Table 2-1). Although brand mangers may influence the messages sent by these tangible attributes, their primary responsibility is to influence a brand's *intangible* attributes, such as its perceived value, its image, the memories associated with the brand, and even the perceptions and impressions of those who use the brand. Intangibles are important in brand building for two reasons: they are hard for competitors to copy, and they are more likely to involve consumers emotionally than tangible attributes.

Brands transform products

Although a company may own a brand name and logo, and greatly influence what people think about its brands, the actual brand meaning that influences behaviour resides in the heads and hearts of customers and other stakeholders. If no one were aware of a brand, the brand would have no value because it would have no impact on anyone's buying decision. Of course, you don't know or care about the brands of some of the products you buy—low-risk purchases such as a broom, milk, or matches. But you can be sure that the retailers who decided to buy and resell these items cared very much about the brands they selected for their stores to sell.

A basic principle of branding is that a brand transforms products—goods as well as services—into something larger than the products themselves. Suppose you want to give your father a watch. This watch is more than a timepiece. What you give him is different when you give him a Gucci watch (I care so much about you, I am willing to spend a lot on this item) from when it is a Swatch (hey dad, wear something more fashionable).

How powerful is branding? A brand and what it represents can affect what people are willing to pay for a product. In blind taste tests respondents were asked which of two samples of corn-flakes tasted better. Unbeknown to the respondents, the samples were identical, yet the number of those who chose sample A over sample B increased from 47 to 59 per cent when respondents were told that sample A was Kellogg's (sample B was not given a recognizable brand name). People *perceived* the "brand cereal" as tasting better even though both the cereals were identical. Another study found that, when identical TV sets were sold, customers were willing to pay $75 more for those branded Hitachi than for those branded GE.[4]

Branding has such impact on consumer perception that, rather than relying solely on manu-facturers' (or name) brands, retailers have worked to create their own brands. A **store brand**

Tangible attributes	Intangible attributes
Design	Value
Performance	Brand image
Ingredients/components	Image of stores where sold
Size/shape	Perceptions of users of the brand
Price	
Marketing communication	

Table 2-1 Brand characteristics

(also called a "house brand" or "private label") is *a brand used exclusively by one chain of stores for a line of products made to the chain's specifications.* For many years store brands were generally lower in price and quality than name brands. Eventually, however, chain stores realized that linking their names directly to low-quality merchandise was transforming the overall perception of their stores in the wrong direction. In recent years, the quality of store brands has greatly increased along with positive perceptions of those brands.

Brands make promises and set expectations

In terms of consumer purchases, the essence of a brand is a promise. This promise sets expectations for what a person considers is likely to occur when using a product. French branding expert Jean-Noël Kapferer explains that "a brand is also a contract, albeit a virtual one, between a company and a customer".[5] Knowledge of what a brand stands for and past experiences with the brand allow customers to make a quick and easy decision. That is what a promise means—you know what to expect.

Consistency, a fundamental principle of IMC, is critical to the establishment of a brand promise. Hayes Roth of the brand design and consulting firm Landor Associates, explains that a "clear and compelling brand promise consistently communicated at all points of touch is the principal benefit of branding".[6] Promises mean little, however, if the product fails to meet expectations. Marketing communication has been used for years to make promises in order to generate sales. Unfortunately, too many businesses do more promising than delivering when managing their brand relationships, because they fail to consider that what they are really doing is setting *unrealistic* customer expectations. However, when a promise is strong and the product delivers, the promise becomes a platform for helping to build a long-term relationship with satisfied customers. This is why it is important to create brand messages that make realistic promises—ones the brand can deliver.

Generally, brands fail to meet expectations for one of two reasons. The first is that expectations are raised too high, usually in overzealous advertising. The second is that products or supporting services are defective. Companies must constantly monitor customer expectations and product performance to make sure there is no gap between them—or that there is a *positive* gap and the product surprises customers by delivering more than they expected. When a *negative* gap exists, either the brand promises need to be restrained, or the managers responsible for product performance need to be made aware that their products are not meeting expectations.

Brand equity

Brands live in the heads and hearts of customers, but shareholders are interested in the money in their pockets. Do brands really contribute to the revenue-generating potential of a company? Yes they do. Interbrand, one of the world's leading brand consulting companies, publishes an annual list of the world's most valuable brands: a list of the best-known brands throughout the globe in financial terms (Table 2-2). In compiling this list Interbrand cleverly integrates the anticipated sales data with proprietary information about the strength of the brands.[7] The value the brand represents is often called **brand equity**, which is *the intangible value of a brand beyond the value of its physical assets* (brand equity is sometimes called **goodwill**). Nokia and Mercedes and other companies that have built strong brands over many years have tremendous brand equity.

The source of brand equity is found in the difference a brand makes in the marketplace. The reason Coca-Cola is on top of Interbrand's list is because, when you find yourself facing a large

1 Coca-Cola, US	11 Mercedes, Germany	72 Rolex, Switzerland
2 Microsoft, US	16 BMW, Germany	74 Reuters, UK
3 IBM, US	18 Louis Vuitton, France	75 BP, UK
4 General Electric, US	24 Nescafé, Switzerland	76 Porsche, Germany
5 Intel, US	33 HSBC, UK	77 Zara, Spain
6 Nokia, Finland	36 SAP, Germany	79 Audi, Germany
7 Disney, US	42 IKEA, Sweden	82 Hermès, France
8 McDonald's, US	43 Novartis, Switzerland	86 Hennessy, France
9 Toyota, Japan	44 UBS, Switzerland	87 ING, Netherlands
10 Marlboro US	45 Siemens, Germany	88 Smirnoff, UK
	49 Gucci, Italy	89 Cartier, France
	52 l'Oréal, France	90 Shell, Netherlands
	53 Philips, Netherlands	92 Moët & Chandon, France
	56 Volkswagen, Germany	93 Prada, Italy
	65 Chanel, France	94 Bulgari, Italy
	66 Nestlé, Switzerland	95 Armani, Italy
	67 Danone, France	98 Nivea, Germany
	71 Adidas, Germany	100 Heineken, Netherlands

Table 2-2 Top 10 of the world's most valuable brands and European brands on the 2005 list
Source: Interbrand and BusinessWeek Brand Ranking 2005 (http://www.interbrand.com/best_brands_2005.asp).

It's not a watch, it's a Swatch

By the end of the 1970s the European watch industry had been marginalized by its Japanese competitors. Superior technology and new management practices made the Asian watches both better and cheaper. In particular, the Swiss industry, the traditional watchmakers of Europe, was suffering badly.

Nicholas Hayek, president of the Swiss SMH watch manufacturer group, decided that a counter-initiative was necessary. The answer to the Japanese dominance was the Swatch, a simple, cheap and sporty watch, with plastic as its main material. It was a huge success, perhaps best illustrated by the stock price of SMH, which rose from 100 Swiss Francs in 1983, the year of the introduction of the Swatch, to 1500 Francs ten years later. In 2003 the Swatch Group was the largest watch manufacturer in the world.

Various factors contributed to this success story, but the key factor was the introduction of the product as a brand, rather than just another watch. Upon its introduction Hayek said: "A $5 watch tells time every bit as well as $30000 watch. The Swatch was not selling time so much as fun and costume jewellery." In an interview in the *New York Times* he added: "We were convinced that if each of us could add our fantasy and culture to an emotional product, we could beat anybody. Emotions are something that nobody can copy." Emphasizing the product's design, image and users rather than its technical performance or durability, new kinds of brand associations were introduced in the watch industry. Of course, the basic performance requirements of the watch were sound—it remained a Swiss product after all—but the look was what differentiated a Swatch from a watch.

IMC in Action

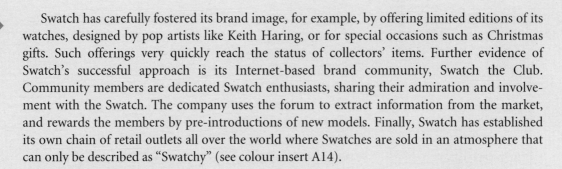

Swatch has carefully fostered its brand image, for example, by offering limited editions of its watches, designed by pop artists like Keith Haring, or for special occasions such as Christmas gifts. Such offerings very quickly reach the status of collectors' items. Further evidence of Swatch's successful approach is its Internet-based brand community, Swatch the Club. Community members are dedicated Swatch enthusiasts, sharing their admiration and involvement with the Swatch. The company uses the forum to extract information from the market, and rewards the members by pre-introductions of new models. Finally, Swatch has established its own chain of retail outlets all over the world where Swatches are sold in an atmosphere that can only be described as "Swatchy" (see colour insert A14).

Think about it

How is Swatch positioned in the watch product market? How do Swatch's name and logo contribute to understanding this position? How can Swatch develop further?

Sources:
Swatch website (www.swatch.com),
Ram Mudambi, Branding Time: Swatch and Global Brand Management, *Fox School of Business and Management (2005)*
Andrew Inkpen and Manish Gulati, Time Marches On: The Worldwide Watch Industry, *Thunderbird, Garvin School of International Management (2004)*

variety of cokes in the supermarket, you buy Coca-Cola because you find it more familiar, better tasting, having a more fancy image, a better reputation, etc. At least, many people behave that way. Kevin Keller, the world's leading branding specialist, calls this **customer-based brand equity**: "customer-based brand equity is *the differential effect that brand knowledge has on consumer response to the marketing of that brand.*"[8] Without customer-based brand equity, there is no financial brand equity of the sort Interbrand reports. And while financial people struggle with ways to monetarize brand equity, this book is about creating customer-based brand equity, the domain of marketers and brand managers; and especially with the role of marketing communications therein.

According to Keller, brand knowledge is the origin of the brand's value. This brand knowledge has two components. On the one hand it relates to the fact *that* you know of the brand, on the other to *what* you know of the brand.

That consumers know of a brand is called **brand awareness**. Brand awareness exists in different degrees. You **recall** a brand when you are able to *bring the brand back from memory without help.* Even recall exists in different degrees. When you can think of only one brand when asked to name brands in a certain product category, this brand is dominant. How many paper tissues brands do you know next to Kleenex? When the answer is none, Kleenex is a dominant brand. **Dominance** seems attractive because it suggests there are no competitors, but brand managers are wary of this kind of superiority. One reason is that dominance more or less implies that consumers perceive the brand to be equivalent to the product category and this makes brand extensions (the use of a brand name in another category) impossible. The most desired position is therefore **top-of-mind awareness** (TOMA). TOMA implies that your brand is mentioned first on a list of all brands when customers are asked for that. For example, 40 per cent TOMA for Nokia means that 40 per cent of the consumers mention Nokia first when asked for a mobile phone brand. When a brand is mentioned, but not first on the list, this is simply called recall. **Recognition** finally is identifying something and remembering that you saw or heard of it earlier. For example, when a brand is only mentioned when asked: "Do you know that Siemens is also making mobile phones?" this is called recognition.

What consumers know of a brand is described by their set of **associations**. Associations in this context has a broad interpretation. It covers both objective knowledge in terms of concrete facts and features, as well as subjective knowledge such as impressions and image. Literally everything a consumer relates (associates) to a brand is part of that consumer's brand knowledge. Indeed, brand knowledge is highly personal, can be biased or even untrue, and will therefore not be the same for every single pair of customers.

The relevance of awareness and associations is illustrated with reference to the consumer decision-making process that is displayed in every introductory marketing textbook[9] and this will be discussed in more detail in Chapter 4. Suppose you want to buy a TV set. According to the standard customer decision-making process, the first thing you do is develop a set of alternatives. Awareness of a given brand is important as this increases the likelihood that that brand is in that set of alternatives. A next step is the evaluation of alternatives, based on the information that is collected. Information collection relies on two sources: the information that is published and available, and the information that is already in the consumer's mind. In other words, all the associations that a consumer already has in connection with the brand. So: how easily does the Philips brand come to your mind when you consider buying a TV set? And what associations do you have regarding Philips?

The **associative network** model is a useful tool for understanding the branding concept. This model depicts (brand) knowledge as a network of nodes that are connected by links. Each node represents a piece of knowledge, and there is a link when the nodes are connected, which means that thinking of one node leads to thinking of the other node. Applied to brands, the associative network displays all associations that come to your mind when you think of that brand. Figure 2-1 shows a simplified associative network for Mercedes.

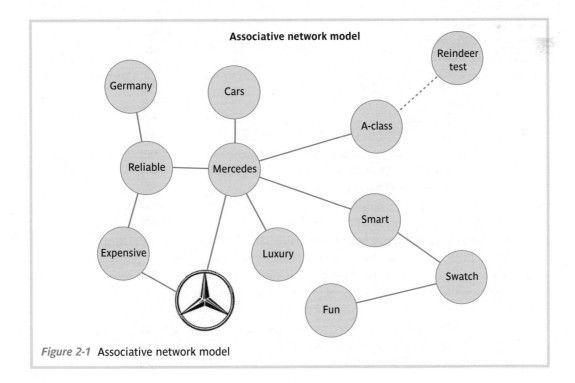

Figure 2-1 Associative network model

Thinking of one node leads to thinking of another, connected node and this is called "activation".[10] The first node activates the second node, and this can be an ongoing process. There always is a first node that is activated and this first node is often referred to as the "cue". So when you are asked to mention brands in product category laundry detergent, the node laundry detergent is the cue, and all brands that are connected to this node are the activated nodes. Sometimes this is also called "retrieving the brands from memory". When you are cued with a brand, associations will become activated.

How many nodes are activated when cued for (academic slang for: how many associations come to your mind when asked to think of a certain brand) depends on two factors: the effort a consumer puts in retrieving all the pieces of information, and the strength of the links. The strength of a link is nothing other than a way of describing how easily a piece of information is retrieved when a connected node is activated. The strength of association is perhaps the single most important concept in branding. First of all, brand managers want a strong connection to the product categories to which their brand belongs. This is in fact the same as the awareness concept discussed above. But they also need positive associations to be easily retrieved when consumers are evaluating alternatives. So they want to establish strong associations. Similarly, they have a huge stake in discouraging unfavourable associations. The clothing brand Lonsdale faced serious difficulties when the brand became associated with neo-Nazis in the Netherlands, to the extent that the brand saw no other solution than to terminate its activities in that country.

How brands are created and maintained

Building a successful brand, whether for a company or for a new product, requires strategic planning and a major investment. With the rise of the mobile telephone market, big telecom players like Deutsche Telecom and France Telecom established new subsidiaries with their own brand names, T-Mobile and Orange respectively, for which they had to spend many euros to create awareness and position the new brand. How is such a branding programme undertaken? Three steps lead to successful brand strategies: (1) selecting the desired brand position, (2) developing the brand's identification, and (3) creating the brand image. This last step is essentially what this book is about, in particular the role of communications in this process. In this section the first two steps of brand creation are briefly discussed.

1 Selecting the desired brand position

A **brand position** is *the standing of a brand in comparison with its competitors in the minds of customers, prospects, and other stakeholders.* The positioning concept was developed by Al Ries and Jack Trout over 20 years ago.[11] According to Ries and Trout, customers who are aware of several brands in a product category automatically compare and rank those brands according to the differences they perceive among them. For example, when people think of cars, they might think of Volvo as the safest, Porsche as the sportiest, and Opel as the most practical.

Although brand positions, like brands themselves, exist in people's heads and hearts, a company's marketing communications can greatly influence how customers perceive a brand in relation to competition. The challenge is to select a position that can be realistically supported by the product, the company, and the marketing communication—and that will be appreciated by customers and prospects.

Consider the athletic shoe category. Rockport has positioned itself as "the leader of the walking fitness movement". Rockport designs shoes for comfort and distributes its products to stores that cater to older customers (who are more interested in walking than competing). Its marketing communications visually and verbally say "comfort" and speak to the older wearer of athletic shoes. In contrast, Nike has positioned itself as the "performance and personal success" shoe, and Adidas has positioned itself as the more down-to-earth yet good-quality athletic shoe.

Because brand position hinges on a brand's meaning, changing a brand's meaning can allow a company to move or enlarge its brand position. Disney, for example, is trying to expand the meaning of "Disney movie", which for many years has meant "classic animated characters that appeal to children". Aspiring to be associated with a broader range of movie types, Disney managers are beginning to release some action-and-adventure films—such as *The Pacifier* (starring Vin Diesel)—as Disney-branded movies instead of marketing them under the company's sister brand, Touchstone Pictures.[12] The question remains how far the meaning of the Disney brand can be stretched.

Positioning strategies

A positioning strategy is generally based on one of several variables: category, image, unique product feature, or benefit. Following is an explanation of positioning strategies along with an example that illustrates how each is used.

Category positioning   This type of positioning is possible whenever a brand defines, creates, or owns a category or subproduct category. Aspirin of Bayer long owned the category of pain relievers. But the connection became so strong that aspirin turned into a product category itself. During the past decade, more pain relievers have entered the market (Advil), so that now Aspirin is a brand name again. Other examples of brands that have, or once had, a category position are Kleenex (tissues), Xerox (copying machines), and Polaroid (instant cameras).

Pre-emptive positioning   This is *brand positioning based on a generic feature that competitors have not talked about.* Pre-emptive positioning is often used by **commodity products**, *goods and services that have very minor or no distinguishing differences.* A good example of what is quickly becoming a commodity is mobile phones. Nokia positions itself as the mobile phones manufacturer that is "connecting people". However, do not all mobile phones connect people? But because Nokia was the first to use this common product feature to differentiate itself, other brands are not able or allowed to use this positioning.

Unique product feature positioning   This type of positioning is based on an element that is unique to the product or company. **Product features** are *tangible and intangible attributes of a good or service,* and they provide a basis for positioning. Price and how it translates into value is a tangible feature that is the basis of Aldi's position as the low-price leader in supermarket retailing. The fact that Aldi has reached this positioning without advertising simply contributes to this positioning: advertising involves costs that the customers would have to meet.

Image positioning   This type of positioning creates differentiation on the basis of a *created association.* It is similar to pre-emptive positioning in that any brand can attempt to create a differentiating image for itself, but, whereas pre-emptive positioning refers by definition to a generic feature—a feature that every competitor could claim because it is inherent in the product category—image positioning is based on deliberately created associations that do not, or do not necessarily, apply to the other players in the market. Often these attempts fail, however, because the image is not realistic, not creatively constructed, or not used long enough to actually build up an association between the brand and the desired image. A very successful example, however, is Marlboro. At one time advertising for Winston cigarettes showed cowboys doing what cowboys do—herding cattle, branding them, and eating beans around a campfire. Nothing really imaginative. The creative people at the Leo Burnett advertising agency in the 1950s, however, decided they could take this attempt at "cowboy" positioning and make it distinctive and inspirational. To do this, they used a solitary cowboy as a symbol of independence, put a tattoo on his arm, and always showed him isolated in dramatic Western settings. As a result, Marlboro became one of the most popular and well-recognized brands in the world.

Benefit positioning   This type of positioning is based on **benefits**, *advantages that allow a product to satisfy customers' needs, wants, or desires.* Axe deodorant for example promises the benefit of being irresistibly attractive to women. Most benefits are experiential, functional or symbolic, any of which can be the basis for brand positioning. Visa credit cards claims that it offers the most places where it is accepted as a method of payment. This claim has both symbolic as well as functional value.

Managing a brand's position

Marketing managers may develop positioning statements, such as Rockport's "Leader in walking fitness", but such statements do not really mean anything if they are not in customers' minds. To determine how customers perceive a brand and its competitors, one thing market researchers do is ask a sample of customers to participate in perceptual mapping. **Perceptual mapping** is *a visualization technique that indicates how customers perceive competing brands on the basis of various criteria.* Figure 2-2 is a hypothetical perceptual map for Nike, Rockport, and L.A. Gear shoes. Maps like this indicate how a sample of customers ranked each brand, from low to high, on selected criteria, which for athletic shoes could be comfort, performance, quality, price, or style. Numerical rankings for each criterion are averaged and plotted. The map enables brand managers to quickly see how their brands compare, in the minds of consumers, with competing brands.

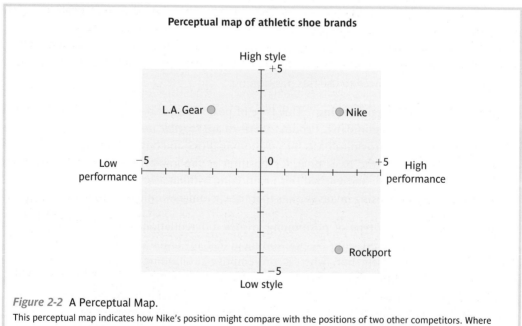

Figure 2-2 A Perceptual Map.
This perceptual map indicates how Nike's position might compare with the positions of two other competitors. Where would you place Adidas on this map?

2 Developing brand identification

The brand name and symbol chosen to represent a brand need to reflect the position of the brand, and they must work as identification cues. Names and brand symbols are what customers look for when shopping, whether in stores, in catalogues, on the Internet, or, in the case of B2B products, at trade shows and exhibits. *Brand names, symbols, logos, slogans and jingles and its packaging* are also referred to as **brand elements**. The more memorable and relevant the brand name and symbol are, the faster and less costly it will be to create awareness of a brand, position it in customers' minds, and develop an image for it. Making it easy to find and repurchase a brand is an important factor in customer retention. Thus, the more specific and less ambiguous brand-identity cues are, the more they help customers save time looking for a product, which adds value to the brand (see colour insert A3).

A brand position is the result of an assessment of the associations related to the brand node in the customer's mind. This brand node is mainly identified by the brand's name and supported by other brand elements of which logos and symbols are the most important. Other brand elements can also be distinctive in identifying brands.[13] The packaging of Pringles chips helps you identify that brand amongst its competitors as Lays, and when you go onto a strange computer you are assured you can work on it as soon as you hear the familiar jingle of Windows.

Brand names

Although choosing a memorable name is more art than science, successful brand names generally are the result of extensive research. For example, when Lucent Technologies spun off its enterprise communication division, marketers wanted a name that would break away from the traditional sound of telecommunication company names. Landor Associates came up with Avaya, inspired by an ancient word for "unity". In market research tests customers commented that the name felt energetic, positive, and "smooth". Landor recommended adding the corporate descriptor "communication" to emphasize the human aspect of Avaya's business. The name and descriptor together reinforce perceptions of a company whose employees are united around a common goal of helping businesses develop strong and seamless relationships with their customers.

Successful brand names share several characteristics that help make them memorable. A good brand name usually communicates one or more of the following characteristics:

- **Benefit:** The name Head & Shoulders says this product is for people who worry about ugly dandruff falling onto their shoulders. Renault chose Espace for its MPV to emphasize the spaciness of this car, unrivalled at the time of its introduction.

- **Association:** Kia from South Korea named its A-class car Picanto, which suggests that this small car is spicy. Unilever named its line of oil and fats products Bertolli to give it an Italian association, which is particularly relevant for its olive oil products.

- **Distinctiveness:** One way to communicate distinctiveness is to use a simple word that is completely unrelated to the product, such as Apple (computers) or Orange (mobile telephony). A distinctive name suggests a distinctive product and ensures that there are no similar brand names with which the product will be confused.

- **Simplicity:** Names that are difficult to say or spell are not likely to be remembered. That is why many brand names are short and phonetically easy: Tide, Bic, Cif, Fa, Fiat. Pronounceability is thus a consideration in choosing a brand name.

For a good overview of brand naming, visit the website of Cintara, an agency that specializes in corporate identity and branding (www.cintara.com/naming.html).

Brand symbols

We live in a visual world. Having a symbol for a brand can greatly increase a brand's recognition. Cattle, for example, are branded with a unique symbol in order to show which ones belong to which ranchers. In the realm of products and companies, a distinctive logo, *a distinctive graphic design used to communicate a product, company, or organization identity* is used to indicate a product's source or ownership. Corporate logos range from a simple name (Coca-Cola in its distinctive Spencerian script) to abstract designs like the Adidas three stripes.

A trademark is similar to but broader than a logo. A trademark is *an element, word, or design that differentiates one brand from another.* The hourglass design of a Coke bottle is a trademark. The literal meaning of *trademark* is "mark of a trade". Some of the first trademarks were initials and other symbols that silversmiths punched into their products. A company has exclusive use of a trademark by using it first and consistently, and by registering it with a government agency. A problem can arise, however, if a trademarked name, such as Kleenex, becomes commonly used for a product category. Though a hallmark of successful branding, the generic use of a brand name may cause the company to lose its exclusive right to the name as a legally protected trademark. This has happened to some brand names. In Belgium, a small photo camera is called a kodak.

In order for logos and trademarks to do their job, they should be distinctive, simple, and consistent with the desired image and positioning of the brand. Further, brand logos are usually enduring symbols, but they may change as the brand matures. Apple Computer's original logo—an apple with rainbow colours—was long considered a classic design because it was not only brightly coloured and youthful (the early image of Apple computers) but also distinctive, simple, eye-catching, and memorable. Recently Apple revised the logo, giving it a solid colour to appear more modern.

3 Creating the brand image

Giving a brand an identity and a position is not enough to make the brand come alive. The final step is the most important one: to create an image in the customers' heads and hearts. Creating this image is what this book is all about. Ideally the identity as aspired to by the company coincides with the image that the customers have of the brand. Brand managers have many tools at their disposal, chief among them the communication instruments.

Although communication is a major aspect of creating an image, other actions under the control of the marketing manager, the brand manager, or the communications manager may be equally important. The role of communications in the brand creation process is described in the next chapter. The remainder of the book then deals more specifically with the way communication contributes to the brand-creation process.

Creating brand equity

According to Regis McKenna, "A successful brand is nothing more than a special relationship."[14] Brand success depends on retaining customers, and good customer relationships lead to retention. A customer relationship programme that builds a brand must be a long-term effort to develop trust, not merely a traditional advertising and promotion campaign that focuses on short-term transactions.

> " A successful brand is nothing more than a special relationship.
>
> *Regis McKenna, relationship marketing expert* "

Brand relationship is the highest level of connectedness brands can achieve with their customers. Kevin Keller has developed an insightful model of how the various levels of relatedness of customers with the brand are related. This "customer-based brand equity (CBBE) building pyramid" is displayed in Figure 2-3. It consists of four levels describing various stages of how customers relate to a brand. On the bottom level the brand is only known to the customer. The brand has salience to the customer, meaning that the customer has some factual understanding of the brand's existence, but nothing more. This, of course, corresponds to the discussion of awareness earlier in this chapter.

At the next level the customer has started to link associations to the brand. Both factual (attributes, features, characteristics), as well as imagery (benefits, impressions). The associative network starts to develop. At the next level, the associations are translated into opinions. Attitudes develop, and again these attitudes can be based on the facts, or on the imagery that was created at the lower level. At this stage the customer actively assesses the brand in consumption decisions, or in any other decision in which the brand is considered. Note that the left part of the pyramid is predominantly based on cognitive processing of information about the brand. The right side in contrast plays on the emotional or affective side of building brands. Indeed, brand building occurs in both heads and hearts.

At the final level, the customer connects to the brand in the form of a relationship. The level of relationships is much more desirable than the previous levels. Customers who attain this level are more valuable, as they typically display loyal behaviour.

The importance of relationships

The importance of brand relationships was illustrated several years ago when Coca-Cola was accused of distributing contaminated products in Belgium and taking too long to respond to the problem. Six months after the news broke—and after Coke's stock had lost nearly one-third

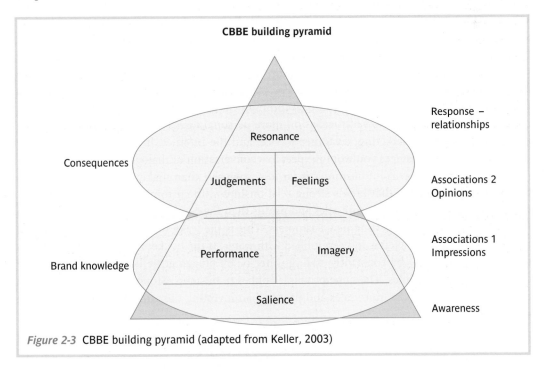

Figure 2-3 CBBE building pyramid (adapted from Keller, 2003)

of its value—a headline on the front page of the *Wall Street Journal* read: "To Fix Coca-Cola, Daft Sets Out to Get Relationships Right". Coke's then-CEO Douglas Daft was quoted as saying, "Every problem we had can be traced to a singular cause: We neglected our relationships." Daft admitted the company had failed to communicate adequately with its European customers and other stakeholders—European Union bottlers, government regulators, and the media.[15] The result? Coca-Cola customers heard and read a lot of negative messages about Coke before the company finally explained the problem and what was being done to fix it. Coke lost the trust of many customers (both consumers and business customers), as well as other stakeholders.

Brand relationships affect bottom-line results, as the Coca-Cola story demonstrates. Because relationships cost money to create and maintain, they had best result in sales or in reduced costs of doing business. Even non-profit organizations have to be sensitive to costs and to their relationships with supporters regarding fund-raising, membership dues, and volunteerism. Unless an organization's brand relationships are profitable, the organization will soon be out of business.

Another important principle of brand relationships is that stakeholders overlap. Although brand messages are aimed at customers, companies must assume that other stakeholder groups will be exposed to those messages as well. For example, employees as well as suppliers can be customers or investors in a company—another reason why message consistency is so important.

A number of principles in addition to bottom-line impact and stakeholder overlap guide the creation of brand relationships. One is the need for managers to shift their mind-set from customer acquisition to customer retention.

Balancing customer acquisition and customer retention efforts

Brand relationships connect customers and brands beyond the first purchase and keep customers coming back. According to Siebel, the leading information technology marketing-support company, repeat sales account for 70 per cent of the average company's total revenue.[16] New companies—or companies launching new products—must inevitably focus on acquiring new customers, but as the shift from acquisition to retention occurs, both the message strategy and the media of communication change. For example, brand acquisition is often seen as a responsibility of advertising and mass media communication, which are good at creating awareness. A retention strategy, however, relies on more personal forms of communication, such as personal sales, direct marketing, customer service, and the Internet. It opens the door for the customer-initiated messages you would expect in a conversation or dialogue.

Making a sale to a current customer is far less expensive than making a sale to a new customer. Thus, a company that builds strong relationships with customers will retain these customers, and the result will be more sales and profits than the company would have experienced from focusing mainly on getting new customers. This is the leaky bucket theory. Suppose you have a bucket, and your job is to keep it filled with water. If the bucket has holes, there are two ways to keep it filled—by constantly adding water or by plugging the holes. Your job will be easier if you plug the holes. The same principle applies to business. Stopping current customers from leaving will result in more sales and profits than investing the same amount in acquiring new customers.

Customer retention is the subject of numerous articles in the marketing press; nevertheless, most companies do not manage it well. One survey of 200 companies found that the vast majority were doing little to create and manage customer relationships. Despite pledges to be customer driven, most were cost driven and on average were losing 20 per cent of their customers each year.[17] The percentage of such loss differs by product category, brand, and company.

Brand loyalty

Just as there are different levels of intensity in personal relationships, so there are different levels of intensity in commercial relationships. The intensity of a brand relationship varies for each customer and product category. The success of the Rolling Stones provides an example of the benefits of strong brand intensity. The group's popularity has lasted 40 years even though the group has not had a number-one hit since 1973. The reason for the band's longevity is the loyalty of its followers. This loyalty is fuelled by the very clear brand image of the brand, carried mainly by the extremely strong personality of lead singer Mick Jagger. Also the logo is very well chosen, both referring to the famous flexibility of Jagger's mouth, the most important instrument for the lead singer (recall his nickname Rubber Lips), and the rebellious image the band still carries successfully. Every concert the band would give will be sold out easily.

Customers have strong emotional feelings for some brands but see other brands as strictly utilitarian. In other words, even loyalty can be based on both the cognitive or affective sides of brand evaluations in Kellers pyramid (see Figure 2-3). A dedicated Pepsi loyalist would not be caught drinking Coke. Someone who regularly uses a Head & Shoulders shampoo because it fights dandruff successfully is not going to feel comfortable using Elvive anti-dandruff. To communicate successfully with customers and exploit their loyalty, a company needs to know reasons for the loyal relationships customers display.

Also the intensity of loyalty can vary from "no loyalty" to "intense loyalty". Customers at the "no loyalty" end of the range are brand-switchers; those at the "intense loyalty" end consistently buy a particular brand. The marketing goal, of course, is to move as many customers as possible to the "intense" end of the range. Not only are the loyal customer relationships cheaper to maintain, but loyal customers also sing the praises of the brand, making positive contributions to the brand's marketing communication efforts.

Knowing customers' level of **brand loyalty**, *the degree of attachment that customers have to a brand as expressed by repeat purchases*, helps companies customize brand messages. One strategy for strengthening brand relationships is to encourage the "connected" customers—through invitations and rewards—to join a brand-user group, thus increasing the intensity of their relationship with the brand. IBM, Microsoft, Apple, and many other computer companies, but also companies like Swatch, or beer brands like the Dutch Brand (no pun intended), have set up user groups. Such groups constitute **brand communities**, *collections of customers who own the same brand and enjoy talking to each other, learning from each other, and sharing new ways of using their products, as well as getting help in solving brand-related problems*. Internet chat rooms likewise create brand communities for a vast array of products. Members of brand communities, like other loyal brand users, often become advocates for the brand, moving to the highest level of brand loyalty.[18]

Why loyalty is rewarding

In most product categories a small number of heavy users account for a large percentage of a brand's sales and profits. Heavy users are sometimes identified as the top 20 per cent of customers based on volume. According to the **Pareto rule**, a rule of thumb found in many economic and business issues, named after Italian economist Vilfredo Pareto, *80 per cent of a brand's sales come from 20 per cent of its customers.* Although the precise ratio varies for every company, the majority of sales and profits almost always come from a minority of a company's customers. These are typically the loyal customers.

A concept companies use in this respect is **share of wallet,** *the percentage of a customer's spending in a product category for one particular brand.* Because few companies can capture 100 per cent of a customer's share of wallet, heavy users are particularly important. A study of 83 grocery chains determined that the top 10 per cent of customers, who were members of the chains' frequent-buyer programmes, spent twice as much per week as the next 10 per cent. The study also found that the "top 30 per cent of shopping-card holders [frequent buyers] account for approximately 75 per cent of a store's total sales, versus only 2 per cent for the bottom 30 per cent".[19] Companies prize brand loyalty, but it is not the only measure of a "good" customer. Some customers who are loyal to one brand only are light users—their total purchases are relatively small. Medium and heavy users, even those who regularly buy two or three brands in a category, can actually be more valuable as customers.

Another benefit of loyal customers is that these people are likely to say good things about the company or brand. Advocates for a brand tend to communicate positively with prospects and thereby generate referrals for the company. Word-of-mouth on behalf of a brand is highly persuasive. Richard Cross and Janet Smith in *Customer Bonding: Pathway to Lasting Customer Loyalty*[20] describe brand advocacy as an even higher level of brand connectedness that would be on top of the brand equity building pyramid of Figure 2-3. Cross and Smith also illustrate that the number of customers at the various levels of attachment with the brand decreases (see Figure 2-4).

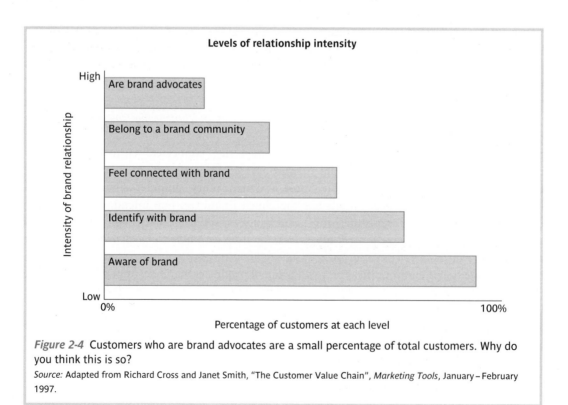

Figure 2-4 Customers who are brand advocates are a small percentage of total customers. Why do you think this is so?

Source: Adapted from Richard Cross and Janet Smith, "The Customer Value Chain", *Marketing Tools*, January–February 1997.

Customer relationship management

Relationships need to be managed. **Customer relationship management** (CRM) is *an approach in marketing that takes relationships as the single most important issue for the marketer.* This stream developed initially in the B2B literature, but has been transferred to consumer marketing.[21] Various definitions of CRM exist. For example, Ruth Stevens, a professor and consultant, says CRM is "a combination of retention marketing and customer service".[22] A much broader definition is:

> Total Customer Relationship Management is the optimization of all customer contacts through the distribution and application of customer information. Simply stated, it is your promise that no matter how your customers interact with you, you will always recognize who they are. Total CRM requires the co-operation of all departments and divisions within an organization around this concept.[23]

Stop! Doesn't this ring a bell? Especially the first sentence of this definition shows how strongly connected CRM and IMC are. The linking pin of this similarity is the topic of branding that is fundamental to both approaches. CRM revolves around brands, although CRM proponents will argue that relationships are maintained with companies, rather than brands. Yet, it has already been said that a brand can refer both to a product and to a company. Similarly, IMC revolves around brands, as has been discussed extensively above.

An important thing to remember about CRM is that most customers do not want to be "managed". However, they usually appreciate a relationship programme that delivers something of value, and relationship programmes do deliver benefits to both customers and the company (see Table 2-3). Again notice the strong overlap with benefits that have been identified as resulting from branding and brands.

An example of using CRM to benefit the customer as well as the company comes from the automotive field. Most automotive dealers understand the importance of maintaining contact with their customers, but few do much more than send notices and perhaps a magazine.

Benefits to the company	
Impact on costs	**Impact on sales/profits**
■ Selling to current customers costs less than attracting new customers	■ Loyal customers buy more
■ Relationships spread the costs of acquisition	■ Loyalty increases long-term customer value
■ Loyal customers are brand advocates, reducing MC costs	■ Fewer defections increase sales
■ Satisfied customers require less hand-holding	
Benefits to the customer	
■ Less risk	
■ Fewer decisions	
■ Fewer switching costs	
■ Greater buying efficiency	
■ Increased association, self-identification	

Table 2-3 Benefits of brand relationships

Daewoo, however, added value to its relationships with its British customers by building a helpful experience around regular servicing. Daewoo offered courtesy loaner cars, flexible scheduling, and follow-ups. Daewoo's programme also helped customers maintain the value of their cars through regular servicing; at the same time its relationship programme brought a positive aura to the brand, a result that is usually rewarded with higher levels of customer loyalty and advocacy.

How brand equity is leveraged

Increasing brand awareness and acceptance means not only selling more products but also finding opportunities to sell even more products by leveraging the equity in the brand. Consider Coleman, the long-established maker of camping equipment. The company decided to expand into the home outdoor grill category. After considering a variety of new grill designs, it decided to go with a traditional design but to differentiate the new product from other grills by colouring it in Coleman's "signature green". To outdoor enthusiasts this colour is almost as well known as the Coleman name. The use of the green immediately communicates that a product is a "Coleman". Because of the brand equity inherent in the new grill, it gained immediate distribution with retailers, and captured a 5 per cent share of the outdoor grill market in its first year.[24]

A variety of strategies allow marketers to take advantage of brand equity. Among these are: adding new distribution channels; extending the product line sold under the brand name; cobranding with another brand; and licensing the brand to other manufacturers to use on their products.

Access to new markets

An established brand name can be instrumental to entering new markets. Expanding internationally is easier when your brand name has already been introduced. When Vodafone renamed its Dutch subsidiary Libertel as Vodafone, it was helped by the recognition of this name due to its sponsorship of Manchester United. McDonald's was so well known that the opening of new outlets in Russia and China needed no real advertising campaigns. Tupperware secured access to new market segments when it decided to change its distribution strategy and also become available through target stores.

Brand extensions

A related way to leverage brand equity is brand extension, which is *the application of an established brand name to new product offerings*. Brand extension is generally most successful when it involves similar products (see colour insert A1). Within the last few years, for example, premium car manufacturers such as BMW, Lexus, and Mercedes-Benz have extended their brands to SUVs (sports utility vehicles), a product category long dominated by Ford, Chevrolet, Nissan, and Toyota. Also extending to more remote product categories is possible. Camel (cigarettes) has extended successfully to clothing and related accessories. The IMC in Action case discusses Virgin's extension strategy.

There are advantages and disadvantages to extending a successful brand to other products. The advantages are savings in time and money when a company introduces new products, because the brand is already known and instantly communicates a certain level of trust (if the brand already has that perception). One disadvantage is the danger of diluting the power and

Virgin: not even the sky is the limit

The all-time champion of brand extensions is Virgin, no doubt. At least, that's how everyone perceives the brand. Starting from a one-man publishing activity back in 1968, in less than 40 years Richard Branson managed to gather over 350 companies under his Virgin label. Does Mr. Branson rewrite branding theory?

Perhaps not. Many Virgin brands are far from successful in economic terms. Only a few of them make a profit, others survive, and there are also categories where Virgin is simply not successful. So, when considered from a business point of view, the success of Virgin is modest at best. Yet, in branding terms, the expansionism of Virgin can be called successful. If acceptance of a brand in a certain product category were the main criterion, Virgin would without hesitation be called enormously successful. The presence of the Virgin label is accepted in every product category it enters; but this is, of course, a very different matter from consumers simply starting to buy Virgin insurance, Virgin golf clubs, or Virgin bicycles. For that matter, it is a limitation of brand extension research itself that it takes consumer evaluation as its main criterion for assessing extendibility.

The Virgin brand does indeed cover the widest range of products you can think of. From wine to galactic trips, you can find a product with the Virgin label on it to satisfy your needs (also see colour insert A13). There is no apparent logic in Virgin's product portfolio. Some argue this absence of logic exactly *is* the logic, but that smells like plain nihilism. Indeed, a closer look at the Virgin brand and its stretching to (literally) outer space, reveals a more subtle logic.

This is evidently not the logic of the theorists. Brand extension theory predicts that brand extension success depends on the presence of fit between the parent brand and the extension product category.[1] Here there is already a flaw in the theory, one heavily and cleverly exploited by Virgin: the parent brand is not related to a single product category, with respect to which a measure of fit could be determined. Ask 50 people what Virgin sells, and you might get 100 different answers.

There is though a more important aspect of the way Virgin challenges brand extension theory. Theory considers an extension category as a given, with fixed characteristics. Not so Virgin! Whatever product Virgin is considering extending to, the question is not: does it fit within our brand, but can we *make* it fit our brand? Is it possible to bring this product to the market, justifying the brand positioning of value for money, quality, innovation, competitive challenge, brilliant customer service and, above all, fun?

What if the competition has already claimed the fun position within the category? Then Virgin makes fun of that! So when Virgin decided to take up the competitive challenge posed by Coca-Cola and Pepsi in 1994, Richard Branson hired a tank, drove down Fifth Avenue to Times Square in New York and, like Boris Yeltsin standing on top of the tank, blew up the huge billboards of the competition in one mighty stroke. Not traditional "British humour" perhaps, but effective, oh so effective!

Think about it

Is there any product category you think Virgin is not likely to be successful in? How important but also how risky do you think is the role of Richard Branson with the Virgin brand?

Note

[1] David Aaker and Kevin Lane Keller, "Consumer Evaluations of Brand Extensions", *Journal of Marketing*, 1990 and many, many others.

Source:
www.virgin.com

IMC in Action

meaning of the brand. If customers associate the brand with a certain product, such as laundry detergent, and suddenly the association is extended to apparel or writing instruments, sales of the laundry detergent could suffer. To be successful, brand extension should result in a compatible fit with the established brand.[25] Another disadvantage is that, if the new product fails, for whatever reason, that failure could reflect negatively on the brand's original products if a strong association developed with the failed product.

Co-branding

Co-branding is *a strategy that capitalizes on using two brand names (owned by separate companies) and provides customers with value from both brands.* Co-branding helps companies that sell commodity products, such as credit cards and air travel, to differentiate themselves. Co-branding involves a contractual relationship between two marketing partners. Often the co-branding partners use a new name for the new product, at the same time widely acknowledging the involvement of the parent brands. For example, it is generally known that the Smart was co-produced by Swatch and Mercedes. Philips and Sara Lee's daughter Douwe Egberts introduced the Senseo coffee machine.

Brand licensing

A strong brand can be licensed. In essence, **brand licensing** is *renting the brand equity to another company, which benefits from the association.* The beauty of brand licensing is that the company owning the brand can continue to use it while also collecting a fee for the brand's use by another company. An example most people are familiar with is the licensing of the names of football clubs or logo to apparel makers. Well-known clubs like Real Madrid and Manchester United generate hundreds of thousands of euros from licensing, a source of income that has become important to many of these clubs. At the time of the transfer of David Beckham to Real Madrid rumours went about that only his name on Real Madrid jerseys would earn the equivalent of the money involved in the transfer (see colour insert C9). Although licensing is a good way to generate extra revenue from a brand, it is a concern for brand managers because it allows a company's brand to be used by marketers who may not keep the brand's best interests in mind. Consequently, monitoring brand licensing is critical to maintaining a consistent brand image.

Ingredient branding

Another way to add value to a brand (and to a brand message) is through **ingredient branding**—*using the brand name of a product component in the promotion of another company's product.* The "Intel Inside" message used by various computer hardware manufacturers is a good example. The manufacturers hope to reinforce the quality of their finished products by featuring the maker of the most important component in the computer: the processing chip. Another example is Gore-Tex. Gore-Tex does not make gloves, shoes, coats, or jackets, but instead the lightweight, warm, and water-resistant fabric from which these items are made. Gore-Tex fabric, however, has become so well known and respected, and has been promoted so prominently (often even more than the apparel brands), that many customers ask for a "Gore-Tex jacket" even though no such brand of jacket exists. Ingredient branding is also used by food products manufacturers. Some dessert mixes, for example, promote the fact they contain Hershey's chocolate chips or NutraSweet.

For ingredient branding to be successful, the ingredient brand must have a high level of brand awareness. When it does, an ingredient brand adds value to the products in which it is used. Manufacturers who use such ingredient branding have found that they can sell their products at premium prices

Managing a system of brands

As companies grow and expand the number of products they make, they sometimes extend their brands to these products and in other cases give these products separate brand names. The specific way in which all brands of a company are named is a strategic issue. A **brand system** is *the systematic description of how all brands that belong to the same company are related*. A brand system is driven by the brand names, but behind that lies the question of positions. When two brands within the same system have the same name, they also have the same position in the customer's head and heart.

There are a few basic models of brand systems.[26] On the one extreme, all brands within a company can carry the same name. Philips is a good example here: whether you buy a light bulb, a TV or a medical system, you always buy a Philips. Unilever on the other hand applies the house-of-brands model: for every product or product category a separate name is used. Sometimes there are even multiple brands within the same product category from the same company: Unilever offers both Knorr and Unox in the dried soup product category. In between there is the category that uses sub-brands or brand endorsements. This is a broad category ranging from situations that resemble the branded house, but where the small identifiers become strong enough to be spoken of as separate brands, to the situation where the endorsement is so weak that a situation of house of brands seems to exist. For example, Mercedes offers only Mercedes cars, but the distinction between the Mercedes A-class, the C-class, and the E-class is still meaningful and goes beyond a simple product description. And McDonald's brands all its products with the familiar Mc-prefix: McChicken, McMuffin, etc. However, they are hardly recognized as individual brands but are mainly perceived as McDonald's chicken-burgers and muffins.

A major role in this discussion is played by the corporate brand. Not only in the case of a branded house strategy, but also in the case of sub-brands and endorsements, and sometimes even when a house-of-brand strategy is applied. For example, for some time the brand Hugo Boss was owned by Unilever. That knowledge is unlikely to have an effect on your appreciation of the brand.

Use of the corporate brand is intended to communicate trust and quality, because the company itself usually has been in existence longer than the product line and has established perceptions of trust and quality. The role of the product brand is to communicate such benefits as performance, reliability, and image. Take Kellogg's Special K, for example. The name Kellogg's says the cereal is well made, well packaged, and fresh—product features that customers have come to associate with Kellogg's products. The brand name Special K is designed to identify the product as a healthy cereal. In three-level branding strategy, a descriptor can be added to identify an even more specific level of performance or other desirable feature, such as in Citroën Xsara Picasso.

Corporate brand names are used for several reasons. One is to take advantage of the value of the corporate name. Another is to strengthen the corporate brand by connecting it with a successful product line. A third is that a product brand helps differentiate the offering from other products sold by the company, as well as from competing products.

A final note: a brand is a relationship

One of the most important effects of using IMC is the building of trust in brands. Remember that a brand is nothing more than a special relationship, and that communication is what drives relationships. Trust is essential for creating the brand relationships that make successful brands. These relationships, however, must provide added value for customers; otherwise, the relationships will soon dissolve. How a company makes its goods or performs its primary services is no longer the number-one factor in establishing a brand's value. The new priority is communication—how a company controls or influences the communication dimensions of everything it does, as well as how it manages the exchange of information between the company and its customers and other stakeholders. Brand communication greatly affects the quantity and quality of brand relationships with all stakeholders, chief among them the customers.

🔔 Key terms

associations Everything that is related to a brand.

associative network Representation of brand knowledge as a network of nodes connected by links.

benefits Advantages that allow a product to satisfy customers' needs, wants, or desires.

brand awareness Whether or not consumers know a brand.

brand community Collections of customers who own the same brand and enjoy talking to each other, learning from each other, and sharing new ways of using their products, as well as getting help in solving brand-related problems.

brand elements Brand names; symbols; logos; slogans and jingles and its packaging.

brand equity The intangible value of a brand beyond the value of its physical assets.

brand extension The application of an established brand name to new product offerings.

brand identity What the brand stands for, how it is described in most fundamental terms, to which all other characteristics and actions can be traced back.

brand image The customer's perception of brand identity.

brand licensing Renting the brand equity to another company, which benefits from the association.

brand loyalty The degree of attachment that customers have to a brand as expressed by repeat purchases.

brand position The standing of a brand in comparison with its competitors in the minds of customers, prospects, and other stakeholders.

brand system The systematic description of how all brands that belong to the same company are related.

branding The process of creating a brand image that engages the hearts and minds of customers.

co-branding A strategy that capitalizes on using two brand names (owned by separate companies) and provides customers value from both brands.

commodity products Goods and services that have very minor or no distinguishing differences.

customer-based brand equity The differential effect that brand knowledge has on consumer response to the marketing of that brand.

customer relationship management (CRM) An approach in marketing that takes relationships as the single most important issue for the marketer.

customer relationships A series of interactions between customers and a company over time.

dominance When brand awareness is limited to only one brand in a certain product category.

goodwill Brand equity.

ingredient branding Using the brand name of a product component in the promotion of another company's product.

logo A distinctive graphic design used to communicate a product, company, or organization identity.

Pareto rule 80 per cent of a brand's sales come from 20 per cent of its customers.

perceptual mapping A visualization technique that indicates how customers perceive competing brands in terms of various criteria.

pre-emptive positioning Brand positioning based on a generic feature that competitors have not talked about.

product features Tangible and intangible attributes of a good or service.

(brand) recall The ability to bring the brand back from memory without help.

(brand) recognition Identifying a brand and remembering that you saw or heard of it earlier.

share of wallet The percentage of a customer's spending in a product category for one particular brand.

store brand A brand used exclusively by one chain of stores for a line of products made to the chain's specifications.

top-of-mind awareness (TOMA) The first brand consumers are aware of.

trademark An element, word, or design that differentiates one brand from another.

Check the key points

Key point 1: More than a product

a   What is a brand? Why is a brand more than just a product?

b   Explain how brands work to transform products.

c   Explain how brands work to create value.

d   Define brand equity. To what extent do you think the Customer-Based Brand Equity concept is related to brand valuation methods like the one reported by Interbrand?

e   What are the different levels of brand awareness?

f   What is the role of associations in branding?

g   Describe the associative network model.

h   Explain what various stages exist for consumers in building brand equity. Which side of Keller's brand equity pyramid is more important?

Key point 2: Brand-building steps

a   List and explain the brand-building steps.

b   What is a brand position?

c   In choosing a brand name and symbols, what principles guide you?

d   What is a trademark? What is the role of a trademark in a brand-identity programme?

e   What is a perceptual map? How are perceptual maps applied in developing branding strategies? What are the limitations of a perceptual map?

Key point 3: Brand relationship characteristics

a   What are the key characteristics of a successful brand relationship programme?

b   Describe the company and customer sides of a brand relationship, and describe the links that forge the relationship.

c   Why do managers need to think about both customer acquisition and customer retention strategies? Is it more expensive to make a first sale or a repeat sale? Why?

d   Explain the concept of "share of wallet".

e   Why is loyalty important, and what rewards does a brand reap from loyal customers?

f   Why are all stakeholders important? What problem is created when the interests of all stakeholders are not considered in brand relationship programmes?

g   Analyse your brand relationships. Do you buy any brands consistently? Are there product categories in which you choose from a set of brands, any one of which is acceptable to you? Are there product categories in which you have no brand preferences at all? Explain the differences among these three types of categories.

Key point 4: Leveraging brand equity

a Explain how the support of each stakeholder group affects brand equity.

b Why is brand extension used? What does it contribute to a brand from an IMC perspective?

c How do co-branding and ingredient branding differ?

d What key problem does brand licensing create for IMC programmes?

e IKEA follows a quite peculiar branding strategy. Under the IKEA flag, hundreds of products are sold that almost all have their own "brand" name. Yet, the retailer does not actively leverage these individual brands. What opportunities do you see for IKEA to make more active use of these individual brands? Why do you think IKEA is not active exploiting these brands?

Chapter Challenge

Writing assignment

Pick a company, and identify what things it does or does not do to help build and maintain a good relationship with customers. Make recommendations for improving the company's relationship-building practices.

Presentation assignment

Select four car brands (e.g. Fiat, Volkswagen, Renault and Saab) and describe the position they take in the market. On what are their positions based? What positioning strategies can you identify? Present a map that displays the positions of the brands in two dimensions that you think best captures the market situation.

Internet assignment

Visit the IKEA website and go to the country you're living in. Study first the company, and what the IKEA brand stands for. Then explore the website and assess how far the website—its design, contents, navigation possibilities—complies with the way you have characterized the IKEA brand.

Case assignment

Pick a store that you frequent that uses loyalty cards. Interview the store manager, and write up a case describing the role of the loyalty card in the retail chain's marketing communication programme. Explain how the store could make the card a more effective relationship-building tool.

Notes

[1] Tom Duncan and Sandra Moriarty, *Driving Brand Value: Using Integrated Marketing to Manage Profitable Stakeholder Relationships* (New York: McGraw-Hill, 1997), p. 16.

[2] Rita Clifton and Esther Maughan, eds, *The Future of Brands: Twenty-five Visions* (New York: New York University Press and Interbrand, 2000), p. vii.

[3] Stan Gelsi, "Detroit's Model Year", *Brandweek,* 1 January 1996, pp. 19–23.

[4] Peter H. Farquhar, "Managing Brand Equity", *Journal of Advertising Research*, August–September 1990, p. RC-7.

[5] Jean-Noël Kapferer, *Strategic Brand Management: New Approaches to Creating and Evaluating Brand Equity* (New York: Free Press, 1994), p. 16.

[6] Hayes Roth, "Wielding a Brand Name", *Latin CEO*, August 2001, p. 64.

[7] Interbrand's website offers a reasonably extensive document in which the procedure is explained. http://www.interbrand.com/best_brands_2005_FAQ.asp

[8] Kevin Lane Keller (2003), *Strategic Brand Management*, 2nd edn, Upper Saddle River: Prentice Hall, p. 60.

[9] See for example Kotler and Keller (2005), *Principles of Marketing*, Upper Saddle River: Prentice Hall.

[10] John Anderson (1983), "A Spreading Activation Theory of Memory", *Journal of Verbal Learning and Verbal Behaviour*, 22.

[11] Al Ries and Jack Trout, *Positioning: The Battle for Your Mind* (New York: McGraw-Hill, 1981).

[12] Bruce Orwall, "Wishing upon a Logo", *Wall Street Journal*, 28 February 2003, p. B1.

[13] Keller (2003) gives a very concise and detailed discussion of the role of all brand elements.

[14] Regis McKenna, *Relationship Marketing* (Reading, MA: Addison-Wesley, 1991), p. 4.

[15] "To Fix Coca-Cola, Daft Sets Out to Get Relationships Right", *Wall Street Journal*, 23 June 2000, p. A1.

[16] "Customer Satisfaction: The Fundamental Basis of Business Survival", a white paper by Siebel eBusiness, February 2001, p. 5.

[17] Quoted in Peter Jordan, "Zero Defections", *Enterprise* magazine, 1995, p. 29.

[18] Fundamental research on brand communities is done by Albert Muniz and Tom O'Guinn (2001) in "Brand Community", *Journal of Consumer Research*, Vol. 27–4, pp. 412–32; and James McAlexander, John Schouten and Harold Koenig (2002) in "Building Brand Community", *Journal of Marketing*, Vol. 66–1, pp. 38–54.

[19] Arthur Middleton Hughes, "The Real Truth about Supermarkets—and Customers", *DM News*, 3 October 1994, p. 40.

[20] Richard Cross and Janet Smith, *Customer Bonding: Pathway to Lasting Customer Loyalty* (Lincolnwood, IL: NTC, 1994), pp. 54–5.

[21] Gummeson is one the most important representatives of this stream. It is noteworthy that this "school" in marketing found its origin in Scandinavia.

[22] Ruth Stevens, "It's Time to Return Meaning to CRM", *iMarketing News*, 20 November 2000, p. 16.

[23] Melind Nykamp and Carla McEachern, quoted in *The New Rules of Marketing* newsletter, published by Seklemian/Newell, October 2000, p. 1.

[24] Stephanie Clifford, "The Grill of Their Dreams", *Business 2.0*, February 2002, p. 96.

[25] There is an extensive body of research on the importance of fit (and other concepts) in brand extensions. See for example David Aaker and Kevin Keller (1991), "Consumer Evaluations of Brand Extension", *Journal of Marketing*, 1991, pp. 27–41; Susan Broniarczyk and Thomas Alba, "The importance of the brand in brand extension", *Journal of Marketing Research*, 1994, pp. 214–228; Paul Bottomley and Stephen Holden, "Do We Really Know How Consumers Evaluate Brand Extensions?" *Journal of Marketing Research*, 2001, pp. 494–500; and Jill Lei, Roger Pruppers, Hans Ouwersloot and Jos Lemmink, "Service Intensiveness and Brand Extension Evaluations", *Journal of Service Research*, 2004, pp. 243–255, to mention just a few.

[26] Aaker and Joachimsthaler (2000) provide a insightful discussion of the concept of brand systems, or brand portfolios or brand architecture as it is also called.

Further reading

Aaker, David A. and Erich Joachimsthaler (2000) *Brand Leadership*, New York: The Free Press.

Austin, Jon R., Judy A. Siguaw and Anna S. Mattila (2003) "A re-examination of the generalizability of the Aaker brand personality measurement framework", *Journal of Strategic Marketing*, Vol. 11–2, pp. 77–92.

Hayes, J. Bryan, Bruce L. Alford, Lawrence Süver and Rice P. York (2006) "Looks matter in developing consumer-brand relationships", *Journal of Product & Brand Management*, Vol. 15–4/5, pp. 306–15.

Kay, Mark J. (2006) "Strong brands and corporate brands", *European Journal of Marketing*, Vol. 40–7/8, pp. 742–60.

Keller, Kevin L. (2003) *Strategic Brand Management*, Upper Saddle River: Prentice Hall.

Ouwersloot, Hans and Gaby Odekerken-Schröder (2007) "Who's Who in Brand Communities— and Why", *European Journal of Marketing*, forthcoming.

Riezebos, R. (2003) *Brand Management—a theoretical and practical approach*, Harlow, England: FT Prentice Hall.

Volkner, Franziska and Henrik Sattler (2006) "Drivers of Brand Extension Success", *Journal of Marketing*, Vol. 70 (April), pp. 18–34.

Touch points: brand communication at work

CHAPTER PERSPECTIVE
Every touch point communicates

The marketplace is a social system in which customers, companies, and media interact. Communication involves the sending and receiving of messages. A company or brand can communicate with, or "touch", customers, prospects, and other stakeholders in many different ways. What many companies overlook and fail to leverage are opportunities for dialogue with customers and prospects.

Companies sometimes believe that if they do not say anything or fail to respond to a customer, they have avoided sending a brand message. Wrong! A company CEO who responds to a question from the media with "No comment", actually communicates a great deal. What most people "hear" is that the CEO is scared to give the right answer or does not know the answer, both of which are bad messages to send. A company that chooses not to respond to a customer's complaint communicates loudly and clearly that it does not care about its customers and is not willing to stand behind its products.

Everything and every person and every message that touches a customer communicates something positive or negative about the organization. The appearance of a service employee, whether neat or sloppy, says something about the company's pride in its work. The design of a product and package says modern, juvenile, feminine, old-fashioned, expensive, dull, or something else. The tone of voice on the phone or the attitude of a clerk or customer-service representative all speak of the personality and friendliness of the organization.

A company and a brand cannot *not* communicate. The challenge, then, is *how* to manage brand communication in order to accomplish business and marketing objectives cost-effectively. To answer this question requires understanding that every touch point communicates, and how marketing communication works, which is what this chapter is about.

IMC in Action

Love and ice cream: the HB story
McCann-Erickson, Dublin, Ireland

Marketing communication consists of the messages companies send and receive and the media involved. It's also about perceptions, how customers interpret the many messages they receive about a brand. In the late 1990s HB Ice Cream, Ireland's number-one ice-cream brand, decided to change its stodgy brand perception. This is the story about how that message was communicated at every possible point of contact with the brand.

With increasing competition facing its ice cream, HB's parent company, Unilever, decided to introduce a new brand identity for HB across Europe. McCann-Erickson Dublin was asked to develop a communication programme to launch the new HB brand identity and test it in Ireland. McCann's communication effort was so successful that it not only achieved high awareness scores in a highly competitive product category but also was a winner in the Advertising and Marketing Effectiveness (AME) international award programme.

The marketing challenge

Traditionally a "poor relation" on the fringe of Europe, the Republic of Ireland earned the tag "Celtic Tiger" through a sustained level of high economic growth during the 1990s. As unemployment rates, stubbornly high for many years, eased downward, larger numbers of Irish young people (18 to 34 years old) opted to stay home rather than emigrate, creating the youngest population profile in western Europe.

Because of its long heritage in the Irish market (since 1926), HB is regarded with great affection by Irish consumers as "our ice cream". It dominates the market despite being bought in 1973 by global marketer Unilever. The HB brand name acts as an umbrella for a wide range of products—three take-home ice-cream brands and five impulse brands (bars and cones bought out of a freezer in a store).

The challenge? Because HB already had a leading share of the Irish ice-cream market, the business objective was to grow the *category* by increasing ice-cream consumption.

Campaign strategy

HB planned to fight for a share of the market in the bigger category of refreshment, using its impulse brands. HB's consumer research had determined that the key target audience for the

HB take-home brands consisted of housewives with children, and that the target for the impulse brands was young adults aged 15 to 34. However, McCann decided that the strategy needed to move beyond these two audiences. Executives wanted a new brand identity with a more contemporary brand perception, especially for the younger people in the HB market. Given HB's ubiquity and broad acceptance, the identity effort could be aimed at *everyone* in the Irish market.

The brand message

For 30 years the HB logo, with its initials (from the original founders, the Hughes Brothers) in script mounted in an oval and printed over four bars, had been a familiar symbol in the Irish media, on signs in the streets, and in shops. The brand also had a high pan-European advertising presence on TV and on billboards. Irish consumers came in contact with HB brands everywhere. It was impossible to walk down an Irish street without seeing HB signage, point-of-purchase displays, branded litter bins, or window stickers on the local corner shop. HB branded freezer cabinets were a prominent feature in shops.

The original logo was appropriate to a relatively undeveloped market in both ice-cream consumption and other refreshments. However, competition had recently become much fiercer as the lines had started to blur between ice cream, carbonated soft drinks, confectionery, and yogurt categories. The time had come to recognize consumers' greater familiarity with ice cream.

The communication effort needed to touch the emotions of the audience. The new design continued to use the familiar HB initials but replaced the oval with a heart shape. The design sought to communicate the values of natural togetherness and love. "Natural togetherness" provided a key emotional benefit by focusing on people enjoying ice cream in a social, interactive environment.

The message strategy utilized a major public event to spearhead the campaign and involve the audience. The big idea was to capitalize on the new heart-shaped logo by using Valentine's Day weekend as a launch platform to create rapid and widespread awareness, excitement, and recognition of the new HB identity. The event would be supported by advertising so that when consumers saw on-pack and in-store changes, they would understand what was happening to the familiar HB brand.

Delivering the message

Fitting a brand of HB's stature and ubiquity with a new identity was clearly a task that needed to go far beyond advertising to engage all possible contact points. Changing all HB's packaging, shop-front signage, point-of-purchase, and freezer cabinet brand messages in every supermarket and grocery store in the country was a logistical challenge.

Rather than relying on a TV commercial to announce the logo, the McCann team felt strongly that the communication should include new media and contact points where appropriate. The core media idea was to create Ireland's first-ever themed weekend on Irish TV. Valentine's weekend was dubbed "The Love Weekend", and themed television programming sponsored by HB included movies such as *Sleepless in Seattle, Truly Madly Deeply,* and *Brief Encounter;* romantic episodes of *The Simpsons, Friends,* and *Golden Girls;* and a special called *An Intimate Evening with Michael Bolton.* In addition, a local television network created a phone-in music video request show called *Cupid's Corner.*

▶ McCann's event-based plan allowed the agency to put in place a completely integrated communication strategy. That meant combining the three elements—the TV spot, a local media launch event, and on-the-street promotional activity—so that consumers were involved with a 360-degree communication programme for the new brand identity. In addition to traditional media time and space placements, the campaign also used sponsorship "stings", short TV spots that announced HB's sponsorship of the Love Weekend. The networks also ran tie-in promotional teasers for the programmes. In newspapers, the TV listings were printed over colour watermarks of the heart logo.

A key element of HB's strategy to compete against the major refreshment brands was to establish a strong street presence in the main urban centres. To get the new HB logo on the street, McCann teamed up with a Dublin film-production company to project video images on large outdoor screens or walls. The Love Weekend TV reminder ads were also projected on large walls at city centre locations on Valentine's night in Dublin, Cork, and Belfast. If the event didn't quite cause national gridlock, it did manage to slow Saturday-night traffic near the light projections. McCann also had "hit squads" at each location distributing HB "Passion Test" cards, short questionnaires that tested the passion in one's life.

In an effort to further bring the event alive, McCann placed a colour ad leading into the TV listings that offered people the chance to win a family holiday. This strengthened HB's ownership of the weekend's TV listings while at the same time the contest generated excitement and enthusiasm.

Evaluation of the HB campaign

Market research conducted two weeks after the Love Weekend but prior to any signage or point-of-purchase changes found that nearly half of all Irish recognized the new symbol. Furthermore, 70 per cent of the 15 to 24 age group were aware of the logo, and 75 per cent of these immediately associated the logo with HB Ice Cream.

Ice-cream sales in Ireland are seasonally biased to the summer months, so another objective was to stretch the impulse ice-cream season so that it starts earlier. Given the success of the Love Weekend with increasing sales in February, it is now part of HB's strategy to launch the new impulse season each year with a Valentine's weekend themed TV event.

Unilever managers were so impressed with the Irish campaign and the results it achieved that they decided to replicate the strategy in all their ice-cream markets. McCann's video of the whole campaign has become the template for similar launch activity in other markets.

Source:
This case was adapted with permission from the Advertising and Marketing Effectiveness (AME) brief for the HB brand-identity campaign prepared by McCann-Erickson Dublin.

Brand–customer touch points

Any situation in which a customer comes into contact with a brand or company is a brand–customer touch point. The touch-point concept suggests that there are many kinds of brand messages, and that media are not the only means by which customers come in contact with a brand message. The touch-point concept emphasizes that *any* occasion on which a customer comes into touch with a brand is a situation that contributes to brand knowledge of the customer, either brand awareness or the composition of the brand's associative network. Indeed, the touch-point framework recognizes that many touch points are not under the brand's control. But just ask yourself what gives you a better impression of a brand: a nice, decent and satisfying reply to a query you had with a brand, or a fancy, glossy, yet unsolicited brochure? Or what makes a longer-lasting impression: the talk of a salesman in the shop, or the experience of your neighbour who has used the product for some time? Understanding how touch points affect customers is critical to managing the customer expectations that drive brand relationships. As the HB Ice Cream story in the opening case illustrates, every touch point contributes to customers' impressions of a brand.

The concept of touch points was first popularized by Jan Carlson, former chairman of Scandinavian Airlines System (SAS). During the time he managed this world-class company, Carlson realized that certain company–customer interactions (touch points) had a significant impact on whether customers chose SAS the next time they flew. He called these touch points "moments of truth". They included on-time departures and arrivals, careful handling of luggage, and courteous interactions with airline personnel.[1] He also discovered that messages delivered at these touch points were often more powerful than anything SAS could say in its marketing communication.

To manage touch points, a company must first identify them. There are four basic categories of customer touch points: company created, intrinsic, unexpected, and customer initiated (see Figure 3-1). The differences between these types of touch points can be sketched in terms of control and intent. Company-created touch points in the first place intend to communicate, and are under the full control of the company. Intrinsic touch points typically have another objective, but nevertheless communicate about the brand. For example, a building primarily houses the activities of a company, but at the same time it also communicates. Or a price is mainly there to raise money, but at the same time this communicates something about the product. Unexpected touch points typically communicate something about the brand, but are by definition not under the control of the company. Customer-initiated touch points are under control, but the outcome is uncertain since it is the customer who takes the initiative and wants to achieve something with the contact. The main role of the company in these kinds of contacts is to respond, as will be discussed later.

Touch points must be integrated to ensure message consistency. Every touch point, to some extent, strengthens, maintains, or weakens the relationship between a brand and a customer. The extended concept of IMC means Integrated Touch Point management.

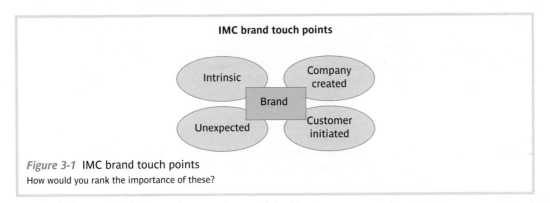

Figure 3-1 IMC brand touch points
How would you rank the importance of these?

Company-created touch points

Company-created touch points are *planned Marketing Communication messages, such as ads, news releases, brochures, and information on packages.* When Lexus or its agency, for example, creates and places an ad in *Time* magazine, it is creating a contact point with the magazine's readers and using the magazine to connect with its target audience. Another creative way of touching customers is described in the IMC in Action box.

One of the advantages of company-created touch points is that, for the most part, they can be planned and controlled. Planning of MC messages requires an understanding of the communication process. Controlling this process implies exerting maximum control over the various stages of this process.

How does communication work?

Conceptually, communication is a fairly simple process: someone—a person or an organization—creates and sends a message to an individual or organization. In every commercial communication situation, companies (or their agencies) that create brand messages do so with certain objectives in mind—to inform, impress, persuade, and/or generate a response. If you have taken a psychology or marketing course you are probably familiar with the traditional sender–receiver communication model. This model has been adapted to show how brand communication works (see Figure 3-2). A good understanding of this model will enable you to understand all the various aspects of marketing communication that are discussed in the remainder of this book.

The communication process starts at the company brand or its agency, thus becoming the **source**, or **sender**—the *initiator of a message.* The first task is to decide what idea or statement the company actually wants to disseminate, and agencies can be particularly helpful here. The next step is to transform this generic message into a concrete one that can be communicated. The creation of an organization's brand messages is generally done by one or more MC agencies. In the basic model of communication, this *process of creating a brand message to convey an idea or statement* is called **encoding**.

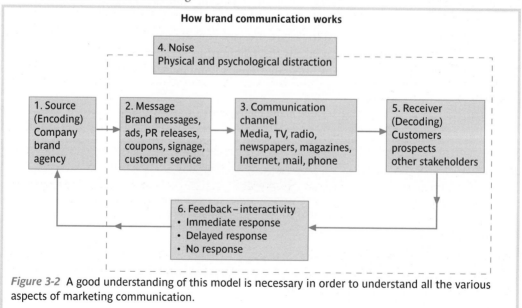

Figure 3-2 A good understanding of this model is necessary in order to understand all the various aspects of marketing communication.

A **message** is *an idea encoded in a combination of words, pictures, actions, symbols, and/or events.* The encoding challenge is to use words, pictures, and other cues whose meanings are shared by members of the intended audience. An **MC message** is *anything that talks about a brand, such as newspaper ads, radio commercials, direct-mail pieces, sales clerks, or customer service.* A communication **channel**, or **media vehicle**, is *the means by which a message is delivered—letter, e-mail, radio, television, newspaper, telephone, an event.*

The **receiver** is *anyone who is exposed to a message.* Once receivers, usually customers and prospects, receive a message, they must decode it. **Decoding** is the *process of interpreting what a message means.* After customers decode a message, they respond in some way, indicating to what extent the message was received, properly decoded, and persuasive. This response is called **feedback**, which is *a response that conveys a message back to the source.*

The communication process occurs in a context or environment where other things are going on—competitive brand messages, people walking by, a telephone ringing, as well as thoughts inside customers' heads. These "other things" are called **noise**—*interferences or distractions that can negatively affect the transmission and reception of a message.* Companies and their MC agencies go to great lengths to create brand messages that have impact—that are attention-getting as well as memorable.

Coffee with car to go

The Volvo Conservatory in Manila, the capital city of the Philippines, is an airy, sparkling-white showroom for Volvo cars that bears no resemblance to any other car showroom you have ever seen. It offers a coffee shop, a bank, music concerts, and art exhibits, as well as lectures on values and on the environment.

The Volvo Conservatory has taken the concept of an entertaining location to an extreme. Except for a display of three Volvo models and one auto accessory shop, there is no obvious sign that this is a car dealer's showroom. The Coffee Beanery, a chic local café, serves customers all day at one end of the showroom; at the opposite end sits a branch of the Urban Bank. People come to the Conservatory to use these facilities, so Volvo becomes part of their daily lives. Many Filipino coffee drinkers become Volvo buyers because of this subtle marketing approach.

The owner of the dealership, Selene Yu, has created a unique culture that appeals to Philippine sensitivities. He explains that the name Conservatory, which suggests an English greenhouse, is relevant because he views the business as a place to nurture the four values that Volvo wants to impart: safety, protection of the environment, social values, and support for the arts. All of these have broad appeal in the Philippines.

In addition to selling cars, the Volvo Conservatory holds concerts by local bands to convey the message that the car is not only for middle-aged executives but for young people as well. It sponsors environmental films to send the message that the Scandinavian automaker is committed to preserving nature. It sends car experts to colleges to educate students on car safety and responsible driving. Volvo brochures are passed around during all these events. The Conservatory works—and sells cars—because it appeals to the values of its Filipino customers.

Think about it

What is a touch point? Why should MC managers be concerned with touch points other than traditional marketing communication? In what ways does the Volvo Conservatory create unusual and effective customer touch points?

IMC in Action

How does marketing communication work?

Now let us reinterpret the basic communication model as a model of how marketing communication works. The numbers 1 to 6 in the subheads correspond with the numbers in Figure 3-2.

1 The source

Company-initiated touch points are about what companies want to communicate. This can be many different things, ranging from creating simple awareness, to an entire new position in the receiver's mind. In between is the creation of an association, a new link in the receiver's associative network. The strengthening of a link can be a goal as well. Deciding on this is not the easiest job. It requires both a long-term strategy and an awareness of short-term effectiveness. Associations are known to exist for a very long time, but can also be very effective when addressing current needs and wants.

An important factor when customers eventually decode a message and form attitudes about a brand is the perceived integrity of the sender. *The extent to which a message sender is believable* is called **source credibility**. Several years ago the scientist and cosmologist Carl Sagan was asked what one invention he would most like to see created. He answered: "A baloney detection kit so that every citizen can tell when he or she is being lied to."[2] Although Sagan was expressing concern about government sources, many customers feel the same way about advertising (and other MC) messages—always wondering what parts of ads are true and what parts are hype. Why do customers feel this way? They know that the sources of advertising are companies that are trying to sell them something. This does not mean customers do not believe anything they see in ads, but rather that they decode ads with caution.

This natural consumer scepticism is the reason why building brand trust is so important. The more customers and prospects trust a company and brand, the more likely they are to decode advertising with less scepticism. One way companies can help overcome source scepticism is by providing multiple "proof" points, or reasons why a brand will deliver on its promise. Another way is for companies to be good corporate citizens and refrain from doing things that affect their reputations negatively.

Knowing what to communicate requires a thorough analysis of the company's current position and what effects it wants to realize. This typically is a strategic issue that goes beyond the creation of advertisements or commercials. Yet, many agencies are playing a part here already.

2 Encoding into a brand message

The encoding step is generally the responsibility of MC agencies. Once the brand position and target audiences have been agreed upon, agencies create MC messages. Agencies must have a thorough understanding of the target audiences to ensure that the words, pictures, and other communication cues used in messages will be decoded with the meanings intended. (Encoding methods are explained in Chapters 6 and 7.)

Encoding and decoding are inseparably connected. Encoding is done with the decoding stage in mind. There are innumerable ways to translate an idea into communicable signs: pictures, words, sounds, gestures, expressions, etc. The art—or science—of encoding is therefore to select that one and only way which is noticed, and understood. In particular for the latter aspect, the encoder should be aware of the frame of reference of the target audience, those people that are assumed to receive and understand the message. For example, one of the most basic encoding decisions advertisers must take is in what language a message is to be disseminated. Or, when an advertiser wants to communicate that her product is meant for persons with high aspirations, encoding this message by introducing a successful person is a good idea; but who is successful critically depends on the frame of reference for the receiver of the message. Hence, the encoding decision to use a successful person is then only step one. The actual person further depends on how the target group will decode the presence of a certain person in the advertisement.

Stephen Manes, a technology columnist for *Forbes*, points out that what a receiver receives may not be what the source intended. Manes is particularly concerned with technological glitches, such as those that sometimes reformat e-mail: "The idea that what you transmit may not be what your correspondent receives—even before allowing for misinterpretation—hasn't yet managed to penetrate the corporate psyche."[3]

> You can never be sure how your message will look or sound to someone at the other end.
>
> *Stephen Manes,* Forbes *technology columnist*

3 Media channels: connecting companies and customers

Media are the channels that connect companies with customers. Most MC messages are carried by TV, radio, newspapers, magazines, Internet, mail, and outdoor boards. Most of these types of media can be used to reach not only mass audiences but smaller, specialized markets as well.

Non-traditional media—including buildings and sports stadiums that have electronic billboards and signage, faxes, kiosks, movies and TV shows (which have product placements), packaging, and even sidewalks—are carrying an increasing number of MC messages. And buzz, the word of mouth that happens when people talk about a product, is also the focus of some non-traditional strategies.

For many years media were considered primarily as vehicles or delivery systems. However, they should be thought of as channels that link companies and customers psychologically as well as physically. Psychologically, media can add to (or subtract from) the intended meaning of a MC message and campaign. Each medium has an image just as every brand has. A message in *Business Week* carries a different significance from one in *Playboy*, *Cosmopolitan*, or *Rolling Stone*. The more positive and relevant the image of a medium is to a brand, the more the medium can enhance that brand's messages. For example, B2B companies like to advertise in magazines such as *Business Week* and *Fortune*, which are seen as prestigious business publications and thus provide a prestigious editorial environment for ads. MacLuhan's statement that "the medium is the message" may be an exaggeration but it nevertheless illustrates an important point in thinking about communication channels.

4 Noise: the clutter that derails communication

In 2003 companies such as Honda and Toyota pulled their commercials from US television during the first days of war against Iraq, even though they knew viewership would be up.[4] These companies believed war reports could stir up tremendous emotional feelings that would make thinking about a new car purchase seem irrelevant. From the marketers' point of view, TV's editorial content was likely to be noise, drowning out the companies' messages intended for customers and prospects.

All communication, including marketing communication, takes place within an environment that contains distractions. Noise can be physical or psychological, and it can come from within or outside the intended communication effort (see Table 3-1). Although zero-defect communication is impossible to obtain, marketers must constantly work to minimize noise.

One of the most troublesome sources of psychological noise is inconsistent brand messages. A past advertising campaign for a popular American beer provides an example. A content

	Noise from a brand's communication process	Noise from outside a brand's communication process
Physical noise	■ Poor print reproduction ■ Distorted sound or visuals (electronic messages) ■ Bad timing of messages	■ Distracting sights and sounds in the environment ■ Recipient's multi-tasking ■ Competitive messages
Psychological noise	■ Mixed meanings of words or visuals ■ Dislike for or distrust of message source ■ Confusion resulting from inconsistent messages about brand promise	■ Irrelevance to recipient's wants and needs ■ Satisfaction with competitive brand

Table 3-1 Types and sources of noise

analysis of the TV commercials found three different selling strategies. Some of the commercials were selling "good taste", others "fun with friends" and still others "high quality". It was not realistic to expect customers to remember all these product claims, but customers who did remember them probably were confused about what this beer was really all about.

One type of noise of particular concern to marketers is **clutter**, which is *competition among commercial messages* (see colour insert A3). Clutter is evident when you open a newspaper and a bunch of ads stares you in the face. Clutter makes it difficult for a particular brand message to get attention. It is important, therefore, to know what competitors are saying, as well as when and where they are delivering their messages. Marketers compete not only for sales, but also for the attention of customers and prospects, as well as other stakeholders.

TV commercial breaks, for example, often contain up to 10 commercials. Magazines' and newspapers' content is 50 to 70 per cent ads. Primacy and recency theories say that the first thing and the last thing you see, hear, or read (in any situation) are more likely to be remembered than all the messages in the middle. Knowing this, agencies negotiate for the first or last place in a print publication or broadcast commercial break, to improve the odds that their messages will be remembered.

5 The receiver and decoding

In marketing communication, the intended receiver is the **target audience**, which is *a group that has significant potential to respond positively to a brand message.* There are three important issues here. The first concerns whether the messages actually reach the receiver mentally. When you look through a magazine or have the TV on, you physically receive many ads. But even though these ads may register on your senses, you probably only *really* read, watch, or listen to a small percentage of them. Second, once the receiver has taken notice of the message, it must be interpreted or decoded. Identical messages may be interpreted differently, and this interpretation is related to many highly idiosyncratic factors. The final question is what the receiver's response is psychologically. In this last stage of decoding, the question is what the effect of the decoded message is. In terms of the associative network model: is awareness increased? Are new associations added to the brand, or are existing links strengthened? Perhaps negative associations are removed?

Decoding is basically the reverse of encoding. Symbols sent by the source must be reconstructed into the original idea or into something close to it. For decoding to be successful, there needs to be shared meaning between the source and receiver. Otherwise, the receiver (the customer) will not understand correctly what the source (the company) is saying about the brand. Shared understanding of symbols is the result of common fields of experience between encoders and the intended audience.

Receivers' fields of experience determined by past activities and observations create the "codebook" used to find meaning in all messages, including brand messages. Fields of experience directly affect how receivers decode messages. They can make an audience more (or less) receptive to a brand message. Suppose your company designs boats and market research indicates that the target market in Europe for yachts tends to be euro-sceptics. You might not want to sub-brand your newest 42-foot sloop *Brussels*. The decoding process is also influenced by the receiver's immediate needs, wants, and concerns. If you are hungry, you will likely respond differently to a sign for pizza than you would if you had just eaten.

Marketers can help ensure that messages are decoded as intended by having a thorough understanding of customers, empathizing with them, and speaking their "literal and emotional language".[5] Even then, the potential for misinterpretation often still exists. For example, when a brand is advertised as selling for half price, the message can be decoded as "a good value" or as "a cheap, low-quality product". To clarify MC messages, companies use **strategic redundancy**, which means *saying the same thing in several different ways*, so that receivers will have several chances to get the message. One of the big advantages of an IMC programme is that it is designed to build in strategic redundancy by co-ordinating all the messages delivered by the various MC functional areas so they reinforce one another. To help ensure that messages are decoded as intended, companies need to be aware of their target audience's field of experiences.[6]

Another technique to help ensure proper decoding is keeping messages simple. An old rule of thumb in advertising says, "Be single-minded". This means that there should be only one main idea in a brand message. A variation on that principle is KISS—"Keep it simple, stupid"— which recognizes that the simpler the message's thought and execution, the easier it is for receivers to grasp the main point.

IMC helps close the gap between intended and perceived messages and thus minimizes the miscommunication, misperception, and misunderstanding that results from inadequate brand communication. It does this by being responsible for the way messages set expectations, and by monitoring the perceptions customers have about the brand. When expectations rise too high, a company must either work to bring its product performance up to that level or create MC messages that make more realistic promises.

Because a perception is the result of communication, a perception provides a window on the success of a message strategy. In other words, tracking customer perceptions is an important source of feedback and the first step in evaluating the success of brand messages.

6 *Feedback and interactivity*

In an attempt to convince 250 000 potential customers to try its Olay Daily Facials product, Olay launched a pilot programme that used the telephone to get prospective customers to respond. In exchange for limited personal information, consumers could obtain a free sample of the new product simply by calling 1-800-TRY-OLAY and interacting with a speech-recognition system. Consumers who called in were also given the option to join Club Olay, a relationship programme that provides consumers with free samples, newsletters, and other benefits. This is an example of how companies are striving to create interactivity with their customers by building a promotional programme around feedback.[7] Feedback indicates that customers, prospects, and other stakeholders have been "touched" by a brand message. There are three types of feedback: immediate, delayed, and no feedback at all.

Immediate feedback is ordering or buying, asking questions, sampling, or interacting in some other way with a brand soon after a brand message is received. Immediate feedback is especially valuable to those doing direct-response marketing (direct mail and telemarketing), which is designed to get the audience to respond immediately with a purchase or some other action. The same is true for most retail advertising, such as grocery and department store ads that include special prices. Other types of immediate response include queries and requests for information, visits to a store, trying a product or using a sample, or repeating the purchase of a product previously tried. Business-to-business marketing often uses feedback to generate leads for personal sales.

Delayed feedback is a response given at a later time. The delay does not mean that a message has had no impact. Image advertising, for example, is designed to work over time, creating and maintaining brand awareness and strong and favourable associations about a brand. The message impact of advertising comes at the point when the consumer is contemplating a purchase and a message impression from the advertising stimulates the selection of the advertised brand. Brand messages are also designed to reinforce brand choice—in other words, to keep current customers satisfied with their brand choice and confirm the wisdom of their choice. This is particularly important for major purchases, such as automobiles.

No feedback is rarely a desired response, but it is meaningful and important. When there is no feedback, a company needs to find out why, because it may indicate a negative impact. If the message was never received, the wrong media may have been used or the message may have been sent to the wrong place or at the wrong time. A non-response could also indicate that there was too much clutter or other noise, or simply that the message was not relevant or persuasive enough to move the target audience to respond. It could also mean that the consumer is not in the market for the product or is loyal to some other brand.

 The promotional monologue of advertising at the seller's convenience is being replaced by dialogue at the customer's convenience.

Anders Gronstedt, author of The Customer Century

If a message is received but misinterpreted, the message may have been poorly encoded. If a message was received and properly decoded but there still is no response, the message may not have been persuasive enough, or receivers may not have been potential customers. When the latter is found to be the case, the company should not waste money designing and sending further messages to this target audience, or should significantly change the message to appeal to the target audience's needs or interests.

Intrinsic touch points

Before investing in company-created touch points (which cost money), a brand should identify and examine its **intrinsic touch points**, which are *interactions with a brand required during the process of buying or using that brand.* Because these contacts are inherent to the buying or using of a brand, these touch points are always sending messages, especially to current customers. A logical way to think about these intrinsic touch points is in terms of the other elements of the marketing mix: the product, its price, and place where it can be acquired. Intrinsic touch points often also refer to the service component of products as well as the **extended marketing mix** for services, including people, physical evidence and the process of service delivery. Here is a list of intrinsic touch points for most car-rental businesses, illustrating the role of the extended marketing mix; it is impossible for a person to rent and use a car without these interactions:

- Company representative who answers freephone reservation number or clerk at rental counter.
- Driver of van to the car holding area.
- Attendant who checks car out of the car-holding area.
- Signage and directions.
- Accessibility of the car rental office.
- Appearance of the car lot and cleanliness of the van and rental office lobby.
- The rental car itself—how clean it is, how well it runs, and its brand name.
- How much does it cost?
- Attendant at car return area.

Product brand messages

United Parcel Service (UPS) makes a point of washing its delivery trucks every evening, knowing that a clean truck sends a message of professionalism and says, "This company takes pride in its work." Also operating on the principle that if something looks good it must be good, companies in the auto industry have always maintained staffs of industrial designers to style cars. The same principle also operates in other industries. In computers and appliances, industrial designers are important members of the product development team. When Apple Computer introduced the iMac, the new computer attracted the attention of computer users and shook up the entire computer industry and its approach to product design. The appearance of the iMac sent a powerful brand message. The extraordinary design of this computer reflected positively on Apple's association with creativity.

In the case of packaged goods, the package itself, such as a piece of Danone dessert, is an intrinsic touch point. How easy it is to open, to reseal and to dispose of all send messages about the brand. Because intrinsic touch points are inherent in the buying or using of a brand, they have the attention of the customer at least for a brief period of time. Recognizing this, companies can use these touch points to deliver a company-created brand message. For example, the Danone yogurt can be printed with a dessert recipe that calls for Danone yogurt, or the box can contain a peel-off coupon which is good for the next purchase. In the case of a car rental agency, promotional signs can be displayed and brochures distributed at the checkout and check-in touch points, as well as in the car.

Price brand messages

The price that is charged for a particular brand is a message indicating how the brand compares with competing brands in quality and status. That is why price is often used to differentiate brands. Other aspects of pricing also send strong messages. The frequency and the extent of brand promotions, for example, say something about a brand. The more a brand is on sale and the more it is discounted, the more ordinary it is perceived to be. When McDonald's unveiled its plan to sell Big Macs and Egg McMuffins for 55 cents (to help commemorate its 55 years of being in business), the company soon found it was sending a negative message. The price cut made some customers perceive the products as cheap and resulted in the financial community slicing a big chunk off the company's share price. One financial analyst commented, "They have transformed one of the great brands in American business into a commodity."[8] Pricing messages, like all others, must be strategically integrated with all other brand messages in order to send customers and other stakeholders a coherent, meaningful message. The IMC in Action box discusses the issue of demand pricing. What kinds of messages does this practice send?

Place (distribution) brand messages

The places where products are distributed can send brand messages. There is a big perceived difference, for example, between cosmetics sold at a French hypermarché and those sold in a boutique in the centre of Paris even when they are the same product or the same brand. The fact they are sold in a "discount" store says they must be a "discount" product. Another "place message" is communicated by where products are displayed within a store. Brands on the bottom shelf are often perceived as being not very popular.

IMC in Action

The customer side of demand pricing

What brand message is being sent when prices suddenly change? Computers and databases have enabled companies to use variations in price to help manage capacity and inventories. This strategy is called *demand pricing*. When capacities decrease, prices are raised to maximize revenue return on products being sold. Oil and gas prices are good examples of demand pricing.

Airlines have been using demand pricing for years. As the date of a scheduled flight comes closer, the airlines' computers automatically raise or lower prices in response to how many seats for that flight remain unsold. Using a database of historical sales, the airlines have good estimates of how many seats should be sold one week out, two weeks out, and so on. When seats for a particular flight are being sold faster than normal, the airlines raise the price for the remaining seats (and vice versa when sales are slower than expected). This is one reason why, for any given flight, the ticket prices paid by passengers on board greatly vary.

Using the same strategy, Coca-Cola is testing vending machines that raise and lower prices in response to changes in the outside temperature. Because more people buy soft drinks on hot days than on cold days, machines are programmed to charge more for a can of Coke when temperatures go up. It is also possible to programme vending machines to increase prices when sales significantly increase in a short period of time (for example, during a special event), in part to prevent the machine from running out before its regularly scheduled restocking.

Demand pricing may help Coke maximize its profits on vending machines, but it may also send a negative brand message to people who regularly use the vending machine. One day a can of Coke may cost 75 cents, and the next day, when the temperature goes up, a can may cost a euro. Will customers think they are getting ripped off? Will customers look for a Pepsi machine, where they know the price doesn't change? Will demand pricing make them switch from Coke to another brand the next time they go to the store and stock up on soft drinks?

Think about it

What is demand pricing? How might it send negative messages to customers? Why is demand pricing less of a problem for airlines than for soft-drink companies?

When the pen company Mont Blanc decided to reposition itself as an upmarket brand several years ago, one of the first things the company did was stop distributing its products in stationery stores that sold cheap pencils, pens, and paper along with paperback books and magazines. The company said those stores did not project the type of image with which it wanted the Mont Blanc brand to be associated.

People brand messages

Suppose you go to a bookstore and ask for the debut novel of Nicci French. In one bookstore the salesperson first takes a sip from his coffee, then glazes around apparently for some help, and then decides to go to the computer to check the inventory. "How do you spell Nicci", he asks. In another bookstore you have the same question. There the salesperson without hesitation leads you to the right corner, helps you identify the intended novel, and also points you to other novels by Nicci French. Further she tells you that if you like the genre, you may also be interested in the work of Liza Marklund.

Do the two reactions described make a difference? Of course they do. And you will not only relate them to the specific bookstores, but to the bookstore's brand as well. And if you were in another city, and were interested in visiting bookstores there, you would certainly know which one to choose.

People brand messages are important because they are very strong. The direct interaction with other people is about the strongest type of messages you can receive. People brand messages are, moreover, particularly important for services. In the absence of a tangible product, people are often the only connection between the consumer and the service brand.

Physical evidence brand messages

IKEA has dramatically changed the world of buying furniture with the introduction of the IKEA warehouses. IKEA broke with traditional ways of selling furniture by introducing the warehouse concept in the industry. The way the shops were designed underlined the basic message of IKEA, that the products need not be as expensive as the traditional retailers suggest. IKEA shops are invariably crowded, not only with people, but also with products. All products have fancy names, and customers are addressed in an informal, yet friendly way. Shopping bags and carts are available for the smaller items, the larger items can be picked up in the stock area. Compare the physical evidence of an IKEA shop with any other traditional furniture retailer.

Not only the interior of the IKEA warehouses communicates, however. The warehouses themselves have a distinct and meaningful architecture, emphasizing the Swedish origins of the company but, more important, also the simplicity and straightforwardness of the whole IKEA concept. On top of that the IKEA outlets are easily recognized in any shopping mall.

Process brand messages

For years, renting a car meant standing in line at a rental office and then filling out a lot of paperwork. Recognizing that this was not a pleasant customer experience (i.e. an intrinsic, negative brand message), rental car companies introduced a special service for heavy users. Hertz's Gold Card service, for example, requires members to provide all their personal information, including credit-card number, only once. From then on, Gold Car members are taken directly to the car holding area where a sign displays members' names and the slots in which their cars are waiting with keys in the ignition and trunks open waiting for luggage. All a Gold Card customer is required to do is show a valid driver's licence and the rental agreement (which is hanging on the review mirror) when exiting the Hertz lot. This type of service sends a positive message to Hertz heavy users: "Hertz cares about you, knows your time is valuable, and will do a little more work at our end to ensure that your experience is hassle free."

Although marketing is often not directly responsible for many of the intrinsic touch points, such as managing service personnel, marketing can make suggestions about how to improve these interactions with customers in order to send a positive brand message. How quickly does a company reply to customer enquiries and complaints? A response seems more positive, regardless of its content, if it is given sooner rather than later. A timely response "says" that the company is concerned and has made the customer's problem a top priority.

As you can see, intrinsic touch points not only send messages, but often provide the opportunity to deliver company-created messages. Also, because intrinsic touch points, by definition, involve current customers, the messages sent at these touch points are some of the most critical in retaining customers.

Unexpected touch points

As their name suggests, **unexpected touch points** are *unanticipated references to a brand that are beyond the control of the company.* They can be either positive or negative. One of the most powerful types is **word-of-mouth brand messages**, or *personal communication between customers or other stakeholders about a brand*, particularly when it is from a dissatisfied customer. A face-to-face personal message from someone you know can be more persuasive than ads and other MC messages, particularly if the point is supported by solid reasons. This kind of personal word of mouth has the power of **third-party credibility**, the believability of *people who are not affiliated with a brand and have nothing to gain or lose from its success or failure.* Third parties are often more believable than company sources because they have no vested interest in a brand.

Other stakeholders—investors and analysts, employees, suppliers, distributors, and government officials—can also be sources of unexpected messages. Although negative comments can be the most damaging messages a brand faces, unexpected positive word-of-mouth messages from any of these sources can be powerful testimony on behalf of the brand.

The media also produce unexpected touch points by writing about a brand or company. In almost all product categories today—from cooking to computers—there are experts who write and talk about products. Publicity releases generate brand touch points, but companies have no control over what stories these releases inspire the media to produce. In the Netherlands public utilities have been privatized. One of the consequences was that salaries of chief executives rose to competitive levels. To the Dutch public this was hardly acceptable and soon the press started to write about exaggerated remuneration for the CEOs while customer service was perceived to decrease. As will be explained in Chapter 12 on PR and publicity, although companies cannot control unexpected touch points, there are things they can do to anticipate and influence them.

Customer-initiated touch points

A communication area that marketing departments often overlook is the **customer-initiated touch point**, *an interaction that occurs whenever a customer or prospect contacts a company.* As the communication model in Figure 3-3 shows, customers and prospects can be the source of brand messages in the same way as a company and its MC agencies. In other words, marketing communication can be two-way communication as well as one way. At first glance, the customer-initiated touch-point model may look similar to the MC model shown in Figure 3-2.

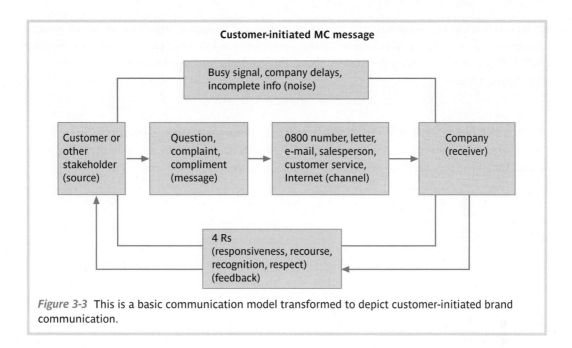

Figure 3-3 This is a basic communication model transformed to depict customer-initiated brand communication.

A close look, however, reveals the differences. The major difference is that the source is now the customer or stakeholder, rather than the brand, which becomes the receiver. Likewise, the messages and the channels of communication are different.

Managing the response to customer-initiated touch points is a critical part of IMC because these contacts, like intrinsic brand contacts, occur primarily with current customers and thus significantly impact on customer retention. Most customer-initiated touch points involve complaints or enquiries about product usage. Contacts are made by angry or frustrated customers who may stop using the brand if they are not satisfied. How a company responds can significantly impact on the repurchase decisions of these customers.

The new communication technologies make it easier for customers to contact a company. At the same time, to show they are customer focused, more and more companies are inviting customers and prospects to contact them by advertising their 0800 numbers and e-mail and website addresses on packages and in many of their other MC messages. Many companies, however, do a poor job of responding to customer-initiated messages. Studies on e-mail and phone contacts have found that the majority of company responses are rated only fair or poor.[9] One of the main problems facing companies today is how to interact with, and have a purposeful dialogue with, customers cost-effectively.

Purposeful dialogue and interactivity

Purposeful dialogue, *communication that is mutually beneficial for the customer and the company*, is a more meaningful concept than the popular term interactivity, *two-way communication that sends and receives messages from customers and other stakeholders*. Interactivity can lead to responding indiscriminately to any customer-initiated contact. For example, one of the early mistakes made by companies using the Internet was inviting everyone to talk to them. Many responders were not customers or potential customers but merely people surfing the Internet looking for something to do. Few companies can afford unproductive interactivity. Similarly, companies talk a great deal about creating a dialogue with customers. But in too many cases their brand communication is intrusive and irritating and thus perceived as self-serving and providing no added value for the customer. For the communication to be mutually useful, the customer must want to hear about the products and must choose to be exposed to this information.

The four Rs of purposeful dialogue

To be successful, interactivity must embody the four Rs of purposeful dialogue that customers are looking for: *recourse, recognition, responsiveness,* and *respect.*

- **Recourse:** A major concern of most customers is how to avoid risk when buying a product. What are their options after buying—that is, what recourse do they have if they do not like the product, if it doesn't work properly, or if it breaks? **Recourse** is *easy access to someone who can solve a problem.* How companies handle complaints, for example, affects repeat purchases. This aspect of marketing communication is second only to product quality in building customer loyalty. The easier it is for customers to get questions answered and problems dealt with, the more likely they are to develop good relationships with a company. The Bombay Company, a furniture manufacturer and retailer, has a no-questions-asked policy. Says President and CEO Robert Nourse, "We'll take the thing back with no hassle, no questions, no guff about 'Where's the receipt?' The cost of that is peanuts compared with what you gain in customer loyalty."[10]

- **Recognition:** Customers and other stakeholders like to be personally recognized; that is one of the first steps in a relationship. In IMC, **customer recognition** means *company acknowledgment of purchases and of the customer's interaction history with the company.* You remember conversations you have had with friends. For a brand relationship to be effective, there must be some way to nurture that same kind of memory. This is also why call centres collect data and ask you for a reference. The initial agony of being treated as a number is soon overcome by the satisfaction that the person at the call centre knows about your history with the company.

  An even better type of recognition occurs when a company not only knows a customer's transaction history but incorporates references to it (when appropriate) into future communications with that customer: customers who are frequent buyers receive special recognition, and customers who had problems with the company receive empathetic attention. Consumers, however, will see through insincere recognition. In direct-mail solicitations, it is wiser to address them "to the occupier", than to address a potential customer by name. Although the former is more impersonal, if the company has had no relationship with the customer, the person being contacted will recognize this familiarity as a ploy.

- **Responsiveness:** Merely providing customers with a freephone number or an e-mail address so they can easily reach the company is not being responsive. Responsiveness occurs when a company representative listens to a customer and stays with the customer until the problem is solved or next steps are agreed to. In other words, **responsiveness** is *a reaction that produces customer satisfaction after a customer-initiated company contact.* The amount of time elapsing between when a product is ordered and when it is received, or between when a complaint is made and when a reply is received, sends a strong message. The shorter the elapsed time, the more responsive a company is seen to be. Texas Instruments receives approximately 200 000 enquiries a year. Over 95 per cent are answered within two hours and nearly all within 24.[11]

■ ***Respect:*** Howard Gossage, a partner in a San Francisco advertising agency in the 1950s and 1960s, has gone down in advertising history as one of the most insightful and intelligent people to work in advertising.[12] Among his many insights was the idea that a marketer's audience is more important than the product or brand. Gossage preached that, without respect for the audience, a company's advertising is sure to be a waste of money. Respect means *consideration* and not hammering customers with advertisements and other messages in which they have little interest.

Companies that have a purposeful dialogue with their customers listen and respond to customers and do not constantly bombard them with "sales" messages. Herb Kelleher, CEO of Southwest Airlines, explains in one sentence why Southwest is known for great customer service: "We don't have a Marketing Department, we have a Customer Department." Southwest's emphasis on the people part of its marketing effort has created a 360-degree view of the whole brand, one that creates a total brand experience based on all brand messages, through all channels, and at all touch points.[13] Southwest understands the importance of company–customer touch points.

A final note: everything communicates

Every time a customer gets into touch with a brand, something is learned about the brand. In all instances the basic communication model of Figure 3-2 has validity. Also, in the case of intrinsic touch points, a message is created, encoded, disseminated, received and decoded. Similarly, word-of-mouth by e-mail will have a different kind of impact from oral word-of-mouth. But the important lesson is that indeed everything communicates.

In the remainder of the book, attention will only be paid to company-created touch points. These are the planned and controlled communication messages, hence the ones that are subject to managerial decision making. However, a Marketing Communications manager should never forget, and should fully understand, the impact other touch points may have on the target audiences, how these other touch points may interfere with the company-created touch points and, finally, seek to exert as much control over the other types of touch points as possible. Everything communicates!

🔑 Key terms

brand–customer touch point Any situation in which a customer comes into contact with a brand or company.

channel/media vehicle The means by which a message is delivered—letter, e-mail, radio, television, newspaper, telephone, an event.

clutter Competition among commercial messages.

company-created touch point Planned Marketing Communication messages, such as ads, news releases, brochures, and information on packages.

customer-initiated touch point An interaction that occurs whenever a customer or prospect contacts a company.

customer recognition Company acknowledgment of purchases and of the customer's interaction history with the company.

decoding Process of interpreting what a message means.

encoding Process of creating a brand message to convey an idea or statement.

extended marketing mix The marketing instruments that explicitly recognize the different aspects of services marketing, consisting of product, price, place, promotion, people, process and physical evidence.

feedback A response that conveys a message back to the source.

interactivity Two-way communication that sends and receives messages from customers and other stakeholders.

intrinsic touch point Interactions with a brand required during the process of buying or using that brand.

MC message Anything that talks about a brand, such as newspaper ads, radio commercials, direct-mail pieces, sales clerks, or customer service.

message An idea encoded in a combination of words, pictures, actions, symbols, and/or events.

noise Interferences or distractions that can negatively affect the transmission and reception of a message.

purposeful dialogue Communication that is mutually beneficial for the customer and the company.

receiver Anyone who is exposed to a message.

recourse Easy access to someone who can solve a problem.

respect Consideration.

responsiveness A reaction that produces customer satisfaction after a customer-initiated company contact.

sender/source Initiator of a message.

source credibility The extent to which a message sender is believable.

strategic redundancy Saying the same thing in several different ways.

target audience A group that has significant potential to respond positively to a brand message.

third-party credibility People who are not affiliated with a brand and have nothing to gain or lose from its success or failure.

unexpected touch point Unanticipated references to a brand that are beyond the control of the company.

word-of-mouth brand messages Personal communication between customers or other stakeholders about a brand.

Check the key points

Key point 1: Touch points

a   What is a touch point?
b   What different types of touch points exist? What are their differences?
c   Which touch points are controlled by a company?

Key point 2: The communication model

a   What are the six elements in the standard communication model?
b   What is encoding? What is decoding?
c   Clarify the difference between a message and a channel.
d   Explain the role of noise in the model.
e   What is meant by "strategic redundancy"?

Key point 3: Interactive communications

a   What does the communication model look like when it is applied to customer-initiated touch points?
b   What are the four Rs of purposeful dialogue?

Chapter Challenge

Writing assignment

You have been asked to advise a local franchise of a large national supermarket chain on how to manage its communication programme. Develop the franchise's own communication model, and explain how the model can help the supermarket identify its communication problems and develop better communication programmes and activities.

Presentation assignment

For your student association, develop a presentation that makes clear what touch points are relevant and should be taken into account in managing the communications function. In an outline, list the key points you want to present. Give the presentation to your class or record it on video to turn in to your instructor, along with the outline.

Group assignment

Have you ever had a bad experience when travelling by air? Or a good experience? Did you make an effort to complain to or compliment the company? For this assignment, you first write a complaint letter, and send it to a classmate. Second, you respond to the letter you received. Take the four Rs of purposeful dialogue into account!

Notes

[1] Roger Hallowell, Leonard A. Schlesinger, and Jeffrey Zornitsky, "Internal Service Quality, Customer and Job Satisfaction: Linkages and Implications for Management", *Human Resource Planning*, 19, no. 2 (1996), pp. 20–32.

[2] Patrick Jackson, *pr reporter* newsletter, 23 January 1995.

[3] Stephen Manes, "Baby, What'd I Say?" *Forbes*, 1 November 1999, p. 410.

[4] Aimee Picchi and Kim Chipman, "Battle Shifts Theme of Ads", *Bloomberg News, Daily Camera*, 21 March 2003, p. E1.

[5] Jon Steel, *Truth, Lies and Advertising* (New York, Wiley, 1998), p. xv.

[6] Ibid.

[7] Patricia Odell, "Olay's Dial-Up Program to Deliver 250,000 Samples", *Direct Newsline*, 17 April 2003.

[8] Greg Burns, "McDonald's: Now, It's Just Another Burger Joint", *Business Week*, 17 March 1997, p. 38.

[9] Jason Riley, "How Companies Handle Customer-Initiated Brand Contacts", *IMC Research Journal* (2001), p. 6.

[10] Jay Finegan, "Survival of the Smartest", *Inc.*, December 1993, p. 88.

[11] Earl Naumann, *Creating Customer Value* (Cincinnati: Thompson Executive Press, 1995), p. 82.

[12] Howard Luck Gossage, *The Book of Gossage*, ed. Bruce Bendinger (Chicago: Copy Workshop, 1995).

[13] Kristine Kirby Webster, *MarketingProfs.com*, 17 September 2002, www.marketingprofs.com.

Further reading

Bitoun, Catherine (2006) "Semiotics, as a tool to understand and take action", *Marketing Review*, Vol. 6–2, pp. 111–21.

Brennan, Ian and Kenneth D. Bahn (2006) "Literal versus Extended Symbolic Messages and Advertising Effectiveness: The Moderating Role of Need for Cognition", *Psychology & Marketing*, Vol. 23–4, pp. 273–95.

Dunn, Michael and Scott Davis (2003) "Building brands from the inside", *Marketing Management*, Vol. 12–3, pp. 32–7.

Hogan, Suzanne, Eric Almquist and Simon E. Glynn (2005) "Brand-building: Finding the touchpoints that count", *Journal of Business Strategy*, Vol. 26–2, pp. 11–18.

Schoefer, Klaus and Christine Ennew (2004) "Customer Evaluations of Tour Operators' Responses to Their Complaints", *Journal of Travel & Tourism Marketing*, Vol. 17–1, pp. 83–92.

Shields, Peggy O. (2006) "Customer Correspondence: Corporate Responses and Customer Reactions", *Marketing Management Journal*, Vol. 16–2, pp. 155–70.

Winkler, Tina and Kathy Buckner (2006) "Receptiveness of Gamers to Embedded Brand Messages in Advergames: Attitudes towards Product Placement", *Journal of Interactive Advertising*, Vol. 7–1, pp. 37–46.

Wu, Bob T. and Stephen J. Newell (2003) "The Impact of Noise on Recall of Advertisements", *Journal of Marketing Theory & Practice*, Vol. 11–2, pp. 56–65.

Consumer response

CHAPTER PERSPECTIVE
Reactions, responses and decisions

Imagine you and two friends of yours were at a party last weekend and you heard a new CD. Your hosting friend mentioned it was by a great new group and she really likes their music. Two days later as you were leafing through *Rolling Stone*, you saw a review of this CD and the group. You read the review noting that is was written by a journalist whom you respect. Next day you were in a record store and you saw a poster announcing the group's new CD release. You asked the retailer to listen to a couple of tracks from the CD and your good feelings about it made you decide to buy.

The next day you met your other friends. All three appeared to have bought the CD, but your stories differed. Michael witnessed that his trip to the record store was the first thing he did the day after the party where he bought the CD without even asking to listen to it. Peter was just marginally less quick. He was in the store one day after Michael. He was there for another CD, but when he saw the poster, he recalled the party and that he really liked the group's music. He asked the store manager to listen to excerpts and what he heard gave him the same good feeling as during the party.

Different people walk different paths but can end at the same place. And various kind of messages (a friend's testimony, an article in a magazine, a poster, sampling) can all play their roles in influencing people's decisions. This chapter seeks to examine systematically the process of decision making by consumers, or more generally the responses that receivers of MC messages can display. Before you can understand how MC messages work to impact on consumer attitudes and behaviours that lead to a particular brand choice, you need a more general understanding of how consumers go about making brand decisions.

Customers love the Starbucks experience

Besides home, school, and work, where do people gather to meet friends and relax in a comfortable environment? Starbucks Coffee has made that place a Starbucks coffee shop for some 22 million customers a week.

Starting with a single coffee shop in Seattle, USA in 1971, Starbucks has now grown into a global brand. With more than 6400 stores worldwide Starbucks has become a major player in the coffee market. On a fast growth track, the company had 10 000 stores by the end of 2005.

Starbucks sells hot and cold coffees, espressos, mochas, lattes, au laits, cappuccinos, frappucinos (a frozen coffee blended with a variety of flavours), and even Chai and Tazo tea, as well as pastries, coffee beans, espresso machines, and other gift items. The product line varies with the location and the climate. But the constant focus is on customer service and on the quality of the coffee—the beans, how they are roasted, how they are mixed and flavoured, as well as how the coffee is rotated out and kept fresh in the stores. All brewed coffee is less than an hour old when it is served. The emphasis on a quality coffee experience makes it possible for the company to charge premium prices for what used to be seen as a commodity product.

Who are these Starbucks customers?

Starbucks originally targeted young college-age people typical of the Seattle coffee house culture. Then those people grew up and became young, upwardly mobile executives. Yuppies and baby boomers—another group that connects with the Starbucks experience—like to celebrate their affluence with little treats like gourmet coffee. Both groups are less interested in the bar scene and more attracted to environments where they can hang out, listen to music, and visit with friends. Both groups seem to value Starbucks as much for the coffee shop experience as for the coffee itself.

How do people decide to go to Starbucks?

Buying a fancy gourmet coffee drink is definitely not a basic need but rather, an expressive choice that reflects customers' aspirations as well as their desire for a relaxing social experience. Starbucks has almost single-handedly upgraded the tired image of the 1960s smoky coffee house into a cozy French sidewalk café or Italian espresso bar. In the US it has created a small cultural revolution in people's social behaviour.

Starbucks also makes the decision to choose Starbucks easy by having lots of convenient locations. The master plan calls for a Starbucks on every corner—or nearly. In New York City, for example, there are more than 300 Starbucks coffee shops. The location of that corner, however, is very important as the company seeks to make convenience part of the Starbucks mystique. You can also find Starbucks at airports, bookstores, and hotels through

IMC in Action

alliances with such companies as Barnes & Noble, Sheraton and Westin hotels, and United Airlines. And the Starbuck's frappuccino beverage is sold in supermarkets, as well as in the coffee shops.

Starbucks appeals to the head and heart

The Starbucks attraction is partly head and partly heart. On the cognitive level (head), Starbucks has transformed customers' preferences by teaching them what good coffee tastes like. Starbucks has established a worldwide standard for great coffee, and its customers simply know that its coffee tastes better. It has also profited from the growing market for gourmet coffee, which has made traditional coffee from long-time coffee brands such as Maxwell House and Folgers seem less desirable.

Customers also choose Starbucks because they like the company's community focus and social responsibility platform. To quickly build a customer base for each new store, a store connects with a local charity and gives free drinks and donates tips and other funds to that organization. The strategy of connecting immediately with a local cause helps overcome the image of Starbucks as a large, impersonal global chain.

Another reason customers choose to visit Starbucks is the staff. Starbucks employees are called *baristas,* Italian for bar server (somewhat like a sommelier in a fancy French restaurant, who helps you choose your wine). The company believes that every dollar invested in employees shows up in customer satisfaction and, ultimately, on the bottom line. The company's generous employee benefits packages include health care, dental care, stock options, training and motivational programmes, career counselling, and product discounts for all workers, full-time as well as part-time. Employees also are encouraged to play an active role in the environment movement, as well as in other local communities causes, and are given time off for these activities.

In line with the environmental awareness of both of its target audiences (boomers and yuppies), Starbucks donates money to the Earth Day Network ($50 000 in 2003) and has in-store promotions for local Earth Day activities. Its customized cup sleeve carries an environmental message and the Earth Day Network website. Starbucks' director of environmental affairs explained that the company tries "to reduce its impact on the planet" through programmes such as giving away coffee grounds for garden compost. In 2003 hundreds of Starbucks partners were involved in Earth Day activities, such as

- Teaming up with Earth Fest in Dallas in a downtown area beautification project.
- Joining with Denver Urban Gardens in an effort to beautify the city's parks.
- Partnering with Friends of Morningside Park, the Columbia University Earth Coalition, and the New York City Parks Department on the seventh annual Morningside Park cleanup project.

Problems in Java heaven?

International success can bring headaches. In some countries, anti-US protesters of Operation Iraqi Freedom made Starbucks a target. Although most of its domestic stores are company owned, its international strategy uses joint ventures or licences to other companies, which own and operate the local stores. This strategy is designed to make the chain responsive to local concerns. Even Arab-owned stores, however, were closed for a while because of anti-US protests over the Iraq and Palestine situations.

Because Starbucks has become a cultural corporate icon, it also attracts critics of large corporations. There is a website entitled "Ihatestarbucks.com". Naomi Klein's book *No Logo* is critical of Starbucks for its coffee-harvesting conditions and some of its employee practices.[1]

The bottom line

Starbucks started as a six-store Seattle coffee-bean retailer. But the vision of its chairman and CEO, Howard Schultz, was to follow in McDonald's footsteps. Schultz has built the Starbucks brand, on a minuscule budget and with little advertising, from a small business to a global corporation with some $4 billion in annual revenues. The company's messages—the ones with the most impact on customers—are delivered in customer service and by employees who operate like ambassadors, creating strong personal relationships with their regular customers. The response by satisfied customers is keeping Starbucks on a roll on Main Streets around the world.

Note

[1] Naomi Klein (2002) *No Logo*, Picador.

Sources:

Helen Jung, *"Starbucks' Growth Risks Backlash in War Protests"*, The Detroit News, *22 April 2003, www.detnews.com/2003/business/0304/22/b04-143736.htm*

"Starbucks Coffee Celebrates Earth Day with $50,000 Commitment", 17 April 2003, CSR Wire, www.csrwire. com/article.cgi/ 1758.html

Rick Aristotle Munarriz, *"Krispy Kreme vs. Starbucks"*, The Motley Fool, *www.Fool.com, 22 April 2003*

Jack Sirard, *"Starbucks Has a Way of Beating Pessimists"*, The Sacramento Bee, *22 April 2003, www.sacbee.com/content/business/v-print/story/6497865p-74*

"Making Customers Come Back for More", Fortune, *16 March 1998, pp. 156–7*

Prospects and customers, consumers and business buyers

The phrase *consumer behaviour* is used to refer to how people and organizations think about, buy, and use products. (Companies *consume* just as individuals do, however, the word "consumer" generally refers to individuals.) Marketing communication managers are particularly interested in how consumers' thoughts and behaviours develop *as a response to MC messages.* For marketers to design brand messages that elicit responses and influence someone's decision-making process, they first need to understand to whom they are talking—current customers or prospects, consumers or businesses—and how those audiences respond to MC messages. Different types of consumers respond to MC messages in different ways, and MC managers must recognize these differences, as well as understand the reasons behind them.

Customers versus consumers

The terms "customers" and "consumers" are often used interchangeably, but making the difference helps in understanding people's and organizations' responses to MC messages. A **customer** in this respect is *the person or organization who takes the buying decision.* In contrast, the **consumer** is the *person or organization who actually uses the product*. Sheth and Mittal even describe three roles in customer behaviour, namely those of the buyer (the customer in the above terminology), the user (the consumer) and the payer.[1] When your mother selects a nice article of clothing for you, which your father pays for, the roles of buyer, user and payer become immediately clear.

Even though the different roles may be performed by the same person, it is nevertheless useful to be aware of the distinction. Later in this chapter it will become clear that the different roles people or organizations play relate to different phases of their buying behaviour. In this book the words consumer and customer will nevertheless be used interchangeably, unless an explicit distinction is deemed useful.

Prospects versus current customers

The brand decision-making process of a person who is considering a brand for the first time is different from that of someone who has purchased that brand before. A **prospect** is *a person who has never bought a brand but might be interested in it*. A **current customer** is *a person who has purchased a brand at least once within a designated period*.

From a company perspective, *motivating a prospect to buy for the first time* is the process of acquiring a customer and thus requires an **acquisition strategy**, an important objective of which is creating brand awareness. *Motivating a customer to make repeat purchases* is a **retention strategy**. Here, rather than focusing marketing communication on brand awareness (since it has already been achieved to some extent), MC messages keep the brand top-of-mind and motivate more frequent purchases. For current customers MC strategies make part of the larger customer–relationship management approach (see Chapter 2).

One of the biggest mistakes a company can make is to take it for granted that current customers will continue to make repeat purchases. Acquisition and retention call for different types of message strategies because prospects and customers use different pathways in making a brand decision. Persuading current customers to make repeat purchases is easier and less costly than motivating a prospect to buy for the first time, but it still requires some strategic marketing communication effort.

Consumers versus business buyers

Prospects and customers exist in both the B2B and the B2C markets. In B2B communication the buying decisions of prospects or current customers call for different levels of involvement and cognitive processing from those in typical B2C communication. Most business decision makers, for example, do more research and analysis than consumers, and they use more of a cognitive approach than an emotional one. Other differences between consumer and business decision making include the following:

- Business buying decisions generally involve inputs from more than one person. The larger the decision is, the more people and departments are involved. Sheth and Mittal's roles of buyer, user and payer referred to above become truly explicit in B2B situations. Some business people have buying authority; others can greatly influence the buying decision. Technical people such as engineers may not actually purchase equipment, but a company's high-tech buyer probably consults them before choosing computer and software systems. Identifying who has the buying authority is usually not as difficult as determining who influences the buying decision. To maximize sales, B2B marketers need to target brand messages to both buyers and influencers.

- Most businesses buy goods in larger quantities than consumers, so the average business transaction is generally worth considerably more than the average consumer transaction. In B2B marketing, the high cost of personal selling—the most expensive MC function—can be justified with other forms of MC messages used to support these personal selling efforts.

- Large business transactions often affect other activities within a company; therefore, business buying carries higher risk than consumer buying. Minimizing risk is always an objective of business buyers and something that B2B marketers must keep in mind when creating brand messages.

- Many business buying decisions are based on responses to requests for proposals (RFPs). A business that wants to make a major purchase invites companies to bid on satisfying a stated need. The Internet makes it possible for companies to send their RFPs to more bidders and makes the response process faster than ever before. RFPs form a common business platform on the Internet and have even moved into B2C marketing with the success of such companies as eBay.

What influences consumer decision making?

Customers and prospects are influenced by a number of cultural and social forces, as well as personal factors. All of these combine to establish the context within which marketing communication is delivered and the way people respond to the messages.

The sociocultural context

Culture—*group values based on traditions and distinctive history*—includes such things as sets of common beliefs, attitudes, and values. Cultural values that relate to clothing, music, food, and drink can determine the appropriateness (or inappropriateness) of marketing certain types of products. For example, marketing bikinis and alcoholic beverages might not be appropriate in Muslim cultures, no matter what the brand message. Society is *a group of people who live together and organize their lives as a community.* Relationships result from intimate bonds, such as family ties, but they are also a product of a sense of community.[2] As was discussed in Chapter 2, forms of community can form around brands.

Companionship is another aspect of the social context that affects how people respond to a message. We know that people respond to, and value, what their family and friends say about brands. For example, in the opening story about the CD, an important message came from a friend who knew the group and liked its music. Word-of-mouth messages can be extremely persuasive to someone considering a purchase decision, especially if they come from a person who is better informed or more experienced with the brand or product.

Social class is *a ranking of people in a society by factors such as family history, occupation, education, and income.* Some societies, such as India, are highly stratified with clearly defined social classes. Other societies, like most in Europe, are more fluid, and to some extent people can move up as a result of their own initiative and accomplishments—and most expect to do so. In Western societies, therefore, aspirational messages—those that present an image or product associated with a group to which the customer *wishes* to belong—usually strike a chord, especially among people roughly identified as being in the middle class. The following list identifies the most common social classes and indicates their typical relative size:[3]

- ***Upper upper*** (1 per cent of the population): The highest class, usually represented by "old money" and well-known families.

- *Upper* (about 2 per cent): Professionals and business people who have achieved financial success.

- *Middle* (about 43 per cent): Professionals, small-business owners, and corporate managers with comfortable incomes.

- *Working class* (about 38 per cent): Lower-middle class or blue-collar workers who earn an average pay.

- *Upper lower* (about 9 per cent): The "working poor", who perform unskilled labour and menial work for minimal wages.

- *Lower* (about 7 per cent): People who dwell in poverty and are often unemployed and on welfare.

Of course, the sizes of the group vary per country, as well as the terms used to denote the various groups. For example, some countries use the A, B, C, etc. categories. But in all these countries the concept of social class is recognized, and the marketing consequences are similar throughout.

Some of the most powerful motivating forces in brand decision making are the people who influence customers' decision making. Sociologists use the term **reference group** to indicate *the associations and organizations with which people identify or to which they belong and which influence their attitudes and behaviours.* For customers, reference groups include family,[4] friends, fellow workers, recognized category experts, as well as well-known people such as athletes, entertainers, and politicians. For businesses, reference groups include professional associations, brand leaders in their product category, consultants, and important customers. Messages from these people, particularly word-of-mouth testimonials, can be an extremely persuasive form of communication.

Reference groups can be grouped into five categories: personal, membership, experts, aspirational, and disassociative:

Reference Group Categories

Personal   Family, friends, co-workers
Membership   Clubs, churches, schools
Experts   Opinion leaders, consultants, leading professionals in category
Aspirational   Famous entertainers, athletes, politicians
Disassociative Counterculture, gangs, antisocial people

That last group is a *negative* reference group: most people generally want to do and buy the *opposite* of what members of a disassociative group do and buy.

A reference group that has caught specific interest of MC specialists are **opinion leaders**, *people to whom others turn for advice or information.* Lawrence Feick and Linda Price developed the concept of "market maven" to describe people who are actively involved in passing on marketplace information,[5] particularly about trends such as new fashions, music groups, and computer programs and games. MC programmes are sometimes designed to reach these people specifically, because marketers know that they will influence others.

Marketing communication often situates a message in a social context that uses the reference group as a cue. For example, a country club or a sports team may connect with an audience's sense of affiliation, the message being, "I want to be like them". Research has shown that reference groups play a big role in the decision to purchase products that are publicly used or consumed—such as clothes, cars, watches, golf clubs, skis, rental cars. Even disassociative groups can be used effectively in marketing, as in the gross-out behaviour of characters in some anti-smoking campaigns.

Personal factors

In addition to age, gender, and education, other personal factors—needs and wants, attitudes, opinions and beliefs, personality, and motivation—affect how people approach a buying decision. Some people are experimenters and rush to try something new; others are risk averse and hold back until a new product has a track record. Because every person is an individual, the closer a marketing communication can speak to a person as an individual, the more likely is the message to ring true. Here are some of the key personal factors that affect how people respond to MC messages.

Needs and wants   Demand for goods and services is motivated by human **needs and wants,** which are *biological and psychological motivations that drive actions*. While both biological needs (such as for food or shelter) and psychological ones (such as for love or respect) require more immediate response, wants command a lot of attention in consumers' minds. Needs are what we feel we *must* have; wants are what we would *like* to have. It must be acknowledged however that in our affluent Western societies the distinction between needs and wants seems hard to maintain.

Marketing communicators have found the hierarchy of needs described by the psychologist Abraham Maslow to be a help in analysing the strength of these needs and wants (see Figure 4-1).[6] **Maslow's hierarchy of needs** is *an arrangement of human needs and wants listed in the order in which, according to Maslow, people satisfy them*. According to Maslow, only when basic, low-level needs are satisfied do people consider wants at higher levels in the hierarchy. At the base

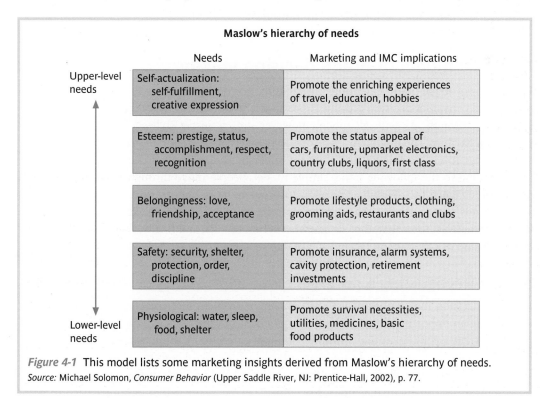

Figure 4-1 This model lists some marketing insights derived from Maslow's hierarchy of needs.
Source: Michael Solomon, *Consumer Behavior* (Upper Saddle River, NJ: Prentice-Hall, 2002), p. 77.

are physiological needs for water, food, clothing, and shelter. Above them are needs for safety, followed by psychological wants for belongingness, esteem, and self-actualization (finding challenge in new ideas and creative impulses).

Marketers must understand needs and wants because the marketing concept is based on the notion that companies should sell products designed to meet customers' needs and wants, not whatever is easiest for the company to produce. The next personal factors are important because they guide brand responses.

Attitudes, opinions, and beliefs   An *attitude* is *a general disposition or orientation toward objects, people, and ideas usually accompanied by negative or positive judgements.* An *opinion* is *a specific judgement that is emotionally neutral.* A *belief* is *a thought or idea based on knowledge.* Unlike attitudes, which are charged with emotion, opinions and beliefs are more cognitively based and tend to be emotionally neutral. Attitudes, opinions, and beliefs reflect a philosophy of life, and marketing communications may be designed to align with various philosophies in order to be relevant to specific types of consumers, who may then respond favourably to the brand message. Changing consumers' attitudes—especially turning a negative attitude about a brand to a more positive view—is a challenging task for marketers, but many campaigns do achieve this result.

Motivations   The response to an MC message also depends on a person's *motivations*, which are *internal impulses that when stimulated initiate some type of response.* Some motivations are temporary—as when you secure a job interview and are motivated at that moment to purchase a new suit to impress your prospective employer. Other motivations are constant. Most people, for example, are consistently motivated by the desire to save money on purchases. MC sales promotion offers such as "Save 25%" and "Free brush when you buy a large bottle of X shampoo" explicitly refer to these kinds of motivation.

A simple model of brand decision making

People do not make brand decisions in a vacuum, nor does everyone act in the same way. To understand consumer decision making, it proves useful to think of it as a sequence of steps consumers go through. As with all models however, this is just a stylized way of representing people's behaviour. The model that is discussed below is not valid for all people in all situations. Nevertheless, it is a valuable starting point for understanding consumer decision making.

According to the following basic, simple model, people move through a five-step decision process (see Figure 4-2). First they recognize a problem or an opportunity. Then they identify a set of brands that can solve the problem or seize the opportunity. Next they evaluate these brand alternatives. After that, they decide what action to take, and finally, they evaluate the purchase decision or other action taken. Each of these steps is explained below.

Step 1: Recognizing a problem or an opportunity

Purchase decision making begins with recognizing a problem that creates a need (or want) or recognizing an opportunity that will provide a benefit not previously thought of or considered possible. Many people plan their summer holidays carefully. A summer holiday is a want for them that they recognize early in the year, after which a careful search begins. Tour operators spark this process by sending out catalogues to their customer base at the start of the holiday planning season, usually by the end of November. Even customers that haven't started to think

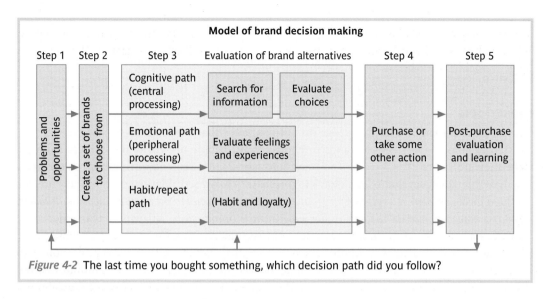

Model of brand decision making

| Step 1 | Step 2 | Step 3 | Evaluation of brand alternatives | Step 4 | Step 5 |

Cognitive path (central processing) → Search for information → Evaluate choices

Emotional path (peripheral processing) → Evaluate feelings and experiences

Habit/repeat path → (Habit and loyalty)

Problems and opportunities → Create a set of brands to choose from → [three paths above] → Purchase or take some other action → Post-purchase evaluation and learning

Figure 4-2 The last time you bought something, which decision path did you follow?

about their holiday plans are triggered to recognize their want for a summer holiday next season.

Another way to go on vacation is to pass by a tour operator who is posting last minute offerings on a billboard outside. Some people that walk by will recognize this as an opportunity to take a break. Their want for a vacation is ignited by the opportunity they are offered.

Marketers use Maslow's hierarchy of needs to analyse and determine which levels of needs or wants their brands are most likely to satisfy. Maslow's theory proposes that consumers will only consider higher-order needs when the lower-order needs are satisfied. This offers a great challenge to marketers: how do they know which levels are satisfactorily satisfied? Can they refer to higher-order levels referring to psychological needs—belongingness, esteem, and self-actualization—or must they refer to lower-order physiological needs to position their brands? Most car manufacturers position themselves by reference to psychological needs, but Volvo has successfully emphasized the safety of their cars as their main brand proposition. Apparently some consumers are sensitive to such safety needs when they are buying a car, while others do not see safety as an issue in this consumption situation.

Step 2: A set of brands to choose from

Once people become aware of a problem or opportunity, they look for ways to solve the problem or take advantage of the opportunity. In this step of brand decision making, customers and prospects begin their search for brands that they consider capable of satisfying their need or want. It is impossible for a brand to be considered if prospects are not aware of that brand. In Chapter 2 it has been explained that you can be aware of brands to different degrees, from dominance to recognition. Here you see the relevance of these notions. When a consumer is cued with a problem and recalls that a specific brand may solve the problem, this brand will be in the set of brands that may be considered. When a brand is dominant, it will likely be the only brand, unless the consumer wants to have more options and looks for help to bring more brands in his consideration set. Recognition is then important.

Knowing that recall is more difficult to achieve than recognition, marketers often design messages that focus primarily on recognition. Sponsoring is particularly powerful in achieving brand awareness, and making sure that brands are at least recognized, even when the brand is not available in some domestic market. Followers of the Tour de France are all familiar with Banesto, a bank that is active only in Spain. But when you are on vacation in Spain and need some cash money, it is not unlikely that you will be actively looking for an ATM of Banesto's.

Evoked sets

Brand awareness and brand knowledge do not guarantee that a brand will be selected. During the step of composing a set of brands to choose from, people narrow brand choices from all those they are aware of (**awareness set**) and have considered (**consideration set**), to the ones they have previously evaluated as "okay" to purchase (*evoked set*). Marketers want their brands included in the **evoked set**, which is *a group of brands that comes to mind when a person thinks of a product category because the person has judged those brands to be acceptable.* This judgement results from prior use of the brand or from brand knowledge gained in some other way (such as from ads, publicity, or word-of-mouth).

Most businesses use something similar to an evoked set—namely, *authorized* brands or suppliers that have been approved to do business with the company. Unlike consumers who casually build their evoked sets over time, most businesses have committees with an ongoing responsibility to evaluate all the different brands and suppliers that provide products to the company. For marketers selling to businesses, the challenge is to have their brands "authorized". This is done through personal selling, ads and articles in trade magazines, and booths at trade shows. The more visible and integrated these messages are in design and timing, the more successful marketers are at getting their brands authorized.

Because most customers use evoked sets, it is no surprise that a study conducted by Grey Worldwide determined that pure brand loyalty is rare.[7] Grey found that customers in the United States, the United Kingdom, and Australia routinely make their choices from a group of brands they consider acceptable—the evoked set. Other research has found this to be true in nearly every product category, which is why striving for complete brand loyalty is not realistic. More appropriate marketing objectives call for getting a brand into more customers' evoked sets (and authorized lists) and increasing the brand's share of customers' category spending (increasing share of wallet).

Step 3: Evaluating brand alternatives

The brands that make it to the evoked set will be assessed. Based on what the decision maker knows about the brands, he will try to come to some preference ordering of the brands. In Chapter 2 it was explained that the set of associations represents the *what* component of brand knowledge. All these associations, or at least the associations that are strong enough to be activated, will be used in the assessment of the brands. At this stage the decision maker performs the role of customer in Sheth and Mittal terminology.

Chapter 2 also showed that there are typically two types of associations. On the one hand there are associations based on facts and figures, on the other there are image factors. These two types of associations are related to the knowledge you have acquired of a brand and the feelings you have about it. Both types of associations play a role in the decision-making process: decisions are made with both head and heart! But how head and heart interact in this process of decision making will be discussed in more depth later in this chapter.

In general terms the outcome of the evaluation process is the attitude taken towards the brand. Applied to brand decisions, and in line with the earlier definition of the term "attitude", a brand attitude is a general disposition towards a brand, usually accompanied by negative or positive judgements. Brand attitudes can be seen as the one-dimensional outcome of the evaluation process that is the input for the next step, the factual decision-making stage.

Step 4: Deciding what action to take

The evaluation step leads to some kind of decision. Most marketers hope that the decision is some kind of behaviour or action. Customers, however, may be confident in their brand choice but remain undecided about the purchase, asking themselves questions such as these: can I really afford this? Will I be disappointed with the product after I buy it? Can I find the product somewhere else for less money? To respond to these questions and motivate action, companies offer money-back guarantees, free samples, and other incentives. Of Sheth and Mittal's roles of the decision maker, the role of payer is most relevant for this stage.

At one time marketers cared only about generating one type of behaviour—a purchase. However, they learned that other behaviours can be just as important. An example comes from the automotive industry. Ninety per cent of new-car buyers visit a dealership an average of three times before they buy. Each visit is a behaviour, the result of a decision to visit or not to visit. Once prospects decide on the brand of car in which they are most interested, they must then decide on a dealer, then which model to buy, what options to select, and what form of financing to use. Smart dealers use an integrated set of messages to encourage prospects to move through this decision process.

The objective of most automotive-related brand messages in the mass media is to get prospects to visit a dealer's showroom. Once prospects come to a showroom, it becomes obvious they are in the information-seeking and evaluation stages. Auto dealers satisfy customers' needs at this point with brochures and well-trained sales representatives. After the initial visit, a smart dealership will send the prospect a thank-you mailing and offer a small premium (such as a pen flashlight, a can of compressed air for inflating a flat tyre, or an emergency flasher) in exchange for making a return visit and taking a test drive. The repeat visit, the result of several brand messages, moves prospects closer to making a buying decision.

Step 5: Evaluating the purchase decision or other action

The last step in brand decision making is brand evaluation by the consumer—to complete the identification of Sheth and Mittal's roles. After making a purchase, customers consciously or subconsciously evaluate their decision and arrive at some level of satisfaction or dissatisfaction. Did the brand meet expectation: "did I make the right decision?" The answer to such questions lead either to a repeat purchase or to a return to the evaluation step to search for a different brand for the next purchase in that product category.

Every company wants prospects to buy once and then become loyal repeat buyers. For that to happen, however, buyers must be satisfied. Thus, a company must follow up a sale, when economically feasible, to make sure the buyer is completely satisfied. Follow-up messages, such as postcards or phone calls from a dealer after a car has been purchased, for example, can provide reinforcement for the decision. They also provide an opportunity for feedback.

An important concept in post-purchase evaluation is what psychologists term cognitive dissonance, which is *the uneasiness that results when two or more beliefs or behaviours are inconsistent with one another.* When such dissonance occurs during the evaluation of choices, customers generally search for more information or look more deeply into their feelings. An example is having to decide between going skiing over spring break or staying on campus to write a research paper due the week after spring break. The tension this decision creates can lead to dissatisfaction with the ski destination as it becomes associated with guilt.

When marketers know that cognitive dissonance may occur, they can create messages designed to lessen the tension. For example, the company trying to sell you the spring-break ski trip could emphasize students' need for a mental break in order to think better and more creatively later. The ski resort could explain that it provides quiet rooms for study early each morning and late each afternoon. Such messages can help alleviate cognitive dissonance.

Different paths to buying decisions

The core of the decision-making process, as illustrated in Figure 4-2 above, is the stage of attitude formation. Eventually the attitude formation may be followed by a buying decision. The buying decision is the most important type of response in marketing, although other types of responses can be important in some cases. Nevertheless, much of the consumer behaviour literature is concerned with the question of how considerations of the head and the heart lead to attitudes and consequently a purchase. These issues are alternatively referred to as hierarchy-of-effects models, decision-making models, think/feel/do models, or cognition/affect/conation models.

The term hierarchy-of-effects model is usually employed in the advertising literature. The best-known model, though a bit outdated, is the AIDA model that posits that *consumers, upon receiving a message go through the stages of Attention, Interest, Desire, and Action*. The background of this approach is the assumption that marketing communication can lead receivers of messages through these stages. This model was originally developed to help sales people do their jobs (Strong, 1925). In personal selling, the sequence of attention, interest, desire and action is a natural one, and prospective buyers might be led through all these four stages in one, or a couple of consecutive and related instances. Now the model is often used more loosely, as a short way of saying that messages can have an effect on various stages of the decision-making process, or, that consumers can have different kinds of responses to messages ("this message is intended to create attention for the product" or "we seek to increase desire for the product").

The AIDA model thus relates strongly to one specific sequence in the attitude-formation stage of consumer buying behaviour, namely the one that starts with think (attention and interest), followed by feel (desire) and is completed by do (action). However, customers can go through these stages in other orders too and the approach of this book is that marketing communications can try to favourably impact on each of these stages, simultaneously or independently. Further, and again in line with the IMC paradigm adopted here, it is not so fruitful to think of what *one* message can achieve, but rather of what an integrated set of messages, few or many, can achieve in the whole sequence of steps in decision making. Therefore, considerable attention is paid to the issue of consumer behaviour models, rather than the more narrowly focused hierarchy-of-effects ones. Yet, ultimately they all turn around the same question: how do consumers come to decisions and where are the possibilities to be found for marketing communication to exert influence on this process.

So the question is: what sequence of think/feel/do do consumers go through in their buying behaviour? You probably, and perhaps cynically, will answer: it depends, and again you are right. But then of course the question becomes: in what situations is any of the sequences most likely? And that question is not so easily answered. First the dominant sequences in decision making will be described, then factors that influence the paths that are taken are discussed.

Various paths to a decision

Technically, six different sequences of think/feel/do can be formed, but four of these paths are found to be most relevant. These paths can be illustrated by a simple example. Think about the different ways in which people approach buying a car. If they choose the **habit/repeat path**, they simply buy the brand that they bought before. Satisfied with the car they are now driving, they have no motivation to change brands. This is the easiest and quickest path to take to a brand decision. It starts with "do" and is followed by "feel" and "think" in any unspecified order. Other people choose the **cognitive path**. They search for information about various brand alternatives and then analyse this information before making a decision. After these cognitive efforts have led them a long way on the decision path, they give room to their feelings in making a decision. Thus the path is "think", "feel", "do", and this links to the AIDA model. Still others prefer the **emotional path**. They look at the styling of various cars, and imagine how each car would make them feel. Only on the basis of these feelings do they make a decision about the purchase. Then after the purchase cognitions will come into play. Hence this is the "feel", "do", "think" path.

> ... many in the [consumer behavior] field are now beginning to embrace the experiential paradigm, which stresses the subjective, nonrational aspects of consumption as well as cultural influences on customer behavior.
>
> *Michael Solomon,* Consumer Behavior

Many scholars, as well as message planners, have considered brand decision making as primarily a cognitive activity. But as Michael Solomon points out, the information-processing model has been overemphasized.[8] The cognitive and emotional approaches are not mutually exclusive. Most brand decisions involve both rational and emotional considerations simultaneously and are made with both the head and the heart (see Figure 4-3). For expository reasons however, the paths will be described as being truly sequentially organized.

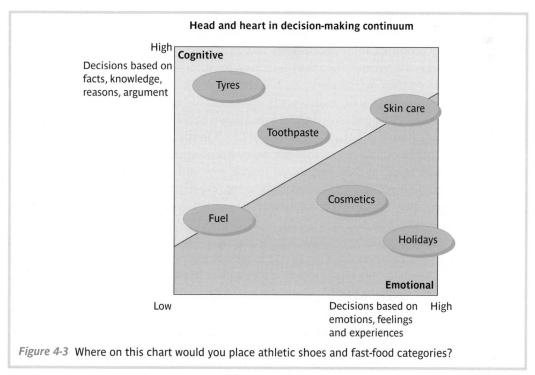

Figure 4-3 Where on this chart would you place athletic shoes and fast-food categories?

The cognitive path   The cognitive path is characterized by the Think-Feel-Do sequence. A consumer on this path first cognitively assesses the information she has about the brands. After the cognition her feelings will be given room to influence the decision. Finally, the brand will be purchased. The key in understanding this sequence is that the dominant influence in decision making is for the cognitive factors, the think factor.

Knowing that some people follow the cognitive path when buying a car, one selling strategy is to equip sales associates with information about competitors' cars (as well as their own-brand cars). The idea is not to argue against competing models but rather to give prospects as much information as possible. Customers will respect salespeople for providing objective information they can use in such a decision.

Because people taking this path usually focus on brand differences, marketers appeal to them by using side-by-side product demonstrations or by explaining unique product features (see colour insert A5). A study of 1000 television commercials found that the most persuasive ones included a brand-differentiating message. In other words, the commercials that helped customers distinguish one brand from another were the most effective.[9]

The emotional path   The emotional path is characterized by the Feel-Do-Think sequence. People who follow the emotional path are driven by feelings and emotions. Although marketers have known for years that buying decisions are influenced by both the head and the heart, they assumed the head consistently played a much more important role.[10] Recently, companies have discovered an important role in marketing communication for messages that stimulate feelings. Such feelings are an **affective response**, which is *a feeling or attitude resulting from emotional processing.*

Typical of this path to decision making is that the decision is only based on emotions. Cognitive evaluation of the alternative is only carried out afterwards. Restaurant visits are often driven by an emotional decision. Does the restaurant give you the right feeling? Afterwards, when the price list has been converted into too high a bill, will the cognitive aspects lead you to a more complete evaluation of your brand choice?

Prospects and customers who have a tendency to take the emotional path in brand decision making recognize problems and opportunities just as cognitive-path decision makers do. But how they respond is different. Rather than searching for information that they then rationally analyse, they focus on their *feelings* about their alternatives. When a person no longer feels good about wearing a particular suit, for example, the experience of "no longer feeling good" can kick in when the person sees a suit ad. Not only will the person be motivated to attend to the ad, but will do so by asking himself or herself: "How would I look in that suit?"

Recognizing that emotional responses drive many brand decisions, marketers are emphasizing the experiential aspect of their brands. As Joseph Pine and James Gilmore explain in *The Experience Economy*, marketers are increasingly using experiences to transform commodity goods and services into brands that engage customers in personal ways and create brand relationships.[11] An involving buying experience, according to Pine and Gilmore, is based on the concept of "marketing as theatre". That's why Volkswagen has built Autostadt Theme Park in Wolfsburg, and Nike has opened a Nike World in several places around the globe. In Pine and Gilmore's elusive language, the retail store becomes a place in which customers are participants in the "staging of the shopping play".

> " Staging brand experiences is not just about entertaining customers but rather about engaging them. "
>
> *B. Joseph Pine II and James H. Gilmore,* The Experience Economy

Pine and Gilmore emphasize that the more customers are engaged, the more likely they are to begin and then maintain a relationship with a brand. Although companies can use an experience-based approach to acquire customers, it is also a way to reach and reinforce the relationship with current customers.

Another reason why the emotional path is being used more is the increase in service products and the importance of service in all kinds of product categories. Because services account for ever-increasing shares of Western economies, brand experiences are becoming an increasingly important MC strategy and tactic. Even goods have experiential brand touch points when you consider events and sampling.

The habit/repeat path   Habit or repeat-purchase decision making starts with the Do phase. Indeed, brands are bought without immediately preceding cognitive or emotional evaluation. Instead, these evaluations have taken place after the previous purchase of the brand, and will again take place after the current buying action. So the sequence becomes Do-Feel-Think or Do-Think-Feel. An important instance of such a sequence is when on a previous occasion a brand has met or exceeded expectations. When a customer recognizes a problem or opportunity similar to the one that prompted the original purchase, there is no searching for information or evaluating alternatives, only recall that the brand previously selected has been meeting expectations and thus can automatically be repurchased.

Impulse buying is another example of a sequence that starts with the Do phase. Lying on a hot beach on a sunny summer afternoon, you need no other incentive than the ringing bell of the ice-cream man to buy an ice cream. Neither high prices, nor feelings of guilt can keep you from buying the biggest Magnum in the man's cart. Only afterwards will you reconsider the situation.

Here is an example in B2B buying. A utility company that operates a fleet of service trucks initially uses a cognitive model to find a brand of fuel that will provide the best performance and the best price and will offer extended credit. Once the utility company makes a brand decision and the brand's performance meets or exceeds expectations, drivers are told always to buy that brand of fuel. If the drivers begin reporting that some of the fuel stations are sometimes out of fuel, or if there are billing problems, the brand selection will be reviewed.

If the fuel company the utility is using is smart, it will use MC functions such as direct mail and personal selling to motivate the utility company to buy not only fuel but also motor oil from the same company. It could also integrate a reward programme that sends premiums to the utility company when its total purchases reach a certain level. This tactic would strengthen the customer relationship and reinforce the utility's decision to remain faithful to the fuel brand even when there are occasional billing and/or supply problems.

The habit/repeat path is an extremely important model because it is the decision-making model that drives customer retention. This "shorthand" decision making turns brand selection into a habit and creates loyal customers. If you ask your parents or friends why they always buy a certain brand, they are likely to tell you, "I've always bought that brand and never been disappointed." Most of the time they cannot remember why they first started buying it. Marketing communication for habit/repeat customers focuses primarily on brand reminders. Some messages, such as those that car dealers send after a purchase, may also be designed to confirm the wisdom of a customer's decision.

The two remaining sequences (think/do/feel and feel/think/do) are less common. The feel/think/do sequence is sometimes associated with actions regarding emotional products that are so expensive that cognitions cannot be ignored, for example with jewellery or fashion apparel (Vaughn, 1980). The think/do/feel sequence has been described as the "low involvement model" (Ray, 1973). According to this model, decisions with respect to low involvement products are based on cognitions only: for example, in the supermarket you only look at the price of various dried soups without wondering how the various brands make you feel. Further, in B2B marketing it is often said that the decision-making unit is composed in such a way as to eliminate any emotional (read irrational) aspects in decision making.

What sequence?

As many examples above illustrate, it will hardly ever be the case that all customers will take the same route to decision making for some given products. No decision maker will invariably take the same route for the same product. When you buy your first mobile phone you will likely spend some time to make a careful evaluation of the various brands. The second time it may depend. When your phone breaks down at an inconvenient time and you urgently need a new one, your path to decision making will be very different from the case in which the phone is still working, but you think the model is outdated and you need a more up-to-date one.

So clearly, the sequence taken in decision making is influenced by many factors. A key factor in this respect is **involvement**, the *degree to which a product decision is important to a consumer.* Involvement is a central concept in marketing, and is often seen as a kind of personality characteristic: either you are involved in buying certain products, or not. However, involvement can also be related to buying situations. It makes a difference to your involvement whether you buy a book as a present to your best friend, or because you are about to make a flight trip of a couple of hours for which you need an easy-reading page turner.

Levels of involvement

Products such as food staples (milk, bread, butter) and utility products (brooms, batteries, detergents, toilet tissue, petrol) are perceived as **low-involvement products**, *products that are relatively cheap, are bought frequently without much consideration, and are low risk.* In contrast, **high-involvement products**, such as cars and computers, are *products for which people perceive differences among brands and are willing to invest pre-purchase decision-making energy.* Typically, such purchases are more expensive and have greater social consequences, and as such are perceived as high risk.

Most people approach *high*-involvement purchase decisions by "thinking" about them first. By contrast, the first response when considering a *low*-involvement product, such as a convenience or an impulse product, is likely to be "feeling" or even "doing". You buy a package of chewing-gum, for example, because you *feel* like having some gum. Or you see a magazine next to the cash register as you are checking out at a food store, and you reach over on impulse and grab it without really thinking or feeling strongly about the decision.

Like decision making, messages can also be described as commanding different degrees of attention, concentration, and involvement. Messages for high-involvement products are likely to be detailed, quality assuring, and so on—if they link a brand promise to important personal goals, such as getting the highest-quality computer or the best price on a car. In contrast, messages for low-involvement products are often designed to stimulate impulsive purchase decisions for products like chewing gum and candy. Such messages are likely to emphasize "fun" or "convenience".

Two factors in particular drive the degree of involvement: relevance and risk.

Relevance   The key to determining the level of involvement is relevance, *the extent to which a product is pertinent and connects with a customer's personal interests.* Relevance need not be the same in all instances. For example, health and fitness products are in relative terms much more relevant after exercising in the gym. A good strategy for marketers of these products, like L'Oréal, Dove, or Nivea, would be to supply gyms with samples of their products or have instructors promote the products before and after classes.

If you need a new pair of glasses, you will be more receptive to brand messages in this product category than you otherwise would be. You will want to make sure that the optician you select can competently provide glasses that match your prescription. You may also be concerned about the look of the glasses and picking out frames of the right style. The brand name on the frame is, for some, an important fashion statement. Personal relevance makes a new pair of glasses a high-involvement purchase.

Risk   High-involvement products, and the MC messages that communicate about them, represent above-average risk and expense. The risk factor, particularly for B2B and expensive consumer products, motivates customers to evaluate brand choices carefully. There are risks that both consumers and businesses try to minimize:[12]

- *Financial risk:* Customers lose money when a brand doesn't work; they have to replace the product or spend extra to make it work.
- *Performance risk:* Product failures can cause other failures such as missed deadlines or the inability to produce other goods or services.
- *Physical risk:* The brand may hurt or injure those who use it.
- *Psychological risk:* The brand may not fit in well with the consumer's or company's self-image or corporate culture.
- *Social risk:* The brand may negatively affect the way others think of the customer.

By recognizing (through research) which of those risks apply to a company's product categories, marketers can design brand messages to minimize the perceived risk. For example, car manufacturers often emphasize the duration of their warranties. By knowing what types of risks most concern customers, companies can relate their brands' features and benefits to these risks and improve their chances of being purchased.

Shifts in decision making because of involvement   Not all brand decision-making situations motivate people to move through a hierarchy in the same way. To understand better how the order of thinking, feeling, and doing can vary, see whether you can determine which order of think/feel/do has been used in each of three scenarios (answers are at the end of the scenarios):

- **Scenario 1:** Bradley stopped at the drugstore on the way home from work to have a prescription filled. While checking out, he bought on impulse a copy of *Time* magazine. When he got home, he found himself reading the magazine rather than watching his favourite Thursday-night TV show. The next day he picked up from the floor one of the subscription cards that had fallen out of the magazine. After looking at the price and recalling that his bank account was in pretty good shape, he realized that subscribing to the magazine would be cheaper in the long run than buying it from a store each week.
- **Scenario 2:** Liz and Mike needed an apartment in Copenhagen, where Mike was being transferred by his company. To make the decision on an apartment, the couple first determined how much they could spend each month on rent, then how much room they

needed, and finally the part of town in which they wanted to live. Next they began looking at what was available that met their criteria. As they went through six different apartment units, they could tell that some were more comfortable and pleasing than others. Finally, after settling on the one that was second-closest to Mike's new office, they signed a contract and made a damage deposit.

■ **Scenario 3:** Lindsay was very frugal with the money she earned. She had a credit card, for example, but made a point of paying off the balance every month to avoid finance charges. But for some time, she had been walking on her lunch hour past a store window close to her office. In the window was a beautiful leather jacket. One day, she was having lunch with a friend and pointed out the jacket. Her friend said she had one similar to it. That did it: Lindsay walked in, handed the salesgirl her credit card, and pointed to the jacket in the window. That evening, when she took the jacket out of its box, the first thing she saw was the price tag. She spent the rest of the evening trying to figure out how she was going to pay the credit-card bill that would come in two weeks and include the cost of the jacket.

(Answers: Scenario 1, do, feel, think. Scenario 2, think, feel, do. Scenario 3, feel, do, think.)

The think/feel/do model sets up for several different message responses that can lead to a brand decision. The route taken depends, to a large extent, on involvement. As not all consumers are equally involved in the same type of decisions, it is evident that for the same products, various routes can be relevant. Besides that, it is not only involvement that determines the decision-making sequence that is followed. Richard Vaughn of Foot Cone & Belding argued that whether a product could be identified as a think or feel product is a second factor (Vaughn, 1980). Combining the think-feel dimension with high and low involvement leads to the FCB (Foot Cone & Belding) grid illustrated in Figure 4-4. This grid suggests that with think products cognition always precedes affect, and with feel products affect precedes cognition. Furthermore, according to the FCB grid, with high-involvement products the sequence is always concluded with the action, while for low-involvement products the sequence always starts with the action. Michael Ray has proposed considering perceived product differen-

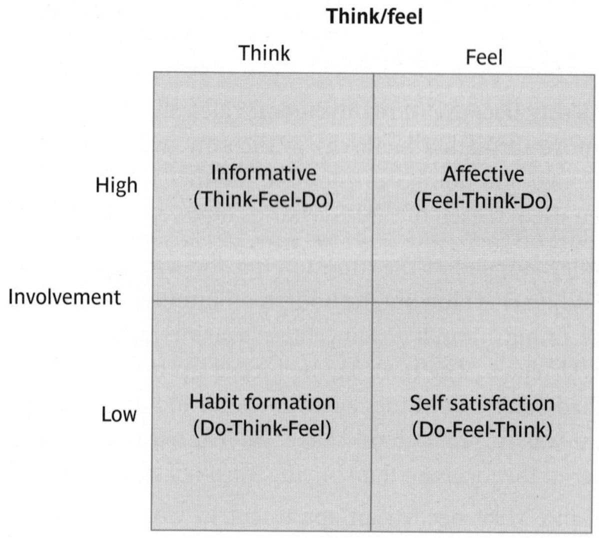

	Think/feel	
	Think	Feel
High **Involvement**	Informative (Think-Feel-Do)	Affective (Feel-Think-Do)
Low	Habit formation (Do-Think-Feel)	Self satisfaction (Do-Feel-Think)

Figure 4-4   **FCB grid**

tiation as a determining factor (Ray, 1973). In case of high topical involvement, high product differentiation leads to the cognitive path, while low-perceived product differentiation and low involvement lead to the do/feel/think path that was captured on the habit/repeat paths above.

What is clear from the discussion above is that not all customers will follow the same paths to decision making, and consequently will not all respond to messages in the same way. MC managers must reckon with that, and design messages that appeal to different aspects of the decision path as the IMC in Action box illustrates. Apart from idiosyncrasies in decision making, the way the messages themselves impact on the decision maker can also differ. That is what the next section is about.

How to ring a bell

Every year New Year's Day is welcomed with tons of fireworks. People enjoy the magic and noise which highlights the beginning of a new year, with new opportunities, leaving behind the old worries. For some, however, the New Year may start as a disaster, through accidents with fireworks, leading to such injuries as burns, blindness, or the loss of a limb.

This is not only a personal tragedy, but also a concern for society. In the Netherlands this has given rise to a series of campaigns to make people aware of the dangers of fireworks, and to bring about a change in behaviour. These campaigns have been initiated by an independent foundation that has persuaded agencies such as TBWA to manage such campaigns free of charge, which they do, sometimes devoting some of their best work to these good causes.

The big concern, however, is how a change in behaviour is to be achieved. Part of the problem is that the target group, i.e. those who are both the most vulnerable and at the same time the most irresponsible in handling fireworks, is young people, who are hard to reach through ordinary campaigns.

The answer is to design uncommon campaigns. And uncommon these campaigns have been. Most of them have been unusually graphic, causing raised eyebrows among parents. Pictures of people who have lost fingers or limbs, or of heavily bleeding victims on hospital stretchers and other visual assaults on the senses, were not readily appreciated by everyone, but they achieved a significant reduction in the number of victims each year. These campaigns that were directed to the cognitive part of people's attitude formation appeared to work better than the softer campaigns that played on consumers' emotions. One campaign showed star football player Dennis Bergkamp scoring a wonderful goal. A repetition of the goal was abruptly discontinued at the very moment of scoring. The message: you'd better have a good look at this goal, because it might be the last thing you ever see; and the screen went black. This suggestion that mishandling a firework can lead to blindness is subtle, but again maybe a bit too subtle for the target audience?

Nonetheless, overall the campaigns have been successful. If anything, this shows that behavioural responses can be the result of advertising that appeals to affect or cognition.

Think about it

What type of advertising would you think is more effective, affect or cognition oriented? Is it important to include groups other than the target group in designing this kind of campaign? Is there an ethical limit to the contents of campaigns like these?

Source:
www.sire.nl

IMC in Action

How MC messages influence consumer decisions

Because the role of marketing communications is to ignite responses or intervene in the decision process, brand messages must be persuasive. **Persuasion** is *the act of creating changes in attitudes and behaviours.* Persuasive MC messages are designed to get customers and prospects to think and feel positive about a brand, and to make that brand their choice when they select a product. MC managers focus on a number of factors—attitude formation and change strategies, brand likeability, credibility and trust, and believable arguments—to trigger the desired consumer response.

Changing cognitions

Changing how people think about a brand is a matter of **learning**, which is *a change in what a person knows that comes from exposure to new information or experiences.* Psychologists have two basic theories about how most people learn. These theories shed light on the post-purchase evaluation and correspond to the cognitive and emotional decision-making models we have been discussing. **Cognitive learning theory** is *a view of learning as a mental process involving thinking, reasoning, and understanding.* According to this theory, we think by comparing new information to what we already know—that is, to thoughts and information filed away in memory (see colour insert A4). When there is discrepancy between our knowledge and the information we try to integrate both—we either adapt our knowledge, or we reject the information. What will happen depends critically on the persuasiveness of the message. **Conditioned learning theory** (also called *stimulus–response theory*) is *a view of learning as a trial-and-error process.* We confront a new situation, respond in a certain way, and something happens. If what happens is good, we are likely to develop a positive feeling about it and respond the same way the next time we are in that situation. If the experience is bad, we are likely to change our response and try something else. Such patterns of behaviour represent the way customers and B2B buyers manage their brand selections.

Learning also intersects with involvement: cognitive learning is especially active in the purchase of high-involvement products; conditioned learning, in the purchase of low-involvement products. Reinforcement advertising is used to remind people of their good brand experiences. Personal two-way communication is used to counter negative reviews when customers complain to a company.

Changing attitudes

Whether they are consciously aware of it or not, most customers and prospects have attitudes about many brands. These attitudes are based on what they have seen, heard, experienced, and learned about brands in the process of evaluating brand choices. Marketers seek to understand and influence these attitudes because they are an important underlying factor in a brand getting into a customer's evoked set and ultimately becoming the customer's brand choice.

Attitudes have two dimensions—direction and degree of conviction. *Attitude direction* is whether the feeling is positive or negative. *Degree of conviction* is how sure customers are about their attitudes, how strong their feelings are—slightly positive, very positive, slightly negative, very negative. Already in Chapter 2 it has become clear that brands are built on strong positive associations—and attitudes are a special and important kind of associations. Hence, marketers should make sure that customers hold positive, and ideally no negative, associations. But it happens.

MC managers can design a strategy based on the dominant prevailing type of attitude (see Figure 4-5). When attitudes are primarily strong and positive, the logical strategy is to reinforce and confirm these attitudes. Weak and positive attitudes are not bad, but are vulnerable and must be reinforced. Strong negative attitudes should be confronted and changed. Weak negative attitudes may be associated with indifference. Enforcement of stronger positive attitudes will bury the weakly negative ones.

Four attitude- and belief-change strategies used in marketing communication are as described here in the selling of ice cream:[13]

1 *Changing beliefs about the consequences of behaviour.* Customers might be persuaded that a new ice cream is not as fattening as they think it is.

2 *Changing evaluations of consequences.* Customers might be persuaded that eating a new ice cream is okay, even if it is fattening.

3 *Changing beliefs about the perceptions of others.* Customers might be persuaded that it is fine to eat a new ice cream because a friend says it's really good.

4 *Strengthening motivations to comply.* Customers might be persuaded to eat a new ice cream because everyone else is eating it.

Elaboration likelihood model and the route to persuasion

When a message wants to change an attitude or a cognition, it has to be persuasive. It will be no surprise that one and the same message is persuasive to some consumers, while others do not adapt their attitudes or cognitions at all. The Elaboration Likelihood Model (ELM) developed by Petty and Cacioppo, is a descriptive model that helps marketers to understand how persuasion works (see Figure 4-6).[14] The ELM describes how receivers of a message process it, and more in particular

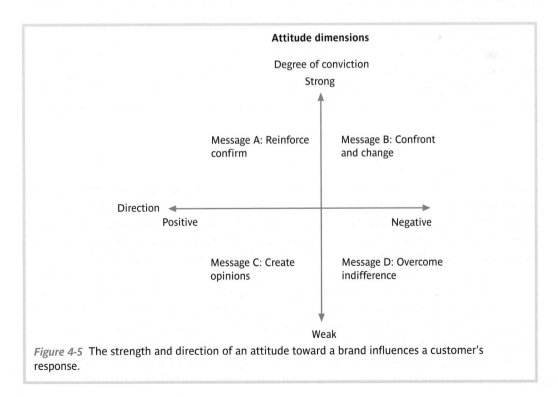

Figure 4-5 The strength and direction of an attitude toward a brand influences a customer's response.

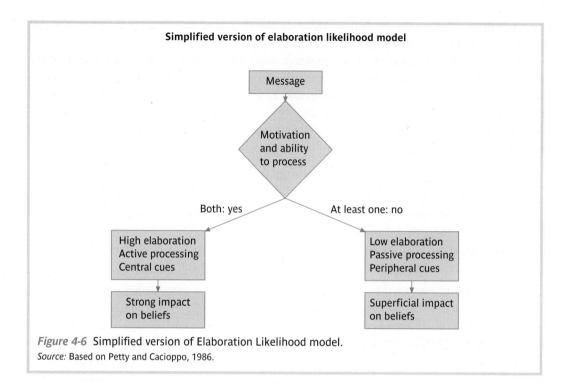

Figure 4-6 Simplified version of Elaboration Likelihood model.
Source: Based on Petty and Cacioppo, 1986.

under what conditions attitude change is likely. The crucial factor in ELM is elaboration. Essentially ELM describes when a message is processed elaborately, or superficially, and what the consequences of this are. Elaboration in this context is *the extent to which the encoded information pieces in the message are processed: in other words, effort is undertaken to understand the message.*

The model goes as follows. When a person receives a message she will (subconsciously in most cases) determine how much effort will be devoted to processing the message. In ELM terminology the distinction is between high elaboration, or taking the central route to persuasion, or low elaboration, called the peripheral route to persuasion. Which route is taken depends on two factors: the motivation to elaborate and the ability to elaborate. These factors are independent, and both have to be satisfied for the central route to be taken. This means that a consumer needs to be both motivated and able to process a message: that is, to give it a high level of elaboration (see colour insert A7).

To illustrate the above point: when you see an advertisement of a bicycle, a product you desperately need, featuring an attractive guy/girl, you may be motivated to process the ad. But when you then find that the ad is written in Russian, a language you do not master, you are not able to process the ad elaborately. Or alternatively, when you come across an ad for a motorcycle but you have no driver's licence for motorcycles, any efforts of the advertiser to motivate you to read the ad will be void.

When elaboration is high, i.e. when the central route is taken, the decoded information is actively processed and integrated with the existing knowledge. Existing knowledge is updated based on **central cues**, *message elements that represent relevant information*, and since the information is carefully assessed, the impact of the new information is strong: updated beliefs are held firmly. When elaboration is low, the peripheral route is taken, the information that is retrieved from the message will be determined by what is called **peripheral cues**, *superficial impressions, based on easily accessible and interpretable message elements.* Peripheral processing has only limited impact on the attitudes of the receiver. The updated beliefs are easily replaced by new pieces of information.

The elaboration likelihood model is an attractive model and has received considerable attention from marketers. One of the reasons is that it has some straightforward implications that make intuitive sense as well. When an advertiser wants her message to be processed elaborately, she has to take care that the message appeals to the motivation of the receivers. In addition, she must take care that her target audience is able to decode the message. The fact that many commercials are not translated these days suggests that advertisers seem to forget this lesson from ELM.

There is more. Inevitably some receivers will not elaborate on the message. Positive effects can then still be achieved when care is given to incorporating positive peripheral cues. The ELM gives a theoretical justification for endorsement by attractive people (see colour insert A9)!

Likeability

A message's likeability can be a critical factor in consumer decision making. If you dislike a brand's advertising—many customers disliked Benetton's controversial social issue advertising—then you may refuse to even put that brand in your evoked set. Likeability is an appeal to the heart: but as the Benetton campaigns illustrated, sometimes the liking response can be driven by cognitive messages, as well as emotional ones.

Many researchers have confirmed your gut feeling that liking an ad is a determinant of liking a brand.[15] Despite this accrued evidence, some advertising managers argue that *liking* a brand message is not important as long as customers *remember* the brand. They say that irritating ads may even attract more attention and stay in the memory longer than appealing messages. Even if that would be true, the associations that are made with this brand are negative. In Chapter 2 it was pointed out that associations have to be favourable to contribute to brand equity. But never forget that not everybody has to like every ad! What may be a disgraceful ad to one group (not the target group) may be attractive to the intended target.

Credibility and trust

Another important factor influencing customers' responses is whether customers find a message to be believable. Consumers generally do not trust advertising, yet they do have more confidence in cognitive ad claims than in ads that try to create an emotional response.[16] Companies that create messages in which arguments and reason are used appeal to people following the cognitive path to a decision.

Marketing programmes use public relations because articles in the news media generally have higher levels of credibility than sponsored messages such as advertising. A factor influencing believability is the perceived credibility of the source, which relates to the trust factor in relationships. Unfortunately, customers are increasingly less trustful of marketing communication messages. To help make messages more believable and counter this lack of trust, companies sometimes use opinion leaders. Such people are generally credible sources, as well as outgoing, likeable, and with higher-than-average social status. Knowing that opinion leaders are credible and trusted, and therefore can influence purchase decisions, companies hire or work with them to support the company's brands. Table 4-1 gives an idea of how various sources of information are trusted, and the effort needed to make use of them.

Source	Effort required	Believability
Past experiences	Low	High
Personal sources (e.g. friends)	Low	High
Marketing communications	Medium	Low
Public sources (e.g. media)	Low	High
Product examination and trial	High	High

Table 4-1 A comparison of information sources

Source: Adapted from Paul Peter and Jerry Olson, *Consumer Behavior and Marketing Strategy* (Burr Ridge, IL: Irwin, 1996), p. 311. Reprinted with permission from The McGraw-Hill Companies.

A final note: there are many routes that lead to Rome

Demetrios Vakratsas and Tim Ambler of the London Business School made a huge effort to have the final say in discussions on the exact Think/Feel/Do sequences and Hierarchy of Effects models.[17] The conclusions of their impressive study were as disappointing as they were obvious: there is no final verdict possible on what the exact order of cognition, affect, and conation is, and it is even hard to predict under what circumstances which orders are most likely. So then, is this whole discussion futile and redundant?

By no means! The researchers Vakratsas and Ambler tried to find generalizations, which is the job of academics. There is nonetheless much practical relevance in thinking about consumer behaviour in Think/Feel/Do sequences. For individual cases marketers simply know what the most logical order for their target group is. Furthermore, even if this is not the case, being aware of these possible aspects of consumer behaviour may help focus the marketers in influencing that particular step in decision making, knowing that its influence is necessarily limited, yet consequential. In other words, basic awareness of the fact that there are possibly multiple steps on the road to decision making is a major and valuable lesson on its own.

🔓 Key terms

acquisition strategy Motivating a prospect to buy for the first time.

affective response A feeling or attitude resulting from emotional processing.

AIDA model Model that posits that consumers, upon receiving a message, go through the stages of Attention, Interest, Desire, and Action.

attitude A general disposition or orientation toward objects, people, and ideas usually accompanied by negative or positive judgements.

awareness set Set of brands consumers are aware of.

belief A thought or idea based on knowledge.

central cues Message elements that represent relevant information.

cognitive dissonance The uneasiness that results when two or more beliefs or behaviours are inconsistent with one another.

cognitive learning theory A view of learning as a mental process involving thinking, reasoning, and understanding.

cognitive path Think-feel-do path in decision making.

conditioned learning theory (also called stimulus–response theory) A view of learning as a trial-and-error process.

consideration set Set of brands consumers consider buying.

consumer Person or organization who actually uses the product.

culture Group values based on traditions and distinctive history.

current customer A person who has purchased a brand at least once within a designated period.

customer The person or organization who takes the buying decision.

emotional path Feel-do-think path in decision making.

evoked set A group of brands that comes to mind when a person thinks of a product category because the person has judged those brands to be acceptable.

habit/repeat path Do-think-feel or do-feel-think path in decision making.

high-involvement products Products for which people perceive differences among brands and are willing to invest pre-purchase decision-making energy.

involvement Degree to which a product decision is important to a consumer.

learning A change in what a person knows that comes from exposure to new information or experiences.

▶ **low-involvement products** Products that are relatively cheap, are bought frequently without much consideration, and are perceived as low risk.

Maslow's hierarchy of needs An arrangement of human needs and wants listed in the order in which, according to Maslow, people satisfy them.

motivations Internal impulses that when stimulated initiate some type of response.

needs and wants Biological and psychological motivations that drive actions.

opinion A specific judgement that is emotionally neutral.

opinion leaders People to whom others turn for advice or information.

peripheral cues Superficial impressions, based on easily accessible and interpretable message elements.

persuasion The act of creating changes in attitudes and behaviours.

prospect A person who has never bought a brand but might be interested in it.

reference group The associations and organizations with which people identify or to which they belong and which influence their attitudes and behaviours.

relevance The extent to which a product is pertinent and connects with a customer's personal interests.

retention strategy Motivating a customer to make repeat purchases.

social class A ranking of people in a society by factors such as family history, occupation, education, and income.

society A group of people who live together and organize their lives as a community.

Check the key points

Key point 1: Who are these people?

a　How do prospects and customers differ? How do MC messages need to be adjusted for these two groups?

b　How do consumers and business buyers differ? How do MC messages need to be adjusted for these two groups?

c　Give an example of how society and culture affect someone's decision to buy a product.

d　What is a reference group? Identify a reference group to which you belong, and explain how that group influenced some buying decision that you have made.

e　How do a need and a want differ? Give an example of a purchasing decision that you have made in which the distinction between a need and a want is apparent.

Key point 2: How does brand decision making work?

a　Which stages does a consumer typically go through in making a brand decision? What roles does this consumer have in the various stages?

b　How does a problem differ from an opportunity? Find an ad that uses the problem approach and another that focuses on opportunities. Explain how the messages work.

c   What is the difference between the awareness set, the consideration set and the evoked set?

d   What are the three dominant paths to a brand decision? Describe each one, and give an example of each.

e   How many decisions have you made in the process of deciding what school to attend? Describe these decisions in think/feel/do sequences. Have any MC messages played a role in these decisions?

f   Have you ever felt cognitive dissonance? How could the brand have relieved the problem?

g   Explain how involvement influences the route that is followed in brand decision making.

Key point 3: How do MC messages affect that decision-making process?

a   Contrast cognitive learning theory and conditioned learning theory.

b   What are the two dimensions of attitude? Choose a product category, and describe the dimensions of your own attitude about that category.

c   Explain the role of persuasion in marketing communication.

d   Describe the Elaboration Likelihood model. Under what circumstances is each route in this model followed? What is the difference in effect between the two routes?

e   What is the difference between liking the brand and liking the ad? Find an example in which the two likeability factors are working at cross-purposes (you like the brand but not the ad, or vice versa).

f   Give an example of a commercial that you find credible.

Chapter Challenge

Writing assignment

A local coffee house has hired you to analyse its customers' behaviour. But first the manager wants you to give him and the store owner a crash course in the basics of brand decision making. Go back through this chapter, and list all the information you can find that seems relevant to using marketing communication to relate effectively to retail customers in a coffee house. Write a three-page document for the store owner and manager on those factors that you think are most important for them to consider. What factors that would influence the purchase of coffee drinks and other products sold in the store do you believe their marketing communication should address?

Presentation assignment

Take a recent advertising campaign and identify all cues that try to persuade the receiver. Analyse what effects these cues will have (one option is "no effect") when the receiver follows either the peripheral route, or the central route to persuasion. Are there elements in the message that either try to increase motivation, or that try to ascertain that receivers are able to process the message?

Internet assignment

Take a look in your pantry and imagine that one of the products there is rotten while it hasn't passed the expiry date. The manufacturer no doubt has a website address on the package. Visit this website and see if there is anything the manufacturer does to address your cognitive dissonance. Alternatively you may call the product's "help-desk" to discuss the problem. Write a short report on your experience and if you think the brand's response could improve, give some suggestions.

Research assignment

Interview a classmate on her or his choice of toothpaste brand. Identify those contextual factors that influence the decision making. Note that this requires a quite in-depth interviewing approach.

Notes

[1] Jagdish N. Sheth and Banwari Mittal, *Customer Behavior: A Managerial Perspective*, 2nd ed. (Mason OH: Thomson South-Western, 2004).

[2] The French sociologist Bernard Cova provides an interesting exposé on the importance of communities in post-modern society, especially referring to the role brands play. Bernard Cova, "Community and Consumption", *European Journal of Marketing*, 31–3/4, pp. 197–316.

[3] Adapted from Richard P. Coleman and Lee P. Rainwater, *Social Standing in America: New Dimensions of Class* (New York: Basic Books, 1978). Such social class statistics are generally hard to obtain. Government census bureaux all seem to have their own, multiple ways to describe the social class structures of their countries. Mostly these are based on income, employment, or education data.

[4] Influence exerted within families, in particular from parents to children, is called intergenerational influences. See for example Elizabeth S. Moore, William L. Wilkie, and Richard J. Lutz, "Passing the Torch: Intergenerational Influences as a Source of Brand Equity", *Journal of Marketing*, 66, 2002, pp. 17–37.

[5] Lawrence F. Feick and Linda L. Price, "The Market Maven", *Managing*, July 1985, p. 10.

[6] Michael Solomon, *Consumer Behavior: Buying, Having, and Being*, 5th ed. (Upper Saddle River, NJ: Prentice-Hall, 2002).

[7] Adam Shell, "Brand Loyalty? Fuggedaboutit!" *Adweek*, 12 May 1997, p. 40.

[8] Michael Solomon, *Consumer Behavior: Buying, Having, and Being* (Boston: Allyn and Bacon, 1992), p. 15.

[9] David W. Stewart and David H. Furse, *Effective Television Advertising* (Lexington, MA: Lexington Books, 1986).

[10] Kevin J. Clancy and Robert S. Shulman, *Marketing Revolution* (New York: HarperBusiness, 1993).

[11] B. Joseph Pine II and James H. Gilmore, *The Experience Economy: Work Is Theatre & Every Business a Stage* (Boston: Harvard Business School Press, 1999), p. 11.

[12] David L. Loudon and Albert J. Della Bitta, *Consumer Behavior: Concepts and Applications*, 3rd ed. (New York: McGraw-Hill, 1988), p. 532. Loudon and Della Bitta adapted this list from Martin Fishbein and Icek Ajzen, *Belief, Attitude and Behavior: An Introduction to Theory and Research* (Reading, MA: Addison-Wesley, 1975), p. 610.

[13] Loudon and Della Bitta, *Consumer Behavior*.

[14] Richard E. Petty and John T. Cacioppo, *Communication and Persuasion: Central and Peripheral Routes to Attitude Change* (New York: Springer, 1986), Ch. 1, 3–23.

[15] Esther Thorson, "Likability: 10 Years of Academic Research", paper presented at the Eighth Annual ARF Copy Research Workshop, New York, 11 September 1991.

[16] Sharon Shavitt, Pamela M. Lowrey, and James E. Haefner, *Public Attitudes toward Advertising: More Favorable Than You Might Think* (Urbana: Cummings Center for Advertising Studies, University of Illinois, 1997).

[17] Demetrios Vakratsas and Tim Ambler, "How advertising works: What do we really know?", *Journal of Marketing*, 63, 1999, pp. 26–43.

Further reading

Coulter, Keith S. (2005) "An Examination of Qualitative vs. Quantitative Elaboration Likelihood Effects", *Psychology & Marketing*, Vol. 22–1, pp. 31–49.

Kempf, DeAnna, Russell Laczniak and Robert Smith (2006) "The effects of gender on processing advertising and product trial information", *Marketing Letters*, Vol. 17–1, pp. 5–16.

Malaviya, Prashant (2007) "The Moderating Influence of Advertising Context on Ad Repetition Effects: The Role of Amount and Type of Elaboration", *Journal of Consumer Research*, Vol. 34–1, pp. 32–40.

Peter, J. Paul and Jerry C. Olson (2008) *Consumer Behavior and Marketing Strategy*, 8th ed., Boston: McGraw-Hill.

Putrevu, Sanjay and Kenneth R. Lord (2003) "Processing Internet Communications: A Motivation, Opportunity and Ability Framework", *Journal of Current Issues & Research in Advertising*, Vol. 25–1, pp. 45–59.

Ray, Michael. L. (1973) "Communication and the Hierarchy of Effects", in P. Clarke (ed.) *New Models for Mass Communication Research*, Beverly Hills, CA: Sage.

Sheth, Jagdish N. and Banwari Mittal (2004) *Customer Behavior: A Managerial Perspective*, 2nd ed., Thomson South-Western.

Strong, E. K. (1925) *The Psychology of Selling*, New York: McGraw-Hill.

Vakratsas, Demetrios and Tim Ambler (1999) "How advertising works: What do we really know?", *Journal of Marketing*, Vol. 63, pp. 26–43.

Vaughn, Richard (1980) "How Advertising Works: a Planning Model", *Journal of Advertising Research*, Vol. 20–5, pp. 27–33.

IMC planning

CHAPTER PERSPECTIVE
Knowing the score

Integrated marketing communication is often compared to an orchestra. Just as an orchestra's performance is guided by a musical score, an IMC campaign must have a written score, or plan. This plan details which marketing communication functions and which media are to be used at which times and to what extent.

An IMC campaign plan is a written document. It can be as minimal as a set of organized notes by a person running a small retail business or as complex as a 100-page document for a multimillion-euro brand campaign. But all good plans, regardless of size, have six basic elements: targeting (designated customers and prospects), SWOT analysis, objectives, strategies and tactics, a budget, and evaluation. The planning process begins with the selection of the desired audience for the brand message. Research then determines the strengths and weaknesses of a company or brand from the perspective of customers and prospects. Planning also takes into consideration marketplace opportunities and threats—the things that companies cannot control but can leverage or address to their advantage.

This chapter explains the differences between objectives, strategies and tactics, and describes the six steps in the planning process. It also clarifies what role the IMC plan has in the company's planning process.

Insights from everywhere
McCann-Erickson, Melbourne, Australia

Holden Ltd. is Australia's premier automaker. The Barina—Holden's smallest model and one of the oldest models in the Australian market—had been a success in the small-car market for many years. However, in recent years, it became clear that the model had lost its way and was on a decline. This situation raised a number of questions for Holden: How do you get a small car back on track and design a marketing communication programme that will help it finish ahead of the competition? Who should be involved in planning the turnaround? Is there a pricing problem? A targeting or positioning problem? A promotional problem? Where do you start?

The McCann-Erickson office in Melbourne saw it as a research problem, one that called for a better understanding of the car's target market in order to create a more on-target creative strategy and communication mix.

The marketing challenge

The Barina was originally launched in the Australian market with an advertising campaign called "Beep, Beep", which used the Road Runner character from the old Warner Bros. cartoon series. This campaign transcended the memorable limits of most advertising and became part of the Australian vernacular. The car was soon affectionately referred to as the "Beep Beep Barina". Even when Holden abandoned the Road Runner visual, the "Beep, Beep" was maintained as an advertising sign-off and a powerful mnemonic device.

However, in the 1990s, the Barina's sales declined by 16 per cent and then by an alarming 43 per cent. There were a number of reasons for this, including an increase in small-car brand alternatives and greater price competition. The most critical change, however, was the decline in interest by the traditional small-car target market—young women.

Segmenting and targeting

McCann-Erickson Melbourne formed a cross-functional task force to gather information about trends important to the Barina's key target market. This task force included personnel from advertising, market research, public relations, and promotions, as well as innovators from other consumer categories such as music producers, magazine publishers, and clothing marketers.

From the research, the McCann task force determined that the primary target audience would be a sub-segment of young women—those in their early 20s who were also characterized as "early adopters", that is, the first to try something and then influence the opinions of others. The broader target audience was identified as "single, female optimists" aged 18 to 34. The third most important segment was all remaining 18- to 34-year-olds, male and female.

The research was also designed to determine why young women had abandoned the Barina. Knowing the *why* is what enables a company to create brand messages relevant to a targeted segment. The McCann task force found that safety was not particularly relevant to young women. Further, Barina's image, which was still associated with the dated "Beep, Beep" campaign, did not match the segment's aspirations—it was considered too young and "girlie". This research also revealed that young women have a great affinity with their cars—they see their car as an "accomplice" in their life. Therefore, a car's image and personality are important to this group. And the car must suit their lifestyle. McCann also found that this segment considered

▶ traditional car advertising dull, uninspiring, and unengaging. What scored high with this segment was unexpected advertising conveyed with wit.

To convince "young female early adopters" that Barina was "cool", the McCann team first had to understand what this group considered cool in general and then anticipate the next trend. To do this, the team conducted innovative multidisciplinary research designed to monitor the lifestyle and attitude trends of this group. This research unearthed two key facts: (1) The target needs to identify with the brand, by identifying with a projected brand user who represents someone she would like to be. (2) The target was interested in Japanese *manga* (a highly identifiable style of comics and animated cartoons), which if translated into advertising could potentially be a very original and unique communication device for Barina.

Objectives and strategies

McCann determined that the Barina campaign's communication objectives were:

- To create a "cool" image of the Barina among 75 per cent of the target audience.
- To have 75 per cent of the target audience associate Barina with two or more of the following attributes: fun, smart, independent, outrageous, and stylish.

The consumer research and resultant understanding of the key target audience indicated that if the McCann team was going to change perceptions of Barina and leave "Beep, Beep" behind, a radically different creative approach was critical. Barina needed to break the rules of traditional car advertising, in terms of both medium and message. The resulting communication strategy recommendations were:

- To develop a character who reflected the identified lifestyle aspirations of the target audience.
- To develop a sense of intrigue and consumer involvement. (The target audience needed to discover Barina for itself, not be told.)
- To build the brand in a consistent supporting manner across all communication expressions.

Message and media strategy

The Japanese cartoon style provided an approach that was fresh and original and in tune with the early adopters' aspirations. The result was an animated character called "BG"—Barina Girl—who represented the target audience's lifestyle, aspirations and personality. The story lines described BG as handling life's highs and lows with intelligence, wit, and determination. For example, a "Bad Hair Day" commercial was inspired by discussions in a focus-group session. In this commercial, BG uses her Barina to deal with her bad-hair problem in an imaginative way.

McCann repositioned Barina as a hip brand by building a strategic street presence prior to the launch of the multimedia campaign. This was accomplished by creating a BG Roller Blading Team, which appeared at selected trendy festivals and gave away premiums branded "BG". Recipients had no way at that point of knowing what "BG" meant, and the simple "BG" logo was reminiscent of a secret underground nightclub symbol. The BG premiums included T-shirts, sun cream, backpacks, stickers, and key rings. Posters designed to look like those for underground bands were hung in selected inner-city areas.

The agency then launched a multimedia advertising campaign that capitalized on the broader target's unique relationship with each medium. The BG commercials appeared only in a select list of television programmes and movies considered to be leading-edge, must-see programmes among the target. The character BG was given her own weekly radio programme on a key radio network. McCann developed new adventures each week to keep the campaign fresh, maintain consumer involvement, and capitalize on topical issues.

A half-page comic strip appeared in another popular medium for the target, a weekly magazine. The strip cartoons were supplemented with full-page colour ads themed around the magazine's special issues such as most beautiful people, celebrity weddings, best and worst dressed, and best bodies.

Evaluation of the BG campaign

Quantitative testing of the BG campaign was positive: 97 per cent of targeted respondents liked the manga-style animation. Findings from ongoing qualitative tracking studies found that the targeted segment was shifting its perceptions of the Barina and its manufacturer, Holden. In approximately 20 focus groups the campaign was discussed spontaneously and enthusiastically. In terms of the behavioural objectives, the campaign had a positive impact on sales. Since the BG campaign launch in 1998, the Barina sales decline has been reversed and sales have grown by 30 per cent. This case demonstrates the importance of segmenting a market, identifying a target, and then learning as much as possible about that target in order to create messages and select media that will have an impact.

Source:
This case was adapted with permission from the award-winning Advertising and Marketing Effectiveness (AME) brief submitted by McCann-Erickson, Melbourne.

Starting at zero with IMC campaign planning

Although managing the acquisition and retention of customers is an ongoing process, once a year most companies do a major analysis to determine what changes need to be made in their marketing communication efforts during the coming year. Each review should start with a clean sheet, as marketers consider how various tools and budgets are used. This process, which is called **zero-based planning**, *determines objectives and strategies based on current brand and marketplace conditions, which are considered the zero point.* That's particularly true when a new product is being launched.

A formal campaign plan is drawn up for several reasons. First, it provides a rational process for identifying the most important communication issues on which the company should focus over the next 12 months—that is, to determine how best to use marketing communication to help the company achieve its sales and profit objectives. Second, it informs everyone involved with MC, including outside MC agencies, what is expected of them. Third, it helps ensure that the MC effort is integrated and focused on the most important communication issues. Fourth, an MC plan tells top management how and why MC euros will be spent and what the company can expect in return for the euros it is investing in marketing communications. Finally, the plan provides a standard against which progress and final results can be measured.

In most cases, the annual plan takes the form of a **campaign**, which is *a set of MC messages with a common theme that runs for a specified period of time to achieve certain MC objectives.* The larger the MC budget, generally speaking, the more pieces and parts an MC plan will have, such as a number of different customer segments being targeted and a number of different MC functions being used.

IMC planning within the organization

Planning occurs at multiple levels within an organization. At the corporate level, it means revising the business plan, which is the company's overall strategy of operating, in order to maximize profits and shareholder value. The business plan is concerned primarily with profit, brand equity, and the company's share price (if the company is publicly owned).

Below the corporate business plan are the plans of individual departments—operations/production, human resources, financial, marketing, and sales. In the case of marketing, the analysis and planning focus primarily on goals for sales and share of market, which can be met through such strategies as launching a new product, a line extension, or expanding the market.

The level below the department level is where analysis and planning take place for marketing communication that focuses on customer relationships (acquisition and retention), brand awareness, brand knowledge, trial, repeat purchase, and overall customer satisfaction. In very large companies with very large MC budgets, the final level of planning is done by each of the major MC functions—advertising, publicity, sales promotion, events and sponsorships, and direct response. The *Integrated* Marketing Communication approach, however, suggests that such a planning at the level of MC functions—as if they were independent—may be suboptimal in terms of loss of effectiveness and missed opportunities for synergies.

MC planning is the planning of activities at a functional level, in contrast to business planning which occurs at the strategic level. MC plans contribute to the realization of the company's goals, and as such MC is a part of the marketing activities. So the process is that corporate goals are translated into marketing goals, which are subsequently translated into MC goals. Hence, the goals as set by the marketing department form the starting point for devising an IMC plan.

This is not the whole story, however. Truly integrated marketing communications does not only integrate the marketing communications functions, it also integrates the communicative aspects of all other marketing actions, and even actions performed by other people in the organization. This point was made more extensively in Chapter 3. Consequently, IMC planning requires a holistic view on the company's actions, and logically this should be reflected in the planning process as well. Ideally business planning is performed in consultation with all departments, including marketing, and the marketing department should base its input on its functional specialists: people focusing on communication, production, etc.

So the role of MC and MC plans is much more complex than the simple sequence: corporate plans, marketing plans, MC plans. The planning process is highly interactive. Nevertheless, at some stage, MC will be set certain goals by the marketing department: brand awareness has to increase by 10 per cent; 15 000 product trials are required by the end of the year; at least 40 per cent of our target must be able to tell the main difference from our competitor. At that stage, the MC department has to make a plan.

This chapter discusses a typical planning process (see Table 5-1) used for an overall MC plan. Planners focus on target audiences, objectives, strategies and tactics, the budget, and the scheduling of MC activities. The plan also describes what ongoing market testing will be done and specifies what measurement methods will be used to determine the effectiveness of the plan

Step	Description
1 Identify target audiences	Analyse the various customer and prospect segments, and determine which to target and to what extent.
2 Analyse SWOTs	Summarize internal (strengths, weaknesses) and external (opportunities, threats) brand-related conditions with respect to communicating with the selected target; determine the success of the MC functions and media used in preceding year.
3 Determine MC objectives	Decide what marketing communication programmes should accomplish.
4 Develop strategies and tactics	Determine which MC functions should be used and to what extent. Choose brand messages and means of delivery. Support each strategy with a rationale. Decide when each MC programme will begin and end.
5 Determine the budget	Decide what the overall MC budget will be and then how money will be divided among the selected MC functions.
6 Evaluate effectiveness	Conduct ongoing MC tests in an effort to find more effective ways to do IMC. Monitor and evaluate all the IMC efforts to determine effectiveness and accountability.

Table 5-1 Zero-based campaign planning

once it has been executed. MC managers working with the people in their departments and with the director of marketing are responsible for putting the MC plan together. Companies that have a good relationship with their MC agencies may ask members of the agency for their ideas and suggestions.

Applying zero-based planning

For years most companies conducted MC planning by looking at a few market research studies and then making some slight adjustments to the plan that had been used the year before. Today this approach is being replaced with the more sophisticated zero-based approach. The "zero" means that planning starts with no preconceived notions about what MC functions or media are needed.[1] Rather than starting with last year's plan, planners select functions and media in the light of current marketplace and brand conditions. For example, advertising may have been heavily used in the preceding year to increase awareness, but now awareness levels are fine and a more important concern is getting trial, which means using more sales promotion and less advertising during the coming year.

Zero-based planning makes sense because competitors and distribution channels are constantly changing, as are customers' wants and needs. With the increase in interactivity and tracking of customer interactions, companies now have more data on which to base MC and media decisions.

Merely because this planning process starts from "zero" does *not* mean, however, that a company will not continue to do some of the things it has done before. Obviously, if there is still need for a promotional effort or an advertising strategy that was used successfully in the preceding year, it should be repeated. One aspect of corporate learning is keeping track of what worked and didn't work. Such learning should help guide annual campaign planning.

The IMC planning process

The six-step planning process that is presented below is equally applicable to B2C and B2B companies; to companies of every size, from the smallest retailer to the largest global brand; to service providers as well as manufacturers; and to non-profit organizations. Each medium and each MC function has its own unique strength. An organization can determine the right mix of media and MC functions only after it has targeted its audience. The first step in zero-based planning, therefore, is to identify key customer and prospect segments.

Step 1: Identifying target audiences

To advertise and promote a product to everyone would be a waste of money because there is no single product that everyone wants or can afford to buy. An analysis of consumer behaviour and customer-response factors (discussed in Chapter 4) will lead to a better understanding of the people and companies most likely to be in the market for the product. Therefore, companies (both B2C and B2B) segment customers into groups based on certain characteristics and the likelihood that group members will buy the product; then companies target messages specifically to these key audiences. The term **segmenting** means *grouping customers or prospects according to common characteristics, needs, wants, or desires.* **Targeting** refers to *analysing, evaluating, and prioritizing the market segments deemed most profitable to pursue.*

Targeting focuses the MC effort on (1) current customers who are most likely to repurchase or influence purchases; (2) customers and prospects who need special attention for whatever reason (they may have slowed their frequency of purchase, have had a serious customer-service problem, have had a dialogue with the brand but have not yet purchased); and (3) prospects who have never bought the brand but might buy it, given their profiles. Other stakeholders who affect or influence these three categories of customers and prospects may also be targeted. Because of its emphasis on consumer insights, account planning helps companies identify and understand their target audiences (see colour insert A8).[2]

Because it is expensive to send out brand messages, the more precise the targeting is, the less the media waste. Also, only by knowing whom to target can a brand do a SWOT analysis (explained next) and develop objectives and strategies that are relevant and persuasive.

Segmenting and targeting is not specific for IMC planning.[3] In fact, the marketing function will have decided on the overall target groups. But within that broader target, selecting a smaller sub-target may be useful for the MC function. For example, when a car manufacturer wants to enter the Danish market (business plan), the marketing department may decide to target the higher-income categories (marketing plan). The MC people may subsequently decide that the best group of customers to which to direct a campaign may be the subgroup of the selected target that lives in the capital of Copenhagen, given the relatively strong presence of the target in this city.

All marketing textbooks have lengthy chapters on segmenting and targeting. The main message in segmenting is that it is better for it to be based on customers' needs and wants. In other words, try to split up a larger group into smaller groups based on commonalities in needs and wants, of course with respect to the product that the company is selling. Usually multiple groups are then identified, all of which, in one way or the other, may be interesting for the company to target. Which target(s) to select is then determined by criteria that relate to the susceptibility of the group to the marketing and communication actions the company can undertake. For example, when it is known that almost all consumers in one of the targets like to watch German *Krimi's*, this common characteristic makes it possible to use the commercial breaks in those programmes to air commercials. In this case the target is selected on the basis of shared television-watching behaviour.

Step 2: Analysing SWOTs

Strategic planning in general is based on an analysis of marketplace conditions. This is what a SWOT analysis does, and this also holds good for the development of a strategic IMC plan. A SWOT analysis is *a structured evaluation of internal strengths and weaknesses and external opportunities and threats that can help or hurt a brand.* SWOT is an acronym for Strengths, Weaknesses, Opportunities, and Threats. In the case of IMC planning a SWOT analysis restricts itself to the communications and brand characteristics that are encountered. For example, a specific sponsorship can be identified as a strength; or a clear media consumption pattern can be seen as an opportunity. Other SWOT elements that may be relevant at the marketing planning level can become irrelevant at the IMC level. A company with a well-qualified workforce as a strength will not call this a strength in the context of IMC planning. Or the threat of entry of foreign companies is usually not seen as a threat when developing a communications plan. So, although SWOT analyses are performed on most strategic planning levels, the contents of the SWOT analyses do not necessarily coincide. Rather a SWOT analysis is unique at its specific level, though it is useful to tap relevant elements from the adjacent levels of planning.

Strengths and weaknesses are internal factors under a company's control (see Figure 5-1). Strengths and weaknesses are determined by asking the target audiences identified in Step 1 of the IMC planning process, colleagues within the company, or by asking a consultant to identify them. Opportunities and threats are external elements—the company has little or no control over them though on occasion it can influence them.

A SWOT analysis that is part of devising an IMC plan concentrates on Strengths, etc. with respect to the two main building blocks of MC: the brand and communication. So, although general developments must not be neglected, emphasis will have to be put on the company's marketplace situation with respect to these two aspects in particular.

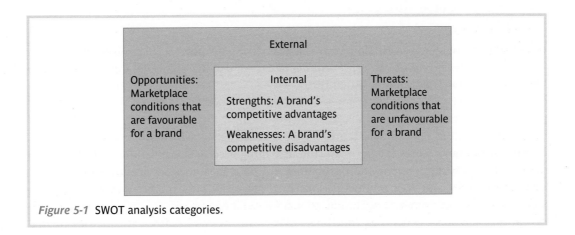

Figure 5-1 SWOT analysis categories.

Recognizing internal strengths and weaknesses

A company's strengths and weaknesses are the elements of a SWOT analysis over which the company has control. Strengths are competitive advantages; weaknesses are competitive disadvantages. Strengths should be leveraged and weaknesses fixed. Mercedes has a strong brand name, associated with robustness, reliability and strength. Mercedes can leverage this brand name when introducing new versions, e.g. the B-class.

Strengths and weaknesses related to the *brand* include such things as how customers and prospects perceive a brand's innovativeness, the convenience of finding and buying the brand (distribution), its pricing compared to competition, the expertise and helpfulness of its sales force, the condition of its physical facilities, and its overall financial strength. Brand image, brand positioning, corporate culture, and core values can also be either strengths or weaknesses. (Although brand images and reputations live in customers' minds, they are considered internal controllable elements because the company can make changes in the 4 Ps (including MC messages) that will in turn affect how these are perceived.)

To determine which are the strengths and weaknesses of *customer brand relationships*, research can have customers rate a brand and its competitors on the following characteristics, or *relationship constructs*, which are dimensions of brand relationships (also see Chapter 2)—whether they:

1 *Trust* the brand.

2 Are *satisfied* with the brand.

3 Perceive the company as *consistent* in its dealings and product performance.

4 Perceive the company as *accessible*.

5 Perceive the company as *responsive*.

6 Feel the company is *committed* to customers and puts them first.

7 Have an *affinity* for the company and its other customers.

8 *Like* the company and enjoy doing business with it.

To determine the strengths and weaknesses of a brand's *communications*, a SWOT analysis should also include how the brand compares to its competitors in each of these areas among the target audience(s):

- Media presence.
- Appreciation of advertising.
- Access to media.
- Possession of an advertising property (an **advertising property** is *an element in advertising that is uniquely related and attributed to one brand*; e.g. the picture of a tiger in action is uniquely associated with the brand Esso).
- A strong sponsorship.

Just as important as *how* a brand scores on these constructs is *why* it scores high or low. For example, if a brand scores low on trust, the first thing a company must do is determine the source of the distrust (among the possibilities are poor customer service, overpromising in planned messages, and poor product performance). Negative performance messages can make millions of euros in marketing communication a wasted investment.

An example of the benefits provided by a SWOT analysis comes from athletic-shoe manufacturer Nike's early experiences of selling to women. In the early 1990s women made up only about 5 per cent of Nike's customer base. Consequently, women became a target for Nike, and when the company did some customer research, it discovered that women did not find advertising that featured Michael Jordan and other male athletes relevant; these messages didn't talk to women. In order to fix this Weakness the company created a separate women's campaign with advertising copy that addressed how women felt about their bodies and themselves, responding to the trend of the 1990s that physical presence was becoming an important aspect in social life (Opportunity). The ads included lines such as "Did you ever wish you were a boy?", "You were born a daughter", and "A woman is often measured by the things she cannot control." Soon after this campaign, women accounted for 15 per cent of Nike's sales.[4] Such success is what led Nike to move further into the women's market, reaching the market niches of girls and young women.

A company can employ many ways to learn of its strengths and weaknesses: by formal market research, but also by analysing service calls, interviewing the sales force and front-line retail employees, doing observation studies of customers shopping, maintaining customer advisory boards, reviewing what the trade press and the popular press are saying about the company and brand, and doing formal or informal surveys of the brand's suppliers and channel members.

Recognizing external opportunities and threats

External factors that companies must live with are a mixture of opportunities and threats. Threats are marketplace conditions that reduce the perceived value or attractiveness of a brand or that result in its being more costly to make or provide. Threats can also be found in changes in the media landscape, both on the consumer side (e.g. people spend less time reading), or on the supply side (e.g. the explosion of television channels consumers can choose from). By definition, threats cannot be controlled, but sometimes a company can lessen their impact. The idea is to anticipate them and make efforts to counteract them.

Opportunities are social and economic conditions and situations in the marketplace that can positively alter customers' attitudes about and behaviour toward a brand or its communication. Smart companies identify and leverage opportunities. Increases in commuter behaviour and the subsequent introduction of tabloid newspapers distributed for free at railway stations in various European countries like Sweden offer distinct opportunities for brands which have those commuters as their target groups (e.g. mobile phone operators).

SWOT analysis

Once the SWOTs have been identified, they need to be analysed. This means that the SWOTs must be assessed in a systematic way. Many things can be taken into consideration when analysing SWOTs, among which the following aspects can be used for most product categories:

1 *Realistic damage* to brand relationships and brand equity if a weakness or threat is not addressed (i.e. anticipated and counteracted).

2 *Realistic benefit* if a strength or opportunity is leveraged (i.e. used to its full potential).

3 *Cost* of addressing or leveraging each SWOT.

4 The *time frame* in which the company has to address or leverage each SWOT.

After the company has analysed its SWOTs, it must use them to set objectives. No company has the time or resources to address and leverage all its SWOT findings, but the analysis can help IMC planners determine where to focus their attention. A SWOT analysis also leads to

Key SWOTs	MC objectives	Best MC function	Rationale
No brand awareness	Create 40% awareness among target	Advertising	Mass media advertising quickest in building general awareness
Identifiable sub-target	Create 70% awareness among sub-target	Direct marketing	Small audience; contact information available
Availability problem	Sell 3500 units in advance of availability	Direct marketing	Use personal contact medium to pre-sell target

Table 5-2 Examples of measurable objectives

decisions about which marketing communication tools to use. Table 5-2 illustrates how a SWOT analysis translates into MC objectives and a choice of MC functions for a fictitious new product launch.

Step 3: Determining marketing communication objectives

The primary purpose of setting objectives is to state what is to be accomplished in order to direct an organization's efforts and allow the organization to evaluate effectiveness. Objectives are *what marketers want to accomplish with marketing communication* (see colour insert A11). They should be measurable if marketers truly want to prove that an MC plan was effective. "Measurable" means that numbers are assigned to the objectives, such as "Increase awareness by 10 per cent" or "Motivate 70 per cent to buy the brand again" (also see the IMC in Action case on Holden's Barina).

Communication objectives versus marketing objectives

Communication objectives should focus on things communication can achieve. Increasing awareness, changes in attitudes, increased knowledge of the brand, response because of the communication. In general the IMC plan will be part of a marketing plan that will have its own *marketing objectives*. Marketing objectives and communication objectives may coincide, but it is more logical to think of marketing objectives that are formulated in higher-order marketing terms. For example, a newly introduced product should sell 12 000 units in its first year. All marketing instruments should play together to reach this marketing objective. Accompanying communication objectives could then be that 20 per cent of the target market should have the brand Top of Mind in this product category, 20 000 requests for information should be collected, the sales promotion must lead 4000 customers to closing the deal, etc. The last objective in particular illustrates that communication objectives and marketing objectives can come very close to each other. Bear in mind that the main distinction is that communication objectives should be within the scope of *only* (integrated) communication activities, whereas marketing objectives are the result of all kinds of marketing actions. When you recall from Chapter 3 that marketing actions such as pricing themselves have communication implications, you start to appreciate the subtleties of the marketing discipline.

SWOT findings determine objectives

Here is an example of how a SWOT analysis can be used to set objectives. Whisky is not a product people learn to drink naturally. So the product category is traditionally facing the problem of attracting new consumers. New consumers are also typically in their thirties, when consumption habits have been established. New products are not so often tried, consumers of that age have to be persuaded and, more importantly, informed. A SWOT analysis may have revealed that potential new consumers are especially scared off by the large variety of choices of whiskies, and have the feeling they cannot see the wood for the trees.

The logical conclusion of this analysis is that potential new consumers should be well informed. So a leaflet may be designed that gives clear and detailed, but easily accessible, information about the various types of whisky, and drinking advice. Objectives may be made concrete, e.g. in one year 50 000 leaflets should be picked up by consumers, of which 20 000 should show serious interest, e.g. by asking the retailer for further information or advice. Or the leaflets should lead to 15 000 visits of a specially designed website.

What makes a good objective?

Because a marketing plan defines the target audience at the outset, objectives do not have to mention the target. Only when the target audience is different from the stated one—for example, because the SWOT analysis led to a focus on a sub-target—is it necessary to define it in an objective. Also, it is assumed that each objective listed must be achieved within the year for which the plan is designed. As with the target audience, the time period is stated only when it differs from the overall plan—for example, "Within the first three months, obtain 75 per cent awareness among the retail trade of the brand's new, improved formula."

Well-written objectives pass the SMAC test. They are

Specific.
Measurable.
Achievable.
Challenging.

The more *specific* an objective is, the better it is. The objective "Increase brand knowledge by 15 per cent" is less specific than "Increase knowledge of the brand's superior warranty by 15 per cent".

Objectives are *measurable*, otherwise it is not possible to determine whether they have been achieved. It is sometimes tempting to state objectives in easy-reading terms: "Brand awareness should increase by 10 per cent", or "25 per cent of our current customers must become loyal customers". When an objective is just this, the objective does not pass the measurability test. The problem is that concepts like awareness and loyalty have multiple interpretations. Chapter 2 has already demonstrated that for the awareness topic: awareness can be defined at different levels, and as far as loyalty is concerned, an important question is whether loyalty is only repeat purchase behaviour, or can also be manifested in a "loyal" attitude. Therefore, the concepts as they appear in objectives must be well defined, and in a way that makes them measurable.

In order to set a realistic and measurable objective, a company first needs a *quantifiable measure of the current situation*. This measure is called the baseline or benchmark. For example, if you want to set a share-increase objective, you first need to know what the current share is. If the current share is 10 per cent and you want to increase it to 12 per cent, then you are proposing a change of 2 share points. This is a 20 per cent increase. But herein lies a problem for most companies: they are not willing to spend the money required to determine the necessary benchmarks. Unless a company knows what percentage of its target audience is aware of its brand, has tried it, has made repeat purchases, and so on, there is little or no basis for setting measurable objectives.

When objectives are *achievable*, those responsible for meeting them will be more inclined to take them seriously. Some managers set objectives too high, hoping to maximize the effort of those involved. Because meeting objectives gives employees a sense of satisfaction, employees are likely to resent managers who consistently set unreachable objectives. Yet objectives should be *challenging* in order to push employees to be creative and do their best work. Objectives need to be set in some interval ranging from minimally challenging, to just achievable.

Using consumer behaviour models to set objectives

As explained in Chapter 4, consumer response models explain how brand messages affect the brand decision-making process. Companies use the steps in these models to guide them in setting MC objectives. The AIDA sequence—awareness, interest, desire, action—for example, suggests that a brand has *communication* objectives for achieving certain levels of brand awareness, certain levels of interest, and so on. Action, the last step in the AIDA sequence, is a *marketing* (behavioural) objective.

In the case of B2B products and high-priced consumer products, MC objectives may address where customers are in their buying process. An insurance company may set an MC objective for its sales representatives as follows: "All customers who request a quote on their home and automobile insurance policies will be contacted personally within 72 hours of their quote requests." This objective would relate directly to customers at the interest step in the AIDA sequence.

Figure 5-2 shows that the percentage of the target audience affected at each hierarchical step gets smaller as customers move toward the last step, action.[5] This illustration gives hypothetical response rates to demonstrate how drastically the percentage of customers affected drops as

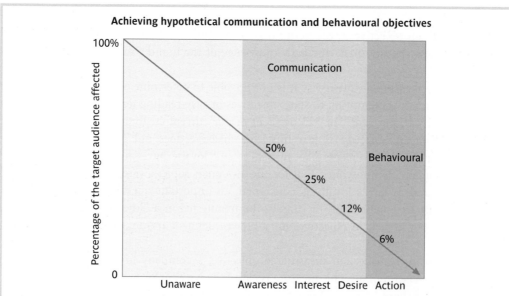

Figure 5-2 Achieving communication objectives is easier than achieving marketing (behavioural) objectives.

customers move through this series of effects. Drop-off happens because making people aware of a brand is much easier than persuading them to buy a brand or take some other action. The level of expected impact obviously varies with the product category, the brand, and the strength of the brand messages.

MC objectives can also be based on the think/feel/do model (Chapter 4). Once a company decides what a target audience should think and feel about a brand, it can determine a desired percentage for thinking and feeling. Examples of "do" objectives were given earlier. Here are examples of "think" and "feel" communication objectives:

"Think" objectives

- Convince 50 per cent of the target audience that Brand X is the most durable.
- Make 35 per cent of the target audience aware that Brand X has the longest warranty.

"Feel" objectives

- Have 40 per cent of the target audience rate Brand X as the brand "easiest to do business with".
- Convince 55 per cent of the target audience that Brand X is the most prestigious of all brands in its category.

The quantitative aspect of an objective—the percentage or raw number to be achieved—often depends on the brand's past performance and how much MC support is available. The more research that has been done on the results of past MC efforts, the more educated the current estimate can be. For example, if customers' measured interest in the brand is generally half of their measured awareness of the brand, and their action is half of their desire for the brand, it would be realistic to set an awareness objective of 80 per cent, an interest objective of 40 per cent, and a desire objective of 20 per cent in order to justify increasing the action objective to 10 per cent.

MC objectives can also be set for one or more of the eight brand relationship constructs listed earlier in this chapter. Knowing that trust, for example, is the most important relationship component, a brand would be smart to have a trust objective, such as "Determine that at least 85 per cent of current customers *trust* our brand more than any other". Other such communication objectives could include the following:

- "75 per cent say our brand is the most *responsive.*"
- "80 per cent say our brand is the most *consistent* in its dealings with customers."
- "90 per cent say our company is more *accessible* than any other competing company."

Some marketers do not focus too much on attitudinal objectives because, they argue, there is no absolute link between achieving them and achieving behavioural objectives. Although it is true that increases in awareness, trust, and other pure communication measures do not guarantee increases in sales, common sense says that if no one is aware of a brand, or if those who are aware of a brand do not trust it, the chances of its selling well are small. The exact relationship between attitudes and behaviour differs by brand and over time as marketplace conditions change, but there is always some level of relationship. This is why it is imperative that brands conduct ongoing evaluations of customer perceptions and behaviour.

Once the objectives have been written in terms of leveraging or addressing the key SWOTs, the next step in zero-based planning is figuring out how to achieve the objectives.

Step 4: Developing strategies and tactics

Every objective should be supported by one or more strategies. **Strategies** are *ideas about how to accomplish objectives.* To accomplish this, various tactics are used. **Tactics** are *specific actions to be taken to execute a strategy.* They are the executional details that bring a strategic idea to life.

The MC agencies are generally responsible for tactics as well as strategies. Artists, writers, producers, and creative directors make the strategic ideas come to life in the form of commercials, brochures, and merchandising kits. Chapter 6 discusses message strategies in more detail; Chapter 7 covers tactics. Here these topics are covered on a more general level for understanding their role in the IMC planning process.

Phases of strategy development

The strategic development of an MC plan generally goes through two phases. The first is determining *which* MC functions and which media to use. This is generally obvious from the SWOT findings, as previously explained. The second phase is more creatively challenging and is the reason why companies hire MC agencies. In this phase, ideas must be created for *how* each MC function and medium will be used.

Phase 1: Selecting the marketing communication and media mixes   Most marketing communication plans use a mix of MC functions because there are always several SWOT-identified areas that need to be addressed or leveraged. A **marketing communication mix** is *the selection of MC functions used at a given time as part of a marketing programme.* Deciding which MC functions can most efficiently and effectively help achieve the MC objectives is not too difficult if marketers stop and think about what each MC function does best. For example, to help achieve the objective "Increase belief of brand claims by 15 per cent", publicity would be used because it has relatively high credibility. If the objective is "Increase trial by 25 per cent", then sales promotion may be the best MC tool because sales promotion adds tangible value to a brand offering. The larger the MC budget is, the deeper a company can go in addressing and leveraging SWOTs; often the result is the use of several of the major MC functions.

The challenge of determining an MC mix is not only deciding which functions to use but how much of each. One MC function may take the lead while one or more of the others are used for support. Many sponsorships are followed up by direct marketing campaigns, explicitly referring to the sponsorship. In such cases the sponsorship creates awareness and an entry point for the direct marketer and, most important, some familiarity with the brand is evoked.

Selecting the right media mix is just as important as selecting the right MC mix. A **media mix** is *a selection of media channels used to deliver brand messages.* Media mix strategies and creative message strategies are interdependent and ideally are developed in parallel. For each target audience, a strategic media mix is determined. In any given campaign, different types of media can be used at different times and to different extents to deliver specific types of messages to specific audiences (media mix is discussed in detail in Chapters 8 to 10). As you can see in Table 5-3, most media are used by most of the MC functions but to varying degrees. For example, sales-promotion offers are most often delivered by mail, magazines, and newspapers, and very seldom by radio and TV (infomercials and home shopping channels are direct-marketing activities). This is why the MC mix and the media mix must be integrated.

MC functions	TV	Radio	Newspaper	Magazine	Mail	Internet	Outdoor
Advertising	XXX	XXX	XXX	XXX	X	XXX	XXX
Publicity	XXX	XXX	XXX	XXX		XXX	
Sales promotion	X	X	XXX	XXX	XX	XX	
Events			X	X	X	X	XX
Direct response	XX	X	X	XX	XXX	XXX	
Sponsorships	XXX	XX			XX		XX	X
Personal selling					XX	XX	

Table 5-3 Extent of media usage by each major MC function

Note: The number of Xs represents to what extent each MC function makes use of each medium: XXX = frequently used; XX = occasionally used; X = rarely used.

Phase 2: Selecting the creative idea   Inexperienced marketers often mistakenly think that selecting a particular MC function or medium constitutes a strategy. The big creative idea however, is a crucial part of a strategy. The big creative idea is an almost enchanting phenomenon in IMC, the element which elevates IMC above a straightforward management task, or an object of study. Thinking of, talking of and analysing creative ideas is the most appealing aspect of studying IMC to many, but, please note, it is nevertheless only a part, and in all honesty, just a relatively small part, of the entire IMC planning process.

Developing a creative idea, and MC and media planning interact. In some instances the creative idea determines which MC functions and media are most useful. In other instances, however, decisions on MC functions and media follow from the SWOT analysis—e.g. the selected target group has an outspoken media profile—so that the creative idea is subject to fitting within these decisions on media usage. Creative strategies and how to execute them are discussed in detail in Chapters 6 and 7. Here, two examples are given.

Assume that a company decides that, given the SWOT analysis, sales promotion will work best to communicate the benefits of an innovative cold-curing medicine. A weak, incomplete strategy would be "Use sales promotion" because it doesn't contain an *idea* about how to use the MC tool. "Use a team of doctors to conduct a media tour explaining the breakthrough qualities of the brand in curing the common cold": this is a much better strategy. Tactical decisions would involve selecting the towns, such as the top 10 markets, for the media tour. This strategy not only implies a MC function—publicity—but states an idea for *getting* publicity.

Another example is the strategy used by Michelin, manufacturer of premium-priced automobile tyres. One of Michelin's communication objectives is to convince car owners that Michelin tyres are the most durable and safest on the market. A weak strategy to accomplish this objective would have been "Use television advertising". Instead, Michelin devised a strong, creative strategy: "Associate the Michelin brand name with protecting families by showing babies sitting on or in Michelin tyres." This strategy links Michelin tyres to babies (who, everyone knows, are precious and have to be protected); the message is: "Michelin is a safe tyre—it protects." Advertising now seems the most appropriate MC function and the use of pictures is essential. This naturally leads to television advertising or print. But another elaboration of this creative idea could have been to sponsor children's playing areas that often use old tyres.

Strategy involves timing and scheduling

An important aspect of MC strategy is timing and scheduling—determining which media placements, promotional programmes, and other MC activities should happen first or last or in between. For example, most brands have seasonal buying patterns—sales are higher during some months and lower during others. Most swimsuits, for example, are sold in late spring and early summer. Strategic planners must decide how far in advance of the buying season to start sending out brand messages and how late into the buying season to maintain marketing communication support.

There is no magic formula for timing promotional programmes. Normally each product category has its own seasonal pattern. Companies can apply some logic, however. Most promotional support for swimsuits, for example, begins in late winter and early spring. This is when people begin to tire of cold weather and begin thinking about the pleasures of summer. During this time, people are most receptive to swimsuit brand messages. Another factor is when retail stores begin displaying the suits. When stores set out new merchandise, they expect manufacturers to have marketing communication programmes running that will help generate sales.

Timing is also important when publicity is part of an MC campaign. Where the publicity angle has news value (for example, a new product or a significant improvement to an old product), it is better to do the brand publicity before advertising. This way, the information is still news and editors will be more likely to run the stories.

A challenge often faced by both B2C and B2B companies is co-ordinating the timing between marketing, production, and sales. Each of these areas needs lead times of several months (sometimes even more). Once a new product has been given the go-ahead for production, three to six months may elapse before the first product is actually manufactured. At the same time, the sales department is making calls and presenting the new product so that when production starts, finished goods will not have to sit in a warehouse for long. To support the sales effort, marketing communication materials—ads, direct-mail pieces, special events, trade-show exhibits—need to be produced, which can take several months. In the case of some consumer products, media time and space need to be bought three to six months ahead to guarantee the best rates and placement.

Timing and co-ordination go together. They are both critical elements of integration. The best way to ensure right timing is to discuss individual department plans in cross-functional meetings, letting everyone know what everyone else is planning to do and when they are planning to do it.

Step 5: Setting the budget

Marketing and marketing communication departments (and their campaigns) are allocated *a fixed amount of money for a fixed period of time*—in other words, a **budget**. Marketing competes with all other corporate departments (such as finance, production, and human resources) for its share of the total corporate budget. Each department brings in a budget along with a projection of what the spending will do to contribute to the company's profits. Management then allocates a portion of the overall corporate budget to each department based on what management feels is the best combination of spending to maximize profits.

In a perfect world these allocations would be done objectively and rationally. Based on a marginal analysis it would be determined which euros would lead to the same amount of euros in return, and those would be the last euros to be allocated to the marketing department. For example, when increasing the budget from 45 000 to 46 000 euros would lead to 1000 additional euros in revenues, the optimal budget would be 46 000. When the additional revenues would be less than 1000, the optimal budget would be below 46 000. But when the revenues would increase by more than 1000 euros, the optimal budget would be above 46 000. But that is the theoretical world of economics and textbook analysis. And although it is important to understand this fundamental concept of marginal analysis, actual budget allocation approaches are much more down to earth,

In fact, the reality is that allocating corporate funds is all too often a highly political process. The more political power certain managers or departments have, the more likely they are to receive more than their objective share. That is why cross-functional management is important. The more others in the company, especially top management, know what the marketing department does and accomplishes, the more political support it is likely to have.

Once marketing receives its budget, it then needs to allocate the money to the various MC functional areas, which, like the departments, compete among themselves for what they feel is necessary to run their programmes. A universal curse of planning is that no one ever has a large enough budget to do everything that needs to be done. This means adjustments need to be made in plans. In the case of marketing communications planning, this adjustment can be made fairly easily if the plan is based on prioritized SWOTs. Managers simply go back to the plan and take out the lowest-priority objective or two—whatever it takes to stay in budget. The remaining objectives and supporting strategies then determine how much money will be allocated to each MC function and to major types of media.

Cost or investment?

From an accounting perspective, MC spending is an expense—one of the many costs necessary to run a business. Most marketers, however, prefer to think of MC spending as an investment. The difference in these two philosophical perspectives is that "costs" are necessary evils but "investments" provide a *return on investment (ROI)*. The better the investment is—the smarter marketers and their agencies are about how MC euros are spent—the greater is the return on the MC investment.

The problem with considering MC spending as an investment is that so many other things besides ads and promotions affect sales. Some of these other variables are support received from channel members, what competitors do regarding making product improvements or changing prices, new government regulations that affect producing or selling the company's product, and social and economic trends that affect how consumers spend their money. Even weather can affect sales: too little snowfall in the winter can have devastating impacts for ski resorts, or a cold spring can reduce swimsuit sales. Consequently, although marketers promise that they can create a certain level of sales, top management knows that these promises are subject to many unknown and uncontrollable factors.

One of the problems with this approach is that a link is sought between MC activities and sales. Recently discussions have started on the possibility of capitalizing MC spending on the financial account under the heading of intangible assets. In particular the question is whether Brand Equity should be accepted as the result of branding activities, including MC. This would definitely do more justice to the principles behind MC, in particular as advocated in this book. It must be acknowledged, however, that other measurement issues have to be solved in order to make this a realistic approach, as discussed in the IMC in Action box.

When a company's top executives consider MC a cost rather than an investment (as most of them do), they are much more likely to cut MC spending when business becomes weak. They argue that by cutting costs, they can maintain profits (profits are what is left after costs are subtracted from total sales revenue). Marketers argue back that reducing MC spending will result in sales being reduced even more. The problem with both arguments is that they can be proved only after the fact—after costs have been cut or after a plan is allowed to run without being cut.

IMC in Action

Balancing brands

Marketers love to say that expenses for brand building like advertising have to be seen as an investment rather than a cost, building the asset brand equity. But do they realize the impact of this statement? Assets are subject to accounting principles and rules: marketers don't live in an isolated paradise but have to recognize the rules of the game. Accountants, strictly monitored by governments or other public bodies, set these rules. What are these rules for intangible assets in general, and brand equity in particular? For years there has been a battle between brand managers and accountants about this very question.

It was in the late 1980s that brand acquisitions (e.g. Grand Metropolitan buying Pillsbury) were popular and that the debate about brand valuation raised awareness. During this time it also became clear that companies were acquired more for their intangible assets and less for their tangible ones. This resulted in high levels of the account "goodwill" on the balance sheet. Shareholders became concerned about this and required reassurance about the real value of this goodwill, needing to distinguish the brand from goodwill in order to know what was really going on. The International Accounting Standards (IAS) tell us that an intangible asset must be identifiable (i.e. must be capable of being separated from the company) when treating it differently from goodwill. Obviously, companies will have no problem when they have to capitalize the cost of a brand purchased in isolation. However, what should they do when brands and goodwill are combined in a business acquisition? And to make the problem even more difficult: how are internally generated brands valued?

Continuing with the rules concerning the accountability of a brand, consider a basic accounting principle like amortization. When buying a car, it is clear how to deal with this principle. However, it becomes again a grey area in the case of intangible assets and, in particular, brands since we cannot know their useful life. And this useful life is in turn needed to estimate the amortization. The IAS say that the useful life of an intangible asset can be short, but it can also be very long or even indefinite. Furthermore, "uncertainty justifies estimating the useful life ... on a prudent basis, but it does not justify choosing a life that is unrealistically short". Moreover, economic and legal factors can influence what is "useful life". Economic factors shape the period over which future economic benefits will be received by the company. Legal factors can restrict the period over which the company controls access to these benefits. Overall, the lack of clarity here leaves some space for a debate. . . .

Fortunately, despite the confusion over the rules, there is no confusion about international differences in accounting practices for intangible assets. There are only a few countries with clearly defined rules for recognition and amortization. Countries such as Australia, New Zealand, Sweden, South Africa, Singapore and Hongkong have simply to match their own national standards with those of the IAS. For example, in the US and Canada the amortization period of brands is, at most, 40 years while in New Zealand it is, at most, 20 years. Finally, in European countries, the rules vary between countries and even between different types of intangibles.

Think about it

Is amortization the only problem of having brands on the balance sheet? How does this story relate to the practice of Interbrand publishing a top 100 of the most valuable brands?

Sources:
Interbrand internal document on the valuation of brands.

International Financial Reporting Standards

*www.emeraldinsight.com/Insight/ViewContentServlet?Filename=Published/EmeraldFullTextArticle/
Articles/0560181006.html*

Determining how much to spend on MC

Many factors, both internal and external, affect how customers respond to MC. Nevertheless, most marketers agree that when all other factors are held constant, the relationship between MC spending and MC impact roughly follows an S curve, as shown in Figure 5-3. The relationship between spending and effect is not linear—that is, increases in euros spent do not generate a constant increase in effect. For the sake of the argument, let us assume the effect is in terms of sales (but in the following sales can be easily replaced by "top-of-mind awareness", or "consumers trusting the brand", etc.). The S curve shows that when a company underspends (situation A), the brand's advertising and promotion are not enough to have a presence and therefore have little impact. Like a choir with too few members, too little spending can hardly be heard. The middle part of the S curve (situation B) is the ideal spending range: incremental spending produces incremental sales. At the top of the S curve (situation C), the return from additional spending has a diminishing effect on increasing sales. Situation C often indicates that the market has been saturated. Everyone who is likely to respond to brand messages has been reached and persuaded to buy. Those who are still not customers would require so much persuading that it would not be cost-effective to do so. The ideal situation would be where the marginal euro spent on MC leads to one more euro of sales: the criterion already introduced as marginal analysis.

Determining the spending level that will correspond with situation B, in which the company gets the best return on the MC euros spent, is challenging, because the "right amount" of spending varies by product category and even by brand. In practice companies use several

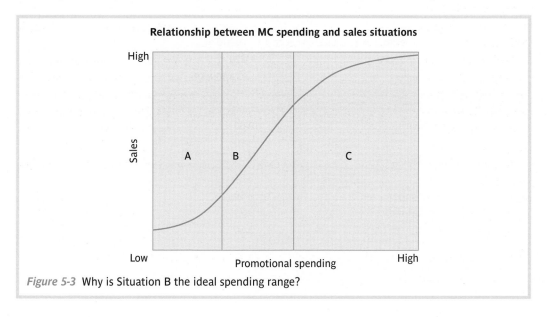

Figure 5-3 Why is Situation B the ideal spending range?

different budgeting methods to determine how much money to allocate to MC, essentially unrelated to the marginal analysis. Recognizing the difficulty of predicting sales results, most companies use a combination of four types of budgeting: percent-of-sales, return-on-investment, objective-and-task, and share-of-voice.

Percent-of-sales budgeting   This method is based on the sales forecast for the coming year and the costs of making and selling the product. This percentage is found in a brand's financial **pro forma**, which is *a breakdown of forecasted sales on a per unit basis*, as shown in Table 5-4 for a fictitious cartridges manufacturer.

To budget for MC, a marketer looks at all the costs involved in making and selling a product, as well as a desired (and realistic) profit. Each area (production, MC, distribution, and so on) estimates how much money it will need to do its job. These amounts are added up, and a total cost per unit is determined. The company then estimates (by looking at competition and examining its own competitive advantages) what it believes is a reasonable selling price per unit. It then subtracts all the costs from this selling price to determine whether enough profit is left to meet desired profit objectives. If there is not, then all the various areas must see where they can reduce costs. Also, the selling price may have to be adjusted as well as the desired profit objectives. Cross-functional management can be helpful in this process.

Variations of this approach exist. Instead of asking the departments what they think they need to achieve their goals, company's management may set a percentage of the sales price as a fixed parameter. Another variation is that instead of looking at expected sales, the total budget is determined as a percentage of last year's sales. Finally, the affordable method works much like illustrated in Table 5-4, with the important difference that the MC budget is not included in the calculations beforehand, but rather follows from subtracting all estimated costs from the expected revenues: what remains can be spent on MC. In other words the MC budget is determined by what the company can afford to spend on MC. What all variations have in common is that they are based on a breakdown of sales figures, leading to a percentage of the sales prices (or revenues at large) to be budgeted for MC.

In most companies, the percentage of sales spent on marketing communication is similar from year to year. Many companies that use this budgeting method also keep their MC and

Forecast number of cases that will be sold next year	1 000 000	
Sales price per case	€25	
Forecasted sales revenue	€25 000 000	

	Euro allocation per case	Percentage of sales
Cost of goods (materials)	10.00	40
Labour	2.50	10
Warehousing and distribution	1.25	5
Sales commission	2.50	10
Marketing communication	**2.50**	**10**
Administration and overhead	3.75	15
Profit before taxes	2.50	10
Total	25.00	100

Table 5-4 Pro forma for cartridge manufacturer

media allocations nearly the same from year to year. For example, if 50 per cent of the MC budget was spent on TV and magazine advertising last year, that is the percentage of the MC budget that will be allocated to TV and magazine advertising this year too. As you might imagine, merely repeating the previous year's spending mix, regardless of changes in the marketplace, is the easiest but not always the smartest way to budget. What is smart is to analyse what last year's budget was able to produce, and to determine which MC functions and media provided the greatest return. These findings, along with an analysis of what it will cost to accomplish specific objectives, should determine how much to spend on MC.

Another drawback to the percent-of-sales method is that it assumes that the creative strategy and execution, as well as the MC functions used, are the same from year to year. The reality is, if a company and its MC agencies are able to come up with a creative idea that is very attention getting, memorable, and persuasive, the company may actually be able to cut back on spending because the brand messages are working harder than normal. (Some would argue that when such a successful campaign is developed, spending should be increased in order to fully leverage its impact. This is an especially strong argument for a brand that has a relatively small share of market and thus a lot of opportunity for growth.)

A more fundamental drawback of percent-of-sales method is that it does not recognize the relationship between MC and a company's performance. Percent-of-sales typically results from seeing MC as a cost. With percent-of-sales the question is "what does MC cost us", instead of "what can MC give us". Further, percent-of-sales tends to be pro-cyclical: when a brand or product is doing badly, automatically the budget for MC is cut, whereas a rise in the budget may be required to recover sales. When indeed the MC budget is reduced, this will do the brand no good, leading to even lower sales which leads again to lower budgets, etc. Breaking this negative spiral is impossible when a company relies on percent-of-sales budgeting.

ROI budgeting   Return on investment (ROI) is *a ratio of income to spending*. Top management likes this method because it comes closest to telling to what extent the company will profit from the euros allocated. There's an old saying: "You have to spend money to make money." To be profitable, however, a company must make *more* money than it spends. If it spends 100 euros, it had better make back more than 100 euros. When it does, it has a positive ROI. One of top management's major responsibilities is to *maximize* the return on the monies the company spends.

Related to ROI budgeting is break-even analysis, which is *a formula for determining the point at which the cost of selling equals the revenue*. Suppose the cartridges company introduced in Table 5-4 has an opportunity to sponsor 10 major festivals in England which will cost 200 000 euros, in addition to its regular activities on which the calculations in Table 5-4 are based. Money for this sponsorship was not included in the budget, so the sponsorships must produce sales in addition to the 1 million cases already budgeted for. The question that marketing must answer is: how many additional cases must be sold to pay for this sponsorship?—that is, to make it worth doing. In other words: how many cases must be sold additionally to make the sponsorship break even.

The answer to this question is found by applying the break-even formula, which reads: promotion cost divided by the dollars per case available. We know that the promotion cost is 200 000 euros. But what are the "euros per case available" to pay for this? To find this, we go back to the company's pro forma (Table 5-4). At first glance, we might say the euros available are 2.50, which is the amount per case allocated to MC. But there is actually more money available. We can add to the MC 2.50 euros the monies allocated to "administration and overhead"

(3.75) and the "profit before taxes" (2.50), because "administration and overhead" is a fixed cost and the 2.50 per case for profit was to generate 2.5 million euro, which is all the company is expecting in profit. Fixed costs, such as electricity, heating, and employee salaries, are those that do not change with slight sales variations.

Euros available per *extra* case sold

Regular MC allocation	2.50
Administration and overhead	3.75
Profit before taxes	2.50
Total per extra case	8.75

We can now determine how many extra cases must be sold as a direct result of the festival sponsorship. We divide €200 000 by 8.75, which equals 22 857 cases, which is the minimum number of cases needed to be sold to break even on an investment of €200 000.

Once the company's marketing and sales force know how many extra cases have to be sold, a judgement call must be made. If they feel confident that the festivals will be able to generate that amount or, better still, *more* than that amount, then the sponsorship would be considered a good investment.

The ROI approach is a straightforward means of comparing alternative budgets. Effectively an ROI analysis asks what the ratio of return to spending is. The key of ROI is that it compares different plans on a common basis. This is definitely a key strength of ROI-type approaches. But there are also at least two important drawbacks to ROI analysis. The first is that the approach depends heavily on the ability to translate all outcomes in common terms (most often in euros or actual sales). As was discussed before, MC goals are not always stated in terms of sales figures. That is an important distinction between marketing objectives and MC objectives. A second drawback is that ROI analysis typically relies on ratios and loses sight of absolute numbers. Sometimes, however, the absolute numbers are important. For example, in an awareness campaign one plan may lead to a 2 per cent increase in awareness for 100 000 euros, while another campaign leads to a 10 per cent increase in awareness for 600 000 euros. According to ROI the first plan is better, but is it also better when looking at the absolute impact of the two alternatives?

Objective-and-task budgeting   This method starts with zero-based planning which determines the marketing communication objectives and the "tasks" that need to be done to accomplish each objective. An **objective-and-task budget** is *an estimate of the cost of each MC task identified by zero-based planning.* Suppose one objective is "To increase customer retention by 10 per cent", and it is decided that the most cost-effective way to do this is to send each customer a New Year's thank-you basket of fruit and candy. This cost can be easily estimated. If this or a similar programme has been used before, *and* if the company kept a record of these programmes and their results, the costs and results can be accurately predicted.

MC agencies often have useful information about the cost needed to achieve certain objectives, particularly if they used similar programmes for other clients and know the costs and results. (Of course, it must be borne in mind that agencies are eager to sell their programmes and thus will sometimes select the most positive results to share with clients.)

The limitation of objective-and-task budgeting is the difficulty of predicting accurately how much spending is needed to accomplish each objective. What worked last year may not work this year.

Share-of-voice budgeting   Share-of-voice spending is *a brand's portion of total media spending in that brand's product category.* The starting point in share-of-voice spending is that this share is compared to a brand's share of market. Thus, if total media spending in the small-battery category is 400 million euros a year, and Duracell is spending 100 million, then Duracell's share-of-voice spending is 25 per cent. If Duracell's share of market is 35 per cent, the brand is underspending. If Duracell's market share is less than 25 per cent, the brand is overspending.

Although this approach to budgeting is almost too simple to be true, thinking in terms of share-of-voice can be very useful. For example, in situations of overspending, the brand should consider the effectiveness of the MC instruments it employs. After all, other brands are more effective in their MC expenditures, at least when it comes to market shares. Or: when a brand wants to grow it can consider whether increasing its share-of-voice spending is the way to achieve this.

Like other methods, share-of-voice spending has its shortcomings. Like percent-of-sales budgeting, it fails to take into consideration the quality of the creative messages. Share-of-voice spending also fails to allow for reactions to changes in the marketplace other than competitors' increases or decreases in their MC spending. For example, if a major competitor gets into profit trouble and greatly reduces its MC spending, share-of-voice budgeting would have all the other brands also reducing their spending levels, when in fact this may be the best time to increase spending and take advantage of a major competitor's weakness.

MC budget allocations

Once the marketing department is told by top management how much the marketing budget will be, marketing must decide how this money will be spent. The first allocation decision is by target market. How will money be divided between efforts to acquire targeted customers and efforts to retain current customers and win a larger share of their category spending? This decision is based on return on spending—in other words, the sales revenue that will result from spending 100 euros to get new customers versus the amount that will result from spending the same amount to retain current customers.

The second allocation is based on geography. Because most companies have different levels of distribution and different shares of market from city to city, the amount of advertising and promotion effort often differs from market to market. Here is an example of a strategy that can be used for geographical budget allocations.

Suppose a brand operates in three geographically distinct markets, one mature, one introductory, and one in its growth stage. As a result of discussions with the company's MC agency it was decided to use the mature market allocation as a benchmark. Introductory markets would be allocated only 50 per cent of what the mature markets were allocated, and growth markets would be allocated 150 per cent. Now, when the total budget is 600 000 euros the result of this approach would be that the mature market would be given a budget of 200 000, the growth market 300 000, and the introductory market 100 000 euros. Note that the point of this last example is not the sophistication of the method, but that it shows how thinking in terms of separate markets may work out.

Step 6: Evaluating effectiveness

Sometimes marketing communication is great: you remember the ad and the brand, the promotion draws people into the store, and the store display motivates people to try the product. At other times marketing communication does not work: the ad is forgettable or the point is unclear, no one remembers the promotion, and the direct-mail piece gets thrown away without being opened. Rance Crain, editor in chief of *Advertising Age*, wonders why it comes as a shock to companies when their advertising doesn't work. After mentioning a couple of examples of ads and promotional pieces that failed to work, he observed that "Companies don't realize the implications of their ads because the managers all think the same." He concludes that "They need to spend more time with ordinary people."[6] In other words, marketing and agency people need to do a better job of research on the effectiveness of their creative ideas as they are developing them.

Market testing

Because the marketplace changes constantly, the only way to know whether something will work is to try it. Good annual plans have some type of testing built in. Procter & Gamble, for example, is always testing new advertising approaches. For most of its major brands, it has three different creative campaigns in the works. One is the main campaign. The second is a campaign that has beaten the main campaign in a laboratory test and is now running in a few test markets to determine whether it does, in fact, produce better results than the main campaign in the "real world". The third campaign is the one being developed to beat the campaign that is in test market.

Another important planning element marketers should test constantly is the level of media spending. How much media spending is too much? How much is too little? Many brands select two or three markets and increase media spending (and other marketing communication support) to see whether sales increase enough to pay for the extra spending and earn the company extra profits. At the same time, companies are always trying to determine the minimal level of spending necessary to maintain their brand's market share.

When a company is considering major changes in marketing communication strategies—such as repositioning, changing the brand name, changing an advertising theme that has been successful for several years—a market test can help determine whether these major changes can be cost-justified.

The downside of test marketing is that it is time-consuming and costly. A test market requires customizing the changes to be tested and then isolating and monitoring these markets to ensure the test is conducted without bias. Most market tests must last at least six months before results are valid. Finally, by the time a test market is conducted, the results analysed and changes suggested by the findings are incorporated into the whole marketing process, from one to two years have gone by. Because the marketplace is constantly changing, the findings and implied changes may no longer be as relevant as they would have been two years before. Chapter 18 goes into greater depth about the various test methods that companies and agencies use to help prevent costly mistakes as well as provide ideas for improving MC efforts.

Campaign effectiveness

The effectiveness of a campaign is evaluated according to how well the effort meets its objectives. This is why a company should define its objectives clearly in measurable terms and specify a time frame within which each objective is to be achieved.

Companies can obtain information regarding the effectiveness of their MC campaigns from corporate and industry reports, as well as by conducting primary research. Evaluation of MC spending must also include measures of relationship strengths in addition to the usual sales, share, and awareness measures. Sales and share are historical measures, but relationship strengths are predictors of future sales. Chapter 18 discusses evaluation in detail and presents some methods for evaluating the effectiveness of marketing communication in brand-relationship building.

The role of feedback

One aspect of IMC that is different from traditional marketing communication is the emphasis on continuous feedback. Current, shared information is critical for decision making by the cross-functional teams. That means companies must have ways of listening to customers wherever contacts with customers occur—particularly contacts with front-line employees. The overnight delivery company Federal Express, for example, tracks performance measures that are distributed daily. In addition, it tracks monthly indicators for all areas, including public relations, and conducts an online employee survey every three months. Managers use the results for discussions with employees and act on the survey information immediately wherever change is needed. Senior managers are required to spend a few days every year in a given sales district to get close to both customers and the front line of the sales and marketing efforts.[7] Continuous feedback programmes help the company become a *learning organization*. The IMC in Action box gives another illustration of the role employees have in designing MC plans.

Using employee input in MC planning

For its SoftBench Suite, a Unix application program sold to businesses, Hewlett-Packard (HP) developed a marketing communication programme based on defining customers' needs. The division began its planning with a product-positioning workshop that defined customers' dilemmas with Unix and identified HP resources that could be used to address these dilemmas.

One result of this customer-focused approach was that planners determined that each HP department—sales, product marketing, engineering, customer support—understood a different aspect of customers' needs. According to an HP marketing manager, "By integrating all perspectives, we were able to think constructively about how our product addressed those dilemmas. Out of all this, we developed a creative strategy focused on customer need."

The creative strategy used the theme "We understand" to emphasize HP's understanding of the issues, pressures, and constraints that software developers and software development managers faced, such as unrealistic deadlines, hidden code errors, simultaneous development of multiple application versions, and transition problems in moving to object-oriented programming. This theme was launched in a print advertising campaign, reinforced in three direct-mail pieces and a trade-show handout, showcased on the company's website, and then later picked up in another division's direct-marketing campaign promoting a product bundled with SoftBench.

As HP managers discovered, true integration goes beyond co-ordinating graphic designs and key messages. Entire divisions or companies need to adopt an integrated attitude to implement an effective marketing communication programme. HP used that approach so that customers would be greeted at all levels with the idea that HP understood their dilemmas. For example, in speaking to customers, all HP employees—from customer-service representatives to sales associates to product marketing engineers—focused on the same thing: understanding and solving the customer's problem.

IMC in Action

Integration as a process makes everyone in the company a salesperson. Integration as an attitude allows employees to offer solutions, not just programmed responses, to customers.

Think about it

Why is it important to use a customer focus in planning an IMC programme? How was this done in HP's SoftBench Suite campaign planning? In what way were cross-functional teams needed to plan, implement, and monitor the "We understand" campaign?

Source:
Adapted from Lindell, P. Griffith, "Lining Up Your Marketing Ducks: Integrated Marketing Communications", Marketing Computers, October 1996, p. 27.

A final note: playing from the same score

An IMC campaign plan defines the way a company does business by creating a customer focus rather than department-focused programmes that can work at cross-purposes and send mixed messages. The more focused a company is on transactions rather than on building long-term relationships, the weaker its relationships with customers will be. In order to create this customer focus throughout the company, it is necessary that everyone plays from the same score: an integration-driven marketing communication plan. This plan also demands internal marketing (see Chapter 1) in order to deliver messages with consistency from everyone who has contact with a customer. The less inconsistent the messages are at these brand–customer touch points, the clearer the brand positioning will be in the minds of customers and other stakeholders.

Integration planning and execution are not easy to accomplish. As more stakeholders are taken into consideration, as more functional areas are used, as different media are used, planning and executing in a consistent manner become very complex. The biggest barriers to integration, however, are egos and turf battles.[8] Because the pay of most managers and executives is proportional to the size of their staff and budgets, it is only natural for them to want the largest staff and budgets that they can get. Consequently, the decision to reallocate MC and media monies to where they can do the most good is often hampered by executives who stand to lose out personally. To overcome this barrier, companies and agencies are beginning to design compensation and reward systems in such a way that people are not penalized when their budgets are temporarily reduced. Although integrated planning isn't easy, it is essential for companies that want to compete in the twenty-first century.

🔒 Key terms

advertising property An element in advertising that is uniquely related and attributed to one brand.

baseline A quantifiable measure of the current situation.

benchmark *see* baseline.

break-even analysis A formula for determining the point at which the cost of selling equals the revenue.

budget A fixed amount of money for a fixed period of time.

campaign A set of MC messages with a common theme that runs for a specified period of time to achieve certain MC objectives.

marketing communication mix The selection of MC functions used at a given time as part of a marketing programme.

media mix A selection of media channels used to deliver brand messages.

objectives What marketers want to accomplish with marketing communication.

objective-and-task budget An estimate of the cost of each MC task identified by zero-based planning.

pro forma A breakdown of forecasted sales on a per unit basis.

return on investment (ROI) A ratio of income to spending.

segmenting Grouping customers or prospects according to common characteristics, needs, wants, or desires.

share-of-voice spending A brand's portion of total media spending in that brand's product category.

strategies Ideas about how to accomplish objectives.

SWOT analysis A structured evaluation of internal strengths and weaknesses and external opportunities and threats that can help or hurt a brand.

tactics Specific actions to be taken to execute a strategy.

targeting Analysing, evaluating, and prioritizing the market segments deemed most profitable to pursue.

zero-based planning Determining objectives and strategies based on current brand and marketplace conditions, which are considered the zero point.

Check the key points

Key point 1: IMC zero-based planning

a   What is zero-based planning? What assumption does it challenge?

b   How do strategies, objectives, and tactics differ?

c   What are objectives and strategies? What does it mean to make integration an attitude?

d   How does the IMC planning process relate to company and marketing planning?

Key point 2: The IMC planning process

a   Clarify the logic of doing a SWOT analysis after having decided on the targets.

b   What internal and external factors are involved in a SWOT analysis?

c   What rules should guide the translation of the SWOT analysis results into objectives?

d   Explain the four different ways to develop a marketing communication budget.

e   How do marketers know whether an IMC campaign is effective?

Chapter Challenge

Writing assignment

Using the six planning steps, create a model that visualizes these steps, showing what other things influence each step. Apply your model to your favourite clothing brand. From information that you find out about the brand from research and from your own personal experience and knowledge of the brand, explain how the brand's marketing communication programme works. Write up your analysis, and use your model to explain your analysis.

Presentation assignment

Research Apple, in particular after it has introduced the i-Pod. What has happened with the brand? What objectives and strategies would you recommend to Apple's current manager to build on the brand's history and the i-Pod's introduction? Using the six-step IMC planning process, develop a marketing communication plan for Apple for next year. Present your plan to the class.

Internet assignment

Consult Nivea's website and check out the historical commercials (www.nivea.com). To demonstrate that the basics have remained the same over decades, find a commercial in the collection that demonstrates any of the following: (1) leveraging an opportunity, (2) addressing a threat, (3) leveraging a strength, or (4) addressing a weakness.

Notes

[1] Tom Duncan and Sandra Moriarty, *Driving Brand Value: Using Integrated Marketing to Manage Profitable Stakeholder Relationships* (New York: McGraw-Hill, 1997), pp. 148–68.

[2] David Soberman, "The complexity of media planning today", *Journal of Brand Management* (2005), pp. 420–30.

[3] For example: David Jobber, *Principles and Practices of Marketing*, 4th ed. (Harlow: McGraw-Hill, 2004); Philip Kotler and Kevin Lane Keller, *Marketing Management*, 12th edn, (New York: Prentice Hall, 2005).

[4] Allan J. Magrath, *How to Achieve Zero-Defect Marketing* (New York: American Management Association, 1993), p. 14.

[5] This figure is based on the path-breaking analysis by Robert Lavidge and Gary Steiner, "A Model for Predictive Measurements of Advertising Effectiveness", *Journal of Marketing*, 1961, pp. 59–62.

[6] Rance Crain, "No Mystery If the Ad Flops: 'Reality Check' Was Missing", *Advertising Age*, 7 April 2003, p. 18.

[7] Anders Gronstedt, "Integrated Communications at America's Leading TQM Corporations" (PhD diss., University of Wisconsin–Madison, 1994).

[8] Tom Duncan and Steve Everett, "Client Perceptions of Integrated Marketing Communications", *Journal of Advertising Research*, 33 (1993), pp. 30–39; Clarke Caywood, Don Schultz, and Paul Wang, *A Survey of Consumer Goods Manufacturers* (New York: American Association of Advertising Agencies, 1993).

Further reading

Hansen, Flemming and Lars Bech Christensen (2005) "Share of voice/share of market and long-term advertising effects", *International Journal of Advertising*, Vol. 24–3, pp. 297–320.

Moorcroft, David (2006) "Linking communication strategy with organizational goals", *Strategic Communication Management*, Vol. 7–6, pp. 24–7.

Murthy, Pushkar and Murali Mantrala (2005) "Allocating a Promotion Budget between Advertising and Sales Contest Prizes: An Integrated Marketing Communications Perspective", *Marketing Letters* Vol. 16–1, pp. 19–35.

Vakratsas, Demetrios and Zhenfeng Ma (2005) "A Look at the Long-run Effectiveness of Multimedia Advertising and Its Implications for Budget Allocation Decisions", *Journal of Advertising Research*, Vol. 45–2, pp. 241–54.

Yoo, Boonghee and Rujirutana Mandhachitara (2003) "Estimating Advertising Effects on Sales in a Competitive Setting", *Journal of Advertising Research*, Vol. 43–3, pp. 310–21.

PART 3

Part contents

Creative message strategies

LEARNING OBJECTIVES

After reading this chapter, you should:

- ☑ Understand how message strategies are created.
- ☑ Understand that knowing your market is essential for fuelling a creative process.
- ☑ Know the different types of selling strategies available.
- ☑ Understand when a creative idea is a "big idea".
- ☑ See that a big idea is not a one-time achievement but is a communication asset.
- ☑ Conclude that creativity is hard work.

CHAPTER PERSPECTIVE
The creative "ROI"

ROI—return on investment? Not for marketing communication specialists. To them ROI refers to relevance, originality and impact.[1] And for good reason. Today, more than ever, if marketing communication is not *relevant*, it has no purpose. If it is not *original*, it will attract no attention. If it does not strike with *impact*, it will make no lasting impression. In developing message strategies, the initials *ROI* (for relevant, original, impact) can be equated with the financial investment made by clients in marketing communication. To be effective, the message strategies must also deliver bottom-line ROI (return on investment). Altogether, relevance, originality and impact lead to return on investment.

Relevant messages that speak to the head and the heart connect with the target audience on a personal level. The message strategies that really ignite consumer responses, however, contain the big O—the *originality* dimension in IMC's ROI formula. The originality factor first springs to life in the "big idea". How this creative concept is developed and executed determines to a great extent how effective the ultimate brand messages stemming from the message strategies will be in having an impact. Advertising awards are nice, but the real victory is making a lasting contribution to the culture. In other words, recognition of originality is appreciated, but the real reward is when the impact is huge. So huge that brand names become iconic, appear in crossword puzzles, feature on greeting cards, or are used by stand-up comedians. That is the ultimate return on the investment in relevance, originality and impact.

MasterCard's "priceless" campaign is priceless

"I wish I had done that one." That's the typical response to a great creative idea. That's also how MC professionals look at the MasterCard "Priceless" campaign, which has been running since 1997 and has won innumerable awards, as well as moved the brand into a more competitive position against market leaders Visa and American Express.

The first "Priceless" ad told the story of a father who took his son to a baseball game for the first time. The format is one that everyone has come to know, starting with items that you can put a price on and ending with some intangible that can't be measured in euros. For example, a more recent commercial shows an attractive young woman preparing for her birthday. "New dress: 160 euros; new make-up, 35 euros; relaxing bath oil: 15 euros." The story then continues in a disco where we see the woman dancing passionately with her friends. "The look in the eyes of your ex boy friend: Priceless".

Background

MasterCard International is a portfolio of credit card companies including Cirrus and Maestro, along with MasterCard. It serves consumers and businesses in 210 countries and territories. With 30 million acceptance locations, 25 000 business partners, and 820 000 ATM locations around the world, MasterCard is the most widely accepted global payment card in the world.

The campaign challenge began when the McCann-Erickson agency was given the charge to turn around the floundering MasterCard brand, which had come to be perceived as an everyday, ordinary credit card—the *other* card you keep in your wallet behind Visa and American Express. The award-winning "Priceless" advertising campaign that resulted can be seen in 45 languages in 96 countries.

The breadth of the campaign

A variety of involving experiences such as sponsorships, sweepstakes, and other consumer and channel marketing programmes were set up to support the campaign. For example, MasterCard has been a long-time supporter of international soccer and is the key sponsor of the sport's five most prestigious events, including the FIFA World Cup. As a sponsor, it gains exclusivity as the official payment system for these events. It also has the right to use the official marks and logos on its advertising, promotions, and merchandising and receives guaranteed on-field perimeter signage.

MasterCard also sponsors soccer great Pelé, who has made more than 150 appearances worldwide on behalf of the company. In a related co-branding effort, more than 2 million World Cup-themed affinity cards have been issued bearing his likeness. (An affinity card carries the image of a particular organization or individual with which people want to identify, such as a university or the World Cup competition.) MasterCard and its sponsoring financial institutions have used Pelé's photo on over 20 million cardholder inserts, mailings, and collateral promotional materials.

To promote its international image, MasterCard used its "Priceless" advertising in the award-winning "Swap" commercial, which featured the tradition of opposing soccer players "swapping" their jerseys following a match as a sign of mutual respect. The commercial was shot in three countries—Prague, Czech Republic; Cape Town, South Africa; and Tokyo, Japan—using a total of 10 locations with 26 actors and more than 200 local extras. More than 30 different "swaps" were filmed with actors representing different nationalities so each region had the option of using a version that best represented its market.

Debra Coughlin, senior VP of Global Brand Building, explained that "[t]he message of true sportsmanship in relation to the FIFA World Cup rings true to our brand position and has broader meaning in relation to the current events of the world." The commercial was shown in more than 50 countries, which leads Coughlin to observe, "We believe the core message communicated in 'Swap' resonates with consumers around the world—regardless of country or nationality." To ensure that the message would work for a global audience, Coughlin's global brand building team worked closely with each local country "to ensure the important nuances of the respective cultures and countries were respected, captured, and communicated".

Alliances like the ones with the FIFA World Cup also benefit the financial institutions, merchants, and other business partners affiliated with MasterCard. In explaining the Universal partnership, Larry Flanagan, MasterCard International's chief marketing officer, explained that the alliance illustrates "MasterCard's ongoing commitment to creating business-building opportunities for our members and merchant partners by aligning the brand with the world's premier properties".

Special promotions also support the "Priceless" theme. When the priceless theme led into a romantic weekend, spending "24 hours in your hotel room", a special promotion was run with a romantic weekend trip in Paris, Marrakech and other places for the prize winners. Another special promotion, the "Priceless Music Promotion" sweepstakes, was launched in January 2006. MasterCard customers are automatically entered for a chance to win a visit to a music concert in the UK, as well as a concert somewhere abroad when they use their MasterCards. For February 2006, for example, the prize was a visit to a Rolling Stones concert in Florida, USA, and a "British legend" concert in Manchester.

Promotions have been equally effective in MasterCard's international marketing. A Puerto Rico promotion won a gold at the 2002 Cannes Film Festival for the way the campaign was integrated into a broadcast of *Titanic*. On-screen captions referred to film elements as "Jack's tuxedo: $900" and "Rose's evening gown: $1500." The last line was: "A reserved space on the lifeboat . . . priceless." In a Malaysian creativity contest, a 23-year-old man won a new Lotus Elise car when his entry on loyalty beat 70 000 other entries. His design featured the word "Priceless" in India ink and Chinese calligraphy with a red hand-drawn signature stamp resembling the MasterCard logo.

Many other examples of how the "Priceless" campaign has been extended can be found on MasterCard's website, www.MasterCard.com. The astonishing variety in the use of the priceless theme is impressive. It shows among others that a really great idea has both wide (in range of applications) and long (in time) extendibility. Finally, on the Internet numerous clips can be found, parodying the campaign in various ways.

Effectiveness of the "priceless" campaign

The success of the "Priceless" campaign has helped MasterCard improve its competitive position. The card has gained market share for five years running. MasterCard's chief marketing officer credits the campaign with helping narrow the gap between MasterCard and Visa. "Five years ago, we had a weak brand . . . We now have a strong brand." A *Brandweek* commentator observed that the campaign has "galvanized the brand, providing energy and vitality within the credit-card association and its constituencies of member banks, merchants, and consumers".

The campaign works because of its soft-spoken creative message, which invokes the basic needs of life and puts MasterCard at the heart of the emotional response to the things that give our lives meaning. It works because of its insight into basic human values, which brings a wandering brand back to consumer relevance. The judges at the Effie Awards said the campaign helped "define a new aspiration that was in tune with emerging consumer values".

Sources:

Business editors, "MasterCard Launches Debit MasterCard 'Priceless Night on the Town' Sweepstakes", Business Wire, 4 March 2003, www.businesswire.com/cgi-bin/cb_headline.cgi?&story_file=. . .

"MasterCard International and Universal Announce Multi-Year Marketing Alliance", 13 February 2002, and "MasterCard Launches Global 'Swap' Advertising Execution in Support of 2002 FIFAWorld Cup Sponsorship", 13 May 2002, MasterCard International News Release, www.MasterCardintl.com/cgibin/newsroom. cgi?id=681

Business editors, "MasterCard Announces Extension of Unprecedented Commitment to Soccer's Five Most Prestigious Events", 12 March 2003, Business Wire, www.businesswire.com/cgi-bin/cb_headline.gi?&story_ file=. . .

Vanessa O'Connell, "MasterCard 'Priceless' Ads Grow Old", Wall Street Journal, 30 September 2002, p. B8.

How to develop a creative message strategy

Anyone can put together an ad, publicity release, sales-promotion offer, event, or any other type of MC message. The challenge is to make these messages creative enough to be noticed, read (or listened to), and acted upon. To do this requires a message strategy, which is one of the primary areas of expertise offered by MC agencies. There are two main steps in producing successful MC messages. The first is developing a creative message strategy, and the second is executing that strategy in the form of ads, publicity releases, sales-promotion offers, events, and all the other MC forms.

This chapter focuses on developing marketing communication strategic ideas—in particular, "creative briefs" that drive the creation of the big ideas that in turn motivate responses. Chapters 6 and 7 go together. This chapter explains why message strategy is important. It focuses on the ideas behind creative messages—*what* to say and why. The next chapter focuses on *how* to say it—the execution of creative message strategies.

A **message strategy** is *an idea about how to creatively and persuasively communicate a brand message to a target audience.* Generally, such strategies blend rational and emotional thinking and integrate them in a creative way. The message strategy for Michelin tyres is to associate the brand with protecting babies. All parents can strongly relate to the responsibility of protecting their children. Consequently, showing that Michelin is good enough to protect parents' most precious possessions—their children—makes this message strategy successful.

A successful message strategy also makes the brand relevant to customers. The long-running campaign for the Dutch insurance company Centraal Beheer played this theme brilliantly. All commercials in this multiple awarded-winning campaign showed ordinary people in suddenly disastrous, sometimes even life-threatening, situations. The slogan said: "Just call Apeldoorn", suggesting that one simple phone call to the insurer's headquarters located in the city of Apeldoorn would solve all problems. The brilliant aspect of this campaign was that the situations in which the characters found themselves were very realistic: watchers of the commercials could easily identify with them. At the same time the disasters that overcame the characters were sheer and clear exaggerations, hilarious in every part. A non-threatening disaster happening to everyday men and women—isn't that a relevant situation in which customers would find an insurance company most useful?

The appeal of a message establishes an emotional or rational link (or both) between the customer and the brand. An **appeal** is *an idea that motivates an audience to respond.* Aspiration, comfort, convenience, economy, efficiency, reduction of fear, love, nostalgia, pride, health, luxury, patriotism, sex, and safety are ideas that engage the minds and touch the hearts of the target audience, and ultimately motivate a response.

In their ongoing competitive war, Coke and Pepsi have searched for strategic ideas that would differentiate the brands in a way that customers would find relevant. Both have had winning ideas, such as "The Real Thing" for Coke and "The Pepsi Generation" for Pepsi, but both continue to search for new appeals to reach new consumers. Recently Coke has tried to portray itself as natural and relevant, using the "Coca-Cola . . . Real" slogan. In one commercial, movie star Penelope Cruz is shown drinking a bottle of Coke in front of a diner packed with men and then accidentally belching. A Coke spokesman said the commercial brings the "natural" strategy to life because it "reflects genuine, authentic moments in life".[2]

The MC industry is constantly searching for creative ideas that are attention-getting and relevant. While major global corporations like Coca-Cola and Pepsi spend millions of dollars annually fighting it out in the "cola wars", smaller companies too must make their marketing messages compelling. Why is creative message strategy so important? Brands need to break through the clutter of commercial messages. Ask yourself why you remember so few ads—and what makes those rare ones that you do remember stand out. The answer: "They were the ones that broke new ground. They told a relevant brand truth in a fresh and original way."[3]

The IMC message strategy brief

When MC agencies create brand messages—whether ads, publicity releases, packaging, or sales-promotion offers—the development of these messages is guided by a document known variously as the creative brief, creative platform, creative plan or work-plan, creative strategy, or copy strategy. This book uses message strategy brief to refer to this document, which consists of *statements about a brand that summarize the research and insights for the creative team.* This helps team members identify the direction and focus for their creative and media ideas.

Over the years many advertising agencies have customized the elements that make up their message strategy briefs. Table 6-1 lists the elements in the message strategy briefs of four major agencies. Although each list contains slightly different elements, there are many similarities. The terms used in these lists, if unfamiliar to you now, will make sense as you go through this chapter.

One technique used to summarize a message strategy in a single sentence is to complete the following statement: The purpose of this MC message is to convince [target audience] _____ that [brand] _____ will [benefit] _____ because [proof]_____. The tone of the message should be [description of message personality] _____.

Ogilvy & Mather	Leo Burnett	DDB Worldwide	Young & Rubicam
1 Product	Target	Marketing objective	Key Fact
2 Key issue/problem	Desired belief	Competitive advantage	Consumer problem
3 The promise	Reasons why	Advertising objective	Advertising objective
4 The support	Tone	Action by target	Creative strategy
5 Competition		Key insight	1 Prospect definition
6 Target		Reward/support	a Product use
a Demographics		Brand personality/tone	b Demographics
b Psychographics		Position	c Psychographics
7 Desired behaviour		Media	2 Competition
8 Target's net impression			3 Consumer benefit
9 Tone & manner			4 Reason why

Table 6-1 Elements of four agencies' message strategy briefs

The strategy for the MasterCard "Priceless" campaign could be expressed as follows:

> The purpose of the MasterCard "Priceless" campaign is to connect emotionally with customers and convince them that they will benefit by using their MasterCards because it lets them enjoy things—most of them intangibles—that you can't put a price on, such as family time. The tone of the message is thoughtful and nostalgic.

As is the case with many management issues, and in particular the creative ones, it is unrealistic to expect that there is one best solution that works for all brands and under all conditions. For example, Citigate Cunningham applied the brief shown in Figure 6-1 to the analysis of software company Freshwater Software. The analysis determined Freshwater's key value propositions, which were found to lie in three areas: "e-business growth" (the Freshwater system is a key to its clients' growth in e-business); "rapid, global scalability" (easy-to-add global customers); and "brand integrity" (the Freshwater system is recognized as trustworthy). Under each of those three propositions are a key message (what the proposition means and what it is all about), proof for the proposition, and a soundbite that restates the proposition in customer-focused language.

Although message strategies should be the foundation of *all* MC messages, the reality is that advertising agencies make greater use of this aspect of brand communications than do other MC agencies.

In genuine IMC, message strategies are broad enough to be executed by *each* of the major MC areas. Coming up with a clever headline that works only in advertising is generally not a good strategy. Michelin's message strategy, previously mentioned, is considered broad because it can be applied to other MC areas such as publicity (with stories about child safety and automobiles), sales promotion (by offering child- and auto-related premiums like car seats), and direct response (in e-mails and regular mail offers that show babies and Michelin tyres).

The three basic steps in developing a message strategy brief are shown in Figure 6-2: (1) determining the MC communication objectives, (2) finding customer insights, and (3) selecting a selling strategy. But the creative planning is not over once the marketing manager has developed a message strategy brief. Sometimes finding a creative way to *present* the strategy for approval—either to agency managers or to clients—is as important as the creative message strategy itself.

Positioning statement	Mercury Interactive is the leading provider of comprehensive Internet growth solutions for e-business		
Value propositions	e-Business growth	Rapid global scalability	Brand integrity
Key messages	Our services, technologies and expertise are critical enablers of e-business growth	We help companies scale their Internet business quickly and globally	We create trust in our customers' Internet brands
Sample proof point	2500 growing businesses outsource website monitoring to Freshwater	Freshwater measures website availability from 11 global networks	Freshwater helps meet unique e-business brand requirements, including 24-hour availability
Sample sound bite	*"We have time and resources to build other areas of our business when Freshwater monitors our Web environment."*	*"As we add customers around the world, Freshwater makes sure they can reliably complete transactions on our website."*	*"Freshwater makes sure my website is available 24 hours a day, seven days a week, so it can support my overall business brand."*

Figure 6-1 Citigate Cunningham's "Positioning Platform" identifies the message strategy for Mercury Interactive. To what extent is this comparable to the outlined briefs in Table 6-1?

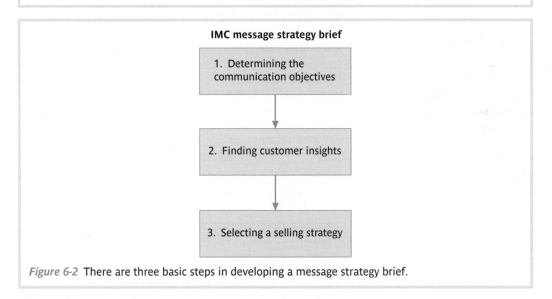

Figure 6-2 There are three basic steps in developing a message strategy brief.

Step 1: Determining communication objectives: what type of impact does the message need to achieve?

The impact of every message strategy must be measured against the message objectives. Therefore, stating appropriate message objectives is an important factor in determining the desired impact. For that reason, marketers often base message objectives on a hierarchy-of-effects model. Recall from Chapter 4 that the AIDA model identifies four consumer decision points (attention, interest, desire, and action) where a message can have an impact. A communication objective can state any of those decision points.

Chapter 4 also discussed consumer decision-making in terms of three paths to a consumer response: cognitive, affective, and behaviour or action—the think/feel/do model. These paths also can be used to craft message objectives for the various functional areas. The list that follows shows typical MC objectives that relate to the three steps on these paths to a consumer response. Responses at each individual step may be the objective—the order in which these steps are taken, i.e. the path that is applicable for the product advertised, does not really matter. Applying sales promotion to induce trial may be equally relevant in a case where the consumer follows a cognitive path, as when the consumer is following the "repeat path". On the other hand, marketers must realize that in the case of the cognitive path, behavioural objectives are conditional on the previous steps. Objectives in a case of repeat buying can be set independently from the cognitive and affective stages, whereas in the cognitive path the degree to which a sales promotion can lead to actual behaviour depends on the extent to which prospective consumers are successfully led through the previous stages. The examples given here are *types* of MC objectives, hence they are not stated in measurable terms; this can be done only when objectives are applied to a specific brand situation. Notice also that these objectives are phrased in terms of consumer response or the effect of the messages on the target audience.

***Sample marketing communication objectives*[4]**
Cognitive responses: Create awareness of brand or of opportunity to use or buy it; educate about brand use, explain how it can solve a consumer problem; create or increase brand knowledge and understanding.

Affective responses: Create or change a brand image or personality; create or change attitudes and brand liking; ignite a desire or need; create or strengthen an association; strike an emotional chord. (This was the focus of the MasterCard "Priceless" campaign.)

Behavioural responses: Increase trial; increase purchase and repeat purchasing; inspire customers to tell others about brand; inspire visiting a showroom, visiting a website, returning a card, or inquiring about the brand.

Remember, we are talking about communication and persuasion objectives, not marketing objectives (sales, share of market, and so forth). Communication objectives focus on the impact that can be delivered through a message that creates shared meaning. Persuasion goes a step further and stimulates impact that leads to attitude formation and change, as well as behaviour.

For example, a communication objective is to increase the awareness of a brand, or have people think a brand is fun to have. When research shows that consumers have become more aware of the brand, or that an increased percentage of the target market now believes that the brand is fun to have, the communication objectives have been reached. It does not say, however, that as a consequence the sales of the brand have grown, which would be a marketing objective. Of course, in the end it is hoped that sales will increase, but then we are talking about a marketing objective, to which the communication (objective) has hopefully contributed.

Step 2: Customer insight: finding diamonds in the data

Once message objectives have been determined, agencies must closely analyse the target audiences. What do they want to hear? What do they care about? How can this brand speak to their wants, needs, and desires? The purpose of this analysis is to find customer insights that enable the choice of a strategy that will relate and resonate with those targeted.

Customer insight describes the *below-the-surface attitudes and beliefs that influence customers' behaviour*. Ogilvy and Mather's Emma Cookson, strategic planning director, describes the search for customer insight as a process of discovering creative gems hidden in the research, or "diamonds in the data".[5] An example is the slogan of L'Oréal, "Because I'm worth it". The slogan is based on the insight that an important driver for women to buy beauty and care products is not because they want to be appealing and attractive to other people, but simple because they are worth it. In this way the slogan refers to the highest level of Maslow's hierarchy of needs, self-actualization, which has proven to be a powerful approach to position L'Oréal. The fact that the slogan is carried by celebrities paradoxically reinforces the message. Also, these good-looking celebrities do not use the brand because it helps them remain attractive, but simply because they are worth it in the first place.

> " . . . we believe in the effectiveness of great creative ideas.
> *Tony Granger, Creative Director, Bozell* "

Back in the 1950s Leo Burnett came up with the idea of associating Marlboro cigarettes with rugged, masculine cowboys working in the wide-open spaces of the American West. The reason for this association, however, was not that cowboys were the primary target. Leo Burnett had the insight that young and middle-aged men fantasize about the freedom and macho independence enjoyed by cowboys. By offering a cigarette that symbolized this romantic idea, cigarette-maker Philip Morris allowed men to escape into this fantasy each time they lit up. Leo Burnett's simple insight made Marlboro one of the top brands in the world.

Finding customer insights for a brand is the responsibility of the account planner, who is considered to be the "voice of the customer". **Account planning** means *using research and brand insights to bring a strong consumer focus to the planning of marketing communication*. An account planner is a researcher and a strategic thinker whose mission is to see the brand through the customer's eyes and to write up those insights for the message strategy brief. The insights uncovered by account planners can reflect or expand on the customer analysis obtained through a SWOT analysis (Chapter 5) (see colour insert B5).

The objective of a message strategy is to connect with the customer in a meaningful way. The challenge is to identify the harbour in the customer's heart or mind where the brand can throw out an anchor. The MasterCard "Priceless" campaign, for example, is anchored by the idea that there is value in the little things in life that we buy, but we cannot put a price on the intangibles—relationships, experiences, emotions—that these things represent.

A good account planner uses observational research and in-depth probing to see how and why customers think and behave as they do. Some account planners get exceptional ideas by listening to their family and neighbours, as well as strangers and heroes. Some argue that good ads and other MC messages are about relationships and real life. When a message is exceptional, it talks to people in ways they find engaging. Target audiences should laugh or feel good when they are exposed to MC messages, not think "what are they trying to sell to me?"[6]

Unfortunately, most definitions of account planning say little or nothing about creating and managing either a dialogue or an ongoing relationship with customers. This will change, however, as more agencies and companies adopt IMC, for the two concepts—IMC and account planning—complement each other.

Account planning insights can be tremendously useful in planning relationship-focused message strategies.

Step 3: Selecting a selling strategy

Over the years, agencies and their clients have developed a variety of selling strategies that are basically strategic templates. One of the most widely used focuses on a brand's main **benefit**, *how a product satisfies customers' needs, wants, and desires.* Most brands offer several benefits, but the one that should be used is the one that is the basis of the brand's positioning strategy (Chapter 2). Inherent in a good position is a promised benefit. A brand's position is how it differs, in a positive and beneficial way, from competing brands.

A benefit-selling strategy can appeal to the head or heart, either of which can experience a benefit from buying and using the brand. People buy cars for both rational and emotional reasons. They like a car's attributes (fuel economy, price, handling, and so forth), but they also may like its looks and the way the car's image reflects their own self-image.

Consider again the MasterCard "Priceless" campaign. It focuses on a benefit, an emotional benefit. To analyse the benefit strategy of that campaign, complete the following sentence: If I use [product]_____, I will [benefit]_____. Your wording will probably read something like: "If I use my MasterCard, I will have a memorable experience."

Sometimes the benefit is referred to as a **promise**, *a statement describing what good things will happen if a person uses a product:* If you buy [brand]_____, then [this is what will happen]_____. Sometimes the promise implies something negative may happen if you *do* or *do not* behave in a certain way. This *fear appeal* is used often in public service announcements, for example in campaigns against AIDS, or around New Year's Eve, to be careful with fireworks.

Because sometimes a promise may stretch believability, the focus of the selling strategy may need to give more weight to the **reason why**, which is *support or proof points that explain why a product will provide the promised benefit.* Generally, "reasons why" refer to important product features: for example, cars supporting a safety claim *because* they have multiple airbags and a cage construction.

Another similar selling strategy focuses on the **features** of a brand, which are *attributes that give a product a distinctive difference,* such as its design or engineering. Although customers buy products for the benefit they receive, sometimes talking about a feature that strongly *suggests* a benefit is more persuasive because it helps answer the question, "How can this product benefit me?" An example of a category that frequently uses a *feature-selling strategy* is disposable nappies. When you tell a new mother that Pampers is the most absorbent disposable, that mother knows right away that absorbency (a feature) means dryness for her baby's little bottom. A dry baby is a happy baby, a state that mothers and babies prefer.

One particularly common feature-selling strategy focuses on price (a feature). This strategy, *value pricing,* is used by discount retailers to make the point that the store offers the best-quality product you can buy *for that price.* Notice that "best quality" is qualified—the quality is best for that price; there may be better-quality products, but they would cost more.

Although price is a feature and an absolute one, value is not. **Value** is *a perception of what something is worth in terms of quality and price.* A selling strategy for value often uses a comparison to put value into perspective. Education is often hard to assess in terms of value. Recently, universities and other educational institutions have started to focus on the value that education may bring to prospective students. This value statement is then formulated in terms of salaries earned by graduates of one institution as compared to graduates of another competing one.

A **unique selling proposition (USP)** is *a product's most distinctive difference from competitive products.* This is another strategy that directly reflects the brand's position. An example is the

USP for Colgate's Total, which states that the toothpaste is *the only one* that offers 12-hour protection.

For most selling strategies, it is important to identify the **support**, which is *reason or proof points on which a claim, benefit, or proposition rests*. The formula for analysing support is: If I use [product]_____, I will [benefit]_____ because [support]_____.

In some industries, such as pharmaceuticals and food, any health claims, as well as any other statements of superiority, have to be supported by research. For emotional selling approaches, the support may come in the imagery. For example, the appeal of the Marlboro cowboy—the independence and manliness of cowboys—is communicated in the Western landscape, the cowboy's horse, and his dress and mannerisms, all of which can be reflected in a consumer's self-image.

Other selling strategies include the following (and it should be no surprise that some of them resemble the brand-positioning strategies discussed in Chapter 2:

- **Generic:** A **generic strategy** *stresses a basic feature or benefit of a product that is not brand specific.* The well-known US white moustache campaign for milk follows this strategy. With this campaign, the consumption of milk is advocated, not one specific brand in the category. Two reasons can lie behind such a strategy. One is that one specific brand is so dominant that it can afford to support the category, rather than the brand. For example, when one brand has a 70 per cent market share, 7 out of every 10 purchases that are the result of a generic campaign end up with the brand anyway. The other rationale for a generic strategy can be that the industry at large finds it more attractive to grow the market, rather than to fight for share of a non-growing market. This is particularly relevant if the feeling is that there is sufficient scope for market growth.

- **Pre-emptive:** A **pre-emptive strategy** *focuses on an attribute or benefit that any other product in the category could have claimed but did not.* This strategy is used in categories with little product differentiation and in new-product categories. Nokia's "Connecting people" approach is basically pre-emptive. Most companies offering wireless devices essentially connect people. By being the first to make that claim and by doing so effectively, Nokia was able to nail down a position as the company that does not sell devices, but connects people: an emotionally more attractive proposition to many consumers.[7]

- **Informational:** An **informational strategy** is *a selling strategy based on giving the facts about the brand and its attributes.* It is used with new products and products that have distinctive features that are strong points of competitive difference. A demonstration or a comparison can be used to prove the claim. Many car brands use this strategy (especially in their radio commercials), although the effectiveness of it may be questioned, as all brands seem to offer the same features at approximately the same discounts.

- **Credibility:** A **credibility strategy** *heightens conviction and decreases the perception of risk.* It is particularly useful with major purchases or products that affect security, safety, or health. Publicity releases that appear as news stories, for example, boost credibility because they have been reviewed by objective reporters and editors. An advertisement that uses endorsements, expert testimonials, or demonstrations to deliver a message is designed to build credibility. When Venus and Serena Williams play with Wilson rackets (for which they are handsomely paid), their choice says this brand of tennis racket is one of the best—otherwise, why would the top players in the world be using it?

- **Emotion:** An **emotional strategy** *connects with customers and prospects at the affective level* and moves them to respond with feelings. A number of emotional appeals are used in marketing communication, such as fear, love, and humour. The "Priceless" campaign is built on an emotional appeal based on family warmth and nostalgia.

- *Association:* An **association strategy** *makes a psychological connection between a brand (its attributes or image characteristics) and its customers and prospects.* Celebrities, for example, are associated with a brand because they lend their glamour to the product and to the user.

- *Lifestyle:* A **lifestyle strategy** is *a type of association strategy that uses situations and symbols of lifestyles that the target audience can identify with or aspire to.* This selling strategy, in which the situation "strikes a chord" or resonates, is used with highly competitive product categories with little differentiation, such as apparel, that rely primarily on images to transform the product into a distinctive brand.

- *Incentive:* An **incentive strategy** is *a selling strategy that creates a sense of immediacy and rewards customers for responding quickly.* It is used in product situations where a quick bump in sales is desired, and as a defensive reaction to counter a competitor's strategy. Sampling and sales promotions, such as telecom providers offering free hours and price discounts, are a type of incentive.

- *Reminder:* A **reminder strategy** *keeps a brand top-of-mind with the target.* It is used with mature brands that have an established brand identity, and it is designed to jog the customer's memory at a point of purchase. Most of the classic Coca-Cola advertising is not focused on attributes or features but rather is designed to keep the Coke brand top-of-mind.

- *Interactive:* The **interactive strategy** is *creating two-way communication in order to open up communication with customers and capture their feedback.* This strategy is used with any product when it makes sense for customers to contact a company.

How do MC managers choose which strategies to use when conceptualizing a message strategy brief? First of all, they recognize that different strategies achieve different objectives. Notice the relationship between the objectives and strategies in Table 6-2, which groups strategies according to the type of consumer response that the objective is trying to elicit.

The work that goes into planning a brief comes together as a statement describing the primary messages to be delivered. With the message strategy brief in place, the next step is coming up with the big idea that is the hallmark of successful MC messages.

Type of response	Message objectives	Message strategies
Think (cognitive)	Awareness, brand knowledge, understanding, conviction	Information, generic, pre-emptive, credibility
Feel (emotional)	Brand image and personality, liking, desire, self-identify	Emotion, association, lifestyle
Do (action, behaviour)	Buy, try, repeat, visit, contact, tell others	Incentive, reminder, interactive

Table 6-2 Objectives and strategies that drive responses

Small cars, big ideas

It is well known that the more mature product categories get, the tougher the competition. And also that it becomes increasingly difficult to find USPs or point of differentiation. The car industry may serve as a prototypical example of this point. First, listen to all the radio commercials coming by. Almost invariably the main point they try to make is that their car is better, offers newer and cheaper accessories and that you should arrange a test drive at your local dealer's. In this way the commercials combine cognitive and behavioural appeals, but the lack of creativity is stunning. Instead of recognizing a Big O, you have to suppress a Big Yawn.

TV commercials hardly have a better score here. The appeals here are not cognitive, but affective instead. Yet, differentiation is hard to find. In the upper segment all cars are exclusive, well designed, luxurious and promise you the good life. Middle-class cars are very effective, offering much more space for the family, and so on. Budget cars are remarkably spacious, offering everything for no money.

Of course, there are exceptions. In 1982 Fiat showed a new campaign for its budget model, the Panda. A classical commercial showed an odd-looking Italian (looking much like the famous actor and director Roberto Benigni in *la Vita è Bella*) demonstrating all the advantages of the Panda: its economy of fuel usage, its effective use of luggage space thanks to clever design, its multi-functionality and its performance when accelerating and flat out. In every shot the actor was laughing at the owners of other cars, who were missing the benefits of the Panda in a way that stayed in watchers' minds for days. In the last scene, in a small but effective joke, the laughter was mimicked by a policeman who was going to ticket the Panda driver for exceeding the speed limit. The idea of this commercial was to connect another type of emotion to cars, namely fun and optimism and enjoyment. A great idea indeed!

Another example of an outstanding car commercial was by Mazda in 1991 with its Amazing Mazda series. These commercials stayed close to the basic idea of listing all the benefits of Mazda cars but, while the Panda case used an affective appeal to add emotion to the brand, Mazda focused on getting the message across in very unconventional ways. One commercial showed a frozen car, bitter cold conditions and a *clochard* hanging on to the car's side mirrors. The man, almost frozen, tried to warm his hands with the help of Mazda's electrically heated mirrors. Another commercial illustrated the car's introduction of a six-cylinder motor performance by a short line-up of midgets who jumped up and down to the rhythm of the running motor (on the sound track). When the motor stopped the midgets came to rest chatting with each other or mopping their brows. The message? Amazing Mazda!

Think about it

How could these two Big Ideas be given legs? Is it necessary that Big Ideas should be related to key features or the benefits of the brand? Or are Big Ideas just a tool to draw attention to the brand in the crowded commercial landscape?

Sources:
www.fiat.co.uk
www.fiat.nl
www.mazda.com

IMC in Action

The big idea takes a creative leap

As the chapter opening indicates, ROI is about not only a financial return on investment but also "relevance, originality, and impact". A big creative idea is *original* because it hasn't been used before and therefore gets attention. It is *relevant* so that it can hold people's attention. And it has *impact* because it affects attitudes or behaviour (see colour insert B4). Part of being original and attracting attention is being unexpected, clever, and often humorous. A good creative idea takes the dull language of the strategy statement and transforms it into an exciting, attention-getting, and memorable message. The move from the business language of strategy to ideas that engage attention has been called the "creative leap" by advertising legend James Webb Young, founder of Young and Rubicam. It's also called concepting, which means *finding the creative concept that will bring a selling strategy to life.*

Concepting is a challenge. Even products that seem dull to customers deserve the investment of creative talent. Stacy Wall, a well-known copywriter and creative director, worked on Nike and other prestigious accounts before starting his own business. One of Wall's first directing tasks was for a pesticide from the FMC Corporation—not a glamorous assignment, but it gave him a chance to test his wings as a director and to prove that he could bring creativity to even the dullest of products. The campaign direction came from the not-too-exciting question "Why don't we give our corn to the rootworms?" Wall's idea was to work with other rhetorical, almost absurd, questions such as "Why don't we give our ice cream to the flies and our sidewalks to the gum?" He brought this strange and big idea to life with interpretive imagery that was as visually interesting as the idea of abandoning a pavement to chewing gum.[8]

The magic of a big idea

The big idea synthesizes the purposes of the strategy; joins the product benefit with consumer desire in a fresh, involving way; brings the subject to life; and makes the reader or the audience stop, look, and listen. In IMC, a big idea translates the strategy into a catchy umbrella theme that unites all the various brand messages and contributes consistency to the various brand messages. That is the business person's way of explaining a creative idea.

For most creative people, getting an original idea is like magic, although it is a product of hard work in backgrounding and becoming informed about the product and its category. Generally, big ideas come to mind after you have immersed yourself in a problem until it dominates your thoughts. Big ideas are not necessarily products of thought but rather of inspiration.

The simplicity of a big idea

A big idea is often one that communicates a simple idea in a simple way. David Ogilvy, a founder of the highly successful agency Ogilvy & Mather, pointed out that campaigns that run five years or more are the superstars; they keep on producing results and memorability because of the strength and simplicity of their big ideas. One superstar campaign is, for example, L'Oréal's "Because I'm worth it".

An effective big idea is often one that takes a simple idea and plays it to its extreme. Nike's "Tag" commercial, for example, which won the Grand Prix at Cannes in 2002, is based on the idea of all the people in a dense urban area involving themselves in a city-wide game of tag. Kash Sree, the copywriter for the "Tag" commercial, explains that the idea originated in those curious, copy-heavy print ads that instruct people on the finer details of playing various games. "It sounds really silly but we just thought, OK, let's do a TV ad off of it, and we wrote it in literally half an hour."[9]

A good idea has "legs"

When professionals say an idea has "legs", they mean that it can be used for different audiences, in different media, in different versions, and over an extended period of time (see colour insert B3). Having "legs" is particularly important in IMC, because big ideas have to stretch across several functional areas.

The big idea is usually associated with advertising, but big ideas can spring from, and are used in, other MC functional areas as well. For example, a Scandinavian campaign for Black Gold beer was unusual because of its use of a big idea for an event that would attract a younger audience and reposition the beer as hip. This particular big idea—a *film noir* festival, which reflected back to the beer's name—demanded both artistic vision and insight into the target audience's interest in participating in such an event.

Although a big campaign idea can come from any MC function, it is logical to search for it primarily within the MC function that is most appropriate to address or leverage the situation. Once the creative team determines what the lead MC function will be, it must select other MC functions to round out the support.

How do you get a big creative idea?

To be effective, marketing communication has to blend rational strategy with inspired and engaging creative ideas. A leading creative person puts it this way: "We always celebrate the intuitive right side of the brain, but the analytical left side is just as important. After all, great advertising isn't about creativity for its own sake. It has to work."[10]

Inspired big ideas are the product of creative thinking. To *create* means to originate—to conceive a thing or idea that did not exist before. Typically, creative thinking involves taking two or more previously unconnected objects or ideas and combining or arranging them to form something new.

Where does creativity come from? Can it be developed? Is it a gift that only special people have? Although most people believe that creativity springs directly from human intuition, creativity is very much a way of thinking that can be learned or at least strengthened. Some people exhibit more creativity than others, but creativity lives within all of us. If human beings weren't creative as a species, we wouldn't have discovered how to harness fire, domesticate animals, irrigate fields, or manufacture tools. And as individuals, we use our natural creativity every time we select clothes from out of the wardrobe in the morning, contrive an excuse, cook a meal, or choose a costume for a party.

 ... great advertising isn't about creativity for its own sake. It has to work.
Linda Kaplan Thaler, president of her own agency

In business, the **creative process** is recognized as *a formal procedure for increasing productivity and innovative output by an individual or a group*. It is used to get ideas and solve problems. Individuals responsible for creating ads, packages, sales promotions, websites, and news releases use various approaches in the development of new ideas. Whatever specific approach you use to get a new idea, the creative process has a fairly predictable set of steps: exploration, insight, execution, and evaluation. Let us look at each step in turn.

Exploration

In the exploration stage, copywriters and art directors begin by assembling the raw materials from which ideas emerge—facts, experiences, history, knowledge, and feelings, plus all the information gathered in the review of the marketing situation that is summarized in the message strategy brief. Brainstorming is useful at this stage. **Brainstorming** is *a formal process in which a small group gathers together for the purpose of generating a multitude of new ideas.* The goal is to record any inspiration that comes into anyone's mind, allowing each new idea an opportunity to stimulate other people's thoughts. Brainstorming is like a series of mini-explosions. One person's idea leads someone else to think of something else.

Brainstorming was developed many years ago by Alex Osborn, one of the founders of the BBDO agency. Although designed as a group activity, the technique can be used in creative teams, usually the copywriter and art director, or even by one person working alone. At the exploration stage, quantity is more important than quality. A basic principle of brainstorming is to get as many ideas on the table as possible, because any one idea may ignite someone else's thinking. Another principle is to not be judgemental while discussing ideas. Every idea is valuable because it stokes the creative fire. Evaluation comes later.

Another exploration approach is based on **lateral thinking**, which means *bouncing from one thought to another in free association.*[11] Playing with metaphors is a good way to jump-start lateral thinking (see colour insert B8). Ask yourself, "What is this product like?" And then, like a dog digging for a bone, search for the craziest possible metaphors. That's how the long-running Absolut Vodka campaign has kept itself fresh. The shape of the bottle, used as a visual metaphor, has been compared to everything from high-rise buildings to skiing tracks (see colour insert C13).

Edward De Bono, an expert on creativity, has described his method of getting ideas as the Six Hats (see Table 6-3). In De Bono's workshops, people are assigned a hat to wear and are asked to respond to a creative problem using the viewpoint that the hat represents.[12]

Whichever creative thinking technique is used, the aha! experience that comes from lighting on a great idea is similar to the way a compelling idea ignites a thought in a customer's mind. In both cases, something magical happens as the idea takes on a life of its own.

During the exploration stage, you hope for inspiration. Some people take a walk through shops, thumb through magazines, or look at award show books. Others look at other people's

White hat:	Facts, data, and information. "What info do we have? What is missing? What information would we like to have? How can we get it?"
Red hat:	Feelings, intuitions, hunches, emotions, and gut feelings. "Here's how I feel . . ."
Yellow hat:	Optimism, the logical positive view of things; focus on benefits. "This might work if . . .; The benefit would come from . . ."
Green hat:	New ideas, alternatives, possibilities. "We need some new ideas here—are there any other alternatives? Could we do this in a different way? Is there another explanation?"
Blue hat:	Analysis of the process being used, priorities, agendas. "We have spent too much time looking for something/one to blame; Let's figure out the priorities; Let's try some green-hat thinking to get some more new ideas."
Black hat:	Cautions and critical judgements. "The regulations say . . .; When we did it before . . .; It would be a mistake to . . ."

Table 6-3 De Bono's six hats

Source: From *Six Thinking Hats* by Edward De Bono. Copyright © 1985, 1999 by MICA Management Resources, Inc. By permission of Little, Brown and Company, (Inc.).

work, not for specific ideas but rather at how they solved a problem, and to unravel their thought process.

What all these techniques have in common is that inspiration is actively looked for. Creative people do not sit still, waiting for the inspirational moment. Instead, they expose themselves to as many stimuli as possible, staying open-minded for that great moment that says: aha!

Insight

In the second step of the creative process, insights are extrapolated through the tedious task of reviewing all the pertinent information, analysing the problem, identifying patterns, and searching for a key verbal or visual concept to communicate what needs to be said. This is the stage at which the search for the big idea—that flash of insight—takes place. It may come all at once, but sometimes it doesn't come until the creative team lets the information stew and simmer for a while.

Techniques that creative people use to stimulate this insight include the following:

- Changing patterns—unexpected juxtaposition.
- Looking at things in different ways—making the strange familiar, and the familiar strange.
- Adaptation—changing the context.
- Imagining—asking "What if?"
- Reversal—looking for the opposite.
- Connection—joining two unrelated ideas.
- Comparison—building a metaphor.
- Elimination—subtracting something or breaking rules.
- Parody—fooling around, making fun of something, looking for the humour.

Typically, the quality of an ad, i.e. how well the commercial is remembered, how well the message gets through, depends significantly on the clarity of the technique that is applied. Thus, the stronger the juxtaposition, the better you will remember it; the more natural and fitting the metaphor, the better the associations are created.

Execution

In the third step of the creative process, the creative team focuses on the execution of the idea, which is sometimes as important as the idea itself. Execution is discussed at length in the next chapter.

One aspect of execution that MC managers don't always think much about is presentation—the selling of ideas. Ideas do not sell themselves; how they deliver on the strategy has to be explained. To get the big idea approved, creative people may have to convince not only the client but others within the agency as well. Winning over the members of the agency account team, for example, can turn them into valuable partners in the presentation to the client. Developing a creative strategy that clearly delivers on the message strategy brief, as well as on the overall marketing communication strategy, will always help.

> How well you sell ideas is as important as how good those ideas are.
> *Bruce Bendinger,* The Copy Workshop

IMC in Action

Playing games

Holland Casino, a Dutch chain of casinos, is a commercial organization which offers gaming opportunities. The company focuses on the growing demand for gambling in a socially responsible matter, making a casino accessible to everybody. With 13 casinos spread over the Netherlands (2006), Holland Casino makes for a popular outing.

For communicating their brand, Holland Casino uses sponsorship as well as advertising campaigns. It sponsored the Dutch Football Premiership League for several years and it won the "Sponsor Ring" award in the sporting category in 2004. One year later the company decided to focus only on the culture and entertainment industries for its sponsorship. In addition to sponsorship, Holland Casino has developed an advertising campaign around the theme "How to play the game". This campaign seeks to link playing a casino game and "playing games" in everyday life. It focuses strongly on getting across the accessibility of the Holland Casino brand. All commercials in this campaign relate to a different theme based on "playing the game".

One example of a TV commercial made by the company to support its football sponsorship is called "Player's number 7". In normal life, the number 7 means luck, but not in this commercial. Different soccer players with the number 7 on their shirts fail to score, fall down at crucial moments or are tackled by the opposition. Towards the end of the commercial, one can hear the voice of Holland Casino saying: "Don't trust only the lucky numbers". Afterwards, you see a soccer player at the gambling table putting all his money on number 13.

"Work on your poker face" is another of Holland Casino's TV commercials. The commercial opens with some women sitting in the waiting room of a cosmetic surgery clinic. They all look up when a man comes in who has just undergone a surgical operation on his face. He can hardly move his lips and has his face set in the same, ridiculous expression. It also means he can barely speak. Leaving the clinic, the man finds out his car was parked wrongly and he is getting his wheels clamped. His mumbled protest doesn't impress the officer. However, at the gambling table in Holland Casino his poker face brings him lots of luck, certainly more than enough to pay the parking fine.

Another TV commercial that is part of the "How to play the game" advertising campaign is "Don't forget the rules of the game". This commercial is about a worldwide beauty contest. After a short introduction by the presenter of the show, Miss Paraguay comes on to the stage and shows off her figure and dress, but then, instead of leaving the stage, she starts to do a striptease in front of the jury. At that moment, the voice of Holland Casino comes in, saying: "Don't forget the rules of the game". Later on, when she is playing in a Holland Casino, she demonstrates that she knows exactly how to play the gambling game.

Think about it

Do you see logic in Holland Casino using this particular appeal and story-telling format? Thinking of the beauty contest example, how far can such a Big Idea be stretched?

Sources:
www.hollandcasino.com
Commercials: www.youtube.com, www.ster.nl

Evaluation and copytesting

In the last step of the creative process, creative people use both judgement and research to evaluate their big ideas. In part, the evaluation is based on the intuition of professionals who serve as creative directors or on an agency's in-house review board.

For clients, evaluating a big idea is almost as difficult as coming up with one. When the agency (or the advertising department in an in-house agency) presents creative concepts, the client is suddenly in the role of a judge—without having gone through the other steps in the creative process. And the problem with a truly creative idea is that no one has done it before, so it appears risky. David Ogilvy recommended that clients ask themselves five questions when evaluating new work:[13]

1 Did it make me gasp when I first saw it?

2 Do I wish I had thought of it myself?

3 Is it unique?

4 Does it fit the strategy to perfection?

5 Could it be used for 30 years?

Evaluation for big-budget MC efforts may also rely on **copytesting**, which is *testing the effectiveness of a brand message, a creative concept, or elements such as a headline, slogan, or visual for creative impact and understandability.* Testing can be conducted at all points during the development of the creative strategy and executions, and even after the completed materials are in use.

Time and money constraints mean that not every idea can be tested. Even though some agencies conduct research to test ideas, a lot of marketing communication go/no-go decisions are based on the judgement of the creative team and the client's marketing staff. They ask themselves questions such as: What's wrong/right with this idea? What if it fails? And, most important, does this idea achieve the message and MC objectives?

Creative ideas, ethics, and sensitivity

Ideas that at first glance seem brilliant sometimes generate criticism for being tasteless, sexist, or racist on second thoughts (refer to the IMC in Action box 'Playing Games'). Obviously, the line between acceptable or not is vague, in particular with respect to taste, but also with respect to sexism and even racism, where some people are more sensitive than others. In 2003 the first author of this text filed a complaint against a commercial by Renault. The ad showed three men enjoying driving a Renault car. The driver especially was having great fun, but when they reached the end point, a big block of concrete was found. The next shot made it clear, though by suggestion alone, that the driver was hung at the block and drowned in the water of the harbour. Tasteless? Yes according to your author, but the court decided that the commercial was obviously a parody on the popular TV series *The Sopranos*, and hence that the commercial used some kind of adaptation technique to make a point. Well, your author is still looking for that point.

Sometimes even clearly offensive commercials make it to the air waves. You may wonder how this can happen, given the long trajectory with many people involved before a commercial is aired. One of the explanations is that during the process, everyone involved is captured by the idea, the big idea, and is carried away by the general atmosphere of enthusiasm. In such situations, people may lose their critical power, and even worse, if they are critical can be overruled or even ignored.

Don't let that happen to you. Both for commercial reasons and ethical reasons alike, always stay critical. Also recall that for many viewers, advertising is truth. Ads tell something about the relationship between companies and clients. And on the larger scale, advertising is a mirror of the society (see Chapter 16). It is one of the most revealing forms of communication, strongly representing the cultural truth of the society in which it finds a place. Great creative ideas should be culturally sensitive in order to add to the integrity of the brand, rather than tarnish it.

A final note: the balancing act

The real art in planning for the creative IMC message lies in balancing the big idea and the selling strategy so they work together. When the creative message overpowers the strategy, the message may be remembered but the brand identification may be forgotten. If the strategy overpowers the creative idea, the message will be dull and never get attention, let alone be remembered. "The agencies that are really great and amazing are those that have some kind of balance", said Tony Granger. "There are agencies that are too creative department-led where the insight is sometimes lacking. There are agencies that are account men-dominated that are full of boring work. The real magic comes when there's a balance."[14]

The stories we tell and remember are the ones that intersect in personal ways with our lives. Achieving that effect calls for both strategic and creative thinking. Brand stories achieve it when they are based on nuggets of insight into how customers feel and think about a brand. Chapter 7 explains how creative and strategic brand stories are brought to life, and how the ideas are executed in words and visuals that grab and stick.

🔑 Key terms

account planning Using research and brand insights to bring a strong consumer focus to the planning of marketing communication.

appeal An idea that motivates an audience to respond.

association strategy A selling strategy that makes a psychological connection between a brand (its attributes or image characteristics) and its customers and prospects.

benefit How a product satisfies customers' needs, wants, and desires.

brainstorming A formal process in which a small group gathers together for the purpose of generating a multitude of new ideas.

concepting Finding the creative concept that will bring a selling strategy to life.

copytesting Testing the effectiveness of a brand message, a creative concept, or elements such as a headline, slogan, or visual for creative impact and understandability.

creative process A formal procedure for increasing productivity and innovative output by an individual or a group.

credibility strategy A selling strategy that heightens conviction and decreases the perception of risk.

customer insight Below-the-surface attitudes and beliefs that influence customers' behaviour.

emotional strategy A selling strategy that connects with customers and prospects at the affective level.

features Attributes that give a product a distinctive difference.

generic strategy A selling strategy that stresses a basic feature or benefit of a product that is not brand specific.

incentive strategy A selling strategy that creates a sense of immediacy and rewards customers for responding quickly.

informational strategy A selling strategy based on giving the facts about the brand and its attributes.

interactive strategy A selling strategy that creates two-way communication in order to open up communication with customers and capture their feedback.

lateral thinking Bouncing from one thought to another in free association.

lifestyle strategy A type of association strategy that uses situations and symbols of lifestyles that the target audience can identify with or aspire to.

message strategy An idea about how to creatively and persuasively communicate a brand message to a target audience.

message strategy brief Statements about a brand that summarize the research and insights for the creative team.

pre-emptive strategy A selling strategy that focuses on an attribute or benefit that any other product in the category could have claimed but did not.

promise A statement describing what good things will happen if a person uses a product.

reason why Support or proof points that explain why a product will provide the promised benefit.

reminder strategy A selling strategy that keeps a brand top-of-mind with the target.

support Reason or proof points on which a claim, benefit, or proposition rests.

unique selling proposition (USP) A product's most distinctive difference from competitive products.

value A perception of what something is worth in terms of quality and price.

Check the key points

Key point 1: A creative message strategy

a   What is a message strategy? How is a message strategy used in marketing communication?

b   Why is relevance an important dimension of a creative message strategy?

c   Why does a message strategy need to be creative?

Key point 2: The message strategy brief

a   What are the three main steps in developing a message strategy brief?

b   Study the agency briefs in Table 6-1. What elements appear most consistently in them? What elements appear infrequently? If you were asked to develop your own outline for a message strategy brief, what would you include?

c   What is a key customer insight? Give an example of what customer insights contribute to the development of message strategy.

d   Find an example in ads elsewhere in this book of a claim, a benefit statement, a reason why, and a USP. Explain the logic behind each one.

e   Write the benefit statements for one of the ads that you like from this chapter. Use the following formula: If I use [product]_____, I will [benefit]_____ because [support]_____.

f   How does the MasterCard story in the opening case exemplify a message strategy brief?

Key point 3: The creative process

a Define *creativity*. What are the key characteristics of creativity?

b What are the four steps of the creative process? Describe an experience you have had in coming up with a creative idea. How was your experience similar to or different from the process described in this chapter?

c Set up a brainstorming session with some of your friends. Ask them to come up with a new idea for a MasterCard ad. Experiment with the brainstorming techniques. Which approach generated the most ideas?

d Find a marketing communication execution that you believe is highly creative and a similar one for a related product that you feel isn't creative. Critique both pieces, and give reasons for your evaluation. Are both on strategy as best as you can tell from the message you see expressed in the materials?

Chapter Challenge

Writing assignment

Find an article in the trade press that describes a new marketing communication campaign or programme. Critique the message strategy, using the information given in the article. What is missing? If you were working on this account as a planner, how would you develop the message strategy brief? Write a memo to your instructor describing the approach you would take.

Presentation assignment

Collect all the MC materials you can find for one of your favourite brands, then re-create what you believe the message strategy brief is for this brand. Analyse the creative idea. Is it a big idea that both grabs and sticks? Is the creative idea on strategy? Does the creative idea have legs? Give a presentation of this idea and add one way in which the idea could be applied other than the way you have found.

TV assignment

Watch a TV channel for two hours and concentrate on the commercials. Analyse the commercials with respect to the leading ideas that are applied and whether they refer to the cognitive, affective or behavioural stages of consumer decision making. Was this a Big Idea? For one commercial, come up with a creative insight that turns the idea into a Big one (that means: maintain the essence of the idea, but fire it with some of your sparkling creativity to make it illuminating and memorable).

Notes

[1] The concept of ROI meaning Relevance, Originality and Impact was originally introduced by Keith Reinhard, former CEO of DDB Worldwide.

[2] "Penelope Cruz Can't Contain Herself in Coca-Cola Promotion", *Denver Post*, 17 January 2003, p. 3F.

[3] Bob St. Julian, "Put Away the Brief and Get Creative", *B&T Marketing & Media*, 8 November 2002, www.bandt.com.au/articles/4f/0c01254f.asp.

[4] Adapted from Sandra Moriarty, "The First Step in Creative Strategy: Creating Customer-Focused Objectives" (paper presented at the annual conference of the Academy of Advertising, Jacksonville, FL, March 2002).

[5] "Diamonds in the Data", *one.a magazine*, 5, no. 4 (Spring 2002), pp. 8–9.

[6] Kelly Pate, "Former NY Ad Man Is Sold on Denver", *Denver Post*, 4 October 2002, p. C1.

[7] Hatfield, "Granger in Effect"; Stefano Hatfield, "Sunshine Supermen", *Creativity Magazine*, 1 April 2002, www.adcritic.com/news/creativity/detail/?q=35188.

[8] Terry Kattleman, "Lwall Power", *Creativity Magazine*, 7 September 2002, www.adcritic.com/news/creativity/detil/?q=36239.

[9] Ann-Christine Diaz, "Kash Sree—Part of Wieden+Kennedy's 'Tag' Team—Moves to the Midwest", *Creativity Magazine*, 29 July 2002, www.adcritic.com/news/creativity/details/?q-=35583.

[10] "A Tip of the Cap to Kaplan Thaler", *Wall Street Journal*, house ad, 14 November 2002.

[11] Edward De Bono, *Serious Creativity: Using the Power of Lateral Thinking to Create New Ideas* (New York: HarperBusiness, 1992).

[12] Edward De Bono, *Six Thinking Hats* (New York: Little, Brown, 1986).

[13] David Ogilvy, *Ogilvy on Advertising* (New York: Random House, 1985), pp. 17–18.

[14] Hatfield, "Granger in Effect"; Stefano Hatfield, "Sunshine Supermen", *Creativity Magazine*, 1 April 2002, www.adcritic.com/news/creativity/detail/?q=35188.

Further reading

El-Murad, Jaafar and Douglas C. West (2004) "The Definition and Measurement of Creativity: What Do We Know?", *Journal of Advertising Research*, Vol. 44–2, pp. 188–201.

Koslow, Scott, Sheila L. Sasser and Edward A. Riordan (2006) "Do Marketers Get the Advertising They Need or the Advertising They Deserve?", *Journal of Advertising*, Vol. 35–3, pp. 81–101.

Till, Brian D. and Daniel W. Baack (2005) "Recall and Persuasion. Does Creative Advertising Matter?", *Journal of Advertising*, Vol. 34–3, pp. 47–57.

Tippins, Michael J. and Robert A. Kunkel (2006) "Winning a Clio Advertising Award and its Relationship to Firm Profitability", *Journal of Marketing Communications*, Vol. 12–1, pp. 1–14.

Toubia, Olivier (2006) "Idea Generation, Creativity, and Incentives", *Marketing Science*, Vol. 25–5, pp. 411–25.

Von Nordenflycht, Andrew (2007) "Is Public Ownership Bad for Professional Service Firms? Ad Agency Ownership, Performance, and Creaticity", *Academy of Management Journal*, Vol. 50–2, pp. 429–45.

West, Douglas C., Emily L. Collins and Alan Miciak (2003) "Management Perspectives of Awards for Creative Advertising", *Journal of General Management*, Vol. 29–2, pp. 23–34.

Yoo, Changjo and Deborah MacInnis (2005) "The brand attitude formation process of emotional and informational ads", *Journal of Business Research*, Vol. 58–10, pp. 1397–1406.

Message execution

CHAPTER PERSPECTIVE
Telling a brand story

Why is Nike such a strong brand? Nike's brand story is known around the world. Peak performance—that is the essence of the Nike brand and the underlying aspiration of Nike customers. The idea comes to life in any number of executions that show athletic superstars nailing the race, the basket, the home run, the hole in one.

A strong brand has a good story; brand communication is all about the telling of the story. The stories we tell and remember are the ones that intersect in personal ways with our lives. Brand stories do that when they are based on nuggets of insight into how customers feel and think about a brand. Figuring that out is the role of the strategies that you read about in Chapter 6. The *execution* of a strategy is the presentation of those insights in stories that ring true with the target audience.

There are essentially two sets of decisions to make in executing a brand message: what elements to use in the brand story and how to structure those elements. The execution elements include all the bits and bytes of a brand message—the words, the sounds and music, the photos and illustrations, the costumes and settings, the lighting—all the many physical details of a production. The structure is the way these elements are combined—the layout, the flow, the form of the message—how everything comes together to deliver the story.

IMC in Action

A sweet romance
Bates Advertising, Auckland, New Zealand

Arnott's is an Australian biscuit (cookie) and cracker manufacturer that has successfully expanded its market to many areas of the Pacific region. In neighbouring New Zealand, however, Arnott's was seen as an "Aussie interloper" and was having a tough time competing against locally entrenched New Zealand brands. If you were assigned to develop a meaningful relationship between Arnott's and current and potential customers in New Zealand, what would you recommend? That was the challenge given to Auckland's Bates Advertising, which created a moving, award-winning campaign for Arnott's. Using IMC, a great creative idea, and an engaging story, Bates was able to involve New Zealand consumers with the brand in an emotional way.

The marketing situation

Arnott's had been in the New Zealand marketplace since 1983 and by the early 1990s had nearly a 30 per cent market share. However, by the mid-1990s, growth had begun to stagnate. Increased competition for shelf space was threatening the profitability and market share of established brands. The biscuit category is characterized by low consumer loyalty. Focus-group research found that consumers had a large repertoire of favorite brands and saw few points of difference among the product offerings.

In addition to the core consumer target market, which Arnott's identified as household shoppers aged 18 to 49 with children, the brand also needed to focus attention on the retail trade target. Competitor Griffin's had come to own the category's primary values (warmth, approachability, trust, caring, everydayness, and friendliness). Arnott's had a perception problem. The company's own research found that the brand was seen as cold and inaccessible and thus at odds with the overall "warmth" of the biscuit category.

Message strategy and execution

Bates decided that the message strategy for Arnott's was to create an emotional connection to the brand. The communication objectives were (1) to improve the brand positioning on key biscuit values (caring and friendly); (2) to increase perceptions of the brand's modernity, quality, and relevance to New Zealand; and (3) to increase trust with the business-to-business audience.

Arnott's was a brand looking for a relationship with the New Zealand consumer. The big idea was to create soap-opera format commercials that featured Michael, an attractive young man, and his search for a meaningful relationship. For two years, the entwined stories of Michael and the Arnott's brand unfolded in the style of a long-running television series, an approach very different from traditional marketing communication in this category. Together Arnott's and Michael won the hearts of New Zealanders.

Bates introduced Michael to the target audience in a lonely-hearts advertisement. In the commercials, his words struck a chord with New Zealand women, thousands of whom responded to his plea for "old-fashioned love". As the campaign evolved, New Zealanders joined Michael in his search for happiness. Arnott's products were featured as integral components of each commercial, providing occasions for meeting and sharing.

The series had three phases. The first phase focused on Michael's experiences as he dated the array of women who answered his advertisement, the second on the development of a significant relationship, and the third on its outcome. The third phase used an interactive approach that involved customers in the campaign. Arnott's biscuits were at the heart of every commercial episode.

In the second phase of the series, Michael bumps into his perfect match in the supermarket parking lot. Not only does he get her name—Jessica—but he also manages to get her phone number. Their relationship begins. During the ensuing episodes, Michael falls hopelessly in love. But for Jessica, Michael's ardour is too much, too soon. Like most divorced women living in the modern world, she has a lot to juggle: her commitment to her son Billy, the challenges and opportunities of her career, and the possibilities that a more independent life can bring. There's also Billy's dad—how does he fit into all of this? Phase two concludes with a cliffhanger: Jessica's ex turns up at the local park, and tension mounts as Jessica seems to be following Billy straight back to his daddy's arms.

The conclusion used an innovative interactive television commercial that allowed viewers to vote on Michael's fate. They were offered four possible conclusions to Michael's search for old-fashioned love:

1 Jessica returns to Billy's dad.

2 Jessica chooses neither man.

3 Michael wakes up to discover that the whole thing was a dream.

4 Jessica chooses Michael, and the two get married and live happily ever after.

These alternative scenarios were launched on television, and the voting forms were available on point-of-sale posters and in magazines. A combination of public relations and an "advertorial" in a women's magazine then took over to build further interest in the outcome.

The winner: a wedding! More than 15 500 consumers participated in this campaign by voting for one of the options. The greatest number of votes was tallied for the wedding. And in a break from convention, Arnott's announced and staged the wedding in a joint venture with the women's weekly magazine. A front cover and an "editorialized" photo spread reported on the event. The wedding took on a life of its own, as New Zealand consumers identified with the fictional Michael and Jessica.

Evaluation of the Arnott's campaign

This highly successful campaign stopped Arnott's share-of-market erosion and changed consumers' perceptions of the brand. Results show that in the space of two years, Arnott's moved from being a brand without meaning or relevance to the New Zealand consumer to being a favourite brand, closing the "preference gap" between itself and competitor Griffin's. Even more important, Arnott's protected its market share while at the same time increasing its average price to 10 per cent above the category average. Finally, as an unusual test of its emotional strength, the campaign was voted "Most Romantic" television commercial by the Romance Writers Guild.

Source:
This case was adapted with permission from the Advertising and Marketing Effectiveness (AME) award-winning brief for Arnott's prepared by Bates Advertising agency in Auckland, New Zealand.

Brand message execution

For Arnott's the integrated campaign told the story of a meaningful relationship and built a caring image for the brand. The strategy of building an emotional connection was executed by using a soap-opera format, attractive stars, an involving brand interaction, and a classic sweet ending. All those executional decisions made the creative idea—romantic "cookie moments"—an award-winning and effective MC campaign.

A big part of the magic of a great idea lies in the way it is executed—and a big part of execution involves creating the right image. A **message execution** is *the format of a completed MC message, such as an advertisement, brochure, or package label.* There is no magic formula for producing good message executions. Four decision areas are key for people on the creative side of marketing communication—writers, designers, and producers—as they seek to bring a big idea alive in an attention-getting and memorable message:

- Message storytelling
- Appeals to use
- How to select and use all the elements of which a message consists
- Consistency

Message storytelling, or the execution framework, defines the type of story that is used to frame the message. The story itself will use one or various appeals to get the message through and try to induce changes in the recipients' cognitions, affects or behaviour (see Chapter 4 on what aspects of consumer behaviour communication tries to influence). To make these appeals work, advertisers use words, pictures, sounds, and people. These are the tools that are available to the creative people. Finally, consistency is of utmost importance in any IMC decision process, both in the execution of single messages and for long-running campaigns.

This chapter discusses the four areas in detail. Since the use of endorsers is of paramount importance in the creative execution of message strategies, a separate section is devoted to this topic.

Message storytelling—the execution framework

The first step in the execution of a brand message is to identify the best way to present the message or tell the brand's story. Experienced creative people look for the technique and style with the greatest persuasive appeal for the idea being presented. Two criteria drive this, and effectively all creative decisions: will this message be noted? Will it break through the clutter? Can it convey the message that is to be communicated? The key characteristic of message storytelling is the execution framework that is applied.

Execution frameworks may be described, in a general way, as either informative or affective, which corresponds to the head and heart approaches. An **execution framework** specifies *the format or approach to be used to tell the brand story.* Some message formats are referred to as "formulas" because they are frequently used. The following list describes eight fundamental message story formats:

1 *News announcement* The simplest form of advertising is just telling that your brand exists, what it is, and what features it has. This is a purely informative framework that will only appeal to the head. It may be useful in introducing new products, or in product categories where other formats have been overused, like detergents or cars. In such an environment

the news announcement format is likely to be perceived as a relief: just getting back to the straight facts without all the hassle. Also, because of this difference, such messages may attract attention. However, this format lacks the potential to add emotion to the brand and is therefore less often used in TV advertising, and only slightly more often in print. In radio commercials, on the other hand, it is more difficult to introduce emotional features, and consequently many radio commercials rely on news announcement formats.

2 *Testimonial* When the message is told by a living person, this is called a testimonial. Such living persons can be celebrities or typical users that deliver a message endorsing a product. By using endorsers the message may more easily attract attention, in particular when celebrities are used. Moreover, the use of a living person adds liveliness to the advertisement. A testimonial, however, still focuses on facts and figures and is primarily an informative type of advertisement. Testimonials by celebrities can add conviction to the message. Research supports the power of Oprah Winfrey or *Consumer Reports* to make people who have no opinion of a product suddenly see it as top of the line.[1]

3 *Authoritative* A special case is when a testimonial is delivered by a person who can claim some kind of authority. There are various bases of authority. Power (politicians), fame (celebrities), morality (opinion leaders), heavy users (sports people), expertise (scientists) all add strength to the message. This may work in two ways. First, the authority may represent an aspiration level on the part of consumers. The authority represents what the audience wants to be, and therefore is believed. Second, the authority is considered much better informed and knowledgeable than the consumer. Politicians and opinion leaders (and sometimes celebrities) do not always appear in person in commercials, but are then played by look-alike actors. Often, though, the conviction of the authority is then at odds with the humour that is often implied by the use of look-alikes. Authority is either related to the product or not. Relatedness adds conviction to the message. An ideal combination is when a famous person is also seen as an expert. Michael Schumacher driving a Fiat is more convincing than the Formula 1 world champion using Vodafone.

4 *Demonstration* Words are just words, and a picture is worth a thousand words. Showing a product, how it works and that it really works well is another way to frame a message. Such messages invite audience members to believe the evidence of their own eyes, and are therefore potentially highly persuasive. Laundry detergents and other cleaning products apply this type of framework extensively. For example, Cillit Bang uses this framework for almost all their products.[2] The drawback is that consumers are so well aware of all the special effects and other tricks that can be applied by ad producers, that they tend not to believe the evidence of their own eyes, at least not when the demonstration is "mediated" by media, in particular television. The real power of demonstration is therefore when it is applied in personal selling, fairs or trade shows. TV commercial makers recognize this and sometimes try to apply the demonstration framework, suggesting that the demonstration takes place at a trade fair.

5 *Slice of life* Showing people in everyday situations using a particular brand is a next step away from mere fact-telling to adding emotion and recognition. Of course, not all everyday situations are useful for advertisements. Creatives focus on everyday situations that help receivers of the message understand the product and create or enforce the right associations. Beer and soft-drink brands make heavy use of this format. They typically show people in desirable states using their product. Those states can be described as happy, exciting, thrilling, romantic, adventurous, satisfied, etc. Not long ago Dutch beer brewer Heineken launched a campaign centred around the Louis Armstrong evergreen "What a

wonderful world". What Heineken did not understand, however, was that beer drinkers usually don't seek the ease and relaxation that is heavily associated with the song. The campaign indeed did not run for long. Often this format shows snap-shots from apparently non-performed situations and have a voice-over or a song telling the core message.

6   *Inherent drama* While slice-of-life advertising reflects everyday life, the possibility of communicating exactly what the advertiser wants is inherently limited by this. Drama, however, offers more possibilities. Drama is a dramatized version of slice of life, and it should be clear that the distinction is sometimes problematic to make. Insurance companies typically dramatize everyday situations exaggerating the misfortune that may happen to people. Sometimes this type of advertising results in true mini-movies that are very well liked and often receive the highest awards from creatives. Sometimes such mini-movies reach cult status. Car manufacturer BMW used the interest of consumers in this kind of mini-movie to attract them to their website.[3] BMW showed a short excerpt from a mini-movie on TV and told the audience that the entire movie could be seen at the company's website. Inherent drama offers the richest possibilities for creatives to disseminate the message. The danger is that the message is hard to decode from the ad. Watching many of the award-winning commercials of the last years demonstrates the point. For example, in 2002 the Nike commercial "Tag" won the Golden Lion award in Cannes with a beautifully designed and shot short movie. The effectiveness of this commercial in communicating anything beneficial for the brand is, however, doubtful.

7   *Fantasy* When drama leaves the realm of reality and enters into the desires and aspiration of the characters in the advertisement, the fantasy framework is applied. This often suggests that the use of certain brands opens doors to worlds that the prospective consumer could only dream of. Philadelphia (cream cheese) took the fantasy theme quite literally, showing people dressed as angels, sitting on heavenly clouds. Two female angels enjoy the pleasures of heaven, one of them referring to the product, the other to an attractive male angel a few clouds apart from them.

8   *Animation/cartoons* Stories can be told by people, but surprising effects can be achieved using animated characters. The possibilities are endless, but using animation is admittedly a step down the ladder of resonance to real life. The trade-off is between this factor and the possibility of telling the story the advertiser wants. Seven-up's animated character Dido starred in one of the more successful animated campaigns.

In addition to these eight ways of communicating a message is the option of using *comparative advertising*. Comparative advertising can be applied with each of the eight formats described above. As the word says, **comparative advertising** means that *one brand explicitly—or sometimes implicitly—is compared to a competitor*. The classic example here is the Pepsi challenge, in which people were asked to taste two or more cola brands blindfold. Of course, the majority expressed preference for Pepsi. Variations in this type of advertising exist depending on whether the competing brand is revealed or not. For a long time revealing the competitor was not allowed in many European countries. This ban has been lifted in most countries in the beginning of the new millennium, but the use of comparative advertising has not shown a dramatic increase. The reason is that comparative advertising has some clear disadvantages. First, by mentioning the name of a competitor the competing brand gains in brand awareness of the expense of the advertising brand. Second, comparative advertising is sometimes perceived as a declaration of weakness: the brand that applies comparative advertising is perceived as not being able to display its point of difference independently. Furthermore, people tend to love underdogs. The brand with which the advertised brand is compared clearly has the role of underdog. And finally, some people simply judge comparative advertising as unethical.

The goal of comparative advertising is to convince consumers that the advertised brand is either superior to some alternative band, or offers benefits unavailable from an alternative.[4] It is most effective when the comparison is based on a concrete attribute or feature, rather than an association or benefit. Associations and benefits are not specific or concrete and are hard to prove in an advertisement. For example, the claim that the advertised brand tastes better than the comparative one is hard to check from the TV screen. Price differentials or other concrete claims, however, can be checked in the shop. Lowest price guarantees further substantiate a claim that the advertised brand has lower prices. Such concrete and verifiable claims offer the best opportunities for comparative advertising. For example, banks can display previously publicized interest rates on mortgages to show that their rate is the lowest. The Pepsi challenge therefore has to be understood not so much as a claim that Pepsi tastes better, but rather that (1) it might be worthwhile to at least try Pepsi once (well that sounds a bit desperate doesn't it?); (2) many other people also like Pepsi, thereby reassuring the social acceptability of drinking Pepsi. The Pepsi challenge, therefore, shows that comparative advertising may serve other purposes than arguing that the advertised brand is outperforming the competition.

Message appeals

Whereas the format describes the kind of story that is used, **appeals** refer to *the cue that should make the advertisement work*. This means that appeals should first and foremost be able to hold the attention of the receiver of the message. Less important, yet also desirable, is that the appeal should relate to the key of the message that is being conveyed. Appeals furthermore try to draw the receivers into the message, and to involve them. Therefore most appeals are emotionally laden, although they may also relate to cognitive states. Five broad and common categories of appeals are discussed here.

1 *Humour* Perhaps the most often applied appeal is humour. There are some clear advantages to this. First, humour inspires to a positive mood. This positive state of mind is, by the logic of classical conditioning, associated with the branded product. Second, humour typically builds up a certain tension in the message to unload in a clue. Third, humour offers a splendid opportunity to convey the core message in the clue. When attention is highest and positive attitudes have developed, the message is revealed.

However, humour also has some potential drawbacks. In particular it can distract the audience from the message. When the joke is too involving, or otherwise requires too much attention, the receiver of the message may not even notice who the sender of the message is. Secondly, humour is quite subjective. What is funny to one kind of audience may be perceived as offensive by another group of viewers. Proper segmentation practice will mitigate the negative consequences of this point.

Various types of humour exist. A recent typology[5] suggested seven such types: comparison, personification, exaggeration, pun, sarcasm, silliness, and surprise. As with the use of humour in general, the sensitivity of the audience to various types of humour is subjective: you like the key idea of exaggeration or you do not. You can stand sarcasm, or you can find it offensive. You can laugh at silliness or you can find it pathetic. Comparison and surprise often seem to be safer types of humour. Punning is a tricky one: when you don't get the clue, the message often loses all its power. Personification—objects or animals in the role of humans—is like exaggeration: you either like it or you do not. Note that personification of this sort is not based solely on humour: young puppies playing with toilet paper like children are not only funny, but also charming.

2 *Sex* While everybody feels attracted by humour (although not everyone enjoys the same kind) there is more controversy about the use of sex appeal in advertising. Presumably there are three kinds of people: those who like it and admit it; those who like it and do not admit it; and those who do not like it. Consequently, the use of sex appeals must be supported by an analysis of the target group (see colour insert B9).

There are three ways in which sex can be applied: nudity, eroticism and subliminal. Nudity refers to the plain use of naked bodies; it is most direct and overt, yet paradoxically usually generates little opposition. Spa mineral waters uses nudity to express the pureness of its products. In fact, nudity is not really an appeal in the way it is defined above, but more of an instrument to use other appeals.

Eroticism refers to the sexual desires between men and women, and sometimes between men, or between women (although this is very rare in advertising). Couples kissing each other or highly suggestive poses may disseminate strong sexual appeal. Alternatively, an advertisement may show people (men or women) in seductive situations, directly relating to the sexual desires of the receiver of the message. Many brands in the body-care product category play this card by combining a demonstration of their product with a sexual appeal in an overt, yet disguised way. Subliminal use of sex appeal means that the appeal is implicitly present. On a superficial level the ad tells one story, but subliminally there is a sex appeal. This in itself makes the technique highly controversial. On the one hand, picking up the subliminal reference to sex is idiosyncratic, on the other, including subliminal reference to sexuality is unacceptable to many people who, for example, do not want children to be exposed to this aspect of life, in particular in this inherently unconscious way.

3 *Feel good* Happiness, success, relaxation: there are many positive states of minds that are attractive for people. They all share a positive quality that is called here "feel good". Obviously the feel-good appeal refers to a desirable situation, and there need hardly be any discussion about the appropriateness of the use of these appeals in advertising. What feel-good appeals lack, however, is the kind of tension that is inherently present in humour or sex, that makes an advertisement not only feel good, but also attracts the audience's attention.

4 *Feel bad* The opposite of feel good appeals is the category of "feel bad". States of mind with a negative quality that fall in this category are, for example, fear and guilt. The use of feel-bad appeals is double-edged. On the one hand, they are more powerful than feel-good appeals because they are stronger and therefore more strongly involve receivers in the message. On the other hand, people do not like to feel bad and may reject the message for that very reason. Insurance companies, by the very nature of their products, often use "feel bad" appeals, for which the insurer has the solution. Some insurers however, focus on the "feel good" appeal that is the result of using their products.

5 *Cognitions* Some advertisements do not seduce you or make you laugh, they don't even make you feel good or bad, they just tell you about the product or brand, what it does and perhaps why it is better than the competition. And indeed, there are categories of people who feel attracted to this kind of advertising. Cognitive appeals are a safe way to tell the message, but using this kind of appeals clearly limits the possibility of adding emotion to the products. But for some product categories, such as grocery shopping goods, emotions are not so important.

It should be clear by now that the choice of appeal is not a matter of what the advertiser likes (see colour insert B11). Instead, the decision is based on the type of product, the target group of the commercial, and the point of difference that is to be communicated. For example, when Volvo wants to strengthen its safety association, a feel-bad appeal might be appropriate. Volkswagen, playing a family car card, could refer to feel good appeals. Mini-Cooper, highlighting the smallness of its cars, might very well benefit from humorous advertising, while Ferrari may wish to emphasize the sex appeal that goes with the car. Finally, a brand like Lada could refer to the fact that it is technically equivalent to other cars in its segment, yet remarkably cheaper, thus using cognitive appeals.

How a shark swims past the secretary

Accenture, formerly called Andersen Consulting, is the world's largest consulting company and, in Germany, one of the most important. Decisions on hiring a business consulting firm of this calibre are made at the CEO level. The problem Accenture faced was how to get a message about Accenture consulting services onto CEOs' desks. It's hard to reach chief executives via traditional media, and their mail is filtered by executive secretaries who function as gatekeepers. Accenture in Germany gave the assignment—to develop a direct-mail message that would get past the secretary—to the Frankfurt office of MC agency Wunderman Cato Johnson, now called Impiric.

To achieve this objective, Accenture had to ensure that the execution of the message would be so interesting that the secretary would pass it on and the CEO would take the piece home. The creative director explained, "If the CEO takes our mailing home and reads it to his [or her] children or grandchildren, then we've surpassed our objectives."

The "Master of Design" campaign, which carried the message that Accenture was a partner in a company's business reengineering, used television commercials and a print campaign that included airport posters. A long-running advertising campaign using a "school of fish" theme had been used by Accenture for the past several years. The evolution followed the company's shift from being a solutions provider on a project basis to being a consulting service that provides ongoing guidance to continuously strengthen clients' business performance.

The key element of the "Master of Design" campaign came to be known as the "Shark" mailing. It was built on a short fairy tale about a school of goldfish living in an undisturbed and peaceful world where they happily perform their work. Suddenly enemies enter the marketplace. Another fish—the Master of Design—becomes the goldfishes' consultant and redesigns the loosely grouped school of fish into a new, more powerful organization with the profile of a shark.

The Shark mailing, which was much more than a brochure, invited the reader to take an active part in the story development. The story could be read at several levels—as a simple fairy tale for children or as a sophisticated metaphor for business executives. It was presented in a blue box with a laser graphic of a fish on its cover that appeared to be moving in water. When the lid was opened, water sounds and music could be heard. The first page showed a school of fish swimming through the streets of a city, many wearing homburg hats. Some of the fish were mounted on magnets, which gave a three-dimensional effect and invited readers to move them around as they progressed through the story.

IMC in Action

Evaluation

Accenture initially sent 140 pieces to its narrow target audience. The mailing generated a 20 per cent response, far above the average. Another important aspect of the Shark mailing was that it integrated into the ongoing "Master of Design" campaign, which successfully repositioned Accenture as a leader in reengineering consulting services.

Think about it

Why do you think this execution was so successful? What elements of the execution separated it from most other direct mailing offers?

Source:
This case was adapted with permission from the Advertising and Marketing Effectiveness (AME) award-winning brief for Accenture prepared by the Wunderman Cato Johnson agency in Frankfurt, Germany.

Message design

The way in which the building elements of a message—e.g. text, visuals, sound—are chosen and combined is called the message design. Thus, choosing a framework is the decision about what kind of story to tell; choosing an appeal is about how to make the connection to the receiver; the design is how to realize all this. When you decide that humour is an appropriate appeal to apply, you still have to come up with a joke. Text, visuals and sound are the three main building blocks; the combination of them is called the "layout" of an advertisement. Other aspects of message design concern tone and style, and the use of endorsers.

Text

Whether copywriters apply their skills to a variety of MC functions or specialize in only one, they need to understand the similarities and differences in writing for print media and writing for electronic media. Writing publicity messages (whether print or electronic) presents special challenges to copywriters.

The goal of text-writing is to present the strategic idea in words that cajole and inspire—but most of all in words that get attention and linger in the memory. One device for creating a memorable impression is a slogan, which is *a clever phrase that serves as a reminder of a brand, company image, or campaign theme.* Philips summarized its renewed branding strategy in the slogan "Sense and simplicity" (see opening case Chapter 2).

Slogans, headlines, and other MC writing use catchy phrases. Catchy phrases are often humorous or clever. However, although humour can be desirable in copywriting, copywriters should be careful not to be *too* funny—that is, not to cross over any line that may make the ad offensive or sound too much like a punch line.

Writing for print

Print text is usually described as either display or body copy. Body copy is *the text of the brand message.* Display copy is *copy in a type size larger than that of the body copy and meant to entice readers into reading the body copy.* The terminology is the same for brochures and direct-mail pieces as for advertisements. In addition to the headline, which is *a line set in large type to get readers' attention and lead into the body copy,* other display copy includes picture captions and subheads, as well as underlines and overlines that either lead into the headline or expand on it, and slogans or tag lines that *wrap up the creative idea at the end of the message*. In general, the objectives in writing display copy are to grab attention, excite interest, build curiosity and get readers to spend time with the message (see colour insert B2).

To be effective, a headline must serve a set of purposes. Attracting attention is the foremost, but it must also engage the audience, explain the visual, lead the audience into the body copy, and cue the selling message. The average MC message has only a couple of seconds to capture a reader's attention.

Ideally, headlines present a complete selling idea. Research has found that, on average, three to five times as many people read the headline as read the body copy. So if the selling premise isn't clear in the headline, the message may be wasting the client's money. In outdoor posters or billboards the headline is the only copy, so it has to communicate, along with the visual, the entire message. The difficulty is that the headline needs to be short and succinct. The traditional notion is that short, one-line headlines are best but a second line is acceptable. In one study of over 2000 ads, most headlines averaged about eight words in length (see colour insert A1).[6]

Publicity writers also pay close attention to creating provocative, newsworthy headlines. The headline will determine how much attention an editor pays to the publicity release. If the editor doesn't find the headline interesting and engaging, the article is not likely to make it into print.

Finally, headlines, particularly in publicity writing, are used to showcase news. Consumers look for new products, new uses for old products, or improvements to old products. "Power words" that imply newness—such as *new, improved*, and *redesigned*—can increase readership and should be employed whenever applicable.

Captions are *verbal explanations of visuals*. Call-outs are *mini-captions positioned around an illustration to help explain or emphasize certain elements in an illustration or picture*. At the end of a printed piece may be found a tag line, which provides either a call to action—for example, instructions on how to respond—or a slogan that serves as a brand or campaign reminder cue. A tag line is often used to summarize, in a catchy way, a campaign's big idea. Brand identification information is typically showcased by a signature at the bottom of the piece. A signature can also be a logo, as in the case of Coca-Cola, whose familiar brand name appears in all planned messages in a distinctive Spencerian script (see colour insert B2).

Writing for electronic media

Most principles that are set up in the context of writing for print media hold true for radio and for television and other types of video, as well. Yet electronic media have some special dictates.

Radio copy has to be clearer than other kinds of copy. The listener cannot reread to find the antecedent of a pronoun, so what the pronoun refers to has to be immediately clear. Language is so full of homonyms (words that sound alike) that listeners can easily confuse the meaning of a word that does not have a clear or sufficient context. Think of the confusion that can result if a listener cannot tell whether a radio commercial is saying *cereal* or *serial*.

TV copy plays a different role from copy for print or radio. For radio the copy—and perhaps some sound effects—has to carry the message on its own whereas TV copy is just one, and perhaps not even the most important, carrier of the message. The role of words is different. In particular, in a TV context it will usually not be the words that catch the attention, but the visuals.

There is more to audio than just TV and radio commercials. Think about how a company answers the phone. How does that "brand voice" differ from the voices you hear when you call its competitors? Advanced speech-recognition technology is making it possible for a customer to have a personal, yet still automated, conversation with a company. Companies strive to make sure that the automated voice reflects the personality of the brand and that the voice system recognizes the emotional dimensions of conversations with customers. Also, the way in which callers are guided through a list of choices when calling a help desk has a strong impact on how the brand is perceived.

Visuals

Video uses the standard techniques of audio; however, its visuals can attract attention and describe something better than words can—by showing it. Video copywriters use action, music, sound effects, settings, casting, and special effects, all of which can add an element of drama to the message.

The word *visual* refers to any kind of art. In print advertising, the art usually consists of a photograph, a computer-generated image, or a hand-drawn illustration (see colour insert C12). In video, the art element may be live-action film, still photos, or animation.

The style of the art is also important. An intimate style uses a soft focus and close-up views. A documentary style portrays the scene without pictorial enhancements such as fancy editing. A dramatic style features unusual angles, distorted colour, fast-paced cuts, or blurred action images. Photos can also smack you right in the eyes or leave you laughing or crying (see colour insert B16).

A powerful visual tool that is sometimes overlooked is *white space*, which is the area in an ad, brochure, or other printed piece in which there are no words or visuals. The next time you are looking at a newspaper, compare the ads. The ads with the most white space are likely to be for luxurious brands or upscale retail stores. White space is an MC message luxury that communicates just that (see colour insert B5).

Typography—the typeface used to present the words in the message—has a design dimension and contributes to the style of the message. When artfully designed and crafted, a typeface—*a set of letters and numbers with a distinguishing design*—evokes a mood. Different typefaces convey different tones (formal, funny, regal, casual) and must be integrated with other elements of the brand message.

Sometimes the visual is not determined until the art director or designer actually "lays out" the ad (designs its look and locates its elements). Advertising managers and art directors often keep an extensive file, or morgue, of noteworthy ads, photos, and illustrations—to serve as idea ticklers. Brand messages use many standard subjects for visuals, both product related and image focused.

Sound

The final element of advertisements is sound, which clearly is not applicable for print advertisements. A major audio element is music, which is used in both radio and television commercials, as well as in corporate videos and the "hold music" you hear when you phone a company. When music is used as a background, its purpose is to help create an emotional tone for the message. Another way music is used is in jingles, which are *short songs that deliver a brand story in an easy-to-sing format*. Jingles are highly memorable, and they offer copywriters a way to repeat a line in a non-irritating way.

Well-known songs can be used to associate a brand with a musical style or period like Tele2 who uses the powerful song "Eye of the Tiger" by Survivor, simply to associate power and drive with the brand. Sometimes songs written for commercials can become a hit success themselves, for example the classic "I'd Like to Teach the World to Sing", which was written for Coca-Cola and then became a pop song.

Radio provides entertainment and news to listeners who are generally busy doing something else—driving, washing dishes, reading the paper, or even studying. To be heard, a message must be catchy and interesting. Radio listeners usually decide within seconds if they are going to pay attention. Therefore, to attract and hold listeners' attention, radio copy must be designed to break through the clutter of other environmental stimuli. To do this, radio copy also uses recognizable sounds—such as the sound of a pop tab opening, then the sound of pouring a drink over ice—to add aural imagery to the message. But keep in mind: intrusive, yes; offensive, no. An insensitive choice of words, an overzealous effort to attract listeners with irritating sounds (car horns, alarm clocks, screeching tyres), or a character that sounds too exotic, odd, or dumb can cause listener resentment and ultimately inattention.

Although text and visuals superficially play the lead roles in advertising, the support of sound should not be underestimated. Sounds and music in particular by themselves can change the meaning of an entire commercial. Just imagine a camera shot of a deserted island. Then think about the impact this shot makes when either a Dixieland type of enjoyable music is played (wow, this is an ideal place for a romantic holiday) or a threatening, heavy sounds kind of music (this is a place to leave quickly). Sport-shoes brand Asics had a strange kind of commercial with futuristic, almost enchanting music. The message was not very clear, but the ad certainly created much brand awareness at the time.

Tone and style

Tone and style are the result of how text, visuals and sounds are expressed. There are many ways in which a particular word can be pronounced, and the subtle differences are decisive for the tone and style of the advertisement. In marketing communication, **tone** refers to the *general atmosphere or manner of expression*. The tone is a cue about the nature of the message and the personality of the brand. Tone of voice—businesslike, solemn, angry, happy, cheering, fearful, sympathetic, frustrated—signals the appropriate emotional response. Tone can also imply conversation—an important dimension of relationship-focused communication.

The personality of the brand speaks through the planned messages, but the style of the language also signals the target audience. Ads with an "attitude", for example, are frequently targeted to young people, particularly the Generation X group, presumed to be anti-advertising. The tone surrounds the message and sets up audience expectations about the brand relationship. Something to remember when setting the tone of a brand message is that the typical marketing language of the strategy statements is rarely appropriate for a consumer audience. Sandra Moriarty warns against "strategy hypnosis".[7] She says that creative people have to understand the strategy, then move beyond it.

Some styles—pedantry, preachiness, and pomposity—don't work very well in marketing communication. Creative teams also try to avoid messages using the corporate "we" when it occurs in so-called brag-and-boast approaches. Negative messages, particularly those that patronize or put down the audience, are also ineffective. Another problem is insensitive or stereotyped images, such as those appearing in much detergent advertising.

Slang is another problem when targeting a younger audience. It is hard for ad folks—even if they are young—to get the nuances right when using slang in a commercial, but the biggest problem is that teen and urban street slang changes so fast that it is often out-of-date by the time the commercial is produced and runs. Should slang be avoided? It can be appropriate if used with sensitivity and tested carefully. Budweiser made slang work with its "Whassup?" line.

Endorsers

Many advertisements, in particular on television, radio and in print, show people in various kinds of relationship to the brand or product. A special kind of people featuring in advertising concerns endorsers. An **endorser** is a *character acting in support of the brand or product advertised*. Not all the people that appear in advertisements are endorsers; many of them just demonstrate the product, act in the dramatized story, are characters in mini-plays, etc.

Endorsers have a special role in the advertisement. The choice of endorsers is therefore an important decision that should not be taken lightly. An important decision is whether the endorser should be a celebrity or not. Choosing a celebrity has both advantages and disadvantages. Celebrities attract attention and associate their personality to the brand. The set of associations that celebrities evoke are automatically transferred to the brand by the mechanisms that are defined by the associative network model.

The disadvantages are that celebrities are expensive, and they live their own uncontrollable lives. This means that the sponsor—the brand that pays the celebrity for the endorsement—has no control over the actions of the celebrity in their private lives (see the IMC in Action box). Celebrities can become unpopular, may behave in ways that run counter to the interests of the sponsor, or can even be accused—or even convicted—of criminal activities. The popularity of Michael Jackson, once the chief endorser of Pepsi, is debatable at best. The story of Cybill Shepherd, a vegetarian endorsing beef, is a classic example. O.J. Simpson's accusation of murder is legendary. Furthermore, compared to celebrities, non-celebrity endorsers, usually unknown actors, have the advantage that they can play a character, perfectly suited and modelled to the needs of the sponsor. Sometimes such characters even reach celebrity status themselves.

Endorsers have to have three key characteristics: they have to be attractive, credible and they should match. Attractiveness in this context does not only refer to physical attractiveness, although that is part of the story. Also sheer fame can make an endorser attractive. Sportspeople are not typically attractive but base their attractiveness on their achievements. Celebrities usually reach high levels of fame, while non-celebrities can be chosen on the basis of physical appearance alone. The combination of fame and good looks wins the first prize, for both the sponsor and endorser for that matter, as the many lucrative contracts of David Beckham illustrate. Attractiveness primarily serves to—literally—attract the attention of the audience.

Credibility, on the other hand, is necessary to give conviction to the message displayed. Credibility can be based on two features: trustworthiness and expertise. Generally speaking, the trustworthiness of celebrity endorsers is deteriorating constantly. The audience is all too well aware of the fact that celebrities are paid vehicles to disseminate a message. In particular, when celebrities endorse many brands, their trustworthiness is at stake (see colour insert C9). On the other hand, expertise is inherent in the role celebrities play in real life. David Beckham endorsing Nike shoes is credible because he is an expert. Justine Henin playing tennis in an Adidas shirt is credible for the same reason, although her endorsement of Wilson tennis rackets is even more meaningful: a racket is a more important attribute for a tennis player than a shirt.

For non-celebrities it is more difficult to be perceived as credible. One tactic advertisers apply is to refer to the profession of the endorsers. Dog breeders have been used to endorse dog food like Pedigree. Another example is the prototypical white coat, suggesting professionalism—for example as a doctor, or as a scientist. Sun washing-machine tablets has used this approach extensively in a series of advertisements, and Calgon used the repairman, telling the equally stereotypical ignorant housewife that she essentially destroyed the heater of her washing machine herself by not using the protection of Calgon. But the problem with the non-celebrities remains. As the audience cannot deduce from other sources that the endorser—who is acting a role after all—has genuine expertise, credibility will remain relatively low.

Finally, the endorsement should match. Matching in this respect refers to two aspects: matching with the brand, and matching with the target audience. A match between celebrity endorser and brand is based on the inherent characteristics of both. This concept of matching rests in the associative network model as well. According to the match-up hypothesis, two entities are accepted to be connected when they match, which means that the two entities have a set of shared associations. When there is no match or a poor one, the consumer will not accept the connection between endorser and brand and the transfer of associations will not take place. Again consider David Beckham as an example. Beckham's endorsement of UK's Vodafone (when he was playing with Manchester United) was a good match; Beckham endorsing German Siemens after his transfer to Real Madrid would match less well. As non-celebrities do not bring a set of associations the concept of matching with the brand is less crucial. However, it should still be clear that there is not really a match when a dog breeder endorses cat food.

The second aspect of match refers to the link that is made to the target audience. Here, celebrities have both an advantage and a disadvantage. Many celebrities represent the aspiration levels of well-defined consumer groups. They match with those groups in the sense that they are recognized, accepted, and admired. But very often, and in particular with sports endorsers, there is also a group which rejects the celebrity. In sports where the intensity of competition is high, e.g. football, an endorsement may lead to a counter-reaction by the opponents. It is a moot point how serious this problem is but the problem may be exacerbated by the endorser's behaviour. When Eric Cantona, a one-time Manchester United player, endorsing Lipton IceTea, showed disrespect to the opponent's fans, this was taken up by all non-Manchester United fans as a statement. This was definitely not in the interest of the Lipton brand. It is less risky, therefore, to strive for matches with non-celebrities. Stereotypes have their role here. In Calgon's advertisement, the housewife is a stereotype to which everyone can relate. Don't we all have washing machines that we fear will break down? And how embarrassing it is to find that the reason is simple, and could have been prevented by using the right product? The stereotypical but characterless housewife in the commercial leaves room for every person using a washing machine. But how differently would we react if it was the machine of Mrs Victoria Beckham that had broken down?

The synergy of text, visuals and sound

Text, visuals and sound play different roles in the logic of a brand message. To illustrate how text, pictures and sound can work together, let us describe a commercial in detail. Champagne producers have tried to persuade people to drink champagne at times other than New Year's Eve. How would you break through this barrier, knowing that people may like the festiveness associated with champagne more than they like the taste? A campaign for Moët & Chandon uses the distinctive pop of the cork to announce times for small celebrations. Rather than focusing on holidays, the campaign shows two intriguing women lying on their backs in a field, an amorous couple in a dark café, a woman rising from a bathtub, and a woman and two men in a rowboat. All the characters become alert as they hear a sound—though the audience doesn't hear it (a technique designed to pique the viewers' interest—"What did those people all hear?"). The ad then uses a voice-over in which a woman asks in a sultry tone, "Is it possible for one sound to do more than break the silence?" The voice-over continues: "Can one sound be inherently French, yet transcend every language?" The spot ends with a visual of a Moët cork being shot toward the viewer, accompanied by an unmistakeable popping sound.

IMC in Action

Finding the right match: the risk of endorsers

The Swedish clothing company Hennes & Mauritz has made use of endorsers for many years. It communicates its brand by the use of two large advertising campaigns each year and some small ones in between. In these campaigns, H&M wants to create a positive and healthy image. Designers like Stella McCartney and Karl Lagerfeld work together with the company to develop the newest trends in clothing for the customers. H&M targets the young-minded, fashion-conscious consumer, aged 18 to 24. It offers hip and trendy clothing for an acceptable price in line with their business concept: "fashion and quality at the best price".

When H&M in 2005 decided to use model Kate Moss for their upcoming ad campaign for its new Stella McCartney line, it seemed to be a good idea. Kate Moss is an attractive woman. She communicates credibility to the target audience, because she is a fashion model and is associated with wearing the newest trends. She and H&M appeared to be a perfect match. However, in September 2005 the UK's *Daily Mirror* published a photo of Kate Moss sitting on a leather couch in a London recording studio, apparently snorting multiple lines of cocaine. This news was of course a big shock for H&M, but at first instance the company decided to give the model a "second chance". Kate Moss signed a written statement promising to remain "healthy, wholesome, and sound". However, in response to public opinion H&M reversed its position a couple of days later, because it did not want to be associated with any kind of drugs. This example illustrates one of the risks of using a celebrity as endorser. Fortunately for H&M, they decided early enough to stop the collaboration with Kate Moss and thus effectively protected their image.

Apart from companies that use different endorsers, one can also observe endorsers related to different brands. Consider the example of Anna Kournikova. This tennis babe earned about $10 million in 2002 and she is probably one of the richest women in sports, thanks to endorsements with companies like Adidas, Yonex, Berlei, Omega, and Lycos. In 2000 Anna Kournikova starred in the new campaign for Berlei's shock absorber sports bras range, and appeared in the highly successful "only the ball should bounce" billboard campaign. This campaign attracted particular attention, but her agents said that sports bras are an essential piece of sporting clothes for women. One year later, in March 2001, the Internet network Terra Lycos announced an endorsement deal with Anna Kournikova. The switch from sport to Internet may seem strange, but according to Terra Lycos' vice-president Steve Fund, she fits perfectly with Lycos. "Anna Kournikova is a perfect match for Lycos," he said. "She is a global superstar and her energy, appeal and hip image are what the Lycos brand is all about."

Apparently, Anna Kournikova's image fitted in with two different types of products as well as in two similar brands.

Think about it

What criteria would you use to decide on endorsements? What about the credibility of Anna Kournikova as endorser? Do you think Anna Kournikova is the appropriate endorser for Lycos?

Sources:
Karimi, S. (2006). "Review of H&M clothing stores. A Swedish brand quickly gains market in the US". www.associatedcontent.com/article/41425/review_of_hm_clothing_stores.html

www.hm.com

www.slate.com

http://advertising.about.com/od/kournikovaanna/

www.emailwire.com/cgi-bin/news/db.cgi?db=ads&uid=default&ID=1019&C1=Advertising&view_r ecords=1&full_view=1

Purnell, S. (2002). "The tennis racket", The Independent, *12 June 2002. Retrieved 11 October 2006, from www.findarticles.com/p/articles/mi_qn4158/is_20020612/ai_n12612594*

The copywriter wrote only two sentences, the visuals caught the attention (did you recognize the use of various appeals in the description?); the initial absence of sound proved to be the key to understanding the commercial. The challenge came in matching the sentences, in style and tone, to the visuals and sounds.

Print layout and design

In print media, "layout" refers to the arrangement of the elements making up an MC message: visuals, headlines, subheads, body copy, captions, trademarks, slogans, and signatures. During the layout process the creative team brings coherence to the visual message and uses style to help create meaning.

By arranging elements creatively—for example, surrounding the text with lines, boxes, shades, and colours—and relating elements to one another in size and proportion, the designer can enhance the message. The design principles of balance, proportion, and movement are guides for uniting images, type, colours, and qualities of the medium into a single communication.

In advertising there are a number of standard layouts. Traditionally, print ads scoring the highest recall have a poster-style format, and a single, dominant visual occupies between 60 and 70 per cent of the ad's total area. Some research shows that ads scoring in the top third for "stopping power" (getting attention) devote an average of 82 per cent of their space to the visual (see colour insert B1).

Figure 7-1 is a hierarchy-of-effects model of creative elements. As the figure indicates, in print messages the visuals and headline attract attention. Subheads and the lead (first) paragraph of body copy spark interest. Body copy and other elaboration devices such as boxes and supporting visuals help build credibility and stimulate desire. The closing paragraph and reminder information such as slogans and tag lines at the end of the piece prompt action. The closing may sometimes include a last line that functions as a call to action—it tells the target audience what to do or gives helpful information such as where the product might be found. Other action items at the end—the logo, slogan, tag line, signature—provide brand identity and reinforce the brand position (see colour insert A11).

Although it is important that the words and pictures work together in creative messages, it helps if the visual adds something to the words and the words extend the idea presented in the visual. If the visual is a literal translation of the words, the concept may be rather predictable, perhaps even boring. But a unique conjunction or juxtaposition of words and pictures results in synergy and creates a richer meaning than either element carries by itself (see colour insert B7).

Video and audio design

A video script is more complex than an audio script because it contains both audio and video instructions, but the principles underlying them are the same. In order to illustrate the visual ideas, a story board is used to provide a pictorial diagram of the scenes. A **story board** is *a series*

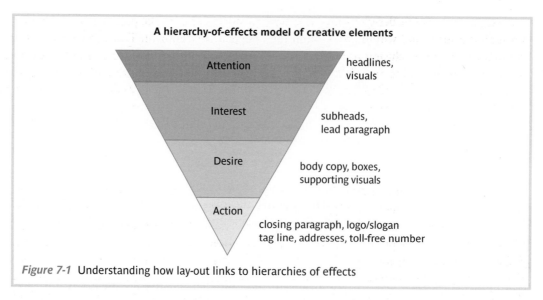

A hierarchy-of-effects model of creative elements

Attention — headlines, visuals

Interest — subheads, lead paragraph

Desire — body copy, boxes, supporting visuals

Action — closing paragraph, logo/slogan tag line, addresses, toll-free number

Figure 7-1 Understanding how lay-out links to hierarchies of effects

of key visuals and accompanying dialogue that explains a TV commercial. The story board co-ordinates the action with the dialogue by showing key frames with their associated audio track underneath the various scenes. Once a TV commercial is produced, photo boards are often made that are similar to story boards, the only difference being the use of photos of actual scenes rather than drawings of them.

The strength of video is its real-life believability and its cinematic qualities, which come from moving pictures and sound. A humorous example that also demonstrates the shock potential of video comes from London, England, where the Borough of Islington ran a public service commercial reminding dog owners to pick up after their pets. The commercial shows a man outside a Georgian home squatting in front of its wrought-iron fence with his pants down. The next shot shows a standard Islington street sign with the words "You Wouldn't". Next is a shot of the man pulling up his pants as a neighbour in a business suit walks by. Then comes a shot of street sign that reads "Don't Let Your Dog". Other commercials, like some of the better Nike commercials, are works of art themselves, and sometimes acclaimed to be a good reason to watch TV in their own right.[8]

Another strength of video that emerges in design and production is special effects. The power of the computer to create fantastic images is opening up new kinds of imagery for film, TV, and commercials. But, as noted before, the use of special effects can backfire: people tend to become more sceptical than ever about the claims of brands, despite efforts to substantiate these claims by visual proof.

Other MC design areas

"Everything communicates" was the message of Chapter 3. Hence, other touch points need the attention of creative designers as well, not only print, radio or TV advertising. Two of the most obvious touch points are exhibits and product packages. Website design is discussed in Chapter 9.

Exhibits

Exhibits, displays, and booths—particularly those used for trade shows—are exciting, visually intensive, three-dimensional formats requiring the creation of a much more complicated design concept than a two-dimensional print ad. All the brand-identity information needs to be easily observable, but exhibit designers may also have to worry about traffic patterns as people move through the space and within and around the designed environment. Trade show exhibits are complicated by the inclusion of message sources such as video screens and computer systems, as well as people staffing and visiting the booth. Most exhibits go beyond sending messages in words and pictures by allowing for actual product demonstration. Models, mock-ups, and actual product demonstrations are showcased to the extent space permits. It is very much a hands-on environment, and the messages are enhanced by the credibility that comes from face-to-face communication.

Packaging

A package, especially for consumer goods, is an important communication vehicle. Its front panel or label defines the product category, identifies the brand, delivers short copy points, and functions as the "last ad a customer sees" before making a purchase decision. A package is more than just a physical container for a product. It reflects the brand image and delivers visual impact. The objective is to generate nearly instantaneous and universal recognition. Consistency of design—between the package design and other brand-design elements—delivers a key visual message. Coca-Cola's hourglass-shaped bottle remained as a brand icon even when the company switched from glass to plastic bottles. Pringles potato crisps made their package their point of differentiation. Chapter 11 tells more about packaging.

The consistency challenge

A challenge in brand communication is to develop MC messages that are strategically consistent with the brand position and image. The more MC messages there are, the harder it is to keep the messages consistent. There are two levels of consistency. *One-voice, one-look consistency* applies primarily to campaigns. *Strategic consistency* applies to all brand messages, not just MC messages.

Executional consistency: one voice, one look

One-voice, one-look consistency is *the type of consistency that occurs when all advertising, sales promotion, sponsorships, publicity, direct response, packaging, and other MC messages have the same look, sound, and feel.* One-voice, one-look consistency indicates that everything is integrated at the execution level. For example, when Philips launched their "Sense and Simplicity" campaign, this was accompanied by a major effort in other MC areas as well, such as their website and packaging. A creative tag line of the campaign was that the high-tech products Philips was delivering should be as simple as the box in which they are delivered. All TV comercials concluded with the same two-tone sound effect. Also, the objective was to have one agency taking care of all MC activities worldwide.

Consistency can be created in an IMC campaign by mirroring the style of a message from one execution to another or from one medium to another. Some of the practices that marketers use to achieve one voice and one look include the following:

- **Visual connections:** a similar format in layout and art style (Absolut vodka ads), or colours (Vodafone red, also on the shirts of Manchester United), as well as the key visual element.
- **Verbal connections:** words, such as slogans, tag lines, and jingles, that can be repeated over and over (De Beers's "Diamonds are forever", Nike's "Just do it").
- **Audio connections:** sounds that work like words to anchor an association, such as the Intel five-tone jingle.

- **Continuing characters:** the same characters (Arnott's—see the opening case) or a continuing endorser (or type of endorser, e.g. L'Oréal is consistently using long-haired beautiful actresses) or a spokesperson character (Ronald McDonald).
- **Symbols and logos:** McDonald's Golden Arches, Adidas's three stripes.
- **Continuity in settings:** the place in which a brand story is set—for example, the Western imagery in the Marlboro campaign.
- **Emotional connections:** Arnott's used emotion as a link among its various executions from ads to magazine stories.
- **Thematic continuity:** simplicity is the key theme of Philips MC activities in all respects.

One-voice, one-look consistency is difficult to achieve when a lot of different departments and MC agencies are creating MC messages about a brand. For example, an IMC brand audit of a major beverage brand found that the marketing services and brand managers were working against 10 different MC objectives. Not surprisingly, a content analysis of a year's worth of planned brand messages found some messages promising quality, some refreshment, and others fun. Because the messages to the same audience were so inconsistent, customers and prospects did not know what to expect from the brand (and poor sales was the result).

A research study into the integration between print advertising and websites looked at message strategy (the objective, promise, or most important message) and at executional consistency (visible in logo, copy and support, product picture, colours, key visual, slogan, and spokesperson). The authors found less integration at the strategy level: only 39 per cent of the 186 brands studied showed consistency in the objectives and the promise between the print ads and the website. There was more consistency, however, at the executional level: 83 per cent of the 186 brands consistently displayed the logo in both print ads and the website.

One of the main things a company can do to achieve "one voice, one look" is to have a cross-functional team of MC managers agree on message standards and then periodically do a content analysis of all the company's recently produced MC messages. The easiest way to do a content analysis is to post all the recent MC messages on a wall and simply step back and see to what extent they are similar.

Strategic consistency

Because companies must communicate with a variety of stakeholders besides customers, it is important to use **strategic consistency**,[9] which is *the type of consistency that occurs when MC messages differ but every message contains certain core elements*. No matter who the audience is, the brand name and logo should be integrated into all messages to leverage the brand identity the company has created for itself. For example, in selling educational toys, the message to parents will be different from the one aimed at the kids. This does not mean, however, that there cannot be certain consistencies in both sets of messages. The brand's personality, positioning, and identification cues, for example, should be consistent, but the individualized selling propositions may differ—for kids: "exciting fun"; for parents: "they learn while playing".

Changing the packaging or even the slogan of a brand over time always creates a consistency dilemma. On the one hand, companies want to have their brands easily recognized and leverage the identity cues they have established. On the other hand, avoiding appearing "old-fashioned" often requires changing the looks of the brand name and its logo.

To achieve strategic consistency, marketers must walk a fine line between tailoring different messages to various target audiences and maintaining a consistent brand image and position. A McDonald's exterior is reasonably easy to recognize worldwide; however, the company uses its interiors to connect with local communities. In Germany, McDonald's serves beer; in Japan, sushi; in France, wine. But everywhere, there is no mistaking McDonald's for any other brand. Why? McDonald's consistently offers a basic standard menu, in spite of the regional additions, and the cost–value ratio of its offerings is predictably always very good.

As Figure 7-2 illustrates, consistency in MC message executions is only the tip of the consistency iceberg. The deeper you go in analysing the brand and corporate strategies, the more important consistency becomes throughout the organization's operations. The foundation on which all communication is built is corporate culture, mission, and core values. What comes next are the various marketing elements of brand strategy: product and service performance, brand identity, and brand position.

Corporate culture means *the shared values and beliefs that structure the way an organization's employees work and interact with each other and with other stakeholders*—or, less formally, "the way we do business around here." A **corporate mission** is *what a company stands for and represents*. A corporate mission is a critical integrative element because coming up with a consistent message is impossible if no one in the company knows what the company stands for. At the marketing level, consistency is signalled by the way the marketing communication reflects the product and service performance messages. IMC recognizes there is more to integration than just having all the pieces in a campaign look alike. IMC impacts a company's total business operations, not just its marketing communication messages.

The consistency triangle

The consistency triangle shown in Figure 7-3 provides a simple way to analyse how all of a company's brand messages relate to each other. Strategic consistency exists when a brand does what it says, from the customer's perspective, and when what the brand says and does are reinforced by what others say about it. In terms of Figure 7-3:

- *"Say" messages* are MC messages that set expectations.

- *"Do" messages* are messages delivered by the company's product and service messages. They are conveyed by how products actually perform, what they actually cost, how convenient they are to get and use, and the brand's supporting services.

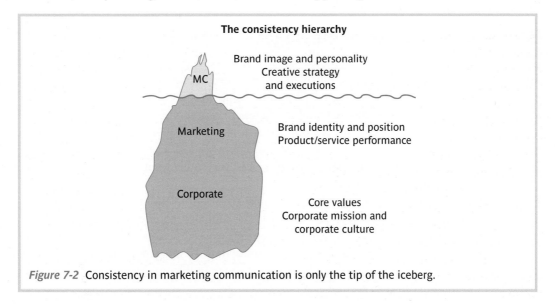

The consistency hierarchy

Brand image and personality
Creative strategy
and executions

MC

Marketing

Brand identity and position
Product/service performance

Corporate

Core values
Corporate mission and
corporate culture

Figure 7-2 Consistency in marketing communication is only the tip of the iceberg.

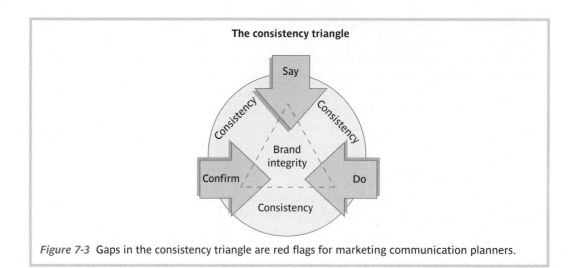

Figure 7-3 Gaps in the consistency triangle are red flags for marketing communication planners.

- *"Confirm" messages* are messages from other people who either criticize or praise the brand or company. Personal and positive third-party communication is considerably more persuasive than most MC brand messages.

The "say" messages delivered by marketing communication must be consistent with the "do" messages about how products and services perform, as well as with what others "confirm" about the brand. Gaps between any of these message types threaten brand relationships.

When an airline puts "special handling" tags on the bags of its frequent flyers, it seems to be promising these customers that they will be the first ones to receive their luggage upon landing. If frequent flyers find that their tagged bags arrive no sooner than anyone else's on the flight, then there is a gap between the "say" and "do" messages. If consistency gaps occur too often or become too large, they will make the brand image seem unfocused. From the customer's point of view, strategic consistency means easy recognition of, and trust in, the brand, as well as "no negative surprises".

A final note: a mess of messages

The full array of MC message executions—all the pieces and parts, bits and bytes—create a mess of messages if they are not carefully planned, executed, and monitored. The communication complexity involved and the reason why most companies are fighting to maintain some measure of consistency in their many brand messages are easy to see. As the chief strategist for General Motors once explained: "Every point of customer contact—from printed material to products to after-sale service—must present the customer with a clear and harmonious impression of the company, its products, and its services. And this unified outward image is a reflection of the company's internal consistency."

Consistency is a means to an end. That end is positive brand relationships. Success at creating this level of consistency is what made the Arnott's campaign an effective message strategy across a variety of executions. The integrated campaign worked because it told a brand story about a meaningful relationship that contributed to building an image for Arnott's as a caring brand. A creative campaign that successfully develops a memorable product image can not only build a new brand but can turn around a troubled one.

🔑 Key terms

appeals The cue that should make the advertisement work.

body copy The text of the brand message.

call-outs Mini-captions positioned around an illustration to help explain or emphasize certain elements in an illustration or picture.

captions Verbal explanations of visuals.

comparative advertising Advertising in which one brand explicitly—or sometimes implicitly—is compared to a competitor.

corporate culture The shared values and beliefs that structure the way an organization's employees work and interact with each other and with other stakeholders.

corporate mission What a company stands for and represents.

display copy Copy in a type size larger than that of the body copy and meant to entice readers into reading the body copy.

endorser A character acting in support of the brand or product advertised.

execution framework Specification of the format or approach to be used to tell the brand story.

headline A line set in large type to get readers' attention and lead into the body copy.

jingle A short song that delivers a brand story in an easy-to-sing format.

message design The way in which the building elements of a message—e.g. text, visuals, sound—are chosen and combined.

message execution The format of a completed MC message, such as an advertisement, brochure, or package label.

one-voice, one-look consistency The type of consistency that occurs when all advertising, sales promotion, sponsorships, publicity, direct response, packaging, and other MC messages have the same look, sound, and feel.

slogan A clever phrase that serves as a reminder of a brand, company image, or campaign theme.

story board A series of key visuals and accompanying dialogue that explains a TV commercial.

strategic consistency The type of consistency that occurs when MC messages differ but every message contains certain core elements.

tag line A line that wraps up the creative idea at the end of the message.

tone The general atmosphere or manner of expression.

typeface A set of letters and numbers with a distinguishing design.

Check the key points

Key point 1: Message executions

a   What are the four key decision areas in brand message execution?

b   Illustrate each of the eight common message story formats with a real life example. Explain how it works.

c   Find an example of comparative advertising. What is compared? Is the other brand explicitly mentioned, or only implicitly referred to?

Key point 2: Message appeals

a   What appeal is applied in each of the messages you found for point b. of key point 1 above? What other appeals does this brand use in other messages?

b   Bring a humorous ad to class and check if everyone finds the appeal equally funny.

c   What is the difference between nudity and eroticism? Illustrate this with an example.

Key point 3: Message design

a   What is the purpose of a headline?

b   How do display copy and body copy differ?

c   Find a copy-heavy print ad. Make a copy of it, and on the copy in red ink identify the headline and the body copy. If any of the following elements appear in the ad, identify them as well: captions, subheads, overlines, underlines, tag lines, call-out quotes. Finally, circle the brand-identification elements, and label them as a logo or signature.

d   What is a script? How do scripts for audio and video media differ?

e   Find an ad that you think is particularly well written and one that isn't. Compare the two, and explain your evaluation.

f   In what ways must a celebrity endorser match? Why? What other two characteristics are desirable for endorsers?

g   Find an example of a celebrity endorser that was not well chosen in your opinion.

Key point 4: Message consistency

a   What is one-voice, one-look consistency? How does it differ from strategic consistency?

b   Collect all the communication materials you can find from a local bank. Analyse them and your experiences with the bank in terms of the consistency triangle. Can you identify any gaps between the "say", "do" and "confirm" messages?

c   Find a product or service that demonstrates inconsistency in the materials developed by the various marketing communication areas. Redesign the materials using a one-voice, one-look approach to create more consistency in these planned messages. Explain your changes.

Chapter Challenge

Writing assignment

Write a text for a radio commercial for your favourite pizza restaurant. Start by thinking what the message is you want to get through. Next choose an execution framework and an appeal. Decide on the other elements that have to find a place in the execution of the framework (sounds?) and then write a text. Finally, make sure that the text will fit in the 30 seconds a radio commercial maximally takes.

Research assignment

Find a series of humorous advertisements, preferably from the same brand. Split your class in two groups and show one group the advertisements to assess the degree to which these ads are considered funny. Then show the ads to the other group and measure to what extent the brand was recognized and remembered, and if the key message was retrieved. Compare the results: were the funniest ads the most or least effective?

Presentation assignment

Take an example of a feel-good advertisement. Redesign this advertisement into a feel-bad format, so that the same message about the brand is conveyed. Present your solution to class and let the class assess how well you succeeded, and what appeal was more convincing.

Notes

1. James Surowiecki, "The Power of the Prize", *The New Yorker*, 18 and 25 June (double issue), p. 67.

2. Cillit Bang shows a nice set of examples on its website www.cillitbang.co.uk. Note how thin the line is between the testimonial and the authorative frameworks.

3. This BMW campaign is described in detail in the opening case of Chapter 9.

4. Shi Zhang, Frank R. Kardes and Maria L. Cronley, "Comparative Advertising: Effects of Structural Alignability on Target Brand Evaluations", *Journal of Consumer Psychology*, 2002, pp. 303–11.

5. Catanescu, Codruta and Gail Tom, "Types of Humor in Television and Magazine Advertising", *Review of Business*, 2001, pp. 92–5.

6. Murray Raphel, "Ad Techniques: Off with the Head", *Bank Marketing*, February 1988, pp. 54–5.

7. Sandra Moriarty, *Creative Advertising*, 2nd ed. (Englewood Cliffs, NJ: Prentice-Hall, 1991), p. 172.

8. "Best Reason for Even TiVo Users to Watch a Commercial", *Time*, 6 January 2003, p. 142.

9. Tom Duncan and Sandra Moriarty, *Driving Brand Value: Using Integrated Marketing to Manage Profitable Shareholder Relationships* (New York: McGraw-Hill, 1997), pp. 69–94.

Further reading

Chingching, Chang (2007) "The Relative Effectiveness of Comparative and Non-Comparative Advertising", *Journal of Advertising*, Vol. 36–1, pp. 21–35.

Garretson, Judith A. and Scot Burton (2005) "The Role of Spokescharacters as Advertisement and Package Cues in Integrated Marketing Communications", *Journal of Marketing*, Vol. 69–4, pp. 118–32.

Kellaris, James J. and Thomas W. Cline (2007) "Humor and ad memorability: On the contributions of humor expectancy, relevancy, and need for humor", *Psychology & Marketing*, Vol. 24–6, pp. 497–509.

Maciejewski, Jeffrey J. (2004) "Is the Use of Sexual and Fear Appeals Ethical? A Moral Evaluation By Generation Y College Students", *Journal of Current Issues & Research in Advertising*, Vol. 26–2, pp. 97–105.

Maciejewski, Jeffrey J. (2005) "From Bikinis to Basal Cell Carcinoma: Advertising Practitioners' Moral Assessment of Advertising Content", *Journal of Current Issues & Research in Advertising*, Vol. 27–2, pp. 107–15.

Schwaiger, Manfred, Carsten Rennhak, Charles R. Taylor and Hugh M. Cannon (2007) "Can Comparative Advertising Be Effective in Germany? A Tale of Two Campaigns", *Journal of Advertising Research*, Vol. 47–1, pp. 2–13.

Media characteristics

CHAPTER PERSPECTIVE
Connecting with customers

Over the years the word *media* has become tightly associated with the word *advertising*, leading many to think that media are used only for advertising. Nothing could be further from the truth! All marketing communication messages are carried by some form of media. Brand publicity, sales-promotion offers, direct-response offers, and sponsorships all use various media to deliver messages to customers. These media include not only the obvious and traditional advertising media—radio, TV, outdoor boards and posters, newspapers, and magazines—but also the Internet, telephone, mail services, coffee mugs, signs, company vehicles and cars, package labels, Yellow Pages, company stationery and business cards, pens, T-shirts, and matchbook covers. These are all *created touch points* (Chapter 3), and they offer a marketer the most control over the way the message connects with the customer.

Another myth is that the media's only job is to provide opportunity for message exposure. The reality is that companies are not satisfied just to have their messages sent or shown to target audiences. They demand that media add value to messages by increasing their impact on attitudes and behaviours; and this can happen only when media are viewed as touch points that create connections with customers.

In IMC the role of media is not only to deliver brand messages but also to help create, sustain, and strengthen brand relationships by connecting companies and customers. The difference between delivery and connection is significant. *To deliver* means "to take something to a person or place"; *to connect* means "to join together". Delivery is only the first step in connecting: it opens the door to touching a customer in a meaningful way with a brand message.

Heineken: repositioning beer in Italy[1]

In June, 1999, the Brand Team[2] of the J Walter Thompson advertising agency in Milan was preparing the launch of a new communications campaign for Heineken beer in Italy. The agency had been handling the Heineken account since 1992 and had succeeded in helping the company to elevate the brand's image to one of the premium beers in Italy and to secure a position as market leader in terms of sales volume. In 1998 Heineken decided that it wanted to gain popularity among a younger adult target market, the 18–24-year-olds. The task for the team had been to design an integrated communications programme that would be able to build on the strengths of the past campaigns yet be more relevant to this new customer base. Today they would review the results of the team's efforts together with the Heineken marketing managers.

The Heineken company

Few people are aware of the fact that modern beer originated in Belgium near the region of Flanders. The Flanders formula incorporated hops for the first time and became a staple of the European diet between the fourteenth and nineteenth centuries.

The Heineken brewery was founded in 1863 in Amsterdam by Gerard Heineken. His goal was to make a high-quality beer and, in only 30 years, he succeeded in making it one of the best-selling beers in the country. For the next century the company maintained its roots in the Netherlands but grew globally. By the 1990s, in fact, Heineken was sold in more than 170 countries and the easily recognized green bottles had become one of the leading brands of beer worldwide.[3]

Beer in Italy

In contrast with the situation in many of its European neighbours where per capita beer consumption reaches as high as 150 litres (Germany) and 139 litres (Denmark) per year (see Figure 1), beer has not traditionally been part of the national culture in Italy. In the 1970s, however, this trend began to change. The younger generations increasingly viewed wine as old-fashioned and became attracted by the exciting advertising campaigns of the large beer producers. The faster lifestyle also favoured beer consumption as a beverage to accompany a quick sandwich at lunch. Yet although a beer culture did begin to develop in Italy during the 1970s and 1980s, for most consumers the choice of brand continued to be based more on image than on an appreciation of the quality of the product itself.

The beer market in Italy consisted of four basic segments:

1 Saving (lowest price, retail segment)
2 Standard lagers
3 Premium lagers (light and clear beer, high quality, higher price; may be drunk alone or with meals)
4 Speciality beers (ales, stouts and bitters; not to accompany meals)

Imports accounted for 25 per cent of beer consumed in Italy and most of this came from other European countries due to the absence of duties and tariffs on beer imported from other countries within the EU. Many international brewers, such as Heineken, also produced locally under licence or through subsidiaries.

Year	Germany	UK	Spain	France	Holland	Belgium	Italy	Denmark
1950	36	85	2	22	11	118	3	62
1956	66	81	6	27	16	113	3	67
1960	91	85	11	35	24	112	4	72
1970	141	103	38	41	57	132	11	107
1973	147	112	43	44	74	144	16	125
1976	151	120	48	49	84	138	14	130
1980	146	118	53	44	86	131	17	131
1983	149	111	59	44	88	128	21	139
1988	144	111	70	39	83	120	22	126
1990	143	110	72	42	90	122	23	127

Figure 1 European beer consumption (litre per capita).
Source: "Note on the Global Beer Industry", Case 9B03M012, Richard Ivey School of Business, 2003.

The turnaround of the Heineken brand in Italy

Heineken entered the Italian market in 1974 through the acquisition of a local brewery, Birra Dreher SpA in Trieste. This acquisition was in line with the strategy of the company to enter new markets through majority interests in local breweries that were responsible for both the production and marketing of its beer in their national markets. This acquisition was followed by another one in 1996 which brought another local brand, Birra Moretti, into the Heineken network. Between the 1970s and the 1990s Heineken's market share in Italy grew through both the sales of the Heineken brand as well as its locally produced brands and the distribution of other imported beers that were part of the international group.[4]

In terms of volume, by 1992 the sales of Heineken beer were in line with those of its strongest domestic competitor (Nastro Azzurro) and greater than those of the other non-Italian brands (Tuborg, Kronenburg, Ceres, etc). In terms of image, however, Heineken was lagging behind many of these same competitors. Heineken was known as an international beer but it was perceived as a beer to be consumed in pizza parlours or bought at the supermarket to take home (savings segment). It was not yet positioned in the bar and restaurant segment nor did it fit clearly into any particular cultural experience captured by many of the other international beer brands in the Italian market such as Corona (Mexican food) or Guinness (Irish pubs).

At this point, the managers of Heineken Italy decided to try to reposition the brand. They hired the JWT agency with a clear mandate to raise the brand image of Heineken and to help establish a position for the beer in new channels of distribution. The target market was identified as adults between the ages of 25 and 36 in the major urban areas of Italy. The specific objectives of the campaign were to:

1 Create a strong and distinctive personality for the brand.

2 Get Heineken into selected bars and restaurants in the HORECA sector with an innovative programme of communications.

3 Develop a new media plan that would include non-traditional channels for beer advertising.

The first task that the agency faced was finding a theme and a personality for the brand in the Italian market that would resonate with this target market. The decision was made for a music theme ("Heineken is music"), but they still had to find the right genre of music to associate with the brand. The agency found the solution in jazz.

This decision was important for several reasons. First, it allowed the brand to take on a new and unique personality that was not tied to any particular "ethnic" identity. No other brand of beer was associated with music, and jazz was the music of choice in a wide variety of public events and social occasions. It was a broad category with a high-quality image and a direct appeal to the sophisticated target market that Heineken aimed to attract. Second, it opened the door to a whole set of integrated marketing communication tools that the agency could use to create this new personality for the brand.

The next step was to create a new advertising campaign through which the world of jazz music would become strongly associated with Heineken. Ads were filmed in jazz clubs around Italy with well-known jazz musicians performing a jingle composed by Sting. The pay-off read: "Where there is feeling, there is Heineken!" As these ads ran on the major television networks, Heineken also organized a series of music events to support and enhance the effectiveness of the message of the campaign. Live jazz concerts at selected clubs were sponsored by Heineken with the use of posters, glasses and other accessories to reinforce the brand image by the public.

The culmination of the campaign came in the summer of 1993 when Heineken became the official sponsor of the Umbria Jazz Festival, the largest and best-known jazz festival in Italy. This sponsorship not only gave credibility to the link between jazz and Heineken, but allowed the campaign to build a greater level of awareness. Television and magazine ads promoting the event were prepared and the Heineken logo and recognizable green colour could be found throughout the venues and materials used to publicize the festival.

In the years that followed, Heineken and JWT continued these initiatives to increase the visibility of the brand on a national level and to establish a strong bond with its core target based on music, and particularly jazz music. Heineken and its agency used several kinds of communication tools including classical advertising, event sponsorship,[5] ads to publicize events, sales promotions and merchandising. The campaign was successful at raising the image of Heineken as a quality beer for social occasions. Moreover, the results of a brand equity study conducted by Heineken during these years clearly showed that the brand had literally become associated with the word "music". By 1998 Heineken had become a leading brand within the "premium" segment of the market and its market share in the HORECA sector rose significantly. While the sales of beer in Italy grew by 6.8 per cent between 1992 and 1999, Heineken's sales increased by 20.5 per cent.

Notes

[1] This case was written by Pamela Adams. It is intended to be used as the basis for class discussion rather than to illustrate either effective or ineffective handling of a management situation. No part of this case may be copied, stored, transmitted, reproduced or distributed in any form whatsoever without the permission of the author.

[2] The Brand Teams of the JWT agency include the Account, the Planner and the Creative.

[3] In 2001, the four largest brewers in the world were Anheuser Busch (US), Heineken (Netherlands), AmBev (Brazil) and Interbrew (Netherlands). Heineken, like most of these large brewers, grew beyond its borders by building or purchasing brewing operations in other countries.

[4] These included Von Wunster, McFarland, Murphy's, Adelscott, Sans Souci, Ichnusa and Amstel.

[5] Event sponsorship was not limited to jazz music at this point, but included such events as the Heineken Jammin' Festivals and specials on television, music programmes on major networks with well-known music personalities such as Nick the Night Fly, as well as the sponsorship of huge international concerts such as those of Sting, Brian Adams, Simple Minds, Phil Collins, and Pino Daniele.

The media business

The selection and use of media can be just as creative as the writing of a publicity release or the creating of a magazine ad. Media planners used to be subservient to the creative team. In IMC, however, media people work alongside the creative people in developing campaigns. The media not only deliver brand messages but can influence a brand's image because they operate as a created touch point. This is the difference between simply delivering an MC message and facilitating the connection of the brand, both emotionally and cognitively, with customers and prospects. Status and luxury brands, for example, often place ads in such magazines as *Cosmopolitan, Vanity Fair* and *Esquire*. Marketers hope that the upscale editorial environment will reinforce the brands' own upmarket images, and they believe that the high production quality of magazine advertising sends an appropriate message. Media can add to or subtract from a brand message, depending on which media are used and in what way.

One of the primary ways in which brands are built is through **media exposure**, which refers to *the number of people who see, read, or hear a medium.* Media exposure, however, does not guarantee *message* exposure. While media planners try to gain the most cost-effective media exposure they can for a brand, it is up to the individual brand messages to attract attention, change attitudes, and motivate behaviour. As shown in Figure 8-1, most brand messages

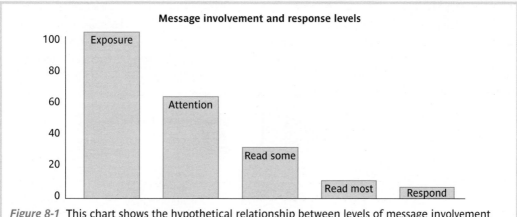

Figure 8-1 This chart shows the hypothetical relationship between levels of message involvement and responses to messages.

generate a response from only a small percentage of those who are exposed to the message. The challenge is to find media whose audiences are most likely to respond and thus narrow the difference between the number exposed (which is what media prices are based on) and the number who respond (which is the return on the media investment).

One of the biggest changes in marketing communication over the past two decades has been media fragmentation and proliferation. They have been a mixed blessing, giving marketers and their agencies more choices in how to reach customers but, at the same time, spreading customers' attention over so many different media that it is much more of a challenge for a company to reach all of its targeted prospects and customers. Despite the increase in media options, however, it is important to note that four media—TV, newspapers, direct mail, and telemarketing—account for over two-thirds of media spending.

Another problem is media clutter. So many brand messages are being delivered by so many different types of message delivery systems that media planners are being more and more creative in trying to find unusual ways to reach their target audiences.[1] Media planners have even launched the idea to project brand logos on the moon: an ultimately extreme example (but don't underestimate the creativity of media-men).[2]

Media classifications

The plural noun *media* is an umbrella term for all types of print, broadcast, out-of-home, and interactive communication (see Figure 8-2). The singular noun *medium* refers to each specific type (TV is a medium, radio is a medium, newspapers are a medium, and so on). A specific publication, TV channel, or radio station is a *media vehicle*. Examples of media vehicles are the *Financial Times*, Eurosport, *BusinessWeek*, and the Google portal on the Internet. When a company "buys media", it is really buying access to the audiences of specific media vehicles.

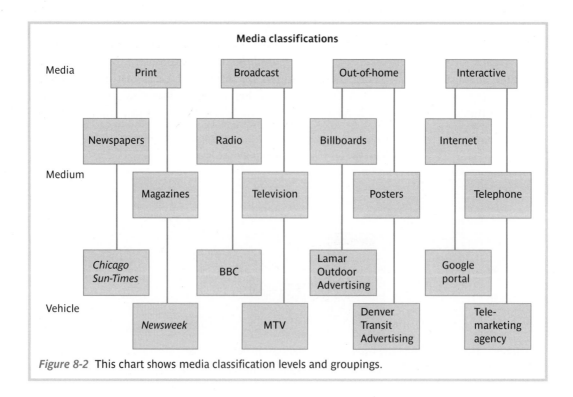

Figure 8-2 This chart shows media classification levels and groupings.

Another way to classify media is by reach and characteristic of media. Here, media planners use such terms as *mass media, niche media, addressable media,* and *interactive media.*[3]

Mass media are *communication channels through which messages may be sent to the "masses"—large, diverse audiences.* **Niche media** are *communication channels through which messages are sent to audiences with a distinct commonality.* Eurosport is a niche medium that reaches sports fans in Europe.

The distinction between mass and niche media is not always easy to make. Although Eurosport is a niche medium, the audience it reaches is still diverse and heterogeneous. The key factor that distinguishes mass media from niche media is that the latter have a clear core characteristic. Eurosport only broadcasts sports events, MTV is all about music and youth culture, TV 5 Europe reaches Francophone audiences. This is the knowledge that advertisers reckon with. Thus, a media planner's primary concern should not be how a medium is labelled but rather to what extent its audience, as defined by its main characteristic, would be interested in what a brand has to offer. Subject, content, and distribution patterns are indicators of an audience's interests.

Media that carry messages to identifiable customers or prospects are referred to as **addressable media** because all can be used to send brand messages to specific geographic and electronic addresses. Addressable media include the Internet (see Chapter 9), postal mail, and the telephone. Addressable media are used primarily to communicate with current customers or with carefully selected prospects.

Two-way media allowing both companies and customers to send and receive messages are called **interactive media**. The benefit of interactive media such as the telephone, the Internet, and salespeople is that they allow an instant exchange of information to take place. More important, they make it possible for a customer to contact a company.

Media intrusiveness

Because of the high level of commercial message clutter, companies need all the help they can get in attracting attention to their messages. Media planners know that media vary in their degree of intrusiveness (see Figure 8-3). The most intrusive medium is personal selling because

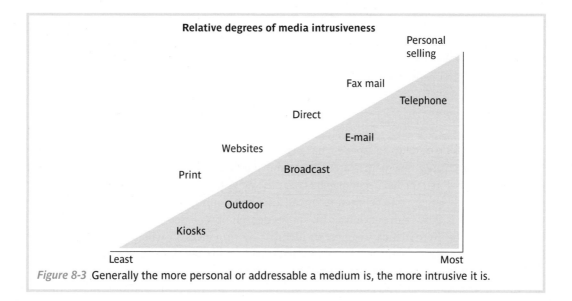

Relative degrees of media intrusiveness

Figure 8-3 Generally the more personal or addressable a medium is, the more intrusive it is.

the sales representative's presence demands attention. The least intrusive media is print because users choose when and to what extent to use these media. The more intrusive a medium is, generally speaking, the more it can be personalized, but also the more costly it is to use.

Admittedly, the word *intrusive* has negative connotations. If a message is too disruptive, it is not exactly something that helps build brand relationships. Companies often find themselves in an awkward position. They know it is to their advantage to get brand messages to customers and prospects, but they also know that many of these messages may not be welcome. There are several ways to minimize the downside of intrusiveness. One is to choose media whose target audience is interested in the product category. Research has shown that one of the benefits of specialized magazines is that readers enjoy learning about new products from the advertising. To help get attention and not be intrusive is one of the reasons why events, sponsorships, and product placements in movies and TV shows have become so popular. Also, giving customers the option to opt-in for receiving brand information means that when MC messages are sent, they are not unexpected and therefore not seen as intrusive.

Media strengths and weaknesses

The strengths and weaknesses of each medium are relevant to any type of brand messages they carry, regardless of the type of marketing communication message—everything from traditional advertising to publicity resulting from a news release. Table 8-1 summarizes the strengths and weaknesses of each medium discussed in this chapter and the next. Terms that may be unfamiliar to you are defined in each discussion.

This chapter further discusses three media types in considerable detail: print, broadcast and out-of-home. Interactive media are treated in the next chapter.

Print media

The print media include newspapers and magazines, directories, mail, brochures, packaging, and all other forms of message delivery that are produced by printing words or images on paper or some other material, such as balloons, T-shirts, caps, and pens. Print messages are relatively permanent compared to broadcast messages, which are fleeting. In this case, *permanence* means that the message can be kept (clipped and saved, for example) and revisited. Sales brochures and product literature (sometimes called *collateral materials*) are designed to assist sales representatives in making calls and taking orders. Training materials may also be available in printed form. Annual reports are a good example of more elaborate publications that are meant to be kept, at least for a year.

Newspapers

Although readership of daily newspapers has been in a slow decline over the last 25 years relative to population increases, newspapers are still a major medium. Generally speaking, three types of newspapers exist. First, the local newspapers cover the news from relatively small regions. What a region is depends largely on the circumstances. In some countries, regions are defined by the major cities and their surroundings. In more densely populated countries like Belgium, Denmark and the Netherlands, regions are defined by provinces in which multiple cities are found. National papers clearly are defined by national boundaries. A special branch of national newspapers are the free circulation papers like *Metro* in Sweden and other countries. The fact that their distribution system is based on free sampling, mainly in railway stations, makes them a

Medium	Strengths	Weaknesses
Newspapers	■ Reader education and income ■ Tangible ■ Reader habit, loyalty, involvement ■ Short lead time ■ Low production cost ■ High one-time reach ■ Good for detailed copy	■ Poor reproduction, especially colour ■ Decreasing readership ■ Clutter ■ Media waste (mass audience)
Magazines	■ Audience selectivity ■ Expertise environment ■ High-quality reproduction ■ Long life ■ High credibility	■ Long lead time ■ Low "mass" reach ■ Costly production ■ Low frequency (weekly, monthly, or quarterly)
Television	■ Impact: sight, sound, motion ■ Good builder of reach ■ Local, national and international ■ Targeted cable channels	■ Broad audience ■ High production cost ■ Intrusive ■ Messages short-lived
Radio	■ Audience selectivity ■ "Theatre of the mind" ■ Frequency builder ■ Relatively low product cost	■ Background (low attention) ■ Low reach ■ Sound only ■ Messages short-lived
Outdoor	■ Localized ■ Frequency builder ■ Directional signage	■ Low attention ■ Short exposure time ■ Poor reputation (visual pollution) ■ Zoning restrictions
Telephone	■ Personalized ■ Real-time interaction ■ Attention getting ■ Measurable results	■ Costly ■ Ugly image ■ Intrusive
Internet	■ Mass and addressable ■ Can be personalized ■ Extremely low cost ■ Can be interactive	■ Clutter ■ Limited reach ■ Limited creative options

Table 8-1 Strengths and weaknesses of major media

separate category. The reach—what audience reads the newspapers—differs for these three types of newspapers, and that defines their usability for advertising purposes. Despite internationalization tendencies European newspapers are scarce. Two examples are the *Financial Times*, and the *Wall Street Journal*—Europe edition. These newspapers are targeted at the business communities, making them of limited use for true mass media purposes. The absence of truly European journals can be attributed to cultural differences, language barriers, and other

L'Oréal and their integrated media mix

L'Oréal, the world's largest cosmetics company, has 17 distinct brands that are distributed all over the world. The company has classified its brands into four categories: consumer products (e.g. Maybelline NY), professional products (Redken), luxury products (Biotherm) and active cosmetics (Vichy). Because of the many brands focusing on different target groups, the use of different media to promote the brands is essential.

In 1998 L'Oréal set its promotion budget to $1.25 billion, almost equal to that of Coca-Cola. With the support of this budget, the company developed a unique promotion policy for all its brands. Brands which were sold in a mass market were advertised and promoted with TV ads that were broadcast internationally. The unique promotion policy for different brands was underlined by the fact that L'Oréal used the tag line: "Because I'm worth it" only for hair care products; Maybelline and other brands did not use this slogan. The tag line: "We're worth it too" was used in a campaign for kid's shampoo. In this campaign, the company targeted the children by advertising on the Cartoon Network channel. Next to TV ads, L'Oréal preferred to advertise in the magazines read by the hip and young consumers—for example in *Elle*. In health and fitness magazines, printed ads were used to promote ColorSpa for men.

A few years ago, in common with many other companies at that time, L'Oréal realized that advertising in the traditional way was not enough. In 2004 the company launched an innovative online campaign, which was supported by outdoor and press advertisement. To promote the Colour Pulse brand (for hair colouring), consumers could use e-vouchers, SMS entry, and be part of an online auction. After online registration, the e-vouchers (worth £1) had to be downloaded from L'Oréal's website, allowing consumers to get a refund when purchasing Colour Pulse. Moreover, consumers could bid online in an auction to win one of a number of prizes. Registered users were allowed to make one bid a day, either via the website or via SMS. To stimulate the purchase of Colour Pulse even further, consumers were informed that they could receive five extra free bids a day when they entered the code found on the product online.

L'Oréal extended the interactive way of dealing with its customers in 2006 to the adoption of a new form of mobile marketing. In this form of advertising the viewers are looking at competitions which are promoted in TV ads. They can vote for the correct answer and in a TV ad later in the campaign, the winners are announced. This encourages consumers to tune in later in the campaign. The use of mobile marketing is an addition to the company's use of traditional media. While TV ads are more appropriate for the mass public, L'Oréal targets the biggest fans of their products by interactive online campaigns and mobile marketing. Why? Because we are worth it!

Think about it

Have you ever used e-vouchers or have you taken part in online auctions? In your country, by the use of which medium is the L'Oréal brand communicated most? To what extent do you think that the different media used complement each other?

Sources:
www.loreal.com
New Media Age *(2006) 'Fox, L'Oréal and MFI adopt mobile-linked TV ad spots'. http://search.ebscohost.com/*
Pearse, J. *(2004) 'L'Oréal launches integrated digital Colour Pulse campaign'. http://search.ebscohost.com/*
Verma, M. *(2005) 'L'Oréal's global branding strategy'. ICFAI Knowledge centre. www.ecch.com*

factors that define the heterogeneity of Europe. Even Europe-wide initiatives like *Metro* publish national versions of their format, making them essentially national newspapers.

Strengths and weaknesses of newspapers

Newspapers boast a number of strengths. They reach a mass audience which is not defined only by circulation numbers as many copies are read by multiple readers. Like magazine readers, newspaper readers are above average in education and income. The fact that newspapers are tangible allows customers and prospects to be exposed to brand messages when and where they prefer, and to read and reread ads at their own pace for better comprehension.

Because most newspaper circulation is daily, frequency can be quickly built among those who regularly read the newspaper. The average newspaper reader spends 29 minutes a day reading a weekday edition, even more reading a weekend or Sunday edition.[4] The newspaper has a designated place in subscribers' daily routines. The fact that newspapers offer a constant supply of information and entertainment means that most subscribers have an emotional involvement with their daily newspaper, which is a benefit to advertisers. Finally, daily newspapers provide marketers with flexibility and short lead times. Newspapers have a quick production process, which allows a company to change the content of its advertising up to 24 or 48 hours (depending on the newspaper) before the paper is published. Interestingly, research has shown that newspaper readers often consider advertising to be news, too.

Newspapers have several weaknesses. Their average life span is only one day. They are printed on low-quality paper. Consequently, when ink is applied, it spreads, which is why newspapers have relatively poor reproduction qualities for any kind of graphics. Clutter is also a problem in newspapers. Not only does a brand message compete with other ads for attention, but it must also compete with all the editorial content. Perhaps the most serious weakness, from an IMC perspective, is that newspapers are a mass medium. Even though an advertiser can quasi-target a message by requesting that it appear in a special-topic section (such as sports or travel), the cost of the space is based on the paper's total circulation. This means that there can be a high percentage of media waste.

Magazines

Magazines are classified by frequency of publication (weekly, monthly, bimonthly, quarterly) and by type of audience (consumer, business, trade, and professional). Magazines are also classified by how they are distributed. *Magazines that sell subscriptions* are classified as **paid-circulation publications**. Even these publications, though, receive approximately three-quarters of their income from advertising sales. In contrast, **controlled-circulation publications** are *trade, industrial, and organizational magazines that are distributed free to those working in a given subject area or affiliated with a given organization.* These magazines make up for the lack of subscription income by selling ads, selling their database of subscribers, and in some cases sponsoring annual trade shows. Although there are some good controlled-circulation publications, most media planners prefer buying space in paid-circulation magazines. Logic tells us that people are more likely to spend more time reading a magazine they have paid for than one they have received for free.

Like newspapers most magazines are nationally focused but international magazines are slightly more common. *BusinessWeek* is perhaps the most internationally oriented magazine, again (as with the *Financial Times* mentioned above) targeted at business communities. Other examples are *Cosmopolitan*, or *Marie Claire*. Despite their international availability most of these magazines come in national editions. Advertisements in these magazines are nevertheless mainly by international, high-status brands.

Strengths and weaknesses of magazines

As mentioned earlier, an advantage of magazines is their high-quality reproduction. These higher production values, however, mean that production takes longer than in newspapers, so more lead time is required to place ads in a magazine (one to three months depending on the magazine). Because most magazines are subject-specific, one of their greatest strengths is their audience selectivity. Subject-specific magazines are seen as being authorities on their respective subject areas. Therefore, brands that advertise in them can benefit from this expertise halo, an added value for a brand message.

Like newspapers, magazines are tangible and thus allow readers to read them at their own pace. Magazines also have strong reader involvement because readers (of paid-circulation magazines) have selected and paid for their magazines, a strong indication that they are interested in a magazine's subject and will spend time with the magazine. Magazines are even more permanent than newspapers because they are kept much longer and are frequently picked up and read more than once, providing additional opportunities for a brand message to be seen, read, and have an effect.

A feature of magazines that many marketers particularly like is the ability to do a **split run**, *a process in which a marketer places one ad in one half of a magazine's circulation and a different ad in the other half.* This allows marketers to test one offer, headline, or creative approach against another. The only thing that is required is that both ads contain a response device such as a toll-free number, coupon, or order form that is coded so that the marketer can tell which ad produced a higher response.

Magazines, too, have weaknesses that concern advertisers. Although highly targeted, most magazines have relatively limited reach of a brand's target audience. This is more true of consumer than of B2B magazines. Magazines also have a long lead time, up to three months before publication. Consequently, magazines do not offer the scheduling flexibility of newspapers and some other media. Another drawback is their lack of frequency. Many appear only once a month or even less often, especially industry magazines and trade journals. Finally, magazine ads are more costly to produce than newspaper ads (but far less expensive than TV commercials).

Broadcast media

As broadcast media, radio and television have several characteristics in common. On average, people spend 85 per cent of their media time with broadcast media and only 15 per cent with print media.[5] This statistic might seem to indicate that broadcast is the best place for brand messages. Keep in mind, however, that people do other things while listening to radio and watching TV, especially when commercials are on.[6]

Radio and television are broadcast via various transmission channels. Airwaves, cable, or satellite distribution are the most common, and they vary in technical aspects and quality. Although the quality issue is of some relevance to brand communicators, the really important issue is that the speedy technical advances also open doors in the direction of interactive communication. Today, television watchers for example are asked to vote for *Idols*-like contests by telephone, and some radio programmes ask their listeners to go to websites, respond in a guest book and messages therein are communicated back during the programme. Indeed, the computer is slowly taking over the functions of the traditional channels, or rather traditional and modern channels are integrating. Interactive television is technically possible, with the traditional television screen largely functioning as a computer terminal, the remote control being used as a keyboard/mouse, as can be experienced in many hotel rooms.

Both radio and television accept news releases; video news releases, especially, can be effective in generating brand publicity. Local stations often cover special events—such as a grand opening of a store or a sports event—by doing on-site broadcasts; thus broadcast media can be helpful in supporting event marketing programmes. Compared to print messages, however, broadcast messages are fleeting. Once a message appears, it is gone until it runs again. (People rarely record commercials in order to watch them over and over.) The fleeting nature of broadcast media is one reason why cable news channels like CNN, or sports channels like Eurosport, have been so successful—they can provide programming 24 hours a day for people who want to tune in for a short while to catch the latest update.

Broadcast commercials are more intrusive than brand messages in print media. Programming and commercials are presented in a stream, one after another. Readers of print media can select stories and ads in whatever order they want and completely ignore whole sections. With broadcast media, this is difficult to do. The remote control and video or DVD recorder make it possible to time-shift programmes and zip past commercials;[7] but the presentation form is still linear, and viewers and listeners have to attend to the information in the order in which it is presented.

Exposure to broadcast media is measured in rating points. A **rating point** is *1 per cent of a communication vehicle's coverage area that has been exposed to a broadcast programme.* If the Champions League final is said to have had a 40 rating in Germany, this means that during an average 15-minute segment of the programme, 40 per cent of all German households were tuned in. At the local level, a radio or TV programme that has, for example, 3 per cent of the households in its market tuned in is said to have a 3 rating (in that broadcast coverage area).

Broadcast ratings are based on a communication vehicle's coverage area, or **marketing universe**, which is *a specified target profile within a geographical area.* This universe can be defined however a marketer wants to define it: all households in the Paris metro area, adults nationwide, or women aged 25 to 49 in Sweden.

Although the price charged for broadcast time is based on ratings, media planners must remember that ratings tell only what percentage of households within an area are tuned to a certain TV or radio programme. Ratings are not a measure of the number of people paying attention to commercials. Media exposure does not equal message exposure. For broadcast media, actual message exposure is only 25 to 50 per cent of programme exposure.[8]

Strengths and weaknesses of radio

Radio is called "theatre of the mind" because listeners must provide their own mental visuals for the words, sound effects, and music they hear. Listeners create mental pictures not only for programming content but also for commercials. Such a high level of mental involvement happens, however, only when the programming or commercial messages are attention getting and the words and sounds are rich in imagery.

Station programming formats provide radio with its most important strength—selectivity. As with magazines, when an audience has a common interest, it is relatively easy for media planners to match the audience to a brand's audience profile. For example, the audience for a golden-oldies station is much older than the audience for a Top 40 station and has different wants and needs. All-news and classical formats have audiences that skew higher in education and income than most other formats.

As with newspapers, there is a short lead time for preparing and running a low-budget radio commercial. A radio spot can be written and produced in a couple of days and placed into a station's schedule in less than a week. Radio spots with custom-written music, special sound effects, and well-known talent, however, can take a couple of months to arrange and produce.

Like TV, radio is intrusive, which is both a strength, and a weakness. On the one hand, intrusiveness is a strength because radio presents brand messages whether the audience wants to hear them or not. On the other hand, some people find the fact that radio does this offensive, and many have conditioned themselves to ignore the messages.

Radio's other limitations are that it has no visuals and is fleeting. Another serious limitation is the fact that radio is used as background entertainment by people who are doing other things. Finally, even with sophisticated audience measurement techniques, it is difficult to determine what percentage of brand messages is actually heard.

Strengths and weaknesses of television

Because TV is so dynamic (due to its ability to carry sound and moving visuals), it is often considered the prestige medium for marketing communication. When retailers consider taking on a new line of products, they often want to know to what extent this line will be promoted on TV.

A major limitation of using TV, especially for small brands, is high production costs. Lead times for TV can also be a limitation, especially at the national level. The best programmes and time slots are often sold four to six months in advance. Another limitation of TV is clutter, both because of content, and the presence of other commercials competing for attention. A **commercial pod**, which is *the commercial break in a TV programme*, can carry 10 or more different brand messages. Although a commonly expressed opinion is that commercials are annoying, irritating, and sometimes even debilitating, many people also realize that commercials are a fair price to pay for being able to watch TV. Many people use commercial pods to do other things, e.g. make some coffee; however, it is remarkable that most consumers know commercials they say they never watch.

Out-of-home media

In addition to print and broadcast, another large group of media are the **out-of-home media**. Billboards and transit posters are two of the most common categories of out-of-home media. Others include theatre and video ads, product placements in movies, aerial advertising, electronic kiosks, ads in elevators or bathroom stalls, banner displays on automated teller machines (ATMs), chalk-and-stencil sidewalk messages, placards on shopping carts—the list could go on and on. Posters and small digital screens are making it possible to reach people almost anywhere they go, and particularly in situations where they have nothing else to do, as when they are riding on a bus.

Outdoor advertising

Outdoor advertising dates back at least to the Roman Empire, when commercial signs were painted on city walls. In modern times, as cars and highways took over the landscape, large signs along highways and streets became message-delivery points. Today the outdoor advertising industry remains strong and profitable. Exploiting the concept of creating effective brand contact points, out-of-home message delivery includes a wide range of locations where brand messages can be posted. Besides traditional outdoor boards, outside signage includes signs on trucks and shopping bags; even uniforms serve as vehicles for brand messages. These are the media we encounter as we go about our daily business.

Sloggi

Sloggi, part of The Triumph International Group, is an underwear brand that has used outdoor advertising extensively since its launch in 1979. The company started by developing ladies' underwear, followed in 1991 by Sloggi For Men. Nowadays, Sloggi is targeting the younger customer, because of the fashionable styles and the comfort one gets from wearing Sloggi underwear.

When advertising underwear, it is not unusual to depict scantily dressed people, since underwear is associated with a touch of sexiness. Sloggi is known for its billboards on which it communicates the brand to the mass public. In 2002 it started with the advertising campaign "Sloggi Bums". On large billboards women were shown from behind, wearing only Sloggi briefs. As expected, most drivers slowed down as they passed the billboards. In this way, the short exposure effect of billboards was avoided ... at least for men! This turned out to be the beginning of a long-running advertising approach.

The Sloggi Bums advertising campaign continued in 2003 and the company again challenged the tolerance of the mass public. A giant billboard featured four models wearing only high heels and G-strings with the slogan "It's string time!". While many men's hearts were beating, the first complaints were not long in coming. In Leeds (UK), for example, where Sloggi placed billboards near to mosques, there were protests from Muslims. Complaints were submitted to the Advertising Standards Authority, who ordered Sloggi to remove all the billboards near to mosques. Interestingly enough, the ASA decided against banning all the Sloggi billboards in the rest of the country, simply because there were no complaints apart from those connected with mosques. Sloggi responded by saying that they would avoid placing similar posters in sensitive sites in the future.

Following the billboards offensive, in 2004 Sloggi came up with another brilliant idea for outdoor advertising: the Sloggi Balloon. The balloon is shaped like a rugby ball and printed all over with a model in her underwear. It can even ascend and descend three times faster than an average balloon (whether that is demonstrating a product feature is unclear, however). A special team, Team Sloggi, is in charge of taking the balloon to racing events around Europe and of brand communication.

After billboards and the Sloggi Balloon, the company continued to use outdoor media—in a third way: posters on trucks. At the end of June 2005 a number of lorries were used to support awareness of Sloggi in the UK's major cities. Driving the trucks on busy streets each day exposed many shoppers to the brand. Logically, the campaign attracted a lot of attention. What should you do when you see ten almost naked women driving by?

Think about it

Do you think that Sloggi communicates its brand effectively by the use of daring posters? What are the advantages and disadvantages of outdoor advertising in comparison with other media? In how far is the Sloggi campaign affected by these disadvantages? Would the campaigns described be (legally) possible in your country? Do you consider them ethically acceptable? Also consider the impact on a driver's concentration.

Sources:
www.theasiannews.co.uk/news/s/191/191248_not_near_the_mosque.html
www.triumph.com/uk/downloads/history.pdf
http://commercial-archive.com/106244.php
www.roadads.co.uk/campaign_sloggi.htm

Advertisers commonly purchase space from public transit authorities. Posters appear on (and inside) buses, subway trains, and taxis, as well as in bus shelters and subway stations (see the IMC in Action box). Other place-based media include shopping malls, stores, health clubs, and libraries, as well as community, student, and senior centres. Posters inside a conveyance or waiting place generally have a captive audience that can spend some time with a message, so those posters are designed to deliver more complex messages.

One of the newest attempts to attract attention to advertising posters (such as those found at bus stops and in subways) is to arm them with sound tracks that deliver short brand messages and atomizers that spray brand-related scents. Proctor & Gamble, for example, used posters to advertise its new Head & Shoulders shampoo, which is billed as "citrus fresh". Pushing a button on the poster activates a whiff of the citrus fresh scent.[9] The benefit of these posters is greater message involvement and, at least for a while, more word-of-mouth discussion. The downside is the cost, which is nearly five times as much as that for a regular poster.

One of the strengths of outdoor advertising is that it is a good way to extend reach and, even more so, extend frequency of a brand message. Outdoor boards also provide geographical flexibility for targeting. Outdoor boards are sometimes used for teaser campaigns, particularly in support of a new-product launch.

Another advantage of outdoor media is that they can attract people with certain commonalties. People attending tennis tournaments obviously have an interest in sports. People in airline terminals are more likely than the average population to be businesspeople or vacation travellers. When advertisers use transit media, the challenge is to select communication vehicles whose audience demographics most closely match those of the brand's target audience. Outdoor boards are used to keep established brands top-of-mind, and their primary function is as a brand reminder. They are also widely used to provide directions: "Shell at next exit". For the most part, outdoor boards are used for consumer brands.

The limitations of outdoor boards are numerous. Outdoor boards have "passing" exposure: most people who are exposed are passing by, often at fairly high speeds! This fact, plus the fact that outdoor boards must fight for attention with all the other visual stimuli that surround them, means they must carry simple yet highly attention-getting messages. The more visual the message is, the more impact an outdoor board will have. Another limitation is that, when used extensively, the messages may suffer from wear-out, as customers ignore boards they have seen several times before.

Outdoor's biggest limitation is its negative perception. Many people consider billboards as nothing more than visual clutter. Environmentalists have referred to outdoor advertising as "visual pollution on a stick".[10]

In these days of marketing accountability, another limitation is the difficulty of measuring the effectiveness of outdoor boards. Most outdoor campaigns are part of larger media plans, and it is next to impossible to break out the incremental impact of outdoor messages. Many people passing by in cars never see or read the posted messages. Most companies that sell outdoor advertising keep detailed case histories showing impact on sales. Media planners must interpret these cases carefully, though, before assuming that the results for one brand will transfer to another brand and marketing situation.

Cinema and video

Besides selling tickets and food, cinemas can generate revenue by running *commercials before movies*, called trailers. Yet these communication vehicles have some inherent problems. Targeting other than by type of movie—action, comedy, or drama—is difficult. Further, people have not paid to see the commercials. As noted above, television commercials are often accepted as a means to pay for the programming, but in the cinema the audience has paid money directly: why be bothered by a set of trailers? On the other hand, it seems an accepted fact that commercials are part of the show: and sometimes an appreciated one too, especially since many trailers are mini-movies themselves.

The advantages of movie-theatre commercials include the captive audience and the lack of clutter. A half-dozen or so commercials presented within a two-hour period in a cinema encounter far less clutter than 60 or more messages appearing within the same time period on television. Moviegoers in the UK may sit through as much as 20 minutes of advertising before the feature film starts.

Videocassette and DVD producers have found that commercials on rented movies can reach a mass audience. Video is playing an increasingly important role in message delivery for both consumer and B2B brands. Unlike cinemas, which still tend primarily to run brand messages for movies only—previews or trailers—rental videos are carrying more and more messages for non-movie products. According to one study, two-thirds of the people who rent videos resent the presence of commercials, yet over half reported that they watched the commercials.[11]

Another type of video advertising is the product video produced by a company as an individual infomercial. Nearly every major brand has a product video, a video catalogue, or a CD-ROM to augment the efforts of its sales staff and to use for prospecting. Many car manufacturers, for example, produce videos of new models that let people take virtual test drives on their televisions at home. These test-drive videos are advertised in the conventional way and then sent to individuals who request them. Their overall cost is extremely high when production and distribution are added together. Yet their impact is much greater than that of a typical television commercial, and the high cost may be justified by the positive reactions of high-potential prospects. Pay-out, or impact on sales, can be easily determined because there is a record of those who received the videos.

Non-traditional media

Non-traditional media—hot-air balloons, pavement painting, cubicle doors in public toilets, painted buses and cars (see colour insert B16), disposable coffee-cup holders (java jackets), mousepads, ATM screens, race cars, rolling billboards pulled through city streets—are increasingly attracting the attention of media people. A company in Paris places ads on the small tables used by sidewalk cafés and bars. The company provides the tables for free, making its money from selling the advertising space. There are dozens of ways that creative people find to carry their messages. In all these situations three variables have to be balanced. One is the cost, the second is effectiveness in reach, and the third is the effectiveness in getting the message through. Effectiveness in reach means that the question must be asked: who are likely to see this message, and how likely is it that they will notice the message? Effectiveness in delivering the message means that the likeliness of receivers of the message understanding it must be assessed. This is the case with all messages, but with non-traditional media, the question in what circumstances people receive the message is crucial.

Although non-traditional media may never achieve the status of major media forms, they should be considered for use in narrowly targeted programmes. The challenge is to use non-traditional media when they fit strategically into a media mix and not merely because they are different. According to the director of out-of-home and non-traditional media at BBDO, these media have several limitations: lack of audience measurement, equipment failure (such as breakdowns of recorders supplying video messages in elevators), and high production and operating costs.[12]

Non-traditional media are frequently used in **guerrilla marketing**, *a marketing approach that reaches people in unconventional ways*—in the streets or in other unexpected places. The idea behind this in-your-face marketing is to extend the impact by creating buzz; the creative delivery of the message has talk value.

Product placement

In Steven Spielberg's 1993 movie *Jurassic Park*, there were more than 1000 marketing and product tie-ins. **Product placement** is *paid verbal or visual brand exposure in entertainment programming*. For years, movie producers took care not to show brand names on the screen. As times changed, both marketers and producers realized that product placement could be an effective means of sending brand messages. Many moviegoers remained unaware of the practice for some time; a situation that has changed and seems to be accepted by the audience. Although product placement is often associated with movies, the biggest showcase for placements is actually popular TV sitcoms. Another form is placements in video games. For example in racing games, the cars may carry brand names and even the boards around the circuit can be used.

Product placements differ in the way they appear. There are three such ways: the brand identifier (name, logo, or any other means by which the brand is identified) may be shown, the brand may be mentioned, or both occur. Research shows that the visual way is most effective.[13] A second factor that influences the effectiveness is the way the placement is related to the plot. In ideal cases the placement is perceived as a natural element in the story, which the episode could not do without. In other instances it is all too obvious that a placement is bought-in: the story could very well do without the placement.

Product placement often results in prominent exposure. In the James Bond movie *The World Is Not Enough* the BMW sports car model Z28 was launched with a starring role. Several scenes had close-ups of Bond driving the car, leaving no question as to the brand (see colour insert C2).

There are two major advantages with product placement. One is that the audience cannot skip the placement. It is integrated in the story; zipping it, or zapping away is not possible. The second advantage is that the brand or product is shown in a natural situation: product usage can be shown, advantages can be emphasized. Another advantage is that the use of brands is seen as natural. In real life people use brands, so why should people in movies not use brands? One research showed that the use of billboards of real brands instead of fictive brands was appreciated by players of a video game.[14]

Disadvantages are in the first place that the brand may remain unnoticed. This is a specific form of clutter: the viewer is watching the story and will pay insufficient attention to the products and brands that are used. Furthermore, the brands run the risk of the director's cut. Movie makers want to retain autonomy of their product and may decide—even in very late stages of the production process—to eliminate certain scenes from the movie. When a Reebok ad was cut from the movie *Jerry Maguire*, the sneaker company sued Sony for violating the terms of the product-placement agreement. The placement had been the centrepiece of a planned Reebok retail promotion that subsequently had to be dumped.[15]

How product placements help in building brands is further discussed in Chapter 11.

A final note: connectivity and creativity

All too often media are seen as just the carrier of the message. Nothing is farther from the truth. There is more than just a point in Marshal McLuhan's famous words: the medium is the message. As was discussed in this chapter, many key issues are related to the choice of the medium: target audiences, reach, intrusiveness (both in its beneficial and detrimental meaning), effectiveness. The choice of the right medium together with the issue of scheduling (discussed in Chapter 10) is one of the key decisions in IMC planning, nothing less.

One way to appreciate this point is to recall the importance of the noise factor, described in Chapter 3. Noise can have a devastating effect on the efforts of brand message creators to communicate. Noise is particularly relevant in the choice of media. Clutter is a form of noise: the detraction caused by content in the surrounding of the brand message, or by other commercial messages all influence the effectiveness of the message. Reaching the wrong audiences is a matter of noise: those people to which the message is not targeted may have difficulty in understanding the message because they have the wrong decoding scheme. The eventual interpretation of the message is unpredictable. Lack of attention is a form of noise. Choosing a medium based on the attention that people may pay to the message will determine the chances of a right interpretation. An ad in a trade magazine will get a greater degree of attention than a product placement.

So, communication is not only interesting in its creative elements. It is also a matter of choosing the right media to communicate the results of creative outbursts. As this chapter has shown to a lot of creativity can also be put in, selecting ways to communicate the message—that is:, to create a connection with the audience.

🔑 Key terms

addressable media Media that carry messages to identifiable customers or prospects.

commercial pod The commercial break in a TV programme.

controlled-circulation publications Trade, industrial, and organizational magazines that are distributed free to those working in a given subject area or affiliated with a given organization.

guerrilla marketing A marketing approach that reaches people in unconventional ways.

interactive media Two-way media allowing both companies and customers to send and receive messages.

marketing universe A specified target profile within a geographical area.

mass media Communication channels through which messages may be sent to the "masses"—large, diverse audiences.

media exposure The number of people who see, read, or hear a medium.

niche media Communication channels through which messages are sent to audiences with a distinct commonality.

out-of-home media Communication vehicles that the target audience sees or uses away from home.

paid-circulation publications Magazines that sell subscriptions.

product placement Paid verbal or visual brand exposure in entertainment programming.

rating point 1 per cent of a communication vehicle's coverage area that has been exposed to a broadcast programme.

split run A process in which a marketer places one ad in one half of a magazine's circulation and a different ad in the other half.

trailers Commercials that run before movies.

Check the key points

Key point 1: Media classifications

a   What are the four general types of media?

b   Explain what the following sentence means: "Media exposure does not guarantee message exposure."

c   What does each of the different types of media sell? On which media do advertisers spend the most money?

d   Explain the difference between a medium and a media vehicle. Give examples of each.

e   What is the difference between mass media and niche media? Between mass media and addressable media? Between addressable media and interactive media?

f   Why is intrusiveness a problem for some one-way media? Give an example from your own experience of a highly intrusive message, and describe your response to it.

Key point 2: Print media

a   List the various forms of print media.

b   Compare the strengths and weaknesses of newspapers and magazines.

c   What are some of the advantages and disadvantages of advertising in the Yellow Pages?

d   You are designing a marketing communication programme for a restaurant near your campus. Would you recommend any print media in your advertising plan? Why or why not?

Key point 3: Broadcast media

a   Explain the concept of image transfer. Give an example of a brand message that you have heard that benefits from image transfer.

b   Compare the strengths and weaknesses of radio and television.

c   You are designing a marketing communication programme for a restaurant near your campus. Would you recommend using any broadcast media? Why or why not?

Key point 4: Out-of-home media

a   Describe the different forms of outdoor boards.

b   What are the greatest strengths and weaknesses of outdoor boards?

c   What problems are associated with cinema- and video-related commercial messages?

d   List and describe some of the non-traditional media, and discuss their role in an overall MC campaign.

e   Explain product placement and what it brings to a brand.

f   You are designing a marketing communication programme for a restaurant near your campus. Would you recommend any out-of-home media? Why or why not?

Chapter Challenge

Writing assignment

Inspect copies of the three types of newspapers identified: local papers, national papers and free circulation papers. What advertisements do they contain? Analyse the differences not only in terms of advertisers, but also in terms of contents: do the ads differ in terms of messages, formats, appeals, etc.?

Presentation assignment

Choose two college-age friends, and develop a media diary for each one. Take them through a typical day, and ask them what they see, read, view, watch, or listen to. Then consult with your parents or two other adults, and develop media diaries for them. Compare and contrast the two sets of diaries. Develop a presentation for your classmates that explains how the media usage habits of these two groups of people differ.

Internet assignment

Check out your favourite gaming site. How many of the games have product placements? How many placements are there in such games? Marketers claim such placements add reality to the game. Do you agree? Also check out some of your PlayStation, X-Box or Gamecube games. What kind of brands do you typically see in there? How far do you think this practice of placements in videogames can stretch?

Notes

[1] Jonathan Bond and Richard Kirshenbaum, *Under the Radar* (New York: Wiley, 1998).

[2] This idea was discussed on http://advertisingindustrynewswire.com/2006/04/23/27_225316.

[3] Tom Duncan and Sandra Moriarty, *Driving Brand Value: Using Integrated Marketing to Manage Profitable Stakeholder Relationships* (New York: McGraw-Hill, 1997), pp. 102–3.

[4] Television Advertising Bureau, as cited on TVBasics website, July 2000.

[5] Radio Advertising Bureau, www.rab.com, June 2000.

[6] "Why big audiences don't always mean big gains for advertisers", Mark Ritson, *Marketing* (UK), 10 March 2002. Comparable research in the Netherlands in 2005 showed the same results.

[7] Philips announced in 2006 that they had invented a technique so that zipping would not be possible any more.

[8] *Dimensions '98* (Media Dynamics, 1998), p. 335.

[9] Erin White, "Advertisers Hope Fragrant Posters Are Nothing to Sniff At", *Wall Street Journal*, 10 October 2002, p. B1.

[10] *No Logo*, Naomi Klein, (Flamingo, 2000)

[11] Scot Hume, "Consumers Pan Ads on Video Movies", *Advertising Age*, 13 November 2000, p. 40.

[12] Rebecca Gardyn, "Moving Targets", *American Demographics*, October 2000, www.americandemographics.com.

[13] Cristel Antonie Russell, "Investigating the Effectiveness of Product Placements in Television

Shows: The Role of Modality and Plot Connection Congruence on Brand Memory and Attitude", *Journal of Consumer Research*, December 2002, Vol. 29 Issue 3, pp. 306–18.

[14] Michelle R. Nelson, *Journal of Advertising Research*, Mar/Apr 2002, Vol. 42 Issue 2, pp. 80–92.

[15] Stefano Hatfield, "Granger in Effect", *Creativity Magazine*, 7 October 2002, www.adcritic.com/news/creativity/detil/?=36238.

Further reading

Bronner, Fred and Peter Neijens (2006) "Audience experiences of media context and embedded advertising: A comparison of eight media", *International Journal of Market Research*, Vol. 48–1, pp. 81–100.

Dertouzos, James N. and Steven Garber (2006) "Effectiveness of Advertising in Different Media", *Journal of Advertising*, Vol. 35–2, pp. 111–22.

Hansen, Flemming, Steen Lundsteen and Jørgen Kai Olsen (2006) "The effects of print vs TV advertising, documented using short-term advertising strength (STAS) measures", *International Journal of Advertising*, Vol. 25–4, pp. 431–46.

Morimoto, Mariko and Susan Chang (2006) "Consumers' Attitudes toward Unsolicited Commercial E-mail and Postal Direct Mail Marketing Methods: Intrusiveness, Perceived Loss of Control, and Irritation", *Journal of Interactive Advertising*, Vol. 7–1, pp. 8–20.

Taylor, Charles R., George R. Frange and Bang Hae-Kyong (2006) "Use and Effectiveness of Billboards", *Journal of Advertising*, Vol. 35–4, pp. 21–34.

Veloutsou, Cleopatra and Claire O'Donnell (2005) "Exploring the effectiveness of taxis as an advertising medium", *International Journal of Advertising*, Vol. 24–2, pp. 217–39.

The Internet and interactivity

CHAPTER PERSPECTIVE
Adding two-way to one-way media

The majority of most companies' sales and an even greater proportion of their profits come from current customers with whom the company has established a connection. To motivate repeat purchases, companies need to continually connect and reconnect with customers. The media most suited for doing this are those that are addressable and interactive. The importance of interactive media is continuously increasing. The most important driver of this is, of course, the Internet that has become a dominant power in today's world. The Internet offers various forms of interactive communications, and its real powers are now gradually being uncovered.

One-way media are used most often for creating brand awareness, helping position a brand, and keeping the brand top-of-mind with customers and prospects. In contrast, interactive media are used not only for generating repeat purchases but also for communicating with prospects who have expressed interest in a brand. Interactive media are extremely valuable in building brand relationships because they enable companies and customers to get to know and trust each other.

This chapter explains the value of interactivity and how the Internet and its communication formats can be integrated into the overall relationship-building efforts. From a general discussion of communication and technology, it moves to an analysis of the Internet and online communication. The final section touches on Internet privacy issues.

IMC in Action

BMW's "films" makes interactivity a winner

The big debate at the international Cannes Film Festival in 2002 was whether to include BMW's *Hire* film series in the advertising award competition. Although the innovative campaign was already a winner of the sales-promotion industry's Reggie Awards and the advertising industry's Clios and the One Show, the Cannes advertising folks simply didn't know what to do with it. Was it advertising or wasn't it?

That debate showcases a trend in marketing communication. Advertising is seeking to redefine itself as marketers use more promotional tools, including the interactive dimensions of the Internet, in innovative ways to strike the right chord with target audiences. In the bmwfilms.com series, the automaker used a series of online films starring British actor Clive Owen, who, in his role as the mysterious driver, tackles a host of dangerous situations in his finely tuned, smoothly performing BMW. The high-quality digital "advertainment" was designed specifically for the Internet.

BMW's marketing research had found that the traditional BMW customer was a middle-age male with a median income of about €150 000. Managers knew that to grow the market, they needed to reach a younger but equally affluent audience. What made the members of BMW's target market different from the customers of other upmarket competitors, such as Mercedes or Lexus, was their active lifestyle. They were engaged in sports as part of their daily routine, not as spectators. They also loved driving and appreciated technology. Their technological orientation was apparent in their high level of Internet use, the highest among all buyers of various upmarket makes and models.

With a small marketing budget compared to the budgets of its competition, BMW had found success in alternative media strategies such as the product placement that featured the new Z3 roadster in a cameo appearance in the James Bond film *GoldenEye*. A second Bond film, *Tomorrow Never Dies*, featured the 7 series and BMW's new cruiser motorcycle.

To further combat a slowdown in sales, BMW marketing executives brainstormed with the company's agency in search of a new marketing communication approach. Two ideas surfaced: (1) to create a series of short films running from five to seven minutes and (2) to incorporate the Internet to reach BMW's websavvy market. These two ideas were merged and became a series of short films for the Internet. The move away from traditional advertising was justified by the expectation that what was lost in terms of audience size could be made up for in terms of involvement. To realize this, the goal was "to produce the most exciting, fun thing people had ever seen come out of their computer."

The story lines all involved a mysterious person who is a professional driver and helps people out of difficult situations. The driver, hired for his superb driving skills and unshakeable poise, encounters unexpected obstacles that test his abilities as well as the various types of BMWs he drives. The Fallon team found directors were more than willing to sign up for the experimental films because the scripts had gripping and creative storylines that blurred the line between cinema and advertising. The BMW 740i sedan, for example, starred in "Ambush", in which a van swerves close to the driver and the door slides open showing masked gunmen who are threatening to fire unless the driver stops and surrenders his passenger. In a dramatic chase with some unexpected twists, the driver and his car save the passenger.

Films in the series were co-directed by various well-known directors including John Frankenheimer (*The Manchurian Candidate* and *Grand Prix*), Ang Lee (*Crouching Tiger, Hidden Dragon*), Guy Ritchie (*Lock, Stock and Two Smoking Barrels*), Ridley Scott (*Bladerunner* and the Apple Macintosh "1984" launch commercial), Tony Scott (*Top Gun*), and David Fincher (*Seven*). In contrast to the usual practice in filming commercials, these directors were given free rein to direct the content and action as they saw fit.

When the campaign was terminated on 21 October 2005, more than 100 million viewers had logged on to the streaming video website. The films could be seen only on www.bmwfilms.com. However, 30-second commercials were developed from them for television commercials designed to work like movie trailers. TV audiences thought the commercials were announcing a movie until the title at the end displayed the BMWFilms logo and directed viewers to the website.

According to Jarvis Mak, a senior analyst at NetRatings, BMW's goal was to rebuild a brand image and develop a relationship with customers while entertaining them. BMW did that effectively while at the same time garnering a lot of attention for the brand and the film series, particularly among its upscale target market. Not only did the series create a lot of buzz—with stories in *The New York Times, Time* magazine and other media—but the films also hit the target: more than half of the visitors to bmwfilms.com were males, had broadband access, and fell into BMW's traditional upscale target market with incomes of €75 000 and higher. As a measure of the "stickiness" of the website, the visitors spent on average more than six minutes at the site.

Some of the 2002 films were underscored by subplots that left more questions than answers, an ideal technique for creating intrigue. In addition to the plot and subplots, the films contained real phone numbers and websites. In one promotion, time and place information was given for viewers to assemble to participate in a BMWFilms live-action experience. Hundreds of people showed up, some travelling up to 500 km to join the event.

The BMW films were so effective because the idea was creative, attention-getting, and intriguing. It also redefined advertising as it moved the genre into the new world of interactive communication. As one expert said: "*The Hire* was an unprecedented example of media convergence that both pushed and crossed boundaries."

The Cannes judges finally decided the campaign belonged in the interactive division, where it walked away with the Gold Lion. But that still begs the question of whether *The Hire* film series is good advertising as well. Randall Rothenberg, who critiques advertising for *Fast Company* magazine, answers the question when he says the series reinvents the genre of advertising: "The BMWFilms advertainments show that creative life remains within advertising."

Sources:

Youngme Moon and Kerry Herman, "BMWFilms", Harvard Business School case, N9-502, 046, 11 January 2002.
Randall Rothenberg, "Ad of the Month", Fast Company, March 2003, p. 40.
Patrick McKenna, "The Long Way to Madison and 23rd", Promo, 1 May 2002, www.industryclick.com/ magazinearticle.asp?magazinearticleid=147314&
Peter Breen, "Hire Education", Promo, 1 May 2002, www.industryclick.com/magazinearticle.asp?magzineid =122&releaseid=
Barbara Gengler, "BMW Back in Showbiz", The Australian IT, 29 June 2002.
"Tune Up Web Film Campaign", CNET News.com, 7 June 2002, www.news.com.com/2100-1023-934052.html
"BMW to Reprise Web Film Effort", 7 June 2002, www.internetnews.com/IAR/article.php/1355321.

Communication and technology

In 2001 the world held its breath. Many Internet-related companies lost up to 50 per cent of their value as displayed on the stock exchange, often leading to bankruptcy. The uncontrolled growth of the virtual world, sometimes referred to as the "new economy", had come to a sudden end. Some expected—hoped? feared?—that the Internet itself would turn out to be a fad, which would soon collapse.

Nothing could have been farther from the truth. The boom now has proved to be a necessary "correction" of the hyper-expectations with which the Internet world had been confronted, often created by the most outspoken proponents of the new reality. But in its fundaments the promises of the Internet have turned out to be realistic. Increased access to information, high rates of interactivity, an essentially borderless world: the Internet makes it all true. Companies have learned how to work with the Internet as well. A company that is not present on the Internet with an easily accessible and searchable website or portal is not taken seriously any more.

This chapter focuses on the impact the Internet revolution has had on the *communications landscape*. From an IMC perspective, the Internet is first and foremost a medium that makes interactivity in a rich information setting possible, at reasonable cost. Notice that the interactivity characteristic as such is not unique to the Internet. Communications by telephone, as well as personal selling, also have this feature. Compared to telephone conversation, the Internet offers a much richer information environment. Compared to personal selling, the decisive feature in favour of the Internet is cost. Compared to both, the Internet does not rely on a human being as the sender of information, which is both an advantage (cost) and a disadvantage (less responsiveness). A third consequence of the absence of a human being on the sender side is that Internet sites are available 24/7, i.e. at any time of convenience to the receiver. That is what is called customer orientation!

Integrating interactivity into relationship building

One of the major changes in today's marketplace is the increased communication between companies and customers. According to an article in *The Economist*, the marketing world was much simpler when all that companies did was *send* brand messages.[1] The increasing use of interactive technology leads customers to expect two-way communication with companies—that is, better customer service. They want to ask questions, place orders, and register complaints 24/7.

Driving this increase in interactivity is increasing access to and use of the Internet. Consumer and business use of the Internet is expanding rapidly because the Internet is both inexpensive and easy to use. Nonetheless, the rapid growth has created a problem for many companies—namely, how to handle and manage the increase in interactivity. In an attempt to better manage and make use of Internet-facilitated interactivity, intranets and extranets have been set up, broadband has been greatly expanded, and companies are experimenting to discover how best to integrate wireless communication into their MC operations.

Different "nets" for different uses

There have been important advances in communication technology throughout history, but from a growth perspective, the most phenomenal is the Internet, which is *a worldwide system of linked computer networks*. Despite the fact that the Internet has only a 30-year' history, it has established a prime place in the lives of most people. In most European countries Internet accessibility reaches 100 per cent levels and use is also high. The type of use differs according to age groups. Younger people (roughly of ages below 40) mainly use the Internet for communication purposes: e-mail, chat, communities, etc. For older cohorts the emphasis shifts to using the Internet as an information source. The Internet is also used as a sales platform, first, for information products like books, music, video, and second, for highly standardized services like ticketing (air travel, holidays, music concerts).

The Internet's greatest characteristic (from a marketing perspective) is being a relatively inexpensive, interactive communication medium. It helps companies connect and build stronger brand relationships with customers, employees, and other stakeholders by employing the power of two-way communication. The Internet has also become a major internal medium for companies that have set up intranets. Companies also use extranets, which connect employees with all key external stakeholders such as MC agencies, suppliers, and distributors. As a medium of marketing communications, the Internet combines the characteristics of many other media—newspapers, magazines, catalogues, TV, and directories.

The Internet is, however, a two-edged sword. Today, a major problem with a brand can be communicated around the world within minutes by dissatisfied customers. The greater the problem, the faster the word will spread. Intel found this out several years ago when a user discovered a problem with an Intel chip. In a matter of days, the faulty chip became a discussion topic in dozens of high-tech chat rooms, and the issue was soon picked up by offline mass media and further publicized.

Television, cable, computer, and phone companies are all scrambling to take leadership positions in the new world of convergence, which is *the combining of telephone, computer, and TV into one interactive communication device.* An example of communication convergence is online streaming video that has the ability to carry live, two-way audio between customers and companies. The primary factor limiting the application of convergence is lack of bandwidth.

Bandwidth *governs the amount of digital information or data that can be sent from one place to another in a given time.* Limited bandwidth is a particular problem for exchanging large data files that contain graphic and video elements. Fortunately, the speed of technological evolution is providing greater and greater data-transmission capacities. This means that as more consumers buy faster computers and have access to more bandwidth through cable and satellite services, companies can deliver more complex brand messages than ever before. The growth in bandwidth is to some extent countered by the increased demand for bandwidth, by the ever-growing complexity of the communications, but in general the technological growth exceeds the growth in demand.

Currently, the Internet still accounts for only a modest percentage of all media spending. This statistic, however, is misleading because the Internet is far less costly to use than most other media. The importance of the role that the Internet plays in acquiring and retaining customers is much bigger than the percentage of Internet spending suggests. Also, in the increasingly *integrated* marketing communications approach spending on individual media is not reflecting the efforts of IMC at all, as the BMW case illustrates nicely. A few million euros (which is a small percentage of major MC budgets) can produce a great deal of online exposure and interactivity with customers and prospects.

The true power of interactivity comes into force when, with the use of sophisticated software, companies can target brand messages to individuals or small dedicated groups and quickly alter message content with customized images and appeals. In particular, the growing presence of communities offers tremendous targeted communications opportunities. At the same time, almost literally, the interactive options of Internet communication can be used to make a company more responsive to its customers by providing easy access to information.

Real-time, targeted, personalized, and interactive brand messages—that is one of the major differences in marketing communication created by the Internet; and it is a powerful tool in building customer relationships.

Another consequence of the Internet that reshapes the world of communication is that customers do not only have access to information controlled by the company, but can consult other customers, competitors and any other source of information with a click of the mouse. The number of unexpected touch points, information sources that are not under the control of the brand, has grown incredibly. Just go to Google and search for an average brand name. The numbers of hits is usually in the millions.

Wireless communication

Wireless transmission of data and information is likely to be the single most significant change in media technology during the first decade of this millennium. China, India, and other developing countries that do not have enough telephone and cable lines to support all the new media are investing heavily in wireless communication, leapfrogging the in-ground stage of communication infrastructure. Customers are now able to access the Internet to send and receive e-mail with mobile phones and more advanced hand-held devices, another indication of the growth of wireless. Although many companies are getting into the wireless business, most marketers of consumer and B2B goods are still waiting to see how viable it is to send brand messages via wireless.

Marketers will be attracted to wireless advertising for several reasons: (1) customers are increasingly mobile, (2) messages can be targeted not only by individual mobile phone number but also by time and location of targeted customers, and (3) wireless provides one more way to reinforce brand awareness and motivate customers to respond. It is expected that wireless messages will be most successful when used to redirect customers to certain websites and to sponsor web pages that are likely to be accessed with mobile devices, and for "click-and-dial". An example of "click-and-dial" is a message that would appear on your mobile phone's message screen asking whether a birthday or special occasion is near and, if so, if flowers would be an appropriate gift. The message would allow you to click through to an online florist to place an order.[2]

Interactive TV

The convergence of computers, television, and the Internet is referred to as **interactive TV**, a technology that allows viewers to respond directly to TV commercials with a click of the remote control or a remote keyboard. Viewers can order movies instantly, for example, rather than having to make a phone call. By clicking on a website address in a commercial, a viewer can go directly to the site to get further brand information or place an order. Interactive TV also allows viewers to obtain information while watching a programme. For example, while watching a tennis game, a viewer can bring a player's profile on-screen as the player is coming to serve. The work to make television a two-way medium has been going on for several decades. Although the technology now exists for interactive TV, customers have been slow to embrace it; many are not yet convinced of its value.

M-commerce is the future of interactive media

One of the most rapidly advancing types of interactive media is wireless digital communication. Its application to business is referred to as *m-commerce* (*m* for "mobile"). Devices for using this medium include mobile phones, some personal digital assistants (PDAs), and global positioning systems (GPSs). The first generation of wireless devices consisted of analogue mobile phones. The second generation consisted of digital mobile phones. The third generation can transmit voice, data, and video. Since 2001, wireless phones have been equipped with wireless application protocol (WAP), an industry standard that allows these phones to receive content from the Internet.

In some countries, such as Finland and Japan, wireless-phone subscribers already outnumber fixed-line subscribers. In destroyed Afghanistan, the number of fixed lines is so small that effectively mobile telephony is the standard. The owners use their phones not only to talk to each other but also to send e-mail messages back and forth, pay for small-ticket items such as soft drinks, and subscribe to text messages such as horoscopes and jokes. And the uses are fast expanding. According to one observer, "People will be accustomed to getting up-to-the-minute personal and customized news, from traffic and weather to sports, stock quotes, and even when movies are playing." Such use, if it becomes widespread, will make wireless communication a particularly attractive way to deliver brand messages.

Retail marketers are excited about the prospect of tying messages to location. A shopper in a mall will be able to request on-the-spot information concerning sales in the mall. A shopper in a grocery store will be able to obtain electronic coupons. A tourist walking past a restaurant can be alerted to a lunch special.

Think about it

What types of brand messages—from what types of businesses—seem the most logical choices for transmission by means of wireless devices? Will the proliferation of brand messages sent by wireless media finally cause customers to revolt against commercial messaging?

Source:
Brad Applegate, "From 'Appointment Viewing' to 'News on Demand'", posted on MediaPost Monitor, *18 July 2000, www.masha@mediapost.com. Used by permission.*

Addressable media and interactive media

Addressable and interactive media are reshaping brand relationships. Besides serving as communication vehicles for product offers to customers, addressable media—e-mail, mail, and phone—can deliver messages asking research questions about level of brand satisfaction, further purchase intentions, and reactions to new promotional offers. With the right messages, these media can help retain current customers and increase a brand's share of their category spending. For major-purchase goods and services, it can often be cost-justified to use addressable media to reach targeted prospects.

Even cable television operators now have digital systems with addressable capabilities, so they can send a customized selection of programmes and brand messages to a particular subscriber's cable address. Pan-European broadcasters like Eurosport offer the opportunity to include local advertisements in their commercial breaks. Technically it is already feasible to submit individualized messages over the cable networks.

Interactive media take a step beyond the ability of addressable media in making more intimate the relationship between brands and customers. Companies have traditionally asked, "How can *we* best send messages to our customers and prospects?" They are now beginning to recognize that another question is just as important: "How can *our customers* easily send messages to us?" Companies that sincerely want customers and prospects to talk to them need to provide options for communicating with the company—phone, e-mail, a portal, or old-fashioned mail. The more flexibility there is to interact with a company, the more consumers are likely to do so.

Interactive media include many of the addressable media previously described. The difference between interactive and addressable media is simply in how they are used. As mentioned earlier, the Internet can be used as a mass medium (banner ads), an addressable medium (e-mail), or an interactive medium (live chat). From a customer's perspective, interactivity means *accessibility, recognition,* and *responsiveness*—all the things people require in a relationship, whether personal or commercial. From a brand perspective, interactivity means the ability to listen as well as speak and then modify corporate behaviour as a result of customer feedback.

Four characteristics set interactive media apart from mass media: (1) they can target individuals as well as customer segments; (2) they can be used by customers and prospects to talk to a company; (3) they are more measurable and accountable than mass media; and (4) they can demand more attention than mass media because of the personalized brand messages they can carry. The ability to deliver tight targeting is a particularly important benefit.

Interactivity can be either active or passive. *Active interactivity* occurs when a company and a customer talk to each other in real time (by means of the telephone or live chat). *Passive interactivity* involves a time delay—that is, it is asynchronous. A customer may get an e-mail on demand or use a company-sponsored kiosk or website to ask questions, retrieve information, and request information that arrives later by mail, fax, or e-mail.

Interactivity allows companies to integrate customers into a company. Customers can and should contribute to product planning and development, as well as to distribution and marketing decisions. Indeed, interactivity is increasingly seen as a customer's "right". If customers can easily ask one company a question or voice a complaint, they expect to be able to do so with every company with which they do business. Companies that do not facilitate customer interactivity risk sending a message that they are antiquated and don't care about customers.

Although phone and mail are the most widely used interactive media in terms of MC spending, the fastest-growing and -changing media are commercial e-mail and company websites. E-mail and websites depend on different technologies and are used differently by both customers and businesses. For these reasons they are discussed here as different media, although both travel over the Internet.

E-mail marketing

The popularity of e-mail is undisputed. This is good news for marketers because e-mail is a less expensive form of one-to-one communication than either regular mail or telephone calls. E-mail has become a popular and effective way to reach customers because it is so simple and inexpensive to use.[3] Unsolicited e-mail (spam) has become a major source of customer irritation which is countered by spam filters that have reached high levels of effectiveness. Some Internet service providers, such as Hotmail, provide customers with free e-mail and Internet services in return for their agreeing to view advertising.

Opt-in and opt-out strategies

Customer receptivity is an important consideration in the proper use of e-mail campaigns. This is why permission marketing is increasingly used. Customers who **opt-in**, *give permission for e-mail from a particular company or brand to be sent to them.* To motivate customers to opt-in, companies often use sweepstakes, games, or the promise of some type of reward. An example of a motivational offer for opting-in is free online planning calendars with e-mail reminders of key occasions so marked. This is done in exchange for personal data, which can be used to drive customized e-mail ads. Opt-in strategies have two benefits. First, they identify the person (or company) as being interested in the product category. Second, when customers sign up, smart companies ask profile questions so they have a better idea of their customers' demographics and lifestyles, which can in turn be used to anticipate needs and wants.

A second strategy is **opt-out e-mail**, which is *a series of messages that a company sends automatically until notified to stop.* For example, when you sign up for an online newsletter, the web page will often have a box, *already checked*, that says something like "Please send me news about special offers". Unless you uncheck the box (opt-out), the company will send you brand messages at regular intervals. This technique, similar to the way book clubs in the offline world lock their customers in, means that unless you tell the company not to send next month's selection, you will receive it. Some customers find this practice tricky and resent it. The strategy that is most respectful of customers is opt-in e-mail.

E-messages that you find in your mailbox that you have not opted-in or -out for are called **spam**, *unsolicited e-mail whose purpose is to sell a product or service.* Spam is not only bothersome to consumers but also a growing concern for businesses and government regulators. In the online environment, spam is seen as an issue of major concern. For companies it is a large cost. According to *Internet News*, it was estimated that in 2005 businesses in the US spent $5 billion to deal with spam (based on lost production time and IT costs).[4] Initially it was thought that self-regulation of spam would work out, but by now it is generally admitted that it is so bad—according to one estimate 41 per cent of all e-mail is spam—that some form of government enforcement is needed. Guidelines say that e-mail should be used only:[5]

1 To solicit current customers.

2 To contact individuals (or companies) who have opted-in.

3 To contact individuals who have not opted-out after being given the opportunity to do so.

4 By marketers who have assurance from list brokers that names supplied conform to one or more of the above.

In Europe regulations are generally more strict than in the United States. This has made it better for consumers but in some ways more difficult for marketers. In Germany, Austria, Italy, Denmark, and Sweden, laws require that customers opt-in before they can be sent any promotional e-mails. EU regulations require that "marketers must tell consumers what data they will collect and retain, exactly how it will be used in the future and then give them the option of opting in or out of the process ... [If] a consumer ... moves or changes any of the initial information given, the whole process starts over." Such rules for collecting consumer information make marketing databases more difficult to create. On the other hand, once databases are created in this way, they are more effective, with return rates up to 40 per cent.[6]

E-mail formats

E-mail marketing can be done in a variety of formats, such as ads, discussion lists, newsletters, and publicity. Which format is best depends on the marketing communication objectives that need to be achieved.

- *Ads:* Companies can send out e-mail advertising as plain text or as **rich media**, which is *e-mail that features audio and/or video*. Rich media e-mails use technology that permits streaming video, among other special effects, to be distributed within an e-mail message rather than in an attachment. They can be extremely effective in attracting people to a company's website. For example, when Warner Bros. sent potential licensees an e-mail message featuring a trailer for an upcoming film, the response rates were exceptionally high.[7]

- *Communities:* Online communities can include hundreds or thousands of people. Companies can participate in these communities and send marketing messages to the members. Companies should do this in an undisguised fashion, as a disguise is not only considered unethical, but also may severely harm the company once it is discovered. But, as noted before, communities are very attractive because they comprise homogenous groups of people.

- *Newsletters:* Marketers send mass e-mailings set up as newsletters on brand-related topics. Unlike members of discussion lists, newsletter recipients cannot communicate directly back to the marketer or to other recipients.

- *Publicity:* News releases are being distributed online not only to editors but also to others who need to know about a company's announcements.

Although distributing e-mail costs relatively little in space, time, or postage, the software and hardware required for handling large e-mail distributions can cost millions of euros. Also, there is the cost of collecting e-mail addresses or renting address lists, as well as of creating the messages to be sent. Nevertheless, the cost is still low compared to the cost of using other media. This is why nearly all companies using e-mail hire services such as MessageMedia and Yesmail, which specialize in helping a brand put together an effective e-mail programme. When the cost of the service is included, it is possible to estimate opt-in e-mail at about €2 per sale. In contrast, banner ads (discussed later in this chapter) have an average cost per sale of €100; direct mail, approximately €71.[8]

Strengths and limitations of e-mail marketing

Research has shown that e-mail is the most effective form of online marketing because it can be personalized and is relatively inexpensive.[9] It is a particularly effective way to retain customers. In one study 63 per cent of companies surveyed said e-mail was their most effective customer retention tool.[10]

Most e-mail ads are designed to encourage **click-through**, *the act of responding by clicking on a link to go directly to a particular website*. Users are 3 to 10 times more likely to click through to a company's website from an e-mail than from a banner ad. Another study found that of those who visited a site, 63 per cent responded to e-mail campaigns, compared to 29 per cent for offline advertising.[11]

Another advantage of e-mail is that once a message has been produced, it has a relatively small distribution cost. Neither the size of the audience nor the size of the message greatly affects the cost. As with direct mail, however, there is the cost of acquiring addresses of other-than-current customers, producing the message, and handling responses. E-mail campaigns also allow for easy testing of offers and how they are presented. Offers and messages that work best can quickly replace those that generate only average or below-average results.

Judging the effectiveness of e-mail is relatively straightforward when the objective is to generate sales: costs are balanced against revenues. But also when other behavioural objectives are set, like click-throughs or website visits, measuring effectiveness is not much of an issue. For other types of responses the same issues count, as are discussed in Chapter 18.[12] A major limitation of e-mail campaigns, even when customers have opted-in, is clutter. Internet research companies forecast that clutter will only get worse. In response, an increasing number of anti-spam software systems are being used by both individuals and companies. Another challenge many companies face is responding to e-mails in a timely manner. The use of e-mail suggests interactivity, and in line with that customers expect a quick response. Studies show that nearly all expect a response within 48 hours, many even within six hours.[13] In particular, people that send messages to help desks want help, often instantaneously. Few companies meet these expectations.

Website marketing

Most of the major MC functions use the Internet, along with the other major media, to connect with customers and prospects. The Internet, and particularly websites or portals, are brand-message *expanders*. In other words, MC messages such as ads, publicity releases, packaging labels, and even events can direct customers and prospects to a brand's website for more information about the brand. Offering this level of brand knowledge was simply not possible before the Internet was integrated into the MC and media mixes.

Websites provide unique brand–customer touch points with online communities and chat rooms. A creatively designed website that is interactive and fun to visit will not only attract visitors but will extend their stay. The website designed for Lexus, for example, is filled with lifestyle information that appeals to Lexus owners and prospects, such as descriptions of luxury hotels, where the best farmers' markets are located, and what a really high-tech home includes. The website plays jazz and "new luxury" music that is heard in Lexus commercials. It also has links to Lexus commercials for visitors who want to learn more about the product.[14]

The most important step for directing customers and prospects to a website is to register it with as many search engines as possible in order to gain visibility and site visits. **Search engines** are *Internet tools that use keywords to find websites*. Web marketers often use common keywords to structure their websites in order to maximize how often the sites turn up in searches.

Online brand communities

A valuable aspect of a website is the ability to bring together customers and prospects to share ideas on how to use a company's products. **Virtual communities** are *groups of people who focus on certain online activities and establish relationships with one another*. Soccer teams, for example, have websites where their fans congregate and communicate with the team as well as with each other. These fans constitute a virtual community based on team loyalty.

For each of its products, Adobe offers user-to-user forums that operate like bulletin boards where customers can post and read notes. At the Kraft Foods website, there is a bulletin board called the "Wisdom of Moms Exchange" where people can post such things as recipes and Mother's Day memories. Such sites not only allow loyal users to share tips with each other but also reinforce their commitment to the sponsoring brand. Also available on some corporate sites are chat rooms that allow people to talk to one another in real time.

Online brand communities bring companies various benefits: aggregating people into addressable target markets; creating bonds, which may deliver goodwill to community sponsors; allowing the company to listen to its customers, providing a type of real-time research. Further, consumers communicate with each other, either to reinforce brand experiences, or to help with finding new product uses. Monitoring the communications in the community gives valuable information to the brand on how the brand is perceived.

Online customer service

Responding to customers is a critical management responsibility and another area in which a website can add value to a brand or company. Customer service is not the last rung on the ladder at the end of the sale, but rather the first—it begins the moment someone arrives on a website.[15] There are three necessary elements for delivering good customer service online:

1 *Thorough and easy-to-use information at the website:* Simple sites may employ a frequently asked questions (FAQ) list, which supplies the answers to commonly asked questions. Websites also offer an index or search engine, which allows users to find help by typing in keywords.

2 *Customizable products and services:* More and more companies are creating websites that allow customers to design the products and services they want. Computer manufacturers like Dell for example, allow both individuals and businesses to design computers to order (see colour insert B6). Customers are presented with an extensive menu of features, and their computers are built to the specifications they choose. Similarly, Nike allows some of its website visitors to order custom-made shoes (see the IMC in Action box). This phenomenon is sometimes called mass-customization.[a1]

3 *Human interaction:* Rarely does a site provide answers to all possible questions. Often there is still a need for a user to communicate with a real person. Companies should provide toll-free numbers so that online users know where to call. They should also allow for easy use of e-mail, although this option should not be provided if the response rate is going to be slow. No online consumer should have to wait more than 24 hours for an answer by e-mail. A quicker solution is a direct online link to a customer-service representative. The user is able to type in questions and receive immediate responses. Another variation allows a user to type in a question and then receive an immediate telephone call back from a customer-service rep.

Online design

There was a time that the majority of business executives said the primary objectives for their companies' websites were to build brand awareness and provide information. These objectives, which are primarily about one-way communication, neglect one of the major relationship-building characteristics of a website: interactivity. A printed brochure can build brand awareness and supply marketing information, but a website can also engage customers and other stakeholders in valuable dialogues. Unless a website is interactive, a major portion of its value goes unused.

Online design is a hot area of design. On the one hand, it is similar to poster design, and, in fact, that is how designers usually approach online ads or the opening page of a website. It is also similar to video design in that both work with a screen as a frame. On the other hand, the content is entirely different. Video offers all the benefits of cinematic techniques as well as realistic action. Online images are often dominated by words—although this is changing rapidly as the technology improves and makes animation and sound easier to integrate into website design.

Because of the magic of digitizing, web design can combine images from all different sources, such as photographs, type, film, sound, and games. The art can be illustrations or photographs that, through animation, can move. Any illustration can be scanned and manipulated through such art programmes as PhotoShop and Flash. Sites should load quickly and be viewable on a variety of browsers. Ease of access is determined by the complexity of the design and the use of animation and multimedia formats.

There are two basic types of online formats. One is online advertising, usually presented as a banner. The other is a website, which in its simplest form resembles an online brochure that gives information about a company, as well as details about its products, brands, and services, and contact information. More contemporary websites are interactive, allowing customers to contact the company with questions, shop online, and link to other products and services, such as chat rooms and product-related reference information. Online advertising is discussed later on in this chapter.

Pimp my shoe

There are only a few companies that define twenty-first-century marketing better than Nike. This worldwide manufacturer of athletic shoes, clothing and sports equipment became Digital Marketer of the Year in 2006. This is not strange, since you can spend hours browsing on their flashy website. But there is more to it than a flashy website. The key point is that consumers can *interact* with the company. Let's see how Nike did it.

"We do not start with the medium," Mr. Edwards, VP global brand and category management, says. "We always start with the consumer and then look for the best ways to connect with them." This outside-in approach was used in the development of the Build Your Own Shoe campaign. On Nike.com, you can "pimp" your own footwear (running, football, basketball shoes) and equipment (bags and balls). For developing your personalized shoe or bag, you can choose your size, favourite colour and personal ID. This campaign was supported in May 2005 by the purchase of a placement on the Reuters Building in Times Square. People passing by with a cell phone could call a toll-free number to get access to the dial pad in order to personalize the sneaker on the sign. In reply, the customer gets an SMS message with the result of the personalization and goes on Nike's website to purchase it. Can that be more interactive?

Yes it can. Recently, Nike decided to work together with Apple, because both companies noticed that running and listening to music (Apple's iPod) was a good combination. A new shoe (that can be "pimped" as well) was born: Nike Plus. This shoe contains a built-in pocket, in which the Nike + iPod Sport kit can be placed. This sensor measures the activity while running and then transfers this data wirelessly to the iPod. After the workout, the workout data can be checked online by connecting the iPod to the computer. In this way, one can compare runs and compete with friends.

An interactive tool that Nike implemented for its World Cup strategy is the use of online communities. Looking at conversations on other social networking sites and blogs, the company saw that this was a great opportunity to let consumers shape the brand and talk about it. The place to be for this community became Joga.com, a networking site for soccer fans, launched in February 2006 (pending the World Cup later that summer) in association with Google. Members from all over the world can participate in fan communities of their preferred teams or players, download videos or post a blog. Months after the World Cup tournament ended, the community continued to exist.

IMC in Action

Having developed such an interactive website, Nike has to cope with several issues related to all these implemented innovations. First, the company faced an increase in marketing expenditure (first quarter 2006). More important, customers are getting used to this interactivity and customer service. Nike may need to run faster to meet the needs of the Internet-empowered customer. Well, let's see how they just will do that.

Think about it

Do you think that Nike's online activity will replace its normal stores? What about the future of Nike's online activities?

Sources:
www.theagitator.net/index.php?/archives/384-Digital-Awards-To-Greenpeace-Nike.html
www.flytip.com/blogs/advertising/archives/2005/05/index.shtml

Gavin O'Malley, "Who's leading the way in web marketing? It's Nike, of course", Advertising Age, *00018899, 16 October 2006, Vol. 77, Issue 42.*

Stanley Holmes, "Nike It's Not a Shoe, It's a Community", BusinessWeek, *00077135, 24 July 2006.*

Website design

The design of a website is a critical issue. The first step in creating a successful website is to set objectives. What is the purpose of the site? There are a multitude of possible answers, including education, conversation and dialogue, feedback and research, entertainment, and sales. The next step is to identify the target audience: Who are they? How long have they been online? What kinds of browsers and computers will they be using? What languages do they speak? Why will they come to the site and with what expectations? How often will they come to the site? Will they want to download, print, or e-mail website information? What are their product needs?

Web-page design begins with an outline of the content and a flow chart that shows how the site will be navigated and how the links will perform. The first page is called the home page, and that is *the place where viewers begin looking at a website.* Usually, the home page offers the viewer a number of options that can be accessed by clicking on a graphic or type element. Most web pages have hyperlinks which are *buttons or other sensitive areas on the page that, when clicked on, move the viewer to another page or site.* Hyperlinks, which have to be plotted into the design, add an interactive or customer-guided element unavailable in any other form of marketing communication (see colour insert B10).

What complicates online design is navigation—*the process by which people access a website, find the information they want, and move around within the site and to other related sites.* Websites are not designed for the linear reading of one page after another. People jump around when they are visiting a site. Therefore, routes have to be mapped that represent typical viewers' patterns of information processing. It should be easy for viewers to go in whatever way they want to go, whenever they want to go there, and easily get back to the home page or other areas in the website.

In the early days of the Web, sites were overloaded with every new graphic trick designers could find. The new credo in website design is to make pages user friendly. Websites can be designed from the very simple to the very complex. Designers worry about adding complicated audio and animation effects that consumers do not want. How often have you watched the entire introductory video of a website? When users are given the option to choose either a multimedia format or a text-and-photos only format, most choose the latter. However, those who choose to look at the video presentations buy significantly more than those who choose not to.[16] The following list contains guidelines for creating websites that work:

- Make the home page work hard to establish your identity and tell what you do.
- Make the interface intuitive. People should not need training in order to use the site; all operations should be obvious.
- Make content prominent. Don't bury the content under a lot of graphics, ads, or complicated site design.
- Make navigation user-friendly.
- Don't create too many levels.
- Make sure menu options are complete.
- Give users a way to return to the main menu.
- Use links rather than long periods of scrolling.
- Put navigation aids at both the top and the bottom of the page.
- Provide a site map.

A good example of a website that is simple yet involving and invites interactivity is one for Pedigree dog food, www.pedigree.com. After selecting a country, you enter a website that has the same layout for every country, although the appearance is adjusted. The home page has an attractive look, and offers a limited number of main sections. Each section is a source of useful information for visitors (what breed of dog appeals to me?) where information on Pedigree's products is integrated. Take a look at the site and click on the Puppy link for example. An important link on the home page is one of the website categories: "Contact Us". This further encourages customers to ask questions, complain, or make suggestions. Despite the high level of standardization Pedigree has adopted, country-specific websites still have their idiosyncratic features. The UK site for example offers a DogBoard, a forum for discussions on anything concerning dogs. When it was a major concern to pet owners, the German website offered information about the bird flu that was at that moment a serious problem in some, but not all, European countries. The French site again has a section devoted to multimedia.

Every element of interactive design should be done with the customer in mind. Building a website that meets the needs of the target audience is difficult, but research is there to help, as Table 9-1 demonstrates. The figures, compiled by Forrester Research, indicate that users are most likely to return to sites that have high-quality content, are easy to use, are quick to download, and are updated frequently. And although the research is somewhat outdated, the results still make intuitive sense.

Integrating online brand communication

The Internet medium can serve many if not all communications functions. In many respects the online world is the virtual mimic of the offline world. But the two worlds do not stand in isolation. Often the IMC activities themselves establish links between the offline and online realities. In the remainder of this chapter specific aspects of Internet marketing communications will be presented.

Factor	Percentage of respondents citing this factor as important
High-quality content	75
Ease of use	66
Quick to download	58
Updated frequently	54
Coupons and incentives	14
Favourite brands	13
Cutting-edge technology	12
Games	12
Purchasing capabilities	11
Customizable content	10
Chat rooms	10
Other	6

Table 9-1 Factors driving repeat site visits

Source: Heather McLatchie, "E-Business Essentials", *clipwebzine*, 23 August 1999.
www.clipwebzine.com/article.cfm?storyid5163

Online advertising growing fast

Although still a fraction of total media spending, online advertising is growing faster than any other type of advertising. Advertising online offers a number of advantages:

- *Interactivity:* Companies and customers can engage in dialogue.
- *Flexibility:* Brand messages can be instantly changed/revised if not producing desired results.
- *Precise targeting:* People who come to a website are interested in that site's topic, product category, or brand and therefore are more likely to respond.
- *Quick results:* Because people are online 24/7, as soon as an offer is placed online, it has a potential audience that can immediately reply.
- *Measurable:* Hits, click-throughs, and purchases can easily be tracked.

Online advertising comes from online companies as well as from offline firms who want customers and prospects to visit their websites. Ad spending on the Internet is still increasing despite the dot.com crash of 2001. As online advertising has become more common, however, users have learned to ignore it. Thus, agencies are always searching for new and better ways to attract attention. Often the result is increasingly intrusive online advertising. As with any other form of advertising it is difficult to find the right balance between attraction and irritation.

Once a company decides to advertise online, it must decide on which sites to place its ads. Some common guidelines are used to select these sites: (1) visitors to the sites must match the company's customer profile; (2) the site must have good viability (it is established and promises to be around for a while); (3) the site's privacy policy must be similar to your company's; (4) site content must be compatible with the image of your company; and (5) the site must have performed well for you or other similar companies in the past. Hewlett-Packard spends approximately 75 per cent of its online advertising budget on sites that have produced results and the remaining 25 per cent on sites that were not used before but meet the other criteria listed above. This strategy is an ongoing process of finding and using sites that produce the best results (as measured by whatever objectives have been established).[17]

Types of online ads

The creativity of the message design is an important factor in attracting attention to a web ad. As an example of the power of a well-designed ad, Scott Kurnit, CEO of iVillage Inc., told this story: "Just the other day I was going through a food site and saw an unbelievable ad for Coca-Cola. I had to use my mouse to take a bottle of Coke and pour it into an empty glass. Then I added ice cubes and a straw. I was so fascinated by it I kept doing it over and over. I spent several minutes of my precious time with this one brand."[18]

Another way to attract attention is with frequency. Although the average number of online ads created for a company's use is about eight (and almost half of all companies are using fewer than two), the 10 largest Web advertisers have averaged 290 different ads. Amazon.com has the most, with some 360 different ads in its portfolio. Production and placement costs in traditional media make such volume prohibitive, but on the Web creating a variety of messages is an important (and less costly) strategy.

Marketers are sure to come up with new ways to deliver brand messages online, but currently the most prevalent types of online advertisements (besides e-mail) include the following:

- **Banner ads:** The first type of online advertising is the **banner**, which is *a small ad on some other company's web page.* These mini-ads function like outdoor boards: they have to grab attention quickly with highly condensed information and interesting animation (see colour insert B9). Buttons on banners that you can click on take the Internet user to the sponsor's website. The function of banner advertising is to tease the viewer into investigating the company behind the banner, and the success of banners is usually measured in terms of their click-through rate. Tracking technology can now be used to instantly identify website visitors and select from a variety of banners to display, depending on the visitor's profile. When two people view the same page at exactly the same time, one can be shown an ad for financial services, while the other may see an ad for an online bookstore. Banner ads that appear vertically on a screen are known as "skyscrapers".

- **Interstitials:** Similar to a banner ad but more intrusive, an **interstitial** is *an ad that pops up in a separate frame on a screen page.* The user has to stop reading and click on the interstitial to eliminate it.

- **Pop-ups and pop-unders:** One step below interstitials in intrusiveness, **pop-ups and pop-unders** are *ads that appear when a viewer closes a page or site.*

Interstitials and pop-ups and pop-unders are controversial because of their relatively high intrusiveness. Customization may be the answer to the intrusiveness problem. The idea is that, based on available customer data, an online advertisement is customized to the needs, wants and interests of the viewer. Technology allows this in a technical sense, and customer data are available in many instances. There are agencies that are specialized in collecting customer data and making them available, under the conditions that were agreed when the data were collected, to online advertisers. As an increasing number of consumers come to understand that making personal data available for such purposes can be to the benefit of the customer—less annoyance and frustration, more relevant information—this is win-win for both customers and advertisers. Nevertheless, there is a constant concern about privacy issues that these intermediaries have to take into account.

One of the first Web advertising design considerations is deciding how intrusive a banner ad should be. Do you need to attract attention, even if that means "clicking off" a few surfers in the process? Or are you concerned about building a brand relationship with your users? According to a presentation co-sponsored by three major online advertising companies, there are five "Golden Rules of Online Branding" regarding banner ads:[19]

- Keep banners simple—the more creative elements (graphics and words) there are, the less ability a banner has to raise brand awareness.
- Maximize size of logo—the bigger the logo, the more likely the banner will send a clear message to customers.
- Maximize size of banner—just as with print ads, the larger the size, the greater impact it has.
- Use frequency—the optimal frequency number differs by product category and banner design, but overall, research findings indicate that a frequency of five impressions is the most efficient.
- Include a human face—the presence of a human face was found to increase attention more than other design elements.

Clearly, not all Web advertisers follow these rules. Some of the new techniques that use a click-or-die strategy can only be described as obnoxious. The idea is to design a site that is "sticky" enough to keep viewers "glued" to it. Web gremlins have been created that hijack your cursor and won't release it until you click on its mother site.

Online display ads look more like small space ads in newspapers and magazines. The same design principles apply: use a headline to catch attention and convey an interesting idea, and keep the body copy (if any) simple. The visual impact usually lies in the overall design of the ad. Art may be used, but graphics consume memory and may be problematic given viewers' various levels of computer and software sophistication. The fancier the art and the animation effects, the harder it will be for users with simple systems to view the graphics.

Because business is driven by customers' wants and needs, it is not surprising that ad-blocking software has been developed. What especially concerns companies that sell online advertising is that some of this ad-blocking software is being installed in modems. If ad-blocking becomes pervasive, many Internet service providers will be forced to increase their fees because advertising revenue will be greatly reduced or even eliminated.[20]

Online ad targeting

Early online advertising simply targeted the broad Web audience. As technology has grown more sophisticated, businesses are increasingly able to place specifically targeted advertisements online (see colour insert C12). Online targeting strategies can be divided into three types:[21]

- *Editorial:* Banners are targeted by site or by page topic. For example, advertisers on the Yahoo! search engine can place ads on any of the more than 100 000 categories featured in Yahoo's Web directory.

- *Filtered:* In the most popular form of professional Web advertising today, advertisers can specify targeting parameters, such as the user's operating system or browser software, time period, country, or even Internet service provider. The selection mechanism on the service provider's server analyses the request and selects for placement only the sites that match the ad's specifications.

- *Personalized:* Next-generation systems will use neural networks and other learning methods to allow personalized content and advertisement selection based on the browsing and interaction history of a particular user, as well as other demographic information. *Ad servers* (computers that control the ad placements) are often run by an independent company which is neither the advertiser nor the content website. These computers can be programmed so that they fine-tune ad placement to reflect response rates.

Integrating the Internet and public relations

For online companies and offline companies that use e-commerce, home pages may function as corporate or brand brochures. They are designed to summarize succinctly a company's business, reinforce the corporate or brand identity, and provide a site map so visitors can easily navigate the website.

Because websites can contain a vast array of information, they can be designed to be useful to all of a company's stakeholders. For media relations, a site can contain a description of a company's business operations, a listing of all its brands and products, a listing of all executives, and, most important, company contact information. Many sites, for example www.siemens.com, also carry selected photos that media representatives can easily retrieve and use. Most companies post their press releases on their websites and maintain a file of them for a certain period of time. The human resources department often uses the company website to publicize job openings and provide prospective employees with easy access to the company.

The websites of public companies can be important sources of information for the financial community. For example, after the story broke regarding defective Firestone tyres on Ford Explorers, which were blamed for dozens of rollover accidents, Ford's stock price declined. To address the concerns of the financial community and other Ford stakeholders, Ford put on the opening page of its corporate website a special button that said: "For official Ford News on the Firestone recall, click here." This link took online users to a listing of news releases and other information that Ford had made public about the recall and the company's future use of Firestone tyres.

Integrating the Internet into sponsorship programmes

Rather than simply placing ads on sites, some companies prefer to sponsor entire sites. The site's content may come from a non-profit association, but it is specifically created to attract target audiences for the corporate sponsor and to promote that sponsor's products. Online educational seminars (just like in-person seminars) represent one of the most common sponsorship opportunities. Other sponsors attempt to create a "halo effect" for their brand by associating it with something positive. Sponsorships are more about building customer relationships long-term than about driving sales short-term.

Measuring online marketing communication

The first step in measuring the effectiveness of online marketing communication programmes is to identify primary target audiences. Visa, for example, has three primary targets—customers, merchants who accept Visa cards, and banks that process credit-card transactions. Visa wants to see an increase in the number of banks that use its for-banks-only website to get answers to frequently asked questions, thus reducing the number of calls to Visa customer service, where each contact is very expensive. A similar objective exists for merchants. In the case of Visa customers, objectives relate to card sign-ups, card usage, and perception of Visa. To determine how well its website is performing, Visa uses the following measurements, which are fairly standard in the industry:

- **Lift:** How many additional transactions were made by Visa cardholders who visited Visa's website?

- **Conversion rate:** What percentage of non-Visa cardholders who visited the site signed up for a Visa card?

- **Brand knowledge and perception:** What percentage of site visitors report knowing more about Visa and thinking more positively about Visa compared to those who did not visit the site?

- **Number of visits:** This commonly used measurement is only of value if the majority of visitors are customers or prospective customers. If people are motivated to visit only for a chance to win a prize, for example, and for no other reason, most visitors may not be prospects.

- **Length of time on site:** The longer people stay on a site, the more likely they are to purchase or learn more about the brand.

- **Number and types of inquiries:** The more a company can engage customers in a dialogue, the stronger the brand relationship should be.[22]

One advantage of using the Internet for advertising, sending e-mail, and posting a website is the measurability of hits and click-throughs. One of the premier media research firms says, however, that such measures can be misleading. For example, although the average click-through on banners is far below 1 per cent, these banners are still creating brand awareness, increasing average customer lifetime value, and, if banners are done creatively, helping to reinforce brand image. Consequently, the actual number of customers that Internet advertising generates is often several multiples above what is tracked.[23]

Internet privacy and security issues

As Internet use has grown, privacy and security have become of increasing concern. **Privacy** is an ill-defined term that according to most laws simply refers to the personal life environment. In practice it is meant as *the control people exert over information they consider personal*. When you give your personal information to a company, you will not feel this as threatening your privacy. What you will feel as affecting your privacy is when this company uses this information for purposes other than you expected; even shares the information with other parties; or when you do not know that a company collects information about you, let alone if you do not want that information to become known.

Security refers to *the situation that personal information may be misused to the detriment of a particular person*. Security and privacy thus both refer to the control over information that relates to the person in question. Privacy, however, is largely a mental issue, while security has to do directly with physical or financial harm that can be incurred. The reason people do not reveal the Personal Identification Number of their bankcard is different from the reason they do not share their sexual preferences. The first is a matter of security, the latter of privacy.

Privacy

There are two major issues with respect to privacy. The first is the concern about information that is made available to one website being given or sold to third parties. The fact that this is an issue is inherent in the nature of data. As data may be copied at practically zero marginal cost, a company that has obtained interesting data must resist the strong temptation to sell the data at almost no cost; the more so, since it will also be able to keep the information itself. Since there are few incentives for organizations not to sell such data, regulation and legislation are in place in most countries. Many websites that ask for personal information do so assuring that the collected information will only be used for certain dedicated issues, often related to the core activities of the company itself. Implicitly this means, however, that organizations that do not display such a disclaimer do indeed have the opportunity to use the data as they wish.

The second privacy issue is the existence of all kinds of tracking instruments that collect information about the website visitor. Often this is hidden from the consumer, and indeed many advanced software applications exist. The simplest form though is called a **cookie**, which is *a simple text file in which actions, movements and data relevant to the site usage are recorded*. Cookies are stored on the user's own computer (so technically they are under the control of the website visitor) and are activated upon the next visit to the same site. Cookies are relatively harmless and in fact useful too. Every time you log on to a website the cookie helps in getting access: it may keep your login name for example, but also your password if you have indicated that. The real concern about cookies and other web tracking tools is that they may be read by marketers for very different reasons from those the website visitor may have intended. This use is not likely to be harmful to the consumer, but it definitely is a matter of privacy: uncontrolled use of information that is in principle personal.

When personal data cannot be traced to a real person, little damage is done. This is the reason why many Internet users use aliases, concealing their offline identity. This is effective to a limited extent only. Much of the use of personal information is not linked to a name, but to the user of a computer, where the computer is identified by its IP address. Consequently, while the uncontrolled spread of personal information may be limited, the impact of it in the online world is more severe. Just think of spam. Lots of unsolicited e-mails enter your mailbox daily. However, this information is always directed at your e-mail address, and for that reason many people use nicknames.

To meet the concerns of web users, companies can adopt various strategies. One such strategy is formulated by the Federal Trade Commission in the USA, and is captured in four recommendations.

Fair information practices

- *Notice:* Give clear and conspicuous notice of what information is collected and how it will be used.
- *Choice:* Let consumers choose whether their information can be used for any purpose besides fulfilling the transaction.
- *Reasonable access:* Consumers should be able to access the information collected about them and have a reasonable opportunity to correct any errors or delete the data.
- *Adequate security:* Companies should ensure proper handling of consumer information to prevent unauthorized access or identity theft.

Furthermore, many companies publish their privacy policy on the website. Another step is to let the company's handling of personal information be controlled by autonomous bodies, in exchange for a seal of approval. This is comparable to certification issues in other domains like safety. And although this is not common practice in Europe, such developments are under way in the US.

Security

Security refers primarily to financial issues that are related to e-commerce transactions. The security of financial transactions is a major concern of online consumers. According to a Gallup poll held in 2000, slightly over half (55 per cent) of all Internet users did not feel confident or totally secure that their credit-card information would remain secure.[24]

When the Web-design firm Interaction-Architect was researching security issues for a major European airline, it discovered "that people's perception of security when doing online transactions depends on the simplicity of the site and on the availability of user support". The company suggested that to increase a sense of security, an online transaction site should be comprehensible, predictable, flexible, and adaptable.[25] In other words, perception of security may extend beyond actual security and reassurances of security. Privacy and ease of use are two issues, but payment is of most concern.[26] Without security, a customer relationship is weakened.

Solving the privacy concerns and even more the security issues is of vital importance to the developments in the online world. When consumers do not feel secure in the online world, they will not develop their activities beyond surfing and chatting. This would seriously hinder the possibilities the Internet offers for e-commerce, and even more for the promise of highly personalized, interactive marketing communications.

A final note: Internet—a world apart

In less than three decades the Internet has taken a central place in most Western societies. Internet access rates of close to 100 per cent are more common than exceptional. To some extent it seems that these days two worlds exist: the online and the offline world (see colour insert B15). Synergy and interaction between these two worlds is still a largely unexplored area.

Most companies are present in the online world now. But the use they make of it differs largely. To some the online world fully replaces their offline activities; those companies are essentially information-processing companies, like banks. For many more companies the online world opens new avenues to sell products. The online world needs to be integrated with offline logistics processes. To all companies however, the online world is a communication medium of increasing importance, the main reasons being its cost-effectiveness and the opportunities it offers for interactive communication.

It holds good for all companies that the Internet is a medium, one of the many that are available to communicate marketing messages. Managing the Internet in the Integrated Marketing Communications approach requires a careful assessment of what kind of messages are best disseminated with the help of this medium, and how the Internet presence interacts with all other messages that are communicated, intended or not.

Internet: it's really a world apart; but not apart from the real world.

🔑 Key terms

bandwidth Governs the amount of digital information or data that can be sent from one place to another in a given time.

banner A small ad on some other company's web page.

click-through The act of responding by clicking on a link to go directly to a particular website.

convergence The combining of telephone, computer, and TV into one interactive communication device.

cookie A simple text file in which actions, movements and data relevant to the site usage are recorded.

extranet A limited-access computer network that links suppliers, distributors, and MC agencies to the company.

home page The place where viewers begin looking at a website.

hyperlinks Buttons or other sensitive areas on the page that, when clicked on, move the viewer to another page or site.

interactive TV The convergence of computers, television, and the Internet.

Internet A worldwide system of linked computer networks.

interstitial An ad that pops up in a separate frame on a screen page.

intranet A walled-off section of the larger Internet to which only company employees have access.

navigation The process by which people access a website, find the information they want, and move around within the site and to other related sites.

opt-in e-mail E-mail from a particular company or brand that has been given permission to be sent.

opt-out e-mail A series of e-mail messages that a company sends automatically until notified to stop.

pop-ups and pop-unders Ads that appear when a viewer closes a page or site.

privacy The control people exert over information they consider personal.

rich media E-mail that features audio and/or video.

search engines Internet tools that use keywords to find websites.

security The situation that personal information may be misused to the detriment of the person in question.

spam Unsolicited e-mail whose purpose is to sell a product or service.

virtual communities Groups of people who focus on certain online activities and establish relationships with one another.

Check the key points

Key point 1: Addressable and interactive media

a   How do addressable and interactive media differ? Why is their use increasing?

b   How do interactive media and mass media advertising differ?

c   How do opt-in and opt-out e-mail differ?

d   Is it accurate to say that there is no cost to e-mail campaigns? Explain.

Key point 2: Internet-based marketing communication

a   How can a company make its website more visible in order to attract more visitors?

b   Explain the attraction-versus-irritation problem with online advertising.

c   How effective are banner ads? How is their effectiveness determined?

d   Why have Web-based companies turned to offline advertising? Find an example, and analyse its effectiveness.

e   Explain how online communities, forums, and chat rooms can be used in marketing programmes. On the Web, find a product-related forum or chat room, and explain what you learned at that site.

f   What are two methods of delivering customized messages on the Web?

Key point 3: Websites

a   What is the first step in creating a website?

b   What are three things to think about when you set up a website?

c   What is the most important consideration in website design? What is the biggest problem?

d   In what two areas of customer service do online companies tend to fall short?

Key point 4: Customer concerns

a   What is the difference between privacy and security?

b   Why should privacy be a major issue for Web marketers?

c   What is the relationship between targeting and privacy?

d   What four privacy practices does the U.S. Federal Trade Commission recommend?

e   What can an online marketer do to increase customers' sense of security?

Chapter Challenge

Writing assignment

Write a short essay with the title: "Personal information I don't mind being ubiquitously available". Start with asking yourself what the consequences of ubiquitous availability might be. If you think that no personal information should be available to this extent, discuss what kind of information might meet what kind of availability. For example, you may argue that information about the study programme you are following might be generally available to prospective employers. Try to be precise: in the example just given, would you think your list of grades is also open to dissemination? But what does it mean if some students make their grades available and others don't?

Presentation assignment

Pick a local company that does Web marketing. Interview its webmaster and analyse its website. Identify its other uses of the Internet. Does it sell products both online and offline? What is its privacy policy? How might this company's Internet use be improved? Prepare a presentation on what you have found out to give to your classmates.

Internet assignment

Compile a list of five queries you would like see answered for three companies. Do a contest in class for which company the queries are answered quickest by Internet use only. What is characteristic of the winner? Does it depend on the experience of the searcher? If so, what does that mean for the company? Have another look at the respective websites. For what public is the website apparently designed?

Notes

[1] "Business and the Internet", *The Economist*, 26 June 1999, p. 17.

[2] Steve Fioretti and Bob D'Acquisto, "Advertising Takes a Ride on the Wireless Wave", *iMarketing News*, 21 August 2000, p. 19.

[3] Jim Sterne, "In Praise of E-Mail", *Inc. Tech 2000*, 15 September 2000, p. 149.

[4] www.Internetnews.com/iar/article.php/1564761, 6 January 2003.

[5] Mylene Mangalindan, "Cut the Spam, Direct Marketers Say", *Wall Street Journal*, 25 February 2003, p. D4.

[6] Lisa Bertagnoli, "E-Marketing Tricky in Europe", *Marketing News*, 16 July 2001, p. 19.

[7] Bill McCloskey, "Rich Email: Part 1", *ClickZ Network*, 24 February 2000, http://gt.clickz.com/cgi-bin/gt/sb/rm/rm.html?article=1357.

[8] Sterne, "In Praise of E-Mail".

[9] McCloskey, "Rich Email: Part 1".

[10] Cara DiPasquale, "E-Mail Effective for Customer Retention, Sales", *AdAge.com*, 3 April 2002.

[11] "Email—Most Effective Online Marketing Tool", *Los Angeles Times*, 27 January 2000, www.nua.net/surveys/?f=VS&art_id=905355553&rel=true; and Sterne, "In Praise of E-Mail".

[12] Sterne, "In Praise of E-Mail", p. 152.

[13] Susan Stellin, "Online Customer Service Found Lacking", *New York Times*, www.newyorktimes.com, 3 January 2002.

[14] Nat Ives, "Marketers Shift Tactics on Web Ads", *New York Times*, nytimes.com, 11 February 2003.

[15] James Daly, "Editor's Note: Service First", *Business 2.0*, 27 June 2000, p. 5.

[16] Bob Tedeschi, "Web Merchants Go Multimedia", *New York Times*, 13 March 2000, www.nytimes.com/library/tech/00/03/cyber/commerce/13commerce.html.

[17] Lori Enos, interview with Shirley Choy-Marshall, director of marketing for HPShopping.com, *E-Commerce Times*, 26 July 2001.

[18] Louis Whitman, "Dotcoms Shaping Up", *BrandEra Times*, 25 April 2000, www.brandera.com.

[19] Jeffrey Graham, "Internet Advertising Best Practices: Five Rules to Brand By", *ClickZ Network*, 25 October 2000.

[20] Terry Lefton, "Blocking Those internet Ads", from *Industry Standard*, reprinted in *Boulder Daily Camera: Business Plus*, 23 April 2001, p. 12.

[21] Marc Langheinrich, Atsuyoshi Nakamura, Naoki Abe, Tomonari Kamba, Yoshiyuki Koseki, *Unintrusive Customization Techniques for Web Advertising*, www8.org/w8-papers/2bcustomizing/unintrusive/unintrusive.html.

[22] Clare Saliba, interview with Gerry Sweeney, VP e-Visa, *E-Commerce Times*, 3 August 2001.

[23] Bob Walker, "System for Measuring Clicks Is under Assault", *New York Times* www.newyorktimes.com, 27 August 2001.

[24] David W. Moore, "Americans Say Internet Makes Their Lives Better", Gallup News Service, 23 February 2000, www.gallup.com/poll/releases/pr000223.asp.

[25] Sim D'Hertefelt, "Trust and the Perception of Security", *Interactionarchitect*, 3 January 2000, www.interactionarchitect.com/research/report20000103shd.htm.

[26] www.forrester.com/ER/Press/Release/0,1769,177,FF.html; "Forrester Technographics® Finds Online Consumers Fearful of Privacy Violations", Forrester Research press release, 27 October 1999.

[a1] Benedict Dellaert and Stefan Stremersch (2004) "Consumer Preferences for Mass Customization", MSI Working paper 04-118.

Further reading

Argyriou, Evmorfia, Philip J. Kitchen and T. C. Melewar (2006) "The relationship between corporate websites and brand equity: A conceptual framework and research agenda", *International Journal of Market Research*, Vol. 48–5, pp. 575–99.

Carroll, Amy, Stuart J. Barnes, Eusebio Scornavacca and Keith Fletcher (2007) "Consumer perceptions and attitudes towards SMS advertising: recent evidence from New Zealand", *International Journal of Advertising*, Vol. 26–1, pp. 79–98.

Grant, Ian and Stephanie O"Donohoe (2007) "Why young consumers are not open to mobile marketing communication", *International Journal of Advertising*, Vol. 26–2, pp. 223–46.

Karson, Eric J., Samuel D. McCloy and P. Greg Bonner (2006) "An Examination of Consumer Attitudes and Beliefs Towards Web Site Advertising", *Journal of Current Issues & Research in Advertising*, Vol. 28–2, pp. 77–91.

Lohtia, Ritu, Naveen Donthu and Idil Yaveroglu (2007) "Evaluating the efficiency of Internet banner advertisements", *Journal of Business Research*, Vol. 60–4, pp. 365–70.

Palmer, Daniel E. (2005) "Pop-Ups, Cookies and Spam: Toward a Deeper Analysis of the Ethical Significance of Internet Marketing Practices", *Journal of Business Ethics*, Vol. 58–1/3, pp. 271–80.

Media planning

Chapter 10

LEARNING OBJECTIVES

After reading this chapter, you should:

- ☑ Be able to describe the media planning process.
- ☑ Understand and appreciate the application of various statistics in media planning.
- ☑ Know the meaning of media objectives, in particular gross rating points (GRPs).
- ☑ Never forget to incorporate costs in media planning.
- ☑ Understand the concept of media scheduling.

CHAPTER PERSPECTIVE
Planning media connections

Media are the bridges that carry messages back and forth between companies and customers. In essence, these bridges are opportunities to create customer contact points. As media choices continue to increase, media planning becomes more precise but also more challenging. And because media are a major expense, there is constant tension between maximizing the delivery of brand messages while minimizing the cost. But media are about more than just delivering a message. Media are *how* customer contacts are created—the media used can enhance or detract from the impact and meaning of brand messages. As a result, media planning can be as creative as designing an ad or event.

In this chapter, the focus is on the tools and the process of media planning. This chapter explains why selecting the right media enables companies to deliver brand messages effectively and to connect to their customers and prospects.

Media planning: what's it all about?

In large companies the media plan is a sub-division of the marketing communication plan (which, as we have seen, is a sub-division of the marketing plan). **Media planning** is a *process for determining the most cost-effective mix of media for achieving a set of media objectives.* The key is to

Jochem's last trick

Jochem de Bruin has been the spokesperson in Rabobank commercials since 2003. He is a smart, charming, young man, representing the modern face of the bank. Over the years he has featured in commercials about a wide variety of services, including mortgages and investments. In 2007 it was decided that Jochem needed to be replaced. At the same time the organization planned to introduce Rabo Mobiel. This coincidence led to a final commercial: Jochem hosts a press conference, giving information and answering questions about the new product, and at the same time announcing that he is leaving the company. His trustworthy and sympathetic appearance certainly played a part in the acceptance of Rabo Mobiel: paying with your mobile phone. What?

Calling with your wallet

Calling with your wallet and paying with your mobile phone. It may sound ridiculous, but this is exactly what Rabobank, a Dutch financial services provider, is offering with its service "Rabo Mobiel". With this service Rabobank customers will soon be able to use their phone not only for calling and sending text messages but also for checking their bank account, transferring money or paying for a cup of coffee in a bar. All this is possible due to the Rabo Mobiel simcard that can connect the customer with the bank instantly. With this service Rabo Mobiel combines the advantages of calling at a reasonable price with the convenience of accessing bank account data any time and anywhere. Linking the customer's wallet to his or her calling device makes Rabobank the first bank in Europe to combine mobile banking and inexpensive calling.

Rabobank Group

The Rabobank Group was established in the Netherlands in the late nineteenth century as a collection of small, co-operative, rural banks. This co-operative basis has led the group to become a financial services provider through independent, local banks. In the Netherlands the Rabobank Group had established 188 local banks by 2007. These banks are all part of a parent organization called Rabobank Netherlands. Rabobank Netherlands advises and supports the local banks with their daily operations and additionally fosters several subsidiary companies. These subsidiaries, together with the local banks, provide a wide array of complementary services including loans, leasing, insurances and mortgages and form the largest all-finance company in the Netherlands serving over 9 million private and corporate customers. Outside the Netherlands, the Rabobank Group now has 289 offices in 38 different countries. This makes the Rabobank Group one of the twenty biggest financial institutions in the world. It is also the world's leading food and agri bank. Additionally Rabobank holds a triple A rating.

Rabo Mobiel

Rabo Mobiel was set up as an independent entity of Rabobank, partnering with telecom provider Orange and multimedia company Talpa to deliver its services. Rabo Mobiel was first offered in November 2006. At the same time a massive advertising campaign was launched. Initially Rabo Mobiel targeted the 2.6 million existing Internet banking customers of Rabobank. But since mobile phones have become a commodity, non-Rabobank customers have also become part of the target market. According to Eric Huygen, CEO of Rabo Mobiel, the goal of the campaign was to firmly position Rabo Mobiel in the market, first as a company but also as a product. Since Rabo Mobiel was a new concept, customer awareness and sales had to be built from scratch. The goal is to attract approximately 150 000 customers by the end of 2007. That is why all possible communication means were used to convince the market of the concept of mobile banking.

Rabo Mobiel campaign

In November and December 2006, during the launch of Rabo Mobiel, communication was mainly used to position Rabo Mobiel and therefore marketing communication was primarily informative. Radio and TV commercials were broadcast several times a day and direct mail was used to tap into the market of existing Rabobank customers. A great part of the promotion was centred on Internet advertising banners. Through these Rabo Mobiel realized a constant online presence. Print ads were also employed, but due to the decreasing effectiveness of this communication tool, they only represented a small part of the campaign and were only used once at the beginning of the campaign. In January 2007 the campaign moved from an informative to a more commercial one, and communication from that time forward covered messages like "calling for 10 cents a minute", and "600 minutes of free calling".

Apart from external marketing communication, internal communication also played an important role in the campaign of Rabo Mobiel. Employees of Rabobank received a USB-stick containing all information on Rabo Mobiel. Also, information on the service was published on the internal web of the company and was available through Raboshops, Rabobank information points located in retail stores. Rabo Mobiel even enticed employees to try the product, by offering them one of the phones sold for Rabo Mobiel purposes at a discount.

Although the frequency of marketing communications during the launch of Rabo Mobiel was very high, promotion for the service from 2007 onwards is scheduled just like any other service offered by Rabobank. Every year the company develops a calendar that stipulates in what period which products or services will be promoted. Frequency of communication is thus very similar for all financial services, including Rabo Mobiel.

Not only the frequency with which media are employed, but also the look, feel, voice and tone of the Rabo Mobiel campaign is similar to those of other Rabobank campaigns. Rabobank's brand values and brand positioning were transferred to Rabo Mobiel and formed the basis for its campaign. A perfect illustration of this equality is the TV commercial of Rabo Mobiel, featuring the Rabobank spokesperson, Jochem de Bruin hosting a press conference. At first the journalists are surprised and sceptical about it, but at the end of the commercial Jochem makes them laugh, signalling that he has managed to win their sympathy for Rabo Mobiel.

The TV commercial as just described was strongly integrated with the other media used in the Rabo Mobiel campaign. They were used to reinforce each other. That is why all media, TV, radio, direct mail, print media, and the Internet, were employed together and at the same time. This ensured the greatest exposure and enabled Rabo Mobiel to position its organization and products firmly in the marketplace.

Results

So far Rabo Mobiel's comprehensive communication plan has brought remarkable results. By April 2007 brand awareness for Rabo Mobiel was around 80 per cent. As CEO Eric Huygen put it: "Rabo Mobiel is pleasantly surprised by the results so far." In order to track results Rabo Mobiel continually carries out research, to assess customer satisfaction, for example, or to test the company's products. This allows the company to uncover inconsistencies and to make the necessary amendments at any time. Hopefully research will continue to show positive results for Rabo Mobiel.

Sources:
www.consumentenbond.nl/thema/elektronica_en_communicatie/553918/rabo_mobiel/6421888/
6422482/?ticket=nietlid
www.rabobank.nl/mobiel
www.ubachswisbrun.nl/xcms/werk/id/1084
http://nl.wikipedia.org/wiki/Jochem_de_Bruin

balance message impact and cost—maximizing impact while minimizing cost. Media are often the largest single cost item in a marketing communication budget, especially for consumer goods and services. If the selected media do not deliver the brand messages and help them have maximum impact, sales will likely suffer, and much of the media money will have been wasted.

Although media planning is numbers driven, it has a significant creative dimension. Media planners must be creative in analysing the quantitative aspect while understanding the qualitative dimensions and how people use media. The science and art of how media connect companies and customers can be captured in the following considerations: the *moment* in which brand messages are delivered, the *mood* of customers or prospects at the time they receive or send brand messages, the *mind-set* of customers and prospects, the *media* that carry the messages, and the *milieu* in which messages are exchanged.[1]

Unless the media budget is extremely small, most companies use more than one medium—for several reasons. First, different media have different message-delivery features, as was explained in Chapters 8 and 9. Second, media strategies often call for a variety of media. Finally, a single communication vehicle can seldom reach everyone in a target audience.

The challenge of media planning is becoming greater because the number of ways to send brand messages is increasing. Recognition of this development, however, has been slow in coming. Not until the late 1980s, for example, did the Advertising Research Association recommend that its 30-year-old model for evaluating media effects be revised to include all marketing communication functions, and not just advertising.

Recall from Chapter 3 that there are four kinds of brand touch points: (1) *intrinsic*, which automatically occur during the course of buying or using a brand; (2) *customer-created*, which are initiated by customers and prospects; (3) *unexpected*, which appear in the media and elsewhere unannounced; and (4) *company created*, which are the planned marketing communication messages. Media are the vehicle for all touch points except the intrinsic ones. Media planning is primarily applicable for the company-created touch points, although the number of customer-created messages is increasing, and companies are considering how best to manage media usage by customers for asking questions, complaining, and making suggestions.

Before media planning begins, the brand messages being delivered and received at intrinsic and customer-created touch points should be reviewed. If these messages are negative, they can outweigh any positive effect of company-created MC messages, and the result may be a waste of media money. Another reason to identify intrinsic touch points is that they can provide additional "media" opportunities at almost no cost. Intrinsic contacts—such as service delivery, packaging, and repairs—represent opportunities to provide brand information and reinforce brand images. Because these brand touch points automatically demand the attention of customers, especially current customers, they provide a captive audience already interacting with the brand in some way.

Media buying is *the execution of a media plan.* Media buyers negotiate with publishers, broadcasters, and other media representatives to arrange cost-effective contracts that will satisfy the media objectives. In media buying, it is not the lowest price that is most important but the return on the media investment in terms of effect on the target audience. Media buyers usually do post-buy analyses to make sure the messages were delivered when and to whom as promised.

One trend affecting media buying is the consolidation of media companies into conglomerates. Each media conglomerate bundles its various vehicles to offer planners "cross-media buys". For example, media companies offer buyers the chance to use a variety of its vehicles to send "integrated messages". A study commissioned by *Advertising Age* found that half of the companies and agencies surveyed said they had taken advantage of these integrated media packages. The main reason given was that they delivered "an integrated marketing message across all [media] platforms".[2]

A four-step planning process

Although important in its own right, media buying is primarily an execution of, and therefore is driven by, the media plan. This chapter focuses on the tools and process of media planning. Because an almost unlimited number of media options exist for producing company-created touch points, media planners must sort through a lot of information when developing a good media plan. The task breaks down into four steps: (1) identifying media targets, (2) setting media objectives, (3) determining media strategies, and (4) scheduling media placements. Each step is discussed in this chapter.

Step 1: Media targeting: finding the target audience

The marketing plan identifies the brand's target audiences. The planner's job is to select the communication vehicles and markets whose profiles most closely match those of the target audiences. The greater the match, the better. The extent of the match is determined by looking at how the target audiences differ from the average population. For example, if the target audience is twice as likely as the average population to own a boat, communication vehicles whose audiences are at least twice as likely to own a boat should be considered. Every target market has such **skews**, or *variations from the general population.* The greater the variance from average, the greater the skew. A skew is also sometimes described as an *index.* For example, demographic analysis might reveal that physicians index, or skew, higher on income than does the general population. Skews and indexes indicate to what extent a number—be it a population, an attribute score, or anything else that can be described numerically—differs from the average. Marketers find this information useful because such differences form the basis on which target audiences can be identified and reached.

The size of a target audience also affects media decisions. In general, the smaller the targeted audience is, the more personalized and interactive a message can be. For example, to reach 5000 households in a city of 100 000, addressable media would be more appropriate than mass media. But if the targeted audience in this same metro area were 50 000, mass media would be more cost-effective.

Planning step	Questions to ask	Tools/sources for answers
1 Media targeting	Who is the target audience? Where is the target audience? How big is the target audience? How much does the average target household consume? How is the brand doing in one market in comparison with other markets?	Customer database CDI (category development index) BDI (brand development index) Internal sales data
2 Media objectives	How much reach and targeted reach? How much frequency and effective frequency? What frequency distribution is acceptable? How much media weight (GRPs, TGRPs)? Should media weight be equal in all markets?	MRI, Nielsen, and other media data sources Agency computer programs for determining ratings and frequency Past history of campaigns and agency's experience Share data from Nielsen
3 Media strategies	Which media and how much of each in the media mix? What is the best balance of one- and two-way media? What is the target customer's buying process? When is the best time (aperture) to reach customers and prospects? How concentrated should the media mix be? How should media be scheduled? Which media are compatible with the creative work? What media environment is most compatible with the brand's image? What are the best CPMs and CPPs?	Media kits from each media vehicle being considered (includes rate card) SRDS (Standard Rate and Data Services) Personal contact with media sales representative for latest costs and availabilities Review past campaigns to see what media weight created what results (must keep in mind other variables)
4 Media schedule	Should media be continuous, flighted, or pulsed? How seasonal is product buying?	Budget Analysis of sales by month, day of week Closing dates (when vehicles need to receive ads) from media kits or sales reps

Media profiles

Many media vehicles profile their audiences in terms of demographics, psychographics (lifestyles), and product usage. That information allows them to analyse their audience in terms of appropriate products to be advertised. However, such detailed information is not always available for many media vehicles, especially those with small audiences. When media vehicles do have audience-profile information, it is generally demographic. Vehicles dealing with particular areas of interest, such as sports, hobbies, or finance, are the ones most likely to have lifestyle and product-usage data in addition to demographic profiles.

Table 10-1 is a hypothetical example of the type of information available on magazine audiences. Such information helps media planners understand the audience of a particular vehicle and how it compares to the profile of their brand's targeted audiences.

This is how to read and make use of the information shown in the sample report (Table 10-1). A report such as this would help media planners who are interested in reaching college students (note data are for "College students currently enrolled"). Assuming the decision had been made to use magazines in the media mix, the question then becomes—"Which magazines?" The data show which magazines are most widely read by college students. Column A is the projected

Category	A (000)	B Horiz. %	C Vertical %	D Index
College students, currently enrolled	15 136	7.46	100.00	100
Men	7182	7.39	47.45	99
Women	7954	7.53	52.55	101
Magazines				
Allure	883	19.19	5.83	257
Better Homes & Gardens	2129	5.65	14.07	76
Boating	176	5.88	1.16	79
Brides	1064	16.64	7.03	223
Family Circle	1068	4.72	7.08	63
Fitness	954	14.38	6.30	193
Glamour	1910	16.09	12.62	216
Good Housekeeping	1238	4.88	8.18	65
Marie Claire	752	23.17	4.97	310
Maxim	2604	26.33	17.20	353
Outdoor Life	460	6.67	3.04	89
Prevention	632	5.85	4.17	78
Reader's Digest	2685	6.27	17.74	84
Shape	1068	18.64	7.05	250
Stock Car Racing	163	4.77	1.07	64
Time	2363	10.31	15.62	138
TV Guide	2330	7.78	15.39	104
Wall Street Journal	364	9.60	2.40	129

Table 10-1 Sample data for readership of magazines by college students

Source: 2002 Doublebase Mediamark Research Inc., extracted from a list of 220 magazines. Used by permission.

number of college students who have looked into the magazines listed. For *Allure* this is 883 000. Column B shows the *percentage of a magazine's readers* who are college students. For *Allure* 19.19 per cent of its readers are college students. Columns A and B contain the basic data on which the more informative numbers in columns C and D are based. Column C shows what *percentage of college students* read each magazine. According to this report, 5.83 per cent of all college students read *Allure*. The last column, D, is an index that shows how likely college students are to read a magazine *compared to the total adult population*. So, whereas college students make up 7.46 per cent of the total population of adults, 19.19 per cent of *Allure*'s readership consists of college students. Consequently, the index is 257 (19.19 divided by 7.46 times 100) which means college students are roughly 2.5 times more likely to read *Allure* than the average adult. In this way, Column C gives an impression of how well a magazine reaches the target audience in absolute numbers, while Column D can be interpreted as a measure of effectiveness, more particularly of implied waste. A high index implies low waste of media euros. In this example, *Maxim* would be the best choice, with both a high absolute reach, and a low waste in the sense of reaching people that are not in the target.

Determining CDIs and BDIs

A major decision in media planning is how to divide media spending among all the markets in which a brand is being sold. To help make such decisions about where to use media to promote a brand most effectively, marketers use a **category development index (CDI)**, which is *a numerical indicator of the relative consumption rate in a particular market for a particular product category*. To understand CDIs, remember that 100 is the average index score: anything above 100 is higher than the average, and anything below 100 is lower than the average. Suppose a city has a CDI of 200 for hot dogs. This means that the average household (HH) in that city consumes twice the national average. If a city has a 50 CDI for hot dogs, that means the average household in that city consumes only half of the national average. Not surprisingly, companies are generally more interested in markets that have CDIs above 100. It is a natural application of the saying "Fish where the fish are."

To determine a category development index (CDI), you first must determine the average household consumption rate for a marketing universe, such as "Western Europe". The **marketing universe**, or simply universe, is a useful concept that can be defined as *the total market of interest*. A marketing universe can differ per company, per brand, per situation. The marketing universe can be defined by a company in any way it wants. The marketing universe represents a basis for comparison in many analyses. Hence, while an analyst has freedom to define it according to her needs, she must be explicit on this definition. And of course, it cannot be changed within the analysis.

The consumption of the marketing universe becomes the base against which the average consumption in a particular marketing area is compared. Let us look at the yogurt category and determine the CDI for France in relation to the Western European market. First, we must figure the average consumption in the marketing universe which is calculated as the total amount consumed—e.g. 1 billion pounds—divided by the number of households in Western Europe—e.g. 100 million households. This shows us that the average household (HH) consumption in the defined marketing universe is 10 pounds per year:

$$\frac{\text{Total pounds sold in Western Europe in a year}}{\text{Total number of households in Western Europe}} = \text{Avg. lbs per HH}$$

$$\frac{1\,000\,000\,000 \text{ pounds sold in Western Europe}}{100\,000\,000 \text{ million households}} = 10 \text{ lbs per HH}$$

The calculation can be made in whatever unit a category is sold—pounds, cases, jars. It should *not* be made in currency, however, because different brands within a category charge different prices.

Once the average household consumption is determined for the marketing universe, the average household consumption must be determined for the market area in question. Thus, the same calculation is made for this market, in this example France:

$$\frac{\text{Total pounds sold in France}}{\text{Total households in France}} = \text{Avg. lbs per HH}$$

$$\frac{375\,000\,000 \text{ pounds sold in France}}{15\,000\,000 \text{ households in France}} = 25 \text{ lbs per HH}$$

Once the average annual household consumption is known for a particular market, such as 25 pounds for France, the CDI is determined by dividing this number by the average household consumption rate in the marketing universe, which is 10 pounds per household. To get an index, this number is multiplied by 100:

$$\text{CDI} = \frac{25 \text{ lbs in France average}}{10 \text{ lbs W-Europe average}} \times 100 = 2.50 \times 100 = 250$$

This CDI of 250 says that the average French household consumes two and a half times as much yogurt as does the average Western European household. For this reason, yogurt companies' media plans generally have more media weight—that is, advertising with higher relative impact—in France than in a market with a much lower CDI. CDIs tell marketers where they are mostly likely to get the best return on their media euros.

The category development index indicates relative development of a product category in a market. The **brand development index (BDI)** is a *numerical indicator of the development of a particular brand within a market relative to all other markets in which the brand is sold.* The higher a market's BDI, the better a brand is doing in that market compared to all the other markets in which the brand is distributed. As with a CDI, a BDI of 100 is average. Let's continue the yogurt illustration to show how a BDI is determined; the Danone brand is used as an example:

$$\frac{\text{Total pounds of Danone sold in Western Europe}}{\text{Total number of HH in Western Europe}} = \text{Avg. lbs of Danone per HH in W-Europe}$$

$$\frac{500\,000\,000 \text{ lbs of Danone}}{100\,000\,000 \text{ HH}} = 5 \text{ lbs Danone sold per HH in W-Europe}$$

$$\frac{105\,000\,000 \text{ lbs. of Danone sold in France}}{15\,000\,000 \text{ HH in France}} = 7 \text{ lbs Danone per HH in France}$$

$$\text{BDI for France} = \frac{7 \text{ lbs in France}}{5 \text{ lb in Western Europe}} \times 100 = 1.40 \times 100 = 140$$

Marketing managers and media planners pay close attention to these numbers in order to track brand performance. A low BDI tells the manager that a brand is doing relatively worse in that market than the brand is doing in other markets. One reason for a below-average BDI could be a weak sales force in that particular market. Another possible reason is greater competition, in which case a media planner may opt for more media weight and promotions in that market. A high CDI signals a market that is well developed and is therefore attractive to be present. However, since all brands in a category use CDIs in their media planning, and all want to "fish where the fish are", high-CDI markets often become promotional battlegrounds in which all the major competitors are buying an above-average amount of media. A low CDI in contrast signals a market where the particular product category is not (yet) large. A manager needs to use his judgement whether this is due to market characteristics that make it unlikely that the market will ever be adopting the product at similar levels as other markets, in which case there is no apparent need to pay specific attention to that market. Alternatively, the reason for a low CDI may indicate unexplored grounds, opening opportunities to grow the market. And in general growing markets are the most attractive to be active in.

If anything, BDI and CDI therefore are indicators, not decision-making instruments. BDI and CDI signal market opportunities, or lack thereof. These numbers, like all numbers, need interpretation and judgement to become truly valuable for managers. (Note that a BDI is different from a market share, although they look similar. Both tell something about a brand's performance in a certain market. Market share, however, is telling how well your brand is doing *compared to other brands in a specific market*. BDI tells how well your brand is doing *compared to your brand in other markets*.)

Step 2: Setting media objectives: what do you want to accomplish?

Media objectives reflect what a company wants to accomplish regarding the *delivery* of brand messages. MC objectives describe what a company wants customers to think, feel, and do about its brand; media objectives describe how a company will expose customers to brand messages in such a way that the messages *have the opportunity* to impact on customers' thinking, feeling, and doing.

In many agencies and companies creative strategy decisions are made before media objectives are determined. When this happens, a company risks missing some opportunities for connecting with customers. As stated before, *integrating* the media and creative planning (by means of cross-functional organization) produces better media plans, for the following reasons:

- There are now more media alternatives than ever before, and some are much better than others at reaching certain audiences.

- Media planners may be able to suggest new ways to reach target audiences that are just as effective as, but less expensive than, the media a company has always used. Media are a major portion of most MC budgets and therefore should not be an afterthought.

- Some media and programming environments are so specialized or have such strong personalities (such as *Bild* or the *Financial Times*) that brand messages can have more impact when especially designed to be compatible with them. Reaching a target audience in a media environment with the same "tone" as the brand message enhances communication.

Media objectives explain what needs to be accomplished in order for customers and prospects to be exposed to the MC message. The two media variables that determine this are *reach* and *frequency*. These variables measure the breadth and depth of message delivery. When *reach (R)* and *frequency (F)* are multiplied together, the resulting number is *gross rating points (GRPs)*, which indicate the weight of the media plan. Reach, frequency, and GRPs are explained in the following pages.

Reach

No matter how good an offer is or how creatively an MC message has been designed, it can have no impact until an audience has an opportunity to see or hear it. MC messages need to reach customers and prospects. In the context of media, the term **reach** refers to *the percentage of an audience that has had the opportunity to be exposed to a media vehicle within a specified period.*

Although reach is a widely used media-planning measure, it is important to keep in mind that it is an *estimate* of communication—almost always an *over*estimate. Why? Reach is an indication of the *opportunity* for exposure to a brand message; it is not an indicator of how many customers and prospects actually are exposed to a brand message. When you buy a magazine, you may read only a portion of it and not even see half the ads. Nevertheless, you have had an *opportunity* to see the ads, so you are counted as having been reached. (These kinds of estimates make steps 2 and 3 of the media planning as much art as science!)

Reach (R) is expressed as a percentage, although advertisers don't use the per cent sign. For example, R = 58 means that 58 per cent of an audience in a defined marketing universe had the opportunity to be exposed one or more times to a brand message in a media vehicle. A related term is *coverage area* that refers to the area where the medium is distributed. For example, the coverage area of a national newspaper is all households in the country. The reach then refers to the percentage of all these households that buy or receive the newspaper. Reach is the more relevant concept for media planners.

Calculating reach

The way in which reach is calculated varies by medium. The reach of radio and television is indicated by the ratings of particular programmes which is basically the same as their reach. One rating point equals 1 per cent of a broadcast vehicle's coverage area. The point to remember is that, for radio and TV, *programmes* determine ratings, not the stations themselves.

The reach of specialized magazines is based on a universe defined by the category of interest or use, rather than by household in a given geographical area. For example, the universe for the trade publication *Golf Course Management* would be all managers of golf courses. The reach of outdoor advertising is indicated by the percentage of cars in a metropolitan area that drive by billboards carrying a particular brand message within a 24-hour period. Most companies using outdoor advertising display the brand message on multiple boards at the same time. If a brand message is posted on 100 outdoor boards spread throughout Brussels, for example, the reach is determined by the percentage of cars driving by these boards. If there are 2 000 000 cars registered in Brussels, and traffic counts show that 2 000 000 cars have driven by one or more of these boards within a 24-hour period, the reach is said to be 100 (100 per cent). In outdoor terms, this is known as a "100 showing". (Unfortunately, traffic counts don't recognize the same car driving by more than once, a problem known as *duplication*, described below.) In the case of direct mail and telemarketing, reach is determined by simply dividing the number of mailings made by the total number of households or companies that make up the defined universe.

Another way to determine reach is by the number of message impressions. An **impression** is *one exposure to a brand message.* Media planners sometimes use impressions as a measure of reach when it is difficult to identify a marketing universe (the basis on which a reach percentage can be figured). Internet brand messages are often figured in terms of impressions because it is still difficult to tell who of visitors is in the marketing universe. The number of visits to websites carrying a particular brand message determines the number of impressions for that brand message.

When the marketing universe, the basis of calculating reach, is defined in terms of a target market, rather than a general market, the outcome is referred to as the **targeted reach**, *the portion of a communication vehicle's audience that is in a brand's target market.* Targeted reach is important to calculate because it shows what a company is actually getting for the money it spends on any given media vehicle. The differential between reach and targeted reach is called **media waste**, which is *reaching people who are neither customers nor prospects*, and is a major concern in media planning and buying. Bear in mind that, while marketers are interested in targeted reach, media usually work with reach; hence, marketers are asked to pay for reach. This makes waste not only a disturbing factor, but also one that cost real money.

Frequency

In media planning, the word **frequency** refers to *the average number of times those who are reached have an opportunity to be exposed to a brand message within a specified time period.* To help ensure that a message gets exposed, most media plans call for a frequency greater than 1. It is common knowledge that exposure to any particular brand message is far less than the exposure to the vehicle carrying that message. This means *message* exposure should be given more attention than *vehicle* exposure.

A second reason for multiple exposures is to increase the chance that a message will be understood. The more complex the message, the more exposures will be needed in order for the target to fully understand what is being communicated. Building associations, for example, requires repetition of the occurrence of the association with the brand according to classical conditioning theory. Finally, and perhaps most obviously, frequency increases the chance that a message will be *remembered.*

Effective frequency

In making media planning decisions a key concept is that of **effective frequency**, *the number of times a message needs to be seen to make an impression or achieve a specified objective.* Guidelines say this is somewhere between 3 and 10. In reality, this is not much of a guideline because the range is so wide. One of the best ways for a company to determine the effective frequency level is to track customer responses, testing various levels of frequency.

Another reason why the level of effective frequency varies with every message is that there are so many variables that determine the impact of a brand message. Some of these variables are:

1 ***The offer's value and complexity:*** Making prospects understand that a local bank now offers "free cheque accounts" does not require nearly as much frequency as getting them to understand that the bank offers four different savings plan options (let alone getting them to remember what those options are and how they differ).

2 ***The attention value of the medium itself:*** Some media vehicles demand more attention than others, or attention of a different kind. For example, an outdoor board may be startling, but a TV commercial generally commands more sustained attention.

3 *The attention-getting power of the message itself:* The more creative and attention getting a message is, the greater is the likelihood that it will have the desired effect.

4 *The target audience's level of need or desire to learn about a brand:* Some product categories are simply more interesting than others and automatically get attention more easily. Most people, for example, find cars more interesting than washing powders. When audience interest is high, less frequency may be needed to be effective.

5 *The MC objectives:* If the communication objective is to increase brand awareness rather than to change behaviour, probably less frequency is needed.

6 *Personal influences:* Word of mouth can greatly affect the impact of a message. If word of mouth is negative, more frequency is needed to help counter the negative messages.

7 *The amount of competitive brand messages:* Generally, the more frequency competitive brand messages have, the more frequency is needed for your brand. **Share-of-voice spending** is *a brand's portion of total media spending in that brand's product category.* This corresponds to share-of-voice budgeting described in Chapter 5. Most marketers and media planners agree that a brand must maintain a competitive share of voice.

Different levels of frequency create difference levels of response. Most media planners agree that there must be a minimum level of frequency before any impact will occur. As frequency continues to increase, however, there comes a time when additional increases have little or no effect. At this point, a marketer's return on frequency becomes zero. One of two things is generally happening at this point. Either most members of the target audience who are going to respond have done so, or **message wear-out**—*brand messages that once attracted attention and motivated the target audience no longer do so*—has occurred.

Frequency distribution analysis

When planning for message frequency, it is important to keep in mind that frequency is an average. More informative therefore, is an analysis called **frequency distribution analysis** (sometimes referred to as a **quintile analysis**), which is *an analysis that divides a target audience into equal segments and establishes an average frequency for each of these segments (quintus* is Latin for "fifth"). The segments are based on the actual frequency for every member of the audience. Thus, the first segment consists of those consumers that report least frequent exposures to the message, etc. For example, a quintile analysis might reveal that the top 20 per cent of those reached have an average of 13 exposure opportunities and the bottom 20 per cent have an average of only 2 exposure opportunities:

Quintile	Frequency (average number of exposures)
Top 20% of audience	13
Next 20%	10
Next 20%	6
Next 20%	4
Bottom 20%	2

In this case, an average frequency of 7 results, but approximately 40 per cent are exposed to the message on average more than 10 times, whereas for 60 per cent the average exposure was less than 6. This of course provides more detailed information than just the average frequency.

Reach × frequency = gross rating points

Reach and frequency are interrelated concepts that when combined produce a measure called *gross rating points*. **Gross rating points (GRPs)** are *a combined measure of reach and frequency indicating the weight of a media plan*. The more GRPs in a plan, the more "weight" the plan is said to have. **Media weight** is *an indication of the relative impact of a media plan*. GRPs are determined by multiplying reach by frequency

When *targeted reach* is applied to a media plan, we talk about **targeted GRPs (TGRPs)**, which is *the number of gross rating points delivered against just the targeted audience*. TGRPs provide a more accurate picture of what a brand receives for its media spending. The difference between a plan's GRPs and targeted GRPs is the number of GRPs that are wasted, a number that always needs to be minimized as much as possible. This can be done by selecting the media vehicles that will reach the targeted audience most accurately.

Ideally, gross rating points should be compared only for mixes of vehicles *within the same medium*. GRPs for TV, newspapers, and direct mail cannot be reliably compared because the different media have different levels of impact. Does a 30-second TV ad have more or less impact than a half-page newspaper ad, an outdoor board, or a 60-second radio commercial? There is no simple answer to this question.

Now that you have some understanding of all the critical media terms, here are some examples of typical media objectives. Like all marketing objectives, media objectives should be measurable, as these are:

- *Reach:* "Have a minimum reach of 65 during each of the first three quarters of the year, and 80 in the last quarter." (This company needs to rid its inventory at year's end, so it needs to advertise special promotions in the fourth quarter.)

- *Frequency:* "Have a minimum frequency of 5 each quarter in markets where share is over 20 per cent; have a minimum frequency of 10 in all other markets." (This brand is in a highly competitive and complex category—vitamins—and recognizes that if it is to increase its share of market, it needs to increase brand knowledge, which requires greater repetition of its message.)

- *Target allocation:* "Allocate 50 per cent of media spend to reach current customers and 50 per cent to reach prospects." (This brand knows that brand loyalty in its category is very thin so it has to put as much effort against keeping current customers as it does in acquiring new ones.)

- *Timing:* "Have 300 GRPs of advertising support within the month preceding each promotion." (This company has data showing that the higher its brand awareness is during a promotion, the greater is the response to its promotions.)

- *Interactivity:* "Respond to 95 per cent of customer/prospect-initiated e-mails within 24 hours." (This company knows that a quick response is an added value to customers because it makes them feel special and important.)

- *Integration:* "Reach 80 per cent of targeted media editors/news directors with press releases 30 days prior to start of new-product advertising." (Brand publicity has a much better chance of being used when the story is news. If a company asks for publicity at the same time a new product is being advertised, the news value is diminished by the ads telling the story.)

Step 3: Determining media strategies: how will you accomplish the objectives?

Media strategies are ideas about *how* media objectives will be accomplished through the selection of various combinations of media. For every media objective there should be one or more strategies. These strategies describe the media mix—that is, which media should be used and to what extent. Cost always determines the selection of strategies. Like every other marketing communication operation, media must operate within a given budget. Because of the large number of media choices, the final decision about which media to use is often influenced by their cost. Media tools used to make objective cost comparisons among media alternatives are cost per thousand (CPM) and cost per point (CPP).

To develop creative cost-effective media-use strategies requires in-depth understanding of each medium's attributes and cost and a thorough understanding of the target audiences. As explained in Chapters 8 and 9, each medium has its own strengths and weaknesses. Table 10-2 (cf Table 8-1) is a summary of how major media compare in attributes that marketers take into consideration when deciding which media can best help achieve media objectives.

Media strategies involve more than just identifying which media should be used. "Spend half the money in TV, a quarter in newspapers, and a quarter in outdoor" is not a particularly useful media strategy. A good media strategy states how media can help create a brand experience and engage customers and prospects—that is, how media will create a connection. This requires a good understanding of the brand's customers and targeted prospects, for people's ideas and interests and what it takes to reach them do not remain constant. An example of changing attitudes about the consumer/media vehicle connection is seen in the area of reality TV shows. They were originally considered too edgy for mainstream advertisers; then the broad success of such programmes as *Big Brother* and *Idols* followed by numerous "makeover" programmes and many more made reality programmes acceptable even to conservative advertisers.

Good media strategies require creative selection and use of media.[3] For example, a strategy can be to use media that reach the target audience at unexpected times (such as late, late night) in communication vehicles whose image is, let us say non-traditional. Another combination of creative and media strategy is to use a **teaser campaign**—*a series of messages that carry no brand identification but are designed to create curiosity*—to build interest in later brand messages. It also allows the target audience an opportunity to "discover" the story and thus become more involved.

Media strategy factors

Type of product

An important consideration in determining media strategies is the type of product being promoted. When advertising low-involvement products such as detergents, paper towels, or industrial cleaning services, planners should consider the more intrusive media. Another strategy, however, is selecting media whose editorial content creates a more receptive environment. For detergent and paper-towel brands, a "shelter" magazine such as *Better Homes & Gardens* or the Home & Garden television channel provides such an environment. In contrast, high-involvement products such as luxury goods and entertainment offers can make use of print media, where readers select the stories and ads they want to see.

Attribute	Magazine (local)	Newspaper	Outdoor	Television	Radio (local)	Direct mail	Tele-marketing	Internet	Phone	Packaging
Target selectivity	good	poor	poor*	broadcast average/ cable good	good	best	best	good/best**	best	best
Reach	low	best	high	high	low	low	low	high	low	best
Message impact	average	average	low	average	low	high	high	low	high	high
Geographic flexibility	poor	poor	good	national poor/local good	good	good	good	low	best	good
Lead time to use	long	short	long	national long/local short	short	medium	short	short	short	long
Ability to control time of exposure	poor	good	poor	best	best	good	best	best	best	poor
Where vehicles used most	home/ some away	home	out of home	home	home/car	home/office	home/office	home/office	home/office/ car	home

Table 10-2 Relative attributes of major media

* But good geographically.
** E-mail is best.

Source: Based on "General Characteristics of Major Media Forms", in Media Planning: A Practical Guide, Jim Surmanek, NTC, 1995. Reprinted with permission from the McGraw-Hill Companies.

Customers' buying decision process

Media strategies should also be driven by customers' buying decision processes (Chapter 4). Recall the basic AIDA model—consumers go through the stages of attention, interest, desire, action. IBM uses the AIDA model to drive its media decisions. Each step in the decision-making process requires a different media strategy. A media strategy for reaching people in the first stage of looking for a laptop computer would be to place image advertisements in business-oriented media such as *BusinessWeek*. For prospects who attended a trade show where they visited an IBM booth and tried a ThinkPad laptop, a media strategy would be to use direct mail to send, immediately after the trade show, an offer for a free 30-day trial (this strategy assumes that names and addresses of booth visitors were captured). An important element of the latter strategy is timing—making sure that prospects receive the offer within a few days of attending the show, before they forget their trial experience.

For mass-consumed products such as computers and cars, a strategy using selected mass media could be useful to create attention and maintain brand awareness and the interest of a broad target audience. However, once a customer enters the desire and action stages for these products, the best media strategy would be to use selected interactive media (mail, e-mail, phone). The closer to the action step, the more personal the message delivery needs to be. The more personal the message and the medium, generally the more impact the two will have (see Figure 10-1). Although interactive and addressable media are expensive, the cost often can be justified because of their ability to motivate behaviour.

The importance of interactivity during the action stage cannot be overstated. In their early phases, e-business companies such as Amazon.com found that people often went to their company websites, filled shopping carts, got ready to check out, then found themselves with a question but no way to get it answered, so they abandoned their shopping carts. That is why many e-commerce companies now make their sites interactive and provide e-mail addresses and phone numbers, as well as hyperlinks to customer service. Making sure that an interested customer can talk to someone in person is vital.

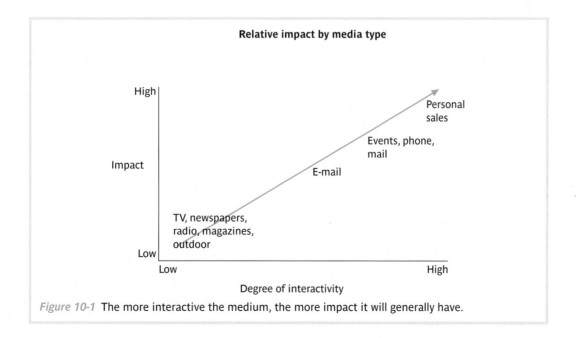

Relative impact by media type

Figure 10-1 The more interactive the medium, the more impact it will generally have.

Apertures

A media strategy used by the advertising agency DDB Worldwide demonstrates understanding of customer touch points and of buyer decision processes. This agency uses the word aperture (which means "opening") to describe *any situation in which the target audience is highly receptive to a brand message*. Literally, an aperture is the opening in a camera's lens. The more open the lens is—the wider its aperture—the greater is the amount of light that passes through. Similarly, the more open a person is to receiving a message, the more impact that message can have. A media strategy that is built by following customers through their daily lives tries to identify and take advantage of apertures. A sports stadium, for example, is an aperture in which people are more open to brand messages related to food, drink, and sporting goods than they are to political messages, dietary aids, and life insurance offers.

Determining the media mix

One of the most important considerations in creating an IMC media mix is to choose media that enhance the messages being delivered. As a DDB Worldwide media executive explained, "It is no longer enough to calculate a cost per thousand or other body-count figures. We also need to think about the qualitative benefits that different media vehicles can provide, such as conveying a message with authority or having the ability to be influential."[4] There is no one best mix. Every brand situation is different, and a mix should be driven by the media and marketing objectives.

In the world of media planning and buying, the media selected for a brand constitute a media mix. Determining the media mix is a major strategic challenge that involves two basic decisions: (1) which media to use and (2) how much of each to use. Most media plans call for both one-way and interactive media but are heavy on one-way media.

Most media plans include more than one media vehicle. In such cases, reach is almost always less than the sum of the individual reach figures, because of duplication. Duplication is *the overlapping coverage of two or more vehicles*. If Deutsche Bank decides to supplement its *BusinessWeek* advertising by also running ads in the *Wall Street Journal Europe*, on a Business Radio channel, and on the CNN cable channel, many members of the audience would receive the message more than once—there would be a lot of duplication. Some small businesses are exposed to two of these vehicles, some to three, a few to all four. Similarly, the use of a mix complicates the concept of frequency. Within one vehicle frequency is equated to the number of insertions. With multiple vehicles it is less straightforward to add the number of insertions. In the following sections the complexities of defining reach, frequency, and consequently GRPs are discussed.

When the objective is in terms of reach, the more media vehicles used, the faster reach will increase. But it is not simply a matter of adding up. Table 10-3 shows how the reach of two media combine into *unduplicated* reach. This table is valid when two different media are used for which reach of the two is independent (which means that the chance a consumer is reached by one medium does not dependent on whether he is reached by the other medium). When reach is independent the unduplicated reach of two media can be calculated as $R_A + (100 - R_A) \times R_B/100$ where R_A and R_B are the reach of A and B respectively. Thus, when medium A has a reach of 45 and medium B has a reach of 55, the unduplicated reach is $45 + (100 - 45) \times 55/100 = 75$. Of course this kind of calculation critically depends on the assumption of independence. When two media have completely separated coverage, combined reach will indeed be the simple sum of the reach of the two media.

Reach of second medium	Reach of one medium					
	25	35	45	55	65	75
25	44	51	59	66	74	81
35	–	58	64	71	77	84
45	–	–	70	75	81	86
55	–	–	–	80	84	89
65	–	–	–	–	88	91
75	–	–	–	–	–	94

Table 10-3 Combined reach of two media

Calculating broadcast gross rating points

In designing a media plan, multiple vehicles are usually employed. The total GRP is then calculated by adding the GRPs of the individual vehicles. This of course may lead to duplication. Recall from the discussion on frequency that this is not necessarily bad, rather the contrary. But buying GRPs is a rough measure.

When a measure of total GRP can be combined with a measure of net reach, i.e. the reach that results from the combined dissemination of the messages in the media plan, the frequency results for the media plan. For example, Table 10-4 shows a media plan resulting in 196 GRPs, based on GRPs (reach times frequency) for individual programmes. What is the frequency for the entire plan? When research shows that the effective reach was 49, it follows that the frequency—in its original meaning—equals 4 ($F = GRP/R$, because $GRP = F \times R$). Thus, in this example, 49 per cent of the households were exposed, on average, four times to the brand message. In reality, of course, some of the 49 per cent were exposed only once or twice, while the very heavy viewing households may have been exposed as many as 18 times (the total number of times the brand message ran). The earlier discussed frequency distribution analysis provides more detailed insight.

GRPs indicate the weight of a media plan; the more GRPs, the "heavier" the plan. Comparing media plans to outcomes in the marketplace often gives media planners and account

Programmes	Programme rating		Frequency		GRPs
9 o'clock news	6	×	5	=	30
Friends	10	×	4	=	40
Law & Order	15	×	6	=	90
Match of the Day	12	×	3	=	36
Total					196

Table 10-4 GRPs based on total US household coverage

managers a good idea of how much weight should be used to introduce a new product, increase the level of brand awareness, and so on. That is why a typical media objective states a certain number of GRPs: "Support the brand's introduction with 3000 GRPs within the first three months." Although the media planners are given GRP objectives, they still have to make a decision as to the balance of reach and frequency. This is because $R \times F = GRPs$. When you have a set number of GRPs, increasing the reach decreases the frequency, just as increasing the frequency decreases the reach.

Media weighting

Understanding consumer decision-making processes influences the weight that may be given to various media. Take, for example, hot dogs: parents buy them but children eat them. A weighting strategy could be 65 per cent of media placed to reach parents and 35 per cent placed to reach children. Companies also figure media weights for competing brands in order to determine how much weight of their own to use in certain areas. For example, if Harley-Davidson found that Honda (motorcycles) was significantly increasing its media weight to reach 16- to 24-year-olds, it might counter by making a similar increase in media weight for this segment.

Media concentration

Media mix strategy is influenced by the degree of concentration needed in a plan, which is basically a qualitative decision. A *concentrated* media mix delivers greater frequency (at the expense of reach) than a *broad* media mix. A *concentrated* media mix uses fewer media and communication vehicles than a *broad* media mix. Furthermore, vehicles themselves differ in the concentration of their audiences. Newspapers and magazines provide greater concentration because most are sent repeatedly (by subscription) to the same audience members; broadcast programmes have audiences who are not as consistent and usually broader in their characteristics.

Concentrated media mixes are used when an audience can be narrowly defined—for example, "females, 13 to 21, living in major urban areas". Another reason for using a concentrated mix is that it may help build strong relationships with a smaller but more important portion of a target audience, those who represent the heavy users. Further, some MC executives believe the argument that if three different sources tell you something, the message will have more impact than if you get the message three times from the same source. In this view, a broad mix of media increases message synergy, although empirical evidence is weak to support this belief. Message complexity also favours a concentrated strategy. Complex messages may require multiple exposures, asking for the high frequency that is associated with a concentrated strategy. A final point to consider is that a broad mix is usually more expensive, since different media require different messages that have to be produced independently.

Calculating media cost

Another strategic decision relates to how the media budget will be allocated. No brand has an unlimited amount of money to spend on media. Cost is always a consideration in any kind of media decision. Although the costs of time and space are important to know, what is even more important to keep in mind is the cost for creating a lead or a purchase. Because media costs are so important, they are discussed at several places in this book (see, for example, Chapters 8 and 9).

Cost per thousand

Because the number of audience members—customers, households, businesses—is different for every communication vehicle, comparing the cost of a unit of time or space is often misleading.

To determine which are the best value among all the many vehicle alternatives that reach the target audience, media planners use a calculation called **cost per thousand (CPM)**, *what a communication vehicle charges to deliver a message to 1000 members of its audience* (the *M* in the abbreviation is the Roman numeral meaning "1000"). CPM is found by using the following simple formula:

$$\frac{\text{Cost of ad unit}}{\text{Circulation or audience}/1000} = \text{CPM}$$

CPM adjusts factual costs for the effect of using a certain vehicle. But it is a rough indicator as it does not take into account the effectiveness of the various media. A more appropriate measure therefore is based on reach, or—even better—targeted reach, leading to a measure called **targeted cost per thousand**, *the cost to deliver a message to 1000 members of its targeted audience*. To calculate TCPM, the CPM formula applies, except that the targeted reach (in actual numbers) is substituted for the vehicle's total audience.

Cost per point and cost per response

Similar to cost per thousand is **cost per point (CPP)**, *a measure used to compare same-medium broadcast vehicles*. In this use, the word *point* is shorthand for *rating point*, which is 1 per cent of a station's coverage area. As with other measures, CPPs should not be used to compare two different types of vehicles—such as radio and TV or newspapers and radio—because different media are best compared on the basis of their different strengths (Chapter 8).

The ultimate objective of any marketing communication programme is to motivate the target audience to respond in some way. Therefore, the best way (where possible) to compare the cost-effectiveness of different vehicles, regardless of their media type, is on the basis of the **cost per response (CPR)** generated by each of the vehicles, which is *the media cost divided by the number of responses generated*. This type of comparison assumes that the message, creative costs, and offer are held constant in all the media used. The desired response needs to be defined in any behavioural way, such as "bought the product", "made a store visit" or "requested more information about the brand or offer". CPR can be determined for media vehicles that have direct and measurable contact with prospects and customers such as e-mail, regular mail, and telephone. When media are used that do not have a built-in tracking mechanism—such as TV, radio, and outdoor—the only way CPR can be determined is by comparing the total cost of the media campaign to all the responses received within a reasonable time period.

Step 4: Determining the media schedule: when and where should media run?

The final decision in the media plan concerns the timing of placing the messages. Three commonly used scheduling strategies are flighting, continuous scheduling, and pulsing (see Figure 10-2). **Flighting** is *a scheduling strategy in which planned messages run in intermittent periods*. Clearly, flighting makes good sense for products whose sales fluctuate seasonally. But it is also used when budgets are limited. Why? Media running in flights are presumed to provide sufficient message impact to maintain a brand's presence. With the huge amount of commercial message clutter that exists today, most media planners believe there must be a certain level of frequency; otherwise, messages will have little or no impact on the target audience. Flighting can help them achieve frequency without draining the budget.

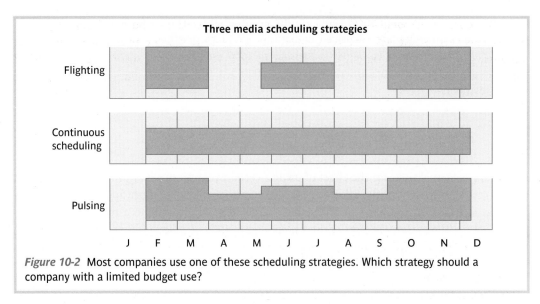

Figure 10-2 Most companies use one of these scheduling strategies. Which strategy should a company with a limited budget use?

The opposite of flighting is **continuous scheduling**, *placing media throughout the year with equal weight in each month.* Continuous scheduling is often used by brands with large budgets and fairly constant sales throughout the year. Brands that desire to maintain a certain level of awareness also use this strategy. Another rationale for continuous scheduling is when a product is frequently purchased or, in the case of B2B products, when the brand decision-making process is relatively long and prospects need constant brand reminders.

Pulsing is *a scheduling strategy that provides a "floor" of media support throughout the year and periodic increases* (it basically combines *flighting* and *continuous scheduling*). Fast-food and beverage companies with large media budgets often use a pulsing schedule. Once a media schedule is worked out, it is detailed in a flowchart such as the one in Figure 10-3.

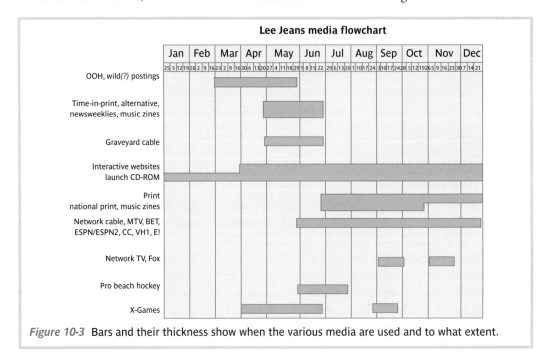

Figure 10-3 Bars and their thickness show when the various media are used and to what extent.

If a product has *seasonal fluctuations*, media planners schedule their buys with similar fluctuations. However, most MC messages, with the exception of sales promotion and direct response, generally have a lag effect, so the media should precede the season. For example, if tennis racket sales start to increase in April then media should begin running in March.

In some categories, such as restaurants and movie theatres, sales vary by day of week, and the majority of sales come on weekends. Media buys supporting these businesses are often scheduled from Thursday to Saturday to reach people when they are making plans for the weekend. Finally, some brands schedule media by time of day. Breakfast foods, for example, may schedule brand messages in the morning to take advantage of an aperture in which customers are thinking "breakfast". The IMC in Action box illustrates that ethical considerations also influence scheduling decisions.

Enjoy Heineken responsibly

How can excessive use of alcohol by young people be fought? It is a question that has been debated for years. On the one hand there are people and institutions who say that alcohol commercials influence alcohol consumption among youngsters, and therefore argue that marketing for alcohol should be regulated. On the other hand there are the producers of alcoholic beverages who cannot deny this statement, but claim that there has never been reasonable proof that advertising is the source of *abuse* of alcohol among this group, and therefore feel regulation is not a solution. Moreover, it does not mean that producers of alcoholic drinks do not take their responsibilities seriously.

In the Netherlands, producers and importers of alcoholic beverages have joined together to set up a foundation called STIVA (Foundation for Responsible Use of Alcohol). Heineken, one of the world's largest beer brewers, was one of STIVA's founders. The foundation's purpose is to contribute actively to the promotion of the responsible use of alcohol and to fight alcohol abuse. STIVA promotes ethical marketing through self-regulation of alcohol commercials. Rules that serve as the basis for this self-regulation are stipulated in an advertising code of conduct, a directive including rules to which promotion for alcohol must adhere. These state, for example, that marketing of alcohol may not be directed specifically at people under 18, and that no more than 25 per cent of the marketing audience may consist of people under 18. Every year STIVA identifies several so-called "young" channels, like MTV. On these channels alcohol commercials are strictly banned.

Apart from its membership of STIVA, Heineken has launched an independent initiative to promote the responsible use of alcohol as well: "Enjoy Heineken responsibly". The initiative was meant to create awareness among customers around the world and help them make informed choices. Via the website www.enjoyheinekenresponsibly.com, the company informs consumers about the effects of alcohol and provides an explanation of what responsible consumption means. The website even features a test to examine consumers' knowledge of alcohol consumption. Additionally, Heineken has integrated warnings for abuse of alcohol in their packaging. By 2006 back labels on nearly all Heineken bottles and cans carried the message "Enjoy Heineken responsibly". In 2006 a commercial with the message was also aired on Dutch television.

Think about it

What kind of media schedule is appropriate for Heineken? What other media could the company employ to reach the target audience?

IMC in Action

Sources:
www.alcoholinfo.nl/index.cfm?act=nieuws.detail&ihnid=636
www.alcoholreclame.nl/alcoholreclame.php3?menu=9&id=32
www.enjoyheinekenresponsibly.com
www.reclamecode.nl/pagina.asp?paginaID=28
www.stiva.nl/
*www.sustainabilityreport.heineken.com/responsible_beer_consumption_and_impact_on_developing_*
markets/responsible_beer_consumption/enjoy_heineken_responsibly.html

In B2B media planning, *support of events* such as major trade shows requires media support both prior to and during the shows in the markets where the shows are held. B2B media planning is also heavily influenced by introductions of new and improved products. Some companies also schedule media according to when *competitors* begin their brand messages. This is generally true of small brands that feel they must "keep up" with leaders.

Media scheduling can also be influenced by the *type of MC message.* An awareness/image message requires weeks of media to have an effect compared to a promotional offering. A seasonal promotional offer, however, should be made only when the target audience is in a buying mood. Swimsuit manufacturer Speedo, for example, might start its brand advertising in February but not run any promotional offers until April and May, when the weather has turned nice and people are ready to buy.

Another factor in determining a media schedule is the lead time available. **Lead time** is a calculation of *the number of days needed to produce the message and allow the vehicle time to prepare it for publication or broadcast* (magazine lead time can be up to three months). Any sudden changes in the marketing plan, which are more the rule than the exception, generally require changes in the media mix. When media budgets need to be kept flexible, it is best not to depend heavily on national TV and magazines. They demand relatively long lead times; and, once contracts are signed for space and time, it is difficult (though not always impossible) to get out of these commitments.

One way brands attempt to retain customers is to continually make improvements and expand product offers. Each major *new or improved product* needs media support. A new product, for example, may call for an initial media blitz with a heavy concentration of media weight preceding or coinciding with the date of the product's launch. The timing for this support varies. In some introductions, companies wait until the product is in distribution; in others, media placement begins ahead of time to build interest and the desire of customers. In the case of products sold through retail, media buys are sometimes scheduled ahead of the product launch to motivate retailers to stock the new/improved products and also to pull the product through the distribution channel by creating consumer demand. Retailers are more likely to want to stock a new product if customers ask for it.

A final note: media integration

Many areas of a company's operations benefit from media scheduling being integrated (see colour insert B1). The most obvious is the overall marketing plan. When a company introduces a new promotion or product, media support is crucial. But unless the planning is integrated with production and distribution schedules, media may deliver brand messages at the wrong time. A common problem in both B2C and B2B marketing is advertising a product too long before it is available.

Media scheduling and the development of creative materials (such as ads, packaging, and publicity releases) must be integrated so that a company does not miss opportunities for reaching the right audiences, at the right time, in dynamic ways. Media also must be integrated with each of the MC functional programmes.

Finally, media scheduling must be integrated into a company's total business operations. A good example is the way in which brick-and-mortar retailers promote their websites, enabling customers to buy online. By integrating the Internet medium with the rest of the media effort, businesses have been able to increase sales. Amazon.com though, has reversed the process, integrating a direct-mail catalogue into its predominantly online business.

🔒 Key terms

aperture Any situation in which the target audience is highly receptive to a brand message.

brand development index (BDI) Numerical indicator of the development of a particular brand within a market relative to all other markets in which the brand is sold.

category development index (CDI) A numerical indicator of the relative consumption rate in a particular market for a particular product category.

continuous scheduling Placing media throughout the year with equal weight in each month.

cost per point (CPP) A measure used to compare same-medium broadcast vehicles.

cost per response (CPR) The media cost divided by the number of responses generated.

cost per thousand (CPM) What a communication vehicle charges to deliver a message to 1000 members of its audience.

duplication The overlapping coverage of two or more vehicles.

effective frequency The number of times a message needs to be seen to make an impression or achieve a specified objective.

flighting A scheduling strategy in which planned messages run in intermittent periods.

frequency The average number of times those who are reached have an opportunity to be exposed to a brand message within a specified time period.

frequency distribution analysis An analysis that divides a target audience into equal segments and establishes an average frequency for each of these segments.

gross rating points (GRPs) A combined measure of reach and frequency indicating the weight of a media plan.

impression One exposure to a brand message.

lead time The number of days needed to produce the message and allow the vehicle time to prepare it for publication or broadcast.

marketing universe The total market of interest.

media buying The execution of a media plan.

media planning Process for determining the most cost-effective mix of media for achieving a set of media objectives.

media waste Reaching people who are neither customers nor prospects.

media weight An indication of the relative impact of a media plan.

message wear-out Brand messages that once attracted attention and motivated the target audience no longer do so.

pulsing A scheduling strategy that provides a "floor" of media support throughout the year and periodic increases.

quintile analysis *see* frequency distribution analysis.

reach The percentage of an audience that has had the opportunity to be exposed to a media vehicle within a specified period.

share-of-voice spending A brand's portion of total media spending in that brand's product category.

skews Variations from the general population.

targeted cost per thousand The cost to deliver a message to 1000 members of its targeted audience.

targeted GRPs (TGRPs) The number of gross rating points delivered against just the targeted audience.

targeted reach The portion of a communication vehicle's audience that is in a brand's target market.

teaser campaign A series of messages that carry no brand identification but are designed to create curiosity.

Check the key points

Key point 1: Media planning steps

a   List and explain the four steps in media planning.

b   What gains are possible by integrating media planning in marketing planning?

c   What is the difference between media planning and media buying?

d   What is the difference between a media objective and a media strategy? Which comes first?

Key point 2: Media objectives

a   What information is included in a set of media objectives?

b   Define *reach* and *frequency*. How do they differ?

c   Marketers ask themselves, "How much reach is enough?" Explain what that question means and how you would answer it. How would you determine how much reach is enough?

d   What is a GRP? How are GRPs computed?

e   What is targeted reach? Why is it important to marketers?

f   What is the difference between a GRP and a TGRP?

▶ g   What is effective frequency? What is message wear-out? What three factors affect the evaluation of effective frequency and wear-out?

h   What is frequency distribution analysis? How is it used in media planning?

Key point 3: Media mix

a   Why is a media mix used in media planning?

b   What are three decisions involved in determining the best media mix?

c   Explain why duplication and waste are problems for media planners.

d   What is the difference between a concentrated media mix and a broad media mix? Give an instance in which each approach would be appropriate.

e   How does the media mix reflect the creative strategy?

f   Explain how media weighting decisions affect the way the media budget is allocated.

Key point 4: Media costs

a   What is a CPM? Why do media planners use calculations such as CPMs in their media plans?

b   How do you compute a cost per thousand? What does CPM tell you about a medium's audience?

c   Why do media planners compare the cost of a unit of time or space rather than just counting the audience?

d   What is the difference between CPM and TCPM? Between CPP and CPR?

Key point 5: Media scheduling

a   In a magazine or newspaper find a print ad that has an obvious seasonality factor. Explain how seasonality drives the media buy.

b   In what ways do the flighting, continuous scheduling, and pulsing strategies differ? How is each used?

c   Give an example of an integration factor that affects scheduling.

Chapter Challenge

Writing assignment

Reach is the percentage of the target exposed to the vehicle or programme, not the percentage exposed to the brand message. In a memo to your instructor, explain this problem, and outline some suggestions about what might be done to make the evaluation of a brand message's reach more reliable.

Presentation assignment

Interview the advertising manager at a large company or retail store in your community. Summarize that company's media plan and media mix. Explain why the various media were chosen. Present this report to your classmates.

Internet assignment

Decide in class on a few products that everybody will try to allocate where to buy on the Web. While surfing and searching, keep track of the commercial messages that you receive, such as banners, interstitials, pop-ups, etc. (see Chapter 9). Back in class, make an overview of all the impressions that everybody has encountered. Determine the reach and frequency in your class (assume your class is the marketing universe). What do these numbers tell you about the effectiveness of Internet advertising?

Notes

[1] Mark Goldstein, speech at University of Colorado IMC Programme, 8 November 2000.

[2] Jon Fine, "Cross-Media Catches Fire", *Advertising Age*, 23 October 2000, p. S2.

[3] Goldstein, speech.

[4] Michael White, personal correspondence with the second author, 17 March 1993.

Further reading

Gritten, Adele (2007) "Media proliferation and the demand for new forms of research", *International Journal of Market Research*, Vol. 49–1, pp. 15–23.

Huang, Chun-Yao and Chen-Shun Lin (2006) "Modeling the Audience's Banner Ad Exposure for Internet Advertising Planning", *Journal of Advertising*, Vol. 35–2, pp. 123–36.

Piersma, Nanda and Jedid-Jah Jonker (2004) "Determining the optimal direct mailing frequency", *European Journal of Operational Research*, Vol. 158–1, pp. 173–82.

Tektas, Arzu and Elif Deniz Alakavuk (2003) "Allocation model: a tool to develop effective media plans for Turkey", *International Journal of Advertising*, Vol. 22–3, pp. 333–48.

Yoon, Carolyn, Michelle P. Lee and Shai Danziger (2007) "The effect of optimal time of day of persuasion processes in older adults", *Psychology and Marketing*, Vol. 24–5, pp. 475–95.

PART 4

Part contents

Chapter 11

Building the brand: product placements, events, sponsorships and packaging

After reading this chapter, you should:

- ☑ Understand how product placements help build a brand.
- ☑ Understand how events help build a brand and what types of events exist.
- ☑ Understand the growing phenomenon of sponsorships and the related topic of cause marketing.
- ☑ Appreciate the role of packaging as a communication function.

CHAPTER PERSPECTIVE
Image building

Brand knowledge is the basis of brand equity. Awareness and image go hand in hand to make the difference in the marketplace. In Chapter 3 it was argued that everything communicates, yet in this and the subsequent chapters it will be highlighted that various communications functions are particularly useful for various aspects of the brand-building process, as well as for various aspects of consumer behaviour and relationship building. Creating brand awareness and building an image, establishing a set of associations with the brand that are strongly favourable and unique in the customer's mind, are the subject of this chapter.

Advertising is the principal instrument in this process, and this has been discussed extensively in the previous chapters. Here we turn to other tools that equally, and sometimes even more strongly, contribute to image building, and that is the link between the (at first sight perhaps) heterogeneous set of topics covered in this chapter.

IMC in Action

A bull with wings and other anomalies

"Often copied, never equalled."[1] This is how Red Bull characterizes its position in the marketing landscape. Wary of demystifying the brand, Red Bull claims it is not interested in understanding why its marketing and communication works. As long as it works and consumers recognize Red Bull as a genuine and authentic brand, the company is satisfied. Let's see what the company did to reach this position, and how it can permit itself to be so ignorant of scientific approaches to understanding its success.

How it all started

Although it looks at first sight that Red Bull originates from the laboratories of some giant multinational, the truth is much more natural. The story is that Dieter Mateschitz was travelling in South East Asia where he found that people there used a drink to keep them alert and give them physically more stamina. The drink was a cheap local product which had a Thai name that was the equivalent of Red Bull. With the local producer he agreed to make the product suitable for the Western market and to produce it in Austria where it was introduced in 1987. The ingredients of the drink made it a candidate for regulation—much to the frustration of Mateschitz, who called the first three years of his entrepreneurship the worst in his life. In some countries such as France and Denmark the beverage does indeed fall under the regulations of the pharmaceutical industry, as if it were a medicine. In most countries, however, Red Bull finally managed to create a product category of its own, where competitors have a hard time winning only a small part of the market. In most markets where Red Bull is active it is market leader with a worldwide market share of 65 per cent, while in some countries this easily reaches the 80 per cent mark.[2] The market size? €2.5 billion a year.

How did he do it?

The phenomenal success of the brand is usually attributed to the marketing genius of Mateschitz. The key, they say, is the uniform, consistent and meaningful way in which the brand was brought. Whatever the company does, it relates to the central themes that are summarized in its slogan: "Red Bull gives you wings". And it does many things. There is advertising, but this makes up only a relatively small part of the company's communication mix. Red Bull is particularly known for its sponsorships. Furthermore, there is free sampling, a distinctive packaging and of course its self-created events.

Packaging, advertising and sampling

In creating the market, Red Bull looked for the right target groups to convince them to try the product. A market research agency concluded that the drink had no chance of ever becoming a success: the colour was unappetizing, it felt sticky in the mouth, the taste was disgusting and its position—stimulates body and mind—was deemed irrelevant.[3] Mateschitz however looked deeper. When the first market reactions were ambivalent, with 50 per cent of a test group going over about the drink and the other 50 per cent saying it tasted terrible, Mateschitz responded that that would at least create market buzz.

However, what was more important was that Mateschitz realized that this lab research only proved how Red Bull would be perceived in the lab. The brand he had in mind did not offer anything to people in an experimental study: its real benefits could only be appreciated in certain circumstances. The benefits were not taste, nor look, smell, or its feel. The Red Bull benefit is that it keeps you going when you otherwise would have stopped. Mateschitz understood that there was a specific scene—parties and raves—where the drink would make a difference. Red Bull was particularly targeted at young outgoing people, visiting bars and clubs. Can you imagine a group for which it is more interesting to keep going, hour after hour?

Free sampling at these outgoing locations was an important element in the marketing approach. This was accompanied by having role models (for the outgoing youth), for example DJs, consuming the drink. Empty cans were put in litter bins at the exits of the clubs. The attention-drawing design of the cans, blue and silver, made sure they would be noticed in any situation, even among trash. A further element in the initial communication mix were the television commercials. One commercial, the viewers' favourite according to Red Bull's website, showed Saint Peter at the gates of heaven, complaining that he lost his job: he was no longer needed to give wings, since a competitor on earth was now doing the job. In its characteristic cartoon style this certainly appealed enough to the target group.

Advertising certainly created awareness, its packaging helped consumers recognize the product on the shelves, or identify it when they saw the DJ take a sip. And the sampling helped to provide the first experience. But more was needed to substantiate the claims that Red Bull "gives you wings".

Up in the air and more

At first glance it does not seem to make sense to combine wings with a bull, or in fact two red bulls, as the logo shows. But that is too narrow an interpretation of the wings theme. Taking a broader interpretation of the verbal "gives you wings" leads to the understanding of endurance, vitality, energy. But also staying closer to the literal wings theme, associations like freedom, force, space and even speed come to mind. And it is in these broad, yet clearly related, elements that Red Bull continually seeks opportunities to give meaning and content to the brand. So let's consider some of its sponsorships and events in more detail.

Flying days and soap box races

The wings theme clearly inspired the agency to propose this self-initiated event. Flying from a 6-metre-high platform as far as you can, in a self-constructed aircraft without mechanical help, to land in the water. That is the basic and simple idea of the Flugtag (flying day), a word that is used even in the US. Spectacular, imaginative and creating great awareness, this event has been around since 1991. Similar in nature are the slightly less famous soapbox races. In self-constructed vehicles, again without engines, the contestants ride round a track.

Sponsorship of Formula 1 team

In 2005 Red Bull entered a new, yet logical scene with its ownership of a Formula 1 motor-racing team. But where most sponsors use their entry to the F1 world to treat their friends and family to a visit to an unforgettable event, for Mateschitz and Red Bull, the objective is different. Says Mateschitz: "For us, the quality of the editorial reportage about our Formula One team is key."[4] In order effectively to reach the Spanish-speaking world, one year later the company decided to start with a second team called Torro Rosso.

Sponsoring/celebrity endorsements of extreme sports

Sponsorship is further realized primarily in the world of extreme sports. This may be further away from the wings theme, yet relates more obviously to the fundamental functional stance the brand has taken: supporting endurance and high performance under extreme conditions. Sponsorships of Red Bull are found in cliff diving, BMX (bicycle moto-cross), skateboarding and skiing amongst others. But the list is endless, and mainly filled with individuals in uncommon sports like free climbing, windsurfing, and paragliding. In a quite different area, but nevertheless linked to the principles of the company, is Red Bull's sponsorship of the Taurus awards, an Oscar-like award for stunt people.

Music academy

Several times Red Bull has organized master classes for DJs where they can meet the heroes of their profession. This academy has been organized on a relatively ad hoc basis, i.e. irregular and at various locations including Berlin, Dublin, Cape Town, Rome, and New York. Remarkably, the visitors of this academy are not asked for a favour in return. Red Bull relies on the word of mouth effect. "Hey Mr. DJ, where did you learn this?" "I was in the Red Bull Music Academy."

Hangar 7 and aircraft

Of a totally different nature is Red Bull's art and cultural centre, Hangar 7, in Salzburg, Austria, to which Hangar 8 has been added. This centre owns a collection of old aircraft that are shown and occasionally demonstrated. At the same time the centre hosts art exhibitions of various kinds. There is a common theme in its artistic policy, however, which is to give space to new, creative and challenging artists. Finally, there is an upmarket restaurant, Icarus, to which famous cooks from all over the world are invited to demonstrate their skills and are given the opportunity to experiment with new recipes.

Explain the success

A red bull with wings that sponsors arts, stuntmen awards, and soapbox races? Red Bull has not only challenged the market for beverages, but in essence the common wisdom of marketing principles itself. Where is the consistency, where the coherence, where is the integration of communication?

But what it does in fact prove is that the execution is less important than the principle (although this is of course not unimportant). The execution cannot be judged without looking at the principles underlying it. When these are adhered to, the tactics follow almost automatically, and by their very nature contribute to the brand positioning.

Notes

[1] www.redbull.com company information.

[2] www.icmr.icfai.org/casestudies/catalogue/Marketing1/Red%20Bull.htm

[3] Wippperfürth, A. (2003) *Speed-in-a-Can: The Red Bull Story*, San Francisco: Plan B. www.plan-b.biz/pdf/Speed-in-a-Can.pdf

[4] http://emagazine.credit-suisse.com/app/article/index.cfm?fuseaction=OpenArticle&aoid=136241&coid=180363&lang=EN

Sources:
www.redbull.com
Red Bull, the Anti-brand brand, (2004) case study by Nirmalya Kumar, Sopie Linguri, and Nader Tavasolli, London Business School
"Red Bull Energy Drink" (not dated), John Simpson, and Bridget Dore, Marketing in South Africa, *Van Schaik publishers*
Speed-in-a-Can: The Red Bull Story, (2003) case study by Alex Wipperfürth, San Francisco: Marketing boutique Plan B.

MC and the consumer decision-making process

A fundamental idea in Integrated Marketing Communication is that everything communicates and hence that everything influences every aspect of the consumer's behaviour. It nevertheless is also true that some communication functions are better suited to influence certain aspects of the consumer's attitudes and behaviour than others. This is not another truth, but another dimension of the same truth. Sales promotion (see Chapter 13), for example, first and foremost influences the consumer's actual buying decision, but it also contributes to the image that is created of the brand.

In this fourth part of the book the focus will be on the various communication functions. The organization of this part follows the logic of which aspects of consumer behaviour are particularly influenced by which communication functions. The organizing principle follows the simple consumer decision-making process: problem recognition, generating alternatives, evaluating alternatives, the purchase decision, and post-purchase evaluation. So in this chapter attention will be directed to those functions that help in generating and evaluating alternatives. Chapter 12 then focuses on auxiliary functions for making the evaluations, i.e. the role of PR and publicity in supporting the generated image by lending it credibility. Chapter 13 continues with sales promotion which is primarily directed at reaching a decision, while Chapter 14 discusses the personal selling process which leads to a closing of the deal. Finally Chapter 15 devotes attention to two instruments that are especially (but certainly not exclusively) useful in the post-purchase evaluation stage: direct marketing and customer service. As is argued in Chapter 15, direct marketing (DM) is a marketing microcosm on its own, yet DM and customer service are the only MC functions that pay attention to the post-purchase evaluation of the consumer.

Advertising is not discussed in this part. In fact, advertising has featured in the previous chapters. Although the topics discussed in Chapters 6–10 in principle hold good for all MC functions, they have been presented in the context of advertising. The logic is that advertising is the most obvious and most visible form of MC. This part of the book therefore emphasizes other MC functions. Nevertheless, issues such as creative strategies and media planning (to name just two) apply equally to these functions as they do for advertising!

In this first chapter of this part attention will be directed to those functions that have as a main objective to create awareness and to build associations. Awareness is essential to make it to the evoked set in the consumer decision-making process; associations are the elements that will be weighed in the evaluation of the alternatives.

Product placements

Creating awareness and building associations is the typical objective of TV advertising, but this advertising faces two extremely challenging issues. First, the advertising landscape is so over-crowded that it is becoming harder and harder to get noticed, let alone heard. Second, consumers are becoming increasingly fed up with advertisements. TV viewers have learned that commercial breaks are very useful to go to the bathroom, get a drink, make a quick phone call, or check e-mail, and if that all is done, a little zapping is preferable to being confronted with the next series of annoying TV commercials. Hence, although advertising still seems to be the backbone for many IMC plans, alternative ways are sought to get in touch with consumers.

A particularly effective way to face the two challenges identified is the exploitation of product placements. A **product placement** is *the paid-for, identifiable appearance of a brand or product in a TV show or movie.* When a brand appears in a programme but it is not paid for, this means that this is a voluntary decision on the part of the producers to include the brand. At best this falls under the heading of publicity, and sometimes this voluntary decision is helped by a brand representative. This is sometimes called "brand plugging". Also, when the brand is unidentifiable, there is no effect on the consumer and the placement serves no purpose, at least from a communication perspective.

The term "product placement" is in fact inadequate; "brand placement" is a better term to describe the idea, but since "product placement" is so common we will keep to it. It is also important to realize it is not restricted to movies or TV shows. Brands also appear in video games, stage plays and books, and when we see that the ball used in a soccer match is from Adidas, the dividing lines between sponsorships and product placements rapidly vanish.

Nevertheless, product placements in movies such as the endless James Bond series (see colour insert C2), and TV shows like *Desperate Housewives* and *Friends* have some specific features that at least make them a special kind of sponsoring, but in fact make them a special instrument in the marketing communication mix.

Objectives of product placements

Product placements share many features with regular advertising in commercials. It is no coincidence that many commercials look like mini-movies with a story line, a plot, main characters, etc. TV commercials that are designed in that way emphasize the creation of associations and demonstrate product usage. Less emphasis is given to brand awareness, although of course every time a brand appears in a commercial the awareness of the brand is increased.

The same principles are applicable to product placements. Brand awareness is supported, but the main objective is to create associations and demonstrate product usage. The associations are created by various connections. The brand is associated with:

- *The programme:* An appearance in a popular sitcom like *Friends* has a different impact from a German Krimi like *Siska*.

- *The use situation:* When a mobile phone is used in a series to call the emergency services, this has a different impact from its use by two friends to make a nonsense call.

- *The characters:* Characters have all the properties of real people and differ in popularity. Some are role models, others are villains. Many are stereotypes and are potentially useful to connect a brand to a specified target group.

■ *The plot:* Products may play an important role in the development of the plot—or not. When the product helps the plot develop to a desirable end, or in contrast relates to "the opposite side", this influences the impression the audience gets from the placement. James Bond's cars are always instrumental and often play a vital role in the story.

The conclusion is that deciding on a product placement is very similar to creating a commercial (see Chapters 6 and 7). But in contrast to making a commercial, however, the advertiser is now dependent on the creativity of the programme or movie director.

How does product placement work?

A product placement means that a branded product appears in the programme or film. This can take different forms, and it is not even necessarily the product itself that assumes the role. The product can be shown, actively used, or the characters can talk about it. In all cases the branded product appears in the show. Furthermore, it is also possible that a related identifier appears in the programme. This can be the logo, the package, or any other element that helps identify the brand. Whenever a large square building in blue and yellow appears, this will be recognized as an IKEA outlet. And if you watch a Western and see a cowboy light a cigarette won't you just believe it's a Marlboro? For such indirect identifiers to work, the brand should have a sufficient level of brand awareness already, and the identifier must be strongly and unequivocally related to the brand.

The question of effectiveness has been further studied by Cristel Russell, a pioneer in product placement research. Russell showed that the effectiveness in achieving an attitude change depends on how the placement appears in the programme, as well on its connectedness to the plot. Placements can appear either visually (you just see the brand) or auditory (characters talk about the brand). According to Russell's results a visual appearance is better when there is low plot connection, otherwise the placement is too intrusive. An auditory appearance on the other hand permits high plot connection. The question remains as to how a placement that is both auditory and visual is perceived by the viewers.[1]

Such academic research leaves many questions unanswered and should always be interpreted with care: will such results hold in different circumstances, in other shows or programmes? What other variables influence the effects? What they make clear though is that the identified factors are important. Other factors that should be considered are for example:

■ Frequency of auditory appearances.

■ The time length of visual appearances.

■ The attitude of the characters with respect to the placement.

■ The relation to the characters.

Apart from the effects of the placements themselves, they are also used for cross-promotions. A **cross-promotion** occurs *when one communication mix element refers to another element.* For example, when in personal selling the salesman refers to the appearance of the newest Aston Martin in the latest James Bond movie, this is an example of cross-promotion. Cross-promotions are a natural aspect of an integrated marketing communications approach. Product placements are especially powerful for cross-promotions because they offer the most natural way to demonstrate the product's usage, in particular highlighting its unique selling points. Another way in which product placements enter the cross-promotions scene is when actors from the show or movie are contracted as endorsers of the product. Finally, and particularly relevant for placements in movies, is the possibility of sales promotions (see Chapter 13) after the show for the brands that appeared in the movie.

IMC in Action

Nokia is in the game

How are Nokia, a world leader in mobile communications, and Tony Hawk, a professional American skateboarder, related? A first reaction would be that there is no relationship between the two; a closer look, however, reveals a different truth.

For years Activision, a publisher of video games, has been marketing video games endorsed by Tony Hawk. Based on Tony Hawk's skills as a skater and the skateboarding scene, a complete series of games have been developed. It started in 1999, when the first game, Tony Hawk's Pro Skater, was released. Since then several games have been marketed, including a game called Tony Hawk's American Wasteland in 2005. In American Wasteland the gamer is brought into Los Angeles, where he or she has to fulfil several tasks in order to build a relationship with a group of local LA skaters. While completing these tasks the gamer encounters several areas in and around LA and developers have put much effort in making this digital copy of the city look as realistic as possible. While gamers make their way through LA they cannot help but run across vehicles and billboards, for example. And this is where Nokia comes in.

Since day one, Nokia has been a partner in producing the Tony Hawk games. This basically means that Nokia has paid for a significant amount of the development costs of the games, in return for brand placement in the games. Together with Chrysler and Motorola, Nokia offset 10 per cent of the development costs of Tony Hawk's American Wasteland. Brand placement in the Tony Hawk games allows Nokia to target hard-to-reach customers, mainly 13- to 25-year-old males who spend an increasing amount of time playing games instead of watching television. And since Nokia phones are generally popular with young men, Nokia billboards fit perfectly into the game scene.

Up until now Nokia has been integrated in the games by means of static advertisements. This means that Nokia billboards were fixed into the game's coding. However with the development of online gaming and the increasing use of the Xbox 360 and Playstation 3, both Internet compatible, dynamic advertisements present a future possibility for brand placement. Dynamic advertisements are ads that are not burned into a game's coding and thus can be changed on an ongoing basis. Dynamic ads include in-game billboards that not only feature a game for a month, but also comprise links to Web content, for example. According to publisher Activision, future Tony Hawk games could even feature Internet phone calls with changing messages from Tony Hawk that result in a differential gaming experience. This presents Nokia with a great opportunity to give its gaming customer the chance to interact with the Nokia products and to experience the brand hands-on, thus moving from mere brand placement to product placement in the Tony Hawk games.

Think about it

What are the advantages of dynamic advertisements over static advertisements? How can dynamic advertisements change the way gamers think about the brands being advertised?

Sources:

http://en.wikipedia.org/wiki/Tony_Hawk%27s_American_Wasteland
http://xbox360.ign.com/articles/667/667130p1.html

David Kiley (2006). "Rated M for Mad Ave", BusinessWeek, Issue 3973, pp. 76–7. Retrieved 12 February 2007, from the World Wide Web: Business Source Premier.

Amy Johannes (2006). "In the Game", Promo, 19 (3), pp. 28–30. Retrieved 12 February 2007, from the World Wide Web: Business Source Premier.

Strengths and limitations of product placements

Product placements have numerous advantages, but also some important disadvantages. Chief among the positive aspects are the reasons why product placements are becoming increasingly popular.

- They cannot be avoided by viewers. Integrating a brand in a show makes it impossible to zap the message away.
- They avoid the clutter of commercial breaks.
- They provide a more natural context in which to show the product, and hence are more acceptable to viewers.
- They can be used to demonstrate the product's usage.
- They allow the brand to be connected to popular shows or actors. Sometimes the characters themselves are desirable to connect to.
- The audiences for the shows or movies are often well defined.

With so many advantages it is clear why product placements are becoming increasingly popular. But now have a look at the following disadvantages.

- They have very long lead times, in particular when movies are the vehicle.
- They remain secondary to the show or movie. Producers and directors often require final autonomy over their product (the show) and what remains after the director's cut is sometimes a disappointing few seconds. Good negotiation skills are indispensable when product placements are pursued. Philips paid a good deal of money to have James Bond use their new Sensotec shaver in *Die Another Day*, but after the director's cut just a few seconds of the scene remained.
- Shelf lives of movies and shows are very long. Occasionally we still watch movies from before the Second World War, and every time a new James Bond is released all the old Bond movies are shown on TV. At first sight this looks to be an advantage, but when a brand has been redesigned, restyled, or just repositioned, the remainder of the product placement is potentially detrimental to such efforts.
- The popularity of the vehicles is an uncertain factor. TV commercials are not popular, but that is a fact. The success of a new movie is never clear beforehand, and the success of TV shows can fade unexpectedly.
- Product placements can backfire when the audience does not accept the placement. When the placement is too prominent, audiences can perceive this as intrusive and artificial.
- Product placements may go unnoticed. A placement in the final scene of an action movie is not very likely to be noticed.

Product placements are a potentially powerful element in the communication mix. Their effectiveness has yet to be proved, and in any case the instrument has to be used with great care, perhaps more than with any other element.

Events

Some of the most powerful brand messages are those that directly involve customers and prospects. Recognizing the impact of these types of messages, marketers are becoming cleverer at creating and using the MC functions that produce this type of brand involvement. Events (both created and participation) and sponsorships are powerful functions. The involvement of customers with the event, or the sponsored object makes them receptive to brand messages.

Event marketing is *a promotional occasion designed to attract and involve a brand's target audience.* According to Claire Rosenzweig, president of the Promotional Marketing Association, "Recent recognition from corporate marketers that event marketing engages consumers with a hands-on, emotionally rewarding brand experience, has caused them to shift budget resources from 'traditional' marketing practices to event marketing, which is the fastest growing practice in the industry."[2] Other reasons for using events are to reach hard-to-reach target audiences, to increase brand awareness, and to provide a platform for brand publicity.

Tupperware pioneered the use of an event as a selling tool—the in-home Tupperware party (see colour insert C10). Door-to-door personal selling had been around for years, but Tupperware creatively turned it into an event that became the cornerstone of the company's marketing and distribution. Sales are driven by lively product demonstrations and socialization. The latter can create peer pressure, as a Morgan Stanley analyst explained: "People at parties do feel a little bit of an obligation to buy."[3] As successful as that approach has been, it is now threatened by online marketing. Some Tupperware sales representatives have set up their own websites, much to the consternation of the Tupperware managers and other sales representatives, who feel the online sales technique will undercut the famous parties. Tupperware has also expanded distribution into some retail stores.

Tupperware parties are unique marketing experiences that represent what has become known as "experiential" marketing. The basic idea is that a brand can differentiate itself by creating an experience around its product. Instead of selling product performance, companies sell the brand experience.[4]

DaimlerChrysler uses an experience-based strategy with its Jeep Camps, which offer vacation, learning, and social experiences. These experiences help define the brand, producing a strong sense of brand community that borders on evangelism. When the campers return home, they are eager to share their experience with friends and associates, creating brand-advocacy messages through word of mouth.[5]

As Joseph Pine and James Gilmore point out in *The Experience Economy*, for a brand experience to be successful it must offer enjoyment, knowledge, diversion, or beauty. The experience can be passive or active. Passive experiences are those that entertain or provide aesthetic enjoyment, such as visits to museums or demonstrations of a product. Active experiences are ones in which customers participate, such as learning driving skills at Camp Jeep. The key to their success is a "sensory interaction", such as a "tasting" during a tour of a food or beverage plant.

Events can have a major impact because they are *involving*. This characteristic makes an event more memorable and motivating than passive brand messages, such as advertising, because the people attending are participating in and are part of the event. Events can also help position or reposition a brand by associating it with a certain activity, such as ABN AMRO's involvement in the Volvo Ocean Race in the opening case of Chapter 1 demonstrates (also see colour insert C14).

Because most events have a single focus, they attract homogeneous audiences. In most cases, events are selected that attract audiences whose profile matches the brand's current customers. To reach women jeans-wearers and reposition Levi's as "youthful, in-style, and sexy", for example, Levi Strauss & Co. sponsored the MTV Video Awards and Levi's Fuse Tour. The Fuse Tour attracted young females who are prime Levi customers. Brand publicity was used to announce the events and extend the events' awareness-building. These events also became part of Levi's local co-marketing promotions, complete with local TV and print advertising and in-store appearances of the celebrities featured in the events—which generated even more brand publicity.

Because events are individually created, they can and should be designed not only to meet involvement objectives but also to generate brand publicity. Such publicity is likely to reach a larger audience than an event itself. Volvo, for example, estimates that its million euros investment in tennis events results in over 1.7 billion consumer impressions. The company estimated that to reach the same number of consumer impressions by advertising, six times the amount spent on the tennis events would have to be invested.

Companies use events in three ways: they create them, participate in them, and sponsor them. In all three instances the point of departure is the event that has a prime objective that is not marketing related. Events exist in their own right, whether or not they are used by a brand to communicate brand messages. The Volvo Ocean Race is a sports event, Levi's Fuse Tour is created to entertain young women with a music concert, and trade shows have a primary objective of bringing businesses into contact with each other. Yet, as discussed, these events are powerful opportunities for brands to communicate their own message.

Created events

Celebrations, concerts, competitions, and other types of happenings are brand-created events (also refer to the Red Bull examples in the opening IMC in Action case). Companies create events to leverage the promotional aspects of such occasions as grand openings, brand or company anniversaries, new-product introductions, and corporate annual meetings. When McDonald's sells a hamburger, it is not an event. But when McDonald's sells its trillionth hamburger, an event can be created—that is what brand-publicity people get paid to do. Such events can bring people together, but they can also be celebrations designed to attract publicity.

Internal marketing uses events frequently to build company morale and exchange vital information. Kentucky Fried Chicken, like most franchise companies, has an annual convention to which all franchisees are invited. The objectives of the convention are to introduce new products, procedures, and cooking and store management processes; to provide a forum for franchisees to network and share ideas; and to enable corporate managers to interact with franchisees in a relaxed, pleasant environment. Most corporate meetings, especially those that involve stakeholders such as franchisees who do not have to attend, are held in "vacation" locations to maximize attendance and provide a reward to employees.

Although events attract and involve customers and other stakeholders, those who participate are likely to represent only a small percentage of a brand's target audience. To make an event pay out, the company needs to include elements that will be of interest to the media, thus creating brand publicity as well. Grand openings and the introduction of new products are publicity events (Chapter 12) designed not only to involve customers, prospects, and other stakeholders (such as employees and the financial community) but also to make the nine o'clock news or food pages. The more creative, fun, and exciting an event is, and the more people are involved, the more likely it is that the event will generate brand publicity. In 2005 Mazda in New Zealand organized an event involving a parade of 249 Mazda cars, which set a world record recognized by the famous Guinness World Records organization.

Specialized companies known as *event managers* develop everything from publicity stunts to internal company morale boosters. Successful events create an interactive experience that engages, educates, and entertains employees, customers, and other stakeholders. When well managed, events generate considerable brand publicity as well. Event management includes organizing the event and its logistics, staffing it, and marketing it to participants, sponsors, and attendees. Event managers also have to set up and run the event efficiently and safely. In other words, managing an event involves many forms of marketing communication, careful planning, and execution. The Red Bull Flug Tagen are an example of a successful created event.

Trade shows and other participation events

Rather than creating an event, companies may choose to participate in an event created by someone else. Examples are trade shows, fairs, and exhibitions. National or regional fairs provide local businesses with an opportunity to demonstrate their products for both consumers and local B2B customers. Most countries also have annual auto, boat, and home and garden shows that attract consumers who are especially interested in these product categories. Companies choose to participate in an event according to the type of people it attracts. The more a show's attendees are similar to a brand's target audience, the more sense it makes to participate. Companies rent exhibit space at these types of exhibitions and trade shows. The larger the space and the larger the anticipated attendance, the more exhibit space costs.

The most important participation events for B2B companies are trade shows. Trade shows are second only to personal selling as the most-used tool in B2B marketing communication. Pro-Team, a manufacturer of industrial vacuum cleaners, employs a full-time trade-show co-ordinator because trade shows are the company's number-one marketing communication function. A **trade show** is *an event at which customers in a particular industry gather to attend training sessions and visit with suppliers and vendors to review their product offerings and innovations.* Suppliers set up booths at which they demonstrate their products, provide information, answer questions, and take orders. A typical industry trade show has 10 000 attendees and includes 400 exhibits. Consumer trade shows, which are used to feature new models and products in such categories as cars, boats, and gardening, average from 45 000 to 50 000 attendees and 200 exhibits.[6]

In planning for a trade-show exhibit, a company must decide what products to feature (there is seldom space or time enough to include all products), who will staff the booth, how to screen and qualify visitors to the booth, and how to capture names of qualified prospects. Some of the strategies used to maximize booth attendance are (1) sending out personal invitations a couple of weeks before the show, (2) designing a booth that is aesthetically inviting and pleasant to visit, and (3) using "borrowed interest", such as an entertainer, give-aways, or a draw for a significant prize, to attract visitors. Of paramount importance is the follow-up to the trade show. The easiest way to do that is to collect business cards. Often this is done by organizing some kind of sweepstake or contest, the winners of which will be approached by the address they leave on their card. The collected addresses must be screened and contacted within a limited time after the show. Table 11-1 contains a checklist for companies planning to have an exhibit at a trade show.

Because trade-show participation is a type of brand communication, the booth should be designed in a way that reinforces the brand/company image and positioning. Some high-tech companies, for example, use laser lights and modern electronic music to help reinforce their position as being on the cutting edge of technology.

Companies participate in trade shows primarily to reinforce relationships with current customers and to create qualified leads for new customers. Trade shows provide opportunities to engage customers in personal communication and relationship-building activities, such as

Several months before the trade show
■ For each major show, set measurable objectives with a cross-functional team of sales, marketing, customer service, and the trade-show co-ordinator.
■ Design (or update) the exhibit booth, making sure that it is interactive and reinforces the brand image.
■ Select products and brands to display in the booth, and determine which ones will be featured (generally the new or improved items).
■ Select an incentive to motivate customers and prospects to visit the booth.
Several weeks before the trade show
■ Decide who will staff the booth (usually members of sales and marketing).
■ Send out personal invitations to current customers and to prospects.
■ Train the people who will be staffing the booth, showing them how to screen, qualify, and capture prospects' contact information.
After the trade show
■ Have the people who staffed the booth fill out an exhibit evaluation form that helps identify changes that need to be made to improve booth productivity.
■ Follow up with sales to see which leads have been contacted and how many sales were made.
■ Determine the return on investment for the trade-show appearance.

Table 11-1 Checklist for exhibiting at a trade show

seminars and receptions. Jim Obermayer, co-author of *Managing Sales Leads*, identifies four reasons why trade shows are so important as a B2B marketing communication tool:[7]

- On average, 83 per cent of trade-show attendees have not seen a salesperson from their suppliers within the last 12 months.
- Over 80 per cent of those who attend trade shows have buying authority or heavily influence brand choices.
- Two-thirds of trade-show attendees plan to make brand buying decisions at the show.
- Trade-show-created leads cost 70 per cent less to close than other leads.

Objectives for trade shows, therefore, should state how many customers and prospects the company wants to see and how many leads it wants to turn into sales. Because of the expense of exhibiting at trade shows, companies need to maximize the number of current customers and prospects that visit their booths in order to cost-justify the participation. The value of participating in a trade show can be determined by several criteria: the number of customers and prospects who visit the booth; the number of orders written at the show; the number of qualified leads obtained; and, most important, the number of sales resulting from these contacts.

Sponsorship

Sponsorship is *support of an organization, person, or activity, financial or in kind, in exchange for brand publicity and association, or other marketing communication objectives.* Although sponsorships differ from events, the two overlap because many events often have several sponsors.

Not surprisingly, many of the use guidelines are the same for each of these marketing communication functions. Another important objective of sponsorships is the chance to entertain business guests. Mixing in a relaxing environment, enjoying the event without the pressure of a business environment, is an important element in building relationships. Business seats in football stadiums are examples of this practice.

Sponsorships both differentiate and add value to brands. Nike, for example, sponsors champion golfer Tiger Woods because Woods is well liked and respected by members of the brand's target audience. The association with Woods helps differentiate Nike from other marketers of sporting goods and also helps increase the status of the Nike brand.

An important element of a brand is its associations. Sponsorship is one of the main ways in which a brand develops associations. The challenge is to find associations that reinforce the desired image of a brand. If the association is inconsistent with the brand's image and with other MC messages, a sponsorship can do more harm than good—customers will be confused about what the brand actually is and who makes it. Concern about the consistency of image association increasingly flows in two directions; groups and events are becoming increasingly selective about accepting sponsors.

Companies can sponsor a variety of things: media programmes, events, individuals, teams, sport categories, cultural organizations, good causes, and so on. It is almost impossible to attend any kind of large function today, such as a rock concert or spring-break beach party, without being inundated by brand banners, posters, and samples. A good example are the annual introductory days of universities, when they welcome their new students, that attract up to 10 000 students to their campuses for music, fashion, games, and social events. During such introductory days, a variety of companies not only sponsor the event, but also give out coupons and samples at their exhibits.

Companies use the following guidelines when choosing sponsorships:

1 *Target audience:* The audience for what is being sponsored should have the same profile as the brand's target audience(s).

2 *Brand image reinforcement:* Sponsorships should be used in an environment that is consistent with a brand's positioning and image.

3 *Extendibility:* The more brand exposure a sponsorship can provide, the more beneficial it can be. If the sponsorship is a multi-year relationship, for example, a company may consider promoting the sponsorship on its packaging, as many Olympics sponsors do. Marketers seek brand publicity that extends beyond the publicity directly provided by the event itself.

4 *Hosting opportunities:* The more privileges a sponsorship provides, the better. Sponsorship of a museum, for example, could include the right to use the museum for a corporate social function, exclusive tours for customers and employees, and invitations to openings of new exhibits.

5 *Cross-selling:* Many events offer the opportunity to sell products. Coca-Cola is not only the exclusive drinks sponsor of the Olympics, but at the venues of the Games only Coca-Cola is on sale, not its competitors. When a credit card provider sponsors a theatre festival, tickets can be bought more easily (or sometimes even exclusively) using the credit card account.

6 *Cost-effectiveness:* Some sponsorships produce enough brand-message exposure that if the cost of the sponsorship were converted to a cost per thousand (CPM), it would be competitive with other media buys.

7 *Other sponsors:* When a company associates with an event or cause, it does so to enhance its own image and positioning. Because some organizations have many sponsors, a company would be wise to know who the other sponsors are. Most companies expect category exclusivity, which means none of its competitors will be a sponsor.

Sports sponsorships

Sponsorships cover a wide range of activities, including arts, culture, broadcasting, education, science, environment, but by far the largest sector is sports. It is estimated that no less than two-thirds of spending on event sponsorship is sports related. As athletes, sports teams, tournaments, and leagues at all levels have increasingly recognized the financial benefit of having sponsors—and, in turn, have realized that they can offer added value to brands—companies have found themselves with an increased range of sponsorship opportunities (see colour insert C5).

The single largest sporting event that attracts sponsors is the Olympic Games. Not only are the Olympics a huge advertising venue, but they also represent a unique sponsorship opportunity. Sponsorships bring in about 28 per cent of the event's revenue—more than €1.4 billion for the 2004 Summer Games in Athens. The lure of the event is its reach: some 3.9 billion people—more than half the world's population—tune in to one or more of the televised games.[8] Almost equally huge are the Winter Games. In 2006 the Winter Games in Torino reached 2.1 billion people in 160 countries.

There are many ways to affiliate with the Olympics as a sponsor. There are sponsors for teams and sports, as well as countries. But there are also sponsors of the Olympic movement. For the 4-year Olympiad, running from 2005 to 2008, eleven main sponsors are connected to the movement: Coca-Cola, Kodak, McDonald's, Samsung, Atos Original, Lenovo, Omega, Visa, GE, Manulife and Panasonic. Together they contribute $866 million for this privilege that encompasses both the 2006 Torino Winter Games and the Summer Games of 2008 in Beijing. Next to these, each of the Games has its own main sponsors, official sponsors, and official suppliers, which of course are all aliases for sponsors that contribute different amounts, and consequently obtain different privileges.

Among the reasons to sponsor a team or event, exposure is the most important. Although sport is inherently performance oriented, good results are not particularly important—although performance will increase exposure, because the best teams get most media attention. Drugs may be a problem, however: various sponsors of cycling teams ended their sponsorship agreements following doping scandals. Phonak ended their sponsoring of a professional cycle team after Floyd Landis of their team, winner of the Tour de France 2006, was accused of doping. Also, external effects may influence sponsorship arrangements. In the Netherlands a small insurer ended the sponsorship of a soccer team in the highest division after supporters' misbehaviour. Again, it is the not the sporting achievements that influenced this decision.

Next to exposure, the association with a sport or a team or individual athlete are relevant criteria. Formula 1 racing is dynamic, high-tech, adventurous, international and sexy. Which modern brand does not want to be associated with such key words (see colour insert C3)? And that also holds good for the individual drivers.

Other reasons for sponsoring are more mundane. In Germany, Volkswagen is the sponsor of Vfl Wolfsburg with an unlimited contract. Volkswagen's main factories are located in this city. Dutch PSV originated as the sports club of Philips who are still the main sponsor of the team. And sometimes clubs are simply owned by a company, or its CEO, as its toy. For example, Juventus in Torino was chaired by the late Giovanni Agnelli, then CEO of Fiat.

Cause marketing

Cause marketing is an important *type of sponsorship that marries philanthropy with marketing.* In cause marketing programmes, a brand promises to donate money or other types of support to an organization or social activity when a customer buys or uses the brand. (To limit their financial liability when promising a contribution for each sales transaction, most brands—in small print—state that donations will be made up to a stated amount of money.) An example is the American Express programme to feed the homeless, which has donated two cents to food kitchens for the homeless for each credit-card transaction made by its cardholders. The effort was supported by an advertising campaign stating, "Every time you use the American Express Card, you'll help provide a meal for someone who is hungry." The campaign was estimated to have helped increase AmEx charge-card transactions by 8.4 per cent, so in the short term, at least, this promotion was highly successful.

When the Internet search engine and navigational portal Lycos found itself struggling to build a brand identity and share of mind among many competitors, it used cause marketing. Observing an important principle of cause marketing, Lycos decided to help a non-profit organization in a way that leveraged and demonstrated its expertise—searching. Lycos agreed to help the National Centre for Missing and Exploited Children. The company learned that the most critical period in finding these children is within the first 72 hours of their disappearance. Because of the short lead time required for using the Internet, Lycos developed a system for distributing information and pictures of missing children as soon as their disappearance was reported. Lycos received positive media coverage for its efforts and saw an increase in the number of visits to its portal.[9] There is no question that such sponsorships can have a significant impact on sales among consumers who appreciate a company's dedication to social responsibility.

Non-profit organizations are increasingly offering themselves as a "cause" in order to tap into this type of corporate support. For a cause to be strategically integrated into a marketing communication programme, it must be consistent with a brand's image and needs a bottom-line pay-out (just as any promotion should do).

Technically speaking, cause marketing is not a form of sponsoring: there are no formulated communication objectives. But it is obvious that cause marketing contributes indirectly to the branding objectives of the company. By selecting causes with care, as the Lycos example shows, certain associations can be reinforced, or new associations created. And of course the association of being philanthropic has its own virtues.

Evaluating events

The evaluation of events moves beyond the usual return-on-investment calculations (ROI, comparing revenue generated against the cost of the promotional effort), which are sometimes difficult to derive from an event, to evaluate instead the impact of a brand-event experience on brand image. In other words, the focus is on customer perceptions of a brand and how these may change as a result of a positive experience at an event. Some B2B events, such as exhibits at trade shows, can deliver hard data, such as sales or sales leads. In consumer marketing, however, effective events are more likely to deliver a more positive brand perception, an effect that needs attitude and likeability measures. These perceptions, in turn, can lead to greater customer loyalty, depending on the level of involvement and how positive the experience was.[10] An event, in other words, should be evaluated both as a relationship-building tool in terms of its long-term impact as well as impact on sales in the short term.

One agency which specializes in event evaluation measures effectiveness in terms of brand impact and audience engagement.[11] The firm offers pre- and post-event Web-based surveys that track the performance of an event and measure changes in brand awareness and image. If other objectives have been set for an event, these also are measured. In addition to the Web-based tracking studies, the company also uses focus groups, interviews at the event, and surveys.

For sponsorship a common way of evaluation is to compare its effects with other types of communication effect, i.e. what has been the reach or frequency of the sponsorship, and how much would that have cost by using traditional media. Where exposure is the main objective of sponsoring, this certainly is a good way of assessing sponsorship's effectiveness compared to traditional media. But, as has been made clear, the effects of sponsorships also occur in creating or sustaining associations and this should be taken into account too.

Strengths and limitations of events and sponsorships

Events and sponsorships enhance a company's or brand's visibility by associating it with something positive, such as a cause or athletic event. Because of the involvement factor, events and sponsorships are also good relationship-building activities that bind customers emotionally to a company or brand, and they can be used to involve a variety of important stakeholders. Sponsors of major events and organizations, such as Formula 1 racing, football games, concerts and museums, often receive season tickets or passes and other special privileges for their customers and employees.

As sponsorships have grown (currently at about 5 per cent per year), so has the need for some way of measuring their impact. Most sponsorships should offer a 150 to 200 per cent return on the cost of the sponsorship in terms of advertising and promotional opportunities, not to mention the goodwill and relationships that will arise from the association.

The biggest limitation of event sponsorships is that, depending on the scope of the event, they tend to involve directly only a small percentage of a brand's target audience. Even sponsorships of big international events are facing this problem, as the viewership is highly unfocused. Everybody watches the Olympics, including those people that are not in the target group. Do you know all the main sponsors of the Olympics listed above? Yet, the cost of being a sponsor is simply based on the event's exposure. An alternative and more sophisticated way to measure the return on investment of event sponsorship is to relate the return not to the event itself but to how well other MC functions leverage the sponsorship. Another problem is the control, or lack thereof, that a company has over the design and management of a sponsored event.

Packaging: the last ad seen

The retail environment is a critical brand touch point that delivers brand messages to consumers about packaged goods and service offerings, not only through sales-promotion efforts but also through product packaging. It is estimated that 60 to 70 per cent of brand decisions about packaged goods are not made until consumers are inside retail stores. Thus MC programmes that reach consumers and drive them into stores have a direct impact on sales only when the two come together in the place where customers make brand decisions. The package delivers the final message that brings the entire message-and-response process that is fuelled by creating awareness and building a brand image to completion.

As the self-service concept in retailing has expanded, the package has become a particularly important brand message for consumer brands. As shoppers move through heavily stocked stores, they scan shelves at the rate of 300 items a minute. Amid all this clutter, a package's job is to attract attention, make consumers recall the brand knowledge they already have, and communicate brand information.

Packaging is not only the last message but also an important part of a brand's identity, particularly for **fast-moving consumer goods (FMCGs)** also called **consumer packaged goods**, which are *products that are usually sold in food, discount, and drug stores in small packages and have a low unit price.* These products are purchased frequently, and their brand identity is conveyed by their packages or labels. In fact, the package is often the only brand message that distinguishes a branded product from a generic one.

A great example of **proprietary packaging** (*a package design that is patented to prevent any other brand from using it*) is the hourglass shape of the Coca-Cola bottle. Another example is Toilet Duck (see colour insert C7). This toilet cleaner is packed in a duck-shaped plastic bottle that not only is well recognized on the shelves, but is functional as well. Pringles potato chips developed a new package that was not only exclusive, but also very economical and protective of the product.

A package is, first of all, a container. But it is more than that. A package delivers a complex message about the product category and the brand's selling points, as well as the brand's identity and image. Just as a store's design sends a strong message about the store, the design and labels on a package communicate important messages about the product it contains. A package is an intrinsic brand message. A person cannot buy (in the store) or use (in the home or workplace) a packaged product without coming into contact with the package. A package, in other words, is a medium for carrying a company-created brand message.

Like merchandising and point-of-purchase materials, a package plays a critical role in brand decision making at the point of sale. There are close links between merchandising and packaging, for both add to, or subtract from, the experience that surrounds a purchase decision.

Objectives of packaging

An important responsibility of package design is to link the product to other brand messages to which the customer has been exposed. One way to do this is through the use of flags on the front of the package that call attention to product features and present reminder messages that tie in with other MC efforts, such as advertising campaigns and special promotional offers.

Brand-message transfer is strongest when package designers make sure the package is shown in all packaged-goods advertising so that customers know what to look for. Message transfer is also conveyed through the stylistics of the package's artwork. Especially in fragrances, packages tend to be pieces of package art that display the distinguished nature of the brand involved.

In addition to establishing brand-identity links, package design has specific attention-getting objectives. To determine which colours, typography, and layout styles will attract the attention of busy shoppers, package designers study which items consumers notice and which ones they actually place in their shopping carts. One of the biggest success stories in packaging has been Pepsi's Twist 'n Go container, introduced in 1999. It is spill-resistant, resealable, and designed to fit most car cup-holders.

Although packages are most often thought of in conjunction with consumer packaged goods, the packaging concept also applies to services. The service "package" is the environment in which a service is delivered. How many times have you based the selection or rejection of a restaurant on its exterior or interior appearance? Likewise, the uniforms worn by and the vehicles driven by service personnel operating away from their place of business are elements of the service "package".

The package is a free medium

Although seldom discussed as such, packaging is a major communication vehicle that companies can use to deliver whatever brand message they wish. Unfortunately, many manufacturers of packaged goods still consider a package only as a container. If you think of a package as a communication opportunity, however, the media cost is zero because the package is "already there".

The number of people who walk down food store, drugstore, and mass merchandiser aisles everyday is in the millions—far more than the number who watch an average prime-time TV show. What this means is that a brand's package is like a miniature outdoor board with millions of potential exposures each day. Wine producers understand this bill-boarding function and design their labels with utmost care. A label on a bottle of wine has to do all the selling to most consumers. The labels are often attractive, ranging from classic to modern. The label instantly builds the brand, conveying all information required, but also designed to be remembered in order to support repeat purchasing.

Companies that fail to make their packages attention-getting and appealing miss a communication opportunity. The design cost to improve and modernize a package label, when spread over millions of exposures, not to mention purchases, is one of the best bargains in marketing communication. A good example is a company that produced a line of thin-sliced lunchmeat that was sold in four-ounce plastic pouches. The company lacked the scale to cost-justify producing and running print or broadcast advertising for the line. The fact that it carried the corporate brand name, as did all the other 150 different products, was the only MC support the line had, which is why its sales increases were minimal year after year. Then, working with a packaging design firm and spending less than €100 000, the company redesigned the packaging, giving the line much more attention-getting power and appetite appeal. The result was a 27 per cent increase in sales the first year after the new package was introduced. The return on the investment (ROI) paid for the cost of the redesign many, many times over.

New technology is bringing innovations to packaging, as well. An Israeli company, Power Paper, is using an ultra-thin flexible battery that can be "printed" on a package like ink to add attention-getting features like music on a compact disc or a tiny video demonstration on a technical product. Such packaging innovations can be educational, as well as attention getting.[12]

The fact that the package is the last brand message that a prospective customer sees before making a brand choice is another strong reason for making package design an important part of an IMC programme. This is particularly true for brands and product lines that have little or no other marketing communication support. Techniques like hangtags are used to provide an additional on-product advertisement.

Strengths and limitations of packaging

Packages both protect a product and facilitate its transport. Beyond those functional objectives, however, packages can also be used to make a strong visual statement that brings the brand personality to life, ties in with other marketing communication efforts, and delivers low-cost brand information and reminders in the critical "buy zone" in a store. Furthermore, a package continues to communicate after the buyer leaves the store. The package can provide important decision information, such as nutrition facts, product claims like "caffeine free", and additional information about the product. It can also showcase promotions with flags like "Official sponsor of the Olympics", or "Free toy inside".

Sometimes the package itself can be a source of added value, particularly when it is designed for convenience. Aseptic juice packages—juice boxes—for example, created an entirely new

IMC in Action

The "X bottle"

"Helping males keep a step ahead in the mating game". This is the promise of Axe, one of the nine personal care brands of Unilever. Axe offers shower gels, deodorants, fragrances and other personal care products. With these products the brand targets young men aged between 18 and 35. In order to deliver on its promise, Axe brings new ideas regularly—for example by marketing a new deodorant fragrance every year. This is why Axe enjoys a reputation as an innovator in the men's fragrance category

For Axe, innovation means more than bringing new products. Axe products are marketed in unique and innovative ways too. Advertising is the main marketing communication tool the brand uses, and Axe products are always accompanied by outstanding commercials. Key features used in commercials include coolness, excitement and seduction. Axe advertisements have brought great returns in terms of awards, including 10 Cannes Lions.

"Getting dressed" is one of the advertisements that was awarded a Cannes Lion. The commercial features a young couple that meet in the supermarket and make their way home while undressing each other. However, the commercial shows the story in reverse order, and so the ad begins in bed and ends in the supermarket. Then the line "Because you never know when" appears, referring to Axe as a deodorant working 24 hours a day.

Another brand element that is subject to Axe's innovative approach is packaging. Axe designs its containers so that they appeal directly to the target audience. Axe shower gels, for example, are packaged in black plastic containers with a rough appearance. The packaging thus communicates the same brand features as the advertisements.

For the marketing of Axe Unlimited, a men's fragrance, packaging played a key role as well. Although the Axe brand promises to keep guys ahead in the mating game, this product targets the more mature customer who is moving towards sophisticated designer fragrances. To extend the brand relevance, the package had to be redesigned. Axe eau de toilette is now packaged in a matte black glass container, called the "X bottle". The bottle has a large "X" engraved in the container and brand labels are positioned on the sides. Because of its matte surface finishing the package appears and feels like rubber and thus evokes a sensual, soft touch, which was one of the objectives in designing the product. Additionally, the matte finishing is resistant to finger marks, a functional benefit of the design. With this packaging Axe combines features that are easily recognizable for existing Axe users with the new appearance of a "designer" eau de toilette. Therefore, the packaging attracts attention but at the same time evokes the memory of brand knowledge and thus completes the process of building awareness and brand image.

Think about it

Why is Axe successful in using its package design as a communication tool? Do you think Axe customers will perceive the Axe package design as a marketing tool? Can you think of other brands that use package design in such a way?

Sources:
www.unilever.com/ourbrands/personalcare/Axe.asp
www.thebrewerydesign.com/pdf/Brewery_cs_axe.pdf
www.lightninglabels.com/innovative-packaging-ideas.htm
www.brandpackaging.com/content.php?s=BP/2006/04&p=13

category in the beverage market because they are not only portable and lightweight but don't have to be refrigerated. Bottles with a special non-drip spout provide added value for products such as syrup and detergent. Packages can even function as a premium when they become collectibles, such as Avon bottles, special holiday liquor bottles and designer cans used to package teas, biscuits, or crackers.

The biggest weakness of packaging is its potential for clogging up landfills. The long box often used to package CDs is one example of what many consider to be overpackaging. The aseptic beverage box used for milk and juices turned out to be a nightmare for environmentalists because the thin layers of paper and plastic and the aluminum-foil lining are hard to separate. A number of companies are redesigning their packages in order to make them more disposable. Carnation has converted its pet food cans to recyclable aluminum. Heinz has replaced its perennial dump filler, the squeezable ketchup bottle, with a bottle that can be more easily recycled.

The greatest challenge from a marketing communication point of view is to educate customers that the package is an ad. For many customers the package remains the container of the product. Creativity and design are necessary here, perhaps more than in any other area of MC, to make packaging the powerful MC instrument that it potentially is.

A final note: adding experiences to a brand relationship

Events, sponsorships, and customer service are critical dimensions of relationship marketing. They provide interactivity, and they create a memorable brand experience. The intensity of involvement that comes from a personal experience is the reason why messages delivered through events and customer service are so powerful. Experiential communication is persuasive because it pumps up the customer's level of attention, interest, and recall of a brand and company.

Marketing communication functions that deliver experiential contact make it possible for a company to develop a positive, highly involving, and memorable link to a brand. They also offer an opportunity to tightly target an audience. Combining the persuasiveness of personal contact with the involvement of experience-focused communication, events, sponsorships, and customer service can be used to create, maintain, and grow more effective brand relationships.

🔒 Key terms

cause marketing Type of sponsorship that marries philanthropy with marketing.

consumer packaged goods *see* fast-moving consumer goods.

cross-promotion When one communication mix element refers to another element.

event marketing A promotional occasion designed to attract and involve a brand's target audience.

fast-moving consumer goods (FMCGs) Products that are usually sold in food, discount, and drug stores in small packages and have a low unit price.

product placement The paid-for, identifiable appearance of a brand or product in a TV show or movie.

proprietary packaging A package design that is patented to prevent any other brand from using it.

sponsorship Support of an organization, person, or activity, financial or in kind, in exchange for brand publicity and association, or other marketing communication objectives.

trade show An event at which customers in a particular industry gather to attend training sessions and visit with suppliers and vendors to review their product offerings and innovations.

Check the key points

Key point 1: Product placements

a   What are the reasons product placements are growing in popularity?

b   What factors influence the effect of product placements?

c   Why is cross-promotion particularly relevant for product placements?

d   What are the strengths and limitations of product placements?

Key point 2: Events and sponsorships

a   How does a created event differ from a participation event? Give an example of each.

b   What departments or MC functions use events? What do they hope to accomplish with the events?

c   What do events contribute to relationship programmes?

d   What is a trade show? Who is its target? What objectives might a company specify for its participation in such an event?

e   How do sports sponsorships work? What are their objectives?

f   Define *cause marketing*. Find an example of cause marketing. How effective is cause marketing at building brand relationships?

g What are the strengths and limitations of event marketing and sponsorships?

h Develop a set of typical objectives (at least three) for event marketing and sponsorship, based on the strengths you identify for each area.

Key point 3: Packaging

a What communication functions does a package perform?

b What does it mean to say that packages have a billboard function?

c What are the key strengths and limitations of packaging design?

d List and explain at least three objectives that you might set for your packaging.

Chapter Challenge

Writing assignment

Visit a supermarket and buy packages of dried soup of at least three brands. Describe their packages, in particular identifying elements that are common, and elements that are different. Next, check other MC messages of the respective brands. In what way do the packages reinforce these other brand messages?

Presentation assignment

Watch an episode of your favourite TV show and identify all product placements in it. Describe and analyse their appearance in terms of the effectiveness factors given in the text. When you tape the episode, show it in class and assess the responses to the placements.

Internet assignment

Consult the website of the international Olympic movement (www.olympic.org) and identify its sponsors. Check what different kind of sponsorships there are, and what companies get in return for their support.

Notes

[1] Cristel Russell (2002), "Investigating the effectiveness of product placements in television shows: the role of modality and plot connection congruence on brand memory and attitude", *Journal of Consumer Research*, Vol. 29–3, pp. 306–18.

[2] "PMA Announces Formation of Event Marketing Council ..." (press release, Promotional Marketing Association, 13 March 2003), www.pmalink.org/about/press_releases.

[3] Quoted in Melanie Warner, "Can Tupperware Keep a Lid on the Web?", *Fortune*, 12 January 1998, p. 144.

[4] Joseph Pine II and James Gilmore, *The Experience Economy: Work Is Theatre and Every Business a Stage* (Boston: Harvard Business School Press, 1999).

[5] A detailed discussion of how such Jeep Camps help create brand communities is given in McAlexander, Schouten and Koenig (2002), "Building Brand Community", *Journal of Marketing*, Vol. 14–2, pp. 61–79.

[6] Melinda Fulmer, "Tricks of the Trade Shows", *Los Angeles Times*, 19 February 1997, p. D1.

[7] Jim Obermayer, "Power Play: Sales Leads Are Why You Exhibit" (presentation at Exhibitor Show, Baltimore, Fall 1999).

[8] David Sweet, "Bowing to TV, IOC Bars Web Use of Audio, Video from Olympics", *Wall Street Journal*, 2 August 2000, p. B1.

[9] Stephanie Zschunke, "Cause Marketing: Lost and Found", *Reputation Management*, February 2000, p. 22.

[10] Kay Harmsen, "Experiential Event Marketing: Building Brand Relationships That Last", *IMC Research Journal*, Spring 2001, pp. 19–26.

[11] Kurt Miller, "Beyond ROI: Using Measurement to Improve Event Marketing Performance" (corporate handout, Jack Morton Worldwide, Boston, n.d.).

[12] "Firm Studies New Features for Packaging", *Boulder Daily Camera*, 12 February 2001, p. 13A.

Further reading

Carrillat, Francois A., Barbara A. Lafferty and Eric G. Harris (2005) "Investigating sponsorship effectiveness: Do less familiar brands have an advantage over more familiar brands in single and multiple sponsorship arrangements?", *Journal of Brand Management*, Vol. 13–1, pp. 50–64.

Christensen, Sverre Riis (2006) "Measuring Consumer Reactions to Sponsoring Partnerships Based upon Emotional and Attitudinal Responses", *International Journal of Market Research*, Vol. 48–1, pp. 61–80.

Crawford, Stephanie Y. and Catherine Leventis (2005) "Herbal product claims: boundaries of marketing and science", *Journal of Consumer Marketing*, Vol. 22–7, pp. 432–6.

Dolphin, Richard R. (2003) "Sponsorship: perspectives on its strategic role", *Corporate Communications: An International Journal*, Vol. 8–3, pp. 173–86.

Hudson, Simon and David Hudson (2006) "Branded Entertainment: A New Advertising Technique or Product Placement in Disguise", *Journal of Marketing Management*, Vol. 22–5/6, pp. 489–504.

La Ferle, Carrie and Steven M. Edwards (2006) "Product Placement", *Journal of Advertising*, Vol. 35–4, pp. 65–86.

Sneath, Julie Z., Zachary R. Finney and Angeline Grace Close (2005) "An IMC approach to event marketing: The effects of sponsorship and experience on Customer Attitudes", *Journal of Advertising Research*, Vol. 45–4, pp. 373–81.

Publicity and public relations

CHAPTER PERSPECTIVE
Managing relationships with publics

Public relations professionals have always understood the concept of relationships—after all, the word *relations* is part of their job title. Unfortunately, many marketing people in the past did not always recognize or appreciate the value of public relations.

Some major steps toward bringing marketing and public relations departments closer came in the early 1990s with the development of a concept called *relationship marketing*, pioneered by PR consultant Regis McKenna.[1] At the same time, courses devoted to relationship marketing began to develop in business schools around the world. Although McKenna's background is public relations, he challenged the marketing industry to become more "customer-centric" and to understand customer relationships better. "Advertising, promotion, and market-share thinking are dead," wrote McKenna, "and what counts are the relationships a company develops with its customers, suppliers, partners, distributors—even its competitors."

IMC is helping to introduce to marketing practitioners some of the concepts that public relations professionals have known about for years, such as the importance of stakeholder relationships. Marketing people are discovering the power and value of marketing public relations—that is, brand publicity—to deliver highly effective, cost-efficient messages. At the same time, public relations people are learning more about marketing and are using marketing concepts such as branding and positioning to build corporate communication strategies.

The Body Shop: Inspired by nature?

Looking for cocoa body butter or mango shower gel? The Body Shop is the place to be for naturally inspired products like these! The first Body Shop store was opened in March of 1976 in Brighton, UK. At that time founder Anita Roddick simply sold body care products to make a living. By 2007 The Body Shop is a global manufacturer and retailer of naturally inspired, ethically produced beauty and cosmetics products and has over 2100 stores in more than 55 countries throughout the UK and Ireland, Europe, the Middle East, the US, Africa and Asia Pacific, and sells over 1200 different products. Throughout its existence the company has not only created a niche market for naturally inspired products, it has also changed the ethical position of the cosmetics industry by not testing any personal care products on animals. Both factors contributed to the fame of The Body Shop and, although competitors have copied all or parts of its concept, the company still enjoys great brand recognition.

"Masstige" brand

Positioning itself as a "masstige" brand ever since 2004, The Body Shop seeks to provide its customers with "a shopping experience that combines excellent service with a comprehensive range of naturally inspired personal care products offering high performance benefits and competitive pricing". This positioning allows the brand to be the cheaper alternative to brands such as Estée Lauder and Clinique, hence differentiating itself. To be able to deliver the "masstige" experience to its customers, The Body Shop first of all focuses on product innovation. New products are introduced across various product categories at a constant rate and are meant to support multiple purchases and higher transaction values. Examples of new products include extensions in the Almond Bath and Body Range, a new range of luxurious home spa products called Spa Wisdom, and a new-look make-up collection.

Another strategic focus of The Body Shop is store development. After years of using the same store outlook, in 2004 The Body Shop developed a new store design and since then has focused on spreading this design throughout its dedicated stores. By the end of 2006 154 stores already embodied the new design. The design is meant to create an improved shopping experience. Another way in which The Body Shop improves the shopping experience for customers is by means of improved customer service. At the heart of this improved service are staff development programmes that help sales associates serve customers in a better way. Not satisfied with providing outstanding customer service in-store, The Body Shop aims to provide dedicated service through multiple channels. The development of a multiple-channel organization thus represents the third strategic goal of the company.

Apart from sales through dedicated stores, The Body Shop also sells its products via the Internet on www.thebodyshop.com, and offers customers an experience similar to Tupperware parties by selling through a channel that is called The Body Shop at Home. Although the Internet channel is currently only available for customers in the US, and The Body Shop at Home is only offered to customers in the UK, the US, and Australia, a multiple-channel strategy is ready to be spread throughout all regions in which the organization operates.

IMC in Action

The Body Shop mission and values

At the heart of The Body Shop's strategy is a mission that stipulates the following commitment: "To dedicate our business to the pursuit of social and environmental change." To live up to this dedication the organization has five core principles: oppose animal testing, support community trade, activate self-esteem, defend human rights, and protect our planet. Each of these values serves as a basis for the company's global campaigns.

A deep-rooted campaign by The Body Shop in the UK has been the fight against animal testing, which started in 1987. By then The Body Shop, together with the British Union for the Abolition of Vivisection (BUAV), ran its first promotional campaign against vivisection, or the dissection of living animals. In 2006 the company backed up the BUAV again, this time campaigning together with others like Marks & Spencer, to stop the EU from bringing back cosmetics tests on animals in a new law called REACH (Registration Evaluation Authorisation of CHemicals). This 2006 campaign featured a nationwide advertising campaign in the UK, to convince the British to fight for cruelty-free cosmetics. The Body Shop's aversion to animal testing is not just the basis of campaigns, but is also a profound part of the company's policies. The company guarantees: "None of our products or ingredients have been tested or retested on animals for cosmetics purposes since December 31 1990." Although The Body Shop is not the only organization fighting against animal testing, the company was the first international cosmetics brand to be awarded with the Humane Cosmetics Standard for its policy against animal testing in 1999.

Apart from its fight against animal testing, The Body Shop is also fully committed to the support of fair trade programmes. In 1990 a footsie roller, produced by Teddy Exports from India in 1986, became the first Community Trade product and marked the establishment of The Body Shop's fair trade programme, called Community Trade. The ultimate objective of this programme has been to "satisfy the demand for natural ingredients, gifts and accessories in a fair way, to maximize the sustainable benefits to the supplier communities and to meet customer's expectations of The Body Shop as an ethical retailer". In 2007 The Body Shop buys from 31 Community Trade suppliers in 24 countries and has created sustainable relationships with communities around the world. By sourcing products from these communities at fair prices, which cover production costs and producer wages, The Body Shop enables the Community Trade suppliers to invest in their future. Currently, more than half of The Body Shop core lines contain one or more Community Trade ingredients.

A close look at The Body Shop reveals many other campaigns in which the company is involved. Think of the "Stop Violence In The Home" campaign, or "Stop HIV: Spray To Change Attitudes", for example. Additionally The Body Shop set up The Body Shop Foundation in 1990. This independent charity funds human rights and environmental protection groups. The charity is funded by The Body Shop by means of yearly donations, which amounted to £700 000 in 2006. All in all, The Body Shop has an impressive record of contributions to socially important issues.

Marketing communication

How is all this communicated to The Body Shop's customers? Although The Body Shop is known as an organization that is not involved in advertising of any kind, the company still enjoys great brand recognition. The company has mainly gained this recognition through the various campaigns in which it has participated. These campaigns have constantly raised awareness of the social issues that are considered important by The Body Shop's customers. The company thus does not advertise its products but instead promotes its ethical image to reach target customers. Communications about campaigns depend to a great extent on publicity, but also consist of in-store messages. For example, customers are updated on successes of the Community Trade programme through in-store posters that tell the personal stories of people involved in the programme. The Body Shop at Home allows a company representative to communicate directly to the customer. Additionally, The Body Shop has a well-developed website that provides extensive information on all campaigns and aid programmes in which the company is enrolled.

The Body Shop takeover

Since The Body Shop has contributed greatly to creating awareness for ethical issues, it is no surprise that the company has enjoyed a strong brand image for years. However, the brand's true identity has recently been questioned.

It was in March 2006 that The Body Shop was taken over by global cosmetics company L'Oréal. The takeover is expected to be beneficial to both companies. The Body Shop will benefit from the financial backing and expertise of L'Oréal in such areas as R&D and marketing, which will provide the brand with opportunities for growth. L'Oréal, on the other hand, will benefit from The Body Shop's experience in dealing with community trade and other environmental and social issues. As such, L'Oréal will be able to improve the way it operates from an environmental and social perspective. However, the great differences in the corporate images of the two companies could also have an adverse effect. The Body Shop has built the image of an ethical company that is against animal testing of any kind. Also, the company is known for its natural products. L'Oréal on the other hand, has been criticized for testing its products on animals in the past. Nevertheless, The Body Shop is not worried that its corporate image will be harmed. During the takeover the two parties agreed that The Body Shop values and the way it operates would be respected. Also, the two agreed upon keeping The Body Shop as a separate entity within the L'Oréal group. The Body Shop thus has not specifically taken any steps to protect its image, but instead will continue operating in the same way it did before. The future will determine whether the natural and ethical The Body Shop brand will indeed remain untainted.

Sources:

www.thebodyshopinternational.com

Buav (2006) "High street joins fight to stop EU forcing lipstick tests on animals". Retrieved 28 February 2007, from www.buav.org/news/2006_news_updates/2006_11_REACH_release.html

Datamonitor (2006) Body Shop International, PLC SWOT analysis.

Entine, J. (1996, 2003) "A social and environmental audit of The Body Shop: Anita Roddick and the Question of Character". Retrieved 28 February 2007, from www.jonentine.com/body_shop.htm

Nguyen, M. (2006) "Consumers boycott Body Shop over 'betrayal'", B&T Weekly, Vol. 56 (2557), Australia: Reed Elsevier Inc.

The Body Shop International PLC (2006) Annual Report and Accounts 2006. Retrieved 28 February 2007, from www.thebodyshopinternational.com

The Body Shop International PLC (2006) Animal testing policy 2006. Retrieved 7 March 2007, from www.thebodyshopinternational.com

The practice of public relations

Public relations covers a wide variety of activities designed to affect both public opinion and the opinion of specific stakeholders whose support a company needs. Public relations can be a concept, a profession, and a management function, as well as a practice. Its objective is to create goodwill and understanding—positive relationships—between an organization and its stakeholders. Many of the bigger companies in the world are constantly struggling with their public image. For example, Shell is facing a few heavy and persistent attacks on their public image, ranging from being rooted in the oil and chemical industry with its highly environmentally unfriendly connotation, to the Brent Spar story, accusations of abuse of the Nigerian people in the Niger delta, to major accounting problems. All of these issues have almost nothing to do with the products Shell makes, yet are detrimental to the general feelings people hold in relation to Shell (see colour insert D5).

Publicity can be interpreted as every instance in which stakeholders receive a message about the brand that is not disseminated by the brand. Publicity has a significant overlap with the concept of unexpected touch points, introduced in Chapter 3. As publicity is not generated by the brand, its credibility in the eyes of the receiver is high, and this makes publicity an important factor in creating brand images. Part of the job of PR managers is to control, or even initiate, publicity. This is a delicate job, where the distinction between publicity and plain advertising is easily lost. When PR fails to do its work of managing publicity with the utmost care, it can easily backfire. Many five o'clock lifestyle shows are paid by companies like Unilever. As long as this is not known publicly, it remains a very successful example of managing publicity. But as soon as it becomes known, the expected response of the public is that they feel cheated, and this backfires on the company. Brands do not want to run this risk and make sure that they are open about this kind of sponsorships (also see Chapter 11).

The interests of public relations and marketing overlap, but in many organizations public relations operates separately from marketing and has different goals. One PR professional explains the difference between the two areas this way: "Whereas marketing and sales have as their primary objective selling an organization's products, public relations attempts to sell the organization itself."[2]

Public relations strategy can be focused on the corporate brand or on a product brand. Public relations departments generally have responsibility for managing the corporate image. Marketing is generally responsible for managing the image of product brands. The distinction between the two is sometimes fuzzy, especially when the corporate name is the same as the brand name (Nike, Mercedes) and when both the corporate and the product brand names are used to identify a product (Sony Walkman).

This chapter begins with an overview of the public relations industry and the types of activities it includes. It then explores brand publicity, whose primary objective from an IMC perspective is building a brand's overall credibility. The third main section is devoted to PR's general working area: corporate communication—building a company's image and reputation and other corporate public relations areas that are particularly important to IMC, such as employee and financial relations and crisis communication.

Defining public relations

Public relations, as introduced in Chapter 1, is *a communication function used to promote mutual understanding between an organization and its various stakeholder groups.* Here is a list of responsibilities and functions of a public relations department:[3]

- To serve as the central source of information about the organization, and as the official channel of communication between the organization and the public.

- To bring to public attention, through appropriate media, significant facts, opinions, and interpretations that will serve to keep the public aware of the organization's policies and actions.

- To co-ordinate activities that affect the organization's relations with the general public or with other stakeholder groups.

- To collect and analyse information on the changing attitudes of key public groups and stakeholders toward the organization.

- To plan and administer informational programmes designed to fulfil most effectively the responsibilities listed above.

- To co-ordinate the public relations activities with other marketing communication efforts within the organization and to bring a relationship perspective to those areas.

The public relations industry

Public relations is one of the fastest growing of all the communication functions used in IMC. Like most of the other functions, it suffered a downturn of the beginning of the twenty-first century, but the industry had experienced a healthy double-digit growth during the previous decade.[4] Although some of this growth was the result of mergers and acquisitions and the dot.com boom, the trend indicates a healthy industry. Public relations is growing because it has the power to cut through message clutter.[5]

Compared to the huge amount spent on mass media advertising, public relations spending is relatively minor since it triggers little or no media cost, which consumes the major portion of an advertising budget. The major public relations expenditures are for personnel and the production of events, newsletters, brochures, annual reports, and corporate advertising.

Types of public relations activities

In an effort to maintain good relationships with all of an organization's important stakeholders, public relations programmes include various "relational" activities. Table 12-1 indicates the range of "publics", or stakeholder audiences, that are targeted by different kinds of public relations activities, from government officials to employees, the financial community, and the media. These areas of expertise may be developed internally within a company, but they are also available from PR agencies. Some public relations agencies provide a full range of programmes, and almost all carry out publicity and media relations. Some specialize in certain communication areas such as marketing public relations and government relations. Agencies may also focus on specific industries, such as pharmaceuticals, agriculture, or high technology. This chapter discusses these areas, beginning with marketing public relations, commonly known as *brand publicity*.

Brand publicity

From an IMC perspective, one of the most important activities in PR is **brand publicity**, *the use of non-paid media messages to deliver brand information designed to positively influence customers and prospects.* It is estimated that up to 70 per cent of the average public relations firm's revenues comes from doing brand publicity.[6] Another indication of the importance of brand publicity is that public relations firms are increasingly being acquired by advertising agency conglomerates, which recognize the importance of this function in the MC mix.[7]

Activity	Description
Publicity	Programmes that support product and brand communication and promotion (brand publicity), and that are directed primarily at customers and prospects.
Media relations	Activities that distribute information to the media creating publicity for an organization; activities that cultivate relationships of trust with key reporters and editors.
Corporate communication	Managed by senior-level counsellors, such programmes focus on corporate identity, reputation management, and strategic counselling for top management. Responsibilities that are sometimes found in corporate relations include: ■ *Issues management:* functions that monitor public opinion and advise senior management, particularly in companies in sensitive or controversial industries such as pharmaceuticals, drinks, and cigarettes. ■ *Community relations:* programmes that involve members of the local community and address their concerns. ■ *Government relations (public affairs):* information programmes for legislators, government bodies, and regulatory agencies. ■ *Industry relations:* activities that address the concerns of the industry in which the company competes.
Employee relations	Internal communication programmes that keep employees informed and build their morale (can also be part of internal marketing programmes); employee relations can also include labour relations programmes.
Financial or investor relations	Information programmes for the financial community—investors, analysts, and the financial press.
Crisis management	A general plan designed to manage how a company responds when disaster strikes. It addresses all relevant stakeholders—the general public, employees, the community, media, investors.

Table 12-1 Public relations activities and their audiences

With the growing interest in relationship marketing, companies are beginning to learn more about relationship management from a public relations viewpoint. To create "more symmetrical relationships", a term used in public relations to describe interactivity, public relations communication must become more data-driven, a point Sandra Moriarty made in *Public Relations Quarterly:*[8]

> As PR people become more proficient with databases and interactive technologies, two-way communication with stakeholders will continue to increase. As it does, there will need to be some serious creative thinking about what it means to participate in communication initiated by a wide range of stakeholders.

As noted earlier, many companies separate marketing and public relations. Public relations managers, particularly those who track issues and public opinions, typically report to the president of the organization. Meanwhile, advertising managers usually report to a vice president of marketing. Where there is no cross-functional organization, advertising managers may have little or no contact with their counterparts in public relations.

An example of the mixed messages this situation can create was demonstrated in a recent edition of the *Wall Street Journal*. On one page was a full-page ad for the high-tech firm Bay Networks extolling the virtues of the company's electronic communication routing and switching capabilities. On the very next page, the lead news story highlighted Bay Networks' disappointing sales, an indication that the company was not satisfying as many customers as it intended.[9] If the company's advertising and public relations departments had talked, perhaps they could have avoided having these two conflicting messages appear at the same time. A negative news story can more than cancel out the effects of a typical "brag and boast" ad.

Turf battles and philosophical differences between marketing and public relations have been referred to as "marketing imperialism". This term reflects the views of some public relations managers and PR professors who fear that, in IMC, public relations will become subordinate to marketing. Although this tension seems to be decreasing, it can still be found in some companies and universities. Some PR professionals and academics argue that if any changes are made, marketing should report to public relations, given the latter's traditional role in managing stakeholder relationships and its emphasis on listening as well as talking to stakeholders. The tension is also reflected in the debates in the academic world on customer equity versus brand equity (Rust, Zeithaml and Lemon, 2000). Brand specialists argue that the brand is the prime concern of the company, whereas relationship advocates argue for relationships to play the lead role. This is to a significant extent an artificial distinction, however. Relationships can only be maintained with the company, and the most important thing companies do with customers is sell products and brands. Brand management on the other hand must recognize that a brand is nothing if it does not connect customers and the company (see Chapter 2). A brand can, for that matter, be seen as a short-cut, a focal concept that captures everything customers and companies connect. Thus, whenever you are confronted with a discussion of who is in the lead, relationship managers or brand managers, you are essentially faced with a political discussion.

Planning brand publicity

Like all marketing communication, an effective publicity effort is guided by a plan. The planning steps are similar to those for other forms of marketing and MC planning: (1) reviewing the situation, (2) setting objectives, (3) developing strategies and tactics, and (4) evaluation (which is covered in Chapter 18).

Reviewing the situation

Reviewing the situation involves background research, which includes finding the traditional information about the company, the marketplace and competitors, the product or service, and consumers. As with advertising, attitude research is particularly important because most publicity programmes hope to affect people's opinions. Attitude research also helps identify key internal strengths and weaknesses and the external problems and opportunities that the publicity programme needs to leverage or address. This step is part of the overall SWOT analysis (Chapter 5).

Setting objectives

Objectives for a public relations plan are similar to advertising objectives in that they seek to build awareness and brand knowledge. However, publicity can also be used to:

- Create or increase brand awareness (visibility).
- Increase knowledge.
- Create or change attitudes.
- Create buzz (word of mouth).
- Influence opinion leaders.
- Stimulate referrals and advocacy.
- Generate a sense of involvement.

In some brand-publicity programmes the objective is to get the brand name mentioned in the mass media in as many different ways, times, and places as possible. The assumption is that the more mentions there are in the press, the more top-of-mind awareness the brand will gain. This shotgun strategy may not be cost-effective because, like advertising, publicity should be targeted as much as possible to reach audiences that will be interested in the brand.

Publicity can often create a deeper level of brand knowledge than advertising because it uses media messages (news releases, brochures, events) that can provide more information than can be put into an ad. Publicity is also used to create positive attitudes. In fact, creating a positive impression of a brand is equally as important as creating awareness.

One small Dutch clothing company used Gsus as a brand name. This was regarded as blasphemous by many consumers, but resonated a sense of rebellion with its core target group. So it definitely helped the talking, driving the kind of positive word-of-mouth comments among friends, family, and associates that creates **buzz**, a term that refers to *excited talk about a brand*. In particular, public relations seeks to reach and affect **influentials**, *opinion leaders and early adopters who influence other people*. From buzz come referrals and advocacy on behalf of the brand by customers and other stakeholders, such as dealers and suppliers. Special events planned as part of a public relations programme can elicit a high level of brand involvement between a customer and a brand.

Buzz is a product of word of mouth. When a brand competes in a crowded and cluttered category, some companies are finding that it might be better—and cheaper—to let customers discover cool new products themselves and talk about those products among themselves. Word of mouth is a powerful tool because of its high level of credibility, and if a topic is hot, it can spread around the world in hours.

Word-of-mouth strategies currently go by several different names: *guerrilla marketing*, which applies to edgy, unconventional campaigns that generate word of mouth, and *viral marketing*, which is online marketing that refers to the way communication spreads on the Internet. Whatever it is called, word of mouth is low cost because it does not rely on expensive media buys. It can be initiated and reinforced by media stories, which is where public relations comes in.[10] Because of its word-of-mouth expertise, the PR department is sometimes responsible for creating both guerrilla and viral communication activities. But word-of-mouth is also an unexpected and therefore uncontrolled touch point.

Spread the word!

"Word of mouth was always the strongest form of advertising from the day that Adam and Eve had somebody else to talk to," says Lester Wunderman in an interview with *VM People*, 2004. Also today many companies recognize that word of mouth is an important tool to communicate the brand message. And that is where *viral marketing* comes in: a special form of publicity that uses existing social networks to generate positive consumer conversations that deliver measurable brand value. It basically is word-of-mouth spread that is enhanced on the Internet. This spread acts like a virus (viral marketing) and therefore can reach a lot of people. Since viral marketing is a new concept, companies are springing up, ready to earn money.

Digital Media Communications (DMC), based in the UK and Australia, is an expert in the field of viral, buzz and word-of-mouth marketing (together called "connected marketing"). The company provides educational workshops, strategic consultancy and implementation of connected marketing campaigns for major brands, including Bacardi, Burger King, Canon, Diesel, MTV, Virgin Mobile and many more. In the education workshops, DMC provides the customer with scientific and practical information about connected marketing. The strategic consultancy part focuses on giving direction in existing strategic brand management activity to the customer. In a half-day brainstorming consultancy session, the customer can learn when to use connected marketing and can receive expert recommendations about how to apply it in specific projects. After the strategic consultancy session, DMC assists the customer in the choice of approach when implementing connected marketing as a marketing communication tool.

Bacardi's "Planet Party" campaign is one of the campaigns where DMC demonstrated its creative ideas. In 2004 the company worked together with CDP-Travissully and The Viral Factory (together with DMC, a member of the Viral and Buzz Marketing Association) to plan, develop, produce, seed and track this campaign for Bacardi. An intergalactic viral film clip, called Sucker, was spread around the Internet to attract party people to The Planet Party website where they could download another viral clip "Come", find the ingredients for cocktails, discover a nightclub and play with more fun activities. Richie di Franco, Project Manager at Bacardi, stated: "We used the online viral and buzz marketing expertise of various VBMA members to extend our famous party spirit theme into a fun new campaign for 25- to 30-somethings—kickstarting awareness exclusively among a wide group of entertainment-seeking, highly active online users." Later, it appeared that within two months this campaign communicated the Bacardi brand to over two million people and caused online conversations around the world, including Germany and the Netherlands.

Think about it

Have you ever taken part in such a viral marketing campaign? Do you think that viral marketing is the marketing of the future? Is culture a determinant in the effectiveness of this concept?

Sources:
www.vm-people.de/en/
www.vbma.net/?page_id=4
www.freepublicity.nu/free_publicity.php
www.dmc.co.uk/about/
www.wikipedia.org

Developing strategies and tactics

Publicity is used to help create visibility for a brand, build brand credibility, launch products, position the brand as a category leader, and reach hard-to-reach target audiences with articles in special-interest and trade publications. In an IMC programme, monitoring and influencing unexpected messages (Chapter 3) is also an important responsibility of public relations.

Brand publicity is particularly useful in launching new products (see colour insert C4). Some successful new-product launches have used *only* brand publicity, which takes advantage of the news value of the new product. Gatorade relied on the on-camera use of the brand by athletes. Publicity can do it alone, however, only when the marketplace isn't too crowded and the product is unique. In a more competitive new-product launch, media coverage in consumer and business media is used to build customer awareness and provide information, as Toyota did when it launched the Prius hybrid car.

The Internet has changed the brand-publicity process and the way public relations departments operate.[11] The Internet can be used to bypass the media when they choose not to carry a news release or they say something negative about a brand or company. Corporate websites, in particular, have become very important sources of public information, providing a profile of the company, its products, its employees, and its business philosophy. E-mail allows PR departments and firms to instantaneously communicate with the media and reach critical stakeholder groups (employees, consumer groups, investment community).

Other aspects of brand-publicity strategy include scheduling and budgeting. The budget is derived from the overall marketing communication budget, but the publicity plan also allocates various amounts to various tactical programmes. For example, to support the launch of a new product, a series of news releases on the breakthrough engineering of a new razor was written; a press conference was held in conjunction with a launch party for media and industry influentials; the launch was supported with an extensive news kit; and a series of local news releases was prepared as the product rolled out. A cost analysis was then prepared for each activity to determine whether the original budget was sufficient.

Scheduling and timing can make or break a publicity campaign. Publicity, when it has to do with a news announcement about a brand, is timed to precede advertising and other marketing communication functions. This is especially true for new-product introductions, whose news value is good for only a short time. Once the advertising begins, news editors reject the product introduction release because it is no longer "news". The challenge is to continue to find different story angles to keep the brand visible and top-of-mind even after its introduction.

Media relations

An important aspect of publicity is media relations, which refers to *maintaining a positive professional relationship with the media*. The people who manage the flow of information through the media channels are called *gatekeepers*. Gatekeepers are *editors and reporters who select (or reject) stories for their publications or stations based on what they think will interest their audiences*—and they are an important target for media relations programmes. The objective of media relations is to get these gatekeepers to run a story about an organization or to cover—attend and write about—an organization's activities.

Media relations professionals become adept at "placing" stories in the media by developing good contacts in the media. They cultivate these key media relationships by helping reporters, providing them with information, and making themselves and the executives of their companies available to answer questions.

The relationship between journalists and public relations people can be prickly. In most cases, organizations have legitimate news stories with strong news values. However, if the PR person is seen as simply trying to manipulate the media into providing coverage of dubious news value, there may be problems with the media relationship. To create a positive and effective media relations programme, public relations professionals must know their media outlets, understand what the media consider to be news, be able to suggest good story ideas, and be available to answer journalists' questions honestly and openly. Media relations works only when both the channel and the source are open to honest communication.

Strengths of brand publicity

In addition to being able to help create brand awareness and knowledge, publicity's other strengths include (1) building a climate of acceptance for a company and its brands, (2) increasing the credibility and believability of brand claims, (3) breaking through commercial message clutter, (4) reaching hard-to-reach audiences, and (5) doing all these things in a very cost-effective way.

Building acceptance

Positive acceptance is a direct outgrowth of corporate or brand reputation. When people think positively about a company or a brand, they are more likely to accept its claims and point of view—that is, they tend to agree with the communication they hear from the company. More important, they agree that the company or brand is essentially good and trustworthy. Even when problems arise, such as a product failure, customers may be more inclined to agree that it is a good product and give the brand a second chance because of their previous positive experiences. Acceptance leads to trust, and trust is a powerful reason to overcome an occasional disappointment. Public relations programmes use ongoing research to track acceptance, as well as reputation and the level of trust and positive attitudes toward an organization or brand.

Increasing credibility

Probably the most important objective of public relations lies in the area of credibility. The media stories that result from publicity efforts benefit from and seem more believable because of **third-party endorsement**, which is *the perspective presented by a reputable media source that has no personal interest in the success or failure of the product being endorsed*. Public relations messages that are carried in the news media are often seen as more believable than ads. Reporters and editors review news stories based on information provided by public relations offices. If the decision is made to use the information, the objectivity of the news medium enhances the credibility of the story. The third-party endorsement strategy with its built-in credibility is the basis for passing out reprints of articles about the brand or a company's executives.

An example of the effective use of third-party endorsements comes from Steve Jobs's reshaping of Apple. Rather than relying on product claims in Apple advertisements, the publicity team relied almost exclusively on comments from industry analysts. Apple provided them with a steady flow of quotes and research data and created chat rooms and user sites on the Internet to generate buzz, which the analysts noted.[12] Another technique is to prepare and distribute an interview with one of the company's top executives.

Clutter busting

All brand messages compete for attention in a very cluttered commercial message environment. Publicity can break through the clutter of other commercial messages when information is delivered in a creative way, such as at an event that features a personal appearance by a celebrity and important company officials.

A brand message is intrinsically more attention getting, interesting, and believable when it has news value or appeals to human interest. Its power to capture attention can be considerably higher than that of an advertising message. World record attempts, preferably under the auspices of the Guinness' *World Book of Records* institute, are a popular way to attract the attention. Richard Branson sponsored Steve Fossett's attempt to solo-fly around the world in 2003, generating a lot of publicity for his Virgin brand.

Reaching the hard to reach

Another strength of publicity is its ability to reach audiences that are difficult to reach with advertising and other brand messages. For example, upmarket and well-educated audiences, such as business executives, spend less time with television, radio, and popular magazines than other groups do and therefore have limited exposure to traditional advertising. Because this group *does* tend to read newspapers, special-interest magazines, and industry publications, publicity helps reach them and get past the institutionalized communication roadblocks (secretaries and answering machines) that often block sales calls and other direct marketing messages.

Cost-effectiveness

Although it costs money to have someone write a press release and distribute it, there is no charge for the time and space such messages occupy in the mass media. That makes publicity considerably less expensive than mass media advertising and most other forms of mass communication. Given the impact of a news story, brand publicity becomes a very cost-effective MC tool. The Internet has made publicity efforts even more cost-effective, a fact reflected in a survey of brand managers, 42 per cent of whom said public relations is the best discipline for brand building on the Internet, as opposed to 32 per cent who preferred advertising.[13]

Limitations of brand publicity

Although marketers control most MC messages to ensure their content, reach, and impact against a targeted audience, they have much less control over brand publicity because the messages are filtered through media gatekeepers—the editors and reporters who make the decision to run the story or not. As with image advertising, the impact of brand publicity is not easily measured because most of it is focused on affecting attitudes and opinions, changes that are difficult to attribute to messages from just one kind of MC function. In public relations, most measurement consists of counting the number of mentions, column inches, or the amount of time a brand or company story receives in the media. It is difficult, however, to link these measures to behaviours and to the bottom line.

Another limitation is that public relations, by its very nature, can go only so far. Editors will not run stories about the same company or brand too frequently (otherwise the communication vehicle loses its own credibility). Consequently, it is more difficult for public relations programmes to create a frequency of mention in the same media vehicle. So, although public relations may offer greater credibility, advertising offers greater control and produces the awareness that comes from repetition. Another problem, and one that drives to the heart of its greatest strength, is public relations' own image. People are increasingly aware of the fact that PR is active, trying to control publicity.

Brand-publicity tools

Media relations experts help reporters and editors identify ideas for stories, provide background information, suggest or "pitch" story ideas to key reporters and editors, and, in some cases, provide the story. This practice is referred to as "placing" a story. A good media relations programme has a media database with addresses and fax numbers for a variety of media outlets, as well as a contact list with phone numbers and e-mail addresses of key reporters and editors who cover the organization or industry.

Media tools and activities that media relations professionals use to gain publicity are listed in Table 12-2. Even programmes that don't directly involve mass media, such as speeches, are designed to get media coverage. To understand how media relations experts handle story ideas, let us look at each form more closely.

Tool or activity	Description
News release (press release)	Any form of print, visual, or broadcast announcement that an organization makes available to the media about its activities; includes video news releases.
News kit (press kit)	A packet of information that includes photographs and drawings, maps, histories, background facts, stories on different aspects of the product or event, speeches, test results, along with the name of the person to contact for more information.
Press conference	A press event in which corporate officials meet with media representatives to inform them about some major company-related story.
Media tour	A series of visits by a spokesperson for a firm to selected cities for meetings with as many local media representatives as possible. The ideal tour includes live appearances on broadcast media.
Media event	A special event, such as a groundbreaking or grand opening, designed to gain media coverage, as well as create an involvement opportunity for stakeholders.
Speeches	Public statements, often ghost-written by PR staff. Reporters are invited to cover the speech, and clips (for broadcast) or quotes are provided to the media.
Pitch letter	A letter, either regular mail or e-mail, written by a PR person proposing a story idea to an editor or reporter. In close working relationships, the pitch may be made by phone.
Fact sheet	A listing of information about a company or brand that provides background data the media can use when doing a story on the company or brand.

Table 12-2 Brand-publicity tools

News releases

A self-serving news or human interest story created by an organization or its PR firm and given to the media to generate brand publicity is known as a **news release** or **press release**. A news release can appear in both print and video forms.

To be accepted and used, a news release must be professionally created and delivered and meet the basic standards of newsworthiness. Central to an editor's decision to use a publicity release or news tip is the extent to which it has a **news peg** (*an announcement of something that is new*) for a news story or a **human interest angle** (*a story idea that appeals to people for reasons other than news*) for a feature story. Once a story idea has been identified, it must be written up in a form that editors can use with a minimum of editing. Here is a list of pointers for writing news releases:[14]

News release checklist

- Ask who, what, why, where, and when, and be sure that these questions are answered in the release.
- Organize paragraphs so that the most newsworthy points are at the top. Get the main news point into the first paragraph and preferably into the first sentence.
- Use short paragraphs with only one point per paragraph.
- Write stories to match the publication's and its audience's interest.
- Keep the copy tight and concise. Draft, redraft, edit, polish, and cut everything superfluous out of the copy.
- Use journalistic style: short sentences, active verbs. Avoid long and inverted clauses, superlatives, pompous phrases, and jargon.
- Be accurate and factual. Never fudge an issue, exaggerate, or create a misleading impression.
- Substantiate any claims; document the facts; quote from reliable sources.
- If it is a news story, is the news angle obvious? Is it timely?
- If it is a feature story, is the human interest angle obvious?
- Can you simplify complex ideas? Is there an example that would help illustrate the idea?
- If you are explaining a process, can you take it apart and describe it one step at a time?
- If the medium uses a style guide, is the story written to that style?

Video news releases (VNRs) are *television news releases, or packages, produced by a company to feature a product or service and designed to run from 30 to 90 seconds on a news programme.* They are most effective when a story has a strong visual impact. VNRs are usually sent to television stations along with a script. VNRs can be distributed by videotape, satellite, or the Internet. Because VNRs are expensive to produce, the following factors should be considered by a company deciding whether to use a VNR:[15]

- Does the story have a strong visual impact?
- Does the video clarify or provide a new perspective on a news story or issue?
- Will the video help a news department create a better story?
- Can the video be used as background footage while a station's reporter discusses the pertinent news copy?
- Can the organization provide unusual visual footage, or an interview, that stations can't get?

Fact sheets, pitch letters, and news kits

Sometimes sending a news release may not be appropriate. Many reporters want an exclusive story. In such a situation, a **fact sheet**, which is *a summary of key information*, can be provided to the reporter, who then writes the story.

A **pitch letter** is *a story proposal sent to a reporter or editor*. Its purpose is to sell a story idea to a journalist who would then follow up and write the story if it's deemed to be of interest to the medium's audience. Often used with a feature story idea, the pitch can be made by regular mail, by e-mail, or (when there is a working relationship between the PR person and the journalist) by phone.

A **news kit**, or **press kit**, is *a packet of information provided by the PR staff to journalists covering a major story such as a special event or a press conference.* The kit includes background information, such as biographies, historical information, maps, drawings and photos, speeches, quotes, contact information, website addresses, and any other supplemental material that might help the journalist cover the event and write the story.

News values

What constitutes "news"? Media relations practitioners are guided by journalism standards for determining what makes a good news story—timely, relevant, topical, accurate, comprehensive, substantiated, concise, unbiased, and, ideally, exclusive, or at least having a special angle that an editor can use to make it a one-of-a-kind story.[16] The following list summarizes the factors that editors and other media gatekeepers use when deciding whether to respond to a pitch letter or to cover an event:

Factors influencing the selection of news and feature stories

- *Impact:* What is the magnitude (past or potential) of the action or event?
- *Timeliness:* Is it a breaking news story or the latest development?
- *Proximity:* How local is the story angle?
- *Prominence:* To whom does the story happen? Who is involved? How important are they?
- *Conflict:* Is tension or drama created by warring viewpoints?
- *Human interest:* How fun, entertaining, or emotionally engaging is the story idea? Does it touch a chord?
- *Novelty:* Is the story unusual or unpredictable?

Publicists are perfectly legitimate in creating news—that is, doing, finding, or creating something that is the first, biggest, shortest, most expensive, oldest, longest, highest, or most unusual. Special events and special promotions such as the Red Bull Flugtage, are specifically created to be news events (see opening IMC in Action case of Chapter 11). Such events are often more important for the publicity they generate than for the number of people directly involved, because the event usually involves a relatively small number of customers (and other stakeholders) but the publicity can reach millions.

In an IMC programme, public relations staff must work closely with sales promotion and event sponsorship planners. For example, Unilever's Sunlight dishwashing detergent partnered with Whirlpool on an innovative way to build brand awareness and make news at the same time. The idea was to find America's messiest kitchen. The contest was promoted through a broad media relations campaign aimed at women's home, lifestyle, and feature editors. A "spring cleaning" press kit mailing, which targeted these editors at newspapers in the top 100 markets and 10 000 local suburban weekly newspapers, generated nearly 125 stories and thousands of entries. Nearly 50 million impressions were delivered, with 100 per cent of the stories communicating the fact that the contest was created by Unilever and its Sunlight brand.[17]

Advertising versus editorial

As with journalists and PR professionals, the relationship between the editorial and the advertising sides of the media is sometimes prickly, and for similar reasons. Advertisers—the companies providing news releases—sometimes feel that a newspaper should use their releases and give them favourable coverage because they spend a lot of money on ads. Even though most media are supported primarily by advertising, editors and reporters strive to maintain their detachment from the advertising department in order to make news judgments based solely on newsworthiness, rather than on advertiser pressure.

Corporate communication

A corporate communication network can be the conduit through which information is disseminated, discussed, debated, and ultimately incorporated into constructive action and long-term knowledge. Calls to action, goal setting, unifying behind a common mission—a company can carry out none of these activities without an effective communication plan.

Public relations carried out by senior executives who advise top management on how the organization presents itself is called **corporate communication**. These executives, and the public relations agencies that advise them, are very much focused on maintaining the corporate brand and corporate reputation. Another term for the work they do is **corporate relations** because it involves creating and maintaining relationships with key stakeholders who can affect the organization's business, such as government officials and regulators.

Corporate communication executives also focus on public opinion and issues management. Because of the powerful effect of public opinion, organizations of all kinds must consider the public impact of their actions and decisions, as well as how changing public opinion can affect the organization's business opportunities. This is especially true in times of crisis, emergency, or disaster, but it also holds true for major policy decisions. Changes in management or pricing, labour negotiations, new-product offerings, changes in distribution methods, and the closing or opening of plants can all affect a community and hence public opinion about the company. Each decision affects different stakeholder groups in different ways. Through effective public relations, managers hope to channel stakeholder opinions toward better understanding of issues and create more positive attitudes, or at least better understanding of the company's actions.

In addition to news releases, the tools used in corporate communications include newsletters and corporate magazines, and communication that affects corporate image and reputation, such as corporate identity programmes and corporate advertising.

Corporate image and reputation

The difference between an *image* and a *reputation* is sometimes confusing because the two are somewhat related. An **image** is more of a facade or *a representation of a brand or organization derived from planned communication, such as advertising and brand publicity*. Reputation reflects how a company behaves, and it is based on what others say about the company. **Reputation** is *the esteem that a company or brand has in the eyes of its stakeholders*. Reputation depends on the organization's behaviours and is reflected in word of mouth and confirmatory statements by others, as well as in personal experiences with a company or brand. Image can be created; a reputation is earned.

According to Paul Holmes, editor of *Reputation Management*, a brand image is what a company believes about its products, and reputation is the brand plus behaviour.[18] Both brand image and brand reputation are important; ideally, they merge to create brand integrity. In Chapter 1 a brand was defined as the net sum of its relationships. Another way of describing a corporate brand, then, is that it is the net sum of its image and reputation. These two elements together drive brand relationships. An example of a company that understands brand integrity is Sara Lee, which recently offered its controversial cut-tobacco unit for sale. The division, though highly profitable, seemed to undercut the meaning of the company's slogan, "Nobody doesn't like Sara Lee."

Corporate branding is *the practice of managing the identity and image of a corporate organization.* In addition to Sara Lee, Sony, Unilever, and Henkel ("a brand like a friend") are companies that work very hard to maintain a strong corporate brand. The corporate brand may be important even if a company has separate brands for its sometimes diverse product lines, such as Unilever's Bertolli, Axe, Dove, Omo and Slimfast show. A strong positive corporate reputation is also a key ingredient in brand equity.

An indication of the need for marketing and public relations to work closely together in managing corporate reputation comes from a reputation question in Thomas L. Harris's study of Fortune 500 companies.[19] Harris found that when corporate public relations managers were asked how involved other executives were in managing the reputation of the firm, marketing and advertising managers were third on the list, behind public relations/public affairs managers and CEOs (see Table 12-3).

Corporate advertising

Corporate advertising is *an ad programme designed to build awareness of a company and explain what it does or believes.* Corporate advertising is most frequently used by large, multi-product companies and by new companies that result from mergers or acquisitions and want to establish a new corporate identity. Firms that specialize in developing corporate identity programmes and marketing communication campaigns claim that these efforts have a positive

Type of manager	Percentage of respondents who cited reputation management as important
Public relations/public affairs	60
The CEO of the firm	51
Marketing/advertising	39
CFO/investor relations	27
Other top management	24
Middle management	11

Table 12-3 Importance of reputation management

Source: Thomas L. Harris/Impulse Research, "Corporate Communications Spending and Reputations of Fortune 500 Companies" (Los Angeles: Impulse Research Corp., 4 June 1999), p. 16.

impact on employees, investors, and other members of the financial community, help attract high-quality employees, and increase sales. Sometimes companies engage in **advocacy advertising,** *advertising that takes a stand on an issue or advocates a certain viewpoint.* Heineken recently ran a campaign that intended to position the company as an advocate of responsible drinking. One of the commercials showed a glass of beer that was spilt on the ground. A dog sipped it up. The next shot showed that the dog was guiding a blind man. Because of the alcohol, the dog forsook its task, leading the man into a hole in the street. The message was: see what alcohol consumption can do to you.

Mission and cause marketing

A **mission** is *the task or objective that a company is striving to accomplish, and that reflects the core values of the company or brand.* A central mission can be an important part of an IMC programme and become the central focus of integrated communication.[20] The mission statement sets forth the corporate purpose above and beyond making money; it indicates the company's raison d'être. Here are three mission statements that energize stakeholders of their respective companies:[21]

- Ikea: "To create a better everyday life for the many".
- Volkswagen: "Continuously improving technique and design".
- Unilever: "To add vitality to life".

Both marketing and PR should not only be involved in setting a corporate mission but also should be responsible for promoting it.

Mission marketing

The missions of some companies reflect core values of social responsibility. For example, Ben & Jerry's bases its business platforms on a complex mission statement, integrating a product, business and social focus (see www.benjerry.com/our_company/our_mission/index.cfm). Generally, companies such as Ben & Jerry's engage in **mission marketing** which is *using the company's mission as a selling strategy in order to differentiate and add value to a brand.*[22] The company's socially responsible mission co-drives all of its business decisions. It is also a platform on which an integrated marketing programme can be built.

A mission does not have to be as overtly philanthropic as the mission of US-based Tom's of Maine, which is to contribute 10 per cent of profits to support environmental causes. Nike's mission is to offer well-engineered athletic shoes (and clothes) that help people achieve their peak performance, and that objective drives everything the company does. Apple Computer's original mission, to be "the computer for the rest of us", unlocked computer literacy for children and for millions of adults who had no interest in learning programming language. Although Apple lost much of its momentum through management problems in the 1990s, it still has a devoted following of customers who believe passionately in the company because of its mission and the easy-to-use products that support its business platform.

To *market* its mission, a company selects sponsorship opportunities that tie the mission with a larger public interest, and builds on the connection for the long term. The objective of mission marketing is to build a good corporate or brand reputation for the long term. In the discussion of consistency in Chapter 7 the say/do/confirm model was introduced. In the "confirm" step, the goal is to have customers and other stakeholders say good things about a brand. When people believe passionately in a brand's mission, as they do in the case of Apple Computers, they are likely to become advocates for the brand. The mission, however, has to be supported by good practices and tie the company directly to its target audience. McDonald's sponsorship of the Ronald McDonald House for families of children in hospitals reflects and leverages McDonald's tradition of being a family-focused restaurant.

Because of the increasing number of product choices and the similarity of many products, companies are looking for ways to give their brands an edge. Mission marketing is one way of doing that. Craig Smith explained this concept well in a *Harvard Business Review* article: "For the first time, businesses are backing philanthropic initiatives with real corporate muscle ... they are funding those initiatives not only with philanthropic budgets but also from business units, such as marketing and human resources."[23] Mission marketing also uses strategic philanthropy to cultivate those points where the company's long-term interest and the public interest intersect.[24]

Cause marketing

Related to mission marketing is **cause marketing**, *company or brand support for a good cause through donations of a percentage of sales.* Cause marketing requires an agreement between a non-profit and a for-profit company that seeks to maximize the benefits to each partner.[25] A famous example in this context is the fund raising by American Express credit card company back in the 1980s. Amex donated 1 cent for every transaction, and $1 for every new card issued. The result was not only a donation of $1.7 million for the restoration of the Statue of Liberty in New York, but also an increase of 28 per cent in the number of transactions made.[26] The integration of social issues and business practices arose in the 1990s and seems to be everything but a passing fad. Rather it represents "a fundamental shift in how the world's leading companies will use cause associations to position their organizations and brands for the future".[27]

The benefit to the company comes from its association with the good cause such as fights against hunger or breast cancer. Cause marketing, however, often reflects a shorter-term approach, as the American Express example cited above shows, than does mission marketing. Both cause and mission marketing make strong emotional appeals, but mission marketing delves deeper because it rests on a long-term commitment.

Employee and financial relations

In many companies employees are the most important audience for PR messages—even more important than customers—because employees are the frontline of the communication system, particularly in service industries. How they interact with customers and prospects speaks more loudly than messages in advertising or news release. **Employee relations** is *an area of public relations that focuses on establishing and maintaining communication systems with employees.* It is sometimes found in, or co-ordinated with, the human resources department.[28]

IMC planners pay attention to employee relations because employee relations intersects with internal marketing, the effort to explain a promotional effort to employees and get their support. Employee communication, therefore, may be an essential first step before any IMC campaign moves outside the company. The tools of employee relations include newsletters, bulletin boards, employee meetings, websites, and intranets which are especially important for large companies with multiple offices or plants, particularly if they are located in many different countries.

Financial relations is *an area of public relations that creates communication directed to—and often developed in collaboration with—investors, analysts, stockbrokers, and financial media.* Because this communication focuses on a company's finances, it is usually handled by a PR professional close to senior management and the company's top financial officer. The legal staff may also be involved in approving any financial communication. Annual meetings with shareholders may also be the responsibility of the financial relations staff.

For a public company, initial communication with investors may be through a letter of welcome, a newsletter, or a brochure about the company's products and brands, philosophy, and history. Brochures are usually developed for major public actions, such as stock offerings. The primary formal communication tool is the *annual report*, a document required for companies that are noted at the stock exchange which discloses details of a company's financial position. Annual reports are also provided by non-profit organizations on a voluntary basis as a means of summarizing the activities of the organization over the previous year.

Crisis communication

A crisis management plan is *a plan for managing a company's response when disaster strikes*. Such plans designate who will provide what information to media and employees during a crisis. Although the responsibility of the director of public relations, designing and managing a crisis management plan should involve the marketing department because a crisis poses a threat to the company's reputation and brand relationships. Response time is one of the crucial variables when crisis happens. Further, in the aftermath of the event, the whole marketing department has to collaborate (see the IMC in Action box).

Proactive companies are realistic; they know that bad things happen. A manufacturing accident or product failure that causes serious injury or death may occur when a company least expects it. The larger a company is and the longer it is in business, the greater is the likelihood that it will face a crisis.

Coca-Cola crisis communication

June 1999: panic in Belgium. After mad cow disease and the discovery of tainted animal feed, the country faces another crisis. And this time none other than Coca-Cola was the cause of the concern.

Several Belgian consumers had complained of an irregular taste and smell in bottled Coca-Cola soft drinks. Shortly after this incident, more than 100 students at six schools were reported ill after they had noticed an unpleasant smell on the surface of the cans too. The victims had symptoms such as headaches, stomach-aches and shivering, and some students needed hospitalization. In response, the Belgian Health Ministry, in co-operation with The Coca-Cola Company, immediately recalled the soft drinks from the market. The same action was taken with Coca-Cola Light, Fanta, Sprite, Nestea, Aquarius, Bon Aqua, Kinley Tonic and Lilt. In total around 15 million bottles and cans were recalled. Moreover, the crisis in Belgium spread over to France, Luxembourg and the Netherlands. This snowball effect caused the recall or restriction of Coca-Cola's products in these countries too.

Inevitably, The Coca-Cola Company realized that a response was necessary; but their first public statement was not until a week after the reported illnesses. Apparently, the company did not seem to realize that their *response time* to this crisis (which is crucial in minimizing the damage of the brand name) was too long. Moreover, the chairman at that time, Doug Ivester, said in this public statement that the highest priority of the company was the quality of the products(!). He reassured consumers, customers and governments in Europe that the company

IMC in Action

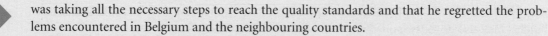

was taking all the necessary steps to reach the quality standards and that he regretted the problems encountered in Belgium and the neighbouring countries.

The Coca-Cola Company identified two specific production and distribution problems: "off-quality" carbon dioxide that affected the irregular taste of the bottled drinks and the unpleasant odour on the outside of the canned drinks. This odour seemed to be stronger when the cans were sold in vending machines. In short, the company denied that its products were contaminated, but admitted that there were some manufacturing mistakes. After the company's public statement, the Belgian Ministry decided to lift the ban on Coca-Cola products, on condition that the company took the necessay steps to strengthen safety measures and conduct an overhaul of the plants.

Analysts complained that the response was too late, and was also lacking in empathy with the victims. In consequence, the costs of the crisis for Coca-Cola were estimated to be more than $200 million in expenses and lost profits and, even worse, its brand image was harmed. These costs could have been far less if the company had responded more promptly to the crisis.

In July 1999, Doug Ivester announced an aggressive marketing campaign to regain the trust of consumers. In the next month, brand-loyal users of Coca-Cola reported the same willingness to purchase the products as before the crisis. Moreover, when tests were conducted in Europe it appeared that the products of Coca-Cola were "normal" and of the "highest quality" and that the symptoms were psychosomatic. The company in turn reacted by stating that this was a wake-up call from which they have learned to be more careful about the quality of the company's soft drinks. And The Coca-Cola Company learned another lesson: the importance of having of an appropriate crisis management plan.

Think about it

Do you think the crisis with Coca-Cola's soft drinks could have been avoided? How? Do you think that, because the symptoms were psychosomatic, the brand name of the company is less damaged? Can you come up with other companies that have faced a crisis like this?

Sources:

Schmidt, Kathleen V., "Coke's Crisis", Marketing News, *00253790, 27 September 1999, Vol. 33, Issue 20.*

"Crisis management in Belgium: the case of Coca-Cola", Victoria Johnson; Spero C Peppas. Corporate Communications: An International Journal, *2003, Vol. 8, Issue 1, pp.18–22 (AN 10003312).*

"Coca-Cola stumbles in Belgium: Response time is critical in crisis management", Strategic Direction, *0258-0543, 2003, Vol. 19, Issue 5, pp. 23–25.*

The need for planning

The secret to managing a crisis is to have everything planned ahead of time. Having a crisis plan worked out *before* a crisis breaks ensures that the company is not forced to quickly improvise a response when emotions are high and the media are knocking on the door with cameras and live video, eager to tell the world how bad things are. During a crisis there is no time to sit back and plan. A company has to respond immediately; otherwise, the media, customers, and others will think the company is trying to hide something.

The crisis plan spells out such things as the names of people to be contacted immediately; responsibilities—who works with which stakeholder group and who talks to the press; guidelines on what can be said and what needs to be checked for legal implications; and recommended actions the company might take to deal with different scenarios. Many companies have disaster scenarios that are used to practise the implementation of the plan.

When a crisis does occur, public relations professionals recommend the following responses from company spokespeople: (1) A reaction should be expressed as early as possible. Don't stonewall, and don't say "no comment". (2) Only designated top company executives—who understand the seriousness of the crisis, as well as the legal liability issues—should talk to the media. (3) The designated spokespeople should explain what happened as they understand it, keeping in mind that people are desperate for explanations. (4) The spokespeople should tell what the company is doing to minimize the damage (such as a product recall). (5) The spokespeople should express sympathy and concern for injured parties and their families. The tone should be humble, and the explanations and concern should be expressed with candour.

What spokespeople should not say or suggest in any way is that the company is responsible for what happened. Such an admission of *liability*—without knowledge of all the related facts, which might take weeks or months to gather and analyse—can result in the company's having to pay millions of euros in compensation. This is not to say that a company should not accept responsibility for its actions, but only that it should take time to accurately determine what its responsibility is. Instead, spokespeople should focus on the company's concern and the actions it is taking to relieve the damage.

Brand image crises

A crisis may hurt a brand because negative associations are created. The more severe the crisis, the stronger the associations become. Various studies by Niraj Dawar and colleagues make clear that other factors are also important. In particular the question if a company or brand is held responsible, i.e. whether the crisis is attributed to the brand, is a decisive factor. Further, the type of response by management is critical. Finally, Dawar found that brands with high brand equity are less vulnerable to crises than brands with less brand equity. "Brand equity works like an insurance in case of crises" (Dawar and Pillutla, 2000).

It makes sense to distinguish between crises at the product level, versus those at the corporate level. Product harm crises occur at the product level: disfunctioning, spoiled, or contaminated products may grow to the size of a crisis when the malfunctioning is systematic and detrimental to the consumers. Crises at the corporate level are of a different kind. They usually have almost nothing to do with the products of the brand, but all the more with the credibility and confidence of consumers with the company behind the brand. Nevertheless, such a crisis can still seriously affect the brand's performance, up until the discontinuation of the company. Worldwide, the Enron scandal has become a standard example of a crisis with the worst of outcomes. Shell's bookkeeping scandals, and systematic over-estimations of its oil reserves is an example of a crisis which has had almost no effect on the brand's performance, whereas its Brent Spar incident almost led to a boycott by car drivers of Shell's filling stations.

Crisis management

After Burger King ran a promotion giving away Pokémon toys packaged inside a plastic ball, the company was shocked when it was reported that a baby suffocated and another child nearly died (half of the ball package had been placed over the mouth and nose of each victim). The company responded by recalling the ball packages (not the toys themselves). To encourage people to act, Burger King gave a free order of fries to each person who returned a ball package. At the time of the recall, the company had distributed over 20 million of the Pokémon toys.

The recall, which was announced in a full-page ad in one of the biggest national daily newspapers in the USA, was not only a responsible thing to do but a smart marketing move because it generated considerable publicity and motivated families to visit their local Burger King once again.

The bottom line of crisis communication is damage control. When a major disaster occurs, especially one resulting in death or serious injury, the damage has been done, and the world will soon be told about it. Look at what happened to Intel when a problem with a Pentium chip was discovered. Even before the mass media made it a big business story, it was being discussed on the Internet, whose audience is very important to Intel's reputation. When the crisis occurred, Intel's initial denial tarnished its previously stellar image. But Intel did learn and act. It has since hired people to monitor all major high-tech chat rooms and immediately report any negative comments about the brand.

A final note: reputation and relationships

IMC programmes that foster positive relationships move beyond image advertising and seek to affect reputation through credible brand messages. According to public relations professional Terrie Williams, putting relationships into public relations is critical because "people are starved for recognition".[29] She referred to psychologist Abraham Maslow's hierarchy of needs (Chapter 4) in explaining that acknowledgment and recognition are important dimensions of self-actualization. That is why customer recognition is an important factor in an IMC programme.

Good citizenship, or social responsibility, is also an important part of a reputation programme. Research shows that consumers will change their buying habits to support companies they perceive as being socially responsible—companies that are environmentally responsible, treat their employees fairly, or work to make their communities better places to live.

🔓 Key terms

advocacy advertising Advertising that takes a stand on an issue or advocates a certain viewpoint.

brand publicity The use of non-paid media messages to deliver brand information designed to positively influence customers and prospects.

buzz Excited talk about a brand.

cause marketing Company or brand support for a good cause through donations of a percentage of sales.

corporate advertising An ad programme designed to build awareness of a company and explain what it does or believes.

corporate branding The practice of managing the identity and image of a corporate organization.

corporate communication Public relations carried out by senior executives who advise top management on how the organization presents itself.

corporate relations *see* corporate communication.

crisis management plan A plan for managing a company's response when disaster strikes.

employee relations An area of public relations that focuses on establishing and maintaining communication systems with employees.

fact sheet A summary of key information.

financial relations An area of public relations that creates communication directed to— and often developed in collaboration with—investors, analysts, stockbrokers, and financial media.

gatekeepers Editors and reporters who select (or reject) stories for their publications or stations based on what they think will interest their audiences.

human interest angle A story idea that appeals to people for reasons other than news.

image A representation of a brand or organization derived from planned communication, such as advertising and brand publicity.

influentials Opinion leaders and early adopters who influence other people.

media relations Maintaining a positive professional relationship with the media.

mission The task or objective that a company is striving to accomplish, and that reflects the core values of the company or brand.

mission marketing Using the company's mission as a selling strategy in order to differentiate and add value to a brand.

news kit A packet of information provided by the PR staff to journalists covering a major story such as a special event or a press conference.

news peg An announcement of something that is new.

news release A self-serving news or human interest story created by an organization or its PR firm and given to the media to generate brand publicity.

pitch letter A story proposal sent to a reporter or editor.

press release *see* news release.

press kit *see* news kit.

public relations A communication function used to promote mutual understanding between an organization and its various stakeholder groups.

reputation The esteem that a company or brand has in the eyes of its stakeholders.

third-party endorsement The perspective presented by a reputable media source that has no personal interest in the success or failure of the product being endorsed.

video news releases (VNRs) Television news releases, or packages, produced by a company to feature a product or service and designed to run from 30 to 90 seconds on a news programme.

Check the key points

Key point 1: Public relations

a   Why is public relations a growth area in marketing communication?

b   What are the key elements of public relations as given in the definitions appearing in this chapter?

c   Which stakeholders are addressed by public relations programmes?

d   Which types of public relations programmes listed in Table 12-2 can also be used in IMC programmes?

Key point 2: Brand publicity

a   Define *brand publicity*. Explain how it differs from public relations in general.

b   Explain how brand publicity can supplement an MC strategy.

c   List five strengths of publicity.

d   What is a media gatekeeper? Why does that person create limitations for publicity's effectiveness?

e   What is third-party endorsement? What effect does it have on publicity? Find an example in which a medium lends credibility to a story about a brand. Explain *how* this credibility is enhanced by the medium.

f   Give an example (besides the examples given in this chapter) showing how each of these brand-publicity tools can be used to promote a company or brand: News release; News kit; Press conference; Media tour.

Key point 3: Corporate communication

a   What is corporate communication?

b   Identify the three main objectives of corporate advertising. Find examples of ads intended to meet each objective, and explain the strategy behind the communication.

c   Why is corporate culture important to corporate communication managers? How does it affect IMC programmes?

d   How does a company's image differ from its reputation?

e   In what way is reputation important to an IMC programme?

f   How do mission marketing and cause marketing differ? Which one is more relevant for an IMC programme? Why?

Key point 4: Crisis management

a   What short-term and long-term risks can result from a crisis?

b   List critical factors in crisis management.

c   Who are involved in crisis management?

d   What is the role of public relations when a crisis occurs?

Chapter Challenge

Writing assignment

Identify a crisis that occurred not too long ago. Document what has been written in the press about the crisis, and also how the company has dealt with the incident. Indicate what the company did well, or where it could have improved. How is the current situation of the company?

Presentation assignment

Analyse your university or college as a brand. How does public relations contribute to the development of the school's brand? Describe the school's identity, image, and reputation. Develop recommendations on what needs to be done to strengthen your school's branding, and present them to your class. Also write a press release aiming to attract new students to your school.

> ### Internet assignment
> Take a brand of your choice and analyse its presence on the Internet. First go to the brand's website and assess how it presents itself, what image the brand wants to communicate, etc. Then go to a public search engine (e.g. Google) and see what the search results are for this brand. How many hits does the brand name generate? How high is the brand's own website on the list? What other hits are there? Do the other sites the search engine finds, contribute to the brand's image or not? What impression does the list of hits make to you? Try to find out how a brand can influence this list that is generated by independent search engines.

Notes

[1] Regis McKenna, *Relationship Marketing* (Reading, MA: Addison-Wesley, 1991), p. 2.

[2] Fraser P. Seitel, *The Practice of Public Relations*, 7th ed. (Upper Saddle River, NJ: Prentice-Hall, 1998), p. 5.

[3] Adapted from Scott Cutlip, Allen Centre, and Glen Broom, *Effective Public Relations* (Englewood Cliffs, NJ: Prentice-Hall, 1985), p. 4.

[4] "2001 Public Relations Industry Revenue Documentation and Rankings Fact Sheet", Council of Public Relations Firms, n.d.

[5] Quoted in Thomas L. Harris, *Value-Added Public Relations: The Secret Weapon of Integrated Marketing* (Lincolnwood, IL: NTC, 1998).

[6] Thomas L. Harris, *The Marketer's Guide to Public Relations: How Today's Top Companies Are Using the New PR to Gain a Competitive Edge* (New York: Wiley, 1991), p. 9.

[7] Richard Rotman, "Why Can't They Get Along?" *Brandera.com*, 30 May 2000.

[8] Sandra E. Moriarty, "PR and IMC: The Benefits of Integration", *Public Relations Quarterly* 39, no. 3 (Fall 1994), p. 41.

[9] David Bank, "Bay Networks' Results to Trail Forecasts", *Wall Street Journal*, 18 March 1998, p. B4.

[10] Paul A. Holmes, "Guerrilla Marketing: The Word on the Street", *Reputation Management*, 6, no. 3 (March 2000), pp. 30–7.

[11] Steve Jarvis, "How the Internet Is Changing Fundamentals of Publicity", *Marketing News*, 17 July 2000, p. 6.

[12] "20/20 Vision", *Reputation Management*, 6, no. 2 (February 2000), p. 40.

[13] "RepBriefs: By the Numbers", *Reputation Management*, 5, no. 3 (May–June 1999), p. 12.

[14] Roger Haywood, "Media Relations", in *Strategic Public Relations*, ed. Norman A. Hart (London: Macmillan Business Press, 1995), pp. 178–9.

[15] Seitel, *The Practice of Public Relations*, p. 283.

[16] Haywood, pp. 178–9.

[17] "Next to Godliness", *Reputation Management*, 6, no. 3 (March 2000), p. 17.

[18] Paul A. Holmes, "Promise Keepers", *Reputation Management*, 6, no. 3 (March 2000), p. 4.

[19] Thomas Harris/Impulse Research, "Corporate Communications Spending and Reputations of Fortune 500 Companies" (Los Angeles: Impulse Research Corp., 4 June 1999), p. 17.

[20] Tom Duncan and Sandra Moriarty, "A Process for Managing Brand Relationships", *Academy Monograph* (New York: PRSA Counselors Academy, 2000), pp. 11–12.

[21] James Collins and Jerry Porras, *Built to Last* (New York: Harper Business, 1994), p. 69.

[22] Tom Duncan and Sandra Moriarty, *Driving Brand Value: Using Integrated Marketing to Manage Profitable Stakeholder Relationships* (New York: McGraw-Hill, 1997), pp. 126–47.

[23] Craig Smith, "The New Corporate Philosophy", *Harvard Business Review*, May–June 1994, p. 48.

[24] Koten, p. 149.

[25] Bill Goodwill, "Cause Marketing Pros and Cons", *Broadcast Café Newsletter*, October 1999, www.psaresearch.com/CRMFEATURE.html.

[26] This story is documented in various places, e.g. www.prwatch.org/node/4965, or in Wikipedia.

[27] Carol Cone, "Cause Branding in the 21st Century", *KG Independent Sector*, www.independentsector.org/mission_market/cone.htm.

[28] "Turning staff into brand ambassadors", *Brand Strategy*, 6–2006, pp. 44–7. Summary of a round-table discussion among seven top brand managers. Says Mark Allatt, Global Brand Director and Director of Brand and Image Development of Deloitte: "Marketing has to work hand and glove with HR all the way through" (p. 44).

[29] Terrie Williams, "Putting Relationships Back into Public Relations" (Vernon C. Schranz Distinguished Lectureship in Public Relations, Muncie, IN: Ball State University, 1996).

Further reading

Carden, Ann R. (2006) "How public relations put the kicks in Route 66—and still is", *Journal of Vacation Marketing*, Vol. 12–2, pp. 130–41.

Dawar, Niraj and Madan M. Pillutla (2000) "Impact of Product Harm Crisis on Brand Equity: The moderating role of consumer expectations", *Journal of Marketing Research*, Vol. 37–2, pp. 215–26.

Edelman, Daniel J. (2006) "The Golden Age of Public Relations", *Public Relations Quarterly*, Vol. 51–1, pp. 20–1.

Gregory, Anne (2007) "Involving Stakeholders in Developing Corporate Brands: the Communication Dimension", *Journal of Marketing Management*, Vol. 23–1/2, pp. 59–73.

Henry, Amy (2003) "How buzz marketing works for teens", *International Journal of Advertising & Marketing to Children*, Vol. 4–3, pp. 3–10.

Robinson, David (2006) "Public relations comes of age", *Business Horizons*, Vol. 49–3, pp. 247–56.

Rust, Roland, Valerie Zeithaml and Katherine Lemon (2000) *Driving Customer Equity: How Customer Lifetime Value is Reshaping Corporate Strategy*, New York: The Free Press.

Starck, Kenneth and Dean Kruckeberg (2005) "Ethical Obligations of Public Relations in an era of Globalization", *Journal of Communication Management*, Vol. 9–3, pp. 29–40.

Sales promotion

CHAPTER PERSPECTIVE
With a little help from my friends

Brands are built by advertising, packaging, PR, publicity and in fact any touch point. In the ideal case, when the top of the brand-building pyramid is reached, the brand is considered a friend. What stays is that the friends engage in commercial relationships, that customers actually purchase the products of the brand. A little help from the brand is often appreciated by the customer. Sales promotions offer this help by adding a tangible benefit to the brand offer.

However, although the primary job of sales promotion is to affect behaviour, it can (and should) also heighten awareness and reinforce a brand's image. In major-purchase product categories, where deciding on a brand may take weeks or months, sales promotion can be used to help move prospects and customers through the decision process. Promotional offers provide tangible added value and are generally available for a "limited time only" to create a sense of urgency.

Sales promotions are mostly one-way, non-personal messages, although when used in direct-response marketing, they can be personalized. Consumer promotions are directed at the end consumer, the persons that literally consume the product at the end of the distribution channel. Alternatively trade promotions are geared towards the next stage in this channel, at wholesalers or retailers. However, both top the often intangible promises of brands with concrete and tangible cream. The real challenge of sales promotion is to have consumers eat not only the cream, but the entire pudding.

Coca-Cola: The Perfect Serve challenge in Germany[1]

On 18 January 2005 Mr. Klaus Faber, founder and CEO of the CMF advertising agency, met with managers of the CCEAG, the distribution company fully owned by Coca-Cola in Germany, to make a final decision on the communications plan that they had developed to raise the quality of the Coca-Cola drinking experience in selected bars and restaurants across the country.

Although Coca-Cola maintained a dominant position in the German carbonated soft drink market, sales had declined in recent years due to, among other things, strong competition from the retail sector with low-priced private label brands. This new programme, called Perfect Serve, was designed to guarantee a standard quality for consumption outside of the home and to revitalize the image of the Coca-Cola brand among consumers. But the team still had worries about whether or not they would be able to convince the on-trade distribution[2] to go along with the plan. There were also concerns that such a programme would not be able to keep the on-trade sector as locked into the Coca-Cola brand as they had been with the use of fountain dispensers.

Coca-Cola in Germany

The Coca-Cola Company, with headquarters in Atlanta, Georgia (USA), manufactures, bottles and distributes non-alcoholic beverages. The company and its many subsidiaries sell more than 400 brands of beverages (soft drinks, coffees, teas, water, fruit juices, sports drinks) in nearly 200 countries. More than 60 per cent of its products are sold outside the US.

Coca-Cola Gmbh (Germany) was the fifth largest subsidiary of The Coca-Cola Company worldwide, accounting for about 3 per cent of global sales and 6 per cent of profits. The company was well established in the country, having entered the market in 1929. Three quarters of a century later Coca-Cola still dominated the German market for carbonated soft drinks with a share of 59 per cent by volume. PepsiCo, Inc, by contrast, accounted for only 6.5 per cent share by volume and Cadbury Schweppes a mere 1.8 per cent.

The company had traditionally subcontracted its bottling and packaging activities to independent bottlers and distributors, as in most other countries. But in 2000 a decision was made to consolidate the German bottlers in order to improve the supply-chain management of its distribution network and to streamline its decision-making processes. In 2002 the company consolidated the Erfrischungsgetraenke (EAG) bottling company which controlled 65 per cent of its bottling business in Germany. By 2004 the new CCEAG held 70 per cent of Coke's sales in the country and the contracts with the remaining nine bottlers were due to expire between 2007 and 2010.

The primary form of distribution of carbonated soft drinks is supermarkets and hypermarkets, which together controlled 41.1 per cent of the consumed volume in 2004. Discount retailers were on the rise with a further 9.1 per cent of the market. The on-trade (HORECA) distribution generated 30.2 per cent of sales. Due to its dominant position in the soft drink market, however, Coca-Cola was not allowed to establish exclusivity contracts with the HORECA sector as beer manufacturers did. Instead, they had to find other ways to try to maintain loyalty to their products in this competitive environment.

Unlike in many other European countries where Coca-Cola was still served in bottles in most (or many) bars and restaurants, in Germany the HORECA sector was served primarily with pre-mix and post-mix fountain systems. The distributors supplied each client with a

▶ fountain which would be fitted onto their bar and which would accommodate only Coca-Cola kegs and mix packages. These systems had allowed the company to maintain a high market share in the sector and to establish close relationships with its customer base.

Market trends

A number of trends in the German market began to worry the management of the CCEAG.

As in other countries, new cold drink product categories were emerging and were being carefully positioned to specific customer targets and experiences (energy drinks, coffee products, flavoured mineral waters, etc). A second trend was the growth of private label brands of colas in the retail sector.

A third and very negative trend concerned the way Coca-Cola was served in the HORECA sector. Some bars began to move away from a consistent use of the fountain system and to mix carbonated water with less expensive brands of cola mix. Often this was done without removing the Coca-Cola logos from their premises and menus. Hence customers who thought they were drinking the "real thing" were actually consuming a different brand of cola. Other bars were increasingly serving cola out of bottles rather than directly from the fountains. For smaller operations, the chance to buy large quantities of 1.5 litre bottles from discounters increased their margins considerably. Yet the quality of the served beverage would depend on the way and number of times the bottle would be opened and closed, the temperature at which the bottle was stored, and the number of servings already made from the bottle. Clearly, the last glass served from a bottle that had been kept open and not chilled properly would be flatter and less refreshing than the first glass poured out of a correctly stored bottle. Again many of these bars displayed the Coca-Cola logo while serving colas from the bottles of other, less expensive brands.

At the same time that these trends were developing, many market research studies were pointing to the importance of product presentation and product quality in the consumer experience especially during "on premise" and "on the go" consumption occasions. These two factors were seen to have an increasing influence on the expectations of consumers and hence, on their decision-making process. It was shown, in fact, that up to 75 per cent of consumer stimulus is visual, but that sound, smell and feel also play important roles in the consumer experience. Many of the high end brands in the HORECA sector, such as Guinness (beer) and Illy (espresso coffee) were using this knowledge to their advantage, creating strict standards for how their product is prepared, stored, and served in bars and restaurants that carry their logos.

The proposal

The proposal designed by the CMF agency to respond to the challenges outlined above was called *Perfect Serve* and consisted of an integrated communications programme for the sales force, outlet owners, bar staff and the final consumer.

The Perfect Serve standard for serving Coca-Cola in bars and restaurants was to consist of six steps:

1 A question from the Server: ask your guests if they'd like a refreshing, ice-cold Coke.
2 Reaching for the glass that matches the original Coke bottle: always serve Coke ice-cold in the original Coke glass preferably poured over two big ice cubes.

3 The optimal taste experience, cooled to the ideal temperature. Ice cold Coke from the cooler for a satisfying and refreshing drinking enjoyment.

4 Salty snacks with Coke. Offer your guests some salty snacks to go with their Coke.

5 Opening the bottle and pouring. Open the bottle in front of your guests and pour it just over half. This will heighten their craving for a Coke.

6 Ask the guest again. One Coke just makes you want more . . . so ask your guests if they would like another one.

This standard was designed to optimize product quality and product service, increase outlet owner (customer) and final consumer satisfaction, and increase the volume of sales: satisfied consumers would purchase more than one Coke at every sitting, come back more often and attract new customers to the premise. The integrated marketing communications plan both targeted end consumers and customers. In order to make consumers aware of the programme and to provide bar and restaurant owners with a signal of quality guaranteed to use in communications with their customers, a basic visual graphic was designed to unite the campaign and all of its elements. The visual contained the traditional Coca-Cola logo together with the name of the campaign, Perfect Serve, and a graphic design of the traditional Coke bottle and contoured glass to be used in the serving experience.

Outlet owners, the customers, were believed to be key in making the Perfect Serve campaign a success. They would be approached with various premiums, incentives and materials to support the campaign. A central element was a specific cooler to be used on their premises to hold the bottles and guarantee a constant temperature of 4° Celsius. Drinking cola at this temperature is commonly appreciated best. Further, the outlet owners were provided with contoured glasses to set drinking the beverage apart and increase the experience. Then they could choose from a list of materials to use to communicate to their customers, such as a bar dispenser, coasters, table stand and a Perfect Serve case (see colour insert C8).

The programme also included a number of incentives for outlets to introduce the Perfect Serve campaign including space in a guide book that was to be distributed to publicize the participant outlets to the target market, and contests with prizes for outlets with the best achievement in sales. Consumer promotions were also envisioned to get the customers to try a Perfect Serve Coke and to reinforce the new image. Finally, a consumer advertising campaign and website were also planned.

Notes

[1] This case was written by Pamela Adams. It is intended to be used as the basis for class discussion rather than to illustrate either effective or ineffective handling of a management situation. No part of this case may be copied, stored, transmitted, reproduced or distributed in any form whatsoever without the permission of the author.

[2] The on-trade or HORECA distribution includes bars, cafés, restaurants, fitness centres and hotels.

Sales promotion: turning attitudes into behaviour

The term *sales promotion* is sometimes misunderstood or confused with advertising, because sales-promotion activities frequently use advertisements to create awareness of promotional offers. Also, sales promotions are often used to complement brand-building advertisements, in order to encourage customers to make their interest concrete. In terms of the AIDA model (see

Chapter 4), when an advertisement succeeds in raising interest and desire, the last step to action is facilitated by the sales promotion. **Sales promotion** is *an MC function that offers a tangible added value designed to motivate and accelerate a response.* Adding tangible value means that people who respond to the promotion will receive more than just the product and its image. Added value includes a reduction in price (for example, 20 per cent off, two for the price of one, no finance charges for a year); extra product (16 ounces of coffee beans for the price of 12 ounces); free samples; premiums (receiving a cosmetic case free with the purchase of $30 worth of cosmetics); and an entry into a sweepstakes.

There are two basic types of sales promotion. *Consumer promotions* target end users. *Trade promotions* target members of the distribution channels such as distributors, wholesalers, and retailers. When sales promotions are designed for *consumers*, a marketer is using a **pull strategy**, which is *the use of incentives to motivate end users to purchase a brand and thus pressure retailers to stock that brand.* These promotions result in consumers "pulling" product through the distribution system. When trade promotions are used, marketers are using a **push strategy**, which is *the use of incentives to motivate the buying and reselling of products.*

Many promotional offers last for a "limited time only". They are used to motivate behaviour, and keeping the promotion short term creates a sense of immediacy, which, marketers hope, speeds up the brand decision-making process. Furthermore, a price reduction that is not for a limited time only, is simply a price reduction, not a promotional strategy.

This chapter first offers an extensive discussion of consumer promotions, and then turns to the topic of trade promotions.

How consumer sales promotion works

The primary objective of sales promotion is to motivate consumer behaviour—that is, to generate some type of active response such as buying a brand's products. Sales promotion is integrated into the MC mix to provide incentives to act at one or more points in the brand decision-making process.

Studies have shown that when sales-promotion tools are used strategically, they can increase sales by as much as 400 per cent. Keep in mind that the usual grocery-shopping trip takes about 27 minutes.[1] During that time, an average shopper selects only 35 to 40 of the 7000 products available in the average grocery store (30 000 items if you include different sizes and flavours). Those selections are driven by a customer's previous experience with the brands as well as marketing communication messages, including sales promotion, used to support these brands.

Advertising creates awareness, interest and desire; sales promotions influence the next step in the consumer decision-making process: action. Remember that action is not restricted to buying. Automobile dealers, for example, offer prospects free drinks and hot dogs just for visiting their showrooms, and companies selling time-share properties offer free dinners and an overnight stay to people willing to listen to a sales pitch. Marketers know that prospects may be aware of and even have some interest in or desire for a brand but may not have enough incentives to seek out the brand or risk buying it. An extra incentive, however, sometimes moves a prospect through the desire, and into the action stage.

To better understand how sales promotion works, we start with a discussion of the typical objectives that this MC function is used to achieve.

Sales-promotion objectives

Sales promotions are intended to turn attitudes into behaviour. Unlike many mass media advertising objectives, most of which have to do with awareness and attitudes, sales-promotion objectives are thus behaviour oriented. Consumer sales promotions are designed to do one or more of the following: (1) induce trial, (2) increase the frequency or quantity of purchases, including repurchase, (3) counter competitive offers, (4) help acceptance of small product modifications, (5) get rid of stock, (6) build customer databases, (7) increase customer retention, (8) cross-sell, (9) extend the use of a brand, and (10) reinforce the brand image and strengthen brand relationships.

Inducing trial

Packaged-goods brands use sales promotions to encourage trial. Sales promotions such as special prices and product samples can motivate prospective customers to try something for the first time. Online service providers often offer a limited period of free Internet access.

Trial is the first step in building a relationship between customer and brand, and is therefore an important one. Only after trial can the experience of the customer be used to further build the relationship. For the consumer her own experience in product usage is the best reference for further decision making. Especially in the case of new products, trial is so important that brands do not hesitate to make a loss on customers' first purchases. When mobile telephones started to conquer the world, handsets were given away free by service providers like T-Mobile and Vodafone. These companies were confident that the cost of the devices would be earned back quickly. Similarly, Internet service providers induced trial by giving away modems.

Another form of trial is the chance to try a sample of a product in supermarkets. New tastes or recipes are introduced to the audience in this way. Again this is based on the idea that there is no more credible source in building brand attitudes than the consumer herself.

Increasing frequency and quantity, repurchase

Because the majority of the people who take advantage of coupons and price reductions are current customers, a good promotional strategy does more than simply offer current customers a discount. It is designed to increase purchase frequency or purchase quantity at each transaction. This is the rationale behind "buy one, get one free" offers. By increasing the purchase quantity, the manufacturer expects that the usage quantity will also increase, but this is not necessarily true. In particular, in the case of products that are easily stocked, sales promotions may just lead to a shift in the timing of the purchases. Nevertheless, this also can be beneficial, for example, because the customer will use the brand for a longer time, increasing the chances that they will become used to the brand.

At the same time, sales promotions remind current customers to keep buying the brand. In particular in product categories where product differentiation is small, customers may be tempted to try other brands every now and then. Sales promotions may help to deter customers from adopting this variety-seeking behaviour.

To increase the frequency of purchases, a company must first calculate the regular purchase frequency in order to set a goal, and must then design a strategy that will encourage customers to buy the product more often. Suppose market research found that the average user of shampoo buys this product every three months. Knowing this, a company might schedule its promotions two months apart, timing that is intended to increase purchase frequency and convince customers that they should keep the brand on hand.

Countering competitive offers

The third objective of consumer sales promotions, countering competitive offers, is used frequently in highly competitive product categories. Airlines, rental car companies, and the manufacturers of soft drinks and breakfast cereals, for example, stay abreast of what competing brands are doing and act frequently to counter these activities. Sometimes this leads to permanent lowering of prices in the whole market, as has occurred in the airline industry.

Helping customers to accept small product modifications

Every change in a product needs the consumer's acceptance. Although the modifications are always meant as an improvement (which manufacturer will change its product for the worse?) consumers are very conservative in their behaviour and are not always willing to try the "NEW" "IMPROVED" "BETTER" "HEALTHIER" variation of their good, old, well-known product. Sales promotions can help to overcome this consumer inertia, just as they may help product trial as described above (see colour insert C6).

A special case is when brands decide to change the packaging. This is sometimes necessary— for example to adjust to fashion, to differentiate from competitors, or simply to modernize. However, particularly in supermarkets, customers do not search by brand names in the first place, but by the packaging. Therefore, a change in package design may need the help of a sales promotion to compensate the (temporary) loss of connection between customer and brand that was established by familiar packaging.

Getting rid of stock

Very obviously, it is sometimes necessary to get rid of old stock. This is, however, not only a matter of facing product obsolescence. Existing stock may also hinder new product introductions, and these product introductions can be the necessary next steps in building the brand. For example, every generation of Apple Macintosh machines meant a renewal of its well-nurtured image of being innovative.

Building customer databases

Companies have great interest in building customer databases. The way such databases can benefit the company is the field of direct marketing, which is covered in Chapter 15. Consumer sales promotion is an effective way to build such databases. Various instruments effectively require the consumer to share contact information (name, address, telephone number, e-mail address) with the firm. The firm needs these to effectuate the reward—for example, a money-back coupon—but much more important are those consumer data for building the customer database.

Naturally, some consumers provide false information to protect their privacy, but many more consumers cannot be bothered and willingly share their data with the company.

Cross-selling and extending the use of a brand

Cross-selling encourages current customers to try additional goods or services provided by a brand. Because customers are already familiar with the brand and trust it enough to make repeat purchases, selling them other products under the same brand or made by the same company can be more cost-effective than selling to those unfamiliar with the brand. In this way, the introduction of brand extensions (see Chapter 2) can be supported.

Reinforcing the brand image and strengthening brand relationships

Although sales promotions by design add something extra to a brand offering, what is added should not only be compatible with the brand's image but also reinforce that image. Members

Sales promotion at Nivea

Skin care brand Nivea (a brand of Beiersdorf) is one of many examples of brands heavily using sales promotions. The brand has several sub-brands such as Nivea Visage, Nivea for Men, Nivea Body, Nivea Sun and Nivea Baby. The company uses sales promotion tools to promote its wide range of sub-brands.

Free product sampling is one of the tools that is used by Nivea, especially to introduce a new product to the market. For example, in 2002/2003, in the UK, Beiersdorf decided to run a Nivea for Men roadshow in order to convince men that skin care was not only for women. Another method to reach the men was a sampling campaign throughout 500 gyms in the UK. A campaign for both men and women was started by Beiersdorf in August 2006, when the company focused on extending its Nivea brand to Eastern Europe. To promote the brand, the company implemented so-called "Blue Walls" in Romania and Bulgaria, a concept that had already been successfully introduced in Austria and Germany. These walls are approximately three metres high and five metres wide, so as to make a strong impression on the consumer. In both countries the walls were built in a hypermarket and free product samples were distributed. Nivea introduced this concept as well to introduce consumers to cross-selling of their different sub-brands: in this case a very logical sales promotion objective.

Sampling, however, is only one tool. Nivea makes use of coupons too, for example, in the United States. If you go to the website www.niveapromo.com, you can click on your favorite product category and after filling in some personal data, it is possible to print a $2 coupon, to be used when purchasing a certain Nivea product. Besides downloading coupons, all the international websites offer brand games to promote the Nivea brand on the Internet. The company offers several online contests as well. In Belgium, for example, you can test your knowledge of the brand by answering questions, filling in personal data and afterwards be given a chance to win prizes.

The newest idea of Nivea is the Nivea house: a three-storey health resort, located in Hamburg (Germany). The house was opened on 27 April 2006 and the concept seems to be successful. In this house customers can try out 500 different Nivea products. Moreover, they can get massages, manicures and consultations on make-up and hairstyling. The director of marketing of Beiersdorf, Pieter Nota, explained the building of the house as a win-win situation. "In our Nivea house consumers can test all our products without obligation and we in turn receive their reaction." One can say that this house is a perfect example of how a company can induce product trial.

Think about it

Will online games be effective to communicate Nivea's brand? Can you come up with other sales promotion tools that Nivea has used before?

Sources:

Dagmar Mussey, "Beiersdorf opens 'oasis' to showcase, test Nivea", Advertising Age, 00018899, 9 January 2006, Vol. 77, Issue 2.

Financial analyst meeting, 7 November 2006.

www.hahlbrock.de/fvk/en/news/meldungen/2006/kugel_nivea_haus.php

www.nivea.com

www.niveapromo.com

www.cosmeticsdesign-europe.com/news/ng.asp?n=69982-beiersdorf-nivea-romania-bulgaria

www.euromonitor.com/PDF/C&T-Beiersdorfag.pdf

of frequent-flyer programmes are rewarded on the basis of miles travelled; and the more they travel, the more special they are made to feel. Major airlines, for example, give their frequent flyers a special toll-free number to call for reservations and flight information. Callers to this number are very seldom placed on hold. McDonald's promotions reinforce the image that McDonald's is a child-friendly place by offering figurines from the latest Disney movie.

Sales-promotion tools

Many sales-promotion tools exist to accomplish the objectives just described. Table 13-1 gives an idea of the relative use of sales promotion tools in the US. Note that price reduction is not included in the table. Although price reduction represents a significant amount of promotional spending, it is impossible to capture industry data for it because of the many different ways in which price reductions are made. Each of the major promotion tools is explained in this section.

Premiums

In the context of sales promotion, a premium is *an item offered free or at a bargain price to reward some type of behaviour such as buying, sampling, or testing.* The most effective premiums are those that are instantly available, such as a free toothbrush attached to a type of toothpaste. Premiums can improve a brand's image, gain goodwill, broaden the customer base (by attracting new customers), produce an immediate increase in sales, and reward customers. A premium may be included in the product's package (in-pack premium), placed visibly on the package (on-pack premium), handed out in a store or at an event, or sent by mail.

Two types of premiums are often used—consumables and collectables. Each of them foster customers' desire for more than one. Consumables are *products that have a one-time use,* such as movie tickets, gasoline, food, and beverages. Collectables are *items of which consumers enjoy having two or more.* Fast-food chains like to have promotional tie-ins with movies whose main

Promotional segment	Percentage
Premiums and specialities	55
POP displays	19
Coupons	8
Speciality printing	7
Fulfilment	5
Internet marketing	2
Games, contests, sweepstakes	2
Product sampling	2
Total	100

Table 13-1 Consumer sales promotion spending, 2002

Source: Consumer Sales Promotion Spending; Adapted from Promotions Trend Report, *PROMO Magazine* supplement, April 2003. © 2003, PRIMEDIA Business Magazines & Media, Inc. All rights reserved.

characters can be reproduced in figurines that children (and some adults) eagerly collect. Items for which customers enjoy having many variations, such as caps, T-shirts, and mugs, are similar to collectables and thus also widely used.

Premiums that can be made unique to a brand can also be attractive to customers. Starbucks' coffee mug is again a good example. The chain's logo on it makes it a unique item, not available in any regular store.

Free is the most powerful sales-promotion word a company can use. Who does not like getting something for nothing? When a premium is being given away, the word *free* is strongly emphasized; it not only attracts attention to the brand message but is also a powerful motivator. The premium is only "free", however, when the item it is supporting is purchased (generally at full price). Obviously a company guards the cost-effectiveness of its premiums. Premiums that cost near the price of the item with which they come put the company on a loss.

The three major challenges posed by premiums are (1) finding ones that a high percentage of a target audience would want; (2) finding one that is cost-effective; and (3) finding ones that can reinforce a product's brand image. When Starbucks offers a free coffee mug after ten purchases, of course with the chain's logo on the mug as a brand reminder, all the challenges are met. Because most people enjoy having more than one mug, this offer is motivating, and because the Starbucks mugs are of high quality and contain the Starbucks logo, they reinforce the brand image. Finally as the mug is available after ten purchases only, the cost of a mug becomes minimal compared to the spending of the customers. As a bonus with this kind of premium, a shallow degree of brand loyalty is also created, shallow because it is not in the first place based on an appreciation of the brand, but on the desire for the mug. Nevertheless, the required repurchasing behaviour is a good step-up to a lasting relationship based on true loyalty.

Specialities

Speciality items do not require any specific behaviour. Specialities are *items given free to customers and other stakeholders to help keep a brand's name top-of-mind*. Unlike with premiums, no purchase is necessary to get a speciality item. Specialities are generally low-cost items such as calendars, rulers, coffee mugs, T-shirts, and pens. B2B marketers may give more costly items, however, such as desk sets, mobile telephones, briefcases, CD players, and watches, to executives or other representatives with whom the company has a relationship.

Spending in the promotional-products category of specialities and premiums is now more than spending on consumer magazine advertising. All types of businesses, including non-profit organizations, use specialities for occasions ranging from launching new products and opening new facilities (where creating a new customer base is an important objective), to rewarding current customers and reminding prospects of the brand.

The rationale behind using speciality items is the belief that people will think more positively about a brand that gives them something of value—the more added value, the greater the impact. Also, because most speciality items are tangible, recipients are exposed to the brand name multiple times (for example, every time they look at the calendar or drink from the coffee mug), and that exposure helps to keep the brand top-of-mind.

Coupons

A coupon is *a certificate with a stated price reduction on a specified item*. Coupons can be used for price reductions or for other merchandise. For example Sara Lee's daughter Douwe Egberts has added coupons to its coffees and teas for decades. This sales promotions programme has evolved into an entirely separate branch of activity for the brand (see www.geschenkenwinkel.nl —in Dutch, but you should get a fair impression from it).

Today, literally a billion coupons are distributed every year, but only about a small percentage of these are ever redeemed. Coupons have to be distributed through some medium—newspapers or magazines, packages, in-store displays, or direct mail. Many reach consumers through colourful **freestanding inserts (FSIs)**, which are *newspaper supplements that contain ads, most with coupons.* FSIs have a slightly higher redemption rate than regular newspaper and magazine coupons, but coupons on or in packages have the highest redemption levels. Why? They are going to customers of the brand.

Electronic coupons are high-tech coupons distributed in-store and online. Online coupons are issued by both individual companies and coupon distribution sites such as Cool Savings (www.coolsavings.com). This site requires that you register and provide a profile of yourself; then it shows you a checklist of lifestyle categories. The company sends coupon offers to you according to the categories you check off. Because customers opt-in and receive offers tailored to their profiles and interests, those coupons are redeemed at a higher rate than are the coupons distributed in newspapers and magazines. Other electronic coupon sites include www.dealcatcher.com, www.couponcraze.com, and www.nocouponclipping.com (see colour insert C15).

The redemption rate of downloaded coupons is 56 per cent, far greater than the average media-delivered coupon rate of 1 to 2 per cent. The reason for the high rate of redemption is that customers go to the trouble to get these coupons for products they want to buy.[2] This high redemption rate suggests that companies should try to acquire the names of persons using these coupons and to make sure that the company is not simply discounting sales to current customers.

Coupons are the best instrument to collect customer data. That is why they are relatively popular with companies. On the customer side the reverse is true. As coupons are cumbersome compared to other promotional instruments, there is a relatively large barrier for customers to engage in the couponing promotion. Consequently the reward promised by a coupon has to be comparatively large in order to have the desired effect.

Price reductions

Short-term price reductions come in various forms: a featured price that is lower than the regular price, free goods ("buy one, get one free"), and enlarged packages ("30 more for same price"). Most price reductions are made to "featured brands", which retailers advertise each week to attract shoppers. These items are generally emphasized in a store's local ad, direct-mail flyers, or TV spots. When retailers receive trade promotion allowances (discussed in the next part of this chapter), they generally pass the savings on to customers in the form of price reductions. Sometimes the retailer even sacrifices some of its own profit margin in order to offer an even lower price on a few featured brands. For a lower price to have meaning, however, it is important that a brand should not be price-featured too frequently. For packaged goods generally featuring a brand not more than one week in every three months will maintain the brand's reference (regular) price.

Another form of price reduction is reduced or extended credit. This incentive is often used with high-priced items such as appliances, furniture, and cars. Typical offers are "No payment till next year" and "Only 0.9 per cent interest". When customers have a strong desire and their only barrier is money, extended-credit offers can be powerful incentives.

Rebates

Some companies offer customers cash refunds known as **rebates**, which are *a type of price reduction*. Rebates are commonly offered for such items as clothing or household appliances. Large rebates, like those given on cars, are handled by the seller. To receive small rebates, like those given for coffee makers, the consumer must send the manufacturer proof of purchase (a receipt and a bar-code label) and a completed rebate form. Many people purchase a product because of an advertised rebate but never collect the rebate because they either forget about it or lose the rebate form or the sales receipt. Failure to take advantage of rebates is called *slippage* and is the reason why marketers can offer high-value rebates: people who do not take advantage of the offer essentially cover the costs of those who do. Yet slippage has also led to a decrease in the motivating power of rebates (customers aren't interested in an offer when they feel that getting the rebate is too much trouble).

As you can see, coupons, price reductions and rebates are three different ways of realizing temporary price reductions. They only differ in the way customers have to act: for coupons they have to act in advance of the purchase; price reductions are achieved during the purchase; and for rebates consumers have to act after the purchase. This largely determines the role these tools play in the communications strategy. Coupons are most useful for inducing trial, increasing frequency, or encouraging repurchase, and especially so for products that consumers are searching for. After all, consumers have to get across the message that brings the coupon, and they are more likely to come across messages for products they are actively looking for. Price reductions on the other hand are better for goods that are bought on the spot. For example, products for which little differentiation exists, the price reduction may be the final and ultimate trigger to buy a certain brand. Rebates then are mostly effective when consumers start to feel connected to the brand. The action required to effectuate a rebate suggests that some degree of involvement with the product, or better the brand, is a prerequisite to establish the contact with the brand.

Sampling

An especially powerful pull strategy, **sampling** consists of *offering prospects the opportunity to try a product before making a buying decision*. Sampling is usually targeted using selected mailing lists or carried out in stores or at events. One of the most costly of all sales promotions, sampling is nonetheless one of the most effective. The proposition is a powerful one: a brand is so good that once people try it they will want to buy it. Sampling offers the greatest credibility of all MC functions because it is based on the product's performance and can instantly move a non-user to become a customer—if the product lives up to the expectation that has been created for it. Sampling is most successful when a product is perceivably different from the competition. Sampling is also particularly useful for products that are experiential in nature. When the benefits of the product are hard to gather from the product information on the package, like food items or perfume, experiencing (tasting, smelling) the product is a very strong communicator of the product's benefits. Maybe this is the reason that one research found that the strategy seems to work better with women (73 per cent positive response) than with men (57 per cent)?[3]

Perfume marketers depend heavily on sampling to win customers. Most perfume counters have sampling bottles so users can try the various fragrances. In major department stores at holiday season there may be as many as 30 competing new fragrance brands, and well-manicured saleswomen armed with spray bottles ask passers-by if they would like a sample spray. To encourage reluctant customers to permit themselves to be sprayed, sellers of Estée Lauder's Black Cashmere offered hand massages as a promotional incentive for the sampling.[4]

"Stink alley", as the perfume aisles are sometimes called, is one place that many customers try to avoid. A more sensitive and less intrusive approach in some stores is to hand out scent cards.

Many in-store sampling programmes are tied to a coupon campaign. Sometimes samples are distributed with related items (such as an on-pack sample of hair conditioner given free with the purchase of a shampoo), but this strategy limits distribution to people who buy the other product. A recent innovation in distribution is *polybagging*, hanging samples on door-knobs or delivering them in plastic bags along with the daily newspaper or a monthly magazine.

In a practice that combines features of both sampling and offering premiums, food and drug marketers use *combination offers*, such as a razor with a package of blades or a toothbrush with a tube of toothpaste, at a reduced price for the two. For best results, the items should be related. Sometimes, a combination offer may be used to introduce a new brand by tying its purchase to an established brand at a special price.

Sweepstakes, contests, and games

A **contest** is *a brand-sponsored competition that requires some form of skill and effort.* A **sweepstake** is *a form of sales promotion that offers prizes based on a chance drawing of entrants' names* (see colour insert C11). Contests and sweepstakes gain attention for a brand message and increase store traffic by requiring those who wish to enter to pick up an entry blank at a store or dealership. To encourage a large number of entries, these types of sales promotion should be kept as simple as possible. By law, the prize structure must be clearly stated and rules clearly defined. Because contests, especially, require some effort, the response rate is extremely low. Furthermore, a portion of those who do respond may be "professional" contest entrants who care nothing about the brand sponsoring the contest. "Professional" contest entrants simply enter for the fun of participating and the chance to win. Although sweepstakes and contests do not generate a high rate of response, they are helpful in setting up customer databases (because entrants have to submit their names and addresses and are often asked to answer other questions). A popular form of sweepstake, which asks participant to complete a slogan about what the brand is, gives further useful insight in how the brand is perceived in the marketplace.

A **game** is *a sales-promotion tool that has the chance element of a sweepstake but is conducted over a longer time.* Grocery stores may design bingo-type games to build store traffic. The marketing advantage of a game is that customers must make repeat visits to the dealer to continue playing. Brand games have become popular tools to promote brands on the Internet.

Contests and sweepstakes must be advertised to be successful, and often they need dealer or retail support. Retailers must be encouraged to build special in-store displays to hold products, help announce a sweepstake or provide entry forms. In this way, sweepstakes are used to get off-shelf product display. Some contests and sweepstakes ask the entrant to name the product's local dealer so that the company may award prizes to the retailers who generate the most entries. This policy gives retailers extra incentive to promote the sweepstake and the brand.

The media of consumer sales promotion

Every sales promotion needs a vehicle to carry it. It should be clear from the review of the different tools of sales promotion that companies use a broad range of ways to deliver promotional offers. Coupons, for example, appear in mass media advertising, in direct-mail pieces, on packages, and on the back of grocery sales receipts. Contests are announced in ads and at events. Samples are handed out in stores, but they are also mailed to homes and businesses.

Many sales promotions, such as displays, are specially constructed and delivered by sales reps or distributors. Sales literature and manuals contain the information that sales reps need about the various types of allowances and discounts they are able to offer customers.

The Internet is increasingly being used to deliver sales-promotion offers and is especially useful for running online contests or games. Visitors to such sites will find a game-playing experience that exposes them to "winning deals" on a variety of merchandise and offers. As site visitors play a game and become interested in brand offerings, they can simply click on the brand mentioned and find out more information and how to order. Because of the game involvement, visitors are motivated to stay at the site longer than they would stay at sites simply offering a catalogue of products. In the same way, packaged-goods marketers are developing free-sample sites that provide them with customer feedback, in addition to an opportunity for customers to try a new product. Promotional efforts are sneaking onto electronic shopping carts as well. A software programme from iChoose Inc. searches its database of coupons and deals to find savings on the exact items customers put in their virtual shopping carts. Fickle shoppers can be teased away with the promise of a 10 per cent saving or a cheaper shipping fee.[5]

Determining consumer sales promotion strategies

Because most consumer sales promotions can show a more direct impact on sales than advertising, sales promotion has a tendency to be overused or misused. Some argue that sales promotions are simply a way to "buy sales" as opposed to convincing people that a brand is good value and moving them strategically through a buying process. Marketers of Coke, Nestlé, Unilever, and Adidas have discovered that traditional retail support in the form of price promotions and coupons drives immediate sales but can also encourage consumers to buy on price—and therefore to switch brands as soon as a competing brand offers a better price. Marketers today are looking for ways to use promotions that will build brand equity, develop long-term customer loyalty, and drive store traffic without being overly dependent on price reductions just to get a short-term increase in sales.

Consequently, marketers need to "forget all that nonsense about consumer promotion being the ugly stepchild of advertising"[6] and focus on its strengths. To that end, the promotion industry is making efforts to become more strategic and less tactical—using promotions to build brands and move customers and prospects through the decision-making process, rather than just reducing the price to move more items. As one marketer stated in responding to a survey on sales-promotion activities: "Increasingly, the gimmicks are gone. We must all step up to the challenge of adding real, brand-building value with promotions—the kind that sparks genuine consumer, retailer, and client interest."[7]

Driving retention through loyalty strategies

Sales promotion is one of the most powerful MC functions for helping retain customers and increasing a brand's share of customers' category spending. *Using promotions specifically designed for customer retention* is called loyalty (or frequency) marketing. In a loyalty promotion, a company offers premiums or other incentives when a customer makes multiple purchases over time. The most simple of these is the coffee or fuel punch card that allows a person a free coffee or a fill-up after a set number of purchases ("buy 10 and get the 11th one free").

When loyalty is based solely on the sales promotion incentive alone, it is spurious at best (Whyte, 2004). Commitment to a brand, the highest level of the brand-building pyramid introduced in Chapter 2, is based on attitudinal loyalty. A main driver of attitudinal loyalty is satisfaction. Satisfaction can only result from product usage, and this completes the argument: product usage is the start of loyalty, but can only be realized after actual consumption of the brand. So, loyalty marketing helps in achieving both repeat purchasing (the behavioural dimension of loyalty) and commitment to the brand (the attitudinal dimension of loyalty) (Chaudhuri and Holbrook, 2001).

A loyalty programme strategy should be set up so that customers remain in the programme even after they redeem a reward. Rewards that are given out should have an expiration date, because outstanding rewards are a financial liability. Also, when a loyalty programme is designed, a company should have an "exit strategy"—how it will end the programme if it is not profitable or no longer fits into the brand's overall marketing strategy. More than almost anything else a marketing communication programme does, a loyalty programme sets specific expectations for its customers. A company should consider how these expectations can be changed when it's time for the programme to end.

The main strength of a loyalty programme is increased customer retention. This not only boosts sales but also lowers selling costs because selling to current customers requires less MC spending. A related benefit is the customer-profile information that loyalty programmes generate. Another benefit is that a good loyalty promotion can help differentiate a brand. Differentiation is especially important in a commodity category, where so many brands are similar in performance and price that customers must look hard to find differences among them. A reward for loyalty may be the only thing that sets one brand apart from another. Rewards make customers feel good, and this feeling can motivate them to become brand ambassadors and to make brand referrals.

The limitations of loyalty programmes are that they can overshadow the brand, and managing and running them requires more resources than do other forms of marketing communication used by the brand. Also, it is difficult to determine whether such programmes are truly cost-effective, especially when competitors offer similar ones. Do they cost more to administer than they are worth in increased revenue? Many companies do not have a clear answer to this question.

Strengths and limitations of consumer sales promotion overall

The earlier discussion of sales-promotion objectives identified the primary strengths of consumer sales promotions as driving sales (increasing trial and repurchase, increasing frequency and quantity of purchase, cross-selling, and extending the uses of a brand), strengthening customer relationships, and reinforcing brand image. Sales promotion clearly has value in a marketing mix; but, of course, it also has limitations.

Although sales promotions can increase sales, the critical decision of whether to use promotions should be based on their cost-effectiveness. Using a process called **pay-out planning** or **break-even analysis**, planners can *evaluate the costs of sales promotions versus the revenue they generate*. In many cases promotions are not cost-effective, although they may deliver on other objectives, such as raising the visibility of the brand. One analysis showed that only 16 per cent of customer promotions were profitable. In other words, in 84 per cent of the promotions, companies spent more than 1 euro to generate an extra 1 euro of profits. One way to counter the risks of sales promotions, in particular when there is considerable uncertainty about the redemption rate, is to take out insurance for excessive situations.

Sales promotions are sometimes criticized for attracting customers who are searching for the best deal, not for a long-term brand relationship. These are customers who always try to buy what is on sale and are not loyal to any brand. In automotive marketing, for example, companies have had mixed experiences with online promotions that have brought masses of unqualified consumers into dealerships to enter sweepstakes and win prizes. Once again, targeting is a critical element.

Another limitation of sales promotion is that as soon as one brand in a category has demonstrated a successful programme, competitors soon follow suit. Price reductions are more vulnerable to this copycatting than premiums, specialities, etc. Competitive actions usually negate the added-value advantage and transform the cost of the programme into just another cost of doing business. Another concern is that overuse of promotional offers will reposition the brand negatively. A brand that is always on sale or always offering premiums will soon be known as the "price brand" or "deal brand", an image that most brands don't want to have. Most companies limit discounts, not only to protect the profitability of the brand but also to protect the retail price. In some product categories—for example beverages or laundry detergents—customers otherwise learn the regularities of the discount programmes and adjust their purchase pattern accordingly.

Two challenges for loyalty programmes are keeping an accurate accounting of customer rewards and managing their disbursement. These programmes can become so much a part of a brand's offering that, if there is a problem, the brand relationship can be weakened by the very programme that was designed to strengthen it.

Targeting promotional offers is a sound strategy, but it needs to be done in a way that does not anger some customers. For example, in an attempt to attract new customers, a mobile phone operator like Orange may offer a substantial benefit to new subscribers. This strategy can attract new customers, but current customers who were never offered this value may feel cheated. When these kinds of new-customer offers are made, it is best to use personalized media so that only non-customers are exposed to the offers.

Sales promotion and the marketing communication mix

For a decade, advertising and sales promotion have engaged in a budget battle, and marketing managers and academics have struggled to determine which works best and when to use various MC mixes. A seven-year study by Procter & Gamble, for example, found that price deals and coupons increased penetration—the number of people buying the brand—but had less effect on customer retention. According to the study, advertising also increased penetration, but its impact was weaker than the sales-promotion tools. The study also found that although advertising was more beneficial for small brands, large brands benefited more from promotion.

One of the major challenges of integrated marketing communication is to get the MC mix right. On the one hand, if too much of the communication mix is allocated to advertising, the brand may gain a high-quality, differentiated image but not enough volume to be a market leader. On the other hand, as Larry Light, Director of Marketing for McDonald's, says, "Too much promotion, and the brand will have high volume but low profitability." Some say that a decline in brand loyalty has been the result of increased sales-promotion spending, which has conditioned customers to focus more on prices than on brands and thus become less loyal. It is possible, however, to use sales promotion effectively to build a brand and reinforce its image.

What is the appropriate balance between sales promotion and brand-building functions such as media advertising and publicity? Extensive research by the Coalition for Brand Equity shows that overemphasis of sales promotions has a negative impact on a brand. The coalition compiled the following findings:

1 Excessive promotion at the expense of advertising may hurt profits. In the consumer packaged-goods field, experts caution that trade and consumer promotion should not exceed 60 per cent of the marketing communication budget. (This can vary from category to category.)

2 A higher ratio of advertising (relative to sales promotion) typically increases profits.

3 A high level of trade and consumer promotion, relative to advertising, has a positive effect on short-term market share but a negative effect on brand attitudes and long-term market share.

4 Without an effective advertising effort to emphasize brand image and quality, customers become deal-prone rather than brand-loyal.

5 Overemphasis on low prices eventually destroys brand equity.

Trade promotions

To get their brands to end users, manufacturers battle against competing manufacturers for the attention and support of members of the distribution channels. For years this goal was accomplished through **trade promotions**, which are *discounts and premiums offered to retailers in exchange for their promotional support.* In recent years, however, companies have taken the more integrated, relationship-building approach known as channel marketing. **Channel marketing** is *an integrated process that combines personal selling, trade promotions, and co-marketing programmes to build relationships with retailers and other members of the distribution channel.* In this book the focus will be on the role trade promotions play in these relationship-building efforts. But to appreciate this role, the broader context of the relationship between manufacturer and other channel members will be sketched.

Members of the distribution channel are called different names depending on their place in the distribution system and the types of products being distributed. The most common distribution channel members are:

- **Wholesalers:** *companies that specialize in moving goods from manufacturers to retailers;* they buy large quantities of a product and then break the quantity down to smaller lots that they then sell to many different retailers.

- **Bottlers:** as in the soft-drink industry, *local companies that buy ingredients in large quantities—for example, the concentrate made by Coke from its famous secret recipe—and then mix them, bottle them, and sell beverages to local stores* (see the opening IMC in Action case).

- **Dealers:** as in the automotive industry, *local companies that buy an inventory of products—for example, cars from Volkswagen or audio equipment from Bang and Olufson—from a manufacturer and assemble a mix of models for sale in their stores or showrooms.*

- **Retailers:** *food stores, drugstores, mass merchandisers, and other speciality stores that sell products and services to consumers.* Sometimes retailers are owned by manufacturers (H&M, Nike), but more often they are independently owned or are members of large chains such as Aldi, Carrefour, and Tesco. In independent stores and chains, manufacturers compete fiercely to have their brands on store shelves and featured in retailers' ads. Most major retail chains have their own brands—*store brands*—which compete with *manufacturers' brands* for shelf space and promotional support.

All distribution-channel relationships are important, but the key relationship for B2C manufacturers is the one with retailers because the retail store is the place where consumers buy products. Retailers are powerful: they control which brands are sold in their stores, where in a store each brand is displayed, how much floor space or shelf space is allocated to each brand, what in-store signage and promotions are used to promote each brand, and which brands are featured in the store's advertising and promotional programmes. Not surprisingly, the majority of trade-promotion euros are spent on retailers.

Trade promotions: the foundation of channel marketing

Moving products from manufacturers to retailers is a complex process that involves warehousing and distribution logistics. The real challenges, however, are: (1) persuading retailers to authorize a brand, which means to *agree to carry a brand*, and (2) persuading retailers to display the product in a positive manner and promote it aggressively to consumers. The majority of trade-promotion spending is used for the latter. However, this is not possible until a brand has been authorized and is displayed on retail store shelves.

Trade promotions for new products

The first step in getting authorization of a brand or of a new product line for the brand is using advertising and publicity to create awareness of the new offering among channel members. Advertising in trade magazines and demonstrating products at appropriate trade shows can accomplish this.

Once trade awareness has been created, the next step is to get authorization by making presentations to retail buyers. Every retail operation, whether an independent store or a chain, has one or more people responsible for buying. In this context a buyer specifically denotes *a person who purchases products for resale and selects which manufacturers' promotions to use.* Before most big chains take on a new brand or a major line extension, a buyer must first be convinced the brand is worth considering; then he or she presents the brand to the chain's buying committee. This committee is made up of senior buyers and other chain executives. Why is it so complicated? Taking on new products requires changes in the retailer's operations (as explained later in the discussion of slotting allowances). In large chains there are several buyers, each of whom handles several product categories.

If a store is interested in a new product or in a line extension, it requires the manufacturer to pay a slotting allowance, which is *a one-time, up-front payment for agreeing to stock a product.* Because the demand for retail shelf space is so great, these fees at large chains can run into the hundreds of thousands of euros and are considered a major trade-promotion expense. Retailers justify this charge because taking on a new brand requires them to allocate one or more "slots" (spaces) in their warehouses, enter the new brand or product items into their computer and scanning programs, and rearrange shelf space within their stores where the new brand will be displayed. Because all stores have a finite amount of shelf space, taking on a new brand generally means dropping or greatly reducing space allotted to a current brand. Some large chains give new products 90 days to prove themselves. If sales do not meet expectations, the products are dropped, and all of the manufacturer's investment with that chain is lost.

Slotting allowances are controversial. Manufacturers say the charges are far greater than what it costs retailers to take on a new brand. Also, these high fees often prevent new brands, especially those not belonging to large companies, from getting distribution in major chains—thereby, opponents suggest, suppressing competition. So far however, slotting allowances have not been considered illegal by the authorities.

When Unilever, Procter & Gamble, Mars (confectionery), and other well-established companies introduce new products, retailers are generally receptive because they know these companies have the knowledge and budgets to create consumer awareness and demand. But usually even these companies must pay slotting allowances. An exception is made only when a brand has achieved such high consumer awareness and demand that the retailer taking on the brand assumes little or no risk. This is a good example of the value of strong brand equity (Chapter 2).

Getting authorization—with or without slotting fees—does not guarantee a brand's success. It is only the first hurdle. The second challenge, persuading retailers to promote the marketer's brand, helps guarantee success—if success means getting ongoing retailer promotional support that complements the brand's MC effort. This calls for a separate trade-promotion campaign, in addition to the launch campaign aimed at consumers. Such an effort involves setting channel marketing and promotion objectives and the strategies to deliver on them.

Trade-promotion objectives

For brands that have been authorized by a retailer, the primary trade-promotion objectives are to (1) increase distribution, (2) balance demand, (3) control inventory levels, (4) respond to competitive programmes, and (5) elicit promotional support by channel members. Before consumers can buy a retail product, it must be available on store shelves. Thus marketers use channel marketing to gain new distribution and motivate the retailers that carry the brand to promote locally.

The most typical trade-promotion objective is to move more products through the channels of distribution. These promotions *increase distribution* by lowering the risk for distributors and retailers to buy in greater quantities than normal. What members of the distribution channel fear most is buying product that they cannot resell. By providing them with special selling materials and promotional discounts and allowances (explained later in the chapter), manufacturers reduce the risk of buying in large quantities.

Knowing how important it is to have products available when customers want them, most manufacturers work hard to make sure product is always available at retail. Service companies, similarly, staff up for traditionally busy times of the day, week, or year. When companies find they have too many goods on hand or service personnel who are not being kept busy, they use promotions to *balance demand* and *control inventory levels*. Rental car companies sometimes offer "three days for the price of two" on Friday-through-Monday rentals because this is a low-demand period. For products that have irregular purchase cycles, an objective of sales promotion can be to help level out the sales peaks and valleys.

Trade promotion can also help a brand *respond to competitive offerings*. To counter the introduction of a new competing brand, for example, a company can use a "loading" promotion, in which retailers are given incentives to buy in larger quantities than usual (to load up on a product). This reduces space and demand for the new brand, making it more difficult for the new brand to get and keep distribution. In high-tech industries, companies continually introduce improved hardware and software. A company that is behind may offer special pricing or product extras in order to prevent current customers from switching to the newer competitive offerings.

Not only does the manufacturer want its products on the shelves of the retailer; in the end, the customer must be triggered to take the products from the shelf again. As has been discussed before, consumer sales promotions are a strong tool in achieving this final objective. But the consumer sales promotions are at the discretion of the retailer. Manufacturers can *elicit promotional support by channel members* by offering trade promotions in the first place. In doing so, the idea is that channel members will pass through the benefits acquired by the trade promotions to the next channel member, e.g. the customer. This can of course also be part of the negotiations between channel members.

Examples of specific trade-promotion objectives are the following (in a plan, these objectives would be stated in measurable terms based on the status of the brand and other relevant marketing input):

- To gain *more* shelf space.
- To gain *better* shelf space. The best shelf space is at eye level and near the beginning of the product category. "Beginning" is defined by the direction from which the majority of customers enter a section—the flow pattern of store traffic.
- To gain *extra* brand displays such as end-aisle displays and complementary product displays, an example of which is having a display of hot dog buns placed above the section of the meat case containing hot dogs.

To help you understand trade-promotion strategies, we next look at the major trade-promotion tools.

Trade-promotion tools

The essence of most trade promotions is a reduction in price, much more so than with consumer sales promotions where tangible benefits can also be offered in other ways. Still, price reductions come in many forms, as the following descriptions of promotional allowances illustrate.

Off-invoice allowances

An **off-invoice allowance** is *a reduction in the wholesale price, with no restrictions, for a limited period*. It is the simplest of all trade promotions and the one that channel members desire most. During the designated promotion period, often 30 days, a brand is discounted a certain percentage, generally between 5 and 20 per cent. Much of the discount, the manufacture hopes, will be passed on to the consumer, although the retailer is not required to pass it on. Manufacturers use this tool to maintain their share of retail shelf space and to enable retailers to price these brands competitively. A problem with off-invoice allowances is that some retailers do "forward buying". Near the end of the promotion period, they buy another month's worth of the product, causing the manufacturer to lose two months of selling products at the full wholesale price.

Volume discounts

As the name implies, a volume discount is based on the amount a retailer buys. The more a retailer buys at a time, the greater the discount. This allowance is designed to motivate retailers to buy more than they normally would. Because retailers have limited warehousing space, manufacturers know that retailers will make a special effort to sell products bought in volume.

Performance allowances

Performance allowances are *price reductions given to retailers in exchange for the retailer agreeing to feature the brand in its advertising or in other promotional programmes*. To receive such allowances, a retailer must submit proof of performance—copies of a newspaper ad or affidavits of performance from radio or TV stations, along with invoices from these media. Most major brands provide retailers with prepared advertising materials—ads, glossy photos, sample radio and TV commercials—insisting that they use one or more of these materials in order to qualify for the allowances.

Display allowances

Another type of performance allowance is an off-shelf display allowance, which is *a price reduction for locating an additional quantity of a brand in a high-traffic area such as the end of an aisle*. In exchange for this allowance, retailers agree to give the brand off-shelf display, which automatically attracts more customer attention and increases sales.

Knowing that most retail stores are always trying to reduce labour costs, some brands periodically use shipper displays in order to get off-shelf display. Shipper displays are *specially designed shipping cartons that when opened become display units complete with signage and a quantity of products ready for sale*. Shipper displays demand little extra labour by retailers. Flaps from the carton stand up to help call attention to the display and carry a brand message. Like end-aisle displays, shipper displays are attention getting and can move several times the amount of product that normally moves from the brand's allotted shelf display. The downside for retailers is that they take up floor space, which in most stores is already being used to the maximum.

Dealer loaders

A dealer loader is *a high-value premium given to a retailer in exchange for the purchase of a special product assortment or a specified monetary volume*. An example is a cooler used to stock soft drinks. After the promotion period, the premium belongs to the retailer, who may raffle it off to employees in each store.

Buy-back allowances

When introducing a new product, manufacturers sometimes offer a buy-back allowance, which is *a payment to buy back the current stock of a brand and replace it with a featured new product*. To further persuade retailers to take on products, some manufacturers guarantee protection from risk by offering to buy back any of their own brand not sold within a specified period.

Dealer contests

To motivate retail dealers and their salespeople to reach specific sales goals or to stock a certain product, companies offer dealer contests, *competitions awarding dealers special prizes and gifts when sales reach a predetermined volume or a stated percentage increase on last year's sales*. Travel-related contests are especially popular. Many chains require that these types of rewards be made to the chain's headquarters and not to individual buyers, so that buyers do not make buying and promotion decisions that are not in the best interest of the chain. The chain then uses the rewards to stage its own internal competitions. On business items such as office supplies, cleaning supplies, and printed forms, sellers sometimes offer trips or other expensive premiums for certain-size orders or multi-year contracts.

In-store demonstrations

Manufacturers of food and beverages, especially new or improved products, use in-store demonstrations, which means *hiring a person to hand out product samples in-store*. Often, in addition to sampling products, these people hand out cents-off coupons to further encourage purchase of the product being sampled. In-store demonstrations not only move many more cases in a day than average but also introduce the product to customers who are not regular users.

Sales training

In many high-tech and other speciality stores, sales assistants help customers by explaining a brand's features and benefits and demonstrating its use. Sales assistants can do this, however, only if a manufacturer provides the store and its sales staff with brand educational materials or, in some cases, holds special training sessions on how to sell the brand. The extent to which sales assistants are motivated to share their knowledge or sell a brand's features and benefits is also a function of the incentives provided by the manufacturer and the retailer. A sale is much more likely to be made when a consumer is approached by a knowledgeable salesperson who is trained about the product's benefits and features, is enthusiastic and tries to sell the product to the consumer because of how well it meets the consumer's needs. The enthusiasm of sales assistants can be sharpened if they are accruing points from a manufacturer to win, say, 500 euros-worth of free merchandise or a free holiday as part of a special trade sales promotion.

Co-op advertising allowances

Many manufacturers have **co-operative (co-op) advertising allowances** in which *a certain percentage of everything a retailer buys is put into a special "co-op" fund.* A co-op fund is typically based on 1 to 2 per cent of annual sales to each retailer. The more the retailer buys, the bigger the retailer's co-op fund is. If, for example, Marks & Spencer department stores purchase 50 million euros in annual wholesale shipments of Nike product, Nike would put 1 million euro that year in a co-op account for Marks & Spencer to advertise Nike products. When the retailer advertises the brand in newspapers, on radio, on TV, or in some other way, from 50 to 100 per cent of the cost is paid for out of that retailer's co-op fund. Such funds allow retailers to promote a brand on their own schedule rather than just during the manufacturer's promotional periods.

Point-of-purchase displays

Point-of-purchase (POP) displays are *in-store advertising displays featuring a product.* If the POP materials are properly integrated, they have the same look and feel as the brand's other advertising and reinforce the brand positioning. Retailers sometimes refer to *in-store promotion activities* as **merchandising**.

It is estimated that marketers spend just slightly less on POP materials than on consumer magazine advertising. Merchandising and POP materials provided by manufacturers (or for franchised stores by corporate headquarters) give the retailer ready-made, professionally designed brand messages. These materials include banners, signs, window posters, counter stands, floor stands, TV monitors, audiotapes for playing over the store's public-address system, shelf signs, end-cap (end-of-aisle) displays, and special display racks. Retail chains typically create many of their own merchandising materials.

The greatest strength of merchandising and POP displays is that they direct attention to a brand at the point of sale. In doing so, they increase customer consideration, positively affecting sales, especially for impulse items. Most important, they can nudge customers from a state of interest or desire to action—making a purchase. One study reported that in-store promotion supported by POP materials increased sales by approximately one-third. In another case, where POP materials were used to support a candy and gum promotion, sales increased nearly 400 per cent in comparison with stores in which the POP display was not used.[5] POP displays can affect sales in all product categories but are especially powerful when used for impulse items.

The second most important strength of these MC functions is that they integrate the out-of-store MC messages that customers have been exposed to and the in-store shopping experience.

It is not uncommon to find big carton soccer players promoting the brands they endorse in supermarkets.

Because display materials can significantly affect sales and are relatively inexpensive to use, most brands prepare them. Consequently, retailers are inundated with them and are forced to be selective. Many retailers are so pressed for time and personnel that roughly half of the promotional materials remain in the stock room, unused and unassembled. Also, because a POP display is place-based—it generally appears in only one location—customers must come to or walk past it in order to be exposed to it. It is estimated that in drugstores and discount stores, only about 20 per cent of store visitors browse most of the aisles.

Integrating promotion strategies

The strategic challenge is to come up with a mix of promotional ideas that minimizes costs to the manufacturer but maximizes support for the retailer. The right mix differs for each retail chain and can be arrived at only by having in-depth knowledge of a retailer's business. The way to determine the right mix is to look at what allowances will best help retailers' meet their objectives, what competitors are offering, what the company can afford, and how retailers have responded to various promotional offers in the past.

One of the first strategic decisions a company must make is how much of its sales volume will be sold on promotion. A brand is either off or on promotion. **On promotion** means *for sale at a reduced price through incentives offered to channel members.* Generally, premium-priced brands are on promotion less than low-cost brands, which sell primarily on price.

Consumer sales promotions are pull strategies because they create consumer demand and thereby "pull" the product through the distribution channel. Push strategies use marketing communication to motivate the trade to buy and make extra efforts to resell products. These efforts thus "push" products through the distribution channels by giving special incentives to get products on retailers' shelves and included in retailers' advertising, special displays, and other in-store merchandising activities.

Most sales-promotion programmes integrate push and pull strategies, using both consumer and trade promotions. The challenge is to integrate both in regards to timing and theme. For example, when Procter & Gamble and other packaged-goods companies introduce a new or improved product, trade-promotion (push) offers precede consumer-promotion (pull) offers such as coupons. This helps ensure that products will be on the shelves when the consumer promotion takes place.

Although push and pull are most frequently discussed in relation to consumer packaged goods, these strategies are also used in selling B2B, service, and considered-purchase products (durable goods). In the case of B2B, often the end users of products are not the same as those who make the buying decisions. Hence, the users become the consumers, and the buyers become the "retailers". Having an integrated promotion programme designed for both can be strategically sound. Buyers can be given certain incentives for buying, and end users can be given incentives to try new or improved brands or to attend training sessions so that their use of the brand will be more satisfying and productive.

The essence of integrating promotion strategies is to realize that both trade promotions and consumer promotions give incentives for the act of actually purchasing products. These acts are by definition consecutive: first, the retailer has to buy the product from the manufacturer; then the consumer buys the product from the retailer. Timing is therefore of utmost importance in designing an integrated promotion strategy, much more so than in the case of MC activities that are directed to building a brand. After all, brands have no expiration date, yet products do.

A final note: the necessity of integration

Today's customers, both consumer and B2B, are extremely value conscious. Therefore, when a brand has a tangible added value (cents off, a premium, a rebate), it helps call attention to the brand and also provides an extra reason to choose that brand. But two major limitations of sales promotions have to be recognized. First, promotions offer tangible value, but it is easy for competitors to add larger values. Second, promotions only work at the moment of purchase; apart from leading to a product experience there is no lasting effect in the sense of building the brand.

This does not limit the effectiveness of sales promotions, however. Yet, it does place an extra challenge to make sales promotions an effective tool in applying integrated marketing communications to build brands. Focusing too much on promotions alone can even hurt the brand. Further, promotional experts can put a lot of creativity in aligning the promotional effort with the brand positioning. In short, sales promotions, perhaps more explicitly than any other MC function, need an integrative approach.

🔑 Key terms

authorize a brand Agree to carry a brand.

break-even analysis A process used to evaluate a plan's costs versus the revenue it generates.

buy-back allowance A payment to buy back the current stock of a brand and replace it with a featured new product.

buyer A person who purchases products for resale and selects which manufacturers' promotions to use.

channel marketing An integrated process that combines personal selling, trade promotions, and co-marketing programmes to build relationships with retailers and other members of the distribution channel.

collectables Items of which consumers enjoy having two or more.

consumables Products that have a one-time use.

contest A brand-sponsored competition that requires some form of skill and effort.

co-operative (co-op) advertising allowances A certain percentage of everything a retailer buys is put into a special "co-op" fund.

coupon A certificate with a stated price reduction on a specified item.

dealer contests Competitions awarding dealers special prizes and gifts when sales reach a predetermined volume or a stated percentage increase on last year's sales.

dealer loader A high-value premium given to a retailer in exchange for the purchase of a special product assortment or a specified monetary volume.

freestanding inserts (FSIs) Newspaper supplements that contain ads, most with coupons.

game A sales-promotion tool that has the chance element of a sweepstake but is conducted over a longer time.

in-store demonstrations Hiring a person to hand out product samples in-store.

loyalty (or frequency) marketing Using promotions specifically designed for customer retention.

merchandising In-store promotion activities.

off-invoice allowance A reduction in the wholesale price, with no restrictions, for a limited period.

off-shelf display allowance A price reduction for locating an additional quantity of a brand in a high-traffic area such as the end of an aisle.

on promotion For sale at a reduced price through incentives offered to channel members.

pay-out planning *see* break-even analysis.

performance allowances Price reductions given to retailers in exchange for the retailer agreeing to feature the brand in its advertising or in other promotional programmes.

point-of-purchase (POP) displays In-store advertising displays featuring a product.

premium An item offered free or at a bargain price to reward some type of behaviour such as buying, sampling, or testing.

pull strategy The use of incentives to motivate end users to purchase a brand and thus pressure retailers to stock that brand.

push strategy The use of incentives to motivate the buying and reselling of products.

rebates A type of price reduction.

sales promotion An MC function that offers a tangible added value designed to motivate and accelerate a response.

sampling Offering prospects the opportunity to try a product before making a buying decision.

shipper displays Specially designed shipping cartons that when opened become display units complete with signage and a quantity of products ready for sale.

slotting allowance A one-time, up-front payment for agreeing to stock a product.

specialities Items given free to customers and other stakeholders to help keep a brand's name top-of-mind.

sweepstake A form of sales promotion that offers prizes based on a chance drawing of entrants' names.

trade promotions Discounts and premiums offered to retailers in exchange for their promotional support.

Check the key points

Key point 1: Consumer sales promotion

a Why is sales promotion referred to as a sales accelerator? Give examples of how sales promotion might work at different points in a consumer's brand decision making.

b List at least three objectives that you might have in designing a consumer sales promotion programme.

c Define *sales promotion*. Explain how sales promotion adds value to a brand offering.

d How do coupons and rebates differ?

e   How do sweepstakes and contests differ? Find an example of one or the other, and explain how it works.

f   How do specialities deliver brand-reminder messages?

Key point 2: How consumer sales promotion works

a   What are the key strengths and limitations of consumer sales promotions?

b   Explain how cross-promotions and tie-ins work. Why are they used?

c   Find a cross-promotion involving a movie. Explain why the two brands are in partnership and what they gain from the partnership. In your estimate, is the partnership effective?

d   How do loyalty programmes work? How do sales promotions contribute to loyalty?

Key point 3: Trade promotion's objectives, strategies, and practices

a   How do push and pull strategies differ? Explain how they should be co-ordinated to be most effective.

b   In what way is channel marketing engaged in creating a push strategy?

c   Explain the main objectives of trade promotions.

d   What is co-op advertising? How does it work?

e   In addition to co-op advertising allowances, explain four other types of allowances used in trade-promotion programmes.

f   What is a slotting allowance? Why do slotting allowances complicate marketing strategies?

g   Explain how price promotions are co-ordinated between a marketer and a retailer.

Chapter Challenge

Writing assignment

Introduce yourself to the manager of a local store, and ask his or her permission to do an MC analysis of the store's promotional activities. Then walk through the store and analyse the use of sales promotions and design. Is a distinctive image and personality presented in these materials and activities? What would you recommend to help the store tighten up its promotional programme and create even greater impact?

Presentation assignment

Collect information about special promotions used by one of the major fast-food chains such as McDonald's, Burger King, or KFC. Explain the objectives of the promotion, how it was set up, and how it worked. Describe all the materials, events, and other MC supporting efforts. Prepare a presentation for your class that summarizes your analysis.

Internet assignment

Check the music section of Amazon.com and the CDnow website. Identify and compare the sales-promotion efforts at both sites. Which one is more effective in its use of consumer sales promotions? Explain why it is so effective.

Notes

[1] *The Art of Sales Promotion, Promotion* (New York: Sibel/Mohr, 1981).

[2] Michelle Slatalla, "Online Shopper: A Path to Redemption (Limited Time Offer)", *New York Times*, 21 June 2001, www.newyorktimes.com.

[3] "The Test Bait", *Brandweek*, 30 March 1998, p. 27.

[4] Sally Beatty, "Block That Spry!" *Wall Street Journal*, 16 December 2002, p. B1.

[5] Ann Mack, "Choose Me", *Brandweek*, 10 April 2000, p. 106.

[6] Peter Breen, "Promotion Trends 2000", www.promomagazine.com/content/report/2000.

[7] Quoted ibid.

Further reading

Bridges, Eileen, Richard A. Briesch and Chi Kin (Bennett) Yim (2006) "Effects of prior brand usage and promotion on consumer promotional response", *Journal of Retailing*, Vol. 82–4, pp. 295–307.

Bruce, Norris, Preyas S. Desai and Richard Staelin (2005) "The Better They Are, the More They Give: Trade Promotions of Consumer Durables", *Journal of Marketing Research*, Vol. 42–1, pp. 54–66.

Chaudhuri, Arjun and Morris B. Holbrook (2001) "The chain of effects from Brand Trust and Brand Affect to Brand Performance: The Role of Brand Loyalty", *Journal of Marketing*, Vol. 65–2, pp. 81–93.

Darke, Peter R. and Cindy M. Y. Chung (2005) "Effects of pricing and promotion on consumer perceptions: it depends on how you frame it", *Journal of Retailing*, Vol. 81–1, pp. 35–47.

d'Astous, Alain and Valérie Landreville (2003) "An experimental investigation of factors affecting consumers' perceptions of sales promotions", *European Journal of Marketing*, Vol. 37–11/12, pp. 1746–61.

DelVecchio, Devon, David H. Henard and Traci H. Freling (2006) "The effect of sales promotion on post-promotion brand preference: A meta-analysis", *Journal of Retailing* Vol. 82–3, pp. 203–13.

Garretson, Judith A. and Scot Burton (2003) "Highly Coupon and Sale Prone Consumers: Benefits Beyond Price Savings", *Journal of Advertising Research*, Vol. 43–2, pp. 162–72.

Palazón-Vidal, Mariola and Elena Delgado-Ballester (2005) "Sales promotions effects on consumer-based brand equity", *International Journal of Market Research*, Vol. 47–2, pp. 179–204.

Simpson, Lisa S. (2006) "Enhancing food promotion in the supermarket industry: A framework for sales promotion success", *International Journal of Advertising*, Vol. 25–2, pp. 223–45.

Whyte, Randall (2004) "Frequent flyer programmes: Is it a relationship, or do the schemes create spurious loyalty?", *Journal of Targeting, Measurement and Analysis for Marketing*, Vol. 12–3, pp. 269–80.

Personal selling

CHAPTER PERSPECTIVE
Lessons from high-powered salespeople

When you look back through history, you see many significant changes brought about by individuals such as social activists Mahatma Gandhi, Lech Walesa, and Martin Luther King Jr.; spiritual leaders such as Mother Teresa; and political leaders such as Charles de Gaulle, Nelson Mandela, and Winston Churchill. All of these individuals were great communicators who knew how to motivate others and change behaviour. In the highest sense, they were doing "personal selling".

Some historians might say that calling these historical figures "salespeople" is insulting because they "sold" ideas rather than goods and services. Nevertheless, selling an idea—getting volunteers, votes and donations—is a form of high-powered personal sales. It is personal because the success of the sales effort often depends on personal one-to-one contact, and such efforts are almost always enhanced by an individual's integrity, credibility and passion.

Unfortunately, over the years the personal selling of goods and services has become associated with manipulation and high-pressure tactics. Although some people still use these practices, today's professional salesperson usually realizes that partnering with customers and prospects in a way that creates a win–win situation is the most effective personal selling strategy.

Although the historical figures mentioned above didn't "sell" for financial gain (as most salespeople do), their success stemmed from their passion for what they believed in, their ability to understand their audiences, and their ability to communicate and persuade. That passion and those abilities lead to the successful selling of goods and services, as well as causes.

Avon's Mark mixes brains and beauty

"Ding Dong! Avon Calling." Avon's famous slogan is now reaching a new and younger audience. The world's largest personal seller of beauty products, Avon, has long been identified with middle-age women and homemakers. Avon's newest MC objective, however, is to tap into the booming market of younger women and teens with a new line of "Mark" makeup.

The Mark line—marketed separately from the regular Avon line to maintain the Avon brand for its loyal customers—strives for a hip, modern image, one that can compete with and appear more sophisticated than Cover Girl. The line is priced a little higher than the regular Avon products but is still competitive with drugstore brands. The name Mark refers to the brand's position as a product designed to help young women "make their mark" in the world. In addition to cosmetics and skin-care products, the line includes bath and body products, fragrances, fashion jewellery, and accessories in sophisticated packaging.

Avon's biggest problem in reaching this target audience is its own dated image, associated with mum and grandma, which is a real turn-off for hip young teens. Indeed, the Mark line might not be able to escape the image of its famous parent brand.

The Mark education

To sell Mark and educate a new generation of sales representatives, Avon has created a new personal selling programme for young women ages 16 to 24. Partnering with the University of Phoenix in Arizona, USA, Avon has integrated an innovative sales force training programme into the launch of the Mark line. New Avon salespeople who complete an online sales training course will receive college credit from the UoP, which specializes in providing practical education for working adults. By positioning Mark as an educational experience, Avon helps to allay parents' concerns about their daughters abandoning their studies in order to "play around with makeup".

Avon says 13 000 young women initially contacted the company about enrolling in the Mark sales training programme. The company hopes eventually to enroll some 500 000 young sales reps in the United States. About 17 million young women in the United States are in that 16- to 24-year-old demographic, and Avon's research has found they spend more than $24 billion annually on beauty-related products.

Avon's research has also found that a typical Mark representative has an average of 13 to 21 young women friends. That means the immediate target audience through the direct-selling channel for the first year would be up to 10 million.

Mark's selling tools

The primary MC tool is the *meet mark* catalogue, with graphics, format, and magazine-style articles designed to reflect the brand's spirited and goal-oriented personality. Like the traditional "Avon ladies", Mark sales representatives hand out catalogues when they make a sales call, rather than mailing them. Avon publishes some 10 million of the large-format catalogues in English and Spanish every six weeks. This makes *meet mark*, described as a "megalog",

IMC in Action

the largest publication reaching this young female audience. In comparison, *Seventeen*, the biggest US magazine aimed at teens, reaches only 2.4 million.

Avon hopes its new sales force will sell the products among groups of friends at slumber parties and other informal gatherings. Beauty rituals such as shopping and learning how to apply cosmetics have long been an important way that teenage girls relate to one another. Avon believes the allure of the products, plus the fun of the parties, will make selling Mark a more attractive opportunity for female teenagers than working behind a fast-food counter. Said Deborah Fine, the former publisher of *Glamour* magazine, who was tapped by Avon to launch the Mark line and run the new Avon Future division, "It's lip gloss with an earnings opportunity."

The Mark line will be supported not only by personal sales calls but by advertising that will run on youth networks including MTV and in beauty magazines such as *Allure*. Avon is also creating partnership programmes with automakers and telecommunication and entertainment companies that will distribute samples and advertise in the Mark catalogue. For other forms of interactivity, the effort is facilitated by a freephone number and a website (www.meetmark.com).

An integrated recruitment campaign targeted at young women at colleges, high schools, shopping malls, and other youth-oriented venues was used to recruit Mark's initial salesforce. In addition to events, the recruitment effort used advertising and other forms of direct marketing to young women. Mark representatives also receive incentives for recruiting other young women.

Mark's vision

Deborah Fine explains that "Our vision for Mark is to provide young women with an engaging product line, a direct-selling opportunity, and a unique brand experience that engages them in a world of community, participation, and empowerment." The phrase "Meet Mark" will be the invitation to both buyers and sellers to enter this new world of beauty and opportunity.

Mark has another educational mission: to teach financial responsibility to the young businesswomen. Instead of buying the product line on credit in advance of sales, as regular Avon salespeople do, Mark representatives will be encouraged to sell the products and solicit the money from friends in advance. They then place their orders online, using their personal credit cards; there won't be extended credit. Avon says the arrangement is intended to keep the process simple; however, it is also designed to teach account balancing and to prevent novices from getting into trouble by ordering more products than they can sell.

The Mark line will eventually join the regular Avon product line as part of Avon's global effort. Avon is marketed in 143 countries through 3.5 million independent sales representatives who produce approximately $6 billion in annual revenues. Andrea Jung, Avon CEO, said, "Around the world, the name 'Avon' stands for aspiration and empowerment. We look forward to engaging young women on a global scale with the Avon earnings opportunity." The effort also will take this innovative integration of education and sales force training around the world.

Sources:

"*Mark Is What You Make It*", Avon Mark website, www.meetmark.com

Sally Beatty, "*Avon Tries Knocking on Dorm Doors*", Wall Street Journal, *28 March 2003, p. B2*

"*Avon Makes Its Mark*", Fashion Windows, *30 March 2003, www.fashionwindows.com/beauty/2003B/ avon.asp*

"*Avon Unveils New Brand, Strategy for Global Business Reaching Young Women*", *17 October 2002,* News.Com

"*Avon Creates Line It Hopes Teens Will Buy and Sell*", *www.cnet.com/investor/news/newsitem/0-9900-1028-20550771-0.html*

Business, *October 2002, www.responservice.com/archives/oct2002_issue2/business/internat.htm.*

Personal selling: the primary two-way marketing communication function

Everyone does personal selling. Children sell lemonade or lottery tickets for their sports clubs. Students sell their used books and yearbook ads. Doctors "sell" exercise and diet programmes to overweight patients. Lawyers "sell" briefs to sceptical judges. The fact is, **personal selling** is *person-to-person interactive communication used to ultimately persuade*. It is the oldest marketing communication function.

The role of personal selling varies by type of business and industry, by the nature of the product or service, and by the business strategy. In B2B product categories, personal selling is one of the most important communication functions. In B2C business, it is often the primary MC function used for expensive goods and services such as cars, insurance, real estate, and mortgages. Personal selling is also used in some retail stores, such as in department stores' cosmetic departments.

Total spending on personal selling is estimated to be close to the amount spent for all media advertising.[1] Personal selling is thus not the remaining element to complete the story of traditional communication functions. On the contrary, because personal selling is such an important function, salespeople are often some of the highest-paid employees in a company.

Today's professional salesperson is supported by information technology and the understanding that creating a good relationship will result in more sales than will the manipulative, hard-sell techniques of the past. Two-way communication, the essence of personal selling, is used to uncover customers' needs and wants and address misunderstandings and objections. In addition, good personal selling today provides product expertise and follow-up service to a transaction and, most important, helps customers to be more successful—that is, it creates value for them. As Table 14-1 shows, personal selling has evolved over the years from focusing on persuasion to creating value through partnering with customers.

Professional salespeople represent one aspect of a total marketing communication organization, and they therefore must conduct themselves in a way that is strategically consistent with all the other brand messages. Where personal selling is used extensively, the salesperson *is* the company in the eyes of customers and prospects. That puts personal selling on high stakes. This function has very high impact, for better or worse. This impact extends beyond the single one-to-one contact in which the sale is closed—or not. The impact of this face of the brand remains long after with the customer. This very customer will become a credible source of mouth-to-mouth communications, one of the most important unexpected touch points for prospective customers.

	Sales era, before 1960	Marketing era, 1960–1990	Partnering era, after 1990
Communication objective	Making transactions	Satisfying needs	Building relationships
Communication strategy	Persuade	Solve problem	Create value

Table 14-1 Evolution of personal selling
Source: Barton Weitz, Stephen Castleberry, and John Tanner, *Selling* (Burr Ridge, IL: McGraw-Hill/Irwin, 1995), p. 12. Reprinted by permission from The McGraw-Hill Companies.

How personal selling works

Personal selling's primary role is customizing brand messages. Generally speaking, MC functions such as advertising, events and sponsorships, and brand publicity can create brand awareness and knowledge. But personal selling, integrated into the MC mix, can customize brand messages on a customer-by-customer basis.

In personal selling, a salesperson asks many questions of a prospective customer in an effort to understand how a product could benefit that customer. During the dialogue, the salesperson can gauge how the customer is reacting to a product offering. If there are misunderstandings, the salesperson can immediately clear them up. If the prospect does not like certain aspects of the product offering (price, credit terms, delivery schedule), the salesperson can address these concerns and perhaps negotiate a solution. This two-way interaction—and the instant customer gratification it can bring—is what makes personal selling the most powerful MC function a company can use.

Acquiring new customers

Average annual customer turnover rates are approximately 15 to 20 per cent, so salespeople must work constantly to acquire new customers to replace those lost. Acquiring new customers at a faster rate than the rate at which current ones leave the brand is one way to increase overall sales. The problem with acquisition, however, is that more time must be spent *locating potential new customers* (or prospects) (i.e. prospecting) than actually making the sale. Sometimes a salesperson may rely on a list (members of organizations, for example). Other marketing communication efforts, such as direct response or advertising, may be used to locate prospects. Customers are motivated to raise their hands as being in the market for a product and to contact the company in some way. Such contacts are transferred into a sales lead: *a person or organization identified as being a prospect—someone able to benefit from the brand being sold.*

However, in many situations prospective customers do not contact the company. Instead, the salesperson must contact them—either acting on some information that identifies individuals as prospects or making contact simply because people's names appear on some list. That is what door-to-door salespeople do when they sell a product or service in a neighbourhood, and it is what telemarketers do when they make their phone calls. *A sales call to a prospect who is not known by the sales rep and has not expressed any particular interest in the company or brand* is known as a cold call. Cold-calling is one of the most difficult forms of personal selling because there is no reason to believe the prospect is in the market for the product and the prospect may show resentment or hostility because of the intrusion.

Retaining current customers

A company's current customers must not be taken for granted. Just because they have been buying from a company for years is no guarantee they will buy from the company next week. As noted, from 15 to 20 per cent of customers "turn over" each year—that is, they leave one brand for another.

Unfortunately, many businesses overemphasize acquiring new customers at the expense of servicing current ones. Marketing communication agencies themselves do this. Top managers—those most responsible for building their agencies—often spend the major part of their time doing personal selling to get new accounts. Once they have sold a company on the idea of becoming a client, however, they assign other people in the agency to work with the new client, and they (top managers) go off to do more personal selling. (They are likely to work on a current account only when the client is dissatisfied and threatening to switch agencies.)

Because customer retention (as opposed to customer acquisition) is at the heart of a brand relationship, salespeople must do things that not only create but also maintain the relationship. A salesperson's number-one personal objective should be to create trust. He or she accomplishes this by demonstrating dependability, competence, a customer orientation, honesty, and likeability.[2] Some sales managers say that current customers should always be treated as new customers—receiving the same level of attention and care as prospects.

As in all areas of IMC, salespeople must create and manage customers' expectations—expectations not only of product performance but of all the services in support of a brand. After closing a sale, the salesperson should make sure the product arrives on time, that invoicing is properly handled, and that the customer knows how to use the product in the proper way. In B2B situations, the salesperson should be analysing the customer's business to see in what ways the brand can further improve the customer's processes, sales, and profit.

Salespeople are often invaluable information resources to their clients. Because they know how other companies use their products, salespeople have a much broader perspective on the product's applications than any single customer can have. They can add value by not letting customers repeat mistakes made by other customers, as well as by sharing ideas that work (as long as those ideas are not proprietary).

Personal selling objectives

You might think that when it comes to setting objectives for personal selling, the main objective would be quite simple: to sell all that you can. After all, the bottom line of personal selling is sales. Though hard to argue with, this objective does not give much direction from a communication standpoint to help ensure that the selling effort is focused and cost-effective. In personal selling as in every other MC function, specific objectives are needed that reflect the salesperson's efforts at every step in the selling process, and these objectives should be driven by a SWOT analysis (Chapter 5).

A brand's personal selling objectives for a newly introduced sub-brand for example are:

- To broaden the brand's market by reaching a new target group.
- To create an appropriate brand identity for the new sub-brand line.
- To sign up a core group of sales reps that relate to the target group.
- To identify prospective customers (and additional sales staff) from within the sales representatives' pool of friends.

Other typical and more measurable objectives for personal selling are:

- To make sales calls on x number of prospective customers each month.
- To identify y qualified sales leads.
- To call on z current customers each month.
- To increase current customers' business by 5 per cent.
- To have product featured in major retail accounts' advertising four times a year.
- To have each account (retailer) that carries the brand, carry at least three or more varieties.
- To handle all incoming complaints within three working days.

Personal selling strategies

One of the most successful personal selling strategies is *helping customers solve problems or take advantage of opportunities*, which is called solution selling or enterprise selling. Too often, salespeople—by nature outgoing, gregarious, and aggressive—become so focused on making a sale that all they talk about is their product's features and benefits. The best salespeople, however, motivate prospects to talk about their businesses and the problems they are having or the opportunities they have not yet been able to take advantage of. Needs assessment, *inquiring about how a business operates*, accomplishes this.

The solution approach to selling focuses on the customer's needs and problems, then shows how a company's product can meet those needs and provide a solution for those problems. In high-tech industries, solution selling often involves integrating the sales and engineering functions to come up with new systems or customizing software to fit the customer's needs.

Another selling strategy is to work with prospects and customers as business partners. A partnering strategy requires that salespeople learn as much about their customers' businesses as they know about their own. A good example of this was Ed, a salesperson with whom the second author once worked. Ed was a salesman for a processed meat company and was responsible for selling to a division of Kroger. He often frustrated the company's marketing department because he refused to present all of the promotions that the department developed. He presented some, but not every one, because he understood Kroger's needs and objectives so well that he knew what was good for Kroger and what was not. He didn't waste the chain's (or his own) time by trying to sell products and promotions that didn't fit Kroger's business plan. As a result, Kroger trusted Ed so much that he was often invited to review *competitive presentations* being made to Kroger. He had developed a partnering relationship based on trust. In the end, Ed was one of the top salespeople in the company.

A partnership starts with a working relationship between senior managers on both the marketer's and the retailer's sides. Dedicated retail marketing teams (located close to key retail accounts in the field) become focused on understanding and meeting the marketing objectives, strategies, and challenges of these key retail accounts. Major marketers, such as Unilever, Procter & Gamble, G-star, and Adidas, operate this way.

Often a field marketing team supports the sales force by developing marketing communication plans tailored specifically for major retailer customers. These plans include account-specific sales and communication objectives as well as strategies for product mix, on-floor merchandising and POP displays, retail advertising, and tie-in events between the manufacturer and the retail chain.

Good salespeople function as a liaison between a company and its customers. Often they sell as hard inside their own company as they do outside, to convince their company to make product and process changes that would best serve their customers. Evidence of such customer focus may result in company executives asking salespeople, "Who are you working for, us or the customer?" The correct answer is "Both".

An important relationship strategy in the sales area, particularly in B2B product categories, is entertainment. This is another instance in which personal selling and trade promotions come together. In addition to sales representatives taking customers to dinner, to sporting events, and on other outings, many large companies have country houses and yachts where customers and prospects are entertained. In some industries such as pharmaceuticals these practices have become excessive, and in response to public concerns have been cut back drastically.

As discussed in more detail in Chapter 11, one reason why companies sponsor motor racing, golf and tennis tournaments, and other events is that these provide a special entertainment opportunity to reward good customers and motivate prospects to become customers. Companies that are sponsors can take customers behind the scenes of these events to meet the celebrities, which is a special privilege.

An increasingly important personal selling strategy involves knowing a customer's history of interactions with a company. The use of this strategy is greatly enhanced by technology—specifically by customer relationship management (CRM) software.

Customer relationship management and personal selling

One of the technologies widely used by sales forces is customer relationship management. CRM is helpful in personal selling in two specific areas. First, it provides individual salespeople with an automated system for organizing sales leads, developing sales presentations, making sales presentations, processing orders, and recording customers' concerns and agreed-upon next steps. Second, having all this information in databases means that it can be easily shared with appropriate departments in the company (production, distribution, marketing, customer service, and accounting) and that customers are *integrated* into the company and customer data are integrated into the MC process. How customers respond to sales offers, their questions and concerns, and what they buy and don't buy are three examples of the valuable information that helps companies communicate with customers.

Because speed is so important in business today, a sale is easily lost if a company spends too much time putting together an offer. Providing salespeople with laptops and modems to access relevant databases can improve the efficiency and effectiveness of the typical sales call significantly. In essence, CRM makes salespeople more productive communicators. A salesperson using CRM can sit in a customer's office with a laptop computer, input that customer's needs, and, with a modem, access company databases to determine product design alternatives, product availability, prices, discounts available based on this customer's past volume, the customer's line of credit, and delivery schedules, among other things. Before leaving the customer's office, the salesperson is able to configure a customized product offering. Being able to do this type of communication quickly and accurately is an added value to customers and therefore a way to be more competitive.

IBM, a major provider of CRM software that provides this capability, has gone so far as to reposition itself as the "ebusiness" company (e-business should not be confused with e-commerce, which is more narrow and relates primarily to online selling). As IBM's ad explains, "ebusiness" integrates many operations.

CRM can also manage customer leads and allow sales force managers to make sure salespeople are doing their jobs. By tracking leads and sales calls, and by keeping customer and prospect profiles complete and up-to-date, CRM enables a company to:[3]

- Know which leads were followed up and when, and what the results were.
- Give the leads that were not followed up to other salespeople, if appropriate.
- Determine why sales were not made (for example, a better competitive offer, dissatisfaction with a brand's current products or services, delivery not soon enough).
- Determine who within the prospect company has influence on the brand decision.
- Keep track of buyers who leave one company and go to another.

A smiling face through the Internet

Imagine the following: the summer vacation is approaching and you are looking for a way to spend your holiday. What would you do? The answer of many people would be that they would go to a travel agency. There, a travel agent would be able to give them a complete overview of holiday options tailored to meet their specific needs. Whether you were looking for a sun holiday in Spain, a safari trip in Africa, or a city break to New York, the travel agent would be able to present you with instant information on any of these trips. Personal selling is the key to this situation; the customer expresses his desires and the travel agent uses her expertise to advise the customer on holiday options that fit the customer's needs. Naturally, the travel agent of course tries to persuade the customer to book the holiday with her agency. Although many people still pursue this strategy for booking their holidays, the number of people booking by phone and through the Internet is growing substantially.

One of the companies that has recognized this trend is Thomson, a tour operator in the UK. Thomson is part of TUI AG, a German enterprise with business divisions in tourism and shipping. The tourism division accounts for 70 per cent of the Group's turnover and has established itself as Europe's market leader in the tourism sector, covering the entire travel-chain from bookings over organizations, to flights and accommodation. The Group comprises five sectors with 3200 group-owned travel agencies, 70 tour operation brands, 120 aircraft, 35 agencies and 279 hotels all over the world. One of these sectors is Northern Europe, the sector of which Thomson is a part.

In 2005 Thomson sold 25 per cent of its holidays online, at the expense of bookings through travel agencies and call centres. In response to this change in customer preference to book holidays via means other than travel agencies, Thomson has set its strategy towards online sales. This is in line with the strategic direction of the parent company TUI, which is targeting direct sales through the Internet, and Web-enabled booking through call centres. Expectations are that the percentage of online bookings will grow to 50 per cent of total bookings before 2009, and Thomson thus recognizes that the Internet is the channel for future growth. Thomson is prepared to go where the customer wants to go, to be able to deliver a holiday experience that elicits a smile, just like their logo.

However, Thomson does not want the role of the travel agents to become obsolete. Instead travel agents are given a different role. Thomson projects that agents will move away from holiday sales, offering instead a greater variety of travel-related products, including foreign language packages, holiday music CDs, digital photo processing, and house-sitting services. Thomson beliefs that there will be a role for travel agents, as long as they are able to create an exciting shopping experience in convenient locations and offer a high level of expertise.

Think about it

Will call centres and the Internet completely replace travel agents in the future? Do you think there will still be a role for travel agents if they move away from holiday sales to offering a wider variety of travel-related products?

Sources:

Prior, L., and L. Huxley, (2003) "Call centres will supplant agents", Travel Trade Gazette UK & Ireland, *Issue 2573 p. 3.*

Searle, R. (2005) "Thomson expects web sales to soar", Travel Trade Gazette UK & Ireland, *Issue 2660, p. 9.*

www.tui-group.com/

The personal selling process

Personal selling, whether to acquire new customers or to sell additional products to current customers, involves generating and qualifying leads, making sales calls, identifying and responding to objections, closing the sale, and following up to build and maintain the customer relationship.

Generating and qualifying leads

Through generating and qualifying sales leads, a personal selling operation can segment and target its market. Sales leads may come from a company's direct-response advertising or from publicity about the company or its brands. They include individuals who call in for information or return a business reply card from a direct-mail piece or a "bingo" card from a trade or special-interest magazine. Leads may also come from referrals—satisfied customers, employees, even competitors who feel a prospect is either too big or too small for them to handle.

When Hewlett-Packard (HP) wanted to motivate corporate customers to upgrade their equipment, the company segmented them by the volume of their previous purchases and then by the job description of the buyers for each of the companies. Specialized mailings were sent to people in each segment, who were then contacted by phone. The calls determined who was most likely to upgrade; those leads were sent to regional sales offices for personal follow-up.

Another way to generate leads is by getting prospects to self-select. When a customer takes the initiative in expressing interest in a product and providing profile information, that behaviour can be highly predictive of future buying, as shown in Table 14-2. Sending brand messages by means of mass media and niche media motivates those interested to identify themselves. Offering premiums can encourage prospects to provide profile information so that a salesperson can decide whether they are *true* prospects.

Managing lead generation sometimes requires mediating the interaction of salespeople and marketing departments, because these two groups often disagree about leads.[4] Marketing often sees a lead as anyone who enquires about the product, while sales defines a lead as someone ready to buy. Marketing people complain that salespeople don't follow up on their leads, and salespeople reply that many marketing-generated leads are not worth following up. The heart of the problem is that each department wants the other to *qualify* the leads (see Table 14-2).

According to research:

60 per cent of all enquirers purchase something within a year.

20 per cent of enquirers have an immediate need.

10 per cent are hot leads.

60 per cent of enquirers also contact your competitors.

50 per cent of all new business starts as an enquiry.

But most companies do not take advantage of these enquiries:

20 per cent of enquirers never receive information.

40 per cent of enquirers receive information too late to use it.

70 per cent of enquirers are never contacted by a sales representative.

Table 14-2 Making strategic use of customer contacts

Source: Arthur M. Hughes, *The Complete Database Marketer* (Burr Ridge, IL: McGraw-Hill/Irwin, 1996), p. 390. Reprinted with permission from The McGraw-Hill Companies.

> " Our conversion-to-lead ratio was extraordinarily high because we were talking to the right people with the right message.[5]
>
> *An HP marketing specialist* "

Once leads are generated, they need to be qualified to determine whether they are genuine prospects. **Qualified leads** are *prospects who seem most likely to buy because of some information that is known about them.* Qualified leads are persons who (1) have a real need or opportunity that the brand can address, (2) have the ability to pay for the good or service, (3) have the authority to buy, and (4) are approachable. A company or person who buys infrequently or demands an unreasonably high level of service may not be a good lead. In the case of estate planning, for example, marketers try to qualify incoming leads by including in the invitation to a seminar a line such as "If your household income is more than 125 000 euro a year, you can benefit from estate planning." They hope that people who may think they want or need estate planning but do not have the wealth to justify it will not waste the time of the company offering the seminar. Not all products are for all people, and potential customers should be assisted in deciding whether a particular product or brand is for them.

Qualifying sales leads is so important because the cost of a personal sales call exceeds the cost of most other company-initiated brand contacts. Although the number varies greatly by product category, the average B2B sales call costs about 500 euros. This figure includes the costs of getting to and from each customer (hotel, meals, entertainment, and transportation) plus salary and commission. In some product categories, such as local media sales, a salesperson can visit half a dozen customers a day, making the average cost per call about 50 euro. By contrast, a person selling airport radar systems may travel halfway around the world to make one sales call, which could cost the company 10 000 euro. Because the average sales call is so much more costly than using advertising or even direct-response marketing media, it is seldom cost-effective for salespeople to make cold calls. Even when a company has a new product, the company's current customers—who are usually the first group of prospects because they already know the company—must be qualified in order to avoid wasting personal selling time.

In B2B marketing, qualifying leads is especially important. The fact that it takes between three and seven personal sales contacts before a major B2B sale is made[6] means a salesperson may have to make several expensive sales calls before closing a deal. The higher the quality of a lead is, the fewer the visits that are required before a prospect responds. The quicker the response rate, the lower is the cost per sale.

Making the sales call

The sales call occurs when the sale presentation is made. The extent and formality of this presentation varies greatly, depending on the offer itself and the relationship between the salesperson and the prospect. Sales presentations can occur during a visit to a prospect's home or office, or during a group meeting, such as the legendary Tupperware parties (see colour insert C10). Generally speaking, the more expensive the product offer, the lengthier and more formal the presentation will be.

In some situations, personal sales calls are made by phone by a company's inside sales force. (This type of selling is different from telemarketing, explained in the next chapter, because these are not cold calls.) **Inside sales** are *salespeople who regularly call on accounts whose average size orders are not large enough to cost-justify an in-person sales call.* The initial sales call on these accounts may be made by a personal sales rep, or the prospect may respond to an ad or direct-mail piece. The follow-up calls are made by the inside sales department. In some cases members of an inside sales force call on the same customers for years and become very good friends although they never meet face-to-face.

Providing current customers and prospects with an appropriate and accurate sales presentation is critical. Successful salespeople script and practise their presentations to make sure they have the key information on the tip of their tongue. Companies often provide sales literature, to help the sales rep make the presentation. Sales literature may include *videos, charts with data and documentation, planning forms to work through with the customer, catalogues, and demonstration materials.* Inside salespeople often refer their customers to the company's website for pictures and other visual demonstrations of a product. Good presentations are interesting, keep the attention of prospective customers, and lead them through their decision process to the point at which they are ready to buy.

In solution selling, the sales representative explains how the brand can help the prospect either solve a problem or take advantage of an opportunity. The presentation should be as much about the prospect as about the brand being sold. All of the details of the offer—such as price, delivery schedule, credit terms, and guarantees—are in the presentation. The end of the formal presentation "asks for the order". Asking for the order means asking the prospect to take action. In most situations, before prospects will agree to make a transaction, they have many questions and objections—reasons for not buying.

Handling objections

If the only thing salespeople had to do was make a presentation and then take an order, they would not be paid very much. Getting a prospect to move through a decision-making process and say "yes" takes a great deal of skill and perseverance. An important skill is getting prospects to voice their objections—that is, to admit the real reason why they are not convinced or why they do not want to buy now—and then responding to the objections. Understanding objections is key to understanding customers. In the best-case scenario, a sales rep learns what the prospect's objections are, is able to satisfactorily address the prospect's objections during the presentation, and goes on to close the sale. In the worst case, a prospect's unknown objections are not addressed, and a sale is lost. A sales rep who has no idea why a prospect did not buy will fail to learn anything valuable that could be passed on to company management or avoided in the next call.

For example, a frequent response to a sales presentation is: "You have a good product and we could really use it, but we just can't afford it now." Good salespeople respond to this type of objection in one of several ways. One way is to offer the prospect credit terms that do not require payment for several months. Another is to point out how the product can reduce costs and therefore pay for itself in *x* number of months. Good salespeople anticipate objections and have answers ready, often in the form of information-filled charts and graphs.

The key in handling objections is to turn them into opportunities. The least a rep has to do in response to an objection is to eliminate it, but this does not lead to an additional reason to buy the product. But turning an objection into another motivator for the sale is making two steps in one. The example of the credit terms is exemplary. Not only is there a solution for a current problem, i.e. not enough resources to buy this product, but by offering reasonable credit terms, a more general problem is likely to be solved: an opportunity is created.

Closing and following up the sale

Once objections have been successfully addressed, the next step is closing the sale, which means *finalizing the terms of the transaction and getting the prospect's agreement to those terms,* followed by issuing a purchase order or signing a contract. Moving a customer to this point of commitment, to actually sign on the dotted line, is the goal of the entire selling process.

Once a sale is made, it is important to keep in contact with customers to make sure all of their expectations have been met. Was the product delivered on time? Was it in good shape? Was the billing correct? Is the customer aware of the next promotional opportunities? Making sure the customer is satisfied requires following up in person or by phone, e-mail, or regular mail.

Some salespeople are reluctant to follow up, believing that doing so is asking for trouble, because when a customer tells them about a problem, the result is extra work for the salesperson. Finding out what went wrong, finding the right people in the company to address the problem, and then making arrangements for the problem to be addressed take time for which a salesperson is not paid anything extra. But avoiding follow-up is a sign of short-sighted thinking. A customer who has a problem that isn't quickly addressed and solved is not likely to remain a customer. Also, follow-ups provide a legitimate excuse for contacting a customer and introducing new products, especially if the customer is satisfied with the first purchase.

Managing the personal selling process

Managing personal selling involves recruiting, training, tracking, compensating, and rewarding sales reps, as well as managing budgets and territory management. How best to integrate personal selling into the company's overall marketing communication programme is also a management concern. Two management issues especially relevant to IMC are (1) how to measure the effects of IMC on sales and (2) how to compensate and reward salespeople. The former interfaces with some of the sales-promotion tools; the latter is similar to spending money on advertising media.

Measuring personal selling efforts

A number of measurements can be used to evaluate personal selling. A *cost per call* is calculated by comparing a salesperson's total costs (salary, commission, expenses) to the number of calls made in a specified period of time (generally one year). A *sales-call-to-close ratio* can be determined by comparing the total number of sales calls made to the number of prospects and customers who actually bought.

Tracking these measurements helps ensure the sales effort is going in the right direction. For example, if the overall company call-to-sale ratio is 5-to-1 this year (meaning five sale calls were made for every sale closed), steps should be taken to reduce that ratio to, say, 4.5-to-1 for the following year. Such ratios can be used to evaluate individual sales representatives, as well. If the company call-to-sale ratio for the average salesperson is 6-to-1, for example, a salesperson with an 11-to-1 ratio should at least be able to explain his or her poor performance. This may well lead to new insights on why the brand performs badly in certain markets, or it may just reveal that this sales rep is simply not doing a good job.

While such sales or outcome-oriented measures are relevant in IMC, other measures are equally important. Some of these behaviour-oriented measures of how well a salesperson performs are (1) the average length of time an individual's accounts have been buying from the company, (2) the average annual sales and profitability of these accounts, and (3) the number of referrals made by these accounts. Clearly these measures are fuelled by the satisfaction of the account with the sales rep performance in meeting the client's needs beyond offering a solution to a specific problem. Because a primary IMC objective is to retain customers, the average customer lifetime should continue to increase if a salesperson is doing a good job. Also, current customers should be motivated to increase the quantity of their purchases from year to year. Finally, customers who have a good relationship with a salesperson and a brand will be more likely to recommend that person and brand to other companies, which means the number of these referrals should be tracked.

Over time, determining how many of a salesperson's customers remain with the company and how many have been lost is relatively easy, as is determining how many sales each salesperson has generated. Sophisticated accounting software can now tell the overall profitability of each salesperson's customers. Using discounts, premiums, and other considerations can make a sale fairly easy, but the best salespeople are those who generate sales without making so many concessions that the company makes little or no profit on the transactions.

Compensation and rewards

Compensation systems are changing in personal selling. Traditionally, compensation was based totally or primarily on sales volume. Some companies still have salespeople working solely on **commission** which is *a percentage of the sales price paid to a salesperson for each transaction*. Often, top salespeople who work on 100 per cent commission are some of the highest-paid people in a company. The problem with commissions being the major compensation factor is that they reward transactions rather than long-term relationships.

To have a customer-relationship focus, companies must balance how they reward salespeople, because people respond to what is measured and rewarded. This is why salespeople are increasingly being evaluated and rewarded not only for sales but also for how long customers have been buying from the company (retention), how much customers are increasing their purchase quantities (customer growth), and how much customers are helped by the salesperson to solve their problems and increase their productivity (customer satisfaction).

Special prizes, such as trips and other high-value premiums, are frequently used to increase sales in the short term. For a new-product introduction, for example, salespeople may receive an extra incentive if 65 per cent or more of their customers buy the new product within the first 90 days of its availability.

In addition to evaluating salespeople according to set objectives, companies nowadays also ask customers to rate the salespeople who call on them. Because the success of personal selling can be so dependent on working with other people in an organization, some companies even ask people in their distribution, accounting, and customer-service departments to rate salespeople. It is critical that the salesperson's performance is consistent with the brand's positioning and reinforces the brand's other marketing communications. What the salesperson says and does will either confirm or contradict the company's other brand messages.

Integrating personal selling and other marketing communication functions

The primary criterion for determining when personal selling should be integrated into the MC mix is whether the margin on each transaction is large enough to cover the high cost of personal selling. Unilever cannot cost-justify having a sales representative sell its Cif and Omo brands to individual consumers because the selling cost would be many times the average purchase price of a few euros. Personal selling is used when a product is complex and the purchase will require assistance to use and maintain the product, such as enterprise software systems, medical imaging devices, and automotive diagnostic equipment sold to auto repair shops. Also, personal selling is integrated into the MC mix when there are a limited number of customers, such as in the beverage can industry, which has only a few dozen major customers (primarily manufacturers of soft drinks and beer).

Personal selling and advertising

In B2C selling, advertising is used by retailers such as car dealers and home furnishing stores to get consumers in the door. These retailers know that the products they sell are major purchases for which advertising can at best only create interest. Most buyers of cars and furniture ask many questions during the information-gathering stage of decision making. Once the prospect is in the store, a salesperson is the best resource for responding to these questions, which can be done while customers closely examine the products being considered.

In B2B selling, advertising's brand awareness and brand knowledge do a certain amount of pre-selling. Advertising can be used to communicate information about the company behind a product as well as key product benefits. Mass media advertising can reach a wide range of prospective customers for far less than it would cost for a salesperson to contact the same number and ask whether they were interested in the brand. Nevertheless, most B2B decision makers have many questions. Complex products, for example, may need to be demonstrated.

Another aspect of advertising that is integrated into the personal selling process is the designing and production of brochures, sales kits, and other materials that salespeople use during sales calls. These sales kits can be anything from a simple set of price sheets, to a fancy glossy binder, to an elaborate box of varied materials. These types of sales kits usually include sections on product selection and pricing, merchandising ideas, retailer advertising aids available, consumer advertising schedules, public relations efforts, consumer promotions, market research, and ways to customize these sales materials for individual retail stores.

Personal selling and public relations

Like advertising, brand publicity in the form of press and video releases can help create brand awareness that makes a salesperson's job easier, as it saves time explaining who the company is and what it stands for. In addition, public relations is especially helpful to the sales force in selling innovative and complex products, particularly when a company's brand is endorsed by a third party such as an industry writer or consultant.

The sales force not only benefits from public relations but also *does* public relations. Salespeople are often the most pervasive public face of the company. Because a salesperson is usually the only person from the company who customers ever see and talk to face-to-face, the salesperson *is the company*. If the salesperson is responsive and helpful, the company is perceived as being responsive and helpful. This is why most companies that provide cars or trucks for their sales force insist that these vehicles be kept clean, because they are constantly seen by thousands of people every day (many different stakeholders).

Personal selling and direct response

Direct response is frequently used to generate leads for sales representatives. It may also be used for follow-up contact with current customers. IBM has embarked on several integrated, database-driven pilot campaigns that have generated three times as many qualified leads as did previous campaigns. A key component of these programmes is asking customers what they are looking for in products and services and how they like to be contacted by the company—by mail, e-mail, phone, fax, brochures, salesperson's visit, or not at all.

Personal selling and sales promotion

A number of sales-promotion tools and techniques can be incorporated into personal selling to strengthen the salesperson's presentation and help close the deal. For example, a sales kit may include free samples, discounts and coupons, or product-related gifts. Trade promotion (Chapter 13) is an important aspect of channel marketing, which relies heavily on personal selling. Finally, sales reps themselves are the target for incentive programmes that are designed to increase their enthusiasm for a product and encourage them to push the product more and sell harder.

Strengths of personal selling

The primary objective of personal selling is building trusting, mutually beneficial relationships. Any brochure or ad can describe the benefits of a brand, but a personal sales call can humanize a brand and a company, particularly when that interaction is supported by CRM.

The greatest strength of personal selling, therefore, is customized two-way communication, which is the ultimate way to integrate a product and its features with customers' wants, needs, and opportunities. Two-way communication is the most powerful form of persuasion—not only to encourage someone to buy but, more important, to encourage that person to remain a customer. By using face-to-face communication, a skilled salesperson can observe a prospect's body language and encourage him or her to express objections. The one-to-one situation facilitates instant feedback to objections (which a good salesperson should anticipate and be prepared to address). Once a relationship is established, motivating sales becomes much easier.

Accountability and measurability, further strengths of personal selling, mean that this aspect of IMC is highly numbers-driven. In most cases, a company can easily measure the sales that each salesperson generates in a specified period. Because most companies use commission-based compensation plans for their sales forces, both companies and salespeople are concerned about how salespeople spend their time and what their selling efforts produce.

Personal selling is the most flexible IMC element. It allows sales messages to be tailored to each customer and prospect, allowing instant changes in a sales presentation as the situation requires. Negotiation is a vital aspect of this flexibility. Personal communication makes it much easier to find the terms that best suit the buyer's needs and to adjust the offer accordingly. If a buyer is primarily concerned with an earlier delivery date, for example, a salesperson may absorb the cost required to meet this date by getting the customer to either buy an additional amount or pay for the merchandise sooner.

Because good salespeople are in constant contact with their customers and know their customers' business, they can collect information and build valuable customer databases. A rich customer database offers vital information to marketing people, allowing them to prepare personalized, targeted messages. Such databases also become very valuable when a customer is assigned to a different salesperson.

Limitations of personal selling

Like all other MC functions, personal selling has some limitations. The most important limitation is its high cost. Maintaining a sales force is costly because it requires not only salaries (or commissions) but also sales call expenses, recruitment, training, and other internal support functions. Because it is basically a one-to-one medium, there are few economies of scale. In fact, two or three salespeople sometimes go to a single important customer's office to make a presentation or make multiple presentations if they represent different product lines. Superficially this looks like an opportunity for combined efforts, but in fact there is a point in this approach as every salesperson represents her own product line, highlighting and selling that single line. Combining efforts runs the risk of offering too limited dedicated information. Yet, it is advisable that salespeople know of each other's efforts to ensure a co-ordinated and integrated communication.

Another limitation is that some salespeople overemphasize making a quick sale and lack the patience to build relationships based on promising long-term leads. A study of 40 000 buyers found that only 11 per cent of those who made purchases did so within three months of their first contact with the company. The study concluded: "It's important to put a relationship marketing programme in place to nurture long-term leads."[7] This limitation, however, is not always the fault of salespeople. Compensation based on commissions fosters the emphasis on transactions at the expense of relationships. Salespeople should be rewarded for generating sales, but when volume is the major portion of their focus, there is a tendency to over-promise in order to make a sale.

The human connection that was described as a strength can also create a dilemma: customers may develop loyalty to salespeople rather than to the company or the brand. As a result, when salespeople change jobs, their customers may move with them. A partial solution to the problem is for the company to maintain a comprehensive database of customer interactions with the company. The database enables a new salesperson to immediately step up and work with each customer intelligently because each customer's history with the company is available. Sometimes, the contracts with salespeople stipulate that when they leave the company, they are not allowed to take their customers with them, but in practice it is often not easy to enforce these terms, in particular when it is the client who takes the initiative to change supplier.

One of the strengths of personal selling is flexibility, but the flip side of flexibility is often strategic inconsistency. When salespeople begin to craft customer-specific sales deals, they may create and deliver brand messages that are at odds with the overall brand strategy. An upmarket, status-brand positioning will not be reinforced if a salesperson continually encourages retailers to run sales.

Just as direct-response advertising is seen as intrusive and often in poor taste, personal selling has developed an image problem over the decades because of so much high-pressure selling and less-than-ethical practices. The "used-car salesman" has become a protopye of the sloppy sales rep that will do almost anything to make the customer buy. Many companies today give salespeople euphemistic titles such as marketing associate, marketing representative, admissions co-ordinator, clinical liaison, professional services representative, or programme manager. The idea is to counteract the rejection associated with the word *salesperson*.

A study of college students in the United States, Britain, and Thailand found that students from these diverse geographical areas all had a very low impression of sales as a career opportunity. Although 72 per cent agreed with the statement "The financial rewards from selling are excellent", 40 per cent said a salesperson's job security is poor. Another sign of the reputation problem comes from an electrical wiring firm that got almost no response to ads in college papers that said, "Looking for entry-level salespeople." When the same company instead ran an ad for marketing people, job applications poured in.[8]

Regardless of the image that personal selling has, this marketing communication function is a huge industry. For many, it offers an entry-level position into marketing; for others, it provides a lifetime career that brings many financial and personal rewards.

A final note: highest cost, greatest impact

Personal selling is the 900-pound gorilla of marketing communication. It costs a lot to feed and care for this beast, but when used for good, its muscle and impact are generally far greater than any of the other MC functions. Integrating personal selling into the MC mix must always be cost-justified, because the cost is significant compared to the cost per sale of all the other ways to reach customers and prospects. When personal selling is the number-one MC function used, efforts should constantly be made to see where less expensive MC functions and media could be used to help salespeople do their jobs, allowing reps to use their time to do only what personal selling does best—engaging in one-to-one dialogue that permits an instant response to the individual questions and concerns of customers and prospects.

🔒 Key terms

closing the sale Finalizing the terms of the transaction and getting the prospect's agreement to those terms.

cold call A sales call to a prospect who is not known by the sales rep and has not expressed any particular interest in the company or brand.

commission A percentage of the sales price paid to a salesperson for each transaction.

enterprise selling *see* solution selling.

inside sales Salespeople who regularly call on accounts whose average size orders are not large enough to cost-justify an in-person sales call.

needs assessment Enquiring about how a business operates.

personal selling Person-to-person interactive communication used ultimately to persuade.

prospecting Locating potential new customers.

qualified leads Prospects who seem most likely to buy because of some information that is known about them.

sales lead A person or organization identified as being a prospect—someone able to benefit from the brand being sold.

sales literature Videos, charts with data and documentation, planning forms to work through with the customer, catalogues, and demonstration materials.

solution selling Helping customers solve problems or take advantage of opportunities.

Check the key points

Key point 1: Personal selling's role and objectives

a   Why is the personal nature of personal selling its greatest strength?

b   Define *personal selling*. What is meant by the statement "Personal selling is more than making a sale."?

c   Explain the evolution of personal selling. How has the focus of the effort changed over time?

d   Explain how personal selling occurs at various points in the marketing process. What roles do sales representatives typically play at each point?

e   Sales calls should be treated like planned communication. What does that mean to a sales rep getting ready to make a call?

f   How is personal selling used to acquire and to retain customers?

g   What is the salesperson's number-one personal objective? Why is it so important? How does that relate to the company's objectives?

h   Explain solution selling and its enterprise dimension.

i   What is CRM? Why is it important in personal selling?

Key point 2: The personal selling process

a   What are the four steps in the personal selling process?

b   What is a lead? Why is it important to qualify a lead?

c   What is inside sales? How might it be used by your college?

d   What is involved in closing a sale?

e   Why is it important to address objections during a sales call?

f   Explain the importance of follow-up for a salesperson.

Key point 3: Personal selling management

a   Differentiate between the cost per call and call/sales calculations, and explain how they are used.

b   Identify one personal selling measurement that is particularly relevant to IMC managers, and explain why it is important.

c   What is the problem with rewarding salespeople through commissions? What can be done to solve that problem?

d   Give an example of how personal selling can be integrated with these MC functions: (1) advertising, (2) public relations, (3) direct response, and (4) sales promotion.

Chapter Challenge

Writing assignment

Visit a local store that has sales assistants on the floor. Analyse how they (1) greet a customer, (2) try to identify the customer's needs and match the needs to merchandise, (3) up-sell, (4) close the sale, and (5) make an effort to build a relationship with the customer. Are their efforts effective? Write a memo to the store's manager explaining what he or she could do to improve the performance of the sales assistants.

Presentation assignment

When an Internet book store sends its books to its customers, the remaining space in the packages is filled with some material that protects the books. Various products are used, and your company sells such fill-up material, based on paper. This has some significant advantages, chief among them environment friendliness. Assume you are a sales rep and have to prepare a presentation to a new lead for packaging materials with the management of such a book store. Give this presentation to your class, and convince them of your product. What is your objective with this presentation?

> ### Internet assignment
> Go to the website for *The Journals of Personal Selling & Sales Management*. Click on "Table of Contents". You will then be given a choice of issues. Keep selecting issues and looking at the recaps of major stories in each until you have found at least two that discuss how personal selling ties in with the rest of a company's marketing communication effort. What were the main point(s) in these stories (as explained in the stories' abstracts)?

Notes

[1] Charles Futrell, *Fundamentals of Selling* (Burr Ridge, IL: Irwin/McGraw-Hill, 1999), p. 5.

[2] Barton Weitz, Stephen Castleberry, and John Tanner, *Selling* (Burr Ridge, IL: Irwin/McGraw-Hill, 1995), p. 386.

[3] Bernaud Liautaud with Mark Hammond, *e-Business Intelligence* (New York: McGraw-Hill, 2001), p. 150.

[4] Bill Herr, "Bridging the Gap between Marketing and Sales", *A&M Review*, April 1996, p. 24.

[5] Martin Evertt, "It's No Fluke", *Sales & Marketing Management*, April 1994.

[6] Jim Obermayer, "Power Plays: Sales Leads Are Why You Exhibit" (paper presented at Exhibition Conference, Baltimore, MD, 4–8 October, 1999).

[7] "Promising Long-Term Leads Are Too Often Lost through Impatience", *Promotional Sense*, 3, no. 1 (Spring 1998), p. 2.

[8] Andy Cohen, "Sales Strikes Out on Campus", *Sales & Marketing Management*, November 1997, p. 13.

Further reading

Anderson, Rolph E. and Wen-yeh (Rene) Huang (2006) "Empowering Salespeople: Personal, Managerial, and Organizational Perspectives", *Psychology & Marketing*, Vol. 23–2, pp. 139–59.

Kidwell, Blair, Richard G. McFarland and Ramon A. Avila (2007) "Perceiving Emotion in the buyer–seller interchange: The moderated impact on performance", *Journal of Personal Selling & Sales Management*, Vol. 27–2, pp. 119–32.

Lynch, Joanne and Leslie de Chernatony (2007) "Winning Hearts and Minds: Business-to-Business Branding and the Role of the Salesperson", *Journal of Marketing Management*, Vol. 23–1/2, pp. 123–35.

Moncrief, William C. and Greg W. Marshall (2005) "The evolution of the seven steps of selling", *Industrial Marketing Management*, Vol. 34–1, pp. 13–22.

Smith, Timothy M., Srinath Gopalakrishna and Paul M. Smith (2004) "The complementary effect of trade shows on personal selling", *International Journal of Research in Marketing*, Vol. 21–1, pp. 61–76.

Chapter 15

Direct marketing and customer service: the dialogue builder

CHAPTER PERSPECTIVE
Making it personal

One of the main things that differentiates IMC from traditional advertising and sales promotion is the increasing use of interactivity. The more personal this interactivity can be, the more effective it is. Direct marketing has been around for decades. However, its use has drastically changed with new communication and information technology. Interacting with customers is easier and less costly now than ever before.

Direct response can be used as the sole business driver or integrated into an MC mix. Direct marketing allows companies to accurately measure the effectiveness of this marketing communication function. When it is done properly, the profitability of *each* customer can be determined. As companies continue to demand more accountability, direct marketing continues to grow. This chapter explains not only the basic principles of direct mail and telemarketing but also how direct marketing can be used to integrate customers and prospects into a company's operations.

Online dating—a whole new (virtual and brave) world

The world has changed, we all know that. The world has also become a lot smaller, with communication tools utilized by the power of the Internet and e-mail. Slow is now a dirty word in our society; a heightened sense of urgency is our new code. We have become so time poor— with ready-made meals, purchasing a house online with a virtual tour and now online dating as the new way to fast-track dating. Our culture has changed.

The Internet, while only just over ten years old, has dramatically changed our lives. Millions of consumers worldwide enjoy it every day. Not only is it used as a search engine and purchasing tool, but online communities, chat rooms and blogging now have strong presence in modern-day society. Even fantasy sports can be played online, including skydiving, riding roller coasters and white-water rafting. A growth in gambling online is another popular pastime, with nearly 2 million poker players gambling online in January 2005 (McCrone 2005).

The little things that were so important, like customer service and our bank knowing our name, seem to have been forgotten by organizations. We are now just a number. If you Google the words "customer service", you will find umpteen organizations that are conducting customer service research, giving advice on what to do and what not to do. It is the buzz word of the moment, and without "it", you could be in danger of losing customers, or worse, losing your business. While many organizations understand the importance of providing a superior level of service to their customers, many are not connecting with their customers. Every organization seems to conduct customer satisfaction surveys, but what do they do with this information?

Much data gathering is undertaken: however, many firms find it a complex and time-consuming process. Point-of-sale, competitions and joining Internet sites are all ways of collecting information for databases. Tracking of individual preferences, surveying customers about their needs and wants is important in our modern world. Amazon.com was one of the first users of tracking and recommending preferences and suggestions to site users. Now we see many online operators engaging in this process.

The online dating phenomenon has grown due to the use of the Internet and marketing communication within our daily lives, with virtual dates a much more practical way of sorting out who you are interested in, and who you don't want to send a virtual kiss to than actually going out and meeting people! Sites such as OKcupid.com, slinky.com.au, rsvp.com.au, match.com and adultxdating.com.eu are just some of the many sites available. While all sites are homogeneous in many ways, they also differ. They all require you to register to be able to use their service. Some are purely for dating and match-ups, others include functions that members can attend depending on their interests. Functions can include dinner, barefoot bowls, put-put golf, wine tasting, "learn to" food courses and cooking classes, horse riding and sailing trips.

Online dating sites can classify you along with their other users to try to determine who is your perfect match! How do they do this? Via collecting your answers to series of questions posted on their sites. While each site differs in what they ask you, some sites have excellent questionnaires that are designed by their members. Web-based customer service elements including web chat or blogs are important elements that can aid better service.

All sites will contact you occasionally—whether it be weekly or fortnightly with potential matches. These matches are designed from their database. The direct mail that is sent to users via e-mail is designed to keep that site "top of mind", build a relationship with you, and also try to find you an online dating partner! Within direct marketing, the term "customer" implies an exchange of value. When a customer gives or joins an online dating site, they want to build a network of possible partners for their own personal reasons. Exchanging such value involves give and take. A site okcupid.com gives you a match test with other members. This allows choosy romantics to create and undertake testing of potential dates. Some recent tests such as the "Get'cho Nerd On!" test, the "What Size Women do Men Prefer" test and the "Obligatory Would-We-Get-Along" test help predict and match your "perfect" partners. This site is rare, as it is totally free, even to send messages! This level of customer intimacy requires a detailed understanding and integrated focus on customers' needs and lifestyles to create meaningful and cultural connections.

An interesting twist to online dating has been undertaken by AirTroductions.com and Virgin Airlines (Virgin seem to give an interesting twist to most of their products!). Remember the days of flying on your own during a long haul flight? Well no longer. Just register with AirTroductions on your particular flight and what you are looking for (male, female and type of relationship and person profile), and presto, the database lines you up with a potential buddy for that flight.

Known as the "find your seatmate before you get on the plane" website, members can pick and choose other members who they'd like to sit next to on any given flight to any destination. You firstly register on the AirTroductions website and fill out a profile. This allows them to start their database and you include your choice of airports and airlines. You list your preferences giving as little or as much information as you'd like. Before taking your flight, you enter your itinerary and AirTroductions e-mails you a list of fellow passengers registered with their service. After viewing their profiles, if you decide there's someone you'd like to meet, you pay a basic $5.00 fee to contact them.

If it's mutually agreeable to both parties, you could change your seating assignments or just meet for drinks. Online or airline dating does not have to be only for romantic interludes. You could network for your own business, get that promotion by drumming up new business, or possibly find the love of your life, who knows? Time is precious, so pass the time with someone you'd actually like to get to know. For $5.00, it isn't much of a cost for a more interesting flight. No more meeting by chance, databases can find your perfect match just about anywhere.

Direct mail via e-mails then remind you that if you are flying again, remember the service offered by Virgin. The points of product differentiation within marketing communication are getting ever more clever to enable and keep relationships with customers by offering meaningful services. Direct marketing allows for marketing communication to obtain favourable responses for online dating services offered. Successful and satisfied customers are grown from databases that can detect loyalty based on the needs of key customers, and providing benefits of value to them more than their competitors. Being close to your customers can help pinpoint new and changing trends, which allows you to stay one step ahead of the competition.

The ability of technology to make possible one-to-one personalization for customer relationships could be the key to better customer service. Tracking individual preferences and polling customers about their specific needs allows companies as mentioned in this case to customize services and products to meet those needs. Databases allow customized direct mail messages which create a powerful tool in creating superior value. While superior customer service and value influences whether customers will purchase (or use) the same company again, for a website or online dating site, customer value is critical for positive word of mouth.

Reference

McCrone, Angus (2005) "How Poker Websites Hold a Winning Hand", *Evening Standard*, 18 February, p. 1.

Personalized and interactive

When a company wants to be in direct contact with its current customers and prospects, it uses **direct marketing**, which is *an interactive, database-driven MC process that uses a range of media to motivate a response from customers and prospects.* Over two-thirds of US adults order products by mail, phone, or the Internet each year.[1] According to a Direct Marketing Association (DMA) study, $1 out of every $17 (nearly 6 per cent) in US sales is due to direct marketing.[2] Moreover, the study found that more than half of all ad expenditures include an offer designed to prompt a potential customer to make a direct purchase, inquire for more information, or visit a store or dealership.

Although direct marketing is frequently part of a company's MC mix, it can be the *only* marketing communication function a company uses to generate business, as demonstrated by so-called catalogue companies such as the Germany-based Otto. Whereas some such businesses are 100 per cent direct (they have *no* brick-and-mortar retail presence), other companies use a combination of retail stores, direct-mail catalogues, and websites. In direct marketing no distributor, wholesaler, or retailer stands between the company making the offer and the prospect. Direct-marketing operations include not only generating the sale but also handling the delivery of the product or the requested information.

In today's customer-oriented marketing philosophy, direct and interactive contact with customers is also used as a means to address customers' needs and concerns. In other words, direct contact is used not only to sell, but increasingly as a way to provide **customer service**, *the process of managing customers' interactive experiences with a band.*

Direct marketing and customer service are called *interactive* because there is two-way communication between the company and prospect; either one can initiate the dialogue. (For that reason, direct marketing is sometimes called *direct-response marketing.*) Although direct marketing is sometimes used to move prospects through the decision-making process—such as motivating a test drive, sampling, or visiting a showroom—most direct-marketing programmes are designed to generate a transaction. Customer service on the other hand focuses primarily on relationships. The main objective of customer service is customer retention.

Direct marketing: integrated on its own

As an all-in-one buying, selling, and distributing operation, direct marketing is a microcosm of the entire marketing process (see Figure 15-1). It begins with a "business organization" and marketing. The direct-marketing function entails research, segmentation, and message creation (called "advertising creation" in the model). As you can see from the model, there is a wide

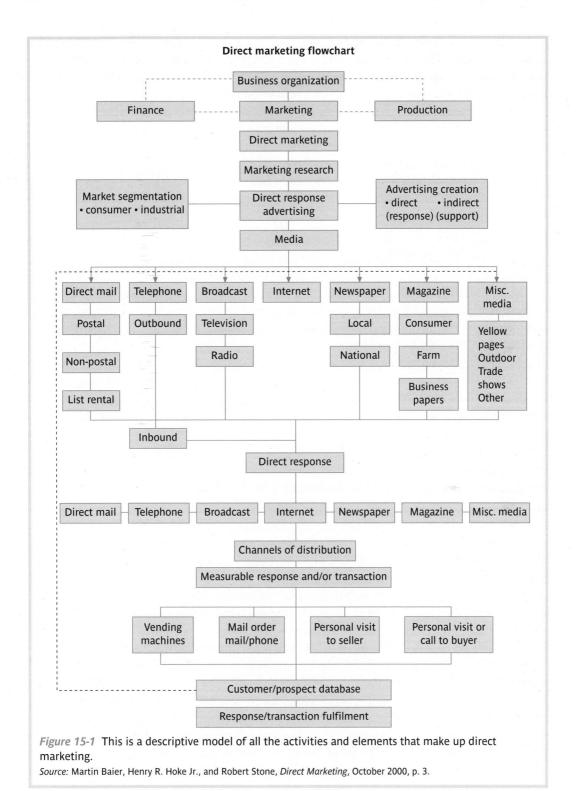

Figure 15-1 This is a descriptive model of all the activities and elements that make up direct marketing.

Source: Martin Baier, Henry R. Hoke Jr., and Robert Stone, *Direct Marketing*, October 2000, p. 3.

variety of media from which direct marketers can choose to deliver their offers. The last section of the model identifies the response process: transaction, distribution, fulfilment, and follow-up. From this process information is extracted to update the customer database. Other marketing mix functions are also integrated into the response step.

Direct marketing's use of intrusive media, such as telemarketing and spam e-mail, has tainted its public image. Nevertheless, direct marketing has a proven track record and is one of the fastest-growing MC functions. Major social and technological changes over the last several decades are fuelling this growth—for example, the growing share of households with both parents holding a job means many families have more income but less time to go shopping. Direct response makes shopping easier and less time-consuming because it can be done from home or office.

The personal dimension

With the extensive use of computers and customer databases, companies are able to be more strategic in the use of direct-response programmes. Analysis of databases may reveal for example that one identifiable group of customers is responsible for a disproportionate share of sales. This group is then a good target for a direct marketing programme, making them customized offers that fit the interests of the group.

Mobile phones (along with traditional telephones), credit and debit cards, catalogues, and access to the Internet have increased opportunities for two-way personal communication between direct marketers and customers and made shopping more convenient. Companies worldwide now provide freephone numbers so customers can place orders or request information regardless of national boundaries. Freephone numbers facilitate immediate, direct responses from customers and help companies collect information to create and refine their customer databases.

Objectives and strengths of direct marketing

One of the primary uses of direct marketing is to generate new sales. However, because its messages can be personalized and individually targeted, direct marketing is also integrated into an MC mix to retain and grow current customers. By its very nature direct marketing is an interactive MC function that creates communication between a company and its customers, which is the foundation of a good brand relationship (Chapter 3).

Another reason why managers include direct marketing in the MC mix is accountability. One of direct marketing's strengths is that it is measurable and its likely effectiveness can be gauged through pre-testing. As explained later in this chapter, determining the cost of generating a lead or a sale as a result of a direct-marketing programme is relatively easy.

Flexibility is another strength of direct marketing: it can be easily adapted to most MC efforts. Direct-marketing messages can be designed and used much more quickly than can many mass media messages. A direct-mail piece can be designed and produced within a couple of weeks; a telemarketing script or an e-mail message can be written and put into use within a few days. In contrast, a TV spot generally takes a couple of months to produce, and the lead time for a magazine ad is several months. Another aspect of direct marketing's flexibility is that the message can be as lengthy as needed, limited only by what the target audience can bear (also see colour insert C12).

When a company needs to produce results quickly, direct marketing, like sales promotion, provides a way to achieve this objective. For offers delivered by e-mail and phone, responses begin coming in immediately; for offers delivered by mail, responses arrive within days.

Direct marketing can help achieve other objectives, including the following (which, if in an actual plan, would be stated in measurable terms):

■ *Producing leads:* Direct marketing does this by inexpensively sending messages that ask people to "raise their hands" if they are interested in a particular product.

■ *Lead qualification:* Whether leads come from other sources or are produced by a direct-marketing effort, they can be qualified with direct marketing. Prospects are contacted and asked several questions to ensure they are worth spending more money on (through a personal sales contact) to generate a sale.

■ *Strengthening brand relationships:* Direct marketing can be used to gather customer-profile data. Customers can be offered a premium or some other incentive in exchange for telling more about their wants, needs, lifestyles, attitudes, and beliefs relevant to the product category. This information in turn is used to create personalized brand messages.

Components and strategies of direct marketing

Direct marketing has what are called front-end and back-end operations. Front-end strategies include *the marketing communication and media mix used to explain and deliver an offer.* Back-end strategies include *operational decisions about how responses to offers will be received and processed, inventory control, shipping of orders, invoicing, handling of returns, and other customer-service functions.* In essence, the front-end strategies set expectations, and the back-end strategies determine how a company meets (or fails to meet) them. When back-end operations fail to meet expectations, the investment in front-end efforts is wasted. So paying attention to *both* ends is crucial.

The important components of the front end are the offer, the database of targeted prospects, and responses. The most important components of the back end are fulfilment, customer service, and privacy protection. The first four components are briefly described below. Customer Service is treated in a separate section at the end of this chapter, since Customer Service is essentially important on its own as a two-way interaction with customers, not only resulting from direct marketing.

The offer

An offer consists of *everything, both tangible and intangible, promised by a company in exchange for money or some other desired behaviour.* Besides the product at a particular price, an offer also includes the terms of payment, the guarantee, the time of delivery, and any promised premiums, as well as the image and other intangibles associated with a brand.

Offers take a prospect through the AIDA sequence of decision steps—attention, interest, desire, and action. In most cases, the offer is good for only a limited time. This restriction gives the offer a sense of urgency. Direct marketers of consumer goods and services know that if customers don't respond within several weeks, the likelihood of their responding at all decreases significantly. Furthermore, an expiration date limits how long a company needs to maintain an inventory of that particular product.

Does this sound similar to sales-promotion programmes? It is. In fact, because the primary objective of a direct-marketing piece is to get current customers and prospects to take some kind of action, sales-promotion devices—premiums, discounts on the product, extended credit terms (Chapter 13)—are common direct-marketing incentives to motivate action. In B2B marketing companies combine direct-marketing offers with sales promotions to stimulate an immediate response in the buying process. For example, an offer might say "Visit our booth at the trade show and enter to win a free holiday"; or "Try our product for 30 days and receive a discount on your first order."

Database targeting

Direct-marketing companies live and die according to the quality of their customer and prospect database lists. Because of the costs of creating and printing a piece, obtaining a mailing list, paying postage, and so on, direct marketers seldom make a profit on their first sales to customers. They must capture customers' names, addresses, and other relevant information so they can send out additional offers and transform first-timers into profitable customers. Also, without a database it is almost impossible to tell which offers perform better than others—another critical piece of information necessary for building a successful direct-marketing business. Finally, a database enables a company to personalize an offer.

No matter how creative a direct offer is, it will not be successful if it is sent to the wrong people. The more carefully a database of customers and prospects is constructed, the higher the response rate will be. A brand's database can be compiled from lists of its customers and prospects, as well as from lists compiled by specialized companies called *list brokers*.

Most companies that use direct marketing have someone responsible for *list acquisition*—renting lists from list brokers—as well as managing the company's own house list (database of customers). Three types of customer lists can be rented. Response lists are *lists of people who have responded to related direct-marketing offers.* Compiled lists are *lists of names and addresses collected from public sources, such as car registrations.* Subscriber lists are *lists of subscribers to magazines.* The subscriber lists of magazines that specialize in one subject—such as golf, tennis, travel, or cooking—are especially valuable to brands within the subject category.

A response list should be evaluated on three critical factors: (1) *recency*, how recently those on the list made a direct-response purchase; (2) *frequency*, how many direct-response purchases they made in the last 12 months; and (3) *money*, how much they spent. The more recent the purchase, the greater the frequency, and the greater the amount spent, the better are the prospects.

List brokers gather names and addresses from a variety of sources—direct-marketing companies, magazines, and companies that collect and process warranty cards. Companies that sell things such as appliances, cameras, luggage, and hair dryers often encourage customers to send in warranty cards that, in addition to purchase date and location, ask about the buyers' interests, hobbies, and ownership of other products. Customers may or may not realize that the information they provide is bought and sold (or rented) by direct marketers. A growing source of lists is e-mail addresses. The most costly e-mail lists include customers who have given their permission to be contacted.

The response

In direct marketing, a response is defined as *something said or done in answer to a marketing communication message.* Like two hands clapping, the response and the offer work together. For example, the value of the offer—including any premiums, awards, or emotional appeals that are promised—is critically important to motivating the customer to respond in the desired way. To respond, a prospect or customer can call a freephone telephone number, visit a showroom, go to a website, send in a contribution to a charity or favourite cause, or become a member.

Although the customer must initiate the response, the company must facilitate and handle the response properly to ensure that the response results in the action desired. Customers who respond by using a free phone call should not be put on hold, waiting for a company representative. The longer the hold time, or the more levels of an automated voice menu the customer must go through, the more likely it is that the customer will hang up and a sale will be lost. When a customer does reach a representative, if that rep is not able to answer questions or is rude, the likelihood that the customer will not complete an order increases. Timely fulfilment is also critical to customer satisfaction and retention. According to the DMA, approximately 10 per cent of all catalogue response orders cannot be immediately filled because the company is out of stock.

First Direct marketing

The United Kingdom experienced a special day on 1 October 1989. This day witnessed the introduction of a new aspect of direct marketing: 24-hour direct banking by telephone. The company First Direct was the first company to personalize the service of banking. It set up a call centre where banking representatives (telephone advisers) performed all the functions of a traditional bank, serving the customer night and day. These representatives verified the identity of the customer, retrieved the account information on the computer screen and handled day-to-day transactions themselves. For special requests, the customer was put through to telephone advisers dealing with the relevant business. In this way customers could always speak to the person in charge and were able to profit from First Direct's high level of customer service. Since the bank had no branches, it claimed that savings were passed on to the customer (for example, interest rates on mortgages, personal loans and Visa cards were offered at a lower price than the competition).

From 1991 to 1995 First Direct used press advertisements as a way to attract new customers through offers of high-quality service and no fees in order to lure customers from other banks. At the same time the company mailed out brochures to an upmarket mailing list describing the mechanisms of telephone banking. The combination of press ads and direct mail led to a great many customer enquiries. Rather than overloading every customer with mail about the different services offered, First Direct decided in 1995 to mail customers only when they needed to. When the company that year added car insurance to its portfolio, it instructed the banking representatives to collect and store car renewal dates from the customer. As renewal dates were approaching, customers received a quotation by mail or by phone. By doing this, the company facilitated a direct response from the customer.

Although online banking was introduced in 1997 and appeared to be a big success, First Direct still has not lost its affinity with telephones. In 1999 the company introduced text message banking for their customers. Customers receive an SMS with current balance texts, mini-statements, alerts when a large payment is made, and so on. The customer can choose which kinds of message he would like to receive and on which accounts; he gets a personalized message.

A final example of how First Direct has used direct marketing to communicate the brand is its launch of (trial) text response press ads in 2003. It was meant for busy people who are interested to respond to a First Direct ad but are at that moment not in a position to make a call. The text response number was written on First Direct's press ads and interested customers were invited to send a text message with their e-mail address. In turn they received an e-mail directly in their mailbox containing a link to the website www.firstdirect.com, where they could apply for products or could ask for further details. How *direct* can a bank be?

IMC in Action

Think about it

Can you think of other companies that have used text response press ads? Do you think direct marketing is the most appropriate form of marketing communication for First Direct?

Sources:

Rayport J. and D. Louie (1997) "First Direct (A)", Harvard Business School

Rayport J. and C. Ardito (1998) "First Direct (B)", Harvard Business School

Larreche, J., D. Parmenter,and C. Lovelock (1997) First Direct: Branchless Banking INSEAD

www.finextra.com/fullstory.asp?id=13225
www.firstdirect.com

Sonya Davda, "First Direct targets people on the move in first text-response trials", Precision Marketing, 18 July 2003, Vol. 15 Issue 40, p. 6.

Fulfilment

The distribution side of direct marketing is called fulfilment—*getting the product or the information requested to the customer in a convenient, cost-effective, and timely fashion.* As noted earlier, this part of direct marketing is often referred to as the *back end* (the term came into use because in many companies the warehouse where products are stored and shipped is in the back end of the building). The fulfilment department is responsible not only for seeing that a product is shipped, but also for managing the inventory, handling the billing, following up on back orders, restocking and issuing credit for returns, and handling exchanges. Another aspect of fulfilment is up-selling or cross-selling. Fulfilment is an important element in building a brand. On the one hand the sale sets expectations about the brand, and meeting these expectations lead to satisfaction, an important driver of customer retention. At the same time, meeting expectations and promises ("we deliver in two weeks") lends credibility to the brand.

Direct-marketing media

Direct marketers deliver their offers using a variety of media including mail, TV, radio, print, catalogues, (mobile) telephone, and the Internet. Marketers often use mass media advertising to encourage people to contact the company—that is, to self-select themselves into the prospect database—and then use direct mail or telemarketing to respond to these prospects. Interested prospects can be identified through a mass media advertising effort for a company-constructed list. Catalogue direct marketers such as Otto, home shopping TV channels such as QVC, and online marketers such as Bol.com are all engaged in direct marketing.

Direct marketers face a basic communication question: what should be the balance of personal and non-personal messages in the marketing communication mix? Varying degrees of message personalization and interactivity are possible (see Table 15-1). At one extreme is real-time interactivity, as in personal selling and telemarketing. Next is delayed-response interactivity: customers must wait, to some degree, to get the information they want. The least interactive media of all are the mass media, which require that customers go to another medium such as the Internet, telephone, or fax to respond.

A brand message in any of the mass media that asks the receiver (reader, viewer, or listener) to respond directly to the sender is called direct-response advertising. Some people confuse

Degree of personalization	Initiation	Interactivity	Response	Message
High	Face-to-face personal selling	Interactive in real time	Personalized communication	Company initiated
	Telemarketing, phone	Interactive in real time	Can be personalized (but often is scripted)	Company or customer initiated
	E-mail, fax	Delayed response	Can be personalized (but often is scripted)	Company or customer initiated
	Electronic kiosks, Internet	Instant information retrieval	Mass message	Customer initiated
	Direct mail	Delayed customer response	Can be personalized but usually treated as a mass media message (telephone response can be personal and interactive)	Company initiated
	Catalogues, videos, CDs	Delayed response	Mass messages (telephone response can be personal and interactive)	Company initiated
	Audiotext (900 numbers)	Delayed interaction	Impersonal mass messages; may or may not have a personal company response	Company initiated
Low	Mass media ads	Delayed response	Impersonal, mass message (telephone response can be personal and interactive)	Company initiated

Table 15-1 The personalization continuum of direct-response marketing

direct-response advertising with direct-mail advertising, incorrectly using the terms interchangeably. Direct-mail advertising is simply one type of direct-response advertising that uses mail rather than other media to deliver a brand offer. The two most widely used types of direct-marketing media are the phone and postal mail, which are described below followed by a discussion of another form of direct-response messaging—infomercials. The use of e-mail direct-response marketing is growing fast but still accounts for only a small portion of total direct-response spending compared to direct mail and telemarketing.

Direct mail

Mail may not be as sexy as newer media such as the Internet, but it is the third largest medium behind TV and newspapers, accounting for approximately 20 per cent of all media spending.[3] The average household receives 18 direct-mail offers a week.[4] People who respond to these offers, and thus find their names on many mailing lists, receive two to three times this number. Mail is a pervasive medium that reaches every business and household. Although mail is primarily considered a one-way medium (i.e. not interactive), it is a medium that customers use extensively to communicate with companies. Because most direct-mail offers contain 0800 numbers, website addresses, or business reply cards along with postage-paid, self-addressed envelopes, it is also generally considered an interactive medium.

The leading mail-order product categories are insurance, financial services, and department stores. Important findings from direct-mail research that should be taken into consideration when direct mail is used include the following:

- Young adults of 18 to 21 are more likely than any other demographic group to respond to a direct-mail offer.
- Offers sent in oversized envelopes have higher response rates than those sent in standard letter-size envelopes.
- The average adult receives 22 pieces of mail per week.
- The higher a person's socioeconomic level, the more pieces of mail he or she receives.
- By month, the highest mail volume comes in December, followed by May and June.

Surprisingly, although direct mail is an addressable medium, the majority of direct-mail offers are impersonal. The labour required to personalize each message is cost-prohibitive for most companies, but there are software programmes that can automatically personalize messages to a certain extent. Even so, this software requires a detailed database of customer transactions plus some profile information for each customer—which many companies do not have. Although the trend is for more and more companies to create and maintain better customer databases, the full power of addressable, personalized direct mail has not yet been explored.

Formats and media

Direct-mail advertising comes in a variety of formats. The two most widely used are the catalogue and the mail package.

Catalogues

Catalogue companies constitute the largest single category of direct marketers. Catalogues describe and usually picture the products offered by a manufacturer, wholesaler, jobber, or retailer. Catalogues are used for both B2B and B2C marketing. Most mail-order companies specialize in certain areas, such as outdoor clothing and equipment, electronic gadgets, and gourmet foods. Originally catalogues were a print format and were delivered by mail to a home or office. Since the introduction of the Internet, a number of companies use online catalogues either instead of or in support of a print catalogue.

The most popular consumer product category making use of catalogues is clothing, followed by home furnishings. This fact reflects the interests of the primary target for consumer catalogues: women.[5] Although a catalogue itself is impersonal, customers can contact the company through a freephone number or online, which opens up an opportunity for one-to-one conversation with a sales representative.

New media are changing the way catalogues look and perform. Some marketers now have a video brochure or catalogue to augment the efforts of the sales staff or to use for prospecting. CDs are increasingly being used to "print" and distribute catalogues, because they are able to store millions of bits of information in a durable yet space-efficient format, can cost less to produce than catalogues, and can feature full-motion sight, sound, colour, and music.

Most catalogue marketers have adapted their catalogues to work on their websites. Because copy, graphics, and layouts for catalogues—like most advertising messages today—are computer-generated regardless of the medium that will be used, moving these bundles of digital data onto a website is easy. More important, having catalogues on a website allows them to be kept up-to-date, unlike a printed catalogue. A company can easily add and subtract items and change prices in response to competitive and other marketplace changes. The catalogue of IKEA used to be its main tool to inform customers of its wide range of offers. Next to displaying IKEA products it provided for a full overview of all the products available. Currently the role of IKEA's catalogue is changing. Increasingly the catalogue demonstrates all kind of IKEA products in nice settings. In this sense the catalogue is becoming more of an advertising tool. Many products are still described in the catalogue, yet the booklet extensively refers to IKEA's website for a complete overview of the products, in particular those that are not displayed in the catalogue.

Mail packages

A traditional direct-mail offer—called a mail package—contains more than one item. Although contents vary, the standard package contains five pieces:

1 *Outer envelope:* The more attention getting and relevant this is, the greater is the chance it will be opened. Tactics proven to increase opening are using coloured envelopes and printing a benefit on the envelope.

2 *Letter:* Years of research have shown that four pages is the optimum length, enough to explain the offer but not too much for high potential prospects to read.

3 *Brochure or similar selling piece:* Generally this is a heavily visual presentation of the product and its benefits.

4 *Insert:* This odd-size envelope or folded sheet talks about key points of the offer, reinforces the offer, and provides an additional element of involvement.

5 *Business reply card and envelope:* The self-addressed, postage paid envelope makes it easy for customers to respond.

Marketers have found that including several items in a mailing helps attract the recipient's attention and is more involving than using only one piece. The more time a person spends with any brand message, the more likely it is that the message will have an impact and generate a response. Therefore, the more creative and involving a mailer can be, the higher the response rate.

Strengths and limitations of direct mail

The number-one strength of mail is its addressability. If a company is able to identify its customers and prospects, mail can be a cost-effective medium because it minimizes waste. Addressability also enables a company to personalize its messages. Although a few magazines offer customized messaging, newspaper and magazine ads generally deliver exactly the same message to each reader. Marketers that use mail can use their databases to customize messages to customers and prospects. Unfortunately, most companies use this addressable medium to send mass messages that are not personalized.

Addressability allows marketers to measure response rates to direct mailings. Thus, mail is much more accountable than most media. Companies can use mail's addressability to test many different offers and send those that generate the highest response rates to targeted customers and prospects.

Despite the perception of direct mail as junk mail, a piece of mail receives more attention than any *mass* media message, especially when it is well designed and inviting. Few people take things from their mailbox and throw them away without first sorting through them. This fact alone almost guarantees that a direct mail envelope will be noticed and given some consideration. Unlike ads in newspapers and magazines, direct mail faces no editorial competition for attention (just other direct mail). According to household diary reports, 52 per cent of unsolicited mail pieces are opened.[6] The percentage of mass media messages that receive similar attention ranges only between 8 and 35.

Another advantage of direct mail is that the brand message can be of any size or configuration. In general, the more complex and expensive looking it is, the more likely it is to attract attention and be opened—although some marketers have found that small postcards inscribed with a "handwritten" message can cut through letterbox clutter.

As you might guess, any medium that has this many advantages is costly to use, and that is one of mail's major weaknesses. Not only is postage costly, but most mailings are considerably more expensive to produce than other types of brand messages. A TV commercial may cost €350 000 to produce; but once it is produced, it can be "delivered" to millions of people without any more *production* costs. In contrast, every direct-mail message to be delivered must be produced. Another weakness is long lead time. It can take weeks and even months to create, produce, and send out a mailing. Generally speaking: the more complex the piece, the longer the lead time.

Telemarketing

Telemarketing is *the practice of using the telephone to deliver a brand message designed to create a sale or sales lead.* The use of telemarketing became so successful that its use increased to the point where the average consumer found it extremely annoying. Consequently, in many European countries the use of telemarketing has been restricted in some way. The success of telemarketing can be understood when considering the following:

1 A company can accurately estimate its return on investment in a telemarketing programme because the results are easy to measure.

2 Telemarketing costs significantly less per customer contact than face-to-face personal selling yet offers many of the benefits of personal selling.

3 Telemarketing is extremely economical for maintaining frequent, personal contact with current customers.

4 Telemarketing by a company that has a customer database is highly targeted.

5 Telephone messages can be personally tailored just as in face-to-face selling.

6 Customers can be reached faster through telemarketing than through most other forms of media.

Phone formats and features

Some people have a problem thinking of the telephone as a marketing communication medium. But it definitely must be included when you think back to the definition of *media* as different means of connecting companies and customers. Like mail, telephony is big business. Marketers divide calls into two categories. *Outbound* calls are the ones we refer to when talking about telemarketing. *Inbound* calls are primarily those made by customers responding to direct-marketing offers (in other media) as well as calls made to customer service.

Outbound calls

Outbound calls are *calls initiated by a marketing organization.* Because it is human participation that makes outbound calls so expensive, some organizations use prerecorded calls, especially to send reminder messages. An example of when prerecorded calls might be a good idea is when a chain of oil-change service centres gives its customer database to a telemarketing call centre that will script and produce a brief recorded message reminding customers when it is time for their next oil change. The fact that this is a message that clearly benefits the customer compensates for the loss of personality in the call. The same can be done for any products that are periodically repurchased.

Inbound calls

Inbound calls are *calls initiated by prospects and customers who are responding to a brand offer or calling with an enquiry, complaint, or request for more information.* Often these come in over a company's 0800 number, so they are free for the calling party. Inbound calls are a critical way in which companies connect with customers (customer-initiated touch points, see Chapter 3) and will be increasing in importance as customer-relationship management (CRM) becomes more widely used.

In response to the increased adversary to outbound calls and legislation limiting that form, companies will make more of an effort to motivate customers and prospects to initiate calls. They will do this by making 0800 numbers and e-mail addresses more prominent in advertising and on packaging. At the same time, companies are also training customer-service representatives and others who handle inbound calls to make sales offers after callers' questions, complaints, or other reasons for calling have been addressed.

Inbound calls are one of the most valuable brand–customer touch points because nearly 100 per cent come from current customers or from prospects who want to become customers. As you will recall, a major principle of IMC is that companies should put at least as much emphasis on customer retention as they do on customer acquisition. Retention is most likely when a company is good at listening and responding. This is why there are companies that specialize in handling inbound calls for other companies.

Most businesses today use some form of automated answering system. Many people regard such systems as "voice-mail jail". Companies use them to save money. Such systems can reduce customer-service operating costs by 20 to 50 per cent.

Automated systems, however, need not be irritating for a company to save money. Capital One Finance Corporation, one of the 10 largest credit-card issuers in the United States, uses an automated answering system that handles customer calls efficiently and effectively. Capital One receives 1 million calls a week from customers who want to check their credit-card balances, question a charge on monthly invoices, ask why their interest rate has changed, and so on. As soon as a call comes in, Capital One's computers (which hold profile data on 17 million customers) go instantly to work. They identify the caller in the customer database (using the telephone number of the incoming call), analyse that customer's profile data, predict why the person may be calling, sort through 50 possible internal call destinations, and even determine what company products may be of greatest interest to the caller. The computers have been programmed to learn all the numbers from which frequent callers usually call (work, home, mobile phone). According to an article on Capital One's system, "All these steps—the incoming call, the data review, the analysis, the routing, and the recommending—happen in just 100 milliseconds."[7]

As the Capital One example illustrates, the "old" medium of telephony has gone high-tech. Because the phone is the primary medium that customers use for initiating communication with a company, how companies choose to receive phone calls can affect customer relationships. There is a range of automated answering systems. An automated attendant (AA) offers a recorded menu from which the caller chooses an appropriate number. An interactive voice response (IVR) system does everything an AA does but, in addition, allows callers to interact with the company. For example, a caller can punch in an account number to find out a bank balance or type in a flight number to find out a departure time. The IVR can handle multiple calls at the same time, so callers are rarely put on hold.

When computer technology integration (CTI) is combined with an IVR system, a call can go into the customer database and bring up the caller's profile, as is done at Capital One. This allows customer-service representatives to know who is calling even before the caller speaks (although most callers still are asked for some form of identification). A CTI system also allows the customer-service rep to transfer the caller's profile to another person or department so the customer does not have to repeat any information after a transfer. This technique, called "screen popping", is part of a good CRM system.

The most advanced automated systems are the automated voice recognition (AVR) systems. With these, customers do not have to punch any buttons but simply give oral responses to questions. Because of accents and different voice levels and manners of speaking, there is still much work to be done in perfecting AVR systems.

Part of a company's media evaluation should be an ongoing monitoring of its automated answering system. After customers learn how to use the system and its short-cuts, its complexity may not seem like a problem for them. But for prospects and new customers, an automated phone system can be intimidating and irritating if not set up with customers' needs in mind.

Integrating call centres into the marketing communication mix

Inbound and outbound calls take place in a **call centre**—*a bank of telephones staffed by sales representatives whose dialogue is guided by computer-generated scripts.* In outbound telemarketing, scripts ensure that all important points are made and that the brand message is consistent. Representatives handling inbound calls have access to scripts with answers to frequently asked questions. Most companies, especially in B2B marketing, also require representatives to make notes of their conversations with customers. Note-taking provides a history of each customer's interaction with the company, which is helpful the next time these customers call.

Although most telemarketing is used for soliciting sales and receiving orders, it can also be used for doing surveys, setting appointments for salespeople, and handling customer service. Companies usually separate customer-service and survey work from solicitations and taking orders, however, because each requires special training. There are exceptions such as Procter & Gamble, whose customer-service representatives sometimes ask a research question after a caller's question or complaint has been addressed.

Strengths and limitations of telemarketing

What makes telemarketing a powerful direct-response tool is its addressability and its occurrence in real time. These characteristics make it more personal than mass media messages. Like face-to-face personal selling, telemarketing personalizes sales calls, making it possible to respond immediately to objections and perhaps generate an instant action. Another advantage is that it demands attention. Although some consumers use caller ID and answering machines to screen calls, most people pick up a ringing phone.

Telemarketing's two major weaknesses are cost, especially when calls are being made by a human being (rather than a computer), and intrusiveness, which leads to the customer resentments discussed earlier. Intrusiveness is the dark side of demanding attention. When used for delivering commercial messages, the phone probably has the worst image of all media because of its intrusiveness. An unwanted phone call from a telemarketer can upset even the gentlest, kindest, and most mature of people. According to the president of a telemarketing company, "learning to live with the new limitations may lead telemarketers to develop higher-quality, less-intrusive outbound call practices".[8]

Infomercials

Marketers' use of TV for making direct offers has increased in the last five years, particularly in the area of infomercials, with programme-length advertisements that may run as long as 30 minutes. They are used to entertain and educate viewers about a product or service and then provide information on how to order that product.

The average cost of producing a top-quality 30-minute infomercial is less than the average cost of producing a quality 30-second TV spot. Why does an infomercial cost less, despite being 60 times longer? Most infomercials use "talking heads" and only one set, and most 30-second commercials use a variety of sets and actors plus complex production techniques. Here is a list of the major steps and items needed in the production of a typical infomercial:[9]

- A shooting script that includes key selling points and how to respond.
- A set, director, and production crew.
- TelePrompter, lighting, and audio equipment.
- Spokesperson.
- Voice-over for describing details of offer not covered by the spokesperson.
- Original or stock music for background.
- Graphics for visual supers (words that appear on a TV screen over the picture).
- Editing and final mix of visual, audio, and graphics.

Like direct-mail offers, infomercials are tested and revised several times before they are used. According to one infomercial expert, "usually the first test is a failure; two or three tests and re-edits is normal". Airtime for testing an infomercial costs about the same as production.[10]

Since most infomercials run on cable stations, often in the middle of the night and during other non-prime-time parts of the day, you might think that few if any people actually see them. Research shows, however, that 15 per cent of all TV sets are on at 1 a.m. and 66 per cent of those who watch cable TV are heavy surfers.[11] And although these are US data, there is no reason to believe that the situation in Europe is very different. Infomercials constantly repeat the important selling points to "catch" surfers who may come across the infomercial and stay for only a minute or two.

Evaluating direct marketing

Measurability is one of the main strengths of direct-response marketing. Although the ability to measure its effectiveness is important, some companies fail to plan far enough ahead to take advantage of this characteristic. Pre-testing takes time, but it can save a company thousands of euros. Smart companies that use direct marketing make testing and evaluation an ongoing activity. Many elements of a direct-marketing offer can be tested. Every test must specify a benchmark against which the results are judged.

Elements that can be tested

As direct marketing has become more widely used, with some offers being delivered to millions of households, testing has become very sophisticated and complicated, because just one percentage point of difference in rates of response can be worth hundreds of thousands of euros. Before executing a direct-marketing effort, especially a large-scale one, the following elements should be tested:

- *List:* The lists that are used have been found to be the single most critical factor affecting the rate of response to addressable media (mail, e-mail, telephone, fax). When a company has a list of 1 million people and mails to all of them at the same time, it is not testing but gambling. Before committing to the costs of contacting a large list, the company should send the planned offer to a small sample (5000 to 10 000 people on the list). If the response rate to this mailing meets or exceeds the planned objective, then the offer can be sent to the entire list with much less risk.

- *Offer:* There are various ways to make an offer. One offer could feature a price of €59.95 along with a free Cross ballpoint pen (which costs the company €5). Another offer could feature a price of €54.95 and no incentive. Both offers would cost the company the same, so the company should use the one that produces a significantly higher response in a test than the other. Each element making up an offer—product, price, credit terms, incentive for responding, guarantee—can be tested. Another opportunity for testing arises when a company decides to change an offer that it has been using for some time. Suppose the product has always had a one-year guarantee and the company decides to change it to three years. The effect of the change on the level of response can be tested.

- *Creative/copy:* An offer can be explained and presented in many different ways. Is a demonstration better than a testimonial? Does a cartoon character work better than a serious, straightforward presentation? Obviously, the creative treatment should be consistent with the overall brand creative strategy. But even within this parameter, there are many alternatives, each of which can affect the response rate.

- *Media mix:* Because different media reach different audiences with different effects, various combinations warrant testing. A company selling a new sun-protection product may test magazines going to three different "outdoor" audiences: hunting and fishing, gardening, and vacationing. Another type of media test is impact. Does a half-page ad generate at least twice the response rate of a quarter-page ad? Unless it does, the company should stick to the quarter-page ad, because a half-page ad costs twice as much.

- *Frequency:* Because current customers are a company's best customers, most companies that use direct marketing send current customers offers throughout the year. Testing the frequency of these offers—how many can profitably be sent within one year—is important. Contacting customers too often not only can be a waste of money (because people stop responding) but also can weaken brand relationships if customers become annoyed.

One basic rule of thumb is used in evaluating direct response: when testing one variable against another, it is critical that the samples for each test be representative of the total target audience. When testing a list, for example, every *n*th name should be chosen, instead of taking the first 5000 names from two different lists. When testing two different offers in print media, split runs should be used: offer A goes into half of the issues printed and offer B in the other half—that is, each goes into every other issue. Making these tests as scientifically pure as possible is a must, because even a quarter of a per cent difference in responses can be important (in a mailing of 10 million, for example, a quarter per cent represents 25 000 responses).

Evaluation methodologies

Although direct marketing can be a stand-alone MC function, integrating it into an MC mix is an especially successful strategy in marketing B2B products or consumer-considered purchases such as financial services, cars, major appliances, and real estate. In these cases, the direct response that is desired may be a step in the buying process, such as taking a test drive or visiting a showroom.

Evaluating the effectiveness of direct-marketing programmes does not require a degree in mathematics. Commonly used measures are the response rate—the number of responses divided by the total number of mailings sent out, expressed as a percentage—and cost per sale—the total cost of the mailing divided by the number of sales that resulted from the mailing. Response rate is a quite precise measure since one of the advantages of direct marketing typically is that response can be relatively well monitored. The cost-per-sale measure already gets trickier, because ascribing sales to a specific DM action is more difficult. Moreover, the IMC paradigm learns that sales is not the only objective of MC functions like direct marketing

Some marketers naively think that if they use a variety of MC functions and media they are practising IMC. The challenge to doing IMC, however, is determining the most cost-effective mix of MC functions and media. A good illustration of how to determine this mix is the following hypothetical example for a manufacturer of telecommunications equipment.[12] This example shows how two different media mixes generate different response rates and different cost per sale numbers.

The objective of the direct-marketing messages in the test campaigns was to generate qualified leads that would result in more sales. Personal selling was used to convert leads into sales.

Both campaigns contained mass media advertising and direct mail, but campaign B also included telemarketing. In the more traditional campaign A, the larger part of media money (70 per cent) was spent on television and print advertising. In campaign B, the larger part (65 per cent) was spent on telemarketing, followed by direct mail (25 per cent) and mass media advertising (10 per cent). As the following table shows, both campaigns spent the same amount of money: €250 000. Nevertheless, the difference in the number of leads generated by each campaign was dramatic: campaign B generated three times as many leads (3750) as campaign A (1250).

Budget allocations (€ 000)				
	Campaign A		**Campaign B**	
TV and print advertising	70%	€175	10%	€ 25
Direct mail	30	75	25	63
Telemarketing	–	–	65	162
Total budget	100%	€250	100%	€ 250
Leads generated by media mix				
	Leads from A		**Leads from B**	
TV and print advertising	438	35%	375	10%
Direct mail	812	65	750	20
Telemarketing	–	–	2625	70
Total leads	1250	100%	3750	100%

In campaign B, telemarketers contacted all those who received the direct-mail offer. Calls were made within 24 to 72 hours after the direct mail was received. (TV and print began running two weeks before the mailing.) The result was that the cost per lead produced by campaign B (€67) was one-third of that produced by campaign A (€200):

Campaign A €250 000 ÷ 1250 = €200 cost per lead
Campaign B €250 000 ÷ 3750 = €67 cost per lead

Although knowing the cost per lead is helpful, the most important number is the cost per sale. As the next table shows, campaign B was also more cost-effective on this measure: €444 versus €6250 cost per sale generated by campaign A. Because the average transaction was €10 000, the MC selling cost for campaign A was over half the price of the transaction—not a good situation to have in most cases.

Cost per sale		
	Campaign A	**Campaign B**
Lead follow-ups	400	2250
Conversion to sale	40	563
Cost per sale	€6250	€444

Only a third (400 of 1250) of the leads produced by campaign A were followed up, and of those, only 40 (10 per cent) were converted into sales. For campaign B these figures were much better: 2250 of the 3750 leads (60 per cent) were followed up and, of those, 563 (25 per cent) were converted into sales. Campaign A produced fewer leads, the leads it did produce were of much lower quality (that is why fewer were followed up), and a lower percentage of those leads resulted in sales.

Why is campaign B so much more effective? Mass media brand messages often produce lower-quality leads because of the limited amount of information they can carry. Direct mail can carry more information, but even these messages are one-way until someone responds. Those who responded to campaign A versus campaign B did not have as much information on which to decide whether they were truly interested in the offer. Furthermore, campaign B's use of telemarketing to follow up and add to the information supplied by the mass media advertising and direct mail allowed prospects to learn more about the offer. The better-informed prospects were able to say whether they were really interested. So campaign B generated not only more leads but also higher-quality leads, meaning a higher percentage converted into sales.

Concerns raised by direct marketing

Direct marketing is criticized for its intrusiveness (phone calls; e-mail and fax spam) and for poor targeting to people who are not interested in the product. That is why direct mail is sometimes called junk mail. Related to the "junk" concept is spam (Chapter 9), a term that applies to bulk e-mail and fax messages.

Privacy is another consumer concern that is aroused by some direct-marketing practices. Consumers today are very concerned about their privacy (Chapter 16). They especially dislike the idea of having their names and other personal information passed around to different types of businesses. As a result, consumers are wary of providing the very information that direct marketers need to segment and target effectively.

While companies must respect and protect consumer information, the good news is that doing so successfully can give a company an edge over its competitors. A study by Kristen Meador found that advertising a privacy policy statement can positively affect brand choice. More important to consumers, however, is how that statement is implemented into a company's business operations. Guidelines or "Ten things to do" type of lists are simple, but often effective tools to help companies and their employees to behave in ways that do not harm the brand.[13]

For marketers, the main disadvantage of direct marketing is its relatively high cost per customer or prospect reached. Direct-mail efforts may have costs per thousand (CPMs) up to €400. By comparison, the CPMs of regular mass media advertising range between €15 and €50, but of course they do not have near the rate of return of direct-mail or telemarketing contacts. Because of their relatively high cost, direct-marketing messages must succeed in creating more than an attitudinal response (which can generally be done much more cost-effectively with mass media messages). Correct targeting is also critical because sending messages outside the target audience, given the high CPM, wastes a significant amount of money. Furthermore, some products simply do not lend themselves to a direct-marketing approach. Certain types of products—such as fresh produce, impulse products (candy bars), and small-ticket, mass-distributed convenience items (toothpicks, ballpoint pens)—have a low profit margin and are therefore not likely to be sold through direct marketing, which must balance the high cost per contact with a high-profit margin on items sold. In addition, consumers are sensitive to the risk that comes from not being able to see, touch, or try on a product before ordering it.

Direct marketing also suffers from clutter. Consumers deluged with junk mail, telemarketing calls, and, increasingly, e-mail are fighting back. In addition to inviting potential government supervision, the result of this clutter is an overall decrease in response rates, which means the average cost per response continues to go up. Because of consumer concerns about the increase in number of unsolicited commercial messages, numerous services have sprung up to screen out unsolicited direct-marketing messages. Subscribers to DMA are encouraged to use this list and remove the names of people who have requested no unsolicited messages.

Customer service: the retention driver

Customer service is everything a company does to take care of customers' needs when they buy and use a brand. Customers' needs and wants are important determinants of consumer behaviour and consumer response to brand messages. Together, customer service and the customer-focused philosophy that it represents form the primary personal communication tool used to address these needs.

Customer service is a key reason for adding two-way to traditional one-way marketing communication. By its very nature customer service is interactive, for it involves a response to customer-initiated brand messages. It permits companies to gather real-time feedback that provides insights into the hearts and minds of customers. Every successful business tries to make the customer-contact experience as positive and rewarding as possible. When customer service is good, brand relationships are strengthened; when it is bad, they are weakened or destroyed. Because customer-service experiences are so personal, poor customer service can outweigh a bundle of great ads and money-saving offers. Therefore, service must be strategically integrated into a company's marketing communication programmes. And like other types of marketing information, customer service is an added value that helps distinguish a brand or company from its competitors.

Some marketers naively think that if a transaction is handled badly, the cost is simply the loss of a single sale. They do not realize that such a loss may represent the loss of a *lifetime* of transactions from a customer—not to mention the cost of the negative word of mouth that such an unhappy customer might spread. Customer service, whether online or handled in the traditional manner, is, from the customers' perspective, a powerful brand message.[14]

Characteristics of good customer service

The phrase *customer service* suggests a number of things—from a department to an attitude. The attitude is the "umbrella" idea, one that means everything a brand or company does is focused on serving the customer. This service mentality can be seen in four areas, all of which deliver intrinsic brand messages (Chapter 3):

1 *Employee performance* during the delivery of a service, such as when a customer rents a car, takes a plane trip, or has an in-home appliance repaired.

2 *A customer-service department* that handles complaints, enquiries, suggestions and compliments.

3 *Technical support* provided by tech-support representatives who answer questions about how to use a product. Tech support reps have product databases with answers to frequently asked questions as well as schematic drawings of products so they can more easily understand how and where customers are having problems. Tech-support representatives are generally more highly trained than regular customer-service representatives.

4 *Facilities, operations, and arrangements*, such as extended hours, play areas for children, and signage that helps customers navigate around a store or through a website. Anything that increases convenience for customers can be considered customer service.

According to a study of 2465 consumers by DDB Worldwide, the top five factors that have a "major influence" on customer retention are (1) product quality/performance (96 per cent rated this important), (2) a company's method of handling complaints (85 per cent), (3) the way a company handles a crisis in which it is at fault (73 per cent), (4) a challenge by a government agency about the safety of a company's products (60 per cent), and (5) an accusation of illegal or unethical trading practices (58 per cent).[15] Notice that dealing with customer complaints was the second most important factor affecting retention. For this and the following reasons, companies are paying more attention to customer service these days:[16]

1 *Competitive advantage:* Customer service offers a way to differentiate brands, although as more competitors improve their customer-service operations, the competitive advantage becomes an even greater challenge to maintain.

2 *Customers' demands:* As more and more brands compete for customers' business, customers can demand better service.

3 *Customers' expectations:* The promise of good customer service is increasingly highlighted in brand messages. The higher that companies raise the expectation of good service, the more customers will demand it from *all* brands.

4 *Relationship maintenance:* When companies use customer service in a proactive way to maintain contact with customers, customers have fewer reasons to go elsewhere.

5 *Increased technological sophistication of product:* As new technology becomes part of more and more products, customers increasingly need technical support and advice about using these products.

Customer satisfaction—and dissatisfaction

Customers do not expect companies to be perfect, but they do expect problems to be corrected quickly. When they are, customers generally stay loyal. When an automaker issues four recalls in a period of a few months, its market share actually may go up. Quick and honest response contributes more than defects hurt a brand's image. Complaints can generate publicity that creates negative brand impact extending far beyond the customer's original bad experience. A good handling of complaints however, may rather increase confidence in the brand, in particular as it demonstrates a true concern in affected customers' welfare.

One reason often cited for poor customer service is that companies try to save money by outsourcing this important customer-handling function. In the words of one industry observer who examined customer-service problems in the pay-TV industry: "To cut costs, most pay-TV providers [have] farmed out customer service functions to vast call centres employing thousands of disaffected workers—low-paid, poorly trained, and lacking any real incentive to care about the plight of their faceless customers."[17] One pay-TV company, DirecTV, however, changed this situation by sending its own managers to each of the outsourced call centres, providing the service reps with company information that enables them to answer more questions, providing free satellite TV to reps after they have worked three months, and inviting them to special celebrity events. These perks, along with more empowerment to make corrections on customers' bills, decreased DirecTV's "churn rate" one percentage point. This may not seem like much, but it saves the company millions of dollars a year.[18]

Poor customer service, especially in a struggling economy can be a factor that affects consumer satisfaction. Satisfaction is known to be a prominent antecedent of customer loyalty, which comes as no surprise.

Objectives and strategies of customer service

The two overriding objectives for customer service are to make customers' interactions with the company a positive experience and to increase customer retention. Stated in measurable terms, these objectives would read something like this:

- To have 97 per cent of customers rate their interactions with the company "good" or "very good" (on a five-point scale).
- To reduce to 10 per cent (from current 15 per cent) the percentage of customers who quit buying from the company each year.

Like all objectives also in this area they should be SMAC—Specific, Measurable, Achievable, and Challenging. Objectives for Customer Service are sometimes straightforward: customer retention is often directly observable in particular when professional CRM software keeps records of individual customer relationships, such as customers' buying behaviour. When also a customer's record of interaction with the brand is filed, it is a relatively simple exercise to evaluate the effectiveness of customer service. Satisfaction however is an attitude which runs into the familiar problems of finding good metrics.

Strategies for making interactions a positive experience include being accessible, demonstrating product knowledge, having a positive attitude, being responsive, and collecting feedback. These activities also are sources of powerful brand messages.

Accessibility

When customers have a question or need help finding something in a store, they want to talk to someone. The challenge is to have employees available to respond to customers who come into stores or who contact a company in some other manner. Companies also need to make it as easy as possible for customers to communicate with the company. They can do so by:

- Providing freephone numbers in all planned messages (such as ads, invoices, on packages, and service manuals).
- Providing multiple ways for the company to be reached—not only a freephone number, but also a mailing address, a fax number, and an e-mail address.
- Cross-training customer-service representatives to handle both phone and e-mail contacts, so that when incoming calls peak, employees assigned to handle e-mail contacts can handle phone calls.

A company sends a negative message whenever a customer cannot get through to an employee by phone, fax, or e-mail or cannot find a sales assistant in a retail store. The more difficult it is to reach someone and get an answer, the less satisfying the customer experience is. If a company cannot afford to maintain an adequate staff during peak call times, it should give customers incentives to call during off-peak hours or provide answering machines that ask customers to leave a message, phone number, and the best time to be reached.

Product knowledge

Knowing how to answer customers' questions is an essential characteristic of good customer service. Representatives need a thorough knowledge of the company's product line and how the products work. This level of knowledge is acquired through a solid training programme. Help-desk staffers should be completely familiar with the products before they hit the marketplace. When companies such as banks and insurers offer multiple complex products, it may not be realistic to assume that all requests can be handled by one employee. In such cases it is crucial to limit the number of connect-throughs to the absolute minimum. Callers don't mind being connected to a more knowledgeable employee—that's in their own interest. But when a second employee cannot answer the request, let alone a third or even a fourth, the company clearly has not organized its call centre professionally. One of the key success factors of First Direct was that it took pains to direct incoming calls to the most knowledgeable person available.

The right communication technology can improve customer-service communication in several ways. It can route a call to the department or representative who talked to the customer before. Computers can be programmed to identify callers automatically (by the number from which they are calling) and transfer them to the last representatives they talked to (if they called before)—all in a fraction of second. Also, having a customer's name, address, and phone number pop up on a screen makes it unnecessary to ask for this information again and avoids recording errors. The right technology allows everyone in the company who touches a customer to provide good customer service.

Attitude

How employees think about and approach customers is as important as technical knowledge. Individuals selected for customer contact need to be upbeat and positive types of people. An employee who is able to project a good mood will put a customer into a better mood and make the customer more receptive to what the representative has to say. Tone of voice and, in face-to-face meetings, body language communicate more effectively than words.

A company can help employees maintain a positive attitude by making sure employee morale is positive. There are many ways to do this. For example a sense of corporate pride can be created by involvement in good causes. In particular when this goes beyond donations, but also involves employees fully in the programme, this will motivate employees to be proud of the brand. Internal marketing (Chapter 1) presents another opportunity to make employees feel good about their company and job. When Philips launched their Sense and Simplicity campaign (see Chapter 2), this was preceded by an internal launch of the campaign, with an extensive motivation for the new positioning. This included a video featuring CEO Kleisterlee explaining the rationale behind the campaign. In this way, the entire company engaged in the new philosophy, and this soon paid off.

Because customer service includes handling complaints from angry customers, representatives can become demoralized or defensive if they do not have a strong positive attitude. The Walt Disney Company, for example, is known for its courteous, enthusiastic staff. The company excels at profiling, recruiting, and hiring the types of people who can maintain a consistently positive attitude, particularly at its theme parks (even though it does not pay significantly more than other companies). Those who are considered good at customer service have the following personality characteristics: professionalism, positive attitude, flexibility, reliability, ability to listen, and empathy.[19] They also receive extensive training.

Responsiveness

A customer bought a VCR at a discount store. The assistant rang up the order incorrectly and then directed the customer to stand in line at the "courtesy" window for a refund, rather than handling the mistake herself.[20] The assistant may have been so unresponsive because she lacked **empowerment**, *the authority to handle customer-relations problems*. Because there cannot be a rule or policy for every imaginable situation, employees must be trained and trusted to respond on the basis of general, rather than specific, guidelines. Employees must be trusted to decide, for example, when taking a short-term loss is likely to result in increasing and extending the lifetime value of a customer—and to differentiate such a situation from a customer's attempt to take advantage of the company.

Feedback

The customer-service function is a tool for listening and gathering customer feedback (see Table 15-2). Customer service provides an opportunity to engage in real-time marketing research—but only if a company has in place a system for not only recording customer comments but also asking customers questions. It's a wonderful opportunity to touch the customer's pulse. A common source of feedback is the customer-comment card. But customer-service representatives and other front-line employees, such as drivers and sales assistants, can be empowered to gather feedback in a structured way.

A company must be able to speedily collect, analyse, and report the data back to managers. In all too many cases, however, customer comments—either from the phone or the ubiquitous comment cards—are not retrieved and used. Although some companies are having success addressing consumer issues promptly, proponents of real-time customer-service feedback acknowledge that it raises customer expectations—a significant issue if companies are not able or willing to truly take action.[21] As Table 15-2 shows, customer service is the number-one gatherer of customer feedback, other than formal market research.

Source	Percentage
Customer-service departments	90
Sales force interactions	87
Point of sale	75
Customer user group	64
Inbound telemarketing	53
Outbound telemarketing	52
Other	30
Warranty cards	27

Table 15-2 Sources of customer information

Source: Reprinted by permission of Harvard Business School Press. From *Customer Connections* by Robert Wayland and Paul Cole. Boston, MA19997, p. 47. Copyright © 1997 by Robert E. Wayland and Associates, Inc., and Ernst & Young LLP, all rights reserved.

Responding to customer-initiated messages: complaints and compliments

The customer-service function is not performed the same way in all companies. In packaged-goods companies, such as Kraft Foods and Unilever, freephone numbers and websites are provided to handle consumer questions. High-tech companies have hot lines to answer questions and provide technical support, as well as provide general information about products and services. In small B2B companies, customer service may be the responsibility of sales or even product managers. In large B2B companies, sales representatives are often the first to hear from a customer with a question or complaint, especially if it is something major.

British Airways (BA) found that half of its customers who had a problem with the airline, and who did not let BA know they were dissatisfied, switched to another airline. However, of those who had a problem and discussed it with BA, 87 per cent continued as customers.[22] A good customer-service department can generally keep customers from defecting if it has the opportunity to talk to them. The lesson here is that companies should encourage dissatisfied customers to contact the company and should make it easy for them to do so (see colour insert C1).

Regaining the loyalty of an unhappy customer can sometimes actually result in a stronger brand relationship than existed before the customer had a problem. According to J. W. Marriott, chief executive officer of the Marriott hotel chain, "Sometimes those customers who you make that extra effort to gain back become the most loyal customers that you have."[23]

A customer-service department can be proactive as well as reactive. Proactive policies—such as notifying B2B customers about anticipated shortages, product recalls, or other problems—are important in keeping current customers and minimizing their calls to the company. When a company knows it will be late shipping orders, for example, customers should be notified of the delay.

For years, call centres were notorious for using low-paid, untrained employees. Unfortunately, many top managers saw customer service merely as something the company had to have rather than as an opportunity to manage customer relationships better. With more emphasis on IMC and relationship marketing, this perspective is changing fast. Not only are companies providing higher salaries and more training to their customer-service representatives, but there is also more interaction between customer service and marketing.

Evaluating the customer service marketing communication function

Two of the most widely used methods for measuring customer service are surveys and mystery shoppers. A common form is the invitation to fill out and return a customer's response card. Customers can take a card and fill it out whenever they like. The effectiveness of this method is questionable. Customers usually do not have an incentive to take the effort to respond in this way. Without extrinsic motivation, the intrinsic motivation becomes crucial. That means that only the very satisfied, or the very dissatisfied customers are likely to respond. Consequently, the customer information retained is biased. From a complaint-handling viewpoint this is not too bad, although dissatisfaction exists in degrees. It is not realistic to assume that all dissatisfied customers will respond in this way. It is likely however, that many if not all of the dissatisfied customers will switch to another brand. As pointed out earlier, accessibility is an essential feature of good customer service. Obviously a better way to collect information on customer service is to administer surveys on a periodic basis with an effort to have a representative sample of customers.

Strengths and limitations of customer service

The more complex a product offering is, generally the more critical the role of customer service. For example, a company providing airplane parts and repairs for private aircraft requires more extensive customer service and technical support than a company making paper clips. Paper clips do not generate a lot of post-purchase questions. Aircraft parts, in contrast, involve unique, project-specific, and sometimes unpredictable situations.

If a company operates with a customer-focused philosophy that permeates the corporate culture and has the commitment of top management, then all of the advantages of two-way communication can be reinforced on the critical customer-service front line. The primary strength of customer service is its contribution to the maintenance of a customer relationship during and after a purchase has been made. Personal encounters, which are more persuasive than mass-media marketing communication, can be used to overcome negative feelings associated with product problems. However, because customer service is rarely managed as part of a marketing programme, the communication dimensions of customer service are usually not integrated into the overall marketing communication approach. Furthermore, training people to work in customer service represents a significant expense to the company, especially when turnover in this area is high.

A final note: communicating with integrity

"Marketing with integrity" was among the issues discussed at a recent forum of direct marketers. Marketers were told that they must self-regulate, give consumers more control, and treat privacy like a customer-service issue; otherwise, they would risk legislation restricting access to the information they desperately need. They were also warned that the result of neglecting these guidelines would be lower response rates (which are already happening).

Although postage rates continue to go up, direct-mail advertising is still widely used. At the same time the cost of e-mail direct marketing continues to decrease while the number of Internet users increases. All this leads to more and more clutter, putting more pressure on creativity in both direct-response message design and knowing when and how to use direct-response media. To find the most cost-effective message and media mix often requires testing several combinations, which is easily done because direct marketing can be easily measured.

🔒 Key terms

back-end strategies Operational decisions about how responses to offers will be received and processed, inventory control, shipping of orders, invoicing, handling of returns, and other customer-service functions.

call centre A bank of telephones staffed by sales representatives whose dialogue is guided by computer-generated scripts.

compiled lists Lists of names and addresses collected from public sources, such as car registrations.

customer service The process of managing customers' interactive experiences with a brand.

direct marketing An interactive, database-driven MC process that uses a range of media to motivate a response from customers and prospects.

direct-response advertising A brand message in any of the mass media that asks the receiver (reader, viewer, or listener) to respond directly to the sender.

empowerment The authority to handle customer-relations problems.

front-end strategies The marketing communication and media mix used to explain and deliver an offer.

fulfilment Getting the product or the information requested to the customer in a convenient, cost-effective, and timely fashion.

inbound calls Calls initiated by prospects and customers who are responding to a brand offer or calling with an enquiry, complaint, or request for more information.

offer Everything, both tangible and intangible, promised by a company in exchange for money or some other desired behaviour.

outbound calls Calls initiated by a marketing organization.

response Something said or done in answer to a marketing communication message.

response lists Lists of people who have responded to related direct-marketing offers.

subscriber lists Lists of subscribers to magazines.

telemarketing The practice of using the telephone to deliver a brand message designed to create a sale or sales lead.

Check the key points

Key point 1: Strengths and components of direct marketing

a Define *direct marketing*.

b Why do we say that direct marketing is a "microcosm" of the entire marketing process?

c What are the main strengths of direct marketing? The main limitations?

d What role do databases play in a direct-marketing programme?

e What media are used in direct marketing?

f How does an infomercial differ from a traditional TV commercial? What are the elements that make an infomercials effective?

g Very few people will watch a 30-minute infomercial for the full time. Why is this type of direct-marketing message successful?

Key point 2: Direct mail and telemarketing

a Explain the strengths and limitations of direct mail.

b How does the cost of mail compare to the cost of other mass media forms? How could you justify using mail?

c How important is mail as a marketing communication medium?

d How important is the phone as a marketing communication medium?

e Compare and contrast outbound and inbound calls in a marketing communication programme.

f What are the key strengths and limitations of telemarketing?

Key point 3: Evaluating direct marketing

a Why can a direct-marketing message be evaluated more accurately than a typical TV commercial or publicity release?

b What elements of a direct-marketing offer can be tested?

c When in the planning and executing of a marketing plan should direct-marketing offers be tested?

Key point 4: Types of customer service

a Why do we say that customer service drives responsiveness?

b What are the two meanings of *customer service*?

c Why is training such an important part of an effective customer-service programme?

d What are the characteristics of a good customer-service programme?

e Explain the central role of the concept of satisfaction.

f What are the strengths and limitations of customer service?

Chapter Challenge

Writing assignment

Take one issue of a magazine, pull out all of the direct-response ads, and separate them into two categories—good examples of direct-response messages and examples that you consider to be weak. Write an analysis of each group, explaining how the good ads differ from the weak ones.

Presentation assignment

Collect a week's worth of direct mail that comes to your letterbox. Analyse how personalized it is. Prepare a presentation to your class in which you describe the continuum of personalization evident in the direct-mail pieces that you received. Which piece is the most personalized? Which is the least personalized? Where in that range would you put the other pieces?

Internet assignment

Find the websites of three companies (addresses appear on packages and in brand messages). Contact these companies with an enquiry or complaint, using the response instructions on each website. Keep track of how long it takes each company to respond. Rate each response on how personal it is (was the response personalized or a stock message?). Record to what extent your question was answered or your complaint was addressed. Record to what extent the company made an effort to find out more about you.

Notes

[1] *DMA Statistical Fact Book 1999* (New York: DMA, 2000), p. 3.

[2] Ibid., p. 287.

[3] Edward Nash, "The Roots of Direct Marketing", *Direct Marketing*, February 1995, pp. 38–40.

[4] Rick Brooks, "Post Office Plan Could Produce More Junk Mail", *Wall Street Journal*, 3 April 2003, p. B1.

[5] *DMA Statistical Fact Book 1999*, p. 72.

[6] Ibid., p. 37.

[7] Brian Steinberg *et al.*, "'Do Not Call' Registry Is Pushing Telemarketers to Plan New Pitches", *Wall Street Journal*, 2 July 2003, p. 1A; Matt Richtel, "Limits to Be Set on Telemarketing", *New York Times*, 20 June 2003.

[8] "About the ATA", www.ataconnect.org/about.htm, 2 July 2003.

[9] www.infomercial-production-marketing-company.com, June 2003.

[10] Paul Niemann, "Infomercials", *Inventors' Digest Online*, www.inventorsdigest.com/magazine, 17 June 2003.

[11] www.infomercial-production-marketing-company.com, June 2003.

[12] Ernan Roman, *Integrated Direct Marketing* (Lincolnwood, IL: NTC, 1995), p. 46.

[13] For example: Ways Companies Can Protect Customers' Privacy; a posting at www.the-dma.org, 10 January 2002.

[14] "Alsop to Sprint: Drop Dead", *Fortune*, 24 July 2000, p. 31.

[15] "Consumers Eager to Know Values That Guide Business Decision", *Marketing News*, 6 November 1995, p. 5.

[16] Thomas Knect, Ralf Keszinski, and Felix A. Weber, "Making Profits after the Sale", *McKinsey Quarterly*, 4 (1993), pp. 79–86.

[17] Bob Parks, "Where the Customer Service Rep Is King", *Business 2.0*, June 2003, p. 70.

[18] Ibid.

[19] Christian Gronroos, *Service Management and Marketing* (Lanham, MD: Lexington Books, 1990), p. 47; A. Parasuraman, V. A. Zeithaml, and L. L. Berry, "A Conceptual Model of Service Quality and Its Implications for Future Research", *Journal of Marketing*, Fall 1985, p. 47.

[20] Mike Cote, "Can't Get No Satisfaction", *Boulder Daily Camera*, 25 February 2001, p. F1.

[21] Dana James "Just Do It: Customer Feedback Ineffective without Action", *Marketing News*, 28 October 2002, p. 43.

[22] Charles Weiser, "Championing the Customer", *Harvard Business Review*, November–December 1995, p. 113

[23] Lovelock, *Product Plus*, p. 214.

Further reading

Coe, John M. (2004) "The Integration of Direct Marketing and Field Sales to Form a New B2B Sales Coverage Model", *Journal of Interactive Marketing*, Vol. 18–2, pp. 62–74.

Mitchell, Shena (2003) "The new age of direct marketing", *Journal of Database Marketing*, Vol. 10–3, pp. 219–29.

Peltier, James, John A. Schibrowsky, Don E. Schultz and Debra Zahay (2006) "Interactive IMC: The Relational-Transactional Continuum and the Synergistic Use of Customer Data", *Journal of Advertising Research*, Vol. 46–2, pp. 146–59.

Sargeant, Adrian, Elaine Jay and Stephen Lee (2006) "Benchmarking Charity Performance: Returns from Direct Marketing in Fundraising", *Journal of Nonprofit & Public Sector Marketing*, Vol. 16–1/2, pp. 77–94.

Scovotti, Carol and Lisa D. Spiller (2006) "Revisiting the Conceptual Definition of Direct Marketing: Perspectives from Practitioners and Scholars", *Marketing Management Journal*, Vol. 16–2, pp. 188–202.

Tapp, Alan, Keith Hicks and Merlin Stone (2004) "Direct and database marketing and customer relationship management in recruiting students for higher education", *International Journal of Nonprofit & Voluntary Sector Marketing*, Vol. 9–4, pp. 335–45.

Trappey III, Randolph J. and Arch G. Woodside (2005) "Consumer Responses to Interactive Advertising Campaigns Coupling Short-Message-Service Direct Marketing and TV Commercials", *Journal of Advertising Research*, Vol. 45–4, pp. 382–401.

PART 5

Part contents

Social, ethical and legal issues

CHAPTER PERSPECTIVE
Managing marketing communication with sensitivity

Because marketing communication is so public by its very nature, it is constantly scrutinized for false promises, misleading statements, and the undermining of social values. In the marketplace of brand messages, constant tension exists among marketers (who want to take advantage of every way they can to persuade people to buy their products), the many laws regulating commercial speech, and the many social mores against which brand messages are measured. Responsible companies want to develop the most effective, attention-grabbing ad campaigns possible, yet they know that if they push beyond acceptable limits—which often are more grey than black and white—they can tarnish their image and risk fines and public humiliation. To make things even more complex, different audiences have different standards against which they evaluate brand messages.

Marketers must continually strive to be competitive while at the same time being legal and ethical in what they say and how they say it. This is why marketing communicators must have a basic understanding of what is and is not socially acceptable, what is legal and illegal, and what is ethical and unethical. This chapter focuses on explaining the issues, standards, guidelines, and regulations that have been put in place by various organizations and government bodies. The chapter's objective is to make you sensitive to the social, ethical, and legal issues that relate to managing the marketing communications that create and sustain customer relationships.

IMC in Action

Ethical consumerism: Fairtrade Foundation

Ethical consumerism is not a new trend but the number of consumers indicating that they are willing to pay a premium for goods that are produced ethically is still increasing. This increase presents evidence that ethical consumerism can indeed generate mass appeal, something the Fairtrade Foundation has been working on for years. The Fairtrade Foundation is a registered charity in the UK that was founded in 1992 by CAFOD, Christian Aid, New Consumer, Oxfam, Traidcraft and the World Development Movement. Later, Britain's largest women's organization, the Women's Institute, also joined. In 2003 membership was opened up to allow other organizations to participate in the governance of the foundation. Thanks to this, the Fairtrade Foundation now comprises 13 member organizations. The foundation is governed by a board that consists of a maximum of 12 trustees, serving up to two three-year terms. Apart from the board, the foundation has 50 staff members and also relies on input from around 30 volunteers. All these people work towards a vision of: "A world in which every person, through their work, can sustain their families and communities with dignity". This vision translates into three objectives. First of all the foundation aims to assist disadvantaged producers and workers in developing countries to improve their social and economic position through better market access, information and terms of trade (see colour inserts D10 and D11). In addition, the organization wants to raise awareness among consumers, enabling them to make more informed decisions about purchases. Lastly, the Fairtrade Foundation attempts to influence UK companies to expand Fairtrade product availability and to develop better trading relationships with suppliers in the South.

With these objectives the foundation has already generated great results. Retail sales of products marked with the Fairtrade label have been increasing for years and in 2005 the estimated sales volume amounted to £195 million in the UK. This growth in sales has enabled a growing number of producers in developing countries to trade within the Fairtrade system. By 2005, 300 producer groups, each representing thousands of farmers, supplied the UK market. 2005 also showed an increase in the number of Fairtrade marked products in the UK; from 972 at the beginning of the year up to 1500 by December.

To realize this increase, the Fairtrade Foundation works with an array of licensees. These licensees provide the foundation with their most important source of income: licence fees. A licence fee typically amounts to 1.8 per cent of net sales value for all products per quarter. In return for this fee, the Fairtrade Foundation allows, but also requires, retailers to use the Fairtrade Mark on specified products and on promotional materials related to these products. Use of the label on any other products is strictly forbidden. In order to be eligible for a Fairtrade Mark, a retailer must sign the Foundation's Licence Agreement. Products from licensees carrying the Fairtrade Mark may only be offered for sale in the UK, and packaging and promotional material featuring the mark must be submitted to the foundation for approval before production. Furthermore, licensees must submit monitoring reports quarterly and must allow for an annual audit, so that the Fairtrade Foundation can ensure that all retailers adhere to the foundation's standards. In December 2005 193 retailers were officially registered as licensees of the Fairtrade Foundation.

Origin

Where did the Fairtrade Foundation originate from? The first attempts to market Fairtrade products took place in the 1960s and 1970s, although sales only really took off with Fairtrade labelling in the late 1980s. While Fairtrade sales were first restricted to relatively small shops selling only a very limited number of goods, distribution expanded dramatically with the launch of the first Fairtrade labelling initiative. This initiative was founded in 1988 in the Netherlands, with the name "Stichting Max Havelaar". The foundation offered disadvantaged coffee producers that adhered to various social and environmental standards an above-market price for their goods. The coffee originated from a co-operative in Mexico, was imported and roasted by Dutch companies and was sold directly to both world shops and mainstream retailers throughout the Netherlands. Thus, the product did not only reach the selective customer base of the world shops but for the first time also reached a larger consumer segment. The initiative was a great success and was soon replicated elsewhere including Belgium, Switzerland, France, Denmark and Norway under the same name "Max Havelaar". In other countries similar non-profit Fairtrade labelling organizations with different names were set up. One of these was the Fairtrade Mark in the UK.

Fairtrade Labelling Organizations International (FLO)

At first all labelling organizations had their own Fairtrade standards, product committees and monitoring systems. However, in 1994 a process of convergence began, which resulted in the creation of Fairtrade Labelling Organizations International (FLO) in 1997. FLO became the umbrella organization of 20 labelling initiatives in Europe, Canada, the US, Japan, Australia and New Zealand. Its main activities comprise establishing Fairtrade standards, facilitating and developing Fairtrade business by supporting, inspecting and certifying producers, and making the case for trade justice. Their efforts are all about harmonizing Fairtrade movements.

Fairtrade Certification Mark

In 2002 the harmonization of Fairtrade movements was extended with the introduction of the Fairtrade Certification Mark. This mark replaced most previous certification marks like "Max Havelaar". The goals of the launch were to improve the visibility of the mark in supermarkets, to facilitate cross-border trade and to simplify export procedures for both producers and exporters. By 2007 all but three labelling initiatives have adopted the new mark. The aim is to replace all individual labels with the Fairtrade Certification Mark.

The Fairtrade Certification Mark displays a cheering person, referring to Fairtrade consumers and producers, enclosed by a black vertical rectangle that stars the word FAIRTRADE. The mark serves as the signature of the FLO and guarantees an extensive process of certifying products as complying with international Fairtrade standards. Certified products include bananas, cocoa, coffee, cotton, fresh fruit and vegetables, rice, sugar, tea, wine, chocolate and many others. Generally speaking, the Fairtrade Certification Mark may only be used on either composite products if more than 50 per cent of the ingredients, by dry weight, are sourced from Fairtrade certified producers, or on commodity products that consist of 100 per cent Fairtrade ingredients. Furthermore, the Fairtrade Certification Mark is only awarded to products and does not make any statement about the companies or organizations selling them. However, indirectly the mark serves as an endorsement of these companies. The Fairtrade Mark is a qualification mark that provides legitimate associations of social responsibility both to the products that carry the mark and to the retailers selling those products. Most important is that the Fairtrade Mark allows consumers to identify products which meet agreed environmental, labour, and developmental standards.

Fairtrade Foundation marketing communications

Although labelling organizations worldwide are united through common standards and a common qualification mark, promotional efforts differ per organization. Let us go back to the UK Fairtrade Foundation. For years this foundation has been trying to reach the mainstream customer. In the late 1990s it seemed that market reach had come to a standstill. Research by Interbrand showed that Fairtrade products were known by customers, but that customers were not yet engaged with the products, and were not buying them. A lot of customers were even at the stage where they had no interest in Fairtrade products. Interbrand argued that this was due to the focus on poor farmers in Fairtrade Foundation advertisements. According to Interbrand, showing products visually would be a more effective way of promotion. In 2001 a chocolate promotion stating "Taste the difference" was launched. Posters were a combination of photography and stylish design and were put up in supermarkets, the place where many people make their buying decision. This way of promotion turned out to be successful and increased awareness from 12 to 37 per cent in three years. However, awareness is still an issue for the Fairtrade Foundation. Their long-term objective, as stipulated in the annual report of 2005, is to reach a level of awareness of 75 per cent.

In order to spread knowledge and create awareness, the Fairtrade Foundation spent £1 041 771 in 2005. Activities comprised promotional merchandise, a Fairtrade newsletter, advertising, events, mark development costs, consumer surveys and so on, signalling that the Fairtrade Foundation uses a lot of different means to communicate to its customers. Most of the awareness raising is focused on the Fairtrade Fortnight, however. The Fairtrade Fortnight is an annual promotional campaign of the Fairtrade Foundation at the beginning of March in the UK and Ireland, which encourages people to buy products carrying the Fairtrade mark. Supermarkets, major development charities, churches, National Federation of Women's Institute members and thousands of supporters around the UK and Ireland promote Fairtrade during this period. Fairtrade is promoted through events that include fashion shows, workshops, Fairtrade food and drink tastings, fairs, festivals etc. The theme of the Fairtrade Fortnight 2007 was "Change Today. Choose Fairtrade".

Although the Fairtrade Foundation markets its brand heavily in its own right, it also relies on outside sources for promotion. For example, the foundation relies heavily on licensees to promote the Fairtrade Mark. By requiring licensees to use the Fairtrade Mark on both products and promotional materials, the foundation benefits from extra exposure of its brand. For licensees the benefits are of course the ethical back-up for their marketing efforts.

Future outlook

Thanks to the many efforts of the Fairtrade Foundation to market its brand, 50 per cent of UK Fairtrade customers could identify the Certification Mark in 2005. Not only do consumers identify Fairtrade products, they also buy them in great quantities. Worldwide Fairtrade certified sales have increased by an average of 37 per cent per year and in 2005 amounted to C1.1 billion. It is expected that Fairtrade sales will reach $9 billion by 2012, and even $20–25 billion by 2020. Let us see how these estimates will reflect on the UK market!

Sources:

Datamonitor (2005) "Ethical consumerism: mass appeal". Retrieved 14 March 2007, from www.datamonitor. com

Griffiths, M. (2005) "Building and rebuilding charity brands: the role of creative agencies", International Journal of Nonprofit & Voluntary Sector Marketing, *Vol. 10, pp.121–32, John Wiley and Sons Inc.*

The Fairtrade Foundation (2005), Annual Report and Financial Statements. Retrieved 14 March 2007, from www.fairtrade.org.uk/about_annual_reports.htm

Uggla, H. (2004) "The brand association base: A conceptual model for strategically leveraging partner brand equity", Brand Management, *Vol. 12, No. 2, pp. 105–23, Henry Stewart Publications.*

www.fairtrade.net
www.fairtrade.org.uk
http://en.wikipedia.org/wiki/Fairtrade
http://en.wikipedia.org/wiki/Fairtrade_fortnight

The role of marketing communication in society

Marketing communications has the power to sell commercial products, as well as socially responsible behaviour (see colour insert D9). Critics ask, however, whether marketing communication has the same kind of power in creating negative social consequences, such as a materialistic consumer culture.

This chapter looks at the various criticisms, ethical issues, and regulatory efforts that surround marketing in general, and marketing communications in particular. The objective is in the first place to learn what those issues are and to get a feel for how far critics are justified, or, on the contrary, criticisms result from a misunderstanding of the marketing function. Furthermore, we will look at how marketing communication can perform a useful and positive role in society and operate in a socially responsible way. The aim of this chapter is to represent critical viewpoints that need to be considered and discussed by anyone who is a student of marketing communication.

The goals of an IMC programme are to inform, persuade, and listen to all stakeholders. The word "persuade" may sound double-edged—like making someone act in a way he or she actually doesn't want—but is used here in the neutral meaning of changing someone's knowledge, associations or attitudes, and possibly behaviour. The relationship component gives IMC a platform on which to build a more socially responsible form of marketing communication than some of the past practices in advertising or direct marketing, which look at consumers solely as targets. Unfortunately, many companies are poor listeners. Many are just now setting up the systems and infrastructure needed for commercial listening and responding. For this reason, there is often a gap between social concerns and business practices on issues such as the environment, social values, overpackaging, and designed obsolescence. For example, here is how one marketing communication function—advertising—has been portrayed by a UNESCO critic:

> Regarded as a form of communication, it [advertising] has been criticized for playing on emotions, simplifying real human situations into stereotypes, exploiting anxieties, and employing techniques of intensive persuasion that amount to manipulation. Many social critics have stated that advertising is essentially concerned with exalting the materialistic virtues of consumption by exploiting achievement drives and emulative anxieties, employing tactics of hidden manipulation, playing on emotions, maximizing appeal and minimizing information, trivializing, eliminating objective considerations, contriving illogical situations, and generally reducing men, women, and children to the role of irrational consumer. Criticism expressed in such a way may be overstated, but it cannot be entirely brushed aside.[1]

For the most part, the criticisms made against advertising can be viewed as criticisms made against all forms of marketing communication because the ultimate goal—to influence buying decisions—is the same for both.[2] Most social critics do not make a distinction between marketing communication functions when it comes to charges of over-commercialization and encouraging conspicuous consumption. To them, *any* brand message that directly or indirectly encourages people to consume is manipulative and, thus, suspect.

Does marketing communication mirror or shape society?

How much influence does MC have on customers and society as a whole? Critics say that advertising in particular, because of its creative skills and pervasiveness, has created a materialistic culture of conspicuous consumption in which not only are people persuaded to buy goods and services they don't want or need, but brand messages present an idealistic profile of glamour, opulent lifestyles, and happiness that supposedly can be had by buying the right brands. In this way, critics argue, marketers shape how we live.

Defenders of MC say that marketers are given far too much credit for persuasive power. They note, for example, that of the hundreds of brand messages that customers see and hear each day, few are remembered. They point out that 9 out of 10 new-product ideas fail, which would not be the case if marketers were as controlling as critics say they are. They also point out that companies spend billions of dollars on research to find out what customers want. If companies could sell anything they wanted to, then why waste money on customer research?

The reality is that MC and society are intertwined and MC does a little of both—mirroring and shaping (see colour insert D8). If MC had no impact on customers, why would marketers spend hundreds of billion euros a year on various forms of MC? At the same time, the whole marketing concept is based on satisfying customer wants and needs. Environmental issues, for example, became a major social concern in the late 1900s not because environmental responsibility was the subject of a strong MC effort, but rather because of an emerging social consciousness. As a result of this new social concern, many companies began to relate their brand messages to the environment.

The purpose of MC, its defenders say, is to provide information and to help customers in the brand decision process. They admit that brand messages are designed to be persuasive, but the fact that much effort is made to send these messages only to people already interested in the product category demonstrates that marketers know they can convince only a very small portion of the total population to buy. In marketplace economies effective communications is an essential part of the game: it is not possible to think of a society based on competition, without the core players on the supplier side informing the other side of why they are competitive. On the other hand, marketers must understand that they are participants of this same society, and have a responsibility to act in ways that are not detrimental to the world they live in. Finding the right balance in this dilemma is in the interests of everyone, both consumers and businesses.

The dilemmas show up in many concerns raised by the consumer side about the behaviours of marketers and their consequences. In this chapter an extensive list of such concerns will be presented. This list is not intended to be exhaustive or final. Society develops over time, as do marketing practices, and every era has its own concerns and issues. After these social concerns two sources of "countervailing power" are discussed. First, the ethical aspects are scrutinized. Ethics is concerned with what most people agree upon as acceptable and unacceptable behaviour. It therefore puts constraints on our behaviour, and obviates any need to be enforced by law, which is the second countervailing power. When ethical issues cannot be enforced, some constraints on marketers' behaviour become a legal matter. Indeed, while some say that "ethics begins where the law ends" it might equally be argued that "laws are needed, where ethics fails".

Concerns about marketing communication

Thoughts of junk mail, telemarketers calling at dinnertime, tasteless TV commercials, and used-car salesmen taint the image of marketing communication. Advertising often ranks at the bottom of many lists of respectable professions. Why is that?

Significant numbers of consumers report that they feel offended by marketing communication "sometimes or often", that they believe that most brand messages insult their intelligence, and that they feel they are occasionally misled by brand messages.[3] The fact that many people have serious misgivings about marketing communication is a result of various perceptions—and sometimes misperceptions. Discussed here are the concerns about MC that are most often heard:

- *MC drives up the cost of products:* Some people feel that MC drives up the cost of goods and services because the cost of marketing is included in the purchase price of products. In other words, customers pay for being sold to. Although it is true that as much as 25 per cent of the price customers pay for some cosmetics goes to marketing, marketing costs are a relatively small percentage of the purchase price of most other products. In fact, mass marketing drives prices down and makes products affordable. In the case of cars, marketing costs generally account for 2 to 4 per cent of the purchase price. Marketers also point out that often the cost of MC is more than offset by price reductions that result from MC encouraging competition in the marketplace. Howard Morgens, former president of Procter & Gamble, says, "We believe that advertising [i.e. marketing communication] is the most effective and efficient way to sell to the consumer. If we should ever find better methods of selling our type of products to the consumer, we'll leave advertising and turn to these other methods."[4] As noted before, competition is the backbone of Western economies, but competition demands that competitors inform the customers about their competitive stances.

- *MC creates a barrier to market entry:* Slotting allowances and the demands of retailers that new products have strong MC campaigns to support new products, constitute a barrier for small, entrepreneurial companies trying to enter the market. In addition, customers have been conditioned to buy popular brands. To become a popular brand on a small budget, however, takes either a really unique product or a terrifically creative message, both of which are difficult to achieve.

■ *MC merchandises too many aspects of our culture:* In an effort to reach prospects and customers, companies have turned an increasing number of public spaces and activities into conveyors of advertising messages (see colour insert A4). Buses used to carry a sign on their sides; now the whole bus is an ad (see colour insert B16). Sports arenas now have brand logos on the playing surfaces besides brand messages on walls, the video monitors, and over the public address systems. Grocery carts are now mobile billboards, and the dividers used on the conveyor belts at checkouts carry brand messages. Some manufacturers place their labels on the outside of clothes, and others splash their brand name across the front of T-shirts and caps—but people pay for the opportunity to wear these branded goods. On some broadcasts of football games, virtual billboards are projected next to the goals, not to mention logos on uniforms of players and coaches. The idea of seeing brands "everywhere" has made some people concerned about the over-commercialization of every aspect of our lives.

■ *MC sells inferior products:* The criticism that MC encourages people to buy inferior products can be especially true of new products. However, few companies make a profit by selling to a customer just once. And there is no faster way to kill an inferior brand than to convince many people to buy it, only to have them find out that they wasted their money. Not only do customers refuse to make a repeat purchase, they also often tell others about the bad experience (negative word-of-mouth advertising).

■ *MC sells unhealthy, dangerous products:* One issue that continues to be discussed is the appropriateness of promoting products that, though legal, may not be good for us, such as tobacco and alcohol (see colour insert C3). Because marketing is a part of selling, some people say it makes no sense to make it illegal to advertise products that are legal to sell. Nonetheless, companies are viewed as having some social responsibility for the behaviour they induce in consumers, be it when executives mislead the public about the known harmful effects of smoking or when retailers serve drinks to customers who then drive when drunk. Anti-smoking advocates continue to push for additional bans on tobacco advertising, and have been quite successful. In the case of alcohol, in some countries, e.g. the Netherlands, advertisers have been forced to add socially responsible messages to their advertising such as "Under 16? Not yet"; or "Enjoy, but drink responsibly".

In the US, but not only there, obesity is a serious problem. In response to the growing concern of people being overweight, especially children, Kraft Foods has changed some of its marketing practices. The maker of such popular food brands as Oreo cookies, Velveeta cheese, and Oscar Mayer has reduced the portions in single-serving packages and greatly reduced in-school promotions for Kraft snack items. Kraft has also said it will work to develop healthier snack foods for children.[5]

■ *MC invites people to overspend:* The "art of seduction" is a nickname for advertising. Consumers are seduced into buying products. When the criticism is that people are seduced into buying products they do not want, this is relatively harmless. Much more serious is the concern that people are persuaded to buy products they cannot afford. Producers of expensive goods like cars and kitchens help consumers to buy these product by offering attractive-looking credit facilities. "Buy now, pay next year". Or: "buy with our 0% loan". Apart from the fact that consumers must be very cautious about accepting the conditions of these loans, the real danger is that consumers can get such loans much too easily, leaving them too heavily indebted. This is made worse by money-lenders who offer their loans on relatively easy terms, but then enforce them very strictly. They suggest that anybody can get these attractive loans, but then tighten the screw. Nevertheless, the message is that virtually everything you want is within reach, and that borrowing money is very easy. Overspending is encouraged, but often ends in bankruptcy.

- *MC is done in bad taste:* In many countries a battle goes on between people who want to establish standards of taste and morality in society and those who feel that open expression must be allowed and defended, even if this means people are sometimes exposed to things they find offensive. Many are concerned about marketers' use of sex and violence to gain attention and sell brands. Even when brand-message content is not offensive to the target audience, it can be offensive to others. Marketers argue that there is freedom of speech and that people are not obliged to watch those commercials or pictures, but that answer is a bit too easy. Moreover, when advertising evokes such responses, even if not in the target audience, the impact on consumers in general should be of concern to the marketer.

- *MC invites censorship:* This can work in two directions: advertisements can be withdrawn to meet the standards of the audience, or the content can be adjusted to reassure the advertisers. Most media strongly protect their right to pick and choose the ads they run. Besides having their own views about what messages are and are not "proper", editors and other media gate-keepers are also responsive to all their advertisers as well as to their audiences. Offending either could result in reduced revenue. Although one could debate the extent to which such practices exist or the impact on the publication of news or ads when the media reject an ad—or a story, for that matter—they are practising a form of censorship.

- *MC creates visual pollution:* You may recall from Chapter 8's discussion of out-of-home advertising that some people consider the proliferation of outdoor advertising to be "visual pollution". As a result, commercial free speech is sometimes restricted for aesthetic reasons and, in some cases, for reasons of safety (restricting the view of drivers, for example). In newer commercial shopping developments, retail store signage is often restricted in size and placement.

- *MC pushes one country's culture onto another:* One thing every global or international marketer exports along with its products is its culture. The increased attention given in recent years to this side of global businesses has led to an increase in protests against this "export of culture". In particular, some countries perceive the pervasiveness of American culture and American values as a threat to their own way of life. A writer in the *South China Post* noted: "Whether it is a case of the French going crazy over Jerry Lewis, the Germans channel surfing for *Baywatch*, or Chinese teenagers idolizing Michael Jordan, there is no denying America's role as the supreme exporter of entertainment"[6]—and entertainment is one very powerful aspect of culture.

  Many countries have sought to keep American culture out. Conservative Islamic countries have barred American television shows and movies. The Chinese have banned direct selling, forcing companies that are grounded in this concept like Avon, to alter the way they do business in China. The European Union requires all TV channels to carry at least 50 per cent European programming. French officials try to limit the number of American films shown in France. In July 1998, there was a two-day meeting of 22 government ministers from around the world to find ways to counter the spread of American culture. What must be sorted out, however, is whether a country is "protecting" its citizens from "corrupting" outside influences or whether it is limiting choices and dictating tastes.

All of these concerns about the effects of marketing and marketing communication are legitimate and deserve debate, but debate that acknowledges that there are two sides to most of these issues.

Ethics and marketing communication

Every society has certain ethics, *moral and value standards that act as behavioural guidelines.* The ethics of organizations and of individuals within a society form the benchmarks for determining what is right and wrong in different situations. Unlike government laws and regulations, which are explicitly stated, ethical codes are generally not written down. Rather, they are held in the social consciousness of an organization or a population, and what constitutes ethical behaviour is determined by public attitudes and feelings. Ethics are important in IMC because they provide the basis for the moral choices that individuals and organizations must make in their relationships with each other.

Marketing practices should be guided by an organization's ethics. Marketers should also ask whether brand messages and programmes are aligned with the ethics of the brand's stakeholders. If they are not, stakeholder relationships will be weakened. In addition, unethical brand messages can reflect negatively on the MC agencies that create them and the media that distribute them.

Establishing what is or is not ethical is not always easy and is inherently subjective. For example, different groups of people hold different opinions of whether salaries for CEOs are justified or not. CEOs often earn millions of euros a year, with bonuses, gratifications and other extras on top. Sometimes these extras are related to the company's performance, i.e. they are given in the form of shares or made dependent on the profits the company makes. In the eyes of consumers the compensation for top officers is often excessive, but the managers involved have reasonable arguments, chief among them being that it is a market they are in, and apparently "the market" is willing to pay them these salaries. In addition, they refer to the international competition where salaries are often even higher. Finally, it is put forward that their income looks impressive—there is indeed no point in denying that, they realize—but that part of this is a compensation for the risks they take by becoming a "public" personality. In particular they claim that the risks of their job are relatively high: when they fail, they fail publicly and it will be much harder for them to find a new job.

Despite such arguments, the issue becomes problematic when the same company has to lay off employees in order to reduce cost, or to raise prices in order to secure profitability. And although every accountant can tell that the links between the CEO's salary and firing people or price increases is weak at best, the communicative impact of such a situation will do no good to the products or brands involved. Hence, it is both an ethical issue—is it morally justified to pay such high salaries?—and a matter of marketing communications.

Because ethics are so subjective, some companies simply say that employees must not do anything illegal. In other words, they let the law define their ethics. However, even law-abiding companies face ethical issues, simply because not all moral decisions are regulated by the law. It is too simple to argue that everything that is not forbidden by the law is *therefore* ethically correct. Companies need to discuss ethical issues and set guidelines for individual and corporate behaviour. Just as brand messages should be strategically consistent, corporate behaviour should be ethically consistent. A cross-functional group responsible for managing brand relationships should be prepared to deal with ethical issues and allow for open discussion.

The best way to explain the ethical issues marketers face is with examples.

Stereotyping

As our societies have become more aware of their diversity, people have become sensitized to cultural, ethnic, gender, and other differences. Although stereotypes sometimes contain grains of truth that may be useful in segmenting a group, the challenge for brands is to develop messages that strike a chord with targeted audiences without reinforcing negative stereotypes (see colour insert D2). For example, the women's campaigns by Nike reach out to women with messages that strike against the stereotyped images of women presented in some fashion magazines.

Even when using careful planning—for example, testing copy with focus groups comprising members from the targeted audience—companies may still alienate some people. Sometimes advertisers are able to use messages that can be interpreted favourably by different audiences. Volkswagen created a highly popular television commercial in which two young men drove around town in a Volkswagen Golf, stopped to pick up an abandoned chair, then stopped again to dump it off because it smelled. Advertising to a niche market like the Gen-X target in the VW Golf ad can be particularly difficult because appealing to one subset may alienate another. Most viewers saw the two guys as cool Gen-X friends or roommates, but older viewers thought they epitomized the aimless, worthless lifestyle of young people. Meanwhile, gay audiences assumed the two guys were a couple and responded positively.

Companies can avoid making some groups uncomfortable or even angry by carefully screening their brand messages and selecting highly targeted media for delivery.

Targeting vulnerable groups

As the population as a whole has become more educated about marketing strategies and tactics, concern has been increasing about messages specifically directed to captive audiences, as well as to less educated or unsophisticated consumer groups.

Feeling that companies take "persuasive advantage" of vulnerable or disadvantaged groups, some critics have mounted efforts to ban the promotion of certain types of products from certain media targeted to certain audiences. Marketing communications aimed at children, and people in developing countries are most critical.

Children

Marketing to children is criticized on several grounds. Some critics worry about children being bombarded with consumer images that glorify the buying of products.[7] Parents see children becoming brand savvy at an early age and demanding certain products and brands. Although some might argue that children need to learn consumer skills, the issue raised by this proliferating consumerism is whether children who are too young to have developed the critical skills needed to separate advertising from other types of directions are being unfairly manipulated. In fact, as one education professor reports, young children have trouble distinguishing TV programmes from commercials, and most children have little or no understanding of the persuasive intention of commercials, so they are particularly vulnerable to advertising claims and appeals.[8]

Marketing to children has come under question because even the most vigilant parents find it hard to screen all, or even a fraction, of the commercial messages their children see. In general, parents prefer to be the ones to shape their children's buying decisions. But companies are free to advertise in and around schools, during children's programming on television, at sporting events, on product packaging and point-of-purchase displays, on the Internet, and in movies and cinemas. Parents cannot possibly be on hand to help their children interpret all of these brand messages.

The more children's tastes appear to be shaped by commercial messages rather than by parental influences, the more support there is for regulation. However, groups that want to shield children from commercial messages have found it difficult to collect valid evidence to support their negative views.

The fact that schools are accepting and displaying brand messages in exchange for money, free equipment, and curriculum materials has met with strong opposition from some parent groups. Companies develop lesson plans and classroom videos that some believe are little more than corporate public relations messages aimed at young audiences. Dow Chemical has prepared an instructional video about the benefits of chemicals, and in an utterly cynical exercise, Exxon has a video using its 1989 Alaskan oil-spill clean-up as an example of environmental success.

According to a study by the non-profit organization Consumers Union, nearly 80 per cent of corporate-sponsored school materials contained "biased or incomplete information [that] favors the company or its economic agenda". The study claimed that these materials are full of "self-interested, incomplete or discriminatory points of view [that] basically teach opinion as if it were fact".[9]

Marketers have learned, however, that if their material is too obviously biased, little or none of it will be used. Ron Schmieder, president of the Plastic Bag Association, describes his organization's booklet entitled *Don't Let a Good Thing Go to Waste*, which is given free to grade-school teachers, by saying: "It's good public relations, plus it takes care of a need. We've tried to give a very balanced view of the solid waste issue."[10]

Developing countries

Companies looking to expand business beyond current markets sometimes see opportunities in countries with fewer trade and product restrictions. Tobacco companies come under criticism for using advertising in Asia, eastern Europe, and South America that was long ago banned in Western Europe and the United States. Free Cigarettes, a Brazilian subsidiary of the international conglomerate British American Tobacco, has used ads that suggest smoking is an appropriate symbol of teenage rebellion. In one, a teen says, "First we go crazy, then we see what happens."[11]

Pharmaceutical companies have been accused of unethical business practices such as using advertising in developing countries to promote drugs that Western regulators have not judged to be safe. Studies have shown that advertisements, as well as labels and package inserts, often overstate benefits and understate risks in countries where government regulations are lacking or are not consistently enforced.[12]

Offensive brand messages

To get a feel for different types of commercial messages, imagine a continuum. At one end are straightforward, objective, safe messages. If a company goes overboard in this direction, it can end up with brand messages that are boring or easily forgotten. At the other end of the continuum are attention-grabbing messages. A company that goes too far in this direction can end up with messages that are too controversial and even offensive.

Even marketing communication that is within legal bounds may not be ethical or socially acceptable. As a promotional stunt a British insurance company sent 77 homing pigeons, each in a cage, to reporters in London to announce a new investment product. The reporters were instructed to release the pigeons and were told that the person whose pigeon returned home first would receive a free case of whiskey. Animal rights groups were outraged, and the Royal Pigeon Racing Association wondered "why a responsible organization would send live birds to people without asking them first if they wanted them". The public relations firm that thought up the idea responded, "It just goes to show how sensitive some people are. We think that it was an innovative and clever idea."[13]

When talking about offensive advertising, people often point to sex and social taboos as two areas where brand messages often cross over the line.

Sex

Sexual images are an attention-grabbing device. That is why bikini-clad women have for years appeared in ads for auto parts and nearly every other male-targeted product you can think of. But using sexual images that are unrelated to product claims may be a poor creative decision because these images can overpower the primary brand message. Also, with the attention comes scrutiny and possible protests from audiences.

The sexual ads that have drawn the most protest are those that exploit women in general as sex objects and those that use under-age models in sexually suggestive ways. However, sexual mores are not the same in all cultures, so it is difficult to develop definitive sexual guidelines. Some ads that are acceptable in European cultures would be considered in poor taste in America. And what is simply a reflection of lifestyle to young people might appear as offensive to the elderly.

Taboo topics

In recent years, clothing manufacturer Benetton has generated a great deal of attention and publicity by using images widely considered by some people to be shocking and inappropriate: pictures of human hearts, a man dying of AIDS, and a priest kissing a nun. But just as people who buy sexy underwear are not generally offended by ads for lingerie, people who are very liberal and often anti-establishment are not offended by Benetton ads. Companies like Benetton are targeting their current customers and likely prospects; they expect these audiences will accept their ads and are thus inclined to ignore the objections of groups who would likely never buy the product anyway. This can be simplistic reasoning, however, because it overlooks other stakeholders who can affect the profits of a company and brand as much as customers do. Brands do not have to offend others in order to appeal to their target audience. One of the basic creative challenges for marketing communication is to find a way to talk to and persuade customers and prospects that does *not* offend other stakeholders.

Manipulation and subliminal advertising

Marketers are expected to influence consumers to purchase goods and services. This influence can take many acceptable forms—product information, pricing, image, and so on. Some individuals and consumer groups suspect that this influence can also assume more insidious forms, akin to mind control and unscrupulous manipulation. Some ads that use strong fear appeals, for example, are criticized for excessive emotional manipulation. Such techniques can result in a negative backlash that turns off the audience.

The most criticized form of manipulative advertising is subliminal advertising—*messages that are received subconsciously, below a person's perceptual threshold, causing a desired response.* The topic of subliminal advertising became popular in 1957 when a market researcher, James Vicary, claimed he had increased the sales of Coke and popcorn in a US cinema by inserting into the main feature film the phrases "Drink Coke" and "Eat popcorn" every five seconds—

but just for a fraction of a second so the words were not consciously seen. Although Vicary's claim caused a major stir in the advertising world, the fact that he refused to disclose the details of his study began to create doubt about the validity of his findings. The marketing community was soon convinced the technique was of no value, and the issue faded.[14]

In the 1970s interest in subliminal advertising was revived with the publication of several books by Wilson Bryan Key, including *Subliminal Seduction: Ad Media's Manipulation of a Not So Innocent America.* The books, long on anecdotes but short on empirical evidence, have generally been dismissed by researchers who have tried to conduct research that proves such a practice exists or is effective. The topic still receives attention occasionally from some researchers and academics; however, a review of research over the years on subliminal messages shows that they are not considered a viable MC tool because there is no proof that they work.[15]

Some people confuse subliminal advertising with the use of colours, music, typography, and design to create a mood or otherwise set the stage for a consumer response. For example, some believe that patrons in a restaurant that uses earth tones on its walls feel especially relaxed and are inclined to linger and order more food and drinks than they would in a gaudier setting. The "message" imparted by the colour of the walls, however, is not subliminal because it is not below the threshold of awareness. Rather, some people merely find earth tones pleasing and choose to extend their stay to enjoy the ambience.

There is another very practical reason why most professionals and academics dismiss subliminal advertising. Even if it worked, any company or MC agency that used it would be running the risk of generating negative publicity for itself. People who worked on the ad would talk about it; the story could not be hidden. Who would want to buy from a company accused of secretly manipulating, even brainwashing, its customers?

A related topic is suggestive advertising. Sometimes ads suggest certain behaviours or situations which as they stand are not ethically acceptable. However, since they are merely suggested, any accusations of unethical behaviour can be rejected by arguing that it is the audience who imagine the suggested things, rather than what is actually displayed. When the link to the disapproved aspects of the ad is not too strong, advertisers will usually get away with this argument.

One example is of a recent Renault advertisement. The scene shows three men in a car. The men are Mediterranean stereotypes. They are clearly enjoying the ride, as is the man in the back seat. The next scene shows the three men in a dockside area, with a heavy concrete weight block visible. The final scene shows two men getting back into the car wearing the same smiles they showed during the ride. The third man has disappeared, but the scene also shows a crane with a rope dangling above the water, leaving no doubt about his fate. A protest against this ad was made to the Dutch regulatory body. In response the agency argued that the scene was clearly a parody on the popular series *The Sopranos* and expected that viewers would have no problem making this link. Since murders were not uncommon in this series they did not see that this advert was an example of bad taste. Another example of advertising at, or over, the edge is for a bath-cleansing product. A little girl and her mother are on two sides of a glass partition and talking in a very emotional way about when they will see each other again. The mother is crying, the girl is very sad and they press their hands opposite each other against the glass. It will clearly take a long time before they will be reunited. Then the camera moves and the reason for their separation is disclosed. The mother is cleaning the bath with some anonymous brand. The pay-off line is "Don't spend your life cleaning" and the advertised brand appears.

Both examples refer to serious issues, of the kind some will claim are not to be used for commercial purposes: murder and (life-long) detention. Yet, as long as it is only suggested, most people will still find this kind of advertising acceptable, and sometimes even entertaining. What is clear though is that this is playing with fire. Either the audience accepts the idea and is charmed by the twist of the ad, or the audience does not accept it, with less favourable consequences, and just as with subliminal advertising, you are left wondering why companies would want to run the risks involved.

Legal issues related to marketing communication

Public opinion or a marketing manager's opinion may not be enough to determine what is and is not appropriate in marketing communication. Ethical concerns are often open to debate. But some behaviours are considered unacceptable to such a degree that legal enforcement is justified. Most societies feel that the threat posed by inappropriate or misleading commercial messages is serious enough to warrant the enactment of laws regulating messages and imposing penalties for violation of those laws. In fact, every form of commercial communication is affected in some way by regulations and watchdog groups that seek to protect consumers and businesses (also see colour insert D6).

Several industry organizations and government agencies monitor commercial messages. They are called on to distinguish between acceptable persuasion, questionable sales pitches, and outright fraud. Responses range from tolerating the messages, to recommending changes, to taking legal action. The following sections discuss the types of legal issues marketers face and describe watchdog organizations' and government agencies' responses to illegal practices.

Misleading claims

Although commercial free speech is protected, to a certain extent, by the general protection of free speech laid down in many constitutions, deceptive commercial speech is not. Factual claims in marketing communication are subject to testing and liable for prosecution if they are determined to be false or misleading. Deceptive advertising has been the focus of many industry and governmental review actions over the years. **Deception** is *the situation if there is a representation, omission or practice that is likely to mislead the consumer acting reasonably in the circumstances, to the consumer's detriment.*[16]

Generating deliberate consumer confusion is one aspect of deception. In a television commercial called "Mr. Quackers", Duracell promised that its Duracell Coppertop brand would keep its robotic duck quacking long after the other robotic contestants in a "Robotic Fight Club", which were powered by "heavy duty" batteries, failed. The claim was technically correct, but what the ad failed to say was that *all* alkaline batteries—including the Energizers that power the legendary bunny—perform better than the old-fashioned zinc "heavy duty" batteries. Although Energizer wasn't mentioned explicitly in the Duracell commercial, Energizer asked regulators to ban the Duracell ad as "false and misleading" because consumers understood the comparison to be against all other batteries, including Energizer's alkaline batteries. Energizer won, and Duracell had to modify its ad by adding the phrase "excluding alkaline batteries".[17]

Dubious health claims are particularly troublesome. To put a stop to such claims, rival marketers often turn to a national advertising review council that most countries have installed. Such a council investigates disputed claims, provides recommendations to the offending companies, and makes its findings public. But it does not fine companies, and compliance by companies is voluntary. These review councils get most of their cases from companies, not from consumers.

In general marketing communication is considered deceptive if messages mislead "reasonable consumers" to such an extent that their buying decisions are influenced—that is, they base a decision on deceptive or confusing information. In other words, both explicit and implicit claims must be substantiated. A good example of implicit claims are those that were used by Publishers Clearing House (a direct-marketing company that sells magazine subscriptions) to mislead people. Personalized letters that contained phrases such as "winners' confirmation form enclosed" and "PCH final notification for tax-free $11 700 000.00 SUPERPRIZE", along with the return address of PCH's "Payments and Disbursements", convinced many recipients that they were winners or could be winners if they bought a minimum number of magazines. These misleading messages prompted so many complaints that several dozen state attorneys-general filed suit against PCH and eventually won the case, including a promise from PCH to refrain from future use of these practices. When brand messages are found to be deceptive, the offending advertiser is forced to stop the advertising or revise the message, as happened with Duracell. In some cases companies making deceptive claims are subject to fines.

IMC in Action

Creative or misleading?

With the overall objective of making offers that are perceived as high value but are of minimal cost to marketers, sales promotions sometimes cross ethical boundaries. How ethical do you think each of the following promotional offers is?

1 **"1/2 Price Sale":** In fine print, the ad says that a customer who buys one pair of shoes at full price can get a second pair of equal or lesser value for half price. Is the headline offer misleading even though the small type explains how the sale works?

2 **End-aisle display of a brand at the regular price:** Shoppers have been conditioned to perceive that products on an end-aisle display are priced below their normal price. Would it be unethical for a retailer to use such a display but price the brand at its regular price?

3 **"Save up to 70%":** Department stores often run promotions with this headline. The reality is, however, that only a few racks of clothes have been reduced by 70 per cent; most items that are on sale have been reduced by only 20 to 30 per cent.

4 **"Fly to Barcelona for only 1 Euro":** What the message does not say is that various taxes and add-ons have to be paid. The true price is not displayed. And also the return trip usually has to be paid for.

5 **"Round Trip to Barcelona only 50 Euro**":** Another typical airline promotional offer is the low-priced round-trip with a small-print** caveat—limited seats available at this price. The airline is selling only 10 seats on selected flights to Barcelona at this low price, and the rest of the seats are priced at regular, and significantly higher, prices.

Think about it

Those offers are legal and used frequently. Even so, some consumers are confused and misled by these offers and feel cheated when they find out what the restrictions or conditions are. What is at stake is the trust and respect of customers. Many companies track brand awareness and trial, but few track image and trust. What can a company that uses these types of promotional come-ons do to monitor the damage that might be done to the company's image?

The key point with deception is the question of whether there is a gap between the product as advertised and marketed and the product as it actually is. Court rulings make it clear that companies would be wise to first show advertisements and marketing campaigns to legal counsel to make sure that the claims do not go too far and leave the company open to liability.[18]

Puffery

Brand messages that are unclear or subject to interpretation are more difficult to regulate. Calling a product the "finest" may be an exaggeration that cannot be proved, but the use of such words is rarely challenged because it is considered to be a legal form of boasting called puffery. Puffery is *the use of hyperbole or exaggeration to promote a brand*. Such hype is acceptable—even if it is a lie—unless a buyer can show that such language *was intended* to be interpreted as a fact or a promise.

In the US, for example, Wal-Mart used a tag line that failed the puffery test. Competitors claimed that Wal-Mart's slogan "Always the low price. Always" implied that Wal-Mart had the *lowest* prices of all retailers. When the ad was reviewed it was deemed misleading. Wal-Mart lost an appeal and changed its slogan to "Always low prices. Always Wal-Mart."[19] Why is puffery allowed? The government, and much of the industry, believes that most consumers know that boastful statements by advertisers are harmless exaggerations. Some experts disagree and argue that even though the law presumes that people do not believe puffery, research repeatedly finds that consumers actually do believe these claims are true.

Questionable business-to-business practices

Retailers often charge slotting allowances (Chapter 13). Some also charge display fees for certain shelf locations (items sitting at eye level are more likely to sell than those displayed higher or lower). Over the years these allowances and fees have escalated so much that small companies cannot afford them. According to an article in the *Journal of Marketing*, "Currently, two schools of thought dominate the debate on these fees. One considers them a tool for improving distribution efficiency, whereas the other proposes that the fees operate as a mechanism for enhancing market power and damaging competition. Managers and public policymakers are uncertain as to the effects of slotting fees and the appropriate strategy to adopt [regarding their use]."[20]

Another example of questionable practices comes from the pharmaceutical industry. Drug manufacturers invite doctors to "continuing education" classes and seminars that sometimes look more like junkets to fancy resorts, golf outings, or cruises. Sales representatives have long provided doctors with product and health information that critics say is too biased toward the sale of the products the reps are selling. Sales reps also provide gifts that some consider to be little more than bribes. Although sales reps play an important role in continuing to inform doctors about advances in the pharmaceutical industry, the question is how best to do the promotion without unduly influencing doctors' decisions on appropriate medical care.

Fraud

More serious in the universe of bad marketing communication practices than any of the previously described questionable tactics is outright fraud at either the consumer or the B2B level. Generally, government agencies aggressively pursue companies that knowingly mislead the public. Companies that have no track record of providing legitimate goods and services are also targeted. Companies engaging in fraud face criminal penalties. One of the most common types of MC fraud is the selling of brand knock-offs—goods that carry a popular brand name but are made by another company and generally are of lesser quality than the brand that has been counterfeited. Most likely to be counterfeited are products that are widely used, such as drugs, cigarettes, casual shoes, perfume, and even golf clubs. The International Chamber of Commerce estimates that approximately C300 billion worth of counterfeit goods are sold each year, 8 per cent of the world trade.[21]

A widely used advertising fraud is the bait-and-switch offer. An example is advertising a car (the bait) at a very low price, telling prospects who express an interest in it that the advertised car was sold and then showing prospects other, higher-priced models (the switch).

Regulatory methods and agencies

A number of different organizations deal with questionable marketing communication messages and practices, including industry self-regulation and government supervisory bodies. In most countries also consumers have organized themselves into consumer leagues, or consumer associations.

Self-regulation

Most of the oversight within the marketing communication industry is handled through self-regulation rather than by government order. It is in the best interests of responsible businesses and trade organizations to maintain high standards, for several reasons. First, the more they do, the less government intervention is called for. Second, industries know from past experience that a few disreputable companies can cause an entire industry to be suspect. Finally, the few companies that do not play by the rules may have an unfair competitive advantage, but only in the short term.

Self-regulation takes place by means of a company's own policies, an industry's own standards, and a review of the media delivering brand messages.

Internal policies

Most companies, marketing communication agencies, and media—not to mention industry associations—have their own professional standards that are used for self-regulating what they do. These standards provide guidelines so employees understand what kinds of messages and interactions with customers are and are not acceptable.

Although marketing communicators are not expected to be lawyers, they should know enough about the laws and government regulations to ask for a legal opinion when programmes and practices may have even the slightest chance of being in violation. Most medium and large companies have legal staff who should be made aware of major marketing communication programmes, especially anything new and different. People working in companies without a legal department must make their supervisors aware of anything out of the ordinary that could be in violation. More than one person has lost a marketing job for failing to get legal advice before initiating a programme that turned out to be illegal and resulted in negative publicity and costly reputation re-establishment.

MC agencies sometimes refuse to accept work from certain organizations, such as tobacco companies. For the work they do accept, media companies may demand proof of claims, for the agencies themselves are responsible for verifying any claims made by their clients before using these in brand messages. Before being distributed publicly, the messages are usually reviewed by agency lawyers. When a claim is found to be misleading, everyone involved—the company making the claim, the agency that produced the ad, and the media running the ad—can face penalties.

Industry standards

Trade organizations also establish guidelines for their members. Several advertising trade organizations have their own codes of practice for their members. More important, they have united to create monitoring groups to deal with questionable advertising practices.

Although many members of trade groups welcome restrictions on marketing tactics as a way to maintain professional standards, some argue that such restrictions are simply a way to preserve the status quo and prevent newcomers from gaining a foothold in the marketplace. Some critics say that the only reason why trade organizations develop codes is to head off government regulations. While this may be true, it is not necessarily a bad thing. Obviously governments will monitor the way self-regulators act. Do they comply with the law? Similarly when the public gets the impression that self-regulation is not effective and does not take complaints seriously, legislation is always the next option.

The European Advertising Standards Authority (EASA) is an independent organization which aims to act in the interest of customers and maintain fair competition for advertisers by monitoring adherence to advertising codes. These codes set out rules for honest advertising, for example, ensuring that ads are not misleading or offensive to consumers, and that companies conduct sales promotions and direct marketing fairly. The authority also has guidelines specific to different areas such as advertising products or brands linked to health, children and financial services. It takes action to rectify cases where these standards are not considered to be met, conducting investigations where necessary as well as dealing with cross-border complaints. Individual countries also have these kinds of regulatory bodies. For example, in the UK, the Advertising Standards Authority (ASA) fulfils a similar role, as does Ofcom, the regulatory body that sets out the statutory requirements that advertising must meet, as informed by the 2003 Communications Act. There are specific requirements for radio, television, print media and wireless communications services, although some are common to all of these mediums.

Media review

Not all magazine and newspaper trade associations have set out advertising guidelines for their members. However, individual media chains and local media outlets often set standards for advertising. Newspapers are more likely than other media to keep out ads that they believe their readers and advertisers might find objectionable.[22] A survey of 321 newspapers found that more than 71 per cent asked for verification or substantiation of ad claims.[23] This same survey also indicated that, while 40 per cent had a written policy outlining the types of ads they would accept or reject, many chose not to give any such explanations. Instead, they inform advertisers that they reserve the right to reject any advertising. A survey of 184 magazines indicated they were most concerned about "good taste", which generally meant rejecting ads with sexual explicitness.[24] For the most part, radio and television broadcasters have been highly active in self-regulation.

Consumer groups

A myriad of special-interest advocacy groups monitor commercial messages related to their causes. They often make their complaints public and organize boycotts when they deem it necessary. Although they have no legal powers, they can pressure companies to change their marketing communication practices.

Marketing communication responsibilities

Managing the social, ethical, and legal aspects of marketing communication is a complex task. MC managers need a general understanding of what they can and cannot do from a legal perspective, as well as what they should and should not do from an ethical on. They also need to know where to go for expert advice, and they should have some idea about what to do when conflicts arise.

Approval processes

To minimize legal and other challenges to brand messages requires an approval process with several message checkpoints. The approval steps vary by company, but in large organizations the process generally includes the following steps:

1 Review by the marketing staff.

2 Review by the public relations department from the perspectives of stakeholders other than customers. Are the messages inconsistent with the social, moral, and cultural standards of these other audiences?

3 Copy testing, not only for communication and persuasion but also for unintended messages.

4 Review by internal and (in the case of major campaigns) by external legal counsel.

5 Review by the MC agency account team and agency lawyers.

6 Review by the media.

Dealing with corporate ethics

To practice ethical behaviour, MC professionals must work in an environment where such behaviour is encouraged and supported. Not all companies give such encouragement or support; too often, companies do the opposite. A company trying to meet certain financial goals may be tempted to cut corners when testing or labelling ingredients, honouring warranties, and providing the promised after-market service. These companies might also allow (or force) marketing communicators to overpromise in order to increase short-term sales.

All companies should have an ethics statement, and new employees should expect to see it. Lack of an ethics policy may be a red flag alerting a new employee to potential problems in the MC programme. Like a crisis plan, an ethics statement should be clearly spelled out and discussed. Problems within the company and incidents outside the company should be used as examples to clarify what is expected of employees. Some companies conduct periodic ethics audits to encourage awareness of various issues that the company is currently facing or might face.

An ethics statement can offer some protection to employees who are being pressured (by middle management) to engage in behaviour that the employees believe is wrong. If such behaviour has already been identified as unacceptable, the employee can point to the official policy as a reason to refuse to co-operate.

Social marketing

Some social groups continually criticize marketing communication practices, but others—such as anti-cigarette and anti-drug groups—embrace MC and use it to promote their own social causes. The same persuasive practices designed to sell products and build brand relationships can be used to help solve social problems or advocate a social-responsible position (also see the opening IMC in Action case). Problem solving is what marketing does, because it is a process that forges a close relationship among strategies, audience, and behaviours.[25] As this neatly fits the objectives of social groups it is just logical that they refer to marketing practices for their own sake. The *use of marketing to address societal problems* is called social marketing.

Social marketing has proved successful in many cases. Thailand dramatically reduced the number of men becoming infected by HIV (the virus that causes AIDS) by encouraging them to use condoms and reduce their visits to prostitutes. Two years after the government-funded campaign began, the frequency of HIV infection in military recruits had dropped fivefold and the frequency of other sexually transmitted diseases had decreased tenfold (see colour inserts D1 and D15).[26]

Direct marketing has also proven an effective tool of social action. In 2002 a young Nigerian woman, Safiya Husseini, was accused of adultery and sentenced in Nigeria to death by stoning. The story attracted international attention because of the harshness of the sentence. Comunicacion Proximity, a Spanish MC agency, was so moved by the story that it launched a campaign, "Amnesty for Safiya", to collect signatures on a petition protesting against the sentence. Having only two weeks in which to work before the sentence was to be carried out, the agency used e-mail and direct mail to collect signatures. The result was over 600 000 signatures sent in by e-mail, 60 000 by mail and fax, and over 40 000 phone calls into a call centre set up for this specific purpose. The result was a reprieve for Husseini.[27] (The agency that created this campaign was awarded a Diamond Echo, the top honour in the Direct Marketing Association's annual Echo Awards competition.)

Social marketing is not without controversy, however. Anti-drug campaigns, for example, have been criticized for targeting the wrong problems (focusing on illegal drugs rather than on alcohol abuse); for glamorizing drug use (by combining attractive actors and actresses with violent images); and wasting taxpayers' money (by having no effect or, worse, being counterproductive). Initiatives to use MC to fight obesity have been criticized too as mere hypocrisy: first fast food advertising makes MC agencies earn lots of money, followed up by campaigns on their side to fight the consequences. The agencies are the only beneficiaries.

A final note: is it the message or the messenger?

The critics are right in some ways: marketing communication can be used to promote stereotypes, target vulnerable populations, and use offensive message strategies to sell products. Brand messages can also be misleading and be used to manipulate and deceive consumers. But marketing communication is also a set of tools that can be used for promoting social issues and public debate, as well as for selling soap and soft drinks. Even the promotion of products can contribute in a positive way to social improvement. Selling toothpaste, for example, has cut back dramatically on tooth decay, and selling soap has created higher levels of hygiene around the world. And Apple's promotional efforts have brought computer literacy to technophobic adults, as well as to schoolchildren whose families could never afford computers.

Furthermore, in a broader context, marketing communication enables the vital exchange of commercial information that makes the economy grow, providing jobs and income as well as an astounding range of product choices. MC itself is not inherently good or bad; it is only the messenger. And the message can contribute to social good as easily as it contributes to social problems.

🔑 Key terms

deception The situation if there is a representation, omission or practice that is likely to mislead the consumer acting reasonably in the circumstances, to the consumer's detriment.

ethics Moral and value standards that act as behavioural guidelines.

puffery The use of hyperbole or exaggeration to promote a brand.

social marketing Use of marketing to address societal problems.

subliminal advertising Messages that are received subconsciously, below a person's perceptual threshold, causing a desired response.

Check the key points

Key point 1: Role in society

a Why is marketing communication a more socially responsible platform than advertising?

b Explain the two points of view represented in the shape or mirror debate.

c What social concerns are raised with respect to marketing? What counter-arguments can be given to explain marketing's role?

d What are the two responses of society to these concerns? How are they related?

Key point 2: Ethical issues

a How would you define *ethics*?

b Whose ethics are relevant for marketers?

c What are sensitive areas in marketing communication?

d What is the difference between subliminal and suggestive advertising?

Key point 3: Legal issues

a What is the limit to free speech? Describe the concept of deception as precisely as possible.

b In how far must claims be substantiated?

c How do puffery and fraud differ?

d Describe the practice of counterfeiting. What kinds of products are most sensitive to counterfeiting?

e What is a bait-and-switch offer? Use this concept to clarify the distinction between ethics and legal issues.

Key point 4: *response to social, ethical and legal concerns*

a   What is self-regulation? What forms can this take?

b   How should marketers organize to respond to social concerns?

c   What is social marketing? What responses to social marketing can you think of?

d   Is MC just the messenger?

Chapter Challenge

Writing assignment

You are the marketing director of a large real-estate company that spends over C1 million a year on advertising in a regional newspaper. You have just received word that the paper is planning a series of investigative articles on the misleading practices used by some estate agents. The story will mention two agents who work for you, whom you had already disciplined for their out-of-line practices. You thought the matter was taken care of, but it is going to be made public and create an extremely negative impression of your company. You know you have "a million euros' worth of clout" with the newspaper. You would like to kill any negative reference to your company, but you realize that the newspaper has a social responsibility to its readers. Write a letter to the editor laying out what you would like the paper to do and why.

Presentation assignment

Pretend you are chairman of an ad agency who is concerned about your creative department using exploitive illustrations of men and women. Prepare a presentation, using both good and bad examples, that demonstrate what is, and what is not, in good taste and acceptable to do.

Discussion assignment

Make groups of about ten students. Identify two advertisements or other MC messages that are controversial. Take the first ad and let every member of your group list arguments why in her/his opinion this is a message that is of social concern, and whether the commercial is ethically or legally acceptable. Discuss the matter and then form into camps, one against and the other in favour of the ad. Then take the second ad. Let the group in favour of the first ad (the group that thought the ad is acceptable) list the arguments against this ad (so take the opposite position); the group against the first ad now lists arguments in favour of this ad. Finally, discuss the issue around whether the arguments against should lead to legal actions against this type of advertising.

Notes

[1] Sean MacBride, *Many Voices, One World: Communication and Society* (New York: Unipub [UNESCO], 1980).

[2] For an introduction to this world of criticism, go to www.adbusters.org or consult *Adbusters*, a magazine that comments on the social responsibility of advertising and marketing communication—or the perceived lack thereof.

[3] Sharon Shavitt, Paula Lowrey, and James Haefner, "Public Attitudes toward Advertising, More Favorable Than You Might Think", *Journal of Advertising Research* 34, no. 4 (1998), pp. 7–22.

[4] Quoted in David Ogilvy, *Ogilvy on Advertising* (New York: Crown, 1983).

[5] www.nytimes.com/2003/07/10/opinion/10THU2.html?th

[6] Simon Beck, "World Gangs up on US 'Culture'", *South China Morning Post*, 5 July 1998, p. 12.

[7] Karen Uhlenhuth, "Ads, Consumer Images Bombard Kids", *Boulder Daily Camera*, 9 October 2001, p. 1D.

[8] Roy Fox, "Hucksters Hook Captive Yungsters", *Mizzou*, Summer 2002, pp. 23–7.

[9] Jim Drinkard, "Lobbyists Trying to Sway Younger Minds", *USA Today*, 23 June 1998, p. 7A.

[10] Lisa Sarkis Neaville, "Molding Young Minds: Firms Spend Big to Get Views into Public Schools", *Plastics News*, 30 October 1995, p. 1.

[11] "Love Is Playing with Fire", *Forbes*, 3 November 1997, p. 39.

[12] David B. Menkes, "Hazardous Drugs in Developing Countries: The Market May Be Healthier Than the People", *British Medical Journal* 315, no. 7122 (13 December 1997), p. 1557.

[13] "First Mad Cows, Now Mad about Pigeons", *Inside PR*, 2, no. 39 (22 July 1996).

[14] Cecil Adams, "The Straight Dope", *Chicago Reader*, 1999 www.chicagoreader.com.

[15] Joel Saegert, "Why Marketing Should Quit Giving Subliminal Advertising the Benefit of the Doubt", *Psychology and Marketing*, 1987, pp. 107–20; Myron Gable, Henry T. Wilkins, Lynn Harris, and Richard Feinberg, "An Evaluation of Subliminally Embedded Sexual Stimuli in Graphics", *Journal of Advertising* 16, no. 1 (1987), pp. 26–31.

[16] "FTC Policy Statement on Deception", issued 14 October 1983, from the FTC website www.ftc.gov/bcp/policystmt/ad-decept.htm, 1 July 2003.

[17] Daniel Golden and Suzanne Vranica, "Duracell's Duck Ad Will Carry Disclaimer", *Wall Street Journal*, 7 February 2002, p. B7; Jack Neff, "Duracell Agrees to Modify Robo-War Duck Ad", *AdAge.com*, 6 February 2002, www.adage.com/news.cms?newsid=33981.

[18] Frank J. Giliberti, "Ads and Marketing Materials Can Lead to Liability", *Marketing Management*, Winter 1999, p. 53.

[19] Diane Richard, "Local Advertisers Turn to Arbitration to Resolve Disputes over Ads", *Minneapolis–St. Paul City Business* 15, no. 9 (1 August 1997), p. 1.

[20] Paul Bloom, Gregory Gundlach, and Joseph Cannon, "Slotting Allowances and Fees: Schools of Thought and the Views of Practicing Managers", *Journal of Marketing*, April 2000, p. 92.

[21] Matthew Benjamin, "A World of Fakes: Counterfeit Goods Threaten Firms, Consumers, and National Security", www.usnews.com/usnews/issue/030714/misc/14counterfeit.htm, 14 July 2003.

[22] Steve Pasternack and Sandra H. Utz, "Newspapers' Policies on Rejection of Ads for Products and Services", *Journalism Quarterly*, 65 (Fall 1988), pp. 695–701.

[23] Herbert J. Rotfeld, Kathleen T. Lacher, and Michael S. LaTour, "Newspapers' Standards for Acceptable Advertising", *Journal of Advertising Research*, September–October 1996, pp. 37–48.

[24] Herbert J. Rotfeld and Patrick R. Parsons, "Self-Regulation and Magazine Advertising", *Journal of Advertising* 18, no. 4 (Winter 1989) pp. 33–40.

[25] "Smoking Guns: PR/Marketing's Role in a Healthier America", *PR News* 53, no. 21 (21 April 1997).

[26] Susan Okie, "Thai Condom Campaign Cuts HIV Infections", *Washington Post*, 3 March 1998, p. Z5.

[27] Dawn Anfuso, "Integrated P.S. Campaign Wins Honors", *imedia connection.com*, 11 November 2002; Beth Viveiros, "Pushing the Envelope: Flight of Fancy", *Direct Marketing Business Intelligence Report*, www.directmag.com, 16 June 2003.

Further reading

Abela, Andrew (2003) "Additive versus inclusive approaches to measuring brand equity: Practical and ethical considerations", *Journal of Brand Management*, Vol. 10–4/5, pp. 342–52.

Beckett, Robert (2005) "Communication Ethics: Principles and Practices", *Journal of Communication Management*, Vol. 9–3, pp. 41–52.

Harker, Debra (2003) "Towards effective advertising self-regulation in Australia: the seven components", *Journal of Marketing Communications*, Vol. 9–2, pp. 93–111.

Maciejewski, Jeffrey J. (2005) "From Bikinis to Basal Cell Carcinoma: Advertising Practitioners' Moral Assessment of Advertising Content", *Journal of Current Issues & Research in Advertising*, Vol.27–2, pp. 107–15.

Preston, Chris (2004) "Children's Advertising: the ethics of economic socialization", *International Journal of Consumer Studies*, Vol. 28–4, pp. 364–70.

Tsiotsou, Radoula (2005) "The Effect of European Union Regulations on Marketing Practices: The Case of European Football Broadcasting Rights", *Journal of Euromarketing*, Vol. 15–1, pp. 75–93.

International marketing communication

CHAPTER PERSPECTIVE
Marketing to the world

Businesses are experiencing phenomenal opportunities to expand internationally. The ease of doing so, however, depends on which countries they choose to enter, what products they are selling, and what methods they choose to build brand relationships. International marketers face many challenges related to different cultures, languages, and levels of economic development. Adapting brand messages while at the same time maintaining strategic brand consistency requires a delicate balance. Cross-functional planning becomes all the more important when brand messages are being sent across national borders.

Most companies today are "international" even if they don't sell outside their national borders, because some or most of their raw materials or equipment comes from other countries. And even if all of their customers and materials are domestic, their competitors may very easily come from other countries. All companies today must therefore consider international issues when analysing their competitive position.

This chapter distinguishes between international marketing and global marketing. It discusses cultural factors in international MC, including cultural sensitivity and social responsibility. Segmenting and targeting are special challenges for international marketers, as are message design and delivery.

Whiskas creates a tiny tiger
BBDO, Düsseldorf, Germany

In the highly competitive cat-food market in the late 1990s, growth rates were nearly zero in most European markets, and all products were seen to perform essentially the same. The Whiskas brand management team at the European office of parent company Mars Inc. decided that the brand needed to differentiate itself and that to do so the emotional core of the brand, on which its relationship with consumers was built, should be emphasized. Enter a brand character: a silver tabby called the Tiny Tiger.

The marketing challenge

Revamping this venerable brand was the challenge given to the Düsseldorf, Germany, office of the international MC agency BBDO. A truly international brand sold worldwide, Whiskas had a 14-country European market. It also had many competitors. In addition to Mars's four other European brands, there were also strong entries from Nestlé and Purina. All these brands were fighting for a share of the market, creating a negative trend in 1997 for Whiskas.

Historically, the differentiating factors in the cat-food segment were health, taste, and nutrition. In the late 1990s all the brands performed essentially the same on these factors. Whiskas had long been successful with the proposition "Whiskas is the preferred food for cats". However, as the competition improved, the Whiskas brand lost its competitive edge.

Campaign strategy

The objectives of the Whiskas "Tiny Tiger" campaign were to differentiate the Whiskas brand from the competition, to make cat owners feel they had a role in the feeding choice, and to make owners feel good about spending more money for Whiskas. Regardless of country, the target audience for Whiskas is universal: female cat-owners between 19 and 65 years of age who are responsible for buying the cat food.

Creative strategy

The "Tiny Tiger" campaign was designed to give the Whiskas brand a heart by focusing on the brand's core essence, which is "care" (see colour insert D13). The Whiskas brand needed to reflect the core benefit of well-being—"the best way to care for your cat"—a benefit that is universally appreciated across the diverse European market. This strategy allowed the BBDO team to focus on those attributes that are most motivating in each market and determine the balance between the nutrition and enjoyment appeals. Caring is an emotional strategy, but this approach also allowed a degree of rationality.

The creative concept was stated as follows: "With Whiskas you can take the best care of your cat. You can see it and you can hear it. Every day." The creative tactics brought that idea to life with a satisfied cat on the lap framed in the Whiskas mask and the sound effect of a cat's purring. In addition, the silver tabby cat character, Tiny Tiger, was created as the hero of the campaign. These three integrated elements—the cat visual, the purring, and the silver tabby—became the Whiskas key brand signals. The simple graphics of the print ads were designed to showcase these brand-identity elements.

Message delivery

The "Tiny Tiger" campaign used a full range of marketing communication functions:

- Television, radio, print, and outdoor advertising.
- In-store promotions.
- Point-of-purchase activities.
- Direct marketing.
- A sales video and sales folder for the sales team to use with the trade audience.
- Internet activities, including a website in Germany (www.Whiskas.de).
- Licensed materials (a silver tabby stuffed toy).

For the advertising, the emphasis was placed on television and, to a lesser extent, print and outdoor. Research determined that cat owners want to see cats in motion, so television provided important visual impact. Print was used in specialized and targeted publications to reach true cat enthusiasts and communicate detailed information about the product. Outdoor offered a unique way to portray the silver tabby cat in a bigger-than-life medium.

Executing an international campaign is always difficult. In this case, the strategy was to use a standardized format with only a change in language for different markets. Because the creative idea was universal, the BBDO team felt that using standardized messages would provide more useful synergy for the brand than attempting to adapt the creative idea to different cultural groups. However, different executions were found to work better in different markets, so the strategy was localized by matching the best-performing executions to each country.

The agency created 11 television spots to launch the "Tiny Tiger" campaign. The campaign also introduced a new single-serve pouch, a line of kitten food, and a cat treat (pocket kibble). The spot "Purr", for example, which used all three of the key brand signals—the satisfied cat on the lap, the sound effect of the cat purring, and the silver tabby—showed high involvement of the owner and performed well in all markets. To see how the executions were targeted locally, consider two of the spots, "Cat Shuffle" and "Mmmeat", which were found from tests to do particularly well in France. "Cat Shuffle" succeeded in communicating functional benefits (taste and freshness) as well as emotional benefits (well-being), and "Mmmeat", which created the highest level of brand awareness in that market, focused more on the functional benefits of the best way to care for a cat.

Other marketing communication strategies

To reach the loyal Whiskas user effectively, BBDO designed a promotion to generate new addresses in the Whiskas database. In Germany, the agency elicited huge responses with two promotion strategies: a 15-second tag to the "It's in Your Hands" commercial and a "kitten starter pack", which included various products essential in the care of a new kitten. Of those customers who called the company as a result of the promotions, 70 per cent were new additions to the database.

Direct marketing was another important part of the MC mix. Whiskas sponsored a quarterly magazine, kitten brochures in stores, and a shop on the Internet site. Other sales promotions included the sampling of dry products and kitten products, and in-store promotions for both the can and the new pouch. Packaging was also part of the mix; a new brand label featuring the silver tabby cat tied the campaign directly to the product on the store shelf.

Evaluation of the Whiskas campaign

Total European sales results from January to August 1998 showed a significant turnaround from a negative growth rate and drop in share to a positive growth rate. An even larger increase in growth rate and share was noted in 1999. The effort was so successful that the campaign was deemed an award winner at the Advertising and Marketing Effectiveness (AME) international award show. More important, it has launched a brand repositioning that has extended beyond western Europe to other regions such as Poland, Hungary, the Czech Republic, the Baltics, Russia, and the UK, as well as Brazil and Argentina. Billboards with the silver tabby have also been used in Mexico. And the Tiny Tiger shows up on the new pouch packages in all markets, including the United States. The increasingly widespread use of the brand character shows how a good idea developed in one country (Germany) for a regional market (Europe) can, if successful, evolve into a global theme.

Source:
This case was adapted with permission from the Advertising and Marketing Effectiveness (AME) award-winning brief for Whiskas prepared by the BBDO agency in Düsseldorf, Germany.

International and global marketing

Marketers today realize that they cannot predict where their competition will arise. For example, China's great Olympic gymnast Li Ning (three gold medals in 1984) now competes against Nike in making performance athletic shoes and other sports gear. His Beijing-based Li-Ning Sports Goods Co. sells more trainers than any other company in the world. Determined to turn itself into an international premium brand, Li-Ning now sponsors national sports teams in France, Spain, Russia, and other countries, as well as China. The Li-Ning brand is seen as the vanguard of China's emerging global brands.[1]

Most companies market their products and compete in the countries where their headquarters are located, as Li-Ning did when he first started out in China. Companies that focus their marketing efforts on their home countries are called domestic (or national) marketers. A national market, then, is an individual country—such as Germany, Australia, or Mexico—and a national brand is one that is sold in only one country.

Companies that market products in several different countries are said to be **multinational marketers**. Most companies engaged in multinational marketing treat each country as a separate market—and one that is "foreign" from the home country.[2]

Then there are the **global marketers**, *companies that consider their market to be just one—the world*. Generally speaking, brands sold around the world are called *global brands*. A company involved in global marketing focuses on world market opportunities, not limiting itself to individual countries or regions. The word **region** is used to indicate *a set of geographically contagious countries*. Sometimes they are politically or economically connected, or by convention, but sometime the grouping is ad hoc. Thus, Mediterranean countries form a region, as do Scandinavia and Eastern Europe. The EU is considered a region from a US perspective. The word "region" is often used in a loose sense, with ad hoc definitions.

Global marketers do not necessarily have to enter every country in the world. The essence of global marketing is "widening the company's business horizons to encompass the world when identifying business opportunities".[3] Most companies start locally, expand nationally, move into international marketing, and then, when their brands have proved themselves, become global brands.

The prototypical example of a global marketer is the American brand Coca-Cola, whose products are distributed in practically all countries in the world. Coke is generally recognized as one of the strongest brands in the world (see Chapter 2). Its enviable global position results in part from the company's willingness to work with local distributors and to support local marketing efforts.[4]

A good runner-up in the list of truly global brands is McDonald's which has brought the Golden Arches to more than 110 countries. Although it saw its franchise tarnished in the 2000s as changing tastes and ageing facilities began to hurt its image, the company is fighting hard to maintain its leading position. The secret of McDonald's global success has been its ability to set up a standardized fast-food restaurant system, with a predictable level of quality anywhere in the world. Its genuinely global character was demonstrated by the introduction of the Big Mac index: an exchange-rate model for international currencies, based on the prices of McDonald's Big Mac.[5] Relying on the high level of standardization of McDonald's products, the prices of the Big Mac are used to gain insight into the issue of purchasing power parity, a measure that compares the value of currencies from the viewpoint of consumers.[6]

Probably the best-known and recognized European brand is Germany's Mercedes-Benz (whose corporate parent is DaimlerChrysler), which is a brand name recognized around the world. Finland's Nokia has profited immensely from developments in mobile telephony. From Japan Toyota and Honda are truly global players, both starting out simply exporting cars from Japan but now investing in manufacturing in numerous countries. In another product category Sony can be mentioned as a truly global marketer, as well as its South-Korean rival Samsung. The following list that identifies the top 25 global marketers and their home countries shows that it is not only global brands that make global marketing companies. Instead many corporations that market various brands are globally active, sometimes with different brand names for similar products in different markets:[7]

1. Unilever—United Kingdom and the Netherlands.
2. Procter & Gamble—United States.
3. Nestlé—Switzerland.
4. Toyota—Japan.
5. Volkswagen—Germany.
6. Coca-Cola—United States.
7. Ford Motor Company—United States.
8. General Motors—United States.
9. Peugeot—France.
10. Fiat—Italy.
11. Renault—France.

12 L'Oréal—France.

13 Kao Corporation—Japan.

14 McDonald's—United States.

15 Mars—United States.

16 Vodafone—United Kingdom.

17 Nissan—Japan.

18 Henkel—Germany.

19 Ferrero—Germany.

20 Sony—Japan.

21 Philip Morris—United States.

22 Danone—France.

23 France Telecom—France.

24 DaimlerChrysler—Germany and the United States.

25 Telefonica—Spain.

In this chapter the international or global marketing landscape will be sketched in four dimensions. First the topic of culture is discussed. Differences between countries are all too often grouped together under the term "culture". Understanding what culture is will enhance the understanding of differences between countries, and the challenges and complications that result therefrom. Second, in international marketing segmenting is an important topic and the international dimension offers new segmentation criteria. As this is the basis of any marketing communication plan, a brief look at segmentation in an international context is included. The chapter continues with two other aspects of the IMC plan: message design and media usage. Finally, the integration of MC efforts in the international arena is described.

Cultural factors

Culture is a major consideration in targeting customers internationally. The word **culture** refers to *the learned behaviours of a people that come from traditions passed on from generation to generation.* It is manifested in how people dress and what they eat, as well as in their music, religion, and entertainment. Culture also includes values and ways of looking at the world. **Values** are *enduring points of view that a certain way of thinking and behaving is preferable to a different way of thinking and behaving.*[8] Values involve judgements of good or bad, right or wrong. In IMC, it can be an important strategy to link values with a company's mission and understand how culture interacts with brand relationships and a customer-focus philosophy. Culture is the glue that binds a group of people together.[9] The question for MC professionals is: How does culture influence customer behaviour in response to brand messages (see colour inserts D3 and D4)?

When planning international marketing communication, companies must assess a country or target group's culture as part of the SWOT analysis. Companies analyse customers' attitudes and beliefs, motivations, and perceptions as they relate to a product category, the brand, and its usage. These culturally embedded traits should affect brand-message strategies differently in each country.

Because culture and communication are closely related, cultural factors are important in planning cross-cultural marketing communication strategies and evaluating their effectiveness. The challenge is to see to what extent there are different response patterns for different cultural groups.

Cultural differences and similarities

Marketers planning international brand messages debate how important cultural differences and similarities are. On the one hand are managers who believe that all cultures are different and that brand messages should always be customized for the local culture. On the other are managers who believe that universals such as love and happiness can be the basis for cross-cultural campaigns, and that the more specific the target (e.g. computer users), the more likely that the target's needs are similar regardless of country or culture. A Procter & Gamble executive explained P&G's approach to the global marketing of its Pampers disposable diapers: "Babies' bottoms are the same everywhere."

In situations of the latter type, brand messages can be standardized around the world. If customer segments are homogeneous between countries and across borders, as in the Whiskas example in the opening case, then standardized strategies make sense. If they are not, however, there is a need for adaptive strategies, which can result in an incredibly complex international marketing programme providing many opportunities for brand inconsistency—obviously a problem for an IMC manager.

Research has found, for example, more differences than similarities in consumer responses to marketing efforts. In many product categories, consumer demographics and behavioural responses vary by country. In a review of research studies into cultural differences and similarities, researchers Onkvisit and Shaw concluded: "The evidence is quite overwhelming that consumer/market homogeneity on a global basis does not exist."[10] Some products are definitely "culture bound", such as local food and some types of entertainment.

It is an important principle that *the degree of cultural difference is often related to the product category*. Some products, such as medicine, computers, and telecommunication, do not differ much by country; other products, such as food and fashion, may have significant differences. In the Whiskas case, the brand's managers used research to determine that owning and caring for a cat were fairly universal factors. Despite these seemingly universal attitudes towards pets, people in various cultures view pets in different ways. This may lead to unusual challenges to international marketers. For example in France cats or dogs are permitted in restaurants, but this practice is not generally appreciated in other countries. Thus an ad featuring a pet in a restaurant, for example, would not have the same impact in both cultures—perhaps touching an emotional chord in France and a humorous chord in the UK.

Consumer products, established products, and products with simple technologies are the most culturally bound, and industrial products and services, new products, and complex new technologies are the least culturally bound. Not surprisingly, business-to-business brand messages from a variety of countries have been found to be relatively unrelated to cultural differences.[11]

Food products are considered difficult to sell globally because of entrenched national eating habits and tastes. Olive oil sells well in the Mediterranean countries but less well in Scandinavia. Cold cereal with milk is a distinctively North American breakfast, but not one that is so commonly consumed in Europe and Asia. For international food marketers, the challenge is whether to develop products suited to local tastes or rather to try to create demand for new "exotic" foods. Many national foods, such as tacos, pita bread, croissants, curry dishes, sushi, gyros, and yogurt, have moved around the world to varying degrees. McDonald's restaurants around the world strike a balance: they offer their standard fare (such as burgers and fries) along with local adaptations such as the McMaharaja (lamb patties) in India and beer in Germany.

So what is an MC manager to do? Obviously the cultural question complicates the practice of one-voice, one-look strategies. Because of the need to plot cultural differences and similarities, international IMC calls for an even more complex plan for strategic consistency than domestic IMC. As Figure 17-1 illustrates, the question of cultural differences is complex because culture consists of many different levels. Even within a country, where one might assume there is a great deal of national identity, there may be different cultures, traditions, and languages. For example, in Spain the Basques and Catalans regard themselves as separate from mainstream Spaniards, who are symbolized by the capital Madrid. In Italy, there are huge differences between the north and the south. In France there are two stereotypes: one for Paris and another for the rural areas.

Dimensions of culture

Studies have found similarities and differences in mass media advertising used in different cultures—including cultures within a country. Generally, these studies have found that ads in Eastern cultures tend to be emotional or symbolic and those in Western cultures tend to be practical, utilitarian, hard-sell, or informative.[12]

Hall's high-context and low-context cultures

Another way of explaining the differences found in cross-cultural studies is in terms of the cultural context surrounding a message. Edward Hall classified countries as being either a high-context culture or a low-context culture. The distinction between "high" and "low" context reflects the extent to which context—*the non-verbal elements surrounding a message*—carries meaning and is a significant part of the message in a culture.[13] A low-context culture is *one in which less emphasis is placed on the social context and more is placed on words, directness, and time (deadlines and schedules).* A high-context culture is *a culture in which meaning is determined by non-verbal cues, social relationships and indirect communication such as metaphors and aphorisms (statements of principle).*[14]

An informational strategy or hard-sell approach in a brand message is likely to be more successful in low-context cultures, such as Germany or the Scandinavian countries, where people rely less on context to interpret the message than they do in, for example, Mediterranean

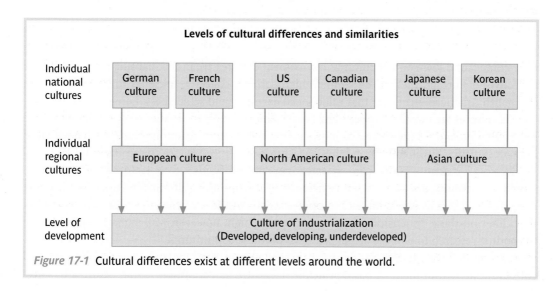

Figure 17-1 Cultural differences exist at different levels around the world.

cultures. Drama and imagery are often more appropriate in high-context cultures, such as Greece and France, where there is more dependence on context to signal the appropriate message. This distinction can be summarized as follows:

> *High-context cultures:* Cultures that pay more attention to the physical environment in which the message takes place. Relatively little information is found in the explicit message. People in these cultures are more sensitive to non-verbal cues.

> *Low-context cultures:* Cultures that rely on the explicit message to carry most of the information. There is relatively little reliance on non-verbal cues.

Hofstede's dimensions of culture

Another approach used in creating international brand messages is to analyse the components of culture as Geert Hofstede has done. In a study of 50 countries, he identified four basic components of culture:[15]

- Power distance: hierarchical versus egalitarian.
- Uncertainty avoidance: tolerance of risk.
- Collectivism versus individualism.
- Feminine versus masculine.

Later a fifth dimension was added, which described the attitude towards time perception, with the extremes of long-term orientation vs. short-term orientation. The differences in business style created by these factors can be major. For example, an individualistic business culture, found in many Western countries, values self-determination, achievement, a future orientation, optimism, and problem solving. In contrast, collectivistic cultures, such as Asian countries, value maintenance of the status quo, harmony, and collaboration.[16]

Even in Asia, however, there are differences in cultural responses to marketing communication. For example, researchers have found that advertising appeals in Taiwan and Hong Kong tend to be dominated more by "Westernized" cultural values than by traditional Chinese ones.[17] In these areas, which have evolved somewhat separately from mainland China, Western goods have a certain cachet. The same also holds true for people in many newly developed countries, where the West is sometimes viewed positively as a bastion of power and prestige.

How can an understanding of the work of Hofstede and Hall help in planning IMC? Researchers have found that Hofstede's individualism–collectivism model corresponds to Hall's high-context and low-context cultures: low-context cultures are individualistic; high-context are collectivist.[18] Further, they have identified high-context, collective societies to be mostly Asian and South American—cultures that value social harmony and selflessness. Low-context, individualistic cultures are mostly European and North American; people in these cultures tend to value self-realization and see themselves as independent, self-contained, autonomous. Such an analysis helps to explain why different brand message strategies are needed (see colour insert D12).

Figure 17-2 adapts Hall's context categories and Hofstede's four factors—each one presented as a continuum—to set up a chart for evaluating the cultural dimensions of a target market. This chart assigns countries to opposite ends of the spectrum in order to demonstrate they differ on these dimensions. In planning a campaign, however, MC managers would need to conduct research to plot the actual positions on these continuums.

Cultural dimensions also can be used to analyse organizations and how people work and communicate within them. A basic principle in most Asian countries is that before a business

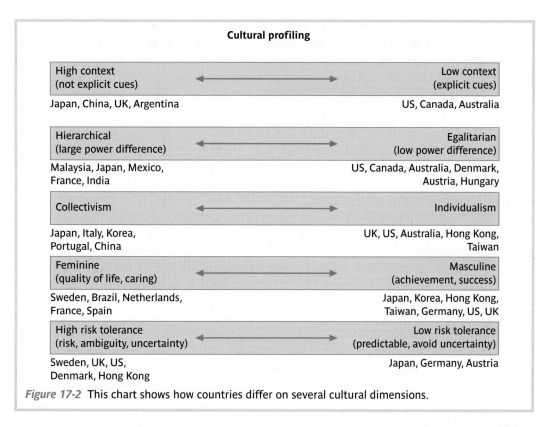

Cultural profiling

High context (not explicit cues)	⟷	Low context (explicit cues)
Japan, China, UK, Argentina		US, Canada, Australia

Hierarchical (large power difference)	⟷	Egalitarian (low power difference)
Malaysia, Japan, Mexico, France, India		US, Canada, Australia, Denmark, Austria, Hungary

Collectivism	⟷	Individualism
Japan, Italy, Korea, Portugal, China		UK, US, Australia, Hong Kong, Taiwan

Feminine (quality of life, caring)	⟷	Masculine (achievement, success)
Sweden, Brazil, Netherlands, France, Spain		Japan, Korea, Hong Kong, Taiwan, Germany, US, UK

High risk tolerance (risk, ambiguity, uncertainty)	⟷	Low risk tolerance (predictable, avoid uncertainty)
Sweden, UK, US, Denmark, Hong Kong		Japan, Germany, Austria

Figure 17-2 This chart shows how countries differ on several cultural dimensions.

relationship, such as that between a client and an agency, is cemented, the people who will be working together must get along socially as well as professionally. So in these countries, part of the brand-relationship building, especially for B2B products, often takes place in restaurants and on golf courses, or in Karaoke bars in Japan.

Cultural sensitivity and social responsibility

A critical competency for people managing cross-cultural communication is cultural sensitivity. One way to develop good relations with culturally diverse people is to become aware of communication styles and the problems and misunderstandings they can create.[19] Having cultural awareness—a sense of cultural differences and similarities—is the first step toward becoming culturally sensitive. Flexibility is a second important factor in a manager's relationship proficiency. Both traits are particularly important when international cross-functional teams are assembled.

Media sensitivity

Global media are magnifying the sensitivity issue. With the development of huge media conglomerates—such as Sony's entertainment division, Columbia TriStar—Western popular culture has spread all over the world. But then something happened: these conglomerates not only discovered local programming but discovered that in many cases audiences *preferred* local shows. So now Columbia TriStar is producing *Chinese Restaurant*, a series in Mandarin Chinese about a young Chinese woman in Los Angeles. The show is carried by 100 Chinese television stations. Columbia TriStar also has become the owner of Super TV, a Mandarin-language channel that reaches 77 per cent of the 5.1 million households in Taiwan. Other Columbia

TriStar production houses are located in India, Latin America, and several Asian cities. Columbia has also set up shop in Germany to go into foreign-language film production in Europe.

Rupert Murdoch's News Corporation learned a painful lesson about the perils of global marketing when it first expanded into Asia. To gain entry into this large emerging market, News Corp bought Hong Kong-based Star TV which gave Murdoch a huge broadcast footprint in Asia. A **broadcast footprint** is *the geographical area in which there is reception from a satellite transmission*. The company intended to blanket the region with English-language channels that would be easy to fill with already-produced programming. Star TV soon found, however, that News Corp's unwillingness to localize programming was a mistake. Since then, Star's real success story has been its Mandarin-language Phoenix channel. In partnership with two Hong Kong companies, Phoenix reaches some 170 million educated upmarket viewers in China, including those in Beijing and the prosperous southern city of Guangzhou.

The model for both television and film is the music industry, where the dominant global companies have discovered two revenue streams by delivering international hits as well as local music. What is emerging is a two-tier production system. English is often the language of international blockbuster films, TV series, CDs, and advertising, but local language hits are equally as important.

The cultural imperialism issue

The headline read: "Brad Pitt car ad is an insult to Asians, says Malaysia."[20] Malaysian authorities were banning a television advertisement that featured Brad Pitt's face in a Toyota ad because they thought the advertisement was humiliating for Asians and represented US propaganda. They saw the use of Western actors and models in a Japanese car ad as an example of cultural imperialism.

The issue of **cultural imperialism** refers to *the impact that a more dominant culture has on another, less dominant culture*. The criticism is most often heard in relation to American companies and their internationalization activities, but applies generally to Western counties. Cultural imperialism is based on the notion that Western movies, television programmes and, especially, advertising promote materialism and a culture of consumption. Brand messages and programme content from Western societies also violate local taboos, such as those of Muslim countries against showing women in bathing suits and other revealing clothing. Opposition to cultural imperialism has led to bans and restrictions on certain brand messages in some countries. In Malaysia, where the Toyota ad with Brad Pitt was banned, all television programmes and commercials have to be produced in the country and use local producers and models. In 1998 China allowed only 10 foreign-made films to be shown in the country; in 1999, it announced that it would ban all unauthorized reception of foreign TV. Both of these policies are nearly impossible to enforce—in any country—because of satellite broadcasting. Nonetheless, various governments, for a number of political, religious, and cultural reasons, are trying to slow the Westernization of their cultures.

A related concern for marketers is boycotts based on protests over political policies. When the US and Britain, for example, initiated the war with Iraq in 2003, consumers in a number of countries boycotted brands from these countries. McDonald's and Coca-Cola were particularly vulnerable because they are seen as symbols of the West at large.[21] But on the other side of the coin, a boycott of French products occurred in the United States because the French government did not support the war initiative.

Exploitation

A dimension of cultural sensitivity that focuses on issues of social responsibility is exploitation in the manufacturing of products. Although manufacturing is not marketing communication, when companies are perceived as being exploitive, this sends a negative brand message that can harm a brand's relationship with its customers and other stakeholders (see colour insert D9). That is why issues that generate protest, such as outsourcing production to Third-World countries where wages and living standards are exceptionally low, may lead to the perception that a company is not socially responsible. Nike, among others, has been attacked for such practices, and protests at World Trade Organization meetings have focused on this issue. In contrast, The Body Shop (personal-care products) and Unilever's Ben & Jerry's (ice cream) are companies committed to protecting the environment and supporting indigenous peoples, goals that each has leveraged to build its brands.

Cultural mistakes

Marketing communication is susceptible to cultural errors if message designers are not sensitive to language and cultural differences. Here are some examples made by various companies:[22]

- In France, Colgate introduced its Cue toothpaste, then found out that *cue* sounds like a certain obscene word in French.

- In Germany, Pepsi's slogan "Come alive, you're in the Pepsi generation" was translated as "Come out of the grave".

- In Thailand, a US-designed ad for Listerine was ineffective because it showed a boy and girl being affectionate to each other in public, a relationship display that violated Thai cultural norms.

- The Danish brewer Carlsberg had to add a third elephant to its beer label in Africa, where two elephants are a symbol of bad luck.

The use of colour can be a sensitive cultural concern, a fact that can create serious problems for global brands that desire consistency in their brand messages. In Japan, China, and many other Asian countries, the colour white is for mourning, as is purple in many Latin American countries. Gold is a strong positive colour for Chinese, but not in combination with black. Ikea uses blue and yellow, the colours of the Swedish flag—but not in Denmark, where that colour combination has a negative connotation because of a period of Swedish occupation.[23]

Don't mistake culture

The understanding of the phenomenon of culture is indispensable for an international marketer. But the concept must be understood and used well. In particular in the behavioural context, in the work of Hall and Hofstede, culture is treated as a set of personality traits. These researchers interpreted culture as a set of shared personality traits that drive behaviour. That is a useful way to understand culture, but one with limitations. Understanding culture this way says that all people, in whatever country, can be classified on the basis of their "score" on these traits. By comparing national averages it tries to prove that, on average, people from different countries differ in the scores obtained on these traits. This is useful information, but it does not tell us that all people in a certain country behave in the way they do. In Italy (generally considered a masculine culture) there are people who could be characterized as feminine, and in Germany (which is characterized as a high-power distance culture) there are people with low power distance. And perhaps it is those feminine Italians or those low power-distanced Germans that are exactly the people interested in your brand.

The message is that the traits that play such a prominent role in discussions about culture are relevant and interesting. And in general, and on average, people of different countries differ in how they score in this trait. Nothing more, nothing less.

Segmenting international target markets

Segmenting markets is a central issue in any marketing strategy. As it is treated in every introductory marketing textbook, it has not been discussed in this text. Marketing communications follows decisions on which markets to target, which again is a result of a segmentation analysis. Thus, market segmentation is done, long before MC comes in sight. Nevertheless, in international marketing communications there are some specific aspects of segmentation that deserve attention, as they influence more directly the IMC strategy and planning decisions. The three ways to classify global or international markets—by geography, by level of market development, and by cohort group—are reviewed in the following pages.

By geography

The distinctions made earlier in defining different types of international and global marketing also describe geographic markets. The most common geographical classifications are local markets (national or domestic) and international markets, which can be regional or global. Regional marketing is carried out in countries that are geographically close, usually within the same continent. In such regions, products are often distributed easily between countries. With the development of alliances such as the EU and NAFTA (North American Free Trade Association, a collaboration of Canada, US and Mexico), regional marketing has gained importance. In Europe, nearly all trade barriers have been eliminated among EU member nations. Similarly, NAFTA was designed to reduce trade barriers between Canada, the United States, and Mexico. In Asia there are several groups of countries with varying degrees of unification. These regional associations and partnerships make it easier for marketers to create and execute MC programmes.

By level of market development

Another way to segment markets is by the level of development of the country. The **developed markets** in most of Europe, North America, Australia, and Japan can be described as *markets in which consumption patterns are focused more on wants and desires than on basic needs*. Consumers in developed countries can easily meet their physical needs (food, clothing, shelter) and thus have money to spend on non-essential goods and services, which include interesting and novel experiences. Developed markets are characterized by:

- High levels of literacy.
- A high standard of living.
- A high level of industrialization.
- An infrastructure that supports health care and education.
- A wide variety of media and high rates of media penetration.

Worldwide expenditures on MC media (not including telemarketing and sales promotion) for 2004 have been estimated to be €440 billion.[24] For decades, Europe has been the focus of many media and marketing efforts. Switzerland, for example, is home to some of the world's

Building brands in the bush

Busi Skenjana is pioneering techniques to build brands in the townships of South Africa by using non-conventional media. She is president of Soweto-based IXesha Marketing Focus, a promotions agency that offers packaged-goods brands an entry into township retailing. Her unusual route to building brand awareness takes her not to traditional media but to dirt roads leading to village social and cultural events, such as weddings and funerals.

She has found that entertainment, celebrations, and social and cultural events provide opportunities for visibility for the brands she represents. She brings in all the equipment, furnishings, food, and other accoutrements needed to stage the event, such as pans and bowls for food, tents, banners, limos, portable stages, even toilets—all of them branded. For example, a branded bridal limousine carries the message "Here comes the [brand X] bride". After all, the same brand sponsors the Bride of the Year award in local newspapers. And Skenjana makes sure that all the little shops in the township are stocked with the brands sponsoring the event.

It's a win–win approach to brand promotion. The celebrants get a larger and more extravagant event at no cost, and the brands get an introduction—and one with positive associations—to a newly developing market. It's an innovative way to reach customers who have access to very few media—and to reach them in a way that is relevant to their lives.

Think about it

What is the key challenge of reaching customers in undeveloped markets? How does IXesha Marketing Focus reach its target markets?

Source:
Busi Skenjana, "Building Brands in a Fragmented Media Society" (paper delivered at the IMM-MASA Conference, Johannesburg, South Africa, 10 March 1998).

truly multinational corporations, many of which have been dominant in their categories since the beginning of the twentieth century.

Although recovering slowly from its 1990s economic slowdown, Japan remains a relatively closed market that is difficult for foreign marketers to enter. Australia is also a difficult market to enter because of fairly tight regulation and its geographic isolation.

Developing markets are *markets in which the consumption patterns are clearly expanding from necessities to wants and desires.* Former Eastern Europe countries are developing as they are recovering from the socialist experiment. For many of these countries entry to the European Union is a crucial step in this development. The benefits of entering this common market are enormous and it is the goal of many governments. The reforms that are necessary for this membership are again important for the economy itself, but of course the EU is principally a political union (despite its origins as a European *Economic* Community).

Many of the Far East or Pacific Rim countries, such as Thailand, Vietnam, the Philippines, Indonesia, and China, are considered developing markets too. Mainland China, with a population of 1.2 billion, is the largest market in this category. Some of the other countries in the Far East region, such as South Korea, Taiwan, Singapore, and Hong Kong, have well-developed economies.

International companies have again been investing heavily in Asia. With its 3 billion people, Asia comprises about two-fifths of the world's population, as well as some of the most promising markets in the world. China in particular has caught the attention of the international business community. The country was closed to marketing until 1978, when economic reforms led to sustained growth and a more open market. After opening up, growth started to enter China's vocabulary hesitantly, but in particular after recovering from the economic slowdown in the 1990s the Chinese economy is sky rocketing. Enormous growth figures, coupled with a population of over 1 billion people, makes this country the El Dorado of internationally oriented companies.

However, doing business in China does involve some adjustments in business practices. Some companies, nevertheless, including Danone, Coca-Cola, and Kodak, have made profits there. Danone has become successful by piggybacking off domestic brands and acquiring local companies. Coca-Cola's sales are growing faster in China than anywhere else in the world. Executives have had to come up with creative solutions to rural markets, including promoting the use of returnable bottles and thus lowering cost. Kodak has prospered by opening up nearly 8000 retail photo stores across China and creating a programme by which local Chinese businessmen can run the business. Although success was initially elusive for many companies trying to prosper in China, a study done in August 2002 revealed that 64 per cent of about 200 companies surveyed in China reported being profitable.[25]

India, too, is a developing market. Developments in India mimic those in China with a few years' delay. India has a big advantage in that English is the nation's shared language (next to the dozens of local languages). Also the Middle East is slowly opening its doors to Western thought and trade. Dubai, capital of the United Arab Emirates, is a key city in the southern part of the Mid-east region. Riyadh, capital of Saudi Arabia, is also a major centre of industrialization. Israel is an exception in this region, of course, because it already has a highly developed economy.

In Africa, Egypt is an expanding economy. Industrialized South Africa offers a stabilized economy and a huge potential for marketers as its African consumer culture emerges. Diverse cultures and closed borders remain in some areas of South America, but strong market opportunities exist in many of the countries, particularly Argentina and Brazil (which it might be more appropriate to call developed), which means product choice is becoming much more important to consumers.

Undeveloped markets are *markets in which consumption patterns remain focused on basic needs.* Challenges to marketers in these regions include lack of media, a relatively high level of illiteracy, low disposable income, and lack of marketing infrastructure such as distribution systems. Modernization itself within these countries—setting up modern transportation and communication infrastructures, as well as distribution channels for adequate health care, education, and food—will provide numerous B2B market opportunities for companies adept at providing these goods and services. As undeveloped countries do modernize, market opportunities will be created for consumer goods, although the consumer orientation will be more focused on meeting basic needs than on wants for some years to come. Much of Africa, outside the big cities, falls into this category.

By cultural cohort group

A **cultural cohort**, a segmentation concept based on anthropologists' cross-cultural studies, is *a group of people from multiple cultures who share a common characteristic.* From a marketer's perspective, a cohort's common characteristic is (or results in) a specific need, want, or desire. For example, new mothers around the world want their babies to be happy. Thus products such as Pampers disposable nappies can appeal to new mothers regardless of nationality. A cultural cohort can be thought of as a global community with a unifying interest.[26]

The cohort approach to international segmentation uses a stratification method in which customers with similar characteristics, and therefore common wants and needs, can be grouped together despite national boundaries. Examples of cultural cohorts include mothers of infants, business travellers, and cat-owners. Recall from the opening case that the target audience for Whiskas was considered universal: female cat-owners who are responsible for buying the cat food. Cultural cohorts are particularly noticeable in the high-tech, fashion, and entertainment industries.

The youth market is one of the most distinct global cohort groups and a particularly important global target for many marketers such as Adidas, Red Bull, Nike, and Nokia. But even within this group, there are still segments based on values, personalities, and lifestyles. In a study of more than 27 000 teenagers in 44 countries, the 500-million member group was divided into six distinct value segments (see Figure 17-3). The study found that teens are not necessarily alike worldwide, even within countries; however, some lifestyle characteristics do cross national borders.[27]

The music video channel MTV is an example of a powerful worldwide media vehicle that reaches the global youth market. It is also a premier platform for marketers trying to reach a cultural-cohort segment. Although most teens listen to the same kinds of music, MTV has found that there are regional and national differences. The channel's managers learned in MTV's early foray into the European market that the world's youth might all say, "I want my MTV!" but they don't want a copycat version of the US channel. For that reason, MTV now airs in more than 20 different feeds around the world, all tailored for their respective markets. All the channels, however, reflect the familiar, frenetic look and feel of the original MTV.

Viacom, the channel's owner, estimates that every second of every day almost 2 million people are watching MTV. In the early 2000s MTV reached 116 million homes in Asia—46 million more than in the United States. Since nearly two-thirds of Asia's 3 billion people are under the age of 35, MTV's growth in the region has been explosive, as it attracts those valuable trendsetting early adopters.

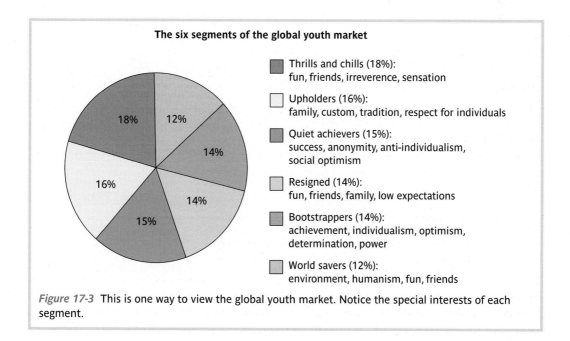

Figure 17-3 This is one way to view the global youth market. Notice the special interests of each segment.

To develop relationships with its viewers in the United Kingdom, Russia, and the Philippines, MTV sponsors parties that are showcases for MTV's advertisers such as Nike, Gap, and Levi's. Compaq's European manager attributes a 12 per cent increase in profit in Europe to the company's presence on MTV. He explains, "Young people trust MTV, and they trust what is shown on MTV."[28]

Message design: the same or different?

The debate about the best international strategy has been going on since the early 1960s. It became a central issue in the early 1980s when Theodore Levitt in an article in the *Harvard Business Review* stated that international companies should use standardized strategies.[29] Research findings consistently show, however, that standardization can be problematic because of differences in national cultures. Nonetheless, corporate managers continue to argue for standardization hoping for better control of the presentation of a brand's image, as well as benefiting from the cost efficiencies of a single campaign (see colour insert D7).

The world may become more nearly a single, homogeneous marketplace, but there will always be economic, geographical, cultural, political, demographic, and technological differences that stand in the way of a truly level playing field. Even if people buy the same products, that does not mean they buy them for the same reasons. International marketers are faced with the challenge of taking advantage of new communication technology to reach millions of customers quickly and cost-effectively while ensuring that they are not sacrificing their desired brand image.

Standardize or localize?

Standardization and localization are the two primary MC strategies used in international marketing communications. A **standardization strategy** (also called a **global strategy**) is *an international MC strategy in which the same basic brand message is used in all countries*. A **localization strategy** is *an international MC strategy in which brand messages are customized to make them compatible with each country's culture and local needs and wants*.

Standardization and localization are at opposite ends of a strategy continuum (see Figure 17-4). Most international MC strategies fall somewhere between these two extremes as marketers aim to "think globally, act locally". A major determinant of whether messages should be standardized or localized is product category as discussed earlier in this chapter.

One problem multinational brands face is that local offices sometimes resent being forced to use global campaigns and make the argument (even when not valid) that the standardized

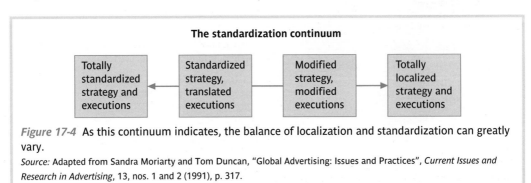

Figure 17-4 As this continuum indicates, the balance of localization and standardization can greatly vary.

Source: Adapted from Sandra Moriarty and Tom Duncan, "Global Advertising: Issues and Practices", *Current Issues and Research in Advertising*, 13, nos. 1 and 2 (1991), p. 317.

campaign fails to adequately address the local market. This situation is often addressed by adopting a strategy that is sometimes called **glocalization**: *having a global strategy that is locally executed*, where the extent of adapting to local circumstances may vary widely. A study of global best practices found that most multinational companies are operating with a combination or two-tier MC strategy: global headquarters determines the broad strategic direction for the brand, and regional or country offices execute the strategy as they see best.[30] Such an approach combines the advantages of both strategies—consistent brand-image development and successful communication accommodating cultural differences.[31]

The language factor

With few exceptions, any sort of localization strategy demands that the language of the marketing communication be translated into the language of the countries where the MC materials are used. Automatically that will create some inconsistencies in how the materials are presented. For international products, language may present both a problem and a creative opportunity.

Online communities are often classified by the languages used as opposed to the geographic region. E-commerce marketers who try to rely on English as an international business language often find that their customers want to do business in their own languages. A study completed in June 2002 identified the percentages of online users by language:[32] The same source observed that by the end of 2005, the use of English had dropped to only 29.7 per cent!

Languages	Number of users (m)	% of internet
English	235	38.3
Chinese	69	11.2
Japanese	61.4	10
German	42	6.8
Spanish	32.7	5.5
Korean	25.2	4.1
Italian	24	3.9
French	22	3.5
Portuguese	19	3.1
Russian	18.1	3
Dutch	12.4	2
Polish	6.7	1.1
Swedish	6	1
Arabic	5.7	1

Internet language use (2002)

Source: www.translate-to-success.com/Internet-language-use.html, retrieved 27 January 2007.

E-commerce companies, such as Bol.com, Amazon.com, and eBay are pushing into international business. They are developing local-language sites across Europe and Asia. Amazon.com operates language-specific sites in Germany and France. It has also exported products to customers in 160 other countries where customers access the site in English. Online auctioneer eBay has a dedicated site for the United Kingdom, but its European rival, QXL, is pioneering a different approach. QXL has moved from nation to nation, launching local sites in some and buying established companies in others, and it now operates in 12 different languages with 12 different currencies.

Language is a main source of marketing mistakes, as some examples mentioned earlier in this chapter illustrate. Translation is a difficult but safer way to introduce brands in other countries therefore. Even the most innocent looking words can lead to embarrassment. When Clairol introduced its curling iron Mist Stick in Germany it failed to realize that the German word *mist* means manure.[33] Translations may lead to results looking strange in the eyes of consumers in the domestic countries. When the phenomenally successful Harry Potter series of children's books was introduced to China, the lead publisher, Scholastic, translated the character's name phonetically as "Ha-li Bo-te" so that Chinese readers would find it easy to say.

One of the most famous examples in this area is the introduction of Chevrolet's *no va* series in Latin American. As Nova means "doesn't go" in Spanish, it seems clear that this is not a fortunate brand name in Mexico and other Spanish-speaking countries. According to Gerald Erichsen, however, this and many other such stories are just legends: it has not really happened, but it is a good story. And for sure the story shows what marketing mistakes *might* happen, when insufficient attention is paid to the language issue.[34]

IMC in Action

La Vache Qui Rit (The Laughing Cow)

A laughing cow. It seems to be quite strange, but this cow has been used to represent a world-renowned cheese brand for many years now. The brand name (called La Vache Qui Rit) was created in 1921 in France and introduced a whole new way of eating cheese. Instead of big pieces of cheese, The Laughing Cow is produced in portions (triangles, squares or rectangles), tubs, slices and snacks. To position itself as a universal brand, it adapted the brand name to the different countries where it was sold: La vache qui rit® in France, Vesela Krava® in the Czech Republic, Krowka Smieszka® in Poland, La vaca que rié® in Spain, A vaca que ri® in Portugal, Con bo cuoi® in Vietnam and Vessiolaia Bourionka® in Russia. The Laughing Cow presents itself as being something special to consumers, in particular to their preferred consumers, children. Her daring red appearance is an important aspect of her identity. Furthermore, in laughing she expresses a human emotion and by wearing earrings, the association with a real cow is made more remote.

What's more, The Laughing Cow has become an advertising legend in itself. The first tools to promote the brand consisted of a humorous range of advertising posters. After that, she was also depicted on decorative plates, exercise books and other school accessories. Her first introduction on the screen took place in 1950. The Laughing Cow featured in a commercial in the cinema, where she was promoted by Pauline Carton. In this commercial Carton presented the cheese spread's virtues and ingredients and she finished the commercial by describing the cheese as "better than ever!". During the fifteen years after the first commercial, the brand message shifted from being product-centred to the use of a more emotional appeal. In the ads families were shown eating and sharing the cheese, representing the personality of The Laughing Cow brand: warmth, friendship and the simple things in life that a family can enjoy.

It is no surprise that humour has always been part of the advertising campaign. In a commercial in the 1980s children were shown growing under the viewers' eyes. In 1984 another TV commercial depicted a range of cartoon-like Laughing Cow portraits to promote the "star of cheese". Guess who was winning. . . . During the 1990s the commercials focused more on one of the core values of the brand: sharing. The ads used scenes of affection in order to bring generations closer together.

One thing about the Laughing Cow remains a mystery: Why is The Laughing Cow laughing? In 2001 the big question was used as the basis of an advertising campaign. People on the street were asked to suggest an answer to this fair question. And even today, there is no answer. However, a community of fans has designed a website devoted to this topic, where one can play games, send e-cards and download screensavers.

Think about it

Do you think the choice of a laughing red cow wearing earrings is appropriate for communicating the brand in every country? What do you think is more effective in delivering the brand message, a product-centred appeal or an emotional appeal? Does this vary per country?

Source:
www.bel-group.com

Maintaining global brand consistency

Planning a message strategy for an international brand is more complex, however, than simply deciding whether to standardize or localize the messages. A brand's imagery and logo, for example, are relatively easy to standardize; language is somewhat less so. But consider the models and settings used in an ad. Such aspects of a brand message can be extremely difficult to standardize. Figure 17-5 breaks out 12 dimensions of strategy and gives examples of the elements that need to be considered in the standardization/localization decision.

One survey of 87 multinational companies that market in China, Taiwan, Hong Kong, and Singapore found that 31 per cent of the advertising used the same strategy as in the home market, while 68 per cent used a different one.[35] Robert Hite and Cynthia Fraser found in 1988 that 66 per cent of the international companies they surveyed used a combination strategy; only 9 per cent used a standardized strategy, and 37 per cent used a localized strategy.[36] Ten years later, a major study of advertising in China by Yin found that little had changed: the majority of the international companies surveyed about their practices in China used a combination strategy.[37]

Yin concluded that the majority of the companies surveyed have abandoned standardization. The only exception was the electronics industry, in which no company used a localized strategy, confirming that high-tech markets are less affected by cultural differences than are other types of markets. Furthermore, she observed that even in the emerging markets of developing countries, some degree of localization is a preferred strategy for most companies, rather than the less costly and more efficient standardization approach. Some researchers have found, however, that although global integration can be done with either a standardization or a localization approach, co-ordination is more difficult with the latter.[38]

The standardization model

Area	Easier to standardize					More difficult to standardize
Product category	Hi tech, hi touch, high fashion	Industrial, computers	Fun services, foods, cigarettes	Homecare, decorating	Food, beer	Contraceptives, bikinis
Product life cycle	New product				Older product with local strategies	
Objectives	Advertising			Media	Sales promotion	
Targeting	International youth market, bus travellers	Industrial buyers	New mothers	Home-makers	Blue collar workers	Subsistence farmers
Positioning	Universal need and target			Culturally determined tastes		
Branding	Common name and image	Modified name or image		Local name or image		Local name and image
Creative strategy	Image		Benefit		Informative	
Advertising message	Creative concept, theme			Execution details		
Production	Central production	Central production and local modifications		Produced locally		
Media	Planning			Buying		
Media availability	Media conglomerates, satellite TV	Intnl. mags, newspapers	National mags, newspapers, TV	Outdoor	PoP, direct response	Local TV, radio, newspapers
Research	Secondary			Primary		

Figure 17-5 Examples of various levels of standardization and localization applications.

Source: Sandra E. Moriarty and Tom Duncan, "Global Advertising: Issues and Practices", *Current Issues and Research in Advertising*, 13, nos. 1 and 2 (1991), pp. 313–41.

The general principle seems to be that it is not so much a question of "Think globally" or "Think locally", more "Think globally and act locally". Companies wishing to launch global marketing campaigns must still play in the local arena of local media, varying government regulations, wide cultural differences, and ever-changing stages of economic and demographic development. Although many of the world's economic and cultural barriers have fallen in recent years, international companies cannot ignore the remaining barriers if they hope to reach their customers on a global scale.

Message delivery: media and technology

Three basic media strategies allow marketers to reach multinational and global markets. One is to localize media mixes to reflect the mix of media available in each country. Another is to use international publications and satellite TV, whose footprints cover various regions of the world. A third way to deliver media across borders is to participate in programmes that have transnational audiences—for example, sporting events such as soccer's World Cup and the Olympics.

Level of media development

Historically it is print advertising—specifically outdoor, magazines, and newspapers—that has offered international advertisers the best way to reach cross-cultural markets. The *Financial Times, Newsweek, BusinessWeek, Cosmopolitan*, the *Wall Street Journal,* and many other publications publish in multiple languages and distribute throughout the world. Or they just distribute their English editions in multiple countries, where their target audiences are English-literate. In developing countries where communication vehicles and literacy are limited, however, radio and posters or billboards dominate the media schedule. In such places, the search is on for non-traditional vehicles and sales promotions that can reach customers in rural villages.

You might not think of outdoor media as being global, but one of the largest outdoor advertising companies in the world, France-based JCDecaux, has nearly half a million display locations spread throughout 1300 cities in 33 countries. JCDecaux is also the inventor of, and world's largest provider of, "street furniture" (bus benches and shelters) and the world leader in airport and subway posters.

Although print is still the advertising vehicle most often used by international marketers, satellite technology is quickly making television the medium for the masses around the world. China has more than 3000 TV and radio stations. Ninety-six per cent of Chinese urban homes have colour television sets. Media growth in China, in general, has been phenomenal as the movement toward a more market-based economy has opened Chinese markets. China has about 2200 general publications, trade magazines, and newspapers. The fastest-growing development, of course, is occurring with the Internet.

Internet: a truly global medium

Marketing communication for many global companies is moving to the Internet because it offers an easy solution to global communication. Nike, for example, uses the Internet to communicate with its customers worldwide.

B2B companies were early users of the Internet to interact with suppliers—many of which are in other countries—as well as to communicate with their own international brand offices.

As a result, B2B companies are ahead of B2C companies in using the Internet to do business internationally. But B2C companies are catching up—particularly in Asia. The situation in South Korea is exceptional, but still exemplary of what the Internet can bring.

E-commerce expanded faster in South Korea than in any other nation around the globe. E-commerce is big business in South Korea, where companies such as E*Trade benefit from the fact that 50 per cent of Korean stock trading is now done online. One particular use of the Internet that is distinctively Korean is the "PC room", a combination of Internet café (without the coffee) and game arcade. There are more than 20 000 PC rooms in South Korea's capital Seoul alone, complete with Web video cameras and rows of computers jammed in as tightly as they will fit. Although many South Koreans have Internet access on home PCs, they come to the PC rooms for souped-up terminals with high-speed links and super graphics, for the camaraderie, and for the help of resident computer geeks who stand by to solve problems instantly. Men tend to spend their time there playing games; women chat online. Computer games also have become a major "sport" marketing arena in South Korea, where at least a thousand professional gamers are sponsored and paid generous salaries by online game manufacturers. The best Korean game players have fan clubs, participate in big game tournaments, and appear on TV shows.

As Internet access continues to grow throughout the world, it greatly expands the marketplace for every company that is prepared to do business online. But there are still many traditional barriers such as differences in language. Taxation, money exchange, and making secure delivery of products are also concerns when selling online outside a company's home country. Another barrier is how and where to resolve legal issues that arise in the course of doing business internationally.

International corporations trying to reach the world's proliferation of Internet users must do so in a targeted, constructive manner, just as they would use any other advertising medium. One of the tools now available to international companies is a new global tracking service for advertisers, launched by ACNielsen. Prior to ACNielsen's research service, marketers relied on market measurements that varied by types of information collected, methods used, and level of accuracy. The research company promises consistently gathered information about the number of people and households per country with access to the Internet, their online browsing and purchasing habits, and the rates of access at home, work, or other locations.

As Internet technology becomes more common throughout the world and more tracking and research services are developed, international advertisers will look to the Internet as an integrated brand message vehicle to carry sales-promotion offers, publicity releases, and ad messages. Most important, companies will use the Internet to develop an online dialogue with customers.

Media convergence

Media convergence is *the bringing together of phone, television and computer, along with a variety of other new technologies, such as smart cards, pagers, personal digital assistants, and satellite navigational systems.* Brand messages may take on an entirely different shape as wireless communication makes use of all these technologies. This is particularly true in early-adopter countries that pioneered the development of wireless communication, such as the Scandinavian countries and Japan.

Picture a butcher's shop in Stockholm, Sweden, where customers are offered a discount for waving their wireless cell phones through an infra-red sensor that records the telephone's number. Near closing time on one particular day, the butcher is anxious to move some prime cuts of Argentine beef. Using the store's customer database, he sends out a special offer by an automated phone message to customers who have ordered Argentine beef before—and who happen to be within, say, 1 kilometre of the shop. The mobile phone network finds these customers and delivers a SMS or MMS message about the special deal, complete with a mouthwatering picture of a sizzling steak. The butcher's wireless company charges a few cents for each message delivered; however, he may recover that cost with the revenue from the Bordeaux ad message delivered at the same time as the beef offer. Customers who buy online get a discount, and the charges are automatically placed on their phone's debit card.

In Japan, Honda is building cybercars that can connect to the Internet. The car's internal navigation system uses a computer satellite mapping system, a modem and mobile phone, Internet browser capability, and a dashboard-mounted, paperback-size screen. It is possible to provide drivers with guides to restaurants, a list of leisure activities, and event schedules.

Media regulation

Developing an international media plan is not simple—not only because of the varied patterns of local media but also because of the different regulations. Although some media are being privatized in countries as diverse as Israel and Russia, governments around the world still own and control most broadcast media, and many still do not permit advertising. In Norway, there is only one commercial Norwegian TV channel. Other countries limit advertising to a certain number of minutes per hour or per day. European Union guidelines allow 12 minutes of commercial messages per hour and mandate at least 20 minutes of programming between commercial breaks. Despite individual country regulations barring or limiting TV advertising, however, households in these countries are increasingly being reached with TV commercials carried by satellite broadcasting companies, such as Columbia TriStar and Sky TV. And there are few restrictions on newspapers and magazines.

Many countries also limit or fully prevent the use of certain media such as direct mail and telemarketing. Good information about media use and audience profiles is not available in every country, especially developing countries. Circulation figures are not always reliable, audience demographics may be sketchy, ad rates may vary greatly, and mailing lists and phone numbers may not exist in a directory or in a database. Also because of costs, the methods used in media research may be considerably different from one market to another, making comparisons almost impossible. Because of the media variations in each country, most international marketers assign national media-planning and -buying responsibilities to in-country media specialists rather than running the risk of faulty, centralized media planning.

Integration at the international level

When companies sell their products outside their home country, IMC practices and principles are even more important than when they sell them domestically. Both international and global marketing call for a complex yet integrated strategy. Building stakeholder relationships with global customers, agencies, media, and channels of distribution can be highly complex and certainly requires cross-functional planning and monitoring. But the same basic integration issues are still driving the strategies.

An example of using an IMC global campaign comes from Microsoft. Its .NET connected software used television, print, and online advertising within a number of countries to showcase studies of how businesses are successfully using .NET software. Because the .NET product line was being promoted globally, Microsoft had to be sensitive to media and global integration issues when adapting the message for other markets. For example, in addition to language, Microsoft also made certain that the examples of .NET use were region specific. For the first half of 2003, the campaign resulted in a 15-point increase in awareness of .NET software among business IT decision makers and a 9-point increase among IT implementers.[39]

The global IMC concept, or GIMC, was developed by Baruch University professors Andreas Grein and Stephen Gould to explain how integration can be managed within a global marketing programme. They identified two critical aspects of GIMC planning: *horizontal co-ordination*, which means co-ordinating a brand strategy across countries; and *vertical co-ordination*, which means co-ordinating a brand message across disciplines. Acknowledging that both standardization and localization (called adaptation by Grein and Gould) are appropriate strategies depending on the product and marketing situation, Grein and Gould then developed a planning model. Table 17-1 identifies the key factors that marketers need to consider when planning a global IMC strategy.[40]

Consistency of branding is the biggest problem for international or global marketers. The English–Dutch global giant Unilever has a vast number of brands in a variety of product

Factor	Standardized strategy	Adapted strategy
Horizontal factors		
Target market	Same and mass; global segments	Different segments; regional markets
Market position	Similar market conditions	Different market conditions
Nature of product	Consumer perceives as similar in use, attributes, and positioning	Consumer perceives as different in use, attributes, and positioning
Environment	Similar physical, legal, political, and marketing infrastructure	Different physical, legal, political, and marketing infrastructure
Vertical factors		
Marketing mix	Same resources allocated	Different resources allocated
Main promotion objective	Build brand equity	Build brand image
Advertising creation	Same theme, appeal, execution	Variations in theme, appeal, execution
Advertising media	Same, possibly global, media use	Different media use; local buys
Sales promotion	Same types and strategies	Different types used
Public relations	Same theme and forms	Variations in theme and forms

Table 17-1 Planning a global IMC strategy

Source: Adapted from Andreas Grein and Stephen Gould, "Globally Integrated Marketing Communications", *Journal of Marketing Communications*, 2 (1996), pp. 141–58. Visit the Journal at www.tanf.co.uk/journal/routledge/13527266.html. Used by permission.

categories. In 2003 in an attempt to develop a more cohesive MC strategy for its detergent brands, a campaign was designed that focused on a universal truth—that kids, no matter where they grow up, think dirt is fun. The "dirt is good" theme is used for Unilever's premium detergent which sells around the world under a variety of brand names, Omo in most of the company's markets, Skip in parts of Europe, and Wisk in the United States.[41]

A final note: think globally, act locally

The goal of most businesses is to market their products or services to the largest group of potential customers at the lowest possible cost with the greatest possible return on their investment. This strategy would suggest that a company should use a standardized or global message to reach large numbers of customers through international markets, as the Whiskas strategy demonstrated.

This standardized international marketing strategy may work for some brands and may offer various efficiency benefits for a company, but in most cases international businesses need to take local economic, cultural, political, legal, demographic, and media factors into consideration, market by market. And this often means that the marketing communication is better served with a strategy that is adapted to the local market.

🔑 Key terms

broadcast footprint The geographical area in which there is reception from a satellite transmission.

context The non-verbal elements surrounding a message.

cultural cohort A group of people from multiple cultures who share a common characteristic.

cultural imperialism The impact that a more dominant culture has on another, less dominant culture.

culture The learned behaviours of a people that come from traditions passed on from generation to generation.

developed markets Markets in which consumption patterns are focused more on wants and desires than on basic needs.

developing markets Markets in which the consumption patterns are clearly expanding from necessities to wants and desires.

global marketers Companies that consider their market to be just one—the world.

global strategy see s*tandardization strategy.*

glocalization Having a global strategy that is locally executed.

high-context culture A culture in which meaning is determined by non-verbal cues, social relationships, and indirect communication such as metaphors and aphorisms (statements of principle).

localization strategy An international MC strategy in which brand messages are customized to make them compatible with each country's culture and local needs and wants.

low-context culture A culture in which less emphasis is placed on the social context and more emphasis is placed on words, directness, and time (deadlines and schedules).

media convergence The bringing together of phone, television and computer, along with a variety of other new technologies, such as smart cards, pagers, personal digital assistants, and satellite navigational systems.

multinational marketers Companies that market products in several different countries.

region A set of geographically adjoining countries.

standardization strategy An international MC strategy in which the same basic brand message is used in all countries.

undeveloped markets Markets in which consumption patterns remain focused on basic needs.

values Enduring points of view that a certain way of thinking and behaving is preferable to a different way of thinking and behaving.

Check the key points

Key point 1: Different types of international marketing

a What are the differences between national, international, and global marketing?

b List three major trends that are driving the move to international marketing. Explain their impact on marketing.

Key point 2: The impact of culture

a Define *culture*. Explain where in the planning of a marketing communication programme culture becomes a factor.

b Summarize the debate about cultural differences and similarities as they apply to creating and delivering brand messages.

c If you were to summarize the difference in values between Western and Asian cultures, what would they be?

d Explain the difference between a high-context culture and a low-context culture. How does context affect marketing communication?

e Explain the concern that some countries have with Western cultural imperialism.

Key point 3: Segmenting international markets

a In what three ways can international markets be segmented and targeted? Explain how these factors make a difference in an MC strategy.

b What are the characteristics of developed markets, developing markets, and undeveloped markets? How does each stage of market development affect a marketing communication strategy?

c What is a cultural cohort group? Why is this concept important in international marketing communication? Give an example of such a group.

Key point 4: Planning international message and media strategies

a What is meant by *standardization*? By *localization*? By *glocalization*?

b What does "Think globally, act locally" mean? How does this advice relate to the IMC principle of being strategically consistent?

c Describe three media strategies used to reach multinational audiences.

d What is media convergence? Give an example of it.

Chapter Challenge

Writing assignment

Identify a product that is sold in your country and in another country. (A good place to start looking is in your school's library in magazines such as *Elle* and *Figaro.*) Collect an ad for the brand in both languages. In a paper, analyse the brand's use of standardization or localization. In how far is this ad reflecting the cultural imperialism critique?

Presentation assignment

Stage a debate between two teams of students. One team supports the idea that standardization is a useful strategy. The other supports the idea that localization is the only way to develop an effective marketing communication plan. Do this twice for distinctly different product categories.

Internet assignment

Pick a product category in which you are especially interested. Then go online to find three companies in that category—one in Europe, one in North America, and one in Asia. Compare the three sites, and see to what extent each site reflects the culture of each company's home area.

Notes

[1] Gabriel Kahn, "Still Going for Gold", *Wall Street Journal*, 28 January 2003, p. B1.

[2] Philip Cateora, *International Marketing* (Homewood, IL: Irwin, 1993), p. vii.

[3] Warren Keegan, *Global Marketing Management*, 6th ed. (Upper Saddle River, NJ: Prentice Hall, 1999), pp. 8–9.

[4] Ibid., p. 9.

[5] The Big Mac index was invented in 1986 by a reporter from *The Economist* and is still reported on today. See: www.economist.com/markets/Bigmac/Index.cfm

[6] Keegan, *Global Marketing Management*, p. 6.

[7] *2002 Fact Pack: A Handy Guide to the Advertising Business* (New York: Advertising Age, 2002).

[8] M. Rokeach, *The Nature of Human Values* (New York: Free Press, 1973), p. 5.

[9] Marieke de Mooij, *Global Marketing and Advertising: Understanding Cultural Paradoxes* (Thousand Oaks, CA: Sage, 1998), p. 43.

[10] Sak Onkvisit and John Shaw, "Standardized International Advertising: Some Research Issues and Implications", *Journal of Marketing Research*, 39, no. 6 (1999), pp. 19–24; and Frenkel Ter Hofstede, Jan-Benedict Steenkamp, and Michel Wedel, "International Market Segmentation Based on Consumer-Product Relations", *Journal of Marketing Research*, 36, no. 1 (1999), pp. 1–17.

[11] John Quelch and Edward Hoff, "Customizing Global Marketing", *Harvard Business Review*, May–June 1986, pp. 59–68.

[12] Jee Young Lee and Trina Sego, "Culture in Advertising on the World Wide Web: Executional Elements of South Korean and US Banner Advertisements", *Proceedings of the 2000 Conference of the American Academy of Advertising*, ed. Mary Alice Shaver (East Lansing: Michigan State University,

2000), p. 198; Gordon Miracle, Beate Bluhm, Juergen Bluhm, Yung Kyun Choi, and Hairong Li, "The Relationship between Cultural Variables and the Amount and Type of Information in Korean and German Television Commercials", in *Proceedings of the 1998 Conference of the American Academy of Advertising*, ed. Darrel D. Muehling (Pullman: Washington State University, 1998), pp. 9–15; and Jyotika Ramaprasad and Kazumi Hasegawa, "An Analysis of Japanese Television Commercials", *Journalism Quarterly*, 67 (Fall 1990), pp. 1025–33.

[13] Edward Hall, *Beyond Culture* (New York: Anchor Press–Doubleday, 1976).

[14] Augustine Ihator, "Understand the Cultural Patterns of the World—An Imperative in Implementing Strategic International PR Programs", *Public Relations Quarterly*, Winter 2000, pp. 38–44.

[15] Geert H. Hofstede, *Culture's Consequences: International Differences in Work-Related Values* (Beverly Hills, CA: Sage, 1980); *Cultures and Organizations: Software of the Mind* (New York: McGraw-Hill, 1991); "The Cultural Relativity of Organization Practices and Theories", *Journal of International Business Studies*, 14, no. 2 (1983), pp. 75–89.

[16] Ihator, "Understand the Cultural Patterns of the World".

[17] Alan Shao, Mary Anne Raymond, and Charles Taylor, "Shifting Advertising Appeals in Taiwan", *Journal of Advertising Research*, November–December 1999, pp. 61–9.

[18] W. C. Gudykunst and S. Ting-Toomey, *Culture and Interpersonal Communication* (Newbury Park, CA: Sage, 1988); and B. C. Deng, "The Influence of Individualism–Collectivism on Conflict Management Style: A Cross-Culture Comparison between Taiwanese and US Business Employees" (master's thesis, Sacramento: California State University, 1992).

[19] T. J. Knutson, R. Komolsevin, P. Chatiketu, and V. Smith, "Rhetorical Sensitivity and Willingness to Communicate: A Comparison of Thai and US American Samples with Implications for Intercultural Communication Effectiveness" (paper presented at the annual conference of the International Communication Association, Acapulco, Mexico, June 2000).

[20] "Brad Pitt Car Ad an Insult to Asians, Says Malaysia", *Straits Times Interaction*, 16 January 2003, www.straitstimes.asia1.com.sg.

[21] Noelle Knox and Theresa Howard, "Anti-War Protesters Take Aim at American Brands", *USA Today*, 4 April 2003, p. B1.

[22] These are compiled from Subhash Jain, *International Marketing Management*, 3rd ed. (Boston: PWS-Kent, 1990), pp. 227–8.

[23] de Mooij, *Global Marketing and Advertising*, p. 56.

[24] Bob Coen, "Universal McCann's Insider's Report", www.mccann.com, presentation to investment analysts at Universal McCann's headquarters in New York, 17 June 2003.

[25] Leslie Chang and Peter Wonacott, "Cracking China's Market", *Wall Street Journal*, 9 January 2003, p. B1.

[26] Tom Duncan, "A Mother's a Mother", *Marketing and Media Decisions*, May 1990, p. 120.

[27] Elissa Moses, *The $100 Billion Allowance: Accessing the Global Teen Market* (New York: Wiley, 2000).

[28] Quoted in Brett Pulley and Andrew Tanzer, "Summer's Gemstone", *Forbes*, 21 February 2000, pp. 107–11.

[29] Theodore Levitt, "The Globalization of Markets", *Harvard Business Review*, May–June 1983, pp. 92–102.

[30] Marilyn Roberts, "2000 International Advertising Pre-Conference: The Global Best Practices Roundtable", *Proceedings of the 2000 Conference of the American Academy of Advertising*, pp. 239–41; Onkvisit and Shaw, "Standardized International Advertising".

[31] Jiafei Yin, "International Advertising Strategies in China", p. 30.

[32] www.translate-to-success.com/index.html, retrieved, 27 January 2007

[33] Kevin Keller, *Strategic Brand Management* (Upper Saddle River, NJ: Prentice-Hall, 1998), p. 138.

[34] http://spanish.about.com/cs/culture/a/chevy_nova.htm gives the Nova story, together with a number of other legends. Fun reading!

[35] Susan H. C. Tai, "Advertising in Asia: Localize or Regionalize?" *International Journal of Advertising*, 16, no. 1 (1997), pp. 48–61.

[36] Robert Hite and Cynthia Fraser, "International Advertising Strategies of Multinational Corporations", *Journal of Advertising Research*, 28, no. 4 (1988), pp. 9–17.

[37] Yin, "International Advertising Strategies in China", pp. 25–35.

[38] Stephen Gould, Dawn Lerman, and Andreas Green, "Agency Perceptions and Practices on Global IMC", *Journal of Advertising Research*, 39, no. 1 (1999), pp. 7–20.

[39] Kate Maddox, "Microsoft Extends 'Agility' Campaign", *BtoB*, 9 June 2003, p. 19.

[40] Andreas Grein and Stephen Gould, "Globally Integrated Marketing Communications", *Journal of Marketing Communications*, 2 (1996), pp. 141–58.

[41] Erin White and Sarah Ellison, "Unilever Ads Offer a Tribute to Dirt", *Wall Street Journal*, 2 June 2003, p. B3.

Further reading

Fengru Li and Nuder H. Shooshtari (2006) "On Toyota's Misstep in Advertising Its Land Cruiser SUV in Beijing: A Distortion of Consumers' Sociolinguistic System", *Journal of International Consumer Marketing*, Vol. 18–4, pp. 61–78.

Hoeken, Hans, Marianne Starren, Catherine Nickerson, Rogier Crijns and Corine van den Brandt (2007) "Is it Necessary to Adapt Advertising Appeals for National Audiences in Western Europe?", *Journal of Marketing Communications*, Vol. 13–1, pp. 19–38.

Kitchen, Philip J. and Li Tao (2005) "Perceptions of Integrated Marketing Communications: a Chinese ad and PR agency perspective", *International Journal of Advertising*, Vol. 24–1, pp. 51–78.

Melewar, T. C. and Claes Vemmervik (2004) "International advertising strategy: A review, reassessment and recommendation", *Management Decision*, Vol. 42–7, pp. 863–81.

Melewar, T. C., Edgar Badal and Joseann Small (2006) "Danone branding strategy in China", *Journal of Brand Management*, Vol. 13–6, pp. 407–17.

Stafford, Maria Royne (2005) "International Services Advertising (ISA)", *Journal of Advertising*, Vol. 34–1, pp. 65–86.

Chapter 2

Measurement, evaluation and effectiveness

CHAPTER PERSPECTIVE
The mandate for accountability

Brand awareness, brand knowledge, customer satisfaction, and many of the other elements that drive brand equity are intangible. Measurement of these concepts is more complicated than simply looking at sales and profits, for which a wide range of information-collecting technology that tracks sales and profitability enables companies to evaluate MC efforts. Scanner data, customer databases, and automated customer-service operations generate enormous amounts of marketing data. In many companies, the primary challenge is not collecting more information but finding the time to analyse and make use of the data that already exists.

One of the most important ways to meet this challenge is to measure and evaluate brand messages by monitoring responses from the different brand messages and campaigns that are used. This chapter also discusses two types of IMC audits: the mini-audit and the in-depth audit. It considers evaluation and measurement of brand messages in general before looking at specific methods. It ends with a discussion of the benefits and limitations of evaluation.

IMC in Action

How Molson Canadian and its agency used evaluation measures to make the brand number one

In the mid-1980s Molson Canadian established itself as the number-one brand of beer in Canada. By the late 1990s, however, its chief rival, Labatt's Blue, had increased its marketing effort while several changes were being made in Molson's advertising. The result, a loss of sales and market share, prompted Molson to hire a new agency, Bensimon-Byrne D'Arcy. Molson's new agency was given this objective: "Make Molson Canadian the undisputed #1 beer brand in Canada." To achieve this objective, it was agreed that the brand had to communicate a sense of sociability, quality, and identity—the top three attributes of a leading brand in the mainstream segment of the beer category.

Bensimon-Byrne D'Arcy knew that the new campaign had to be more than a series of cute, attention-getting ads. The campaign had to touch the target audience emotionally and deeply. It was agreed the new message needed to build on the brand's strong heritage of being "Canadian". Past executions had consistently used scenes of patios, cottages, and road trips. They were aesthetically pleasing but lacked the emotional attitude that would motivate the brand's target, LDA (legal drinking age) to 24-year-old males. (Because Canadian provinces have different drinking age limits, one specific age at which drinking becomes legal is not used in marketing planning; instead, marketers refer to the "legal drinking age".)

As with all new major assignments, Bensimon-Byrne D'Arcy used a disciplined research approach for developing and testing new creative ideas. This approach has three steps: (1) exploratory, (2) diagnostic, and (3) evaluative.

Stage 1: Exploratory research

As Jack Bensimon, president of the agency, explained: "In this stage you look for things you don't know you are looking for." To get a good understanding of the target audience—what those young men thought about, what they did in their spare time, what music they liked, what they thought about life, and so on—the agency did on-the-street interviews. Interns and other young agency people were given video cameras and told to find and talk with members of the target audience. The purpose of these "chats" was to record how this group of consumers thought and talked about a wide range of topics (not just about beer).

As members of the agency team watched hours of video, what they found helpful was not *what* the young men talked about but rather *how* they talked about different subjects—especially about being Canadian. On most topics the dialogue consisted of brief, unemotional comments reflecting typical youthful ambivalence. When topics directly or indirectly related to Canada and nationality, however, respondents became more animated and emotional. Because Canadians, especially young men, are usually reserved when talking about national pride, especially in comparison with Americans, the agency felt it had discovered an interesting customer insight.

Before proceeding, however, the agency knew it needed more confirmation of this finding. Two relevant research studies were found on the Internet. A University of Chicago study measuring national pride in 23 countries showed that Canada ranked third (after the United States and Austria). A study by Ekos Research Associates (a Canadian research firm) found "national pride" to be the second most important "attachment in our lives" after family. These two studies helped convince the agency team that what it had seen in the videotapes was not a fluke but deep emotion that could provide the foundation for a long-term brand positioning and creative platform. (Notice that instead of doing costly primary research, the agency made use of secondary research, saving the client thousands of dollars.)

Final confirmation that "Canadian pride" was a solid concept came from a review of current events (another low-cost but productive research effort). The most important of these events was the 30-year anniversary of Woodstock. It took place in upstate New York in 1999 and drew hundreds of thousands of young people for three days of music, fun, and celebration. Because many of the attendees were Canadians, pictures from the gathering proved to be especially informative. Pictures of many participants showed backpack patches, body tattoos, and T-shirts bearing the slogan "I am Canadian". Conclusion: Young men were proud to be Canadian and were not embarrassed to publicly express their pride. ("I Am Canadian" had been the brand's previous advertising slogan, and though discontinued three years earlier, it had moved into the target audience's vernacular as a form of self-expression.)

Based on these exploratory research findings, the brand's creative positioning was determined to be: "Molson Canadian is the only beer that lets me be as Canadian as I feel." The next challenge was to execute this into compelling brand messages.

Stage 2: Diagnostic measurements

In this stage, the positioning statement was presented to focus groups of the target audience. Also, first drafts of TV copy were read by the writer (without showing any photos) to focus-group participants to see how well the copy communicated. These focus groups indicated that among this target audience, beer was the only product category that tapped into national pride.

Focus groups were also used to see how advertising messages could be fine-tuned to be more attention getting, involving, and persuasive. Six TV spots were selected to be tested by AdLab. Commercials were made into animatics, which are videos of a series of still photos plus a sound track. (Animatics can be made for about $15 000, less than 5 per cent of the cost of a finished commercial.) The animatics were shown to a sample of the target audience. These respondents used a device containing five buttons numbered from 1 to 5 to indicate to what extent they liked or disliked each and every scene (1 – dislike very much; 5 – like very much). Every scene in "Rant", the first commercial tested, received a high rating except for a scene that talked about putting ketchup on macaroni and cheese. It was replaced with a picture and line about the beaver being a "proud and noble animal".

The final copy evaluation was done by mall intercepts in which 150 of the target audience were individually exposed to the animatics test commercials. After viewing, respondents were asked questions about the brand, their intent to purchase, and their anticipated purchase frequency of Molson Canadian. These scores were compared to the average scores of previously tested commercials in the beer and alcohol category. Test commercials scoring significantly better than average were produced and run on-air.

Stage 3: Evaluation

Once the TV commercials and print advertising were developed, the agency made presentations of the campaign to Molson's other MC agencies—packaging, public relations, website development, and channel marketing. This road-show enabled these agencies to co-ordinate and integrate their work with the advertising, the predominant MC function used by the brand.

▶ Two weeks prior to the television launch, the ad agency co-ordinated live performances of "Rant" and other commercials, without notice, in movie theatres. This garnered tremendous word of mouth and media coverage.

The public relations agency responded by making the "Rant" commercial come alive in various sports venues. Taking advantage of the National Hockey League's play-off games, which were happening at that time, the agency had "Joe", the spokesperson in the "Rant" commercial, make his speech live before hockey audiences in five major markets. These performances were so well received by the audiences that they began to be covered by the media. As a result, the brand received over four times more exposure from publicity than was generated by the advertising media schedule.

At the same time, the website people put the new commercials on a specially developed brand website and asked site visitors to write their own "I am Canadian" commercials. Over 40 000 did so! Once the campaign began running, the collective effectiveness of all of Molson's brand messages was measured by changes in brand awareness and market share. Tracking studies were used to determine brand awareness. In this type of research, randomly selected respondents are screened for product usage, and those who qualify are asked with what brands of beer they are familiar. The responses indicate the level of brand awareness for each brand in the beer category.

Results

Twelve months after the beginning of the campaign, the brand's awareness had increased 3 per cent. Three percentage points may not seem like much, but they produced an increase of 2.5 market-share points. In the beer category, each share point is worth millions of dollars in sales. What makes these results especially impressive is that during this time Molson reduced its level of spending from the previous year and had a lower share-of-voice than its chief competitor, Labatt's Blue.

Source:
Information provided by Jack Bensimon, president of Bensimon-Byrne, Toronto, March 2003.

Evaluation and measurement of brand messages

Throughout this book we have talked about the importance of setting objectives. Measurable objectives enable companies to quantify the effectiveness of MC efforts. Measuring and evaluating MC programmes is done to see whether objectives have been met and MC programmes have been effective. Meeting or exceeding objectives shows that the company's money has been spent wisely.

Accountability is a must in business today. Starting all the way at the top—with the board of directors, who answer to shareholders—and extending down to managers of the smallest departments, there is always someone wanting to know how and why money was spent, how the spending helped generate more sales and profits, and whether the money was spent in the most effective way. Yet according to a study by Accenture management consultants, 70 per cent of marketing executives report that they don't really know what kind of return they are getting on their marketing investment.[1] MC managers who lack this knowledge find it very difficult to defend their budgets, let alone justify a budget increase. Keep in mind that marketers are constantly competing internally against all other departments for their budgets.

Being accountable and knowing whether objectives have been met are not the only reasons to do evaluations and measurements. Just as important is finding out *why* MC efforts worked or didn't work. Evaluation and measurement provide feedback. If questions are constructed in the right way, if the correct observations are done, if the right people are interviewed, marketers will receive diagnostic feedback, a critical component of marketing communication (Chapter 3). When objectives are or are not met, finding out *why* provides important corporate learning.

Another important reason for measuring MC efforts is to determine the gap between MC expectations and reality. **Gap analysis** is *an analysis of the difference between what customers expect from a brand (based on brand messages) and what they actually experience.* A gap can lead to all kinds of undesirable results like dissatisfaction, decreasing sales and negative word-of-mouth.

An example of the importance of knowing what kind of return a company is getting from its MC budget is demonstrated by a provider of mobile phone services. When sales of this company began to decrease, it used data mining to learn which of the MC functions it had been using were producing the best returns. The analysis quickly showed that Web advertising had been the most cost-effective in producing sales leads. Based on this finding, the MC spending allocation plan was revised. The company decided to spend all of its MC budget online—on full-screen pop-ups and special offers. The revised plan not only increased the number of calling plans sold but also reduced the cost per sales lead by 70 per cent.[2]

There is ongoing pressure to evaluate and measure brand communication efforts and their effects. Evaluation must include critical areas such as cross-functional planning and monitoring, brand-message creation, media planning and buying, and listening to customers and capturing their complaints, suggestions, and compliments. These are the IMC processes that strengthen the brand relationships which drive profitable brands.

MC evaluation and measurement programmes are conducted both during the development of brand-message strategies and after the completion of a campaign. The basic objective is to predict or determine *results*—that is, the changes in behaviour or attitudes created by an offer, a promotion, a campaign, a company response, or some other type of brand message. Objectives of evaluation and measurement include (1) reducing risk, (2) providing direction, (3) determining to what extent marketing communication programmes met objectives, and (4) determining to what extent the communication effort proved to be a good investment of the company's money.

Important as they are, however, MC measurement and evaluation must be put into perspective. The vast majority of brand messages has never been, and never will be, formally measured or evaluated. Most decisions about whether to use a particular brand message are based on the judgement of a marketing manager (or some other client or agency executive) because there is not enough at risk to justify spending money to evaluate every single message. The decision to measure and evaluate itself is subject to common managerial criteria: what are the possible benefits when we measure? What risks do we run when we do not measure? And what costs (money, time) are involved in measuring?

Generally speaking, MC measurement and evaluation is done primarily when companies (1) have large enough media budgets and (2) stand to suffer significant financial losses if the brand messages fail to achieve the MC objectives. Although some marketing executives feel their personal judgement is sufficient to evaluate brand messages and campaigns, most *smart* executives in these situations prefer to base their use/don't use decisions on some type of objective evaluation.

Although the majority of individual brand messages are never formally evaluated, the selling concept or creative strategy on which a brand message is based may have been rigorously tested.

Once an idea for an advertising campaign has been tested and has proved itself, that idea may be executed for a couple of years with no further testing other than tracking studies (explained later in this chapter).

When an evaluation is deemed necessary, several questions need to be answered to justify the expense:

- What should be evaluated?
- What information already exists?
- At what stages should the MC message or campaign be evaluated?

What should be evaluated: the cost/value factor

Evaluation is generally undertaken for critical decisions that involve a lot of money, resources, or staff time, such as changing a logo or launching a year-long campaign. The idea is to determine the probability of success up-front, before the money is spent. In particular, marketers want to know whether the level of success will be high enough to justify the programme's cost, an analysis that shows the return on investment (ROI). The more that is at risk, the greater the number of developmental evaluations and measurements that should be used. This is also clear from the opening case. The decision by Molson to look for a new and appealing brand proposition was not taken overnight. Once this decision was taken, the way the advertisements were executed were less critical, as long as they fitted into the newly chosen theme.

Evaluation always has costs. Designing and testing questionnaires, conducting interviews or observations, tabulating and coding the findings, and then analysing these findings are all labour-intensive. When focus groups are used, a company hires research firms to recruit and provide facilities for conducting the focus groups. Focus-group leaders are handsomely paid and today most respondents are paid for participating in focus groups. In the case of mail surveys, there is the cost of printing and mailing questionnaires.

Some MC measurements, however, can be made with very little cost, e.g. split-runs, explained in Chapter 8. For a few hundred euros extra, two versions of a print ad can be run in a magazine or newspaper to measure the difference in response for two different offers, headlines, illustrations, or other message components. The same technique can be used in direct mail or with other types of promotional brochures and offers. Although the risk of using one offer versus another without prior research may not be great, the cost of measuring is relatively small and thus the cost/value ratio of the measurement is very good.

Evaluations should measure only those things that can be changed. One car manufacturing company asked its dealers how satisfied they were with a number of operational areas. Three areas of the business always received low scores, but no changes were made. When the president of the company was asked why not, he explained that making such changes would be too costly. Unfortunately, the company continued to ask the questions, not only consuming time and money but also reminding the dealers of things they didn't like about the company.

What information already exists?

Many companies have enormous amounts of data that could be (but have not been) used for evaluative purposes. A good example is a situation that occurred at a public health organization several years ago. When the level of public discussion of AIDS was very high, the organization hired a major advertising agency to conduct focus groups to see what major questions the average person had about this disease. At the same time, the organization hired a consultant to evaluate the organization's call centre, which was set up to answer health questions from medical personnel and the general public. In the course of his audit the consultant noticed that the representatives made notes on most of the calls they handled. When he asked about the purpose of the notes, he was told they were to help the representatives keep track of the number of calls handled and the subject of the calls so they could do their weekly performance reports. Once the weekly reports were written, the notes were thrown away.

In further observations, the consultant found that the notes often included the questions being asked by the people who called in to the centre. Not surprisingly, many of the calls were about AIDS. Those within the organization who had requested the AIDS focus groups did not realize this information was coming in to the organization's call centre each day. The problem was that the people who asked for the focus groups were separate from the call centre people. Because there was no cross-functional organization involving these two groups, the organization paid thousands of euros to gather data that it was already collecting.

Similar situations exist in many companies. For example, marketing departments seldom work closely with customer-service departments and consequently have little knowledge of what customers are saying about the brand and company. Also many companies that issue product warranty cards never tabulate those that are returned—and thus never collect the valuable customer-profile information the cards contain. Before a research project is started, it is wise to make sure that the information desired does not already exist.

Research is the infrastructure behind creative ideas

How do you pique the interest of business executives with a message about the infrastructure behind e-business? This was the challenge presented to the IBM WW IMC teams and that was the assignment given to Ogilvy & Mather, IBM's advertising agency. A business-to-business problem, the award-winning "E-Business Infrastructure" campaign was built on a solid research foundation led by IBM's WW market intelligence team with contributions from Ameritest Research, The Maya Group, and Perception Research Services.

IBM recognized that a new business opportunity existed in the previously unrecognized area of e-business infrastructure—an opportunity that IBM could address by leveraging its strengths in this area. IBM's objective was to define this new category, generate interest in it, and position IBM as the leader in providing infrastructure solutions.

Ameritest, for example, provided IBM with television advertising research and a strategy loop that resulted in a continual refinement and shaping of the strategy, as well as a consistent focus on meeting the campaign's objectives. Rather than a research "silo", where researchers are brought in to test and report their results, the research team was an ongoing integral part of the MC team and their insights were drawn upon to provide ideas, as well as wisdom, in managing the shifting thrusts of the campaign. Two things made this campaign an award winner:

1 The expanded authority that research findings were given in the campaign's development.

2 IBM's insistence that research be used to drive campaign decisions at every step in the development of the campaign.

The initial qualitative exploratory research found that in the post dot-com era, infrastructure was a nebulous subject that many executives didn't think about until they faced a problem or breakdown. Ogilvy & Mather developed a series of TV ads around "Moments of Truth".

IMC in Action

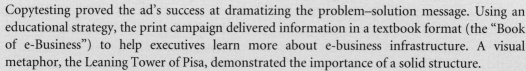

Copytesting proved the ad's success at dramatizing the problem–solution message. Using an educational strategy, the print campaign delivered information in a textbook format (the "Book of e-Business") to help executives learn more about e-business infrastructure. A visual metaphor, the Leaning Tower of Pisa, demonstrated the importance of a solid structure.

The campaign and the research on which it was based were so effective that the campaign was a winner in the 2003 Grand Ogilvy Research Award competition sponsored by the Advertising Research Foundation. In terms of impact, IBM's unaided association with e-business infrastructure rose to an index of 113 from 100, while its primary competitor's association dropped from 80 to 60. In just over nine months, the campaign exceeded IBM's objectives for new-business generation by 354 per cent with more than 1600 new contracts from sales leads directly attributable to the campaign.

Sources:
"Ameritest Shares the 2003 Grand Ogilvy Research Award with IBM, along with First-in-Category Win!",
www.ameritest.net IBM's 2003 Grand Ogilvy Research Award winning case study; e-business Infrastructure
campaign. Used by permission.
"Spotlight Shines Brightly on IBM Research", 11 April 2003, press release from The Advertising Research
Foundation. Used by permission.
Amy Shea, "IBM e-business Infrastructure", May 2003, PowerPoint presentation by Ameritest.

When should evaluation be conducted?

Evaluation can be done at several stages during the development and execution of MC campaigns. The first stage is market research into customer perceptions to determine whether the brand's position needs reinforcing, changing, or repositioning. Then, after message ideas have been generated, comes concept testing, which consists of *tests that measure the effectiveness of the rough ideas that become brand and campaign themes.* Next is copy testing, which was mentioned in Chapter 7 as a type of research that evaluates brand-message executions in a rough form before they are finally produced. Then there is concurrent testing, which is *testing that tracks the performance of messages as they are run.* Some companies test at only one stage, others at more than one—depending on how much the company wants to invest in minimizing its risks.

Finally, there is evaluative testing, which is *testing that measures the performance of brand messages against their objectives at the conclusion of the programme.* The closer a message is to its finished form and the more realistic the testing environment is, the more predictability a measurement generally has, as shown in Figure 18-1. (Some of the terms in this figure may be unfamiliar to you; they are explained later in this chapter.)

The critical role of objectives

An effective marketing communication programme is one that meets its objectives. MC planners must set measurable objectives. The more closely these objectives can be related to sales and profits, the better they are. But only in the areas of direct marketing, personal selling, and sales promotion is it possible to easily measure message effectiveness by sales.

The problem with using sales results alone to evaluate the impact of all marketing communication efforts is that MC represents only one set of variables that affect sales. Product performance, pricing, distribution, and competition have an effect on sales, share, and profits. Consequently, in an effort to try to isolate the effectiveness of MC activities, changes in brand

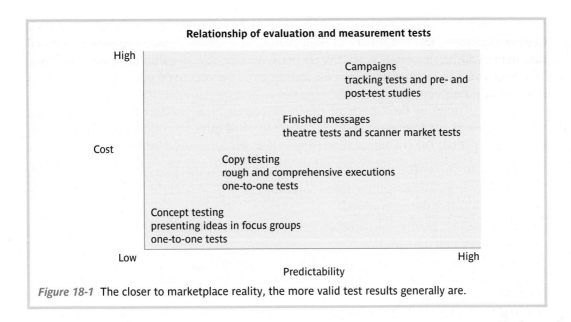

Figure 18-1 The closer to marketplace reality, the more valid test results generally are.

awareness, brand knowledge, and attitude change are measured. Although these measures are also influenced by other factors, they are the ones most widely used to evaluate MC efforts. This does not mean that MC departments and agencies have no responsibility for sales and profits. It means that other variables must be taken into consideration when sales and profits are the primary measures.

Measuring objectives

Although every MC plan is different, most plans have communication objectives to increase one or more of the following: level of brand awareness (awareness); understanding and recall of brand information and image (knowledge); the creation of attitude change and preference (persuasion); trial and repeat buying (behaviour); and the development of customer acquisition, retention, and growth (relationship building). If an objective calls for a 10 per cent increase in brand awareness, for example, then brand awareness should be measured.

If the objectives are behavioural results, such things as requests for more information, trial, and showroom visits are the easiest to measure. As explained in Chapters 13 and 15, one of the main strengths of both sales promotion and direct response is their measurability. The number of prospects and customers who respond to a promotion or offer (by buying, sampling, requesting more information, or visiting a store or trade-show booth) can be compared to the targeted population to ascertain a response rate or percentage.

Measuring changes in attitudes and opinions is more difficult because these changes exist only in people's heads. Also, researchers do not agree about whether attitude changes lead to behaviour changes—or, if they do, to what extent. Nevertheless, most marketers and academics agree that increases in such things as brand awareness, knowledge, and brand preference are indicators of communication effectiveness and are therefore worth measuring and evaluating.

Baselines

An important factor in setting measurable objectives is knowing the baseline—that is, *the beginning point, or where things stand before an MC effort begins.* For example, if you want to increase awareness by 10 per cent, you have to know what the current level of awareness is in order to gauge the amount of change—10 per cent of what? If 60 per cent of the target audience is aware of a brand, and the objective is to increase awareness by 10 per cent, then the desired outcome would be an awareness level of 66 per cent. The objective would be stated like this: "The objective is to increase the awareness level from 60 per cent to 66 per cent, an increase of 10 per cent, within a one-year period."

A tracking study of the launch of the Bella Napoli Pizza product by the Italian food company Buitoni, for example, found that the product had gained a critical level of penetration in its launch period. The communication effectiveness was determined by the following:[3]

- *Awareness:* The 43 per cent level of awareness at the pre-launch stage rose to 98 per cent two years later, surpassing the main competitor, Findus, which held an 84 per cent awareness level during the same period.

- *Brand usership:* Buitoni's penetration went from 11 per cent during the prelaunch phase to 59 per cent after the launch.

Because of the communication support provided by the launch of Pizza Bella Napoli, Buitoni Pizzas registered a 61 per cent growth in sales volume and a 76 per cent increase in shareholder value in the following two years.

Measurement and evaluation methods

Advertising and other MC functions are evaluated using a number of different methods. In this section we'll discuss some of the major methods that include determining if the media bought actually ran, concept testing, and pre- and post-copytesting. You will note that the more finished MC messages are and the more real-life the environment is when message effectiveness is measured, the more valid results are likely to be.

Media: measuring message delivery

One focus of MC evaluation is the delivery of the message. If the message is an advertisement, for example, did it run as scheduled? If the message is a public relations message, clients want to know how much "play" the news release received. In both cases, monitoring services can track performance and report back to clients. Press releases are often monitored by collecting clips—print and broadcast mentions of the brand or of the news release topic. In addition to simple counts, message exposure is also measured in terms of centimetres in print and seconds in broadcasts.

Internet services track hits, the number of times a website is visited. Some online monitoring services are able to track a visitor's activity before, during, and after the visit in order to tell the client where visitors came from, what they did while they were visiting the site, and where they went after leaving the site.

Nielsen Media Research is the primary audience service that monitors the play of commercials and estimates consumer viewing patterns based on panels it runs in many countries. A new service offered by the personal video recorder company TiVo is designed to provide advertisers with moment-by-moment reports on the viewing patterns of their customers.[4]

Testing concepts and creative strategies

Advertising concepts and strategies that are supported by large media budgets receive the lion's share of developmental evaluation and measurement. If a company makes three TV commercials, spends €15 million on media time and space, and then finds that the messages are not

Element to be tested	Measurement methods	Message-testing format
Concept, creative strategy	Focus groups, intercept surveys, projective tests	Idea statements, visuals on display boards
Awareness, brand knowledge	Surveys	Phone, e-mail, customer-service interactions
Communication and persuasion	Focus groups, one to one, laboratory, e-mail	Rough layouts, comps
Recognition, recall	Magazine portfolio, day-after phone survey, theatre	Finished executions, animatics
Physiological responses	Eye tracking, galvanic skin response	Laboratory one to one
Packaging impact	Tachistoscope, observation	Laboratory one to one, in store/aisle
Pilot test	Scanner test-markets	Finished executions
Customer knowledge, attitudes, behaviour	Tracking studies	Phone, e-mail
Copytesting (post-test)	Split-run, scanner data, awareness, attitude change, sales	Finished executions

Table 18-1 Measurement and evaluation methods

communicating or persuading, it has wasted the production costs and €15 million. Table 18-1 lists the elements and developmental stages of brand messages most frequently measured, the measuring methods used, and the format in which the evaluations and measurements take place. (Again, terms that may be unfamiliar are explained in the following sections.) Qualitative research is often used in account planning to find a customer insight that can be addressed with an MC message to deliver on a stated objective.

The first step in developing a campaign is to identify the most compelling message concept, creative theme, or primary selling proposition. An example of a concept test comes from a frozen-food company. Its food technicians developed a frozen pasta sauce that consumers could make from a package containing chunks of frozen vegetables and a packet of seasoning and thickener. All the consumer had to do was place the ingredients in a pan, add some water and oil, and cook for 20 minutes. The challenge was to come up with a message concept that accurately described the product and its benefits in a believable and persuasive manner.

The company did not know whether to focus on the convenience of preparation, the great taste, or the ingredients. Working with its advertising agency, the company wrote the following three concept statements, which were shown to three focus groups of the target audience—women who had families and who liked to cook. Each statement was printed in large letters on poster board. In each focus group, the order in which the three concepts were presented was changed to avoid order bias.

Concept A: Now, in only 20 minutes you can conveniently prepare a delicious-tasting pasta sauce made from flash-frozen vegetables and a secret mix of Italian spices.

Concept B: A rich, thick pasta sauce that is so delicious, your family will not believe you made it yourself.

Concept C: Because it is a unique blend of flash-frozen Italian tomatoes, onions, celery, peppers, and hearty Italian spices, this is the finest-tasting pasta sauce you will ever make.

After all three concepts were displayed, participants were asked to write down and then discuss which one best described a product they would be most likely to buy and why. The "whys" are the most important aspect of concept testing. The key finding about the pasta sauce was that few focus-group members believed that a great-tasting sauce could be made in only 20 minutes. As a result the final copy promised "a great tasting sauce that you don't have to cook all day".

Creative concepts can be tested in several ways. One is to use an **intercept survey**—*a survey in which people in a shopping centre or at an event are stopped and asked to respond to a short questionnaire.* The questions ask respondents to compare various concepts and comment on them. Intercept surveys are not scientifically reliable studies but rather offer a way to get a quick response for diagnostic purposes. They indicate whether the people being interviewed understand a concept and, if they do, whether they like it.

Focus groups are also used to test creative concepts. A **focus group** is *a group of 8 to 12 members of a brand's target audience who, led by a moderator, discuss some aspect of a brand, product category, or message strategy.* Most focus-group discussions last one to two hours, and participants are paid for participating.

The main benefit of focus-group research is diagnostic. The idea is to learn more about a category, competing brands, and message strategies from the user's perspective, and to "diagnose" any problems. When a participant says that a brand is "not easy to use", a good discussion leader probes to find out why this is so and what could be done to improve the brand's ease of use. Some people call focus groups "red flag" research, signalling their belief that focus groups are a good place to hear about problems. Sometimes when people are working closely on a project, such as a commercial or a set of print ads, they overlook the obvious. Focus groups help catch these oversights.

Focus-group findings should not be projected to a brand's total population because (1) the number of participants is too small, (2) the participants do not represent a randomly selected sample, and (3) quite often two or three "strong" people in a group dominate the discussion, often biasing the expressed views of others. Despite these shortcomings, however, focus groups can provide valuable customer insights.

Copy testing to predict communication effects

Copy testing can be used either while the brand message is in development or after it appears. A key concern with copy is that people involved in the development of a creative idea may see its potential differently from the audience for whom it is intended.

All brand messages should, to some extent, do two things—communicate and persuade. To make sure these two message objectives are achieved, companies use several different measuring techniques. As explained in Chapter 3, communication happens when the receiver of a message arrives at the meaning intended by the sender who encoded the message. Persuasion takes place when recipients of a message change their attitudes or behaviour in the direction desired (see Chapter 4). Copy testing measures both of these.

Copy testing can be used to evaluate several aspects of communication: attention, brand awareness and knowledge, emotional responses, and physiological responses.

Attention

One way to test the attention-getting power of a package, ad, or other brand message is by using a **tachistoscope**, *a device that exposes a brand message briefly to test participants so that researchers can measure how long it takes for a certain message or element to be communicated.* Tests using a tachistoscope are called *t-tests.* Respondents are seated before a screen containing a small hole that they are asked to look through. Behind the screen, but in complete darkness, is the ad or other stimulus—such as a logo, package, or promotional flag on a package—that is to be tested.

Suppose a company wants to evaluate several package designs. A number of competitive packages and the test package are arranged behind the screen in the way they would be displayed in a store. Respondents are asked to look through the hole and find the brand being tested. Once the light comes on, it stays on until respondents say they see the test brand and can correctly say where it is displayed (upper left, lower right, and so on). This is called a *find-time test.* By testing several different package designs, this test can help marketers determine which package is the most attention getting. Because the average shopper spends only 20 to 30 seconds making a brand selection in most categories, the quicker a package can be spotted, the more likely it is to be purchased.

Brand awareness and knowledge

Companies commonly measure two types of brand awareness—recognition and recall (Chapter 2). **Recognition** is *the act of identifying something and remembering that you saw or heard of it earlier.* Identifying a person you know within a crowd of people is recognition. **Recall** (or *unaided awareness*) is the more difficult process of *bringing something back from memory.* You may recognize a person in a crowd, but you may not be able to recall the person's name. Researchers measure recall by asking respondents to name all the brands they can think of in a particular product category. The researchers then give the respondents any brand names they did not mention and ask whether they have heard of those brands (a process called *aided awareness*). As you might expect, aided awareness (recognition) scores are always higher than unaided awareness (recall) scores.

A measure of magazine-ad recall is provided by Gallup & Robinson's Impact Test. Respondents are given a magazine to take home and read. The following day the respondents are called and asked to recall as many ads as they can from the magazine. For the ads that are recalled, respondents are asked what brand claims they remember and eventually how likely they are to buy the brand.

Recall measurements of TV commercials—called *post-tests* because the commercials have already been made and are on air—are done in a similar way. Respondents are called and asked whether they watched a certain show the day before. If they say yes, they are asked whether they saw a commercial for a product in a particular category (such as hair sprays, cars, brokerage services, computers). If the answer is yes, they are asked what the brand was and what they recall about the commercial. Those who don't recall the particular commercial being studied are then asked whether they remember a commercial for the brand being measured (a recognition question).

Some of the concerns with post-tests are that programme content can influence a score, as can the number of competitive commercials running at the same time. And, as with the print tests, there is always a question as to what is actually being remembered—the message execution or the brand claims. It has also been found that well-known brands normally have higher scores than do new and less well-known brands just because of the familiarity factor.

Brand knowledge requires a more in-depth measurement than does brand recall. To measure how much respondents know about a brand and to what extent they see it as different from its competitors, researchers use phone and e-mail surveys. Brand knowledge can also be measured with one-to-one personal interviews, but this expensive method is often not cost-justified. Measurements of brand awareness and brand knowledge are frequently used to evaluate a new or revised campaign effort. Measurements are done as pre- and post-tests—that is, before and after a campaign runs.

Emotional responses

Recognizing the power of emotions in brand decision making, and also the fact that emotions are difficult for many people to express, MC agency BBDO Worldwide developed a test that measures emotional responses to brand messages. The agency's proprietary Emotional Measurement System lets respondents communicate their emotions by selecting photographs of individuals with various emotional expressions. After respondents are shown a set of brand messages, they are asked to select from dozens of these individual-expression photos (which have been extensively studied and categorized) the images that best illustrate how the brand messages made them feel. The selected photos are used to "emotionally profile" each set of brand messages shown. This allows the agency and client to select the brand message that comes closest to creating the desired emotional response.

An important emotional response that can be measured is likeability. Traditionally many MC managers felt that it didn't matter whether customers liked an ad as long as the ad built awareness. More recently, a study of different pre-testing methods found that likeability is a powerful predictor of sales success. The likeability of a brand message can be measured along a 5- or 7-point semantic differential scale ranging from "I loved the message" to "I hated the message". Likeability tests consider related factors such as these:

- Relevance (personally meaningful).
- Believability, credibility (convincing and true to life).
- Interest (intriguing, fascinating, engaging).
- Enjoyment (entertaining, warm).
- Familiarity (comfortable).
- Surprise (pleasantly surprising).

The likeability issue, particularly with advertising, is whether people who like a message will transfer that liking to the brand. In a relationship-focused marketing communication programme, likeability is presumed to be a key determinant of the continuation of the relationship.

Physiological responses

Sometimes how we feel emotionally about something affects how we respond to it physically—whether or not we are aware of those responses. According to neurologist Richard Restak, "We have reason to doubt that full awareness of our motives, drives, and other mental activities may be possible."[5] Because people sometimes are not willing to express, or capable of expressing, what they really think or feel about a brand message, measures of physiological responses have been developed. Companies seldom use these tests, so they are described only briefly here. The reason for their limited use is that they are relatively expensive to conduct and the findings are often difficult to interpret.

Probably the most widely discussed physiological test is the *galvanic skin response test*. It uses a galvanometer—the same basic instrument used in lie detectors—to measure minute electrical currents. Marketers use the test to measure to what extent respondents are stimulated or aroused when exposed to a variety of brand messages. Researchers have found that there can be a correlation between level of stimulation and purchase behaviour.[6]

Two other tests have to do with eyes—pupil dilation and eye tracking. The *pupil dilation measure* follows the same concept as the galvanic skin response measurement. The more the pupil dilates, the greater is the indication of involvement in the brand message being shown. The *eye-tracking instrument* uses an infra-red beam to follow the eye, converting its movement to traces on the ad being tested. Measurements show which ad elements attract most attention. This information can be helpful in measuring what is known in the MC industry as "vampire creative"—message elements that detract from the purpose of the brand message.

Tools used to measure persuasion

Focus groups, often used to test an ad's communication effects, are not as reliable for testing persuasion. The reason is that there is a low correlation between what people say they will do and what they actually do, especially when it comes to brand selection. "Intend-to-buy" scores—another name for persuasion scores and preference measures—have fooled many companies. Therefore, several levels and methods of persuasion testing have been developed, each providing a little more validity than the one before: (1) theatre tests, (2) theatre tests with purchases, (3) (scanner market) tests, and (4) trading studies. The more a test simulates real life and includes behavioural responses, the more validity the persuasion score will have.

Theatre tests

After focus groups, companies sometimes use **theatre tests** to measure persuasion effects. These are *tests in which people are invited to a location for the purpose of evaluating their response to a brand message.* Before the showing, participants are asked to complete a questionnaire that asks what brands in certain categories they prefer, and asks as well for some demographic data. Respondents are then shown the programme, which contains from six to eight commercials. Three or four are the commercials being tested. After the showing, respondents are asked about the programme; they are also asked what commercials they remember seeing (a measure of advertising recall). They are then shown a second programme, also containing the test commercials. Following this, they are asked to indicate their preference for brands in a variety of categories similar to the first questionnaire they completed. The difference in the preference scores indicates the level of persuasion.

Theatre tests with purchases

The next level of persuasion validity involves forced purchases after the theatre showing of a brand message. Instead of having participants complete the second questionnaire described above, respondents are given tokens and are taken into a room that is set up as a small store. The shelves are stocked with all the major brands in each of the product categories of the test commercials. Respondents are told to use their tokens to buy whichever brands they want. By recording each person's brand choices and comparing these choices to those indicated on the initial brand-usage questionnaire, researchers can determine how many respondents switched brands. The more who switch, the higher is the persuasion score for the respective test commercial.

One advantage of theatre tests is that animatics (*rough video footage used in ad testing*) can be used instead of finished commercials. Although finished ads are preferred so they don't look out of place or inferior, animatics save companies a great amount of production costs. A weakness of theatre tests is that, because participants are aware they are being tested, they can project intend-to-buy responses that do not necessarily correspond to their normal behaviour. Also, forced-purchase decisions provide only directional answers about persuasion (an ad is persuasive or not persuasive); they cannot be used to say that the test commercial would increase sales by any certain percentage. In the test respondents are forced to buy, to spend the tokens they received, which is not a situation mimicking reality, where consumers always have the option not to buy anything at all.

Test marketing

Test marketing is probably the most valid persuasion test because it takes place over a longer period in a competitive marketplace. Test marketing is *a research design in which an MC campaign is run in two to four markets for anywhere from 6 to 12 months*. Brand sales are compared to sales in similar control markets (those in which the brand has about the same share and is faced with the same major competitors). Three problems are associated with the use of test marketing: (1) It takes a long time. (2) Testing exposes new ideas to competitors. (3) Market tests are expensive. In test marketing, all MC materials must be in finished form, and at least 200 customers need to be interviewed in each of the test and control markets both before and after the market test runs. Scanner market tests and tracking studies are types of test marketing measures.

A scanner market test is *a tracking of a household's purchases by means of scanner data*. The ideas are similar to test marketing in general, but whereas test marketing often relies on self-administered reports, scanner data provide more reliable test measures based on actual buying behaviour. Tests like these are executed in several selected small- to medium-size markets. In each market, researchers have recruited a panel of household members who agree to have a buyer identification card (like a frequent-buyer card) scanned every time they go shopping so that their purchases can be tracked. Ideally, within each market's panel, participants are divided into two groups, the test group and the control group. Often, though, the various test markets are compared. Each group or market receives different commercials or other MC messages: the test group the messages that are tested, the control groups the old messages, or no message at all, depending on the objective of the research. Scanner data are collected and analysed to find the differences in effects

Scanner market tests can be used in a short time-frame to evaluate sales-promotion offers, which, if successful, generally increase sales within days of running. These tests can also be used for longer-term evaluation of a brand's repositioning or a new campaign theme. One of the benefits of scanner tests is that, by tracking weekly (or even daily) sales, researchers can determine how long it takes for marketing communication to have an effect. The more frequently a product category is purchased, the more telling such a test generally is and the less time it requires. Differences in purchases between test households and control households determine the extent of the promotional impact.

Participating households know they are members of a research panel, but they have no idea what brands are being tested. Because brand selections are made in real stores and respondents use their own money, there is nothing other than the test MC messages to influence the results. Also, results are based on actual sales data, not on scores that have to be translated into sales. Furthermore, this type of test has the advantage of not being obvious to competitors.

There are a couple of shortcomings, however. Scanner market tests have high costs—several times the cost of theatre tests. Not only must researchers use finished brand messages, but households must be compensated for participating, stores must be paid for providing scanner data for the test and control groups, and the cable and newspaper media charge a premium for special handling of the test messages. Another limitation is that the percentage of the test panel that makes purchases in the test brand's product category can be relatively small, making projections to a national market difficult although this is of course an issue that goes with most of the research approaches.

Tracking studies

Used most frequently by companies that have multimillion-euro MC budgets, tracking studies are *periodic surveys that measure brand awareness, trial, repeat, and customer satisfaction with a brand and its competitors.* Because tracking studies are ongoing, they offer test-and-control as well as pre- and post-test measures of new campaigns and other major changes in the marketing and marketing communication mix. When the tracking panel is used to test MC materials in a couple of the markets being tracked, using the others as control markets, this is essentially a test market approach. But panels are also used to measure changes on national, or even international level, i.e. for the complete market the company is in.

Tracking studies are one of the best methods for evaluating long-term marketing communication and relationship-building results. Most tracking studies are done by phone or online in several different markets every three to six months. Brands that can afford to do so often track a sample of their strong, weak, and new markets. Unless a company has a database of category users, random dialling is used to find respondents. In the case of service brands, customer-satisfaction tracking studies are often ongoing, with customer interviews being conducted each day or week.

What is asked in a study that tracks awareness, trial, and repeat? Figure 18-2 lists typical questions that a rental car company might ask. To the right of each question is an explanation of the question. Following the screening question, the questions dealing with awareness, trial, and repeat are standard on tracking studies. The remaining questions are customized for each brand and each survey wave (each time the panel is surveyed is called a *wave*). These diagnostic questions help explain why a brand is growing or declining in sales and share. One processed-meat company conducted a tracking study that always included questions on quality and taste. When it was found that the scores for "tastes great" were falling, the TV advertising (which was the primary MC function) was revised to include more shots of taste satisfaction—close-ups of delicious-looking sandwiches and of people smiling while eating. Within six months after the new advertising began running, taste satisfaction scores began to increase.

Although a tracking study is designed to show trends over time, the results of just one wave of interviews often provide valuable insights into the strengths and weaknesses of a brand's marketing programme. Both absolute numbers and the relationship between the various numbers need to be analysed. Obviously, many brand messages—MC, intrinsic, unintended, and customer created—affect tracking scores. Nevertheless, analyses of tracking studies can often help companies spot MC problem areas.

Table 18-2 is a hypothetical set of tracking scores that could be obtained from the questions

Sample tracking study questions

Questions and answers	Explanation
Q: Have you rented a car within the last six months? A: Yes.	*Screening question.* This question is asked first to make sure the respondent is a category user. If the answer is no, the interview is terminated.
Q: Please tell me all the brands of rental cars you can think of. A: Brand A. Brand B.	*Recall question.* The first brand name mentioned is tabulated as the top-of-mind (TOM) brand. There is generally a high correlation between a brand's TOM score and the brand's market share. This is because customers are more likely to mention first the brand they use most. All others mentioned are classified as "unaided" mentions. These are brands that the respondents can recall.
Q: Which of these brands are you familiar with: Brand C, Brand D, Brand E? A: Brand C. Brand E.	*Recognition question.* Interviewer asks for each of the brands being measured that the respondent did not mention in the answer to the recall question. The brands with which the respondent is familiar are classified as "aided" mentions. These are the brands that were not recalled but were recognized.
Q: From which of these companies have you rented a car at least once during the last 12 months? A: Brand A. Brand B.	*Trial question.* The answer to this question indicates which brands the respondent has tried/sampled.
Q: From which of these companies have you rented a car more than once during the last 12 months? A: Brand A.	*Brand menu question.* This answer indicates those brands the respondent feels are OK to use, the ones to which the respondent is loyal.
Q: On a scale of 1 to 5, with 5 being the highest rating, how would you rate Brand A's customer service? How would you rate Brand B's? A: Four for Brand A; two for Brand B.	Here begin the *customized questions.* This particular one is measuring the perceived level of customer service.
Q: On a scale of 1 to 5, with 5 being the highest rating, how would you rate the quality of car that you rented from Brand A? From Brand B? A: Four for Brand A; two for Brand B.	This might be asked to see if the perceived difference in car quality is enough to be used as a copy point in brand messages.
Q: On a scale of 1 to 5, with 5 being the highest rating, how likely would you be to recommend Brand A to someone else? Brand B? A: Four for Brand A; two for Brand B.	This type of question is generally considered as being the most predictive of brand loyalty. If a customer is very likely to recommend a brand to someone else, that customer is very likely to make a repeat purchase.

Figure 18-2 Which are recall and which are recognition questions?

in Figure 18-2. The numbers for Brand A are what brand managers dream of—they are very good. The 40 per cent top-of-mind is the percentage of respondents who mentioned Brand A first when responding to the recall question: "Please tell me all the brands of rental car brands you can think of." This score is close to the brand's market share and shows that Brand A is by far the number-one car rental brand. The fact that nearly two-thirds of the people aware of Brand A rented at least once in the last 12 months is a good ratio and suggests that there are

	Brand A	Brand B	Brand C
Top-of-mind (TOM) awareness	40%	20%	15%
Unaided awareness	62	62	38
Aided awareness	90	85	70
Trial	65	65	20
Repeat purchase	38	10	15
* Numbers are hypothetical.			

Table 18-2 Tracking study scores*
* Numbers are hypothetical.

few, if any, marketing communication concerns. The fact that over half (38/65) rented more than once in this period is also healthy, especially in a competitive category such as rental cars, where actual product differences are minimal.

The numbers for Brand B have both good and bad news. The fact that Brand B's top-of-mind awareness is only half of Brand A's suggests that Brand B may need greater brand-message frequency or more memorable brand messages. The conversion from awareness to trial numbers is very good, as nearly three out of four (65/85) of those aware have tried Brand B. That only one out of six (10/65) makes a repeat purchase, however, indicates a severe problem. One explanation is that expectations were set too high and renters were disappointed. Another more likely explanation is that the brand was inferior: long lines, unavailability, or dirty or underperforming cars may account for the product's low repeat-purchase score.

Because Brand C's top three scores are considerably lower than the scores for Brand A and Brand B, it could be that Brand C is not spending enough on marketing communication. If competitive spending reports show that Brand C is, in fact, spending nearly the same as the other two brands, the low scores would indicate that the brand messages are not communicating or not persuading (fewer than one out of three respondents familiar with the brand has even tried it in the last 12 months). The low top-of-mind scores and unaided-awareness scores could also suggest poor media selection—not reaching the target audience. The good news in these scores is that three-quarters of those who tried Brand C repeated, a much higher percentage of conversion than either Brand A's or Brand B's. This suggests that Brand C should also invest much more in promotion in order to motivate trial, because the findings show that once customers try Brand C, the majority make repeat rentals.

Real-time tracking

The biggest problem with most traditional customer satisfaction tracking studies is that planning and executing them and analysing and reporting the findings take so long that the findings are not up-to-date. Who cares what customers were saying three or six months ago? The Internet is helping solve that problem because it allows almost instantaneous data reporting. Immediate feedback from a website provides information on a real-time basis that can be used to monitor and change strategies. An "intelligent" online reporting system also can alert managers about customer-satisfaction problems as they develop and point to the sources of these problems.[7]

B2B measurement

Because most B2B marketing communication budgets are not as large as the budgets for consumer brands, B2B companies generally do less copy and media evaluation. Tracking studies, for example, are most typically used for consumer products, although nothing other than cost prevents B2B brands from using them.

Because a much larger portion of most B2B budgets goes into personal selling, B2B companies often use forms of measurement such as advisory boards, customer-evaluation forms, and surveys of industry consultants and members of the trade press. Advisory boards are generally made up of customers (both channel members and end users) but can also include suppliers, consultants, and academics who specialize in relevant areas. The purpose of these groups is to tell companies what they are doing right and what they could be doing better.

IBM ThinkPad, for example, has a marketing advisory board made up of marketing directors from non-competing companies, suppliers of marketing services, and academics who specialize in marketing and IMC. Each year, for two days, the group is presented with a variety of ideas—everything from marketing plans to special promotions and packaging ideas, to new-product ideas and creative work—and is then asked for reactions and suggestions.

Customer and other types of advisory groups can provide helpful feedback to companies, but there are limitations to this type of MC evaluation. Normally, the customer advisory groups are quite small and not representative of the company's customer base. Also, some members of these groups may have their own agendas and therefore slant their comments to suit their own company needs and desires.

Online measurement and evaluation

Online evaluations make sense not only for measuring online marketing efforts but also for replacing or complementing mail and phone surveys. Online research has been growing dramatically over the past decade. The *rate* of growth has slowed, however, as response rates continue to drop. The two aspects of online research that hold the most promise are *panel surveying* (sending out questionnaires to people who agreed beforehand to participate) and *data delivery* (distributing measurement findings online). Three major benefits of doing online measurements are timeliness, low costs, and narrow targeting.

Some MC professionals are concerned that findings from online measurements are not as valid as those from offline phone surveys. Because a significant proportion of consumers are still not active Internet users, some argue that samples are not representative of the total population. This suggests that online surveys should be used only when the majority of a product's target audience uses the Internet. There is increasing evidence, however, that online measures are as valid as offline ones.[8]

Although most e-commerce companies that undertake MC measurement focus on sales, other meaningful online measurements can be taken. Online tests can measure:

- Number who requested brand information.
- Number who completed a customer profile.
- Number who made complaints.
- Types of people who visit the site.
- Frequency of visits.
- Number who participate in chat sessions.

- Number and quality of website mentions in the media and by other third parties.
- Type and popularity of other sites that request to be linked to the company's site.

Having this type of evaluative information can help companies improve their websites, online offers, and other online relationship-building efforts.

Online panels versus spam surveys

Spam mailings of research questions can quickly generate a large number of responses, but it is difficult to know who responded. It is known that even if respondents are required to provide personal profile data, approximately 25 per cent provide false data. Another problem of spam research is that, just as telemarketing has made phone survey work difficult to do (the participation refusal rate is now close to 50 per cent), it will make online research more difficult and costly to do. People ignore unsolicited surveys because they either confuse them with sales offers or are annoyed by receiving too much unsolicited e-mail in general.

The concept of permission marketing, mentioned in Chapter 9, applies to doing surveys. The most successful surveys invite people to participate. Not only do people need to give their permission to be sent surveys, but they also must provide personal profiles in order to be in a research panel. This not only ensures a much higher response rate but also provides a database of customer profiles that can be used to match survey respondents to the target audience of a brand for which the research is being done.

Most research companies today own an online research panel. To motivate consumers to participate, various incentives are offered, Recruiting panel members is an ongoing job and requires advertising and tie-in promotions with a variety of websites.

Holding focus-group discussions online offers several advantages, such as saving the cost of renting a research facility and paying high fees for participation, and the possibility of covering wider geographical markets. Operationally, an **online focus group** is *a chat room to which selected people have been invited to meet at a specified time with a moderator.* These groups are most successful when participants are either customers or prospects selected from a highly controlled panel. This helps ensure that participants are who they say they are and are motivated to participate. Because online participants are not sitting across from each other as in a traditional focus-group setting, the timid are more likely to respond, and people are more likely to challenge and disagree with the more outspoken and aggressive participants. At the same time, there are disadvantages. Face-to-face groups provide a certain amount of body language that is lost online. Online discussions also lack the display of dynamics and emotions that can be a measure of how relevant a certain brand aspect is.

Internet research is also used to track online media usage. Participants sign up to participate in a panel and give permission for their online activities to be recorded. Software for doing the tracking is downloaded by the participants, and their activities are uploaded and sent to the research agency for analysis. Such panels provide online marketers with a way to measure who is participating and what other online sites attract their customers. Also, changes of website content and presentation or changes in the mix of links with other sites, for example, can be evaluated with the data.

In sum, MC planners who intend to use online evaluation should consider the following:

- *Use respondents from a pre-recruited panel:* This provides several advantages: respondents are known (online users are notorious for disguising their identity). Respondents can be chosen who best match the brand's target profile. The questionnaire is not perceived as intrusive, and respondents feel an obligation to respond.

- *Ensure quick download:* Because respondents are doing the company a favour, the questionnaire should download quickly, and the instructions should be very clear.

- *Limit questionnaire length:* Companies must respect respondents' time. Experts suggest that questionnaires must take no more than 15 minutes to complete.[9]

- *Make navigation effortless:* The more work it takes for respondents to complete a survey, the lower the response rate will be.

- *Limit contact frequency:* Because most online surveys are done with panels, if members of the panels are asked to participate too often, they may drop out of the panel. The right frequency depends on the incentives offered, the product category, and the length of the questionnaires. The effect of frequency on response rate is something that can be easily tracked and evaluated. When the response rate begins to decrease and all other conditions are the same, frequency should be reduced.

Advantages and disadvantages of online surveying

Online surveys have both advantages and disadvantages when compared to mail and telephone surveys. Online surveys are faster to prepare and distribute, and responses are received faster—days instead of weeks for the return of mail questionnaires. The number of questionnaires completed in a day is not limited by the number of phone interviewers. Theoretically, thousands of online questionnaires can be completed at the same time because they are self-administered and automatically reported. Online surveys provide more flexibility. They can show not only print messages but also audio and video; offline studies can do so only in certain expensive locations. Unlike mail questionnaires, online surveys can be quickly changed when questions are found to be unclear or misleading. Also, data are cleaned as they are collected. For example, if respondents are asked to do a ranking and they assign the same number to two factors, they are instantly made aware of the error and asked to correct it. Finally, as finished questionnaires are returned, unlike mail questionnaires, they are instantly coded and tabulated without need for entering data manually.[10]

Despite its (by now) widespread use, online research does have its limitations. Random sampling produces very low returns. As mentioned earlier, online respondents can hide their identity. Although phone respondents can also do this, area codes and some phone-number prefixes indicate a geographical location for which there are demographic profiles against which respondent profiles can be compared. Also, because respondents can hide their identity, competitors can opt-in to a brand's research panel, hide their identity, and learn what products and ideas the brand is studying. Other concerns are that online samples are not representative and that the research frame (the population from which the respondents are drawn) is not well defined.[11]

Evaluating the IMC process

Processes are more important in IMC than in other areas of marketing. IMC requires more interaction with customers and other key stakeholders, more internal sharing of information, and more cross-functional planning for, and monitoring of, brand relationships. These critical processes need to be effectively managed, which can be done only if they are periodically evaluated and monitored.

IMC audits

An **IMC audit** is *an in-depth research method for evaluating IMC relationship-building practices.*[12] It examines organizational structure, the extent of understanding of MC objectives and strategies within the organization, and the extent to which people agree with those objectives and strategies. It also measures to what extent company-created brand messages are strategically consistent. The IMC mini-audit in Figure 18-3 identifies the various areas covered in a full

---

IMC mini-audit

Circle the number that best describes how your organization operates regarding each of the following statements. If you don't know how well your organization is doing for a given item, circle DK (Don't Know). If a question does not apply to your organization, leave it blank.

Organizational infrastructure   Never   Always

1. In our company, the process of managing brand/company reputation   1 2 3 4 5 DK
   and building stakeholder relationships is a cross-functional
   responsibility that includes departments such as production,
   operations, sales, finance and human resources, as well as
   marketing.

2. The people managing our communication programmes demonstrate   1 2 3 4 5 DK
   a good understanding of the strengths and weaknesses of ALL
   major marketing communication tools, such as direct response,
   public relations, sales promotion, advertising and packaging, when
   putting marketing communication plans together.

3. We do a good job of internal marketing, informing all areas of the   1 2 3 4 5 DK
   organization about our objectives and marketing programmes.

4. Our major communication agencies have at least monthly   1 2 3 4 5 DK
   contact with each other regarding our communications programmes
   and activities.

Interactivity

5. Our media plan is a strategic balance between mass media and   1 2 3 4 5 DK
   one-to-one media.

6. Special programmes are in place to facilitate customer enquiries   1 2 3 4 5 DK
   and complaints.

7. We use customer databases that capture customer enquiries,   1 2 3 4 5 DK
   complaints and compliments, as well as sales behaviour
   (e.g. trial, repeat, frequency of purchase, type of purchases).

8. Our customer databases are easily accessible (internally)   1 2 3 4 5 DK
   and user-friendly.

Mission marketing

9. Our organization's mission is a key consideration and is evident in   1 2 3 4 5 DK
   our marketing communication plans.

10. Our mission provides an additional reason for customers and   1 2 3 4 5 DK
    other key stakeholders to believe our messages and support
    our company.

11. Our corporate philanthropic efforts are concentrated in one specific   1 2 3 4 5 DK
    area or programme.

Figure 18-3 This 20-question mini-audit is an easy way for an organization to quickly test its level of integration.

		Never			Always		
Strategic consistency							
12.	All of our company-created brand messages (e.g. advertising, sales promotion, PR, packaging) are strategically consistent.	1	2	3	4	5	DK
13.	We periodically review all our brand messages to determine to what extent they are strategically consistent.	1	2	3	4	5	DK
14.	We consciously think about what brand messages are being sent by our pricing, distribution, product performance and customer-service operations, and by persons and organizations outside the control of the company.	1	2	3	4	5	DK
Planning and evaluating							
15.	When doing our marketing communication planning, we use a SWOT analysis to determine the strengths and opportunities we can leverage, and the weaknesses and threats we need to address.	1	2	3	4	5	DK
16.	We use a zero-based approach in marketing communication planning.	1	2	3	4	5	DK
17.	When doing annual marketing communication planning, we make sure intrinsic brand-contact points are sending positive brand messages and that these contacts are being fully leveraged before we invest in creating new brand-contact points.	1	2	3	4	5	DK
18.	Our company uses some type of tracking study to evaluate the strength of our relationships with customers and other key stakeholder groups.	1	2	3	4	5	DK
19.	Our marketing strategies maximize the unique strengths of the various marketing communication functions (e.g. public relations, direct response, advertising, event sponsorships, trade promotions, packaging).	1	2	3	4	5	DK
20.	The overall objective of our marketing communication programme is to create and nourish profitable relationships with customers and other stakeholders by strategically controlling or influencing all messages sent to these groups, and encouraging purposeful dialogue with them.	1	2	3	4	5	DK

Add scores (minus blank items and DKs) and divide by 20.　　　Score _____

Figure 18-3 Continued

audit. This mini-audit can be administered to company managers to help them decide whether an in-depth audit is needed.

Brand metrics

The tracking of a brand's performance occupies a major part of a brand manager's time. Also tracked is the performance of brand communication. Such efforts rely on quantitative and qualitative methods, as well as the tracking and regular reporting of sales, share of market, and costs.

Brand metrics are *measures of brand image and brand impact*.[13] The brand-impact metrics are the usual business measures of sales and brand share. Brand-image metrics measure the various parts of the brand-building pyramid, introduced in Chapter 2. Thus, brand metrics measure the following:

- Brand recognition.
- Overall awareness of the brand.
- Understanding of the brand position.
- The imagery people have of the brand
- Brand relevance—how important and meaningful the brand is.
- Brand preference—including the level of customer purchase intent.

The relationships aspects of the brand, the top of the pyramid, are discussed below. Brand metrics help companies to develop rich profiles of stakeholders and their relationship to the brand, and that information enables companies to develop appropriate contact points and message strategies.[14]

Sense and simplicity: it does make sense!

In September 2004 Philips introduced its new brand promise: "Sense and simplicity". As was discussed in the opening case of Chapter 2, the brand promise was meant as a commitment to advanced technology that is easy to use and designed around the way people live and work. After years of branding around "Let's make things better", Philips launched this rebranding initiative as part of a programme to create a truly market-driven company. The "sense and simplicity" advertising campaign revolves around a white box and reflects technology that is "as simple as the box it comes in". Print, outdoor, online and other advertisements all show simple pictures that are supported with straightforward lines explaining how Philips' products make life simpler and sensible.

However, as was explained in Chapter 2, the "sense and simplicity" promise goes beyond advertising. The commitment is, among others, also embedded in Philips Design. According to CEO Gerard Kleisterlee, products like the Philips' Heart Start defibrillator and the Perfect Draft beer dispenser are the products that best demonstrate the simplicity claim. Whether product design makes sense to customers is tested as well in consumer test centres around the world. In these centres products are evaluated and critiqued by consumers, sometimes leading Philips to delay product releases to make the suggested changes.

Next Simplicity events are another way for Philips to showcase concept products. The Next Simplicity initiative was set up at the beginning of 2005 and was meant to be a tangible and inspiring way of communicating Philips' new brand promise. On the basis of worldwide research into consumer needs, five themes, namely care, glow, play, share and trust, and four innovative product concepts per theme were created. Concept models were first showcased at the Simplicity Event in Paris in September 2005. They were designed to include almost no buttons or switches, and were therefore extremely easy to use. Also, the models were experiential, meaning that visitors could experience and interact with them. The product concepts were a demonstration of Philips' vision to "deliver simplicity-led design, to improve the quality of life and contribute to a healthy lifestyle".

The opening case of Chapter 2 has already shown that the renewed brand positioning has brought Philips considerable external recognition. The annual global brand study by Interbrand, resulting in a yearly list of the 100 Best Global Brands, awarded Philips the 48th position in 2006. In 2005 Philips had been ranked 53rd, moving up from 65th position on the list in 2004. This improved ranking signals an increase of 14 per cent in the value of Philips' brand

IMC in Action

▶ and made Philips one of the top gainers in 2006. In response to this result Philips Chief Marketing Officer Andrea Ragnetti said: "The improved Interbrand ranking confirms that our brand promise 'sense and simplicity', which is also the framework for our future growth, is making a difference to the way the world sees and experiences Philips, and is reinvigorating faith in the Philips brand." This signals the importance of the Interbrand ranking for Philips as a measure for success.

A success like this is likely used for follow-up marketing communications. For example, Philips' website features the Interbrand ranking as a means to promote a career with the company. Also, Philips spokespersons now proudly include the improved ranking in company presentations for investors. In addition, press releases concerning the stunning increase in the Philips' brand value have been numerous. Maybe this media attention will result in another increase in brand value that might be shown on future Interbrand Global Brands ranking lists.

Think about it

Do you think the Interbrand list of the 100 Best Global Brands is a good way for Philips to assess the success of branding campaigns? What other ways of measurement can you think of? How would you use the improved ranking in 2006 for upcoming marketing communications?

Sources:

Capell, K. (2006) "How Philips Got Brand Buzz", BusinessWeek, London. Retrieved on 4 April 2007, from www.businessweek.com/globalbiz/content/jul2006/gb20060731_037693.htm?chan=innovation_innovation+%2B+design_top+stories

Interbrand, 2006. "Best Global Brands 2006, A Ranking by Brand Value", BusinessWeek. Retrieved on 4 April 2007, from the www.interbrand.com

www.careernews.philips.nl/e_article000654490.cfm
www.design.philips.com/About/Design/newvaluebyOneDesign/Section-13795/Index.html
www.philips.com
www.philips.com.my/About/News/press/Section-13634/article-14423.html

Relationship metrics

For the most part, measurements of brand awareness, knowledge, attitudes, trial, and repeat purchases are diagnostics that help explain why brand relationships are strong or weak. To give these findings more meaning, researchers combine them with direct measures of brand relationships, called **relationship metrics**. These are *output controls developed specifically for IMC programmes to track the development of brand relationships.*[15] They help explain sales and share trends and provide diagnostic information as a basis for more accurate forecasting.

Some companies feel that brand relationships can be evaluated by simply asking customers whether they are satisfied. Yet more than 70 per cent of customers who defect may have been "satisfied". Research has found a large gulf between satisfied customers and *completely* satisfied customers. The key to generating superior long-term financial performance is to turn the former into the latter.[16]

In order not to overlook the obvious, companies should continually ask customers whether their wants, needs, and concerns are being addressed. But for several reasons this line of enquiry should not be the extent of measuring "satisfaction". The idea of asking what customers want and need seldom opens the door to any creative ideas or competitive advantages. Most customers are not trained to be creative in their responses to satisfaction surveys. As one pundit puts it: "The biggest lie in the restaurant business is the answer to the question: 'How was your dinner?'" A company must look for underlying problems, as well as future wants and needs. As a former senior vice president of Hewlett-Packard says, you need to have an "imaginative understanding of the user's needs".[17]

The key to success here is to adopt a marketing orientation in the business. This means that in designing strategies and programmes, including brand strategy and IMC programmes, companies should listen carefully to their stakeholders, but also build on their own knowledge, expertise and experiences. The truth is in the middle, but it sometimes is tough to get there, starting from your own company perspective.[18]

Among the relationship metrics that companies use most successfully are customer lifetime value (CLTV); recency, frequency, and monetary indexes (collectively referred to as RFM analysis); referral index; and share of wallet. Several of these are discussed in previous chapters but are summarized here to allow you to compare and contrast these measures.

■ *Lifetime customer value (CLTV):* The purpose of this measure is to show a company what an average customer is worth in revenue. CLTV is determined by multiplying the average number of years customers do business with a company by the average amount they spend each year. This figure is then discounted on the basis of current interest rates to determine "net present value". Once a company knows what an average customer is worth in revenue, it can estimate how much to spend to acquire a new customer and how much to spend each year to retain current customers.[19]

■ *CLTV quintile analysis:* Somewhat similar to a customer-profitability measure but with a longer-term perspective, CLTV quintile analysis divides customers into five equal groups based on their customer lifetime value. In the top group are the 20 per cent with the highest CLTV; in the bottom group, the 20 per cent with the lowest CLTV. Tracking the average CLTV of each of the five groups profiles a company's source of revenue. Ideally, the averages in all five groups would continue to increase over time. A red flag could be an increase in the top group and a decrease in all the other groups, indicating that the basis of support is shrinking even though total revenue may be unchanged or even slightly increasing.

■ *Recency, frequency, monetary (RFM) analysis:* The direct-response industry has discovered that the more recently people have bought, the more often they buy, and the more they spend, the better customers they are. In particular, average purchase frequency—the percentage of customers who purchased within the last 30 days (the period varies depending on product category)—indicates to what extent acquired customers are becoming loyal. Sales could be increasing, but if the average customer is buying less frequently, the support base may be weakening (cf. CLTV quintile analysis). Similarly, the more a customer spends, the more likely it is that the customer will continue the relationship.

■ *Referral index:* This index tracks the percentage of new business resulting from a customer or some other stakeholder recommending the brand. It applies best to large-ticket and service products where it is possible to ask new customers what motivated them to choose the brand. Referrals are confirmation that marketers are doing what they are saying they will do for customers. Because referrals are one of the key behaviours of brand advocates (the highest-level brand relationship), a rising referral index score generally indicates an increase in the number of brand advocates—a good indication that relationship-building practices are working.

■ *Share of wallet:* Because the most profitable customers, especially in packaged-goods categories, buy multiple brands, one brand objective is to get an increasing percentage of these customers' category purchases. Scanner data is helpful in spotting this share trend.

When any of the relationship metrics shows a negative trend, a company needs to find out, first, which areas of the company are sending the messages that are causing the negative trend and, second, what needs to be done to correct these messages. The same diagnostic approach should be used when a trend makes a significant jump. Determining why it jumped may enable a company to leverage certain brand messages still further.

Benefits and limitations of evaluation

Evaluating the processes and results of marketing communication has many obvious benefits, but it also has several limitations. In most cases, the point of evaluation is to increase the productivity of brand messages. Although there are limitations, measuring and evaluating is a good idea overall. Companies, however, will never have the time or money to evaluate everything they do. Awareness of the benefits and limitations helps companies decide when *not* to measure or evaluate.

Benefits

Important benefits of evaluation are that it reduces risk, enriches planning, provides controls, and helps document the contributions of the MC programmes and activities:

■ *Reducing risks:* One of the ongoing expectations of marketing communication is creativity. By definition, being creative means doing things differently, in new ways. Predicting results, however, is especially difficult when things are done in new ways. But if new creative strategies, media mixes, and brand messages can be evaluated before they are produced or used throughout a brand's marketing area, the risk of failure can be reduced.

■ *Enriching planning and managing:* Without information about how a brand is performing, it would be impossible to make intelligent decisions about managing relationships and the communication that drives these relationships. Think about the important role that measurements play in the simple task of driving a car. Imagine trying to drive safely without a speedometer to show how fast you are driving, without a gauge to show how much fuel is left, or without a temperature gauge to show whether the engine is overheating. The more measurements you have about the status of your car and its performance, the better you can manage the car's performance and upkeep. The same is true of any aspect of business, including marketing communication and brand relationships.

■ *Providing controls:* Generally, the larger a brand is, the more people, departments, and outside agencies are involved in its marketing communication activities. The more people involved, the more controls are needed to make sure plans are being properly executed and procedures followed. One of the characteristics that helps build trust is consistency. Through constant evaluation of brand messages and interactions with customers and other key stakeholders, a brand can work to maintain consistency. Tracking studies and audits are important ways to control processes. Scores for awareness, communication, and persuasion are often the basis for agency compensation.

■ *Documenting MC contributions:* Because much of what MC does cannot be directly linked to sales and profit, it is necessary to have surrogate measures that can be correlated to sales and profits. For example, by tracking increases in awareness and trial and showing a correlation with increases in sales, an MC department can justify the budget it has been allocated. Often, it can use these findings as a rationale for requesting budget increases.

Limitations

The limitations of evaluative measurements are several: cost, time, validity and projectability, wrong incentives, reduced creativity, and overdependence on research and numbers.

■ *Cost:* Costs for staff time, along with payments to outside measurement services that operate facilities and equipment and often actually do the measurements, can run into thousands of dollars for the simplest of tests. For companies with multimillion-euro budgets, these costs are usually not a concern, but for a medium-size or small business, the costs can be prohibitive. This is why most copy testing is done only for national and international advertising TV and print campaigns.

■ *Time:* Evaluation takes time. Conducting focus groups in three or four cities can take a couple of months from the time they are first thought of to the analysis of findings. The shortcoming of all evaluation efforts, and especially measurements of marketing communication efforts, is that customers, competitors, and other elements in the marketplace are always changing. So even if an advertisement, a publicity action, or a promotional programme tests well, conditions can change by the time the messages and programmes are rolled out to the brand's entire marketing area. When this happens, the results may not turn out as predicted.

■ *Validity and projectability:* All measurements are done on *samples* of respondents. Sometimes, getting a sample that is representative of a brand's customers and prospects is difficult. Talking to a mix of customers different from those in the target audience means that the two groups will probably respond differently. If companies try to save money by reducing sample sizes, this can also lower validity. Another danger is looking at sub-sample responses when the total sample size is just big enough to project answers to questions asked of the total sample only. For example, findings from a representative sample of 200 teenagers can be projected with a fairly high degree of confidence. However, if a company wants to look at the responses of only the girls in that sample, this number may be only 70; and statistically speaking, 70 is not large enough to project to all teenage girls.

■ *Wrong incentives:* Some marketers strongly believe that if brand messages are measured on the basis of, for example, advertising recall, creatives will work to make the advertising memorable and show little concern about increasing brand knowledge and awareness of brand benefits. Thus, when creatives know that they will be evaluated on one aspect, they might tend to focus on only that aspect, leaving other potentially desirable outcomes of their creative work unaddressed.

■ *Reduced creativity:* Some creatives feel that copy testing, especially when done under laboratory conditions, does not indicate how brand messages would perform in the marketplace. They argue that creative work cannot be reduced to numbers. Consequently, when told that their work needs more brand mentions, more pictures of the package, and so on, they may become discouraged and put in less creative effort.

■ *Overdependence on research and numbers:* Too much of a good thing can be bad. An MC department that insists on researching everything, and doing so until the results are exactly what it wants, may lose many opportunities. Just as some managers prefer to make decisions without research, others are so risk-averse that they are afraid to make any major decision without a lot of measurement support. For the latter, calling for more and more measurements to be done can become a way to avoid having to make a decision.

A final note: are you ready?

Measurement and evaluation involve more than the accumulation of data and the monitoring of sales. If used strategically, evaluation becomes an important source of feedback information used in planning marketing communication efforts as well as making sure they are being executed properly.

Although the saying "knowledge is power" is more than a cliché, knowledge does come at a price. In school it is tempting to argue that measurement is always good, but in school you are not confronted with the real world of paying salaries, hiring consultants, time going by in which your competitor approaches all your interesting prospects, etc. Once again: the key is balancing the benefits and drawbacks in decision making in this area. But isn't that the ultimate job description of any manager, including the job you are heading for? When you have got this message, and apply that to all the knowledge that you acquired by studying this book, you are ready to become an Integrated Marketing Communications manager.

🔑 Key terms

animatics Rough video footage used in ad testing.

baseline The beginning point, or where things stand before an MC effort begins.

brand metrics Measures of brand image and brand impact.

concept testing Tests that measure the effectiveness of the rough ideas that become brand and campaign themes.

concurrent testing Tests that track the performance of messages as they are run.

evaluative testing Tests that measure the performance of brand messages against their objectives at the conclusion of the programme.

focus group A group of 8 to 12 members of a brand's target audience who, led by a moderator, discuss some aspect of a brand, product category, or message strategy.

gap analysis An analysis of the difference between what customers expect from a brand (based on brand messages) and what they actually experience.

IMC audit An in-depth research method for evaluating IMC relationship-building practices.

intercept survey A survey in which people in a mall or at an event are stopped and asked to respond to a short questionnaire.

online focus group A chat room to which selected people have been invited to meet at a specified time with a moderator.

recall Bringing something back from memory.

recognition The act of identifying something and remembering that you saw or heard of it earlier.

relationship metrics Output controls developed specifically for IMC programmes to track the development of brand relationships.

scanner market test A tracking of a household's purchases by means of scanner data.

tachistoscope A device that exposes a brand message briefly to test participants so that researchers can measure how long it takes for a certain message or element to be communicated.

test marketing A research design in which an MC campaign is run in two to four markets for anywhere from 6 to 12 months.

theatre tests Tests in which people are invited to a location for the purpose of evaluating their response to a brand message.

tracking studies Periodic surveys that measure brand awareness, trial, repeat, and customer satisfaction with a brand and its competitors.

Check the key points

Key point 1: Brand-message research

a   Why is it important to evaluate brand messages before they run?

b   How does evaluation reduce risk? What other benefits does brand message research bring?

c   How and why is the cost/value factor important in conducting evaluation research?

d   What role do objectives play in evaluation?

Key point 2: Methods

a   What is concept testing? Why is it used?

b   When copy testing is used to evaluate the communication impact of a brand message, what kinds of effects are investigated?

c   Describe three tests that evaluate the persuasiveness of a brand message.

d   Explain how online interactions can be used for research purposes.

e   How are awareness and perception studies used in the evaluation of marketing communication?

f   What is the difference between pre- and post-testing?

g   You work as a creative person in an agency. The person sitting next to you works as the marketing manager for a company. Explain how the two of you might differ in your views about copy testing.

h   Explain the debate in the industry about the use of sales and brand share to evaluate the effectiveness of advertising and public relations.

Key point 3: Evaluating IMC metrics

a   Why would you want to conduct an IMC audit? What would you learn?

b   How does an IMC audit differ from a communication audit?

c   Explain the underlying logic behind lifetime customer value quintile analysis.

d   What does RFM stand for? What is included in this type of evaluation?

Chapter Challenge

Writing assignment

Pick a local company, and develop an evaluation programme for its marketing communication programme. In a two-page memo, outline and explain all the various types of research and evaluation methods that you would recommend.

Presentation assignment

Develop a programme to evaluate relationships for your favourite restaurant. Present to your class a set of relationship metrics. Explain what information they uncover and how that information can be used to develop MC strategies.

> ### Internet assignment
> Visit InsightExpress's website (www.insightexpress.com) for an example of the types of services that online research companies provide. Prepare a report for your instructor on how and when to use the services of this company.

Notes

[1] John Gaffney, "The Buzz Must Go On", *Business 2.0*, February 2002, p. 49.

[2] Ibid.

[3] Information taken from the Advertising and Marketing Effectiveness (AME) award-winning brief for Buitoni by the McCann-Erickson Italiana office in Milan, Italy.

[4] Jane M. Von Bergen, "Her Job Is Monitoring Every Cable Infomercial", *Philadelphia Inquirer*, 16 February 2003, p. A1.

[5] Quoted from Richard M. Restak, *Brainscapes* (New York: Hyperion,1995), by David Wolfe in "What Your Customers Can't Say", *American Demographics*, February 1998, p. 24.

[6] Priscilla LaBarbare and Joel Tucciarone, "GSR Reconsidered: A Behaviour-Based Approach to Evaluating and Improving the Sales Potency of Advertising", *Journal of Advertising Research*, September–October 1995, p. 35.

[7] Karl Weiss, "Internet Research: Harnessing the Power of the Internet with Online Data Reporting", *Alert 38*, no. 6 (June 2000), pp. 1–3.

[8] Ibid.

[9] Geneva J. King, "Today's Marketing Data Research Companies: The News You Need, When You Need It", *Online Newsletter*, 7 July 2000.

[10] Adapted from Phil Levine and Bill Ahlhauser, "Internet Interviewing—Pro", *Marketing Research*, Summer 1999, p. 35.

[11] Dale Kulp and Rick Hunter, "Internet Interviewing—Con", *Marketing Research*, Summer 1999, p. 36.

[12] Tom Duncan and Sandra Moriarty, *Driving Brand Value: Using Integrated Marketing to Manage Profitable Stakeholder Relationships* (New York: McGraw-Hill, 1997), pp. 261–78.

[13] Jeff Smith, comments on the MarketingProfs.com listserv, 5 April 2002.

[14] Ibid.

[15] Duncan and Moriarty, *Driving Brand Value*, pp. 262–3.

[16] Thomas O. Jones and W. Earl Sasser, Jr., "Why Satisfied Customers Defect", *Harvard Business Review*, November–December 1995, pp. 88–99.

[17] Gregory H. Watson, *Strategic Benchmarking* (New York: Wiley, 1993), p. 10.

[18] Day, George S, (1998), "What does it mean to be market-driven?", *Business Strategy Review*, 9 (Spring), 1, 1–14.

[19] Gupta, Sunil, Dominique Hanssens, Bruce Hardie, William Kahn, V. Kumar, Nathaniel Lin and Nalini R.S. Sriram (2006), "Modeling Customer Lifetime Value", *Journal of Service Research*, 9–2, pp. 139–55.

Further reading

Cramphorn, Spike (2004) "What Advertising Testing Might Have Been, If We Had Only Known", *Journal of Advertising Research*, Vol. 44–2, pp. 170–80.

Hall, Bruce F. (2004) "On Measuring the Power of Communications", *Journal of Advertising Research*, Vol. 44–2, pp. 181–7.

Reid, Mike (2003) "IMC–Performance relationships: further insight and evidence from the Australian marketplace", *International Journal of Advertising*, Vol. 22–2, pp. 227–48.

Reid, Mike (2005) "Performance Auditing of Integrated Marketing Communication (IMC) Actions and Outcomes", *Journal of Advertising*, Vol. 34–4, pp. 41–54.

Rosenberg, Karl (1998) "Should the Language of 'Testing' be Abolished?", *Journal of Advertising Research*, Vol. 38–3, pp. 73–6.

Walvis, Tjaco (2003) "Avoiding advertising research disaster: Advertising and the uncertainty principle", *Journal of Brand Management*, Vol. 10–6, pp. 403–9.

Index

A1 Dove spreads its wings (Chapter 2)

Questions

Is this new Dove product a line or a brand extension?
Does the difference matter?
How does this ad fit in with other communication efforts of the brand, in particular with its 'real beauty campaign'?
(also see D2 in part 4).

A2 H&M magazine promotion (Chapter 4)

Questions

What element(s) of attitude formation does this ad refer to?
Do you think this advertisement is internally consistent (in other words, do all the copy elements send you a similar, or complementary message)?
Take into account the target group that H&M is aiming at.

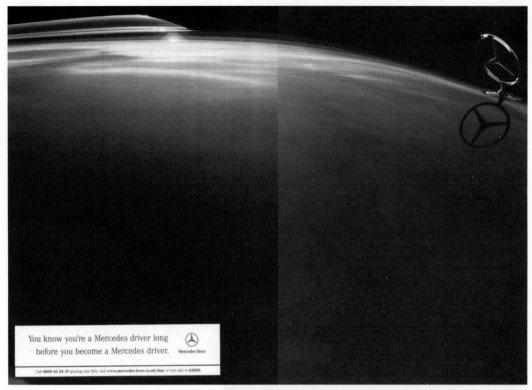

You know you're a Mercedes driver long before you become a Mercedes driver. Mercedes-Benz

Call 0800 66 54 19 quoting star 024, visit www.mercedes-benz.co.uk/star or text star to 64500.

A3 Mercedes takes the long road (Chapter 2)

Questions

What brand elements appear in this ad?

Which one made you recognize which brand the ad is for?

In what way does this ad contribute to brand equity?

A4 Marketing communications are everywhere (Chapters 1 and 16)

Questions

Take a look at which major brands are included on this image of Piccadilly Circus in London and note some that are *not* included. What does this say about these brands in your opinion? Could you imagine Piccadilly Circus with no advertisements?

What is your reaction to this kind of street advertising?

Is there a saturation point?

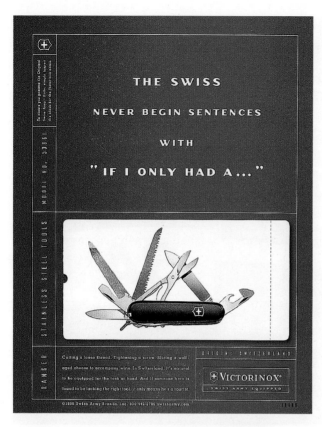

A5 Inviting you to think about it
(Chapter 4)

A6 Print ad for the blockbuster movie *Lord of the Rings* (Chapter 1)

A7 Information processing (Chapters 4 and 11)

Questions

What is the message of this ad?
How much effort does it take to process information in this ad, so that you get the message?
What factors normally determine whether or not you will be willing to pay this effort?
Does it make a difference whether the ad is seen in the context of the Olympic Games or not?

A8 Hit your target (Chapter 5 and 7)

Questions

How does BlackBerry try to contact its target in this advert?
Is this a planning tactic you can appreciate?
Are there alternatives?
Imagine the brand name as BlueBerry. What might this ad look like?

A9 How curious are you? (Chapter 4)

Questions

What is needed to make you elaborate on this message?
Does the ad itself help you to elaborate?
What happens if you only peripherally process this message?

A10 UPS reinforces its brand promise (Chapter 7)

Questions

How do the ad's copy and UPS' slogan interact?
How is the graphic related?
What support does the main text give to the ad's message?

Watch the television version of this advertisement on the OLC! www.mcgraw-hill. com/textbooks/ouwersloot

A11 Real life (Chapters 5, 7 and 18)

Questions

What objectives can you identify behind this ad?
What storytelling is applied here?
What appeal?
Are objectives and ad format consistent?
How can the effectiveness of this ad be measured?

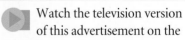 Watch the television version of this advertisement on the OLC! www.mcgraw-hill. com/textbooks/ouwersloot

A12 Making the connection (Chapters 2, 4, and 7)

Questions

Identify all brand elements used in this ad. Is any one of them making you interested or motivated to elaborate on this message?
Do you think Penelope Cruz is a good endorser for this product? Can you think of other endorsers that might be a good choice for you?

Watch the television version of this advertisement on the OLC! www.mcgraw-hill. com/textbooks/ouwersloot

A13 Can you have it simpler? (Chapter 2)

Questions

Would you expect this new extension of Virgin to be successful, given the theory of brand extensions?

How would you describe the message conveyed in this ad?

Identify what aspects of the ad lead to this description.

A14 (S)watch! A Swatch outlet at the Carrousel du Louvre, Paris (Chapter 2)

Questions

Do you know of other brands that have their own retail chain?

Why do Swatch and these other companies have their own chains? Is it so that you can only buy Swatches there and nowhere else? Where do you typically find these outlets?

Part 2

B1 Levi's uses advertising to support its media planning (Chapter 10)

Questions

Would you call this integrated marketing communication as well as media planning?

What kind of commercial would you expect in this context?

What do you think Levi's wants to achieve with this advertisement?

B2 Diet Coke with Cherry, that's clear (Chapter 7)

Questions

Use this ad to identify various elements of print ads discussed in Chapter 7. Is this ad consistent with other advertising for Coke? What elements of the parent brand (Coca-Cola) do you find in this ad?

B3 Orange is a bright colour (Chapters 6 and 8)

Questions

In what way is the text linked to the Orange slogan?
Why is this ad suitable for outdoor advertising?
Consider how this ad can be cross-referenced in a tv commercial.

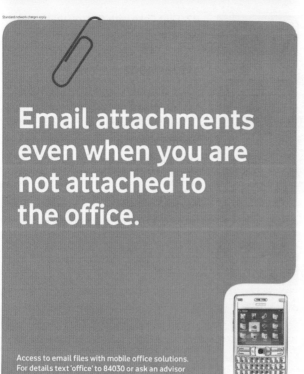

B4 Attached! (Chapters 6 and 8)

Questions

What is the big idea behind this ad?
How can Vodafone elaborate on this idea?
Is this also applicable with other media?

 Watch the television version of this advertisement on the OLC! www.mcgraw-hill.com/textbooks/ouwersloot

B5 Small is powerful (Chapters 6 and 17)

Questions

Why is this ad displaying a great idea?

Would it be as effective in Europe as in the US (from which this ad originates)?

(Also look at the colour insert in Part 3 (C4) showing the effectiveness of PR when Volkswagen launched the New Beetle).

Think small.

Our little car isn't so much of a novelty any more.

A couple of dozen college kids don't try to squeeze inside it.

The guy at the gas station doesn't ask where the gas goes.

Nobody even stares at our shape.

In fact, some people who drive our little flivver don't even think that about 27 miles to the gallon is going any great guns.

Or using five pints of oil instead of five quarts.

Or never needing anti-freeze.

Or racking up about 40,000 miles on a set of tires.

That's because once you get used to some of our economies, you don't even think about them any more.

Except when you squeeze into a small parking spot.

Or renew your small insurance. Or pay a small repair bill. Or trade in your old VW for a new one.

Think it over.

B6 Dell Marketing (Chapter 9)

Questions

How does Dell communicate with this website?

What other marketing uses does Dell make of its presence on the Internet?

In what way is this Integrated Marketing Communication?

B7 Would BASF use chemicals to make such colours? (Chapter 7)

Questions

How do the various elements in this ad relate?

Do they complement and reinforce each other?

B8 Three in a row (Chapter 6)

Questions

Analyse the greatness of this creative idea. What is conveyed with this message?

How could Land Rover vary this theme, using other animals?

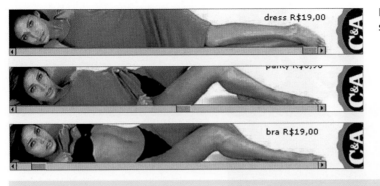

B9 Banner ads can also have sex appeal (Chapters 7 and 9)

Questions

How effective is banner advertising today?

Describe how banner advertising has evolved over the last couple of years.

What other forms of Internet advertising do you know?

B10 Nike on the Internet (Chapter 9)

Questions

In what way does Nike make an effort to integrate its communication?

 Watch the television version of this advertisement on the OLC!
www.mcgraw-hill.com/textbooks/ouwersloot

B11 An appealing brand (Chapter 7)

Questions

What appeal is applied in this ad?
Does it appeal to you?
In what execution framework is it operating?
What is the message conveyed?

B12 Nokia's effort to connect (Chapter 8)

Questions

What specific features of print ads is applied by Nokia?
Why do you think they have lines in different languages?
How much do you learn of Nokia from this advertisement?
How do the slogans(!) relate?

B13 It's not only about what 'you can' (Chapter 8)

Questions

What media are used here? Think of how still other media could be integrated.
What is Canon trying to achieve with this ad?

B14 It depends on your frame of reference (Chapter 8)

Questions

Is this also your idea of "not so high prices"?
In what kind of magazine would you expect to see this ad?
The coupon can be seen as an anachronism. Or is there a more subtle reason behind it?

B15 There's no life like Second Life (Chapter 9)

Questions

How are brands present in the virtual world of Second Life (SL)?

What does their mere presence in SL mean for these brands, in other words is this an example of the catch phrase "the medium is the message"?

What specific features of SL makes it interesting as a communication medium?

What drawbacks do you see of using SL as medium?

Is SL as a medium restricted to certain product categories? For instance, would it make sense for laundry detergents to advertise in SL? For cars? Universities?

Copyright 2007, Linden Research, Inc. All Rights Reserved.

B16 Don't be afraid to get on the bus (Chapter 8)

Questions

Who is the advertiser here?

How does the advertiser make use of the features of the bus?

What is the essence of the message?

Part 3

Xtra wide

In response to a wide body of opinion, Airbus has created an aircraft with an extra-wide body. The A350 XWB. Inspired offspring of the A380. Its revolutionary cabin gives passengers a completely new experience of space and comfort - in every class. This is the future of flight.

The A350 X~~~
XTRA WIDE BODY
For the Xtra experience

AIRBUS

C1 Airbus does something Xtra (Chapter 15)

Questions

Identify why this is an example of customer service. What is the first association you have with this ad?
Does it correspond to what the message says?
Comment on the art design that puts the plane in the narrowest part of the "X".

C2 What car does James Bond drive this time? (Chapter 11)

Questions

What is the effect of a product placement?
If a character like James Bond drives different cars in different movies, what does this mean for the differentiation of the brands involved?
Why, in general, is product placement attractive?
Can you think of another car yet, that Mr. Bond might drive next time?

C3 Renault is the proud owner of a Formula 1 racing team (Chapters 11 and 16)

Questions

In what ways does Renault exploit its sponsorship?

What is your opinion of the fact that Renault uses its sponsorship for this particular model of the brand?

Identify how Renault responds to social concerns about the environment. Is this consistent with its F1 sponsorship?

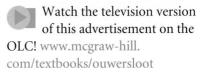 Watch the television version of this advertisement on the OLC! www.mcgraw-hill. com/textbooks/ouwersloot

C4 Publicity at work (Chapter 12)

Questions

In what way could Volkswagen help achieve appearing on the cover of *BusinessWeek*?

Guess how much advertising would be needed to get the same results as this cover story achieves.

Is publicity always good?

(Recall the ad in Part 2 (B5) for the introduction of the Beetle)

C5 Wrrroemmm&m (Chapters 11 and 16)

Questions

How does sponsorship work?
What impact does sponsorship have on the brand?
Can every brand sponsor any object?
Are there ethical limitations to sponsorship?

C6 Price reductions are often used to introduce a new product (Chapter 13)

Questions

Why wouldn't Gillette just introduce the MACH 3 at a $3 lower price?
What other forms of promotions can you think of for the Gillette razors?

C7 The Duck family (Chapter 11)

Questions

Why is this package so important from a branding point of view?

C8 Tools for sales reps to use to promote the Perfect Serve campaign (Chapter 13)

Questions

What stakeholders have been targeted in this IMC campaign?
Why does Coca-Cola not use price incentives in this case?
What could be the role of advertising in this situation?
Is Coca-Cola using a pull or push strategy, or a mix?

 Watch the television version of this advertisement on the OLC!
www.mcgraw-hill.com/textbooks/ouwersloot

C9 On the faithfulness of celebrity endorsements (Chapters 7, 11, and 16)

Questions

In how far is shirt sponsorship of football teams comparable to endorsements, in particular when star players like Beckham are involved?

Do you believe that a series of pictures like these hurt the sponsors, or the celebrity?

How far do you believe that sponsors influence decisions made by top teams (for example it was suggested that Beckham's transfer to Real Madrid was primarily a commercial stunt)? Would you consider it ethically wrong if this were the case?

C10 Personal selling the "Tupperware way" (Chapters 11 and 14)

Questions

Which of the two pictures gets closest to your predisposition of personal selling?

Which one is more appealing to you?

Which one would you think is closest to reality?

C11 Sales promotions add value to a purchase (Chapters 2 and 13)

Questions
What is your first impression on seeing this ad?
Which is the leading brand, and which one is the premium?
Interpreting this ad as a co-branding effort, do the brands fit?
What do they gain by being connected to each other?
What is the real value of the sales promotion to consumers?

C12 It depends on what it tries to sell; I'd say (Chapters 3, 9 and 15)

Questions
What does this advertisement try to say? If you don't get the message, check the context on: www.apple-marketing.co.uk/. How effective would it be in a magazine, or billboard?

C13 Absolutely top of the list (Chapter 6 and 11)

Questions

Absolut has used the shape of the bottle as the leading theme for its advertising for many years. Why has this proven to be a great idea?

What do the ads in fact convey?

Recently the company decided to abandon this theme—why do you think that is?

What arguments could you put forward to try to convince Absolut to stick to its campaign?

C14 Sponsorship all over the world (Chapters 1 and 11)

Questions

Why is sponsorship so effective in many cases?

ABN AMRO emphasized that it was participating in the race, rather than sponsoring a boat: Is there, from IMC perspective, a difference?

Team ABN AMRO I won the race; would the effects of the sponsorship be different if the team's performance would be worse?

C15 Free for free (Chapter 13)

Questions

How often do you make use of sales promotions?

What impact does a sales promotion have on your perception of the brand?

Has the appearance of websites like freeukstuff.com changed the use of sales promotions by consumers?

Have they had an impact on the use of the instrument by companies?

Do these kind of websites change the effectiveness of the instrument?

Part 4

Thinking about yourself is thinking about others.

THIS CARD IS DESIGNED TO HELP ELIMINATE AIDS IN AFRICA

1% of your total spend goes to the Global Fund,
to help fight the AIDS emergency in Africa.
DO THE (RED) THING™ – apply today. Call 0800 700 717
or visit AmericanExpressRED.co.uk

Typical 12.9% APR Variable

D1 American Express applies cause marketing (Chapter 16)

Questions

Why would American Express apply cause marketing?
Do you actually believe that American Express will live up to the promise they make?
What does this do to your perception of the brand?
And what does it do to your perception of American Express' competitors?

 Watch the television version of this advertisement on the OLC! www.mcgraw-hill.com/textbooks/ouwersloot

If you take the time to talk, we promise to listen.

At Dove, we believe our products should be tested by the people they were made for – real women. Try our products and tell us what you think. Good or bad, we just want to hear your thoughts.

By sharing your views, you will get the chance to win a year's supply of our most loved Dove products as a thank you for your time.

Join our biggest ever beauty survey.
Talk to us at dove.co.uk

D2 Dove shows "real beauty" (Chapter 16)

Questions

In what way does this ad by Dove respond to social concerns?
What do you think the brand wants to achieve with this?
Do you believe this is a good proposition for the brand?
Considering that associations have to be strong and favourable (see Chapter 2), how would you assess this ad?

PERONI

ITALY

peroniitaly.com

D3 They brew beer in Italy too
(Chapters 16 and 17)

Questions

Why is this a typical Italian way of advertising for beer (imagine Guinness using the same picture—would that work)?

How well do you think this ad succeeds?

How far is your opinion determined by your own cultural background?

Imagine you are the brand manager of Perrier. Would you be happy with the Peroni brand?

D4 Rover makes use of cultural differences
(Chapter 17)

Questions

How long did it take you to get the point of the joke?

Would this kind of ad (making fun of one's own cultural peculiarities) be equally effective for French or German brands?

D5 Shell as an environmental friend (Chapter 16)

Questions

Do you consider Shell as environmentally friendly or (less demanding) environmentally concerned?

Do you think this kind of advertising helps?

What else is needed to make consumers believe that Shell is environmentally responsible?

Don't just read about it, travel.

Hotels • City Breaks • Holidays • Flights • Car Rental

opodo.co.uk
let the journey begin

D6 Just watch it (Chapter 16)

Questions

Why isn't Nike's famous slogan infringed with this Opodo's slogan?

Suppose that the slogan read: "Travel: Just do it!" Would that harm Nike? Would it benefit Opodo?

D7 Where are we? (Chapter 17)

Questions

How many different countries does this ad refer to?
Can you possibly identify a Country of Origin effect?
Is the integration of cultures successful in your opinion?

D8 IBM and the other (Chapter 16)

Questions

Who is the "other"?
Do you think IBM wants to come across as a socially concerned company with this ad?
Do you hence find this a socially/ethically acceptable ad?

D9 Advocating a good cause? (Chapter 16)

Questions

What is the message of this ad?
Who is the sender?
Is it acceptable to you that a commercial organization makes use of this kind of advertising for its own benefits?

D10 Business is about numbers (Chapter 16)

Questions

Who is the sender of this ad?
Why would this organization send this particular message?
Do you believe the message is trustworthy?
What percentage (the 60 or the 100) is making up for a unique association?

Questions

Compare this ad to the one discussed in D10. What differences do you see?

Which coffee would you expect to taste better?

What is meant by Nescafé's catch line "It's all about you"?

Why is Nescafé using their Fairtrade mark in this way?

 Watch the television version of this advertisement on the OLC!
www.mcgraw-hill.com/textbooks/ouwersloot

D12 Some like it smooth, some like it rough (Chapters 7 and 17)

Questions

What does this ad communicate to you?
How far is this influenced by your cultural background?
Would the ad be different if another colour, e.g. yellow, had been used?

D13 If cats could have pocket money (Chapter 17)

Questions

Where on the globalized, localized continuum would you place Whiskas' approach?

Does the suggestion that cats would choose this brand interact with the authority dimension of Hofstede?

 Watch the television version of this advertisement on the OLC!
www.mcgraw-hill.com/textbooks/ouwersloot

D14 What will in fact give you a pain in the stomach? (Chapters 6 and 17)

Questions

How culturally sensitive do you believe this ad is?

Can you think of other executions of the same Big Idea, referencing to other countries (e.g. in this series of ads, one shows a pizza with Alka Seltzer pain relievers as a topping).

ABCDEFG JKLMNOPQRSTU WXYZ

Together we can eliminate HIV

THE GLOBE AND MAIL
Well written. Well read.

D15 What's missing? (Chapters 4 and 16)

Questions

Who is the advertiser in this case?

What message does this brand communicate?

It will take you some time to have realized what the message is. How does that influence your appreciation?

Will you always be in a situation to elaborate on the message in this way?